U.S. ARMY WAR COLLEGE
GUIDE TO NATIONAL SECURITY ISSUES

VOLUME I:

THEORY OF WAR AND STRATEGY

3rd Edition

Revised and Expanded

Edited by
J. Boone Bartholomees, Jr.
Department of National Security and Strategy

June 2008

*****

The views expressed in this report are those of the authors and do not necessarily reflect the official policy or position of the U.S. Army War College, the Department of the Army, the Department of Defense, or the U.S. Government. This report is cleared for public release; distribution is unlimited.

*****

The Department of State Public Affairs Office reviewed the manuscript for Chapter 13 and poses no objection to its publication. The views expressed are those of the author and do not necessarily represent the official policy or position of the Department of State.

*****

Comments pertaining to this report are invited and should be forwarded to: Director, Strategic Studies Institute, U.S. Army War College, 122 Forbes Ave, Carlisle, PA 17013-5244.

*****

All Strategic Studies Institute (SSI) publications are available on the SSI homepage for electronic dissemination. Hard copies of this report also may be ordered from our homepage. SSI's homepage address is: *www.StrategicStudiesInstitute. army.mil*.

*****

The Strategic Studies Institute publishes a monthly e-mail newsletter to update the national security community on the research of our analysts, recent and forthcoming publications, and upcoming conferences sponsored by the Institute. Each newsletter also provides a strategic commentary by one of our research analysts. If you are interested in receiving this newsletter, please subscribe on our homepage at *www.StrategicStudiesInstitute.army.mil/newsletter/*.

ISBN 1-58487-356-6

CONTENTS

VOLUME I: THEORY OF WAR AND STRATEGY

FIGURES - VOLUME I

Chapter 16

Chapter 19

Chapter 21

INTRODUCTION

J. Boone Bartholomees, Jr.

The *U. S. Army War College Guide (USAWC) to National Security Issues* is the latest edition of the *U. S. Army War College Guide to National Security Policy and Strategy*, which the college has published sporadically under different titles since 2001. This edition of the *Guide* is in two volumes that correspond roughly to the two core courses that the Department of National Security and Strategy (DNSS) teaches: "Theory of War and Strategy" and "National Security Policy and Strategy." Like its predecessors, this edition is largely an expansion of the existing materials, although over 40 percent is new, and the previously published chapters have been updated as necessary. The authors, with one exception all current or former members of the faculty, represent each of the four primary teaching departments of the college. The exception is the inclusion this year of a chapter on space power by a recent graduate—the chapter was his research project while a student. The appendix on the USAWC strategy formulation model in the second volume reflects the alterations in that fundamental document made for the 2008 academic year (2007-08).

Although DNSS uses several of the chapters in this volume as readings for its core courses, and at least one other department uses chapters in its core instruction, this is not a textbook. It does reflect, however, both the method and manner we use to teach the theory of war and the formulation of national security strategy to America's future senior leaders. As we continue to refine and update the *Guide*, we intend to increase course-oriented essays, and several of the new chapters were written specifically to support instruction. The book is also not a comprehensive or exhaustive treatment of either the theory of war, strategy, or the policymaking process.

The *Guide* is organized in broad clusters of chapters addressing general subject areas. Chapters are placed in general blocks for convenience, not as a rigid framework. I made no effort to constrain or shape the authors' work based on where I saw the chapter fitting in the book. Thus, some chapters might have been placed in several blocks, and their presence in a specific block should not be considered a restrictive form of categorization. Volume I starts with theoretical issues on war and strategy. The second block examines power both conceptually and in terms of the elements of power. The volume concludes with studies on specific theoretical issues. The second volume on national security strategy and policy opens with a look at the U.S. security community and its functions. The second block expands to multinational issues and considerations. The volume concludes with studies of specific policy issues or considerations.

PART I

STRATEGIC THEORY

CHAPTER 1
WHY IS STRATEGY DIFFICULT?

David Jablonsky

Colonel (Ret.) Arthur Lykke taught an entire generation of U.S. Army War College students that strategy at any level consists of ends or objectives, ways or concepts, and means or resources. This three-element framework is nothing more than a reworking of the traditional definition of strategy as the calculated relationship of ends and means. Yet the student response is always overwhelmingly favorable, with Lykke's framework invariably forming the structure for subsequent seminar problems on subjects ranging from the U.S. Civil War to nuclear strategy. This is due, in part, to the fact that students weaned on the structural certitude of the five-paragraph field order and the Commander's Estimate naturally find such structure comforting in dealing with the complexities of strategy. But those students also know from their experience in the field that there are limits to the scientific approach when dealing with human endeavors. As a consequence, they can also appreciate the art of mixing ends, ways, and means, using for each element the part subjective, part objective criteria of suitability, feasibility, and applicability—the essence of strategic calculation.[1]

The ends-ways-means paradigm also provides a structure at all levels of strategy to avoid confusing the scientific product with the scientific process. The former involves production propositions that are logically related and valid across time and space. The search for these immutable principles over the centuries by students of war failed, because they looked at classical strategy as something like physical science that could produce verities in accordance with certain regularities. This was further compounded by military thinkers who made claims for scientific products without subjecting those products to a scientific process. Both Jomini and Mahan, for instance, ignored evidence in cases that did not fit their theories or principles of strategy.[2] The strategic paradigm, then, serves as a lowest common denominator reminder that a true scientific product is not possible from the study of strategy. At the same time, however, that paradigm provides a framework for the systematic treatment of facts and evidence—the very essence of the scientific process. In this regard, Admiral Wylie has pointed out:

> I do not claim that strategy is or can be a "science" in the sense of the physical sciences. It can and should be an intellectual discipline of the highest order, and the strategist should prepare himself to manage ideas with precision and clarity and imagination. . . . Thus, while strategy itself may not be a science, strategic judgment can be scientific to the extent that it is orderly, rational, objective, inclusive, discriminatory, and perceptive.[3]

All that notwithstanding, the limitations of the strategic paradigm bring the focus full circle back to the art involved in producing the optimal mix of ends, ways, and means. Strategy, of course, does depend on the general regularities of that paradigm. But strategy does not always obey the logic of that framework, remaining, as the German Army Regulations *Truppen-fuhrung* of 1936 described it, "a free creative activity resting upon scientific foundations."[4] The purpose of this chapter is to demonstrate why, despite increasingly scientific approaches to formulation and implementation, strategy remains principally an art rather than a science, and why within that art the "creative activity" of blending the elements in the strategic paradigm has become progressively more difficult over the centuries.

From Revolutions to Total War.

In the wake of the Napoleonic Wars, there was a growing recognition of the increased complexity of strategy, summarized in Karl von Clausewitz's warning that "there can be no question of a purely military evaluation of a great strategic issue, nor of a purely military scheme to solve it."[5]

At the tactical level, the Prussian philosopher wrote, "the means are fighting forces trained for combat; the end is victory." For the strategic, however, Clausewitz concluded that military victories were meaningless unless they were the means to obtain a political end, "those objects which lead directly to peace."[6] Thus, strategy was "the linking together (*Verbindung*) of separate battle engagements into a single whole, for the final object of the war."[7] And only the political or policy level could determine that objective. "To bring a war, or any one of its campaigns to a successful close requires a thorough grasp of national policy," he pointed out. "On that level, strategy and policy coalesce."[8] For Clausewitz, this vertical continuum (see Figure 1) was best exemplified by Frederick the Great, who embodied both policy and strategy and whose Silesian conquests of 1741 are considered to be the classic example of strategic art by demonstrating "an element of restrained strength, . . . ready to adjust to the smallest shift in the political situation."[9]

Figure 1.
The Policy Continuum.

With his deceptively simple description of the vertical continuum of war, Clausewitz set the stage for the equivalent of a Copernican shift in the strategic ends-ways-means paradigm. Now that paradigm was more complex, operating on both the military and policy levels with the totality of the ends, ways, and means at the lower levels interconnected with the political application at the policy level of those same strategic elements. This connection was the essence of Clausewitz's description of war as a continuation of political intercourse (*Verkehr*) with the addition of other means. He explained that

> We deliberately use the phrase "with the addition of other means" because we also want to make it clear that war in itself does not suspend political intercourse or change it into something entirely different . . . . The main lines along which military events progress, and to which they are restricted, are political lines that continue throughout the war into the subsequent peace. . . . War cannot be divorced from political life; and whenever this occurs in our thinking about war, the many links that connect the two elements are destroyed and we are left with something pointless and devoid of sense.[10]

The Industrial and French Revolutions.

This growing complexity in dealing with the strategic paradigm was compounded by two upheavals. Clausewitz was profoundly aware of one, the French Revolution; he was totally ignorant of the other, the industrial/technological revolution. Prior to the French Revolution, 18th-century rulers had acquired such effective political and economic control over their people that they were able to create their war machines as separate and distinct from the rest of society. The Revolution changed all that with the appearance of a force "that beggared all imagination" as Clausewitz described it,

> Suddenly, war again became the business of the people—a people of 30 millions, all of whom considered themselves to be citizens. There seemed no end to the resources mobilized; all limits disappeared in the vigor and enthusiasm shown by governments and their subjects. . . . War, untrammelled by any conventional restraints, had broken loose in all its elemental fury. This was due to the peoples' new share in these great affairs of state; and their participation, in its turn, resulted partly from the impact that the Revolution had on the internal conditions of every state and partly from the danger that France posed to everyone.[11]

For Clausewitz, the people greatly complicated the formulation and implementation of strategy by adding "primordial violence, hatred and enmity, which are to be regarded as a blind natural force" to form with the army and the government what he termed the remarkable trinity (see Figure 2). The army he saw as a "creative spirit" roaming freely within "the play of chance and probability," but always bound to the government, the third element, in "subordination, as an instrument of policy, which makes it subject to reason alone."[12]

It was the complex totality of this trinity that, Clausewitz realized, had altered and complicated strategy so completely.

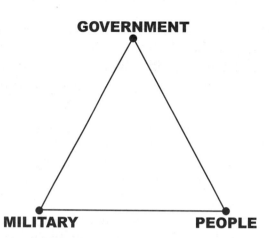

Figure 2. The Remarkable Trinity.

> Clearly the tremendous effects of the French Revolution . . . were caused not so much by new military methods and concepts as by radical changes in policies and administration, by the new character of government, altered conditions of the French people, and the like. . . . It follows that the transformation of the art of war resulted from the transformation of politics.[13]

But while that transformation had made it absolutely essential to consider the elements of the Clausewitzian trinity within the strategic paradigm, the variations possible in the interplay of those elements moved strategy even farther from the realm of scientific certitude. "A theory that ignores any one of them or seeks to fix an arbitrary relationship between them," Clausewitz warned in this regard, "would conflict with reality to such an extent that for this reason alone it would be totally useless."[14]

Like most of his contemporaries, Clausewitz had no idea that he was living on the eve of a technological transformation born of the Industrial Revolution. But that transformation, as it gathered momentum throughout the remainder of the 19th century, fundamentally altered the interplay of elements within the Clausewitzian trinity, further complicating the formulation and application process within the strategic paradigm (see Figure 3).

In terms of the military element, technology would change the basic nature of weapons and modes of transportation, the former had been stable for a hundred years, the latter for a thousand. Within a decade of Clausewitz's death in 1831, that process would begin in armaments with the introduction of breechloading firearms and in transportation with the development of the railroads."[15]

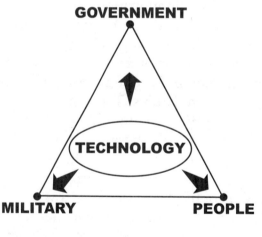

Figure 3. The Impact of Technology.

Technology had a more gradual effect on the role of the people. There were, for example, the great European population increases of the 19th century as the Industrial Revolution moved on to the continent from Great Britain. This trend led, in turn, to urbanization: the mass movement of people from the extended families of rural life to the "atomized," impersonal life of the city. There, the urge to belong, to find a familial substitute, led to a more focused allegiance to the nation-state manifested in a new, more blatant and aggressive nationalism.

This nationalism was fueled by the progressive side effects of the Industrial Revolution, particularly in the area of public education, which meant, in turn, mass literacy throughout Europe by the end of the 19th century. One result was that an increasingly literate public could be manipulated by governments as technology spawned more sophisticated methods of mass communications. On the other hand, those same developments also helped democratize societies, which then demanded a greater share in government, particularly over strategic questions involving war and peace. In Clausewitz's time, strategic decisions dealing with such matters were rationally based on Realpolitik considerations to further state interests, not on domestic issues. By the end of the 19th century, the *Rankeian Primat der Aussenpolitik* was increasingly challenged throughout Europe by the need of governments for domestic consensus—a development with far-reaching implications for the conduct of strategy at the national level within the basic ends-ways-means paradigm.[16]

During much of that century, as the social and ideological upheavals unleashed by the French Revolution developed, military leaders in Europe generally attempted to distance their armed forces from their people. Nowhere was this more evident than in the Prussian *cum* German military, where the leaders worked *hard* over the years to prevent the adulteration of their forces by liberal ideas. "The army is now our fatherland," General von Roon wrote to his wife during the 1848 revolutions, "for there alone have the unclean and violent elements who put everything into turmoil failed to penetrate."[17] The revolutions in industry and technology, however, rendered this ideal unattainable. To begin with, the so-called *Technisierung* of warfare meant the mass production of more complex weapons and forever-larger standing military forces. The key ingredients for these forces were the great population increases and the rise of nationalism, as well as improved communications and governmental efficiency—the latter directed at general conscription of national manhood, which, thanks to progress in railroad development, could be brought to the battlefield in unlimited numbers.

At the same time, this increased interaction between the government/military and the people was also tied to other aspects of the impact of technology on the Clausewitzian trinity. Technological innovations in weaponry during this period, for example, were not always followed by an understanding of their implications, societal as well as military. Certainly, there was the inability on the part of all European powers to perceive the growing advantage of defensive over offensive weapons demonstrated in the Boer and Russo-Japanese wars. That inability was tied in with a trend in Europe at the time to combine elan with a military focus on moral force, bloodshed, and decisive battles. The result was that the military leaders of France, Germany, and Russia all adopted offensive military doctrines in some form.[18]

The fact that these doctrines led to the self-defeating offensive strategies of World War I ultimately had to do with the transformation of civil-military relations within the Clausewitzian trinity in their countries. In France, as an example, the officer corps distrusted the trend by the leaders of the Third Republic toward shorter terms of military service, which it believed threatened the army's professional character and tradition. Adopting an offensive doctrine and elevating it to the highest level was a means to combat this trend, since there was general agreement that an army consisting primarily of reservists and short-term conscripts could only be used in the defense. "Reserves are so much eyewash," one French general wrote at the time, "and take in only short-sighted mathematicians who equate the value of armies with the size of their effectives, without considering their moral value."[19] Although these were setbacks for those who shared this sentiment in the wake of the Dreyfus Affair and the consequent military reforms, it only required the harsher international climate after the Agadir crisis of 1911 for General Joffre and his young Turks to gain the ascendancy. Their philosophy was summed up by their leader, who explained that in planning for the next war, he had "no preconceived idea other than a full determination to take the offensive with all my forces assembled."[20]

Under these circumstances, French offensive doctrine became increasingly unhinged from strategic reality as it responded to the more immediate demands of domestic and intragovernmental politics. The result was France's illconceived strategic lunge in 1914 toward its former possessions in the East, a lunge that almost provided sufficient margin of assistance for Germany's Schlieffen Plan to work, another result of military operational doctrine driving policy. In the end, only the miracle of the Marne prevented a victory for the Germans as rapid and complete as that of 1870.[21]

There were other equally significant results as the full brunt of technological change continued to alter the relationship between the elements of the Clausewitzian trinity in all the European powers. The larger, more complex armies resulted in the growing specialization and compartmentalization of the military—a trend that culminated in the emulation of the German General Staff system by most of the European powers. It is significant that Clausewitz had ignored Carnot, the "organizer of victory," for Napoleon, when considering military genius. Now with the increase in military branches, as well as combat service and combat service support organizations, the age of the "militaryorganizational" genius had arrived. All this in turn affected the relationship in all countries between the military and the government. For the very increase in professional knowledge and skill caused by technology's advance in military affairs undermined the ability of political leaders to understand and control the military, just as technology was making that control more important than ever by extending strategy from the battlefield to the civilian rear, thus blurring the difference between combatant and noncombatant.[22]

At the same time, the military expansion in the peacetime preparation for war began to enlarge the economic dimensions of conflict beyond the simple financial support of Clausewitz's era. As Europe entered the 20th century, new areas of concern began to emerge ranging from industrial capacity and the availability and distribution of raw materials to research and development of weapons and equipment. All this, in turn, increased the size and role of the European governments prior to World War I—with the result, as William James perceptively noted, that "the intensely sharp competitive preparation for war by the nation is the real war, permanently increasing, so that the battles are only a sort of public verification of mastery gained during the 'peace' intervals."[23]

Nevertheless, the full impact of the government's strategic role in terms of national instruments of power beyond that of the military was generally not perceived in Europe, despite some of the more salient lessons of the American Civil War. In that conflict, the South lost because its strategic means did not match its strategic ends and ways. Consequently, no amount of operational finesse on the part of the South's great captains could compensate for the superior industrial strength and manpower that the North could deploy. Ultimately, this meant for the North, as Michael Howard has pointed out, "that the operational skills of their adversaries were rendered almost irrelevant."[24] The Civil War also illustrated another aspect of the changes within the strategic paradigm: the growing importance of the national will of the people in achieving political as well as military strategic objectives. That social dimension of strategy on the part of the Union was what prevented the early southern operational victories from being strategically decisive and what ultimately allowed the enormous industrial-logistical potential north of the Potomac to be realized.

The Revolutions Joined: The Age of Total Wars.

Strategy changed irrevocably with the full confluence in World War I of the trends set in train by the Industrial and French revolutions. In particular, the technology in that war provided, as Hanson Baldwin has pointed out, "a preview of the Pandora's box of evils that the linkage of science with industry in the service of war was to mean."[25] How unexpected the results of that linkage could be was illustrated by a young British subaltern's report to his commanding general after one of the first British attacks in Flanders. "Sorry sir," he concluded. "We didn't know it would be like that. We'll do better next time."[26]

But of course there was no doing better next time, not by British and French commanders in Flanders, not by Austrian troops on the Drina and Galician fronts in 1914, not by the Russian officers on the Gorlice-Tarnow line in 1915. The frustration at this turn of events was captured by Alexander Solzhenitsyn in his novel *August 1914*. "How disastrously the conditions of warfare had changed," he wrote, "making a commander as impotent as a rag doll! Where now was the battlefield . . ., across which he could gallop over to a faltering commander and summon him to his side?"[27] It was this milieu that demonstrated the inadequacy of classical strategy to deal with the intricacies of modern warfare. Napoleon had defined that strategy, as the "art of making use of time and space."[28] But the dimensions of these two variables had been stretched and rendered more complex by the interaction of technology, with the elements of the Clausewitz's trinity. And that very complexity, augmented by the lack of decisiveness it the tactical level, impeded the

Figure 4. The Continuum of War.

vertical continuum of war outlined in Clausewitz's definition of strategy as the use of engagements to achieve policy objectives. Only when the continuum was enlarged, as the Great War demonstrated, was it possible to restore warfighting coherence to modern combat. And that, in turn, required the classical concept of strategy to be positioned at a midpoint, an operational level, designed to orchestrate individual tactical engagements and battles in order to achieve strategic results (see Figure 4). Now, a military strategy level, operating within the ends-ways-means paradigm on its own horizontal plane, was added as another way station on the vertical road to the fulfillment of policy objectives. This left the concept of strategy, as it had been understood since the time of Clausewitz, transformed into:

> the level of war at which campaigns and major operations are planned, conducted, and sustained to accomplish strategic objectives. . . . Activities at this level link tactics and strategy. . . . These activities imply a broader dimension of time or space than do tactics; they provide the means by which tactical successes are exploited to achieve strategic objectives.[29]

At the same time, the full impact of technology on the Clausewitzian trinity in each of the combatant states during World War I substituted the infinitely more complex concept of national strategy for that of policy. To begin with, the growing sophistication and quantity of arms and munitions, as well as the vast demands of equipment and supply made by the armies, involved the national resources of industry, science, and agriculture—variables with which the military leaders were not prepared to deal. To cope with these variables, governments were soon forced to transform the national lives of their states in order to provide the sinews of total war.

Looking back over 50 years later on the totality of this change in what Clausewitz had termed policy, Admiral Eccles defined the concept of national strategy that emerged in World War I as "the comprehensive direction of all the elements of national power to achieve the national objectives."[30] The U.S. Department of Defense (DoD) is more explicit, defining the new level of strategy that emerged at the national level after 1914 as the "art and science of developing and using the political, economic, and psychological powers of a nation, together with its armed forces during peace and war, to secure national objectives."[31]

National strategy, then, involves all the elements of national power. Those elements, in turn, can be conveniently broken down on a horizontal plane into the categories described in the DoD definition of national strategy: political, economic, psychological, and military (see Figure 5).

The linchpin in this horizontal design is the military instrument of power at the national strategic level, the apex, as we have seen emerging in World War I, of the vertical continuum of war (see Figure 6).

Thus, the mix of ends, ways, and means at the national military strategic level will directly affect (and be affected by) the same paradigm operating at each level of the vertical continuum. Adding to the complexity is the interplay on the horizontal plane of national military strategy with the other strategies derived from the elements of national power, each operating within its own strategic paradigm and all contributing to the grand design of national strategy, as that strategy evolves within its own overall mix of ends, ways, and means. That this horizontal and vertical interplay has rendered the formulation and implementation of strategy at every level more difficult has become increasingly obvious. "Because these various elements of power cannot be precisely defined, compartmented, or divided," Admiral Eccles concluded about the "fog" of strategy, "it is normal to expect areas of ambiguity, overlap, and contention about authority among the various elements and members of any government."[32]

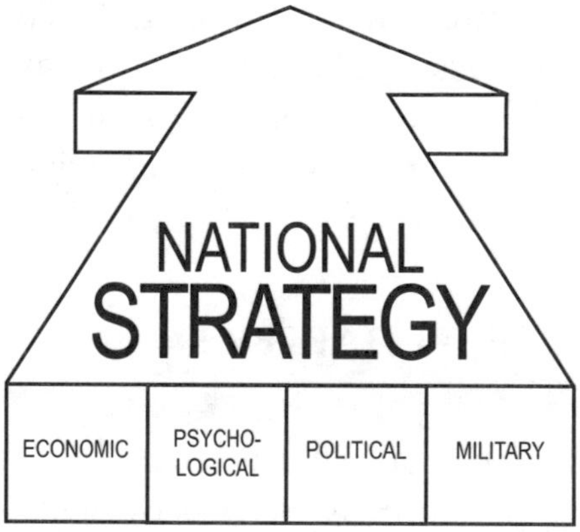

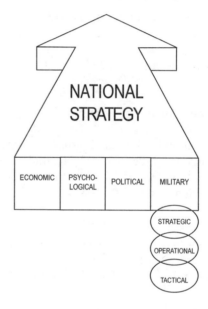

Figure 5. National Strategy: The Horizontal Plane.

Figure 6. National Strategy and the Vertical Continuum of War.

Conclusion.

The United States is in an era in which the strategic landscape has changed and is continuing to change. Nevertheless, the core problems that make strategy so difficult for a global power remain essentially the same as they did for earlier powers ranging from Rome to Great Britain. To begin with, there are challenges to U.S. interests throughout the globe. In a constantly changing strategic environment, however, it is difficult in many cases to distinguish which of those interests are vital, not to mention the nature of the challenge or threat to them. In any case, there are never enough armed forces to reduce the risk everywhere; strategic priorities have to be established.

In addition, like the leaders of earlier great powers, U.S. governmental elites have to grapple with the paradox of preparing for war even in peacetime if they wish to maintain the peace. The dilemma in the paradox that makes strategy in any era so difficult is that to overdo such preparations may weaken the economic, psychological, and political elements of power in the long run. The solution is to so balance the total ends, ways, and means that the natural tension in national security affairs between domestic and foreign policy is kept to a minimum while still securing the nation's vital interests with a minimum of risk. This solution, as the leaders of the great global powers of the past would assuredly agree, is not easy to achieve. In an ever more interdependent world in which variables for the strategist within the ends-ways-means paradigm have increased exponentially, strategists are no nearer to a "Philosopher's Stone" than they ever were. Strategy remains the most difficult of all arts.[33]

ENDNOTES - CHAPTER 1

1. Arthur F. Lykke, "Defining Military Strategy," *Military Review*, Vol. *69*, No. 5, May 1989, pp. 2-8, and his testimony before the Senate Armed Services Committee, *National Security Strategy*, hearings before the Committee on Armed Services, U.S. Senate, One Hundredth Congress, First Session, Washington, DC: U.S. Government Printing Office, 1987, pp. 140-145. See also *Sound Military Decision*, Newport, RI: Naval War College, *1942*, pp. 32, 34, 164, 165; and Henry E. Eccles, *Military Power in a Free Society*, Newport, RI: Naval War College Press, 1979, p. 73.

2. John Shy, "Jomini," pp 173-175, and Philip Crowl, "Mahan," p. 454, both in *Makers of Modern Strategy*, Peter Paret, ed., Princeton NJ: Princeton University Press, 1986. See also Stephen M. Walt, "The Search for a Science of Strategy," *International Security*, Vol. 12, No. I, Summer 1987, pp. 144145; John I. Alger, *The Quest for Victory*, Westport, CT: Greenwood Press, 1982; Admiral J. C. Wylie, *Military Strategy: A General Theory of Power Control*, Westport, CT: Greenwood Press, 1980, p. 20.

3. Wylie, *Military Strategy*, p. 10.

4. Martin van Creveld, "Eternal Clausewitz," in *Clausewitz and Modern Strategy*, Michael I. Handel, ed., London, U.K.: Frank Cass, 1986, p. 41. The formulation of strategy is the creative act of choosing a means, an end, and a way to relate a means to an end." Carl H. Builder, *The Masks of War: American Military Styles in Strategy and Analysis*, Baltimore: Johns Hopkins University Press, 1989, p. 50.

5. Original emphasis. Carl von Clausewitz, Two *Letters on Strategy*, Peter Paret and Daniel Moran, ed./trans., Carlisle, PA: U.S. Army War College, 1984, p. 9.

6. Karl von Clausewitz, *On War*, Michael Howard and Peter Paret, ed., Princeton NJ: Princeton University Press, 1976, pp. 142-143.

7. Michael Howard, *Clausewitz*, New York: Oxford University Press, 1986, p. 16; Clausewitz, *On War*, pp. 127-132.

8. Clausewitz, *On War*, p. 111. "In the highest realms of strategy . . . there is little or no difference between strategy, policy, and statesmanship." *Ibid.*, p. 178. Winston Churchill relearned these lessons in World War I. "The distinction between politics and strategy," he wrote at that time, "diminishes as the point of view is raised. At the Summit, true politics and strategy are one." Winston S. Churchill, *The World Crisis 1915*, New York: Charles Scribner's Sons, 1929, p. 6.

9. Clausewitz, *On War*, p. 179.

10. *Ibid.*, p. 605.

11. *Ibid.*, pp. 592-593.

12. *Ibid.*, p. 89.

13. *Ibid.*, pp. 609-610.

14. *Ibid.*, p. 89.

15. Michael I. Handel, *War, Strategy and Intelligence,* London, U.K.: Frank Cass, 1989, p. 63; Howard, *Clausewitz,* pp. 3-4; and van Creveld, "Eternal Clausewitz," p. 36.

16. Handel, *War,* p. 82. See also Dennis E. Showalter, "Total War for Limited Objectives: An Interpretation of German Grand Strategy," in *Grand Strategies in War and Peace,* Paul Kennedy, ed., New Haven, CT: Yale University Press, 1991, pp. 110-111.

17. Gordon A. Craig, *The Politics of the Prussian Army 1640-1945,* New York: Oxford University Press, 1956, p. 107; Michael Howard, "The Armed Forces as a Political Problem," in *Soldiers and Governments,* Michael Howard, ed., Westport, CT: Greenwood Press, 1978, p. 16.

18. Martin van Creveld, "Caesar's Ghost: Military History and the Wars of the Future," *The Washington Quarterly,* Winter 1980, p. 81. See also Michael Howard, "Men against Fire: The Doctrine of the Offensive in 1914," in *Makers of Modern Strategy,* p. 521; and Handel, *War,* pp. 21, 64-68.

19. Howard, "Armed Forces as a Political Problem," p. 17. See also Jack Snyder, "Civil Military Relations and the Cult of the Offensive, 1914-1984," *International Security,* Summer 1984, p. 109.

20. Theodore Ropp, *War in the Modern World,* New York: Collier Books, 1962, p. 229; Snyder, "Civil Military Relations," pp. 110-111, 130, 132-133.

21. The French military elite made a mirror image of their disdain for reservists in their estimates of German strength. The German General Staff made extensive use of German reservists, however, and instead of the 68 German divisions that had been expected in the implementation of French Plan XVII, there were 83. Howard, "Armed Forces as a Political Problem," p. 17. Joffre's failure to use French reservists more fully in 1914 proved to be, as Douglas Porch has pointed out, "like going to war without your trousers on." See Porch, "Arms and Alliances: French Grand Strategy and Policy in 1914 and 1940," in *Grand Strategies in War and Peace,* p. 142. See also Snyder, "Civil Military Relations," pp. 108, 133. It is true, of course, that had the French Army remained on the defensive instead of plunging into Alsace, it could have brought its full weight to bear on the German Army at the French frontier. Stephen Van Evera, "The Cult of the Offensive and the Origins of the First World War," *International Security,* Summer 1984, p. 89. It is also true, however, that the French offensive ultimately caused Moltke to weaken the right flank that was supposed to "brush the channel with its sleeve." Moreover, as Michael Howard has pointed out, the general concept behind Plan XVII—that France should take the strategic initiative rather than passively await the German offensive—did provide the flexibility that enabled General Joffre to recover rapidly from his opening reverses and redeploy his forces for the battle of the Marne. Howard, "Men against Fire," pp. 522-523.

22. Handel, *War,* pp. 60, 79. "The interchangeability between the statesman and the soldier," General Wavell stated later in summarizing these developments, passed forever . . . in the last century. The Germans professionalized the trade of war, and modern inventions, by increasing its technicalities, have specialized it." Archibald Wavell, *Generals and Generalship,* London, U.K.: Macmillan, 1941, pp. 33-34.

23. Handel, *War,* p. 58.

24. Michael Howard, "The Forgotten Dimensions of Strategy," *Foreign Affairs,* Summer 1979, p. 977. See also Gordon A. Craig, "Delbruck: The Military Historian," in *Makers of Modern Strategy,* p. 345.

25. Hanson W. Baldwin, *World War I: An Outline History,* New York: Harper & Row, 1962, p. 159.

26. Gordon A. Craig, *War, Politics and Diplomacy,* New York: Frederick A. Praeger, 1966, p. 197.

27. Alexander Solzhenitsyn, *August 1914,* New York: Bantam Books, 1974, pp. 330-331.

28. David G. Chandler, *The Campaigns of Napoleon,* New York: Macmillan, 1966, p. 161.

29. *Joint Chiefs of Staff (JCS) Publication (Pub) 1-02, Department of Defense Dictionary of Military and Associated Terms,* Washington, DC: U.S. Government Printing Office, December 1, 1989, p. 264.

30. Henry E. Eccles, *Military Power in a Free Society,* Newport, RI: Naval War College Press, 1979, p. 70.

31. *JCS Pub* 1-02, p. 244. This is what Andre Beaufre long ago termed total strategy: "the manner in which all—political, economic, diplomatic, and military—should be woven together." Andre Beaufre, *An Introduction to Strategy,* New York: Praeger, 1965, p. 30.

32. Eccles, *Military Power*, p. 70.

33. Kennedy, "Grand Strategy in War and Peace: Toward a Broader Definition," p. 7. During the Roman Republic, for example, Roman foreign policy was affected by the distrust and fear felt by the ruling patricians for the plebians of Rome on the domestic front. Barr, *Consulting the Romans*, p. 6.

CHAPTER 2

A SURVEY OF THE THEORY OF STRATEGY

J. Boone Bartholomees, Jr.

A common language is both the product of and basis of any effective theory; people conversant in the theory habitually use words in the same way to mean the same thing. Such meanings may be unique to the theoretical context even if the word has other nontheoretical usages. Thus, the word passion used in a Christian context has an entirely different meaning than in secular usage. Similarly, doctrinal military terms, while hopefully used consistently by military individuals and organizations, may differ slightly (or even radically) in common usage. "Strategy" is such a word. Defining it is not as easy as one would think, and the definition is critical.

Part of the problem is that our understanding of strategy has changed over the years. The word has a military heritage, and classic theory considered it a purely wartime military activity—how generals employed their forces to win wars. In the classic usage, strategy was military maneuvers to get to a battlefield, and tactics took over once the forces were engaged. That purely military concept has given way to a more inclusive interpretation. The result is at least threefold: 1) Strategists generally insist that their art includes not only the traditional military element of power but also other elements of power like politics and economics. Most would also accept a peacetime as well as a wartime role for strategy. 2) With increased inclusiveness the word strategy became available outside the military context and is now used in a variety of disciplines ranging from business to medicine and even sports. 3) As the concept mutated, the military had to invent another term—the U.S. settled on operations or operational art—to describe the high-level military art that had once been strategy.[1] All this, of course, effects any survey of strategy. Thus, this study acknowledges that strategy is now commonly used in nonmilitary fields, and both the definition and overall theory must be compatible with such usage. Nevertheless, this discussion focuses on the national security arena and particularly on grand strategy and military strategy. In that context, we also follow the modern interpretation that strategy involves both military and nonmilitary elements of power and has equal applicability for peace and war, although much of the existing theory we discuss deals exclusively with war.

Surprisingly for such a significant term, there is no consensus on the definition of strategy even in the national security arena. The military community has an approved definition, but it is not well known and is not accepted by nonmilitary national security professionals. As a consequence, every writer must either develop his or her own definition or pick from the numerous extant alternatives. We begin by surveying some of those alternatives.

Clausewitz wrote, "Strategy is the use of the engagement for the purpose of the war. The strategist must therefore define an aim for the entire operational side of the war that will be in accordance with its purpose. In other words, he will draft the plan of the war, and the aim will determine the series of actions intended to achieve it: he will, in fact, shape the individual campaigns and, within these, decide on the individual engagements."[2] Because this is a classic definition, it is not satisfactory—it deals only with the military element and is at the operational level rather than the strategic. What Clausewitz described is really the development of a theater or campaign strategy. Historian Jay Luvaas used to say that because Clausewitz said something did not necessarily make it true, but did make it worth considering. In this case we can consider and then ignore Clausewitz.

The 19th century Swiss soldier and theorist Antoine Henri Jomini had his own definition.

> Strategy is the art of making war upon the map, and comprehends the whole theater of war. Grand Tactics is the art of posting troops upon the battlefield according to the accidents of the ground, of bringing them into action, and the art of fighting upon the ground, in contradiction to planning upon a map. Its operations may extend over a field of 10 or 12 miles in extent. Logistics comprises the means and arrangements which work out the plans of strategy and tactics. Strategy decides where to act; logistics brings the troops to this point; grand tactics decides the manner of execution and the employment of the troops.[3]

This again is military only and theater-specific.

Civil War era soldier and author Henry Lee Scott had an interesting definition derived from the basic Jominian concept: ". . . the art of concerting a plan of campaign, combining a system of military operations determined by the end to be attained, the character of the enemy, the nature and resources of the country, and the means of attack and defence [*sic*]."[4] This actually has all the elements we look for and states them as a relationship that is more conceptually complex and satisfying than Jomini's. However, reflecting the classic paradigm Scott still limited strategy to military endeavors and to theaters.

Military historian Basil H. Liddell Hart had another unique approach to the subject. Because he wrote as the concept of strategy was expanding to include more nonmilitary aspects, his definition is more modern. Liddell Hart defined strategy as: "the art of distributing and applying military means to fulfill the ends of policy." Also "Strategy depends for success, first and most, on a sound *calculation and coordination of the ends and the means*. The end must be proportioned to the total means, and the means used in gaining each intermediate end which contributes to the ultimate must be proportioned to the value and needs of that intermediate end—whether it be to gain an object of to fulfill a contributory purpose. An excess may be as harmful as a deficiency." He was talking specifically about military strategy, and he thought strategy was something akin to but different from the more expansive concept of grand strategy.

> As tactics is an application of strategy on a lower plane, so strategy is an application on a lower plane of 'grand strategy'....While practically synonymous with the policy which guides the conduct of war, as distinct from the more fundamental policy which should govern its objective, the term 'grand strategy' serves to bring out the sense of 'policy in execution'. For the role of grand strategy—higher strategy—is to coordinate all the resources of a nation, or a band of nations, towards the attainment of the political object of the war—the goal defined by fundamental policy.

Liddell Hart went on to say,

> Grand strategy should both calculate and develop the economic resources and man-power of nations in order to sustain the fighting services. Also the moral resources—for to foster the people's willing spirit is often as important as to possess the more concrete forms of power. Grand strategy, too, should regulate the distribution of power between the services, and between the services and industry. Moreover, fighting power is but one of the instruments of grand strategy—which should take account of and apply the power of financial pressure, of diplomatic pressure, of commercial pressure, and, not the least of ethical pressure, to weaken the opponent's will....Furthermore, while the horizon of strategy is bounded by the war, grand strategy looks beyond the war to the subsequent peace. It should not only combine the various instruments, but so regulate their use as to avoid damage to the future state of peace—for its security and prosperity. The sorry state of peace, for both sides, that has followed most wars can be traced to the fact that, unlike strategy, the realm of grand strategy is for the most part *terra incognita*—still awaiting exploration, and understanding.[5]

That is very close to modern doctrine, although the use of words is different. But Liddell Hart's entire exposition was really a means to get past all this uninteresting grand strategic stuff and on to his pet theory of the indirect approach—a technique of implementation that we will consider later.

Contemporary strategist Colin Gray has a more comprehensive definition. "By strategy I mean *the use that is made of force and the threat of force for the ends of policy* [emphasis in original]."[6] The problem with that definition is that Gray ties himself down when he links the definition of strategy to force—in actuality he is mixing definitions of war and strategy.

The U.S. military has an approved joint definition of strategy: "The art and science of developing and employing instruments of national power in a synchronized and integrated fashion to achieve theater, national, and/or multinational objectives." Unfortunately, that definition only recognizes strategy as a national security function, and although it is significantly better than earlier definitions, it remains fairly broad. The explanation in the Joint Encyclopedia goes a little further: "These strategies integrate national and military objectives (ends), national policies and military concepts (ways), and national resources and military forces and supplies (means)." That is more satisfactory, although still focused exclusively on national security issues, which is understandable considering the source. However the joint definition of national military strategy shows that the joint community is divided or at least inconsistent on this subject. "National Military Strategy. The art and science of distributing and applying military power to attain national objectives in peace or war." That is a pure "how to" definition—at best a correlation of objectives with methods with the emphasis on methods. There is no consideration of or recognition of the importance of developing means; there is also no consideration of developing military objectives to accomplish national objectives. The encyclopedia's further explanation on that term goes into the formal document of the National Military Strategy rather than the concept.[7]

The U.S. Army War College defines strategy in two ways: "Conceptually, we define strategy as the relationship among ends, ways, and means." Alternatively, "Strategic art, broadly defined, is therefore: The skillful formulation, coordination, and application of ends (objectives), ways (courses of action), and means (supporting resources) to promote and defend the national interests." The second definition is really closer to a definition of grand strategic art, but if one cut it off after "means," it would be essentially the same as the first definition.[8]

In my own view, strategy is simply a problem solving process. It is a common and logical way to approach any problem—military, national security, personal, business, or any other category one might determine. Strategy asks three basic questions: what is it I want to do, what do I have or what can I reasonably get that might help me do what I want to do, and what is the best way to use what I have to do what I want to do? Thus, I agree with the War College that strategy is the considered relationship among ends, ways, and means. That sounds deceptively simple—even simplistic. Is it actually more than that relationship? Is there some deeper secret? I do not believe there is; however, the relationship is not as simple as it appears at first blush. First, a true strategy must consider all three components to be complete. For example, if one thinks about strategy as a relationship of variables (almost an equation but there is no equal sign) one can "solve" for different variables. Ends, which hopefully come from a different process and serve as the basis for strategy, will generally be given. If we assume a strategist wants to achieve those ends by specific ways, he can determine the necessary means by one of the traditional exercises of strategic art—force development. If a strategist knows both the ends to be achieved and means available, he can determine the possible ways. People, particularly military writers, often define strategy in exactly that way—as a relation between ends and means—essentially equating strategy with ways or at least converting strategy into an exercise of determining ways. That was the traditional approach of classic strategists like Jomini and Liddell Hart, who unabashedly thought of strategy as ways. That is also the typical short-term planning process that a theater commander might do. He cannot quickly change the means available, so he has to determine how to best use what is on hand to accomplish the mission.

Before we proceed, it is useful to address the issue of whether strategy is really necessary. It is certainly possible to conduct a war without a strategy. One can imagine very fierce combat divorced from any coherent (or even incoherent) plan for how that fighting would achieve the aims of the war—fighting for the sake of fighting. Alternatively, preemptive surrender is always an option for the state interested in avoiding strategic decisions; the only drawback is that preemptive surrender is incapable of achieving positive political objectives other than avoidance of conflict. Rational states, however, will always attempt to address their interests by relating ends with ways and means. Given the fact that they are fighting for some reason—that is, they have an end—there will be some (even if unconscious) design of how to use the available means to achieve it. Thus, while strategy may not technically be necessary, it is almost always present—even if poorly conceived and executed.

TESTS FOR STRATEGY

One can test a possible strategy by examining it for suitability, acceptability, and feasibility. Those three nouns test each of the three components of strategy. Suitability tests whether the proposed strategy achieves the desired end—if it does not, it is not a potential strategy. Acceptability tests ways. Does the proposed course of action or concept produce results without excessive expenditure of resources and within accepted modes of conduct? Feasibility tests means. Are the means at hand or reasonably available sufficient to execute the proposed concept? A strategy must meet or at least have a reasonable expectation of meting all three tests to be valid, but there is no upper limit on the number of possible solutions. The art becomes the analysis necessary to select the best or most efficient or least risky.

Of the three tests, suitability and feasibility are fairly straightforward and require no further explication. Acceptability, however, has some complicating features. The morality and legality of strategies is an obvious case in point—morality and legality vary widely by nation, culture, and even individual. But those are not the only complicating features of acceptability. For example, Colin Gray talks about what he calls the social dimension of strategy ". . . strategy is made and executed by the institutions of particular societies in ways that express cultural preferences."[9] That is really an expression of the relation of the acceptability of a strategy to the Clausewitzian trinity. Beyond morality and legality, a truly acceptable strategy must fit the norms of the military, government, and people. Strategies that only meet the norms of one or two of the legs are possible if they are not in major conflict with deeply held norms of the other legs, but they must be achievable very quickly to avoid possibly disastrous conflict over acceptability.

The U.S. invasion of Panama in 1989 is an example of this phenomenon. It was an invasion of a sovereign foreign nation justified by fairly innocuous (certainly not vital) political issues. That was against the norms of all three legs of the American trinity; however, the government had convinced itself that action was necessary, and the military agreed or at least obeyed orders. The potential glitch was the response of the American people. Initial reaction was the predictable support for troops being deployed in harm's way. That support could have quickly turned into opposition had the operation not been extremely rapid and relatively casualty-free.

Even though one might occasionally get away with violating norms, one cannot safely violate deeply-held norms even briefly. Thus, the United States has a norm against assassination (reinforced by a self-imposed presidential directive that adds a legal dimension). Our current mode of declaring that the people of an adversarial country are good but their leader is evil screams for a decapitation strategy executed by assassination. That will not happen. Beyond the question of legality, it would never pass the acceptability test of any of the trinitarian elements.

It is also important to note that these tests are not designed to determine if a strategy is either good or will work. The tests are for appropriateness, and they are not even conclusive in that respect. Although failure to meet the requirements of suitability, acceptability, and feasibility is often obvious, passing those same requirements is a matter both subjective, open to interpretation, and inconclusive. The best analysis may suggest that a strategy is suitable, feasible, and acceptable, but that absolutely does not guarantee success. There will always be risk and unforeseen consequences of action with which the strategist must cope. The best the tests can do is weed out inappropriate strategies.

CATEGORIZING STRATEGY

There are several ways to categorize strategies. One has a conceptual basis: strategy can be declaratory, actual, or ideal. Declaratory strategy is what a nation says its strategy is. Declaratory strategy may or may not be the nation's true strategy, and the nation may or may not actually believe it. A good example is America's Two Major Theaters of War (MTW) strategy. For years the official (declared) U.S. strategy was to be able to fight two near-simultaneous MTWs; however, most analysts and many military personnel were convinced such a strategy was impossible to execute with existing means. Regardless, the United States must maintain some form of a Two MTW strategy, despite recent modifications and adjustments, as its declared strategy even if the administration in power determines that it does not have and is unwilling to buy the resources to execute the strategy. A nation with pretensions to world power cannot easily change or back down from long-declared strategies, and a declared Two MTW capability provides useful deterrent effect. Actual strategy addresses the difference between the declared strategy and reality. It asks the question, "Assuming the United States cannot execute its declared Two MTW strategy, what is its real strategy?" That real strategy would be an actual strategy. An ideal strategy is what a strategist would prefer to do if he had unlimited access to all the necessary resources (both quantitative and qualitative). It is a textbook strategy and may or may not correspond to reality.

A second method of categorization is based on the pattern of execution: sequential, simultaneous, and cumulative. This paradigm attempts to make distinctions between strategies based on whether the strategist is attacking objectives progressively, simultaneously, or in essentially random order. Thus, a typical sequential campaign would involve actions to gain control of the air, followed by efforts to defeat the enemy's fielded forces, and culminate in the attack on or occupation of political objectives. A simultaneous campaign would include near-simultaneous attacks on each of those target sets. A cumulative strategy produces results not by any single action or sequence of actions but by the cumulative effect of numerous actions over time. A commerce raiding strategy is a classic example. The loss of a single ship is not especially significant; there is no need to sink ships in any order; while specific types of ships (like tankers) might be more valuable than others, the loss of any ship contributes directly to victory. The effectiveness of the strategy comes from cumulative losses over time. Although cumulative strategies have never taken on the luster that Admiral J. C. Wylie, the man who first recognized them as a separate category of strategy, hoped, they do allow conceptualization or categorization of strategy based on the pattern of execution.[10]

Attrition, exhaustion, and annihilation are standard strategic categories, although Joint Pub 1-02 does not mention them. The late 19th century German military historian Hans Delbrück made the distinction between exhaustion and annihilation. Attrition is sometimes used synonymously with exhaustion, but they are actually different concepts. Annihilation seeks political victory through the complete destruction (often in a single battle or short campaign) of the enemy armed forces. Attrition seeks victory through the gradual destruction (by a long campaign or series of campaigns) of the enemy's armed forces. Exhaustion seeks to erode the will and resources of the enemy nation/

state rather than the armed forces. Recently, Russell Weigley has opined that, at least in his classic book *The American Way of War*, he should have replaced attrition with erosion as a characterization of U.S. strategy. He believes the term is less confusing and actually better portrays certain aspects of American strategy. Erosion would be closer in meaning to exhaustion than attrition, except that—and this is only a tentative interpretation of Weigley's brief and incomplete explanation of the concept—it would aim more directly at the political or governmental will than at popular support or resources.[11] It is not clear how the term erosion fits into the paradigm, but it would seem to be either a new category or a sub-set of exhaustion. Regardless, Professor Weigley's modification to the traditional categories of attrition, exhaustion, and annihilation is neither widely known nor accepted.

Historian Michael Howard postulated a strategic paradigm based on deterrence, compellence, and reassurance. Military power can deter other states from doing something or it can compel them to do something. "Reassurance provides a general sense of security that is not specific to any particular threat or scenario." *Pax Britannia* is the best example. The British navy provided world-wide security through its control of the seas. That security translated into general peace.[12] Howard proposes these as the broad categories of the ways in which military force can be used. Although deterrence and compellence are widely accepted concepts, the addition of reassurance to create a general paradigm is not widely known or accepted.

Another way, as mentioned briefly above, to categorize strategy is organizational or hierarchical. That is the method that talks about grand or national strategy at one level and theater, campaign, or operational strategy at another level. The term operational strategy is one that theorist Andre Beaufré and historian Alan T. Nolan use, but it is confusing, unnecessarily mixes terms, and is uncommon at best in the literature. We will omit it from further discussions, but it does highlight one significant issue. There is a basic theoretical question about the legitimacy of strategy at the operational level—we are purposefully mixing apples and oranges for no discernable gain in clarity, utility, or comprehension. This confusion only expands as operational art edges more into the strategic realm. While I personally oppose calling theater plans strategic, current U.S. joint doctrine accepts it, and I will follow that doctrine.

Grand or national strategy is associated with actions at the state/national level. The U.S. Army War College defines it as "... a country's broadest approach to the pursuit of its national objectives in the international system."[13] Good grand strategies include or at least consider all elements of national power. These are the means of grand strategy. One could develop a lopsided grand strategy that was purely military or purely economic, but that is not ideal even if some elements contribute only minimally to the final product. This broaches the subject of elements of power—a simple but useful way to classify or categorize power.

Current U.S. military doctrine recognizes four categories of power available to a nation or strategist: diplomatic, informational, military, and economic (often referred to using the shorthand DIME). Other potential candidates include social/psychological, which was an accepted category until recently, and political. While political and diplomatic appear to be similar and are frequently used synonymously, I believe they are actually different. To me, political refers to the power generated internally or domestically while diplomatic refers exclusively to power in the international arena—the ability to influence adversaries, allies, and neutrals. Political power is important for generating or sustaining support for the policy/strategy or popular will. Regimes with little domestic support (and thus little political power) have difficulty executing their international policies. Social/psychological power was very similar to political power in some respects, but also contained elements of informational power. Since its major components were subsumed in other terms, social/psychological power fell into disuse.

In a war, the other elements of power (and the strategies developed for their employment) tend to support the military element; however, there is always a symbiotic relationship between the elements. Thus diplomatic strategy may support military strategy, but military success may be an essential precursor for diplomatic success. Similarly, economic strategy may be designed to provide military means, but the military capture or loss of economic assets may directly influence the effectiveness of the economic strategy. Additionally, different types of warfare emphasize different elements of power. For example, in a civil war, the political element becomes especially important. It is for just this reason that the Washington community dealing with the War on Terrorism (WOT) has adopted a new model to think about power. Besides the traditional DIME elements, the counterterrorist community has added intelligence, legal or law enforcement, and financial to their list of elements of power—giving the acronym MIDLIFE or DIMEFIL. Those are useful tools to consider in the WOT, although it remains to be seen if the expanded categories of national power will gain broad acceptance.

STRATEGY AND THE TYPE OF WAR

Does (or should) one's strategy necessarily change based on the type of war he is fighting? If strategy is a function of ends, then it ought to change or be different as the political ends change. The alternative view, however, is that destroying the enemy's military force is always the best (to some theorists the only legitimate) objective for the military regardless of political goals. This gets to what Clausewitz called the supreme judgment about a war—its nature. "The first, the supreme, the most far-reaching act of judgment that the statesman and commander have to make is to establish by that test the kind of war on which they are embarking; neither mistaking it for, nor trying to turn it into, something that is alien to its nature. This is the first of all strategic questions and the most comprehensive."[14] Based on the characteristics of the war, the military's objective may or may not have anything to do with destroying the enemy's military force. For example, one might have political goals that make avoiding battle at all costs, and instead maneuvering to seize specific locations, not only a viable but a desirable strategy. The strategist will only recognize this if he or she understands the kind of the war they are waging, recognizes when that changes, and adapts strategy accordingly.

The inclusion of potential changes in the nature of a war during its conduct raises another important question. If the nature of a war can change, then is not trying to shape that nature into a form that suits the strategist a legitimate strategic exercise? Is Clausewitz overlooking a useful strategic tool when he warns against trying to turn a war into something alien to its nature? Strategists should certainly try to control or influence the nature of a war as much as possible. The problem is when they do not recognize that their efforts have failed and persist in fighting the wrong kind of war. Thus, in the 1960's the U.S. might legitimately have tried to turn the Vietnam war into a conventional international war between North and South Vietnam—that was the war the U.S. military was best prepared to win. However, when that effort failed, the strategists should have recognized that fact and adapted to the true nature of the war they were fighting. Unfortunately, that did not occur until it was too late to win that war, and paradoxically, the nature of the war changed again in 1975, and the war became precisely the conventional international war the United States had initially wanted.

EXECUTING STRATEGY

Next we need to consider a few theories on potential ways to execute strategy. Knowing that strategy is a considered relation among ends, ways, and means is a necessary first step, but it does not help one actually do anything. Fortunately, hundreds of authors have given their thoughts on how to conduct strategy. Some are better than others. Most are "ways" determinations rather than comprehensive ends-ways-means analyses. Still, they are worth consideration. As a minimum a competent strategist should be aware of each.

Sun Tzu.

The ancient Chinese philosopher Sun Tzu did not define strategy, but he offered pointers on its practice. At times, Sun Tzu can be so straightforward he is simplistic. For example, the statement, "Victory is the main object of war" is not especially informative. One can make all the tortuous interpretations one likes, but the statement is blunt and obvious in its intent. That is not to say it is trivial—in fact, it is well for anyone involved with war to remember that the object is to win—it is just wrong as an absolute. The object of war is not victory, but as Liddell Hart says, "a better peace—even of only from your own point of view." One can strive so hard for victory that he destroys the subsequent peace. Liddell Hart again says, "A State which expends its strength to the point of exhaustion bankrupts its own policy, and future. If you concentrate exclusively on victory, with no thought for the after-effect, you may be too exhausted to profit by the peace, while it is almost certain that the peace will be a bad one, containing the germs of another war." Victory is certainly better than the alternative, but it cannot be the exclusive aim of war. I expound on that for two reasons. First, Sun Tzu should be treated like Jay Luvass recommended using Clausewitz—the fact that he said something only makes it worthy of consideration. Second, the fact that Sun Tzu is both an ancient and an Asian author does not automatically mean he had all the answers or even addressed all the questions. There is a tendency to read volumes into fairly straightforward passages of Sun Tzu on the assumption that there must be something of deep significance behind each phrase of the book. In many (if not most) cases, the phrases actually mean exactly what they say. Sun Tzu was not saying that war is a political act when he said, "War is a matter of vital importance to the State"—reading the rest of the quote makes it quite apparent he was simply saying war is important and must be studied.[15] That does not need tortured interpretation to be significant.

It is commonplace to acknowledge that Sun Tzu advocated deception and winning without fighting. For example, he wrote, "For to win one hundred victories in one hundred battles is not the acme of skill. To subdue the enemy without fighting is the acme of skill." Sun Tzu has become the intellectual father of a school of warfare that advocates winning by maneuver or by psychologically dislocating the opponent. Although undesirable, the ancient Chinese soldier might not be as pleased about that paternity as his advocates believe. Sun Tzu expended lots of effort explaining how to maneuver and fight. In some respects, he is very like Jomini (of all people). For example, Sun Tzu advocated attacking portions of the enemy with your whole force: "If I am able to determine the enemy's dispositions while at the same time I conceal my own then I can concentrate and he must divide. And if I concentrate while he divides, I can use my entire strength to attack a fraction of his." Sun Tzu thought that the defense was the stronger form of warfare but that offensive action was necessary for victory. "Invincibility lies in the defence [*sic*]; the possibility of victory in the attack.... One defends when his strength is inadequate; he attacks when it is abundant." He sometimes did incomplete analysis and thus provided advice that might be wrong depending on the circumstances. For example, Sun Tzu said, "To be certain to take what you attack is to attack a place the enemy does not protect." It is easy to use that quote as an advocacy for Liddell Hart's indirect approach. That is, attack where the enemy does not expect. The problem is that there is almost always a reason why the enemy does not defend a place, and it usually has to do with the limited value of that place. However, Sun Tzu was not setting up Liddell Hart. The line after the original quote changes the meaning of the entire passage: "To be certain to hold what you defend is to defend a place the enemy does not attack."[16] We now have a statement on chance and uncertainty in war—that is, the only certain way to take a place is if the enemy is not there—not advice on the indirect approach. Nevertheless, Sun Tzu is known as the advocate of deception, surprise, intelligence, and maneuver to win without fighting. He is mandatory reading for the strategist.

Clausewitz.

Clausewitz is generally more useful for his philosophical musings on the nature of war than his "how to" strategic advice. In that arena, much of what he preached was either commonplace or Nineteenth Century specific. The exceptions are three. First was his advocacy of seeking battle. This obviously sets him apart from Sun Tzu and many others, and Clausewitz is quite specific about his expectations of decisive battle. He wrote,

> . . . the importance of the victory is chiefly determined by the vigor with which the immediate pursuit is carried out. In other words, pursuit makes up the second act of the victory and in many cases is more important than the first. Strategy at this point draws near to tactics in order to receive the completed assignment from it; and its first exercise of authority is to demand that the victory should really be complete.[17]

Next, Clausewitz originated the concept of attacking what he called the enemy's center of gravity. The center of gravity comes from the characteristics of the belligerents and is "the hub of all power and movement, on which everything depends. That is the point against which all our energies should be directed."[18] He offered several possibilities but decided that attacking the enemy's army was usually the best way to start a campaign followed by seizing his capital and attacking his alliances. The concept, which the U.S. military adopted almost verbatim until the most recent doctrinal publications, has caused interminable debate both in the active force and the schoolhouses. Tactically the U.S. military has always identified and attacked vulnerabilities—now, some dead Prussian is telling us that strategically we should attack strengths (for whatever else one might believe, it is clear that a center of gravity is a strength not a weakness). We thus see attempts to mix the two concepts and essentially do both—usually described as attacking strengths through vulnerabilities.

Clausewitz's final significant "how to" idea is the concept of the culminating point. "There are strategic attacks that have led directly to peace, but these are the minority. Most of them only lead up to the point where their remaining strength is just enough to maintain a defense and wait for peace. Beyond that point the scale turns and the reaction follows with a small force that is usually much stronger than that of the original attack. This is what we mean by the culminating point of the attack."[19] Although Clausewitz only discusses culmination in terms of the attack (his later discussion of the culminating point of victory is a different concept), modern U.S. doctrine also identifies a culminating point for the defense—essentially a breaking point.

Jomini.

The Baron Antoine Jomini, a contemporary of Clausewitz with service in the French and Russian armies during the Napoleonic wars, also gave modern U.S. theory and doctrine several terms. He was much more specific in his "how to" analysis than Clausewitz. Jomini believed war was a science and consequently one could discover by careful study rules about how it should be conducted. He offered the results of his study. Jomini is often criticized for being geometric—although such a depiction overlooks some aspects of his work, it is not totally unfair. Jomini was specific about how to plan a campaign. First one selected the theater of war. Next, he determined the decisive points in the theater. Selection of bases and zones of operation followed. Then one designated the objective point. The line of operations was then the line from the base through the decisive points to the objective point. Thus, the great principle of war "which must be followed in all good combinations" was contained in four maxims:

1. To throw by strategic movements the mass of an army, successively, upon the decisive points of a theater of war, and also upon the communications of the enemy as much as possible without compromising one's own.

2. To maneuver to engage fractions of the hostile army with the bulk of one's forces.

3. On the battlefield, to throw the mass of the forces upon the decisive point, or upon that portion of the hostile line which it is of first importance to overthrow.

4. To so arrange that these masses shall not only be thrown upon the decisive point, but that they shall engage at the proper time and with energy.[20]

Jomini's maxims remain good advice if not elevated to dogma, and his terms, such as lines of operations, decisive points, etc., form the basis of much of the language of modern operational art.

Liddell Hart.

B. H. Liddell Hart had his own approach to strategy that has become famous as the indirect approach.

> Strategy has not to overcome resistance, except from nature. *Its purpose is to diminish the possibility of resistance*, and it seeks to fulfill this purpose by exploiting the elements of *movement* and *surprise*....Although strategy may aim more at exploiting movement than at exploiting surprise, or conversely, the two elements react on each other. Movement generates surprise, and surprise gives impetus to movement.[21]

> Just as the military means is only one of the means of grand strategy—one of the instruments in the surgeon's case—so battle is only one of the means to the end of strategy. If the conditions are suitable, it is usually the quickest in effect, but if the conditions are unfavorable it is folly to use it. . . . His [a military strategist's] responsibility is to seek it [a military decision] under the most advantageous circumstances in order to produce the most profitable results. Hence *his true aim is not so much to seek battle as to seek a strategic situation so advantageous that if it does not of itself produce the decision, its continuation by a battle is sure to achieve this.* In other words, dislocation is the aim of strategy."[22]

The strategist produces dislocation physically by forcing the enemy to change front or by threatening his forces or lines of communication. Dislocation is also achieved psychologically in the enemy commander's mind as a result of the physical dislocation. "In studying the physical aspect we must never lose sight of the psychological, and only when both are combined is the strategy truly an indirect approach, calculated to dislocate the opponent's balance." Although Liddell Hart would be appalled at being compared with Clausewitz, this statement is similar to the Prussian's comment, "Military activity is never directed against material force alone; it is always aimed simultaneously at the moral forces which give it life, and the two cannot be separated."[23]

Liddell Hart and his indirect approach have won a wide following among strategists. However, the issue of direct versus indirect is actually a smoke screen. The indirect approach is a tactical concept elevated to the strategic level, and it loses some of its validity in the transition. Strategically, it is sometimes (if not often) advantageous to take a direct approach. This is particularly true in cases when the contending parties have disproportionate power—that is, when one side possesses overwhelming force. In such cases, the stronger side invariably benefits from direct action. The concept of the indirect approach is also a downright silly notion when talking about simultaneous operations across the spectrum of conflict. Advocates will cry that I have missed the point. Liddell Hart seeks an indirect approach only because what he really wants is the mental dislocation it produces. I would counter that his real point was the avoidance of battle and winning without fighting. Surprise, which Liddell Hart acknowledges is how an indirect approach produces mental dislocation, is a tremendous advantage; however, designing strategies purely or even primarily to achieve surprise overlooks the rest of the equation—surprise to do what? Surprise for what purpose? If a strategist can accomplish his purpose in a direct manner, it might be more desirable than contending with the disadvantages inherent in achieving surprise. Nevertheless, the indirect approach is a recognized strategic tool that has tremendous utility if used intelligently.

Beaufré.

French general and theoretician Andre Beaufré provided another way to think about strategy. He made significant contributions to deterrence theory, especially in his skepticism of the deterrent effect of conventional forces and his advocacy of an independent French nuclear force; however, his main contribution was in the realm of general strategy. Beaufré published an influential trilogy of short books in the mid-1960's: *An Introduction to Strategy, Deterrence and Strategy,* and *Strategy of Action.*[24] He was generally Clausewitzian in his acceptance both of the political and psychological natures of war and his characterization of war as a dialectic struggle between opposing wills. He was adamant that wars are not won by military means alone (destroying the enemy army) but only by the collapse of will.

Beaufré recognized the criticality of nonmilitary elements of power—political, economic, etc. He also recognized that strategy was neither an exclusively wartime activity nor restricted to planning against an enemy—one might have strategies for relations with friends or allies as well. Beaufré is sometimes credited with expanding the concept of strategy beyond the purely military, although contemporaries were already doing that under the rubric of grand strategy—a term Beaufré disliked and replaced in his own writing with "total strategy." Total strategy defined at the highest national level how the war would be fought and coordinated the application of all the elements of power. Below total strategy was a level Beaufré called overall strategy, which allocated tasks and coordinated the activities for a single element of power (essentially national-level sub- or supporting strategies like a National Military Strategy or a National Economic Strategy). Below overall strategy was operational strategy, which corresponded fairly closely to the modern concept of operational art.[25]

All these strategic levels directed strategies that fell into "patterns" depending on the levels or resources available and the intensity of the interests at stake. The first pattern Beaufré called the direct threat; it occurred when the objective was only of moderate importance and the resources available were large. A threat of action was often sufficient to achieve the objective. If the objective was of moderate importance but resources were inadequate to back a direct threat, nations usually resorted to indirect pressure operationalized as political, diplomatic, or economic pressure. If freedom of action was restricted, resources limited, and objectives important, a third pattern resulted. That pattern was the use of successive actions employing both direct threat and indirect pressure—often with a limited use of military force. The fourth pattern was another possibility if freedom of action was great but the resources inadequate and the stakes high—"*protracted struggle, but at a low level of military activity* [emphasis in original]." If military resources were sufficient, a nation might try the fifth and final pattern: "*violent military conflict aimed a military victory* [emphasis in original]." Strategic analysis based on synthesizing both material and psychological data, rather than habit or "the fashion of the moment," should dictate the selection of the pattern and the specific strategies.[26]

According to Beaufré, there were two general principles of strategy, which he borrowed from Foch: freedom of action and economy of force. There were also two distinct but vital components to any strategy—"1. *Selection of the decisive point* to be attacked (this depends on the enemy's vulnerable points). 2. *Selection of the preparatory maneuvers* which will enable the decisive points to be reached [italics in original]."[27] Beaufré then developed a list of nineteen components of maneuver: eight offensive—attack, threat, surprise, feint, deceive, thrust, wear down, follow-up; six defensive—on guard, parry, riposte (counterattack), disengage, retire, break-off; and five related to force posture—concentrate, disperse, economize, increase, and reduce. All of these aim at gaining, retaining, or depriving the enemy of freedom of action. Retaining the initiative was vital in every case.[28]

For Beaufré, total strategy might be executed in one of two modes: direct or indirect. All elements of power played in both modes, but the direct mode emphasized the military instrument. Indirect strategy, which he carefully distinguished from Liddell Hart's indirect approach, used primarily the nonmilitary instruments to achieve political goals. Beaufré also developed a universal formula for strategy: $S=KF\psi t$. S represented strategy, K was any specific factor applicable to the case, F equated to material force, ψ represented psychological factors, and t was time. That formula is too general to be useful beyond illustrating the point that in direct strategy, F is the predominant factor while in indirect strategy ψ prevails.[29] Fortunately, that is all Beaufré really tried to do with his formula.

Another of Beaufré's major concepts was the strategy of action. This was a counterpart to deterrence. When deterring, the state wanted its opponent to refrain from doing something, while an action strategy aimed at causing someone to do something. The aim of one was negative and the other positive. Other authors at the time and since have called this coercion, and Beaufré used that term, but he thought coercion too often implied use of military force and wanted action to include a broader range of options.[30] His broader interpretation and insistence on the high nature of total strategy actually pushed his strategic theory into potential collision or overlap with policy, which Beaufré had difficulty explaining away other than the different mindset of the practitioner of each (intuitive, philosophical, and creative for policy; pragmatic, rational, and policy subordinate for strategy).[31]

Beaufré's work is not well known in the United States. His books are not in modern reprint in English (a French reprint of one came out in 1998), are difficult to locate, and are not frequently consulted. He was innovative, but his ideas were not unique. His insistence on coining new language with which to discuss familiar topics probably worked against his long-term acceptance. Much of his thought has come to modern U.S. theory from, or at least through, other sources.

Luttwak.

Edward Luttwak, an economist and historian who has written extensively on strategic theory talks about attrition and maneuver as the forms of strategy. For Luttwak, attrition is the application of superior firepower and material strength to eventually destroy the enemy's entire force unless he surrenders or retreats. The enemy is nothing more than a target array to be serviced by industrial methods. The opposite of attrition warfare is relational maneuver—"action related to the specifics of the objective". The goal of relational maneuver, instead of physically destroying the enemy as in attrition, is to incapacitate his systems. Those systems might be the enemy's command and control or his fielded forces or even his doctrine or perhaps the spatial deployment of his force, as in the penetration of a linear position. In some cases it might entail the attack of actual technical systems—Luttwak uses deception of radar rather than its destruction or jamming to illustrate the final category. [32]

Instead of seeking out the enemy's concentration of strength, since that is where the targets are to be found in bulk, the starting point of relational maneuver is the avoidance of the enemy's strengths, followed by the application of some selective superiority against presumed enemy weaknesses, physical or psychological, technical or organizational.[33]

Luttwak recognizes that neither attrition nor relational maneuver are ever employed alone—there is always some mix of the two even if one or the other is decidedly dominant. Relational maneuver is more difficult to execute than attrition, although it can produce better results more quickly. Conversely, relational maneuver can fail completely if the force applied is too weak to do the task or it encounters unexpected resistance. Relational maneuver does not usually allow "free substitution of quantity for quality." There is always a basic quality floor beneath which one cannot safely pass. Only after that floor has been exceeded will quantity substitutions be possible.[34]

Luttwak also says that strategy is paradoxical.

> The large claim I advance here is that strategy does not merely entail this or that paradoxical proposition, contradictory and yet recognized as valid, but rather that *the entire realm of strategy is pervaded by a paradoxical logic of its own*, standing against the ordinary linear logic by which we live in all other spheres of life (except for warlike games, of course).

He believes paradoxical logic pervades the five levels (technical, tactical, operational, theater strategic, and grand strategic) and two dimensions (vertical across levels and horizontal in levels) of warfare.[35]

At the most basic level, Luttwak demonstrates both the presence and the desirability of choices in war that defy peacetime logic. His base example is the choice of an approach road to an objective. The alternatives are a wide, straight, well-surfaced road and a narrow, winding, poorly-surfaced road. "Only in the conflictual realm of strategy would the choice arise at all, for it is only if combat is possible that the bad road can be good *precisely because it is bad* and may therefore be less strongly held or even left unguarded by the enemy." Thus, commanders make choices contrary to normal logic because they produce valuable advantages—advantages arising directly from the nature of war. Like Clausewitz, Luttwak believes the competitive aspect of war, that it is always a competition between active opponents, is one of the defining aspects of war. "On the contrary, the paradoxical preference for inconvenient times and directions, preparations visibly and deliberately incomplete, approaches seemly too dangerous, for combat at night and in bad weather, is a common aspect of tactical ingenuity—and for a reason that derives from the essential nature of war."[36] Commanders make paradoxical choices primarily to gain surprise and thus reduce the risk of combat.

> To have the advantage of an enemy who cannot react because he is surprised and unready, or at least who cannot react promptly and in full force, all sorts of paradoxical choices may be justified. . . . Surprise can now be recognized for what it is: not merely one factor of advantage in warfare among many others, but rather the suspension, if only briefly, if only partially, of the entire predicament of strategy, even as the struggle continues. Without a reacting enemy, or rather according to the extent and degree that surprise is achieved, the conduct of war becomes mere administration.[37]

Gaining surprise, therefore, becomes one of the key objectives of strategy. In fact, whole schools of strategy (Luttwak refers specifically to Liddell Hart's indirect approach) have been founded on the principle of surprise. The problem is that paradoxical choices—those necessary to achieve surprise—are never free or even necessarily safe because every "paradoxical choice made for the sake of surprise must have its cost, manifest in some loss of strength that would otherwise be available." The choice itself may make execution more difficult (it is harder to fight at night);

secrecy can inhibit preparations and is almost never total; deception may contain relatively cost-free elements (like false information leaked to the enemy) but as it becomes more sophisticated, complex, and convincing it soaks up resources (units conducting feints are not available at the main point of contact). At the theoretical extreme, one could expend so much force gaining surprise that insufficient combat power remained for the real fight.[38]

> Obviously the paradoxical course of "least expectation" must stop short of self-defeating extremes, but beyond that the decision is a matter of calculations neither safe nor precise. Although the loss of strength potentially available is certain, success in achieving surprise can only be hoped for; and although the cost can usually be tightly calculated, the benefit must remain a matter of speculation until the deed is done.[39]

All of this, of course, is complicated by friction, which Luttwak calls organizational risk. Also, acting paradoxically can become predictable. Thus, by 1982 in Lebanon the Israelis had established such a reputation for paradoxical action that they were unable to achieve surprise until they broke their established paradigm and conducted the obvious frontal attack down the Bekka Valley. Luttwak recognizes that some situations call for straightforward, logical solutions. "If the enemy is so weakened that his forces are best treated as a passive array of targets that might as well be inanimate, the normal linear logic of industrial production, with all the derived criteria of productive efficiency, is fully valid, and the paradoxical logic of strategy is irrelevant."[40]

While he has some interesting and valid points, especially in the details, Luttwak's insistence on the paradoxical nature of war is too broad a generalization. There is much that is paradoxical in warfare; however, if war were completely paradoxical as Luttwak asserts (his exceptions are too trivial to be significant), war would not yield to study. In fact, much of warfare—including its paradox—is very logical. In a sense, Luttwak's argument proves that proposition and refutes itself.

Van Creveld.

Martin Van Creveld's The *Transformation of War* is, according at least to the cover, "The most radical reinterpretation of armed conflict since Clausewitz." He represents a segment of modern scholars that believe Clausewitz no longer explains why, how, or by whom wars are fought. To Van Creveld, war is no longer a rational political act conducted among states—if it ever was. He points out that warfare waged by nonstate actors dominated conflict in 1991 rather than the organized, political, inter-state warfare between great powers that the international community seemed to expect (and Clausewitz seemed to predict). War is no longer fought by the entities we always assumed fought wars. The combatants in modern wars no longer fight for the reasons we always believed. Finally, they do not fight in the manner we always accepted as standard.[41]

Modern war takes many forms—the Clausewitzian trinitarian form of war being one of, but by no means the dominant one of, them. For Van Creveld, Clausewitz does not apply in any case that does not involve exclusively state-on-state warfare. Since he sees a resurgence of "Low-Intensity Conflict," he believes war will be dominated by nonstate actors. "We are entering an era, not of peaceful economic competition between trading blocks, but of warfare between ethnic and religious groups." Currently fielded military forces are irrelevant to the tasks they will likely face. Should the states in question fail to recognize the changed reality, they will first become incapable of wielding appropriate force at all and eventually cease to exist as recognizable states.[42]

The nature of the participants dictates the nature of the reasons they fight. Because the participants are not states, they will not be fighting for state-like reasons. This follows logically from Van Creveld's assertion that politics applies only to states—not a more broadly defined interest in a more broadly defined community. Nonstate actors fight wars for abstract concepts like justice or religion. Frequently, groups feel their existence is threatened and lash out violently in response. In any case, reasons are highly individualistic and do not yield easily to analysis—especially analysis based on the inappropriate model of the Clausewitzian universe.[43]

Finally, Van Creveld believes that Clausewitz did not understand how wars are fought—at least his assertion that they would tend naturally toward totality is wrong. He cites international law and convention, among other factors, as major inhibitors on the drift toward totality in state-on-state war. More significant is his critique of strategy. Like Luttwak, Van Creveld sees strategy as paradoxical. He believes pairs of paradoxes define strategy. If the object of war is to beat our opponent's force with our own, then we must design maneuvers to pit strength against weakness. Because war is competitive, our enemy is doing the same thing, and we must conceal or protect our weakness from the opponent's strength. Thus, the essence of strategy is "...the ability to feint, deceive, and mislead." Eventually one can work so hard on concealing that he and his side may be deceived—where the distinction between feint and main effort is unclear. Van Creveld also discusses the paradox in time and space using the same argument as Luttwak that the shortest distance between two points may not be the straight line. Other paradoxes include that between concentration and dispersion (concentration is necessary to apply power, but concentration increases the chance of discovery) and between effectiveness and efficiency (the more economical, streamlined, or efficient a military organization becomes, the more vulnerable it is).[44]

Perhaps uniquely in the field of strategic theory, Martin Van Creveld has provided a critique of his own thesis. In a chapter of a book published in 2003, Van Creveld finds, not surprisingly, that on balance his earlier work, written in 1988-1989, holds up very well. The Gulf War was an aberration—the outcome of which was almost preordained. Otherwise, ". . . the main thesis of *The Transformation of War*, namely that major armed conflict between major powers is on the way out, seems to have been borne out during the ten years since the book's publication." Conversely, nontrinitarian wars are on the rise and conventional forces do not seem able to bring them to satisfactory closure. ". . . [T]he prediction that history is witnessing a major shift from trinitarian to nontrinitarian war seems to have fulfilled itself and is still fulfilling itself on an almost daily basis." He believes information warfare might be a wild card that could disrupt his predictions; however, on balance he sees information as advantageous to (or at least an equalizing factor for) nonstate actors, and hence a confirmation of the trend toward nontrinitarianism. Thus, Van Creveld sticks with his criticism of Clausewitz and essentially every element of his original thesis.[45]

MISCELLANEOUS ALTERNATIVES

There are also whole categories we can only classify as miscellaneous, alternative, possibly-strategic concepts.

Denial, Punishment, and Coercion.

These are proposed replacements for attrition, exhaustion, and annihilation. They actually describe the ends of strategy (or perhaps a limited set of ways) rather than a complete strategic concept. Their utility is limited and their acceptance as a group by the strategic community is minimal at best. Coercion, of course, is a recognized strategic concept on its own; it is just not commonly grouped with denial and punishment as a paradigm.

Jones. Historian Archer Jones has a unique approach to strategy:

> The object for military strategy used herein is the depletion of the military force of an adversary. The definition

of political-military strategy, a companion term, is the use of military force to attain political or related objectives directly, rather than by depleting an adversary's military force. Of course, military strategy usually endeavored to implement political or comparable objectives but sought to attain them indirectly, by depleting the hostile military force sufficiently to gain an ascendancy adequate to attain the war's political goals.[46]

Jones does not use attrition because of its association with a particular form of military strategy. Instead, he asserts that military force can achieve its objective of depleting the enemy through one of two methods. Combat strategies deplete the enemy by directly destroying his force in the field. Logistic strategies deprive the opponent of supplies, forces, weapons, recruits, or other resources. Either of these strategies can be executed in one of two ways. One can use "a transitory presence in hostile territory to make a destructive incursion," which Jones labels a raiding strategy, or one can conquer and permanently occupy significant segments of enemy territory, which he calls a persisting strategy. The two pairs—combat and logistics and raiding and persisting—define comprehensive strategy.[47]

Jones then puts the factors into a matrix and uses them for all kinds of warfare—air, land, and sea. Air war, however, can really only be raiding because of the nature of the medium. This is a military only, ways only approach to strategy that works best as Jones applies it—in retrospect to analyze historical campaigns. The separation of a purely political strategy from military strategy based on whether or not the aim is depleting the enemy force is awkward to say the least. Jones has an interesting concept of "political attrition." This means that victory in battle raises morale and engenders optimism about winning in a reasonable time with acceptable casualties. Conversely, defeat in battle makes victory look less certain, farther away in time, and attainable only at high cost. He does not think that political attrition necessarily works in reverse—that is, you cannot store up good will during good times to tide you over during the bad times. (Although presumably you would start the bad times at a higher overall level of morale.) Elsewhere, Jones compares popular will to win with the classic economic supply and demand theory of elastic and inelastic demand.[48] That is a much less satisfying explanation. While perhaps of little use to practical strategists, Archer Jones' concepts are creative and not completely without merit. His ideas show up with increasing frequency in historical works.

Decapitation.

An attractive recent concept is a strategy we might characterize as decapitation where one targets specifically and selectively the enemy leader or at least a fairly limited set of upper-echelon leaders. This has most recently found expression in the expressed strategic objective of regime change, which tends to automatically focus on the enemy regime leadership regardless of the potential scope of the mission. Strategic treatises like the Quadrennial Defense Review and the National Defense Strategy that use regime change as an evaluative factor, hint at a widening acceptance of the concept. A primary assumption, generally implied or asserted without proof, is that the current leader (perhaps aided by a small group of accomplices) is the whole cause of the international dispute. A corollary assumption is that eliminating the current evil leadership will result in its replacement by a regime willing to grant the concessions demanded by the opposing state or coalition.

There are several problems with this approach—most related to the validity of the assumptions. First, the assumption that the common people of a country are good and could not possibly support the policies of their evil ruler is (as a minimum) unproven in most cases and palpably false in many. Thus, decapitation will not solve the problem. In Clausewitzian terms, taking out the government does not automatically destroy or break the will of either the people or the military. Second, a potential follow-on regime can be either better than, about the same as, or worse than the current leadership. Hence, the odds of achieving one's policy objectives by decapitation are actually fairly poor. The U.S. experience in Iraq after successfully removing Saddam Hussein's regime demonstrates these caveats. The old saw about contending with the devil one knows may be worn, but that does not make it any less worthwhile advice; and while decapitation may work, it is neither easy nor a panacea.

Boyd. U.S. Air Force Colonel John R. Boyd talks about the "OODA loop"—that is the decision cycle of observation, orientation, decision, and action. The concept is derived from a fighter pilot in a dogfight. Like the pilot, a strategist wins by out-thinking and out-maneuvering his opponent; by the time the opponent decides what to do and initiates action it is too late since you have already anticipated and countered his move or made a countermove that makes his action meaningless. One accomplishes this by possessing sufficient agility to be able, both mentally and physically, to act a step or more ahead of the enemy. Thus, the successful strategist always works inside his enemy's decision cycle.[49] This theory describes a way, and really is a new and unnecessarily complicated rephrasing of the ancient concept of the initiative. Initiative is not critical or essential, and alone it is not decisive. Robert E. Lee had tactical, operational, and even strategic initiative at Gettysburg and lost tactically, operationally, and strategically. However, initiative is a tremendous advantage—if Boyd's paradigm makes it more clear or obvious to the strategist, it has provided a service. The caution is that one can think and act so swiftly and outpace the enemy so dramatically as to actually create friendly vulnerability. The OODA loop concept predicts that the enemy will not be able to react effectively to an action; however, it does not postulate enemy paralysis and complete immobility. One can envision circumstances where a confused enemy reacting to information or situations hours or days behind its opponent makes a devastatingly successful move that its opponent has long since discounted or thought negated.

Warden. Another U.S. Air Force Colonel, John A. Warden III, translated his targeteering experience into a strategic theory, thus elevating the tactical process of allocating aircraft sorties to specific targets to a strategic theory. Warden views the enemy as a system of targets arrayed in five strategic rings; the innermost and most important is leadership. One can win by striking that inner ring so frequently and violently that the enemy is essentially paralyzed and never able to mount an effective defense. It is unnecessary to take on the outer and much more difficult target rings like the enemy's armed forces, although modern advances like stealth technology make simultaneous attack of the entire target array possible (instead of the traditional sequential attacks where one array had to be neutralized before proceeding to the next).[50] This is often considered an air power theory—and Warden used it to push the decisiveness of air power—but the conceptual approach has broader application. Its major drawback as a general theory of strategy is that it works best (if not exclusively) when one side has or can quickly gain total dominance of its opponent's airspace.

UNDERDOG STRATEGIES

There are also a number of alternative strategies that seem to be intended specifically for, or at least be most appropriate for, weaker powers or underdogs:

Fabian. Quintus Fabius Maximus Verrucosus was a Roman general during the Second Punic War. He advocated avoiding open battle because he was convinced the Romans would lose, which they proceed to do when they abandoned his strategy. Thus, Fabian strategy is a strategy in which one side intentionally avoids large-scale battle for fear of the outcome. Victory depends on wearing down (attriting) one's opponent over time—usually by an unrelenting campaign of skirmishes between detachments. Somewhat akin to a Fabian strategy is a strategy of survival. In that case, however, the weaker power does not necessarily avoid battle. Instead, one reacts to his opponent's moves rather than making an effort to seize the initiative. The object is to survive rather than to win in the classic sense—hopefully, sheer survival achieves (or perhaps comprises) one's political aim. This is a favorite alternative strategy of modern critics for the Confederate States of America. Scorched earth strategies are another variant of the basic Fabian strategy. The concept is to withdraw slowly before an enemy while devastating the countryside over which he must advance so he cannot subsist his force on your terrain. Attrition will eventually halt the attack—it will reach what Clausewitz called a culminating point—and the retreating side can safely assume the offensive. This is actually the addition of a tactical technique to the basic Fabian strategy and not a major new school of strategy.

There is a whole subset of doctrine under the general heading of strategies for the weak that advocates guerrilla warfare, insurgency, and/or terrorism:

Lawrence. T. E. (Thomas Edward) Lawrence was the first of the theorist of insurgency or revolutionary warfare. His Seven Pillars of Wisdom, originally published in 1926, recounted his experiences with Arab insurgent forces fighting the Turks in World War I.[51] The title—a reference to Proverbs that Lawrence carried over from an earlier incomplete book about seven Arab cities—is misleading since Lawrence did not have seven theoretical pillars of guerrilla war. Lawrence's narrative explained the war in the desert by clearly defining the objective, carefully analyzing the Arab and Turkish forces, describing the execution of raids to maintain the initiative, and emphasizing the importance of intelligence, psychological warfare, and propaganda. The objective of the guerrilla was not the traditional objective of conventional forces—decisive battle. In fact, the guerrilla sought exactly the opposite—the longest possible defense.[52] Lawrence believed that successful guerrillas needed safe bases and support of at least some of the populace—perhaps as little as 20 percent, although an insurgency might be successful with as little as two percent of the population in active support as long as the other 98 percent remained at least neutral. A technologically sophisticated enemy (so the guerrilla could attack his lines of communications) that was not strong enough to occupy the entire country was also advantageous. Tactically, the guerrilla relied on speed, endurance, logistic independence, and at least a minimal amount of weaponry. Lawrence compared guerrillas to a gas operating around a fixed enemy and talked about them as raiders versus regulars. Their operations were always offensive and conducted in precise fashion by the smallest possible forces. The news media was their friend and tool. Lawrence thought the Arabs were ideally suited for such warfare, and that "granted mobility, security, time, and doctrine" the guerrillas would win.[53] His theory got entangled in his flamboyant personality, so although he was a society darling, he had less impact on military circles.[54]

Mao. Mao Zedong developed the most famous and influential theory of insurgency warfare. His concepts, designed initially for the Chinese fight against the Japanese in World War II, have been expanded and adapted by himself and others to become a general theory of revolutionary warfare. Mao emphasizes the political nature of war and the reliance of the army on the civilian population, especially the Chinese peasant population. He advocated a protracted war against the Japanese; victory would come in time through attrition. He believed the Chinese should avoid large battles except in the rare instances when they had the advantage. Guerrillas should normally operate dispersed across the countryside and concentrate only to attack. Because the Chinese had a regular army contending with the Japanese, Mao had to pay particular attention to how guerrilla and regular operations complemented each other. He postulated a progressive campaign that would move slowly and deliberately from a stage when the Chinese were on the strategic defensive through a period of strategic stalemate to the final stage when Chinese forces assumed the strategic offensive. The ratio of forces and their tactical activities in each stage reflected the strategic realities of the environment. Thus, guerrilla forces and tactics dominated the phase of the strategic defensive. During the strategic stalemate mobile and guerrilla warfare would compliment each other, and guerrilla and regular forces would reach approximate equilibrium (largely by guerrilla forces combining and training into progressively larger regular units). Mobile warfare conducted by regular units would dominate the period of strategic offensive. Although guerrilla units would never completely disappear, the regular forces would achieve the final victory.[55] Mao has had an enormous impact on the field of revolutionary warfare theory.

Guevara. Ernesto "Che" Guevara de la Serna based his theory of revolutionary warfare on the Cuban model. He offered a definition of strategy that highlighted his variation of the basic guerrilla theme—especially his divergence from the Maoist emphasis on the political nature of the conflict and reliance on the people. Che wrote, "In guerrilla terminology, strategy means the analysis of the objectives we wish to attain. First, determine how the enemy will operate, his manpower, mobility, popular support, weapons, and leadership, Then, plan a strategy to best confront these factors, always keeping in mind that the final objective is to destroy the enemy army." To Che the major lessons of the Cuban Revolution were that guerrillas could defeat regular armies; that it was unnecessary to wait for all the political preconditions to be met before beginning the fight—the insurrection itself would produce them; and that the countryside was the arena for conflict in underdeveloped Latin America. Gradual progress through the Maoist stages of revolution was unnecessary—the guerrilla effort could not only establish the political preconditions of revolution but also win the war on its own. Parties, doctrine, theories, and even political causes were unimportant. The armed insurgency would eventually produce them all.[56] That was incredibly naive and even dangerous as an insurgent strategic concept, but Che became very well-known—if unsuccessful—pursuing it.

Terrorism.

Although there is no outstanding single theorist of terrorism, it is not a new strategic concept. Often used as a tactical part or preliminary stage of a larger campaign or insurgency, terrorism can if fact be a strategy, and sometimes even a goal in itself. Many ideological terrorists—perhaps the best examples are ecological terrorists—have no desire or intent to progress militarily beyond terrorism. Although political, most are not interested in overthrowing a government or seizing control of conventional political power. They simply want their espoused policies, ideologies, or political agendas adopted. Alternatively, anarchists, who traditionally have used terror, just want to destroy government without replacing it. They have no positive goal whatever.

The theory behind terrorism is fairly straightforward. A weak, usually non-governmental actor uses violence, either random or carefully targeted and often directed against civilian targets, to produce terror. The aim is to make life so uncertain and miserable that the state against which the terror is directed concedes whatever political, social, economic, environmental, or theological point the terrorist pursues. The technique has not proven particularly effective as a stand-alone strategy in changing important policies in even marginally effective states. It is, however, comparatively cheap, easy to conceptualize and execute, requires minimal training, is relatively safe since competent terrorist groups are extremely difficult to eradicate, and is demonstrably effective in gaining the terrorist publicity for himself and his cause.

COUNTERUNDERDOG STRATEGIES

If there are strategies for the weak, the strong are sure to develop counterstrategies. Opponents generally fight a Fabian strategy by trying to exert enough pressure or threaten some critical location or capability to bring about the battle the Fabian strategist is trying to avoid. There is (and needs to be) no body of theoretical work on countering Fabian strategies. The same, however, cannot be said of countering insurgencies and terrorism.

Formal modern counterinsurgency theory developed as a result of the insurgencies that sprang up after World War II in the decolonizing world. It tended to be symmetric in the sense that it analyzed insurgencies and then attempted to beat them at their own game and in their chosen arena. Modern counterinsurgency theory tends to recognize the political nature of most insurgencies and approach them holistically rather than from a primarily military point of view. That is a fairly big break with traditional counterinsurgency techniques that concentrated on locating and destroying the guerrillas and often relied heavily on punishing the local population for guerrilla activity as the sole means of separating the guerrilla from his base of support. Discussion of some representative modern counterinsurgency theorists follows.

Caldwell.

British Colonel Charles E. Caldwell wrote *Small Wars — Their Principles and Practice* at the end of the 19th century. This was a guide for the conduct of colonial wars. Caldwell distinguished three broad categories of small wars, which he defined as any war in which one side was not a regular army. His categories were: campaigns of conquest or annexation; campaigns to suppress insurgents; and campaigns to punish or overthrow dangerous enemies. Each was fundamentally different from any form of regular warfare. Small wars could take almost any shape—the most dangerous of which was guerrilla warfare. Caldwell gave sound tactical advice about fighting a colonial or guerrilla enemy, but from a theoretical or strategic point of view is of limited value. He recognized that colonial enemies could be skilled and dedicated warriors and recommended treating them as such—a refreshing change from standard colonial views. However, Caldwell thought the small wars experience was both exclusively military and unique to the colonies. He thus both did not develop the multi-disciplinary approach common to modern counterinsurgency strategy and did not recommend translating the colonial military lessons into lessons for the big wars of the European colonial powers. He thought the strategic aim of counterinsurgency was to fight because the counterinsurgents had the tactical advantage but were at a strategic disadvantage. Caldwell, while still touted today and worth a look for his tactical precepts, was a theoretical dead end for the strategist.[57]

Trinquier.

Roger Trinquier published *Modern Warfare: A French View of Counterinsurgency* in 1961. Trinquier served with the French paras in Indochina and Algeria. Those experiences shaped his views, and his theory heavily reflects French counterinsurgency practice in the 1950's. Trinquier argued that nuclear weapons were decreasing the significance of major traditional wars and replacing them with guerrilla war, insurgency, terrorism, and subversion. He approached the study of counterinsurgency by examining how the goals and techniques of insurgents differed from traditional warfare. His conclusion was that traditional methods and organizations would not work in counterinsurgencies. Trinquier's concept of modern warfare sought to destroy the insurgent organization as a whole, not simply its military arm. For him the central tenet of counterinsurgency was winning the support of the people. He advocated an interlocking system of political, economic, psychological, and military actions to undermine the insurgents' strategies.

Trinquier suggested three principles: separate the guerrilla from the population, occupy the zones the guerrilla previously used to deny him reentry, and coordinate actions over a wide enough area and long enough time to deny the guerrilla access to the population. Following the successful technique of quadrillage used by the French in Algeria, Trinquier advocated a gridding system to divide up the country administratively and to facilitate sweeping and controlling the nation sequentially. He was also a strong advocate of eliminating safe havens both inside and outside the national borders.[58] Trinquier's basic approach is found in all modern counterinsurgency theory.

Galula.

David Galula wrote *Counterinsurgency Warfare: Theory and Practice* in 1964. He postulated a simple construct for counterinsurgencies that emphasized the political nature of the conflict, especially the relationship between the insurgent and his cause. His definition of "[i]nsurgency is the pursuit of the policy of a party, inside a country, by every means" was designed to emphasize that insurgencies could start before the use of force. Insurgencies are by their nature asymmetric because of the disparity of resources between the contenders. The counterinsurgent has all the tangible assets — military, police, finance, court systems, etc., while the insurgent's advantages are intangible — the ideological power of his cause. Insurgents base their strategies on powerful ideologies, while the counterinsurgent has to maintain order without undermining the government. The rules applicable to one side do not always fit the other. The logic of this asymmetric power relationship forced the insurgent to avoid military confrontation and instead move the contest to a new arena where his ideological power was effective — the population became the seat of war. Politics becomes the instrument of war rather than force, and that remains true throughout the war. Politics takes longer to produce effects, so all insurgencies are protracted.[59]

The counterinsurgent warrior must begin by understanding the political-social-economic cause of his opponent. Large parts of the population must be able to identify with that cause. The cause must be unique in the sense that the counterinsurgent cannot co-opt it. The cause can change over time as the insurgency adapts. The power of the cause increases as the guerrilla gains strength and has success. Good causes attract large numbers of supporters and repel the minimum number of neutrals. An artificial or concocted cause makes the guerrilla work harder to sell his position, but an efficient propaganda machine can do that.[60]

Galula discussed several approaches to immunizing the population against the insurgent cause or message. Counterinsurgents must: continuously reassess the nature and scope of the problem with which they deal; address problems proactively; isolate the battlefield from external support; and work to increase support for the regime. They must be vigilant — do not interpret a strategic pause by the insurgents as victory. Intelligence is critical. The counterinsurgent organization must have the authority to direct political, social, economic, and military efforts. The military cannot have a free hand — it must work within and be subordinate to the overall political campaign. Like Trinquier, Galula recommended a systematic division of the country and sequential search, clear, and hold operations. Counterinsurgent propaganda should focus on gaining and maintaining the neutrality of the population.[61] Galula is having a major influence on the development (or rediscovery) of U.S. Counterinsurgency theory in 2006.

Kitson.

Frank Kitson wrote *Low Intensity Operations: Subversion, Insurgency, and Peacekeeping* in 1971. He added details to the basic structure of counterinsurgency theory already constructed by the French. Like the other theorists Kitson recognized that counterinsurgency is a multi-discipline job. He warned against abuses, but recommended that heavy force be used early to squash an insurgency while still in a manageable state. The military campaign must be coordinated with good psychological operations. Kitson conceptualized two kinds of intelligence — political and operational.

Political intelligence is an ongoing process while operational intelligence supports specific military operations. The military must be involved in the intelligence gathering process (political as well as operational). Counterinsurgency forces must be attuned to the environment, able to optimize resources by phases of the campaign, and able to coordinate all the resources at their disposal.[62]

STRATEGIC ADVICE

There are also numerous advice books that give leaders and decisionmakers more or less specific advice about what to do or how to do it without necessarily offering a comprehensive strategic or theoretical paradigm. Examples include Niccolo Machiavelli's *The Art of War, The Discourses*, and *The Prince* written to influence Sixteenth Century Florentine leaders and Frederick the Great's *Instructions for His Generals*, the title of which explains its intent. Alternatively, there are collections— like *The Military Maxims of Napoleon* — of military advice culled from the writings of great soldiers. As historian David Chandler noted in his introduction to a recent reprint of that work, "The practical value of military maxims can be debatable. . . . Consequently the collecting of his [Napoleon's] *obiter dicta* into any kind of military rule-book for future generations to apply is a process fraught with perils and pitfalls." In a more modern vein, *QDR 2001: Strategy-Driven Choices for America's Security* (Michele A. Flournoy, ed.) is essentially an advice book that presents a specific strategic solution without developing an overarching strategic theory.[63] Advice books are often beneficial; however, their generally narrow focus and frequent bumper sticker quality limit that utility.

Deterrence.

During the Cold War the nuclear weapons field developed its own set of specific strategies based on deterrence theory. Deterrence theory itself is a useful strategic concept. Conversely, concepts like mutual assured destruction, counterforce or countervalue targeting, launch on warning, and first strike versus retaliation are terms of nuclear art that will retain some relevance as long as major nations maintain large nuclear stockpiles, but they no longer dominate the strategic debate as they once did. According to the Department of Defense, deterrence is "the prevention from action by fear of the consequences."[64] It is altogether different from compellence where one is attempting to make another party do something. Theoretically, one party can deter another either by threat of punishment or by denial. Threat of punishment implies performing an act will evoke a response so undesirable that the actor decides against acting. Deterrence by denial seeks to avert an action by convincing the actor that he cannot achieve his purpose. In either case deterrence theory assumes rational decision makers with similar value systems. To be deterred, one must be convinced that his adversary possesses both the capability to punish or deny and the will to use that capability. Demonstrating the effectiveness of deterrence is difficult, since it involves proving the absence of something resulted from a specific cause; however, politicians and strategists generally agree that nuclear deterrence worked during the Cold War. It is not as clear that conventional deterrence works, although that concept has numerous advocates and is deeply embedded in modern joint doctrine.

Deterrence theory had many fathers, but some of the most prominent deserve mention. Albert Wohlstetter established his credentials when he wrote *The Delicate Balance of Terror* for RAND in 1958. Bernard Brodie wrote, among other things, *Strategy in the Missile Age* in 1959. Herman Kahn's *On Thermonuclear War* was ground breaking in 1960. Thomas C. Schelling published *The Strategy of Conflict* in 1960 and *Arms and Influence* 6 years later; both remain classics.[65]

SEAPOWER

Mahan.

There are also schools of single service strategies devoted to sea power or airpower. In the sea power arena the most famous strategic theorists are Alfred Thayer Mahan and Julian S. Corbett. American naval officer Mahan wrote several books and articles around the turn of the 20th century advocating sea power. Perhaps the most famous was *The Influence of Sea Power Upon History 1660-1783*. Mahan developed a set of criteria that he believed facilitated sea power, but his major contribution was in the realm of the exercise of that capability through what he called command of the sea. His study of history convinced Mahan that the powerful maritime nations had dominated history, and specifically that England had parlayed its command of the sea into world dominance. At the grand strategic level, Mahan believed that countries with the proper prerequisites should pursue sea power (and especially naval power) as the key to prosperity.

To Mahan oceans were highways of commerce. Navies existed to protect friendly commerce and interrupt that of their enemies. The way to do both was to gain command of the sea.[66] For Mahan the essence of naval strategy was to mass one's navy, seek out the enemy navy, and destroy it in a decisive naval battle. With the enemy's navy at the bottom of the ocean—that is, with command of the sea—your merchantmen were free to sail where they pleased while the enemy's merchantmen were either confined to port or subject to capture. Diversion of naval power to subsidiary tasks like commerce raiding (a favorite U.S. naval strategy in the early years of the republic) was a waste of resources, although in his later writing Mahan acknowledged some contribution from such tactics. The key to Mahanian naval warfare was thus the concentrated fleet of major combatants that would fight for and hopefully win command of the sea. Ideally, that fleet would have global reach, which required secure bases for refueling conveniently located worldwide. Although Mahan's theories actively supported his political agenda of navalism and imperialism, they contained enough pure and original thought to survive both the author and his age.

Corbett.

British author Julian S. Corbett had a different interpretation of naval warfare. A contemporary of Mahan, Corbett saw British success not so much as a result of dominance of the sea as from its ability to effectively wield what we call today all the elements of national power. Corbett differentiated between maritime power and strategy and naval power and strategy. Maritime strategy encompassed all the aspects of sea power—military, commercial, political, etc. Naval strategy dealt specifically with the actions and maneuvers of the fleet. Like Mahan, Corbett saw oceans as highways of commerce and understood their importance. However, he emphasized not the uniqueness of sea power but its relationship with other elements of power. For Corbett, the importance of navies was not their ability to gain command of the sea but their ability to affect events on land. He believed that navies rarely won wars on their own—they often made it possible for armies to do so. The navy's role was thus to protect the homeland while isolating and facilitating the insertion of ground forces into the overseas objective area. Neither command of the sea nor decisive naval battle were necessarily required to accomplish either of those tasks. Although Corbett admitted that winning the decisive naval clash remained the supreme function of a fleet, he believed there were times when that was neither necessary nor desirable.[67] His theories most closely approximate current U.S. naval doctrine.

Jeune Ecolé.

Another school of sea power was the Jeune Ecolé that was popular on the continent in the early 1880's. Its primary advocate was Admiral Théophile Aube of the French Navy. Unlike the theories of either Mahan or Corbett, which were intended for major naval powers, the Jeune Ecolé was a classic small navy strategy. It was a way for land powers to fight sea powers. Advocates claimed that a nation did not have to command the sea to use it. In fact, modern technology made gaining command of the sea impossible. And one certainly did not have to have a large fleet of capital ships or win a big fleet battle. Rather than capital ships, one could rely on torpedo boats and cruisers (later versions would emphasize submarines). The naval strategist could either use those smaller vessels against the enemy's fleet in specific situations like countering an amphibious invasion, or more commonly against his commerce (to deny him the value of commanding the sea). Either use could be decisive without the expense of building and maintaining a large fleet or the dangers inherent in a major naval battle.[68] The Jeune Ecolé was an asymmetric naval strategy. It had a brief spurt of popularity and faded. Its advocates probably chuckled knowingly during World Wars I and II as submarines executed their pet theory without the benefit of a name other than unrestricted submarine warfare. It is still available as an asymmetric approach to war at sea.

AIRPOWER

Douhet.

The basis of classic airpower theory—although paternity is debatable—is *The Command of the Air* published first in 1921 by Italian general and author Giulio Douhet. Reacting to the horrors he saw in the First World War, Douhet became an advocate of airpower. He believed that the airplane could restore decisiveness to warfare that ground combat seemed incapable of achieving. It could fly over the ground battlefield to directly attack the enemy's will. Because of technical problems with detection and interception, stopping an air raid would be impossible. Big bombers carrying a mix of high explosive, incendiary, and poison gas weapons could target enemy cities. Civilian populations, which were the key to modern warfare, would be unable to stand such bombardment and would soon force their governments to surrender. Although civilian casualties might be high, this would be a more humane method of warfare than prolonged ground combat.

There were a few strategic dicta beyond that. First, a prerequisite for success was command of the air—a theory closely related to command of the sea. Command of the air granted one side the ability to fly where and when it desired while the enemy was unable to fly. Next, because the airplane was an offensive weapon, one gained command of the air by strategic bombardment—ideally catching the enemy's air force on the ground. Recognizing the technological limitations of his day, Douhet believed there was no need for anti-aircraft artillery or interceptors since neither worked effectively. In fact, resources devoted to air defense or any type of auxiliary aircraft (anything that was not a large bomber) were wasted. The resource argument also featured shifting funding from the traditional land and sea services to the air service—a position not designed to win friends in the wider defense community. Like other airmen, Douhet believed that airplanes were best employed in an independent air force.[69]

Douhet captured the imagination of early airmen with his vision of decisiveness through command of the air. Generations of later airpower enthusiasts continue to seek to fulfill his prophecy. Nuclear weapons were supposed to have fixed the technological shortfalls that prevented airpower alone from winning World War II. That they were unusable made little difference. Precision guided munitions are the current mantra of the airpower enthusiast—they have finally made decisive air attack possible. There may actually be something to the precision guided munitions claim; only time will tell. Douhet's assertion of the futility of air defense proved wrong when radar made locating aircraft possible and fighters became capable of catching and shooting down big bombers. Douhet's assertion of the fragility of civilian morale under air attack also proved false. Nevertheless, he still has a major influence on airpower doctrine and is the father of all modern airpower theory.

Other Airpower Theories.

Douhet may have been the father of airpower theory, but others followed him quickly. Most of the later airpower theorists worked on one or both of two primary issues that Douhet had first surfaced: the most efficient way to organize airpower, a debate generally about an independent air force, or the proper mix of fighters, bombers, and ground-attack aircraft. The debate about separate air forces was important but not a true strategic issue. Conversely, the issue of proper mix of aircraft got directly to the issue of the proper role of airpower. The early theorists presented a variety of views on the issue. William "Billy" Mitchell saw America's strategic problem as one of defense against sea-borne attack. A Douhet-like offensive air strategy was inappropriate. He also believed that aerial combat could provide effective defense against air attack. Thus, he developed a strategy based on a mix of fighters and bombers. In terms of both the necessity of command of the air and the potential strategic decisiveness of airpower, Mitchell agreed completely with Douhet.[70]

Another early airpower theorist was British Wing Commander John C. "Jack" Slessor. Slessor served a tour as an instructor at the Army Staff College at Camberley. His book, *Air Power and Armies*, is a collection of his lectures at the War College. Slessor was a believer in strategic bombing, but, perhaps because of his audience, he also emphasized the relationship between airpower and ground operations. The first requirement was gaining command of the air. Next, airpower could interdict the enemy's lines of communication. Using airpower in direct support of committed troops (the flying artillery/close air support concept) was ineffective. Slessor did believe that both aspects of the air campaign could occur simultaneously—one did not need complete air superiority to begin interdiction. From the standpoint of the ground commander, supporting airpower was most effective in facilitating a breakthrough, in the pursuit, and in the defense.[71]

Slessor's advocacy of interdiction was not, however, the only way one might approach the air-ground support issue. German Chief of Air Staff during the interwar years Helmut Wilberg was a pioneer in direct air-ground support. He wrote some of and edited and approved all of Germany's immediate post-war studies on air force operations. Those studies concluded that strategic bombardment did not work, but that close air support did. Thus, it is not surprising that unlike either the British or the Americans, the Germans developed a tactical air force oriented on close support of ground forces. The opportunity for Germany to develop a strategic air force or doctrine occurred during the tenure of Walter Weaver as Chief of Air Staff between 1934 and 1936. Weaver was a bomber advocate of the Douhetian ilk. However, when he died in an airplane crash in 1936, the Luftwaffe canceled Weaver's pet four-engine bomber development program and slipped comfortably back into its ground support doctrine.

CONCLUSION

Which of these approaches to strategy is the best? What is the approved solution? The answer is simple—there is no best solution. All the above have utility for specific purposes but are lacking as generalizations on strategy. They tend to be 1) war-oriented rather than general (i.e., military strategy rather than strategy in general); 2) too narrowly focused even within the wartime realm (that is they address military-specific strategies rather than more general grand strategies and in some cases represent single service approaches); and 3) even in the military arena are too focused on one aspect of a multidimensional problem (i.e., they attempt to skip the basic ends-ways-means relationship and go straight to the solution). They are generally concerned with the how, while ignoring the what or why. The exceptions were the broad concepts like attrition, exhaustion, and annihilation and nuclear strategy that always aimed at deterrence and clearly linked ways with means to achieve that end.

So, why present all these strategic concepts if they do not work? Remember that although none of the paradigms works as a generalization, each has merit in specific circumstances. The strategist needs to be familiar with each so he can select the best approach or combination of approaches for the situation he faces. In that respect strategy is much like carpentry. Both are skills intended for solving problems. The carpenter uses a saw to cut, a hammer to drive, sandpaper to smooth, and myriad other tools depending on the need—there is a tool for every job. Similarly, the strategist needs to have a wide assortment of tools in his kitbag and be able to select the proper one for the task at hand. There is an old saying that if the only tool one has is a hammer, all problems look like a nail. That is as bad a solution in strategy as it is in carpentry.

ENDNOTES - CHAPTER 2

1. See Hew Strachan, "The Lost Meaning of Strategy," *Survival*, Vol. 47 No. 3, Autumn, 2005, pp. 33-54.

2. Carl von Clausewitz, *On War*, ed. and trans. by Michael Howard and Peter Paret, Princeton, NJ: Princeton University Press, 1976, p. 177.

3. Antoine Henri Baron de Jomini, *The Art of War*, trans. G. H. Mendell and W. P. Craighill, 1862, reprint The West Point Military Library series, ed. by Thomas E. Griess and Jay Luvass, Westport, CT: Greenwood Press, 1971, p. 62.

4. Henry Lee Scott, *Military Dictionary: Comprising Technical Definitions; Information on Raising and Keeping Troops; Actual Service, including Makeshifts and Improved Materiel; and Law, Government, Regulation, and administration Relating to Land Forces*, 1861, reprint The West Point Military Library series, ed. by Thomas E. Griess and Jay Luvass, Westport, CT: Greenwood Press, 1968, p. 574.

5. Basil H. Liddell Hart, *Strategy*, 2nd edition, 1954, reprint New York: Frederick A. Praeger, 1967, p. 335-336.

6. Collin S. Gray, *Modern Strategy*, New York: Oxford University Press, 1999, p. 17.

7. U.S. Department of Defense, The Joint Staff, Joint Publication 1-02, *DOD Dictionary of Military and Associated Terms* (hereafter Joint Pub 1-02), available at *www.dtic.mil/doctrine/jel/new_pubs/jp1_02.pdf*, pp. 507, 357; U.S. Department of Defense, The Joint Staff. Joint Doctrine Encyclopedia, available at *www.dtic.mil/doctrine/joint_military_encyclopedia/ htm*, pp. 731, 542.

8. Robert H. Dorff, "A Primer in Strategy Development" in *U.S. Army War College Guide Strategy*, Joseph R. Cerami and James F. Holcomb, Jr., ed., Carlisle Barracks, PA: Strategic Studies Institute, 2001, p. 11; Richard A. Chilcoat, "Strategic Art: The New Discipline for 21st Century Strategists" in *U.S. Army War College Guide to Strategy*, Joseph R. Cerami and James F. Holcomb, Jr., ed., Carlisle Barracks, PA: Strategic Studies Institute, 2001, p. 205.

9. Gray, p. 28.

10. J. C. [Joseph Caldwell] Wylie, *Military Strategy: A General Theory of Power Control*, New Brunswick, NJ: Rutgers University Press, 1967, reprint Annapolis, MD: Naval Institute Press, 1989, p. 22-27.

11. Russell F. Weigley, "Response to Brian McAllister Linn by Russell F. Weigley," *The Journal of Military History*, Vol. 66, No. 2, April 2002, p. 531.

12. Michael Howard, "Lessons of the Cold War," Survival, Vol. 36, No., 4, Winter 1994-95, p. 165.

13. Dorff, p. 12.

14. Clausewitz, pp. 88-89.

15. Sun Tzu, *The Art of War*, trans. Samuel B. Griffith, 1963, reprint New York: Oxford University Press, 1973, pp. 73, 63; Liddell Hart, p. 366.

16. *Ibid.*, pp. 77, 98, 85, 96.

17. Clausewitz, p. 267.

18. *Ibid.*, pp. 595-596.

19. *Ibid.*, 528.

20. Jomini, pp. 61-63.

21. Liddell Hart, p. 337.

22. *Ibid.*, p. 339.

23. *Ibid.*, pp. 339-341; Clausewitz, p. 137.

24. Andre Beaufré, *An Introduction to Strategy, with Particular Reference to Problems of Defense, Politics, Economics, and Diplomacy in the Nuclear Age*, New York: Praeger, 1965; Andre Beaufré, *Deterrence and Strategy*, New York: F. A. Praeger, 1966; Andre Beaufré, *Strategy of Action*, London: Farber and Farber, 1967.

25. Beaufré, *Introduction to Strategy*, pp. 30-31.

26. *Ibid.*, pp. 26-29.

27. *Ibid.*, pp. 34-35.

28. *Ibid.*, p. 36.

29. *Ibid.*, p. 129.

30. Beaufré, *Strategy of Action*, p. 28.

31. *Ibid.*, p. 132.

32. Luttwak, pp. 92-93.

33. *Ibid.*, p. 94.

34. *Ibid.*, pp. 94-95.

35. *Ibid.*, pp. 4, 87-91.

36. *Ibid.*, p. 7.

37. *Ibid.*, p. 8.

38. *Ibid.*, pp. 9-10.

39. *Ibid.*, p. 10.

40. *Ibid.*, pp. 10-15, 17.

41. Martin Van Creveld, *The Transformation of War*, New York: The Free Press, 1991, p. ix.

42. *Ibid.*, pp. 57, ix.

43. *Ibid.*, pp. 125-156.

44. *Ibid.*, pp. 63-94, 119, 120-220.

45. Martin Van Creveld, "The Transformation of War Revisited," in Robert J. Bunker, ed. *Nonstate Threats and Future Wars*, London, U.K.: Frank Cass, 2003, p.. 5, 7-14.

46. Archer Jones, *Elements of Military Strategy: An Historical Approach*, Westport, CT: Praeger, 1996, p. xiii.

47. *Ibid.*, p. xiv.

48. Archer Jones, *Civil War Command and Strategy: The Process of Victory and Defeat*, New York: The Free Press, 1992, p. 35; Jones, Elements of Military Strategy, pp. 201-204.

49. Boyd never published his OODA loop theory. It is available in John R. Boyd, "A Discourse on Winning and Losing," unpublished paper Air University document number MU43947, August 1987. The best summary is David S. Fadok, "John Boyd and John Warden: Airpower's Quest for Strategic Paralysis," in *The Paths of Heaven: The Evolution of Airpower Theory*, Maxwell AFB, AL: Air University Press, 1997, p. 141-143.

50. John A. Warden III, "The Enemy as a System," *Airpower Journal*, Spring 1995, pp. 41-55.

51. T. E. (Thomas Edward) Lawrence, *Seven Pillars of Wisdom: A Triumph*, New York: George Doran Publishing Co., 1926 reprint New York: Anchor Books, 1991.

52. *Ibid.*, pp. 104-105, 143-145; Robert B. Aspery, *War in the Shadows: The Guerrilla in History*, 2 vols., New York: Doubleday & Co., Inc., 1975, p. 1:262-264.

53. T. E. (Thomas Edward) Lawrence, "Guerrilla Warfare" in *Encyclopedia Britannica*, 1957, Vol. 10, as quoted in Aspery, p. 1:263 and p. 1:269.

54. Peter Paret, ed. *Makers of Modern Strategy: from Machiavelli to the Nuclear Age*, Princeton, NJ: Princeton University Press, 1986, p. 831.

55. Mao Tse-Tung, *On Protracted War*, Peking, China: Foreign Language Press, 1960; *Mao Tse-Tung: An Anthology of His Writings*, Anne Fremantle, ed., New York: New American Library, 1972.

56. Ernesto "Che" Guevara de la Serna, *Che Guevara on Guerrilla Warfare*, Introduction by Major Harris-Clichy Peterson, USMCR, New York: Frederick A. Praeger, 1961, p. 10; Ernesto "Che" Guevara de la Serna, *Guerrilla Warfare*, New York: Monthly Review Press, 1961, p. 15.

57. Charles C. Caldwell, *Small Wars – Their Principles and Practices*, 3rd ed., London, U.K.: His Majesty's Stationary Office, 1898, 1906; reprint East Ardsley, England: EP Publishing Ltd. 1976, pp. 25-33, 85-90, 125-148, 23; Asprey, pp. 1:204-206.

58. Roger Trinquier, *Modern Warfare: A French View of Counterinsurgency*, trans. by Daniel Lee, New York: Frederick A. Praeger; 1964, p. 43-98.

59. David Galula, *Counterinsurgency Warfare: Theory and Practice*, New York: Frederick A. Praeger, 1964, pp. 6-10.

60. *Ibid.*, pp. 17-26.

61. *Ibid.*, pp. 74-79, 87-93, 96-106.

62. Frank Kitson, *Low Intensity Operations: Subversion, Insurgency, and Peacekeeping*, Harrisburg, PA: Stackpole Books, 1971, especially pp. 67-143.

63. Niccolò Machiavelli, *The Art of War*, trans. by Ellis Farnsworth, New York: Da Capo Press, 1965; Niccolò Machiavelli, *The Discourses of Niccolò Machiavelli*, trans. by Leslie J. Walker, Boston, MA: Routedge and Paul, 1975; Niccolò Machiavelli, *The Prince*, trans. Luigi Ricci, revised by E. R. P. Vincent, New York: New American Library, 1952; Frederick the Great, *Instructions for his Generals*, trans. by Thomas R. Phillips, Harrisburg, PA: The Stackpole Company, 1960; The Military Maxims of Napoleon, trans. by George C. D'Aguilar with Introduction by David G. Chandler, 1831, reprint, New York: Da Capo Press, 1995, p. 14; Michèle A. Flournoy, ed., *QDR 2001: Strategy-Driven Choices for America's Security*, Washington, DC: National Defense University Press, 2001.

64. See for example Bernard Brodie, *Strategy in the Missile Age*, 1959, reprint Princeton, NJ: Princeton University Press, 1971; Joint Pub 1-02, p. 156.

65. Albert Wohlstetter, *The Delicate Balance of Terror*, Santa Monica, CA: RAND, 1958; Bernard Brodie, *Strategy in the Missile Age*; Herman Kahn, *On Thermonuclear* War, Princeton, NJ: Princeton University Press, 1960; Thomas C. Schelling, *The Strategy of Conflict*, Cambridge, MA: Harvard University Press, 1960; and *Arms and Influence*, New Haven, CT: Yale University Press, 1966.

66. Alfred Thayer Mahan, *The Influence of Sea Power Upon History 1660-1783*, 1890, reprint Boston, Mass.: Little, Brown and Company, 1970, pp. 29-88, 25, 26.

67. Julian S. Corbett, *Some Principles of Maritime Strategy*, London, U.K.: Longman, Green, 1911.

68. Theodore Ropp, *War in the Modern World*, 1959, reprint New York: Collier Books, 1973, p. 208-209.

69. Giulio Douhet, *The Command of the Air*, trans. by Sheila Fischer, Rome: Rivista Aeronautica, 1958.

70. William Mitchell, *Winged Defense: The Development and Possibilities of Modern Air Power — Economic and Military*, New York: G. P. Putnam's Sons, 1925.

71. John C. Slessor, *Air Power and Armies*, Oxford, England: Oxford University Press, 1925.

CHAPTER 3

TOWARD A THEORY OF STRATEGY:
ART LYKKE AND THE U.S. ARMY WAR COLLEGE STRATEGY MODEL

Harry R. Yarger

Gregory D. Foster argues in a *Washington Quarterly* article that there is no official or accepted general theory of strategy in the United States. In fact, he notes that as a people Americans seem to regard theorizing in general as a futile intellectual exercise. If one were to construct such a theory, Foster continues, it should incorporate those elements found in any complete theory: essential terminology and definitions; an explanation of the assumptions and premises underlying the theory; substantive propositions translated into testable hypothesis; and methods that can be used to test the hypotheses and modify the theory as appropriate.[1] Foster may have this theory thing right. There is little evidence that collectively as a nation there is any agreement on just what constitutes a theory of strategy. This is very unfortunate because the pieces for a good theory of strategy have been laying around the U.S. Army War College for years—although sometimes hard to identify amongst all the intellectual clutter. Arthur F. Lykke, Jr.'s U.S. Army War College strategy model, with its ends, ways, and means, is the centerpiece of this theory.[2] The theory is quite simple, but it often appears unduly complex as a result of confusion over terminology and definitions and the underlying assumptions and premises.

One sees the term strategy misapplied often. There is a tendency to use it as a general term for a plan, concept, course of action, or "idea" of a direction in which to proceed. Such use is inappropriate. Strategy is the domain of the senior leader at the higher echelons of the state, the military, business corporations, or other institutions. Henry Eccles describes strategy as ". . . the comprehensive direction of power to control situations and areas in order to attain objectives."[3] His definition captures much of the essence of strategy. It is comprehensive, it provides direction, its purpose is control, and it is fundamentally concerned with the application of power.[4] Strategy as used in the U.S. Army War College curriculum focuses on the nation-state and the use of the elements of power to serve state interests. In this context, strategy is the employment of the instruments (elements) of power (political/diplomatic, economic, military, and informational) to achieve the political objectives of the state in cooperation or in competition with other actors pursuing their own objectives.[5]

The underlying assumption of strategy from a national perspective is that states and other competitive entities have interests that they will pursue to the best of their abilities. Interests are desired end states such as survival, economic well-being, and enduring national values. The national elements of power are the resources used to promote or advance national interests. Strategy is the pursuit, protection, or advancement of these interests through the application of the instruments of power. Strategy is fundamentally a choice; it reflects a preference for a future state or condition. In doing so, strategy confronts adversaries and some things simply remain beyond control or unforeseen.[6]

Strategy is all about *how* (way or concept) leadership will use the *power* (means or resources) available to the state to exercise control over sets of circumstances and geographic locations to achieve *objectives* (ends) that support state interests. Strategy provides direction for the coercive or persuasive use of this power to achieve specified objectives. This direction is by nature proactive. It seeks to control the environment as opposed to reacting to it. Strategy is not crisis management. It is its antithesis. Crisis management occurs when there is no strategy or the strategy fails. Thus, the first premise of a theory of strategy is that strategy is proactive and anticipatory.[7]

A second premise of a theory of strategy is that the strategist must know what is to be accomplished—that is, he must know the end state that he is trying to achieve. Only by analyzing and understanding the desired end state in the context of the internal and external environment can the strategist develop appropriate objectives leading to the desired end state.

A third premise of a theory of strategy is that the strategy must identify an appropriate balance among the objectives sought, the methods to pursue the objectives, and the resources available. In formulating a strategy the ends, ways, and means are part of an integral whole and if one is discussing a strategy at the national (grand) level with a national level end, the ways and means would similarly refer to national level concepts and resources. That is ends, ways, and means must be consistent. Thus a National Security Strategy end could be supported by concepts based on all the instruments of power and the associated resources. For the military element of power, the National Military Strategy would identify appropriate ends for the military to be accomplished through national military concepts with national military resources. In a similar manner a Theater or Regional Combatant Commander would have specific theater level objectives for which he would develop theater concepts and use resources allocated to his theater. In some cases these might include other than military instruments of power if those resources are available. The levels of strategy are distinct, but interrelated because of the hierarchical and comprehensive nature of strategy.

A fourth premise of strategy is that political purpose must dominate all strategy; thus, Clausewitz' famous dictum, "War is merely the continuation of policy by other means."[8] Political purpose is stated in policy. Policy is the expression of the desired end state sought by the government. In its finest form it is clear articulation of guidance for the employment of the instruments of power towards the attainment of one or more end states. In practice it tends to be much vaguer. Nonetheless policy dominates strategy by its articulation of the end state and its guidance. The analysis of the end state and guidance yields objectives leading to the desired end state. Objectives provide purpose, focus, and justification for the actions embodied in a strategy.[9] National strategy is concerned with a hierarchy of objectives that is determined by the political purpose of the state. Policy insures that strategy pursues appropriate aims.

A fifth premise is that strategy is hierarchical. Foster argues that true strategy is the purview of the leader and is a *"weltanschauung"* (world view) that represents both national consensus and comprehensive direction. In the cosmic scheme of things Foster may well be right, but reality requires more than a *"weltanschauung."* Political leadership insures and maintains its control and influence through the hierarchical nature of state strategy. Strategy cascades from the national level down to the lower levels. Generally strategy emerges at the top as a consequence of policy statements and a stated National Security Strategy (sometimes referred to as Grand Strategy). National Security Strategy lays out broad objectives and direction for the use of all the instruments of power. From this National Security Strategy, the major activities and departments develop subordinate strategies. For the military, this is the National Military Strategy. In turn, the National Military Strategy leads to lower strategies appropriate to the various levels of war.

The U.S. Army War College (in consonance with Joint Pub 1-02) defines the levels of strategy within the state as:

- *National Security Strategy* (also referred to as Grand Strategy and National Strategy). The art and science of developing, applying and coordinating the instruments of national power (diplomatic, economic, military, and informational) to achieve objectives that contribute to national security (Joint Pub 1-02).
- *National Military Strategy*. The art and science of distributing and applying military power to attain national objectives in peace and war (Joint Pub 1-02).
- *Theater Strategy*. The art and science of developing integrated strategic concepts

and courses of action directed toward securing the objectives of national and alliance or coalition security policy and strategy by the use of force, threatened use of force, or operations not involving the use of force within a theater (Joint Pub 1-02).

The hierarchical nature of strategy facilitates span of control. It represents a logical means of delegating responsibility and authority among senior leadership. It also suggests that if strategy consists of objectives, concepts, and resources each should be appropriate to the level of strategy and consistent with one another. Thus strategy at the national military level should articulate military objectives at the national level and express the concepts and resources in terms appropriate to the national level for the specified objective.

At some level planning and action fall below the strategic threshold. Under the National Military Strategy the Combatant Commanders develop Theater Strategy and subsequent campaign plans. At this juncture the line between strategy and planning merges with campaign planning that may be either at the theater strategic level or in the realm of Operational Art. Graphically the relationship between strategy and the levels of war appear as:[10]

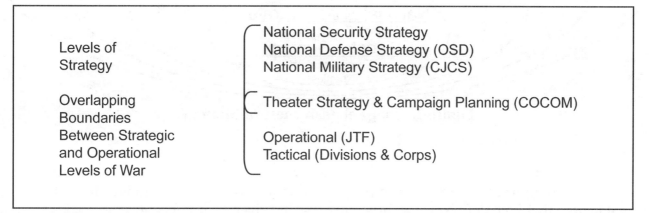

Figure 1. Strategic and Operational Art.

Strategy differs from operational art and tactics in functional, temporal, and geographic aspects. Functionally and temporally, tactics is the domain of battles, engagements of relative short duration. Operational art is the domain of the campaign, a series of battles occurring over a longer period of time. Strategy is the domain of war which encompasses the protracted level of conflict among nations, armed or unarmed. Tactics concerns itself with the parts or pieces, operational art with the combination of the pieces, and strategy with the combinations of combinations. Geographically, tactics is narrowly defined, operational level is broader and more regional in orientation, and strategy is theater-wide, intercontinental, or global. It should also be noted that with the advances in transportation and communications there has been a spatial and temporal convergence of strategy, operational art, and tactics. Increasingly, events at the tactical level have strategic consequences.[11]

A sixth premise is that strategy is comprehensive. That is to say, while the strategist may be devising a strategy from a particular perspective, he must consider the whole of the strategic environment in his analysis to arrive at a proper strategy to serve his purpose at his level. He is concerned with external and internal factors at all levels. On the other hand, in formulating a strategy, the strategist must also be cognizant that each aspect—objectives, concepts, and resources—has effects on the environment around him. Thus, the strategist must have a comprehensive knowledge of what else is happening and the potential first, second, third, etc., order effects of his own choices on the efforts of those above, below, and on his same level. The strategist's efforts must be integrated fully with the stategies or efforts of senior, co-equal, and subordinate elements. Strategists must think holistically — that is, comprehensively. They must be cognizant of both the "big picture," their own institution's capabilities and resources, and the impact of their actions on the whole of the environment. Good strategy is never developed in isolation. (See Figure 2.)

Figure 2. Comprehensiveness of Strategy.

A seventh premise is that strategy is developed from a thorough analysis and knowledge of the strategic situation/environment. The purpose of this analysis is to highlight the internal and external factors that help define or may affect the specific objectives, concepts, and resources of the strategy.

The last premise of a theory of strategy is that some risk is inherent to all strategy and the best any strategy can offer is a favorable balance against failure. Failure can be either the failure to achieve one's own objectives and/or providing a significant advantage to one's adversaries.

Art Lykke gave coherent form to a theory of strategy with his articulation of the three-legged stool model of strategy which illustrated that strategy = ends + ways + means and if these were not in balance the assumption of greater risk. In the Lykke proposition (model) the

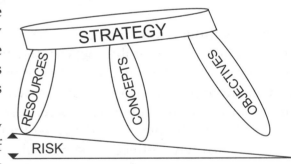

Figure 3. The Lykke Model.

ends are "objectives," the ways are the "concepts" for accomplishing the objectives, and the means are the "resources" for supporting the concepts. The stool tilts if the three legs are not kept in balance. If any leg is too short, the risk is too great and the strategy falls over.[12]

It should be evident that the model poses three key questions for strategists. What is to be done? How is it to be done? What resources are required to do it in this manner? Lykke argues that if any leg of the stool is out of balance then one accepts a corresponding risk unless one adjusts the legs. One might add resources, use a different concept, or change the objective. Or, one might decide to accept the risk. The theory is quite clear—a valid strategy must have an appropriate balance of objectives, concepts, and resources or its success is at greater risk.[13] Lykke's theory, like all good theory, does not necessarily provide a strategy. It is a paradigm that describes the questions to ask and the rules to follow. His strategic theory is supported by the underlying premises and assumptions above and its practice is facilitated by the sharing of common definitions and formats.

Art Lykke wrestled with his proposition for many years and taught thousands of Army War College students to use his model properly through definition and illustration. These definitions and illustrations are important because they provide the common understanding by which strategists communicate. They include:

- *Ends (objectives)* explain "what" is to be accomplished. Ends are objectives that if accomplished create, or contribute to, the achievement of the desired end state at the level of strategy being analyzed and, ultimately, serve national interests. Ends are expressed with verbs (i.e., deter war, promote regional stability, destroy Iraqi armed forces).

- *Ways (strategic concepts/courses of action)* explain "how" the ends are to be accomplished by the employment of resources. The concept must be explicit enough to provide planning guidance to those who must implement and resource it. Since ways convey action they often have a verb, but ways are statements of "how," not "what" in relation to the objective of a strategy. Some confusion exists because the concept for higher strategy often defines the objectives of the next lower level of strategy. A simple test for a way is to ask "in order to do what?" That should lead to the real objective. Some concepts are so accepted that their names have been given to specific strategies (containment, forward defense, assured destruction, forward presence are illustrations). But note that in actual practice these strategies have specific objectives and forces associated with them and the concept is better developed than the short title suggests.

- *Means (resources)* explain what specific resources are to be used in applying the concepts to accomplish the objectives and use no verb. Means can be tangible or intangible. Examples of tangible means include forces, people, equipment, money, and facilities. Intangible resources include things like "will," courage, or intellect.

- *Risk* explains the gap between what is to be achieved and the concepts and resources available to achieve the objective. Since there are never enough resources or a clever enough concept to assure 100 percent success in the competitive international environment, there is always some risk. The strategist seeks to minimize this risk through his development of the strategy—the balance of ends, ways, and means.

Ends, ways, and means often get confusing in the development or analysis of a specific strategy. The trick is to focus on the questions. Objectives will always answer the question of what one is trying to achieve. Concepts always explain "how" the resources will be used. Resources always explain what will be used to execute the concept. If the objective is "defend the United States (what?)"; "to develop, build, or establish a larger force" is a way (how?); and, "national manpower reserves, money, and training facilities" are examples of the means (resources to be used to support the "how"). The rule of thumb to apply here is that resources are usually physical and countable: Army, Air Force, Navy, units and armed forces of United States; personnel; dollars; facilities; equipment— trucks, planes, ships, etc.; and resources of organizations—Red Cross, NATO, etc. Means might also include such intangibles as "will, industrial capacity, intellect. etc.," but state them as resources. Do not use means to describe concepts and do not articulate resources as ways or concepts. In a very simplified manner "diplomacy" is a *way* to promote regional stability (*objective*), but diplomats are the *means*. In the same manner Clausewitz preferred "overthrow of the enemy's government" as the end, to fight a decisive battle as the way, and a larger army as the means. He saw the larger army as an appropriate resource to support his way—the decisive battle. To say "*use of* a larger army" infers a different concept for success and is an inappropriate statement of means (resources).

Over time, thousands of students at the U.S. Army War College have tested Art Lykke's theory of strategy using the historical case study approach. His proposition is a common model for analyzing and evaluating the strategy of historical and current strategic level leadership. By using the theory to break a strategy into its component parts Art Lykke argued any strategy can be examined for suitability, feasibility, and acceptability, and, an assessment made of the proper balance among the component parts. In addition, his lecturing and presentations have led to the adoption of the basic model by a cohort of military and political strategists. This has, in turn, led to the proactive evaluation of strategy during development against the same standards of:

- Suitability—will its attainment accomplish the effect desired (relates to objective)?
- Feasibility—can the action be accomplished by the means available (relates to concept)?
- Acceptability—are the consequences of cost justified by the importance of the effect desired (relates to resources/concept)?[14]

Not only has the basic proposition been tested in historical case studies and practical application, it has also proven itself adaptable to explaining differing aspects of strategic thought. Art Lykke's argument that nations engage in two distinct types of military strategy concurrently—operational and force developmental—illustrate the theory's adaptability. Operational strategies are based on existing military capabilities. Force developmental strategies are based on future threats and objectives and are not limited by existing capabilities. In fact, their primary role is to help determine and develop future capabilities.[15] Thus, the theory lends itself to both warfighters and force developers within the military.

Art Lykke's theory of strategy is an important contribution to strategic thought. In encouraging the strategist to use the term "strategy" correctly while applying the strategy model and its four parts—ends, ways, means and risk, he provided a viable theory of strategy. The assumptions and premises of this theory have proven valid for analyzing and developing strategy. Above all a valid strategy must find a balance among ends, ways, and means consistent with the risk the nation is willing to accept. Art Lykke's theory of strategy provides the basis for clearly articulating and objectively evaluating any strategy.

ENDNOTES - CHAPTER 3

1. Gregory D. Foster, "A Conceptual Foundation for a Theory of Strategy," *The Washington Quarterly*, Winter, 1990, p. 43. Foster's analysis of the assumptions and premises of strategy is particularly thought provoking.

2. Arthur F. Lykke, Jr., "Toward an Understanding of Military Strategy," chap. in *Military Strategy: Theory and Application*, Carlisle Barracks, PA: U.S. Army War College, 1989, pp. 3-8. This document is the best written explanation of his ideas. Also used in this paper are the author's notes and recollections from Professor Lykke's lectures.

3. Henry E. Eccles, *Military Concepts and Philosophy*, New Brunswick, NJ: Rutgers UP, 1965, p. 48.

4. Foster, p. 50.

5. David Jablonsky, *Why Is Strategy Difficult?* Carlisle Barracks, PA: Strategic Studies Institute, U.S. Army War College, 1992. Professor Jablonsky's work, of which this is representative, gives the best explanation. He lists the elements of power as economic, psychological, political, and military. Socio-psychological is another term used as an instrument of power instead of psychological or informational. Note also that elements of power is more inclusive than instruments of power and includes demographic/geographic elements. Dr. Jablonsky raised Art Lykke's proposition to the political level.

6. Foster, pp. 47-48.

7. *Ibid.*, p. 55.

8. Carl von Clausewitz, *On War*, ed. and trans. by Michael Howard and Peter Paret, Princeton, NJ: Princeton University Press, 1976, p. 87.

9. Foster, p. 50.

10. This chart is adapted from an older version commonly used to explain the overlapping. Abbreviations used: CJCS (Chairman, Joint Chiefs of Staff); COCOM (Combatant Commander); and JTF (Joint Task Force).

11. Foster, p. 56.

12. Lykke, pp. 6-7.

13. *Ibid.*

14. Henry C. Eccles, "Strategy—The Theory and Application," *Naval War College Review*, Vol. 32, No. 3, May-June 1979, pp. 11-21.

15. Lykke, p. 4.

CHAPTER 4

THE STRATEGIC APPRAISAL:
THE KEY TO EFFECTIVE STRATEGY

Harry R. Yarger

Strategy is best understood as the *art* and *science* of developing and using the political, economic, socio-psychological, and military powers of the state in accordance with policy guidance to create effects that protect or advance the state's interests in the strategic environment. The strategic environment is the realm in which the national leadership interacts with other states or actors and the possibilities of the future to advance the well-being of the state. It is inclusive, consisting of the facts, context, conditions, relationships, trends, issues, threats, opportunities, and interactions that influence the success of the state in relation to the physical world, other states and actors, chance, and the possible futures—all effects or other factors that potentially affect the well-being of the state and the way the state pursues its well-being. As a self-organizing complex system (a system of systems), the strategic environment is a dynamic environment that reacts to input but not necessarily in a direct cause and effect manner. Strategy is how the state exerts purposeful influence over this environment. Thus, strategy is a disciplined thought process that seeks to apply a degree of rationality and linearity to an environment that may or may not be either, so that effective planning can be accomplished. Strategy does this by identifying strategic ends (objectives), ways (concepts) and means (resources) that when accomplished lead to favorable effects in regard to the state's well-being.[1] It explains to planners what must be accomplished and establishes the boundaries of how it is to be accomplished and the resources to be made available. However, to formulate a proper strategy, the strategist must first determine the state's interests and the factors in the environment that potentially affect those interests. Only from such a strategic appraisal can the strategist derive the key strategic factors and determine the right calculation of ends, ways, and means.

The purpose of the strategic appraisal is to quantify and qualify what is known, believed to be known, and unknown about the strategic environment in regard to a particular realm of strategy and identify *what is important* in regard to such strategy's formulation. It represents a rational, scientific approach to acquiring what Carl von Clausewitz referred to as *coup d'oeil*—the ability to see what is really important.[2] But while displayed below as a linear process to assist the reader's understanding of the concept, in reality the appraisal is always an iterative process wherein each new piece of information must be considered with reference to what is already known, and what is already known revalidated in light of the new information. In this process, the strategist determines pertinent desired end states (interests) that facilitate the well-being of the nation and evaluates the environment to determine what factors may preclude or assist realization of these interests. Based on his assessment of these factors, the strategist chooses key strategic factors on which to formulate ends, ways, and means that address or make use of these factors to create effects that favor the realization of the interests.

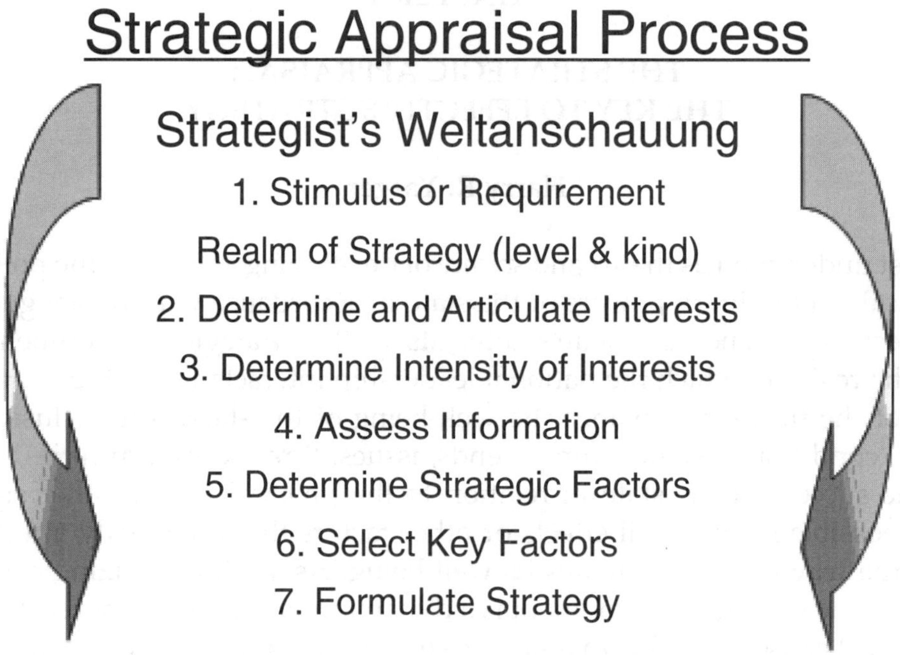

Strategic Appraisal Process

Strategist's Weltanschauung

1. Stimulus or Requirement

Realm of Strategy (level & kind)

2. Determine and Articulate Interests

3. Determine Intensity of Interests

4. Assess Information

5. Determine Strategic Factors

6. Select Key Factors

7. Formulate Strategy

Figure 1. Strategic Appraisal Process.

Through constant study and analysis the strategist maintains a holistic world view that gives meaning and context to his understanding of the strategic environment and the forces of continuity and change at work in it. Consequently, the strategist's *Weltanschauung* is both an objective view of the existing current environment and an anticipatory appreciation of the implications of continuities and change for his nation's future well-being. Appreciating that the strategic environment possesses the characteristics of a system of systems and exhibits some of the attributes of chaos theory, the strategist accepts that the future is not predictable but believes it can be influenced and shaped toward more favorable outcomes.[3] His *weltanschauung* makes the strategist sensitive to what national interests are and the threats, challenges, and opportunities in regard to them. However, a new, focused strategic appraisal is conducted when circumstances demand a new strategy, or the review of an existing strategy is undertaken. Understanding the stimulus or the requirement for the strategy is the first step in the strategic appraisal. It not only provides the strategist's focus and motivation, but it will ultimately lend legitimacy, authority, and impetus to the appraisal and strategy formulation processes and the subsequent implementation of the strategy.

The levels and kinds of strategy fall in different realms. Realms reflect both the hierarchical nature of strategy and its comprehensiveness, thereby allowing the state's leadership to delegate responsibility for strategy at different levels and in different domains while maintaining control over a complex process. The strategic appraisal focuses on serving that realm of strategy undertaken—both the kind and level. For example, the term Grand Strategy encompasses both level and kind, implying an overarching strategy that integrates the use of all the state's power in service of all the state's interests. National strategies are at the national level, but they may apply to all elements of power and the associated departments and agencies as the National Security Strategy does, or they may focus on one element as is the case with the National Military Strategy. Strategies may also have a regional focus, a force developmental focus, an organizational focus, and other foci as illustrated in Figure 2.

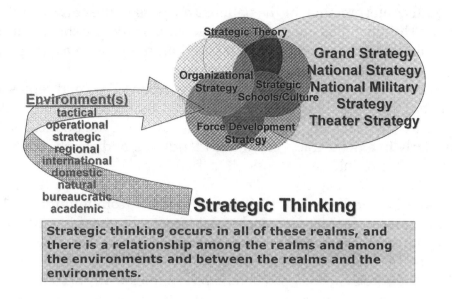

Environment(s)
tactical
operational
strategic
regional
international
domestic
natural
bureaucratic
academic

Strategic Theory

Organizational
Strategy

Strategic
Schools/Culture

Force Development
Strategy

Grand Strategy
National Strategy
National Military
Strategy
Theater Strategy

Strategic Thinking

Strategic thinking occurs in all of these realms, and
there is a relationship among the realms and among
the environments and between the realms and the
environments.

Figure 2. Realms of Strategy.

Thinking about the kind and level of strategy helps develop specificity in the articulation of interests and better focuses the strategy in regard to the desired end states. It also clarifies and assigns responsibility, authority, and accountability. Nonetheless, the strategist at every level and in every domain must still maintain a holistic perspective.

Determining and articulating interests is the second step in the strategic appraisal process. The *DOD Dictionary of Military Terms* defines national security interests as: "The foundation for the development of valid national objectives that define U.S. goals or purposes. National security interests include preserving U.S. political identity, framework and institutions; fostering economic well-being; and bolstering international order supporting the vital interests of the United States and its allies."[4] The nature of the strategic environment suggests a more generalized definition, such as the perceived needs and desires of a sovereign state in relation to other sovereign states, non-state actors, and chance and circumstances in an emerging strategic environment expressed as desired end states.[5] This broader definition encapsulates the dynamism of a strategic environment in which multiple actors, chance, and interaction play, and both external and internal components are recognized. Interests are expressed as general or particular desired end states or conditions. For example, "U.S. economic well-being" would be a generalized interest; while "international access to Middle Eastern oil" illustrates a more particular economic interest. While some interests may change over time, general interests such as free trade and defense of the homeland are persistent.

Interests are founded in national purpose. National purpose is essentially a summary of our enduring values, beliefs, and ethics as expressed by political leadership in regard to the present and the future they foresee. At the highest level, political leadership uses policy to identify state interests and provide guidance for subordinate policy and strategy. Such policy may appear as general as a vision statement that proclaims a desired future strategic environment, or as a more specific statement of guidance with elements of ends, ways, and means. It is found in various documents, speeches, policy statements, and other pronouncements made on behalf of the government by various officials, or it may be provided by leadership as direct guidance for the development of specific strategy. Policy may be inferred as well as stated. It may be the result of a detailed strategic appraisal or arrived at intuitively. Regardless, state policy flows from the formal and informal political processes and the interpretation of the national purpose in the current and desired future strategic environments. Thus, national interests are the general or specific statements of the nation's desired end states within the strategic environment based on the policymakers' understanding of what best serves national well-being.

Interests may be expressed as physical or non-physical conditions. They may represent continuities or changes—things to be protected, things to be promoted, or things to be created. Ideally interests flow logically from the policy formulation process, but the nature of the political and bureaucratic environments, particularly in a democracy, can make identifying and clearly articulating interests and their relative importance or intensity a difficult task. As stated above, in the real world policy appears in many formats, often is not clearly stated, and may not be comprehensive in its statement of interests and guidance for serving interests. It may also come from multiple and contradictory sources, such as the executive or legislative branches, and it may be emerging from the interagency process at the time a strategy is demanded. While strategy is subordinate to policy, the strategist must search out and clarify policy intentions and appropriately identify and articulate interests. In cases where policy intentions or interests statements conflict with the reality of the strategic environment and clarification is appropriate, the strategist provides appropriate recommendations to the approval authority.

Theorists have proposed various methodologies for determining interests and levels of intensity. Sometimes, presidential administrations impose their own methodologies to express categories of interests and their associate levels of intensity. In recent years, course material at the Senior Service Colleges, such as the U.S. Army War College, has focused on three that are termed core U.S. interests: physical security, promotion of values, and economic prosperity. In the U.S. Army War College process model these three interests lead directly to three grand strategic objectives: preserve American security, bolster American economic prosperity, and promote American values.[6] In a much earlier argument, Donald E. Nuechterlein referred to these "core" interests as categories and listed four: Defense of the Homeland, Economic Prosperity, Favorable World Order, and Promotion of Values. Nuechterlein suggested these four end states were so general in nature that their primary utility lay in considering them as categories to help organize thinking about interests, and that actual interests must be stated with more specificity to be of any use in strategy formulation. He also noted that such categorization is somewhat artificial, and interests tend to bleed over into other categories.[7] Nuechterlein was right in both regards. Specificity is critical to good strategy formulation. Specificity in interests lends clarity to policy's true intent and aids in the identification of the strategic factors important in regard to the interests. In addition, since in the strategic environment everything is interrelated, greater specificity helps define the nature and context of the interest and clarifies the level and kind of strategy appropriate for addressing an interest.

Interests as statements of desired end states do not imply intended actions or set objectives—policy guidance and strategy does that. Consequently, interests are stated without verbs or other action modifiers. As argued above, interests are expressed with an appropriate degree of specificity. For example, "access to oil" is an expression of a desired end state, but is very general. It could apply anywhere in the world. "Access to oil in the Middle East" is a regionally stated interest, focusing strategic efforts on a specific region; however, it still allows the use of various elements of power and a wide range of objectives and concepts. "Freedom of navigation in the Persian Gulf" as an expression of a specifically stated interest in the CENTCOM theater military strategy gives an even more narrow focus to the desired end state and emphasizes the military instrument. Hence, statements of interests in strategies achieve specificity by word choice, directing the focus and narrowing the context. Expression of interests, like most things in strategy, remains a matter of choice, but the strategist should be aware of the fact he is making a choice and the potential implications of his word selection—a matter worthy of deliberation and discussion! Therefore, strategists often achieve the right degree of specificity through an iterative process in which they articulate an interest and then restate it as they learn more about the implications of pursuing that interest.

Specificity in interests serves the multiple purposes of clarifying the intent of policy in different realms, focusing attention on the appropriate strategic factors, enabling better strategy formulation, and helping to identify responsibility, authority, and accountability. For example, a military strategy would logically, but not exclusively, focus on end states that could be accomplished through the application of the military element of power. Not exclusively so, because as Nuechterlein observed interests tend to bleed over into other categories, and the military instrument may also facilitate accomplishment of diplomatic, economic, or informational focused interests. In a similar manner, other instruments of power may play crucial roles in support of military strategies.

Having determined and articulated the interests, the third step in the strategic appraisal is to determine the level of intensity of each interest. Different methodologies and models have also guided the determination and expression of levels of intensity. Both Nuechterlein and Army War College methodologies advocate applying levels of intensity to interests to indicate criticality and priority. Levels of intensity at the U.S. Army War College include: Vital, Important and Peripheral.[8] Nuechterlein labeled the important level as "major" and argued for the existence of a fourth intensity— survival—aimed at those threats or changes that challenged the very existence of the nation as we know it.[9] Dropped from most methodologies with the ending of the Cold War, Nuechterlein's survival level deserves reconsideration in light of the increase of weapons of mass destruction (WMD) proliferation among nation-states and the potential access and use of WMD by terrorists. Various actors can pose an imminent, credible threat of massive destruction to the U.S. homeland if their demands are not met. In a period of globalization such as the world is currently experiencing, an imminent, credible threat of massive disruption to the transportation and informational systems that under gird national existence and a stable world order may also reach survival intensity. Thus, interests must have both specificity relative to the realm of the strategy being formulated and a means to identify criticality and priority in order to provide focus in determining strategic factors and formulating strategy.

Levels of intensity indicate criticality and priority of interests in regard to the well-being of the state. They help the strategist understand the relative importance and urgency among interests, but do not imply that any should not be considered or addressed in some manner—all interests are worthy of some level of concern. Levels of intensity suggest relative importance and have temporal, resource, and risk acceptance implications, but the decision to act or how to act in regard to them flows from the whole of the strategy formulation process—not the assignment of the intensity. Intensity levels are transitory in that they are subject to change based on the perception of urgency associated with them at any time. Intensity is dependent on the context of the strategic situation and the policymaker or strategist's interpretation of the context and the importance of the interest to national well-being. The definitions of the four intensity levels of survival, vital, important and peripheral are provided in Figure 3.[10]

Levels of Intensity
Survival - If unfulfilled, will result in immediate massive destruction of one or more major aspects of the core national interests.
Vital - If unfulfilled, will have immediate consequence for core national interests.
Important - If unfulfilled, will result in damage that will eventually affect core national interests.
Peripheral - If unfulfilled, will result in damage that is unlikely to affect core national interests.

Figure 3. Levels of Intensity.[11]

The fourth step in the strategic appraisal is to assess the information relative to the interests. In doing this the strategist casts a wide net. Information includes facts and data relating to any aspect of the strategic environment in regard to the interest(s), including: both tangible and intangible attributes and knowledge; assumptions; relationships; and interaction. He considers all information from friendly, neutral, and adversarial perspectives, and from objective and subjective perspectives in each case. While his emphasis is logically on his realm of strategy, he applies holistic thinking that looks both vertically and horizontally at other realms and across the environment. From this assessment the strategist identifies and evaluates the strategic factors that affect or potentially affect the interests—whether promoting, hindering, protecting or threatening them. From his evaluation of the factors he selects the key strategic factors—the factors on which his strategy's ends, ways, and means are based.

The determination of the key strategic factors and the strategist's choices in regard to them is one of the most poorly understood aspects of strategy formulation. It represents a major shortcoming in theoretical consideration of a strategic mindset. Clausewitz' use of *coup d'oeil* describes this aspect. He argues "the concept merely refers to the quick recognition of a truth that the mind would ordinarily miss or would perceive only after long study and reflection."[12] It is the "inward eye" that leads to sound decisions in a timely manner. What Clausewitz is referring to is the ability to see what is really important in the strategic situation and being able to devise a way to act in regard to it.[13] In strategy formulation "what is really important" are called strategic factors—the things that determine or influence the realization of the interest. Not all information or facts are strategic factors. Strategic factors have meaning relative to the expressed interests. From these the strategist will determine the key strategic factors on which the success of the strategy potentially rises or falls. The figure below outlines the distinctions between information, strategic factors, and key strategic factors.

Information	Facts and data relating to any aspect of the strategic environment in regard to the interest(s), including both tangible and intangible attributes and knowledge; assumptions; relationships; and interaction.
Strategic Factors	The things that can potentially contribute or detract causally to the realization of the specified interests or other interests.
Key Strategic Factors	Factors the strategist determines are at the crux of interaction within the environment that can or must be used, influenced or countered to advance or protect the specified interests.

Figure 4. Strategic Factors.

Seeing what is really important flows from a thorough assessment of the realities and possibilities of the strategic environment—tempered by an understanding of its nature and strategic theory. Strategy in its essence is about creating a more "favorable future" for the state than might exist if left to chance or the actions of adversaries and others. It is proactive, but not predictive. Thus in dealing with unknowns and uncertainties of the future, the strategist forecasts from a knowledge and understanding of the systems of the strategic environment—what they are (facts and assumptions) and how they interact (observation, reason and assumptions) within the various dimensions of interaction. He considers these in terms of continuities and change—thinking in time streams to see how the present can be affected by change and how continuities of the past and changes today may play out in the future. From this assessment the strategist derives the strategic factors—the things that can potentially contribute to or detract causally from the realization of the interest. Factors may be tangible or intangible, representing any aspect of the environment. The existence of other states and actors, geography, culture, history, relationships, perspectives, perceptions, facts, and assumptions all represent potential factors that must be considered in the strategic appraisal. What the strategist understands they are, and what others believe them to be are both important.

Having identified strategic factors, the strategist continues his assessment to determine which are the key strategic factors—those critical factors at the crux of interaction within the strategic environment, representing the potential critical points of tension between continuities and change in the system of systems where the strategist may choose to act or must act to realize the interest. In strategy formulation these critical strategic factors are the "keys" to developing an effective strategy, because using, influencing and countering them is how the strategist creates strategic effects and advances or protects interests. The strategist seeks to change, leverage, or overcome these, in effect modifying or retaining the equilibrium in the strategic environment by setting objectives and developing concepts and marshaling resources to achieve the objectives. When successfully selected and achieved, the objectives create strategic effects that tip the balance in favor of the stated interests. The strategist's assessment of how to best do this is reflected in his calculation of the relationship of ends, ways, and means—the rationally stated output of strategic thought. The calculation and each of its components are based on the strategist's assessment of the relationship between the desired end state and various key factors. It is his appraisal of the strategic environment and selection of the key strategic factors that sets up the calculation.

Hence, the biggest conundrum confronting the strategist in strategy formulation is identifying the key strategic factors. By definition, the strategic environment is big, and there is a lot of information and VUCA in it—the conundrum is to determine what is really important in an overwhelming amount of information and possibilities. How do we determine strategic factors? How does the strategist achieve the focus that enables him to disregard the unimportant and not overlook something critical? Of the strategic factors, how does the strategist choose those that are key and should be addressed by strategy? How do key strategic factors lead to the rational expression of strategic thinking as ends, ways, and means? The thought processes to answer these questions are the heart of the strategic appraisal. Models and insights offered by theorists and practitioners provide guides to assist and discipline the appraisal process, but it starts with an open mind that seeks inclusive answers to broad questions. From there the strategist applies his strategic thinking competencies to narrow the focus through a successive series of questions and answers that lead to the distillation of the key factors.

Postulating broad questions creates the mindset necessary to see what is important. What are the U.S. interests and levels of intensity are broad questions and are steps 2 and 3 in the appraisal process. Factors flow from analysis and synthesis of information relevant to the interests and their intensities. What do I know in regard to facts—actors, geography, culture, history, economics, relationships, perspectives, and perceptions, etc.? For example, who else has relevant interests, what are they and what is the level of intensity? What do I not know, what can I find out, and what must I assume? What presumptions are at work in my thinking or that of others? Where can change be introduced to favorable effect? What or what changes create unfavorable effect? These are all big questions, and to answer them the strategist draws on his *weltanschauung*, focused individual research and study, and the expertise of others.

Factors are defined as pertinent facts, trends, threats, conditions, or inferences that imply an effect on the realization of the interest. Thus, factors are not accumulations of information or statements of simple facts. And their scope exceeds that of "facts bearing on the problem" in the problem solving staff study because they are concerned with what has occurred in the past, what might occur in the future, and multi-ordered effects of any changes. Factors are distinguished from information by the strategist's assessment of their potential causal relationship with the interest. While some may have a visible direct cause-and-effect relationship, many will be less obvious, and their importance lies in their second, third, or further multi-ordered implications in regard to the interest.

Consequently, factors are stated to show their bearing on the interest. For example, if the stated national interest is "a stable, peaceful China," the fact the Great Wall is 4,000 miles long is interesting, but it is only information and not a factor in regard to the interest, because the wall no longer plays a part in China's internal stability or defense. It is also a fact that the population of China is in excess of 1.3 billion. One could argue that it is a strategic factor because the sheer magnitude of the numbers involved has implications for the stated interest. However, in and of itself, the fact is of little help to the strategist other than no strategy in regard to China could ignore the inferences of such a large population. As stated, it has no real context in regard to the interest. A population-related fact better expressed as a factor potentially affecting the stability interest is: "The Chinese government is struggling to sustain adequate job growth for tens of millions of workers laid off from state-owned enterprises, migrants, and new entrants to the work force."[14] This trend could potentially threaten domestic stability in China and has a causal relationship with the interest. If the strategist considered this a key strategic factor, his strategy in regard to China would establish objectives or pursue strategic concepts that mitigate this trend. *The National Security Strategy of the United States of America* (September 2002) sought to influence global peace and domestic stability in China and elsewhere by promoting prosperity and reducing poverty around the world with an objective to "Ignite a New Era of Global Economic Growth Through Free Markets and Free Trade." It argued market economies were better than "command-and-control" economies.[15] The strategy helped encourage China toward a more viable economy and subsequent job creation.[16] Numerous other strategic factors influenced this national strategy, but the growth of the Chinese economy and its successful integration into the American-led global economy did promote a more "stable, peaceful China."

Determining strategic factors is difficult, and ultimately, like most aspects of strategy, the selection of key strategic factors is a matter of choice by the strategist. Sorting through the VUCA of the strategic environment in search of what is really important requires the strategist to approach the appraisal from multiple perspectives using his understanding of strategic theory and applying all his strategic thinking competencies. Such strategic thinking competencies act as lenses to assist the strategist in his evaluation of the strategic environment, reminding the strategist of the dimensions of the intellect that should be applied to seek and sort information and to recognize which factors are key.[17] The U.S. Army War College identifies five such competencies.

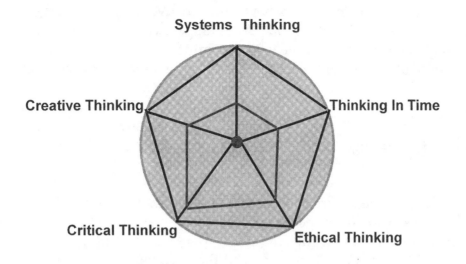

Figure 5. Strategic Thinking Competencies.[18]

Critical thinking processes are applicable to both problem solving and strategic thinking, suggesting a rational way to determine the interest and the related strategic factors. The major components of the process—clarify the concern, evaluate information, evaluate implications, and make decisions/use judgment—lead to an understanding of the facts and considerations relative to the interest and their implications. The assessment of points of view and the clarification of assumptions and inferences, as well as argument analysis and consideration of the impact of biases and traps, when applied to other actors and internally, clarify what is important in the strategic context internationally and domestically. By design, the critical thinking process seeks hard facts, forces consideration of the unknowns and the role of chance, and recognizes the strategic environment consists of both physical and humanistic systems.[19] It is one thinking lens that has great application in the strategic appraisal process.

Richard E. Neustadt and Ernest R. May in *Thinking in Time: The Uses of History for Decision Makers* also place emphasis on determining all the factors and selecting the key factors as a basis for decision making. While their focus is on issue policy, and the terminology does not use the word "factor," their first step in asking for the identification of key elements that are known, unclear, and presumed is obviously focused on determining factors. One insightful approach to this they use is to identify multiple past situations that appear analogous and list similarities and differences. Again, this process logically leads to identifying not only what is known and important in the current situation, but leverages history to get insights into potentially unrecognized factors and relationships among factors. Neustadt's and May's concept of "thinking in time" connects discrete phenomena over time and is able to relate the connections to potential futures and choices for a desired future—hence this thinking process identifies factors that matter in a strategy seeking a more favorable future.[20] Thinking in time is a disciplined process that helps mitigate uncertainty, complexity and ambiguity.

Other strategic thinking competencies also offer insights into how to think of and identify strategic factors. Systems thinking focuses on comprehending the whole, but the process identifies systems, interdependence among systems, individual aspects of particular systems in regard to their roles or functions within the whole, and the effects of any changes induced on the whole.[21] It is synthesis-centric, rather than using analysis—asking how things come together as opposed to breaking them apart and addressing them individually as a planner might. Creative thinking processes offer new and different ways of looking at information and relationships among data, actors, and events.

They help strategists view information in new and creative ways.[22] Ethical thinking processes force the examination of moral factors.[23] From each perspective and process, the strategist acquires information and insights; the processes reveal what is important in regard to interests. The strategist seeks factors relative to his own state's interests, factors relative to his adversaries' interests, factors relative to others' interests, and factors relative to the physical world and chance—looking for what is important that must be addressed or affords an opportunity to serve the state's interests. By disciplining his thinking to consider the five different lenses the strategist precludes blind spots and creates opportunities for looking at things differently; thereby increasing the probability of seeing what is important.

Structural analysis models can also assist in sorting what is important in the vast information available, and thus, lead to the identification of the key strategic factors. One simple structure to use is to look at the information from the perspective of the elements of power. Facts or trends that indicate or affect balance and relationships in power are potential strategic factors. Hence, focusing on the natural and social determinants of power of the various actors serves as a filter for sorting through the overwhelming volume of information to see what is important. The elements of power are listed below.

Natural Determinants	Social Determinants
Geography	Economic
Population	Military
Natural Resources	Political
	Socio-Psychological

Such a filter works because there are casual and interdependence relationships among interests, power, and strategy that become apparent under disciplined consideration. Power is relative, dynamic, and contextual, and the examination and weighing of information in regard to power reveals relevant factors and suggests which are key.[24] Again, the strategist considers this from the multiple perspectives of self, adversaries, others, the physical world, and chance.

Since the strategic environment is a system of systems, and people and other human entities depicted below are part of the interaction, an actor structural analysis is another way to filter information to see what is really important in regard to specific interests. Individual personalities and collective mentalities matter in the pursuit of interests. Here the strategist poses broad questions such as: who is affected by this interest and how; who else shares or opposes this interest and why; how will others act or react in regard to this interest and how and why; and what influences others' actions in regard to this interest and why? Answers to these questions reveal factors that must be considered.

Actor Structures

Individual	Movements
Leadership	States
Groups	International Business Organizations
Organizations	Private Organizations
Institutions	International Governmental Organizations
Interagency/Bureaucracy	Society/Culture

Since factors relate strategy to the interests and a proper focus of strategy is interaction, the dimensions of interaction in the strategic environment are another important information filter. In this construct, the strategist uses the dimensions as lenses to focus attention on what is important amongst the profusion of information. These dimensions are in play to a greater or lesser extent at all times. Colin S. Gray identifies some 17 strategic dimensions as depicted below, but acknowledges there may be many more. The strategist must consider factors derived from analysis using these dimensions both individually and holistically — that is each distinctly but at the same time in context with each other. Since particular dimensions play a greater role or are more critical at particular times in history, the strategist must be attuned to this potential and the fact that none of the dimensions can be ignored over time. A dimension of strategy approach is a valid methodology for identifying what is important in regard to an interest because it allows the question: "What is important relative to this interest in this dimension and how does it interact with the whole of the environment?"

Dimensions of Strategy[25]

People	Strategic Theory and Doctrine
Society	Technology
Culture	Operations
Politics	Command
Ethics	Geography
Economics and Logistics	Friction/chance/uncertainty
Organization	Adversary
Administration	Time
Information and Intelligence	

Different realms of strategy may suggest other constructs for discerning what is important in the vast array of information available to the strategist. Regardless, the appraisal process is similar. From his assessment and synthesis of the information, the strategist determines the relevant factors — facts, issues, assumptions, presumptions, threats and opportunities — that *act or interact to affect the interest.* These factors are written as simple factual statements in a manner that makes clear how they affect, and if they assist or hinder U.S. interests. From this broad understanding and list of factors, the strategist develops a refined list of key strategic factors by asking a new series of questions. What can most likely detract from or preclude the realization of the interest? What best supports or can be leveraged to realize the interest? What does policy guidance allow or preclude? What assumptions are inherent to my understanding of the situation and realization of the interests? Can these assumptions be made factual? What changes in facts or assumptions would affect the realization of interests and how? What role does chance play — are there wild cards? These questions lead to the selection of the key strategic factors — the factors the strategy must account for or that the strategist thinks provides the key to successful pursuit of the interest.

The strategist is now poised to formulate a specific strategy. Using the strategic appraisal framework he has applied strategic thinking competencies and various models to clarify interests and levels of intensity, he has culled out strategic factors relevant to the realization of the interests from an overabundance of information, and he has further refined this broad list of factors into a more focused list of key strategic factors on which to base a strategy. However the strategic appraisal framework has done much more than this. It has immersed the strategist in the strategic environment from the perspective of specific national interests. It has identified what is important relative to those interests, forced the strategist to distinguish between fact and assumption, and alerted him to the consequences of change. Thus, the framework focuses the strategy formulation process on the key strategic factors, and suggests where flexibility is needed and how strategy might be made adaptive. Further, it provides indicators for potential future issues and prepares the strategist for considering changes in strategy.

Once the strategic appraisal is complete, the strategist uses his understanding of the key strategic factors to influence the strategic environment favorably without inadvertently creating other unfavorable effects. These factors suggest suitable objectives, suggest or limit concepts, and identify appropriate resources. In addition, the key strategic factors both suggest and bound what is feasible, acceptable, and suitable in strategy formulation. The assessment of the factors also provides the basis for the consideration of risk in a strategy. Through his formulation of appropriate ends, ways, and means to leverage and account for these factors, the strategist creates favorable strategic effects leading to the realization of the interest. Which factors to act upon, what objectives to set to create favorable strategic effects, what concepts to use to achieve those objectives without adverse effects, and what resources to provide to implement the concepts are all choices made in strategy formulation from the knowledge gained in the strategic appraisal. To the extent this is done well, the strategist creates more favorable effects and brings the strategy closer to the realization of the interest.

The strategic appraisal framework serves to discipline the strategist's thought process and codify its output. Like all theory, it educates but does not dictate—the human mind must make the choices. Yet through education, it leads to potentially better appraisals and a more careful consideration of what the interests are and the factors to be considered in regard to them. Through codification, it allows critical review and a shared understanding of how a strategy is expected to work. As such, the framework is a useful tool, but a healthy *weltanschauung* is essential to retain the proper perspective on the validity of a strategy and to recognize when and whether modification or a new strategy is necessary. Theory can aid the practice of strategic *coup d'oeil* and strategy formulation by offering a framework for identifying and considering the relevant factors, but the strategist's choice of what to do, how to do it, and the resources to be made available remain a creation of the active intellect.

ENDNOTES - CHAPTER 4

1. Arthur F. Lykke, Jr., "Toward an Understanding of Military Strategy," chap. in *Military Strategy: Theory and Application*, Carlisle Barracks, PA: U.S. Army War College, 1989, pp. 3-8.

2. Carl von Clausewitz, *On War*, ed. and trans. Michael Howard and Peter Paret, Princeton: Princeton University Press, 1976, p. 102.

3. Harry R. Yarger, *Strategic Theory for the 21st Century: The Little Book on Big Strategy*, Carlisle, PA: Strategic Studies Institute, U.S. Army War College, February 2006, pp. 17-29.

4. Joint Staff, J-7, *Joint Publication 1-02, Department of Defense Dictionary of Military and Associated* Terms, Washington, DC: United States Joint Staff, April 12, 2002; amended through September 14, 2007, p. 360.

5. Donald E. Nuechterlein, *America Overcommitted: United States National Interests in the 1980s*, Lexington: The University Press of Kentucky, 1984, p. 4. This is a modification of Nuechterlein's definition.

6. Department of National Security and Strategy, *Course Directive: National Security Policy and Strategy Academic Year 2007*, Carlisle, PA: U.S. Army War College, 2006, p. 106.

7. Nuechterlein, pp. 8-14.

8. *National Security Policy and Strategy Academic Year 2007*, pp. 106-108.

9. Nuechterlein, p. 10.

10. *Ibid.*, pp. 9-14, 17-28. Nuechterlein identifies vital interests in regard to various value and cost/risk factors, discussing eight of each. These are still useful, but not inclusive.

11. *National Security Policy and Strategy Academic Year 2007*, pp. 106-108.

12. Clausewitz, p. 102.

13. *Ibid.*

14. *The World FactBook*, Central Intelligence Agency, available at *www.cia.gov/library/publications/the-world-factbook/print/ch.html*.

15. George W. Bush, *The National Security Strategy of the United States of America*, Washington, DC: The White House, September 2002, pp. 17-18.

16. *Ibid.*, p. 26. Here the administration takes credit for success.

17. Richard M. Meinhart, "Leadership and Strategic Thinking," in *Strategic Thinking*, Carlisle, PA: U.S. Army War College, 2007, pp. 36-37.

18. *Ibid.*

19. Colonel Stephen J. Gerras, Ph.D., "Thinking Critically About Critical Thinking: A Fundamental Guide for Strategic Leaders," in *Strategic Thinking*, Carlisle, PA: U.S. Army War College, 2007, pp. 47-75.

20. Richard E. Neustadt and Ernest R. May, *Thinking in Time: The Use of History for Decision Makers*, New York: The Free Press, 1986, pp. 232-240, 252-256.

21. George E. Reed, "Systems Thinking and Senior Level Leadership," in *Strategic Thinking*, Carlisle, PA: U.S. Army War College, 2007, pp. 158-162.

22. Colonel Charles D. Allen, "Creative Thinking for Individuals and Teams," in *Strategic Thinking*, Carlisle, PA: U.S. Army War College, 2007, pp. 47-75.

23. Meinhart, p. 44.

24. David Jablonsky, "National Power," in *U.S. Army War College Guide to National Security Policy and Strategy*, 2d edition, J. Boone Bartholomees, ed., Carlisle, PA: Strategic Studies Institute, U.S. Army War College, June 2006, pp. 127-142.

25. Colin S. Gray, *Modern Strategy*, Oxford, U.K.: Oxford University Press, 1999, pp. 23-44.

CHAPTER 5

MANAGING STRATEGIC RISK

James F. Holcomb

In a tactical situation one is able to see at least half the problem with the naked eye, whereas in strategy everything has to be guessed at and presumed.[1]

Carl von Clausewitz

The hierarchical chart of the Army War College strategy formulation model at Appendix I shows a final block labeled "Risk Assessment." The implication of the diagram is that risk assessment is peculiar to the development of military strategy. Indeed, it figures prominently in that process, but not uniquely so. Policy and strategy properly arrived at, demand a continuous and thorough assessment and reassessment of risk throughout the total process.

Strategists and strategic theorists throughout history have grappled with the concept of risk and methodologies for its assessment. The motivation to eliminate uncertainty in policy and strategy development as well as execution is natural if at times chimerical. There will always be uncertainty. It often will be unmeasurable. The very nature of war and conflict and the increasingly complex strategic environment ensures that this is so. Where then does this leave the aspiring student of strategy? Is risk assessment simply the "comfort level that senior planners experience as they assess key variables?"[2] It is this and more. The concept of risk assessment is worth examining in more detail to put some substance to the form.

DEFINING RISK

Defining risk is a relatively simple task. John Collins, in his primer on grand strategy, reduces it to its essentials: "Discrepancies between ends, which we have identified as interests and objectives, and means—available resources—create risks, which can rarely be quantified."[3] At its core, risk arises when ends and means are not in consonance. This is known as an "ends-means mismatch." Collins is on solid ground with this definition, the legacy of which springs from Clausewitz and his discussion of "the political object of war and the effort to be made."[4] B. H. Liddell Hart also focused on this basic truth: "Strategy depends for success, first and most, on a sound calculation and coordination of the end and the means. . . . An excess may be as harmful as a deficiency."[5] Strategic risk then is the probability of failure in achieving a strategic objective at an acceptable cost. The concept is simple to articulate and easy to understand. But, as in war, the simplest things in strategy are the most difficult.

The first difficulty is in understanding what Clausewitz and others meant by "means" in the ends-means equation. Current use of the term generally accepts that means constitute resources, that is, personnel, treasure, equipment, political will, time and so on. Clausewitz also intended a larger meaning that includes concepts or courses of action to achieve particular objectives; these coupled with resources constitute the means or "effort to be made."[6] It has become increasingly useful to separate these two components of Clausewitz' "means" for consideration in strategy formulation without confusing Clausewitz' original intent. Consequently, risk can be represented by a mismatch in ends and ways or means.

Art Lykke makes the case for this approach, developing a model comprising three variables: ends (objectives), ways (concepts, options or courses of action for achieving them) and means (resources). Using a simple metaphor of a three legged stool, he points out that if the ends, ways and means (the legs of the stool) are not of equal length then we are left with a stool (and a strategy) that is out of balance. Continuing the analogy, he defines this angle of imbalance as risk. The greater the mismatch between ends, ways and/or means, the greater the risk of achieving ones objectives.[7] This is a subtle but important addition to the simple ends-means equation. One can correctly and accurately identify the objective to be achieved and provide adequate resources to achieve it. However, if the "way" of achieving it is not in balance then there is an inherent risk of failure to achieve the strategic objective. For example, during the Cuban Missile Crisis the objective of the Kennedy administration was fairly straightforward: Get the missiles out of Cuba. The means available were adequate and deliverable. However, there were several different ways to achieve the objective. Graham Allison identifies six major categories of possible response: Do nothing, apply diplomatic pressure, secretly approach Castro, conduct an invasion, conduct air strikes, or blockade.[8] One can also see this in the continuing debate over the strategy for Kosovo and the use solely of airpower to achieve particular political objectives. In the Lykke model of the stool, the balance varies depending on which option is chosen. The degree of lopsidedness or imbalance defines risk. Choosing the right policy option (or way) to achieve the strategic objective is therefore a critical consideration even assuming a clear objective and adequate means. That is, an adequately resourced "way" that is inappropriate to the "end" would still create risk of failure to achieve the strategic objective.

Thus, the definition of risk is the degree to which strategic objectives, concepts and resources are in or out of balance. Since strategy is a dynamic process, one must understand that all three elements are variable and subject to change over time. The formulation of effective strategy for any endeavor is a constant quest to ensure balance among the variables. The definition applies to all aspects of strategy development whether dealing with national security (grand) strategy, defense, military or theater strategies, business strategy or even personal strategies.

WHY IS STRATEGIC RISK ASSESSMENT DIFFICULT?

The subtitle is borrowed from David Jablonsky's piece "Why is Strategy Difficult?"[9] The very nature of war and conflict presupposes a relationship between thinking adversaries. This, in turn, ensures that a degree of ambiguity, uncertainty and yes, risk will exist in any developed strategy. Indeed, Clausewitz devotes the central theme of *On War* to this very premise; that is what distinguishes his work from his predecessors and ensures its continued relevance to the present day. Clausewitz was not the only one to recognize the subjective nature of war, but he was the first to mark that characteristic as preeminent. Throughout his work, there are allusions to "chance," "luck," "guesswork," "uncertainty," "probabilities" and so on. The search for hard truths is a frustrating one. This in itself is a lesson. The analogies and metaphors the Prussian philosopher provides to help understand the nature of war are not based on chess, but reflect "a duel on a larger scale," "a pair of wrestlers," "commerce," a "collision of living forces" or a "game of chance." Formulating strategy presupposes "an animate object that *reacts*," and moreover, reacts unpredictably. This equates to Andre Beufre's definition of strategy as the "art of the dialectic of two opposing wills using force to solve their dispute."[10] Just as one actor identifies objectives, develops concepts and allocates resources, so does the potential or actual adversary. The variables in the strategic equation have now doubled, further complicating the task. Moreover, ambiguity and uncertainty *increase* as one climbs up the strategic ladder as moral factors gain primacy over material ones.[11] The problem is that these moral factors can only be guessed at.

Clausewitz explicitly refers to this transition from certainty to uncertainty in strategic analysis:

> At this point, then, intellectual activity leaves the field of the exact sciences of logic and mathematics. It then becomes an art in the broadest meaning of the term-the faculty of using judgement to detect the most important and decisive elements in the vast array of facts and situations.[12]

The strategist now faces a prospect "that Newton himself would quail before the algebraic problems it could pose."[13] Risk assessment is difficult because strategy is difficult; strategy is difficult because war is the most complex of human undertakings and filled with unknowns. Liddell Hart concludes in this regard: "This complicates calculation, because no man can exactly calculate the capacity of human genius and stupidity, nor the incapacity of will."[14] It is the inherent nature of war itself that sets the student adrift in a strategic sea of uncertainty.

GENIUS AND UNCERTAINTY

Despite this uncertainty, there is comfort in the knowledge that others have navigated these waters before. The challenge is to somehow structure or frame the strategic problem to minimize the unknown or more importantly, to account for it. The effective strategist strives for the "closest approximation of the truth" knowing that full knowledge is an impossibility.[15]

Clausewitz identifies two preeminent qualities in a successful strategist that bear consideration:

> If the mind is to emerge unscathed from this relentless struggle with the unforeseen, two qualities are indispensable: first, an intellect that, even in the darkest hour, retains some glimmerings of the inner light which leads to truth; and second, the courage to follow this faint light wherever it may lead (emphasis in the original).[16]

These are the elements that define what Clausewitz terms "genius." The aspiring strategist should not be misled or discouraged by the use of the term however. Clausewitz does not refer to the result of good genetics, but to the development of a mind through study and experience. He is clear on this point as he continues his discussion: "It is the *average result* that indicates the presence of military genius."[17] In other words, "genius" as Clausewitz describes it is not solely the unique gift of a Napoleon or Gustavus or Hannibal. It is an achievable skill and the "inner light" can be taught and learned.

Von Moltke the Elder took up the same theme several generations later:

> What is necessary is to discover the situation, such as it is, in spite of its being surrounded by the fog of the unknown; then to *appreciate soundly* what is seen, to *guess* what is not seen, to *take a decision quickly, finally to act with vigour*, without hesitation[18]

The message is that an education in strategic subjects, followed by continuous historical study to maintain mental suppleness combined with vicarious experience through exercise, and actual experience, all contribute to acquiring the skills necessary for finding the "closest approximation of the truth." Strategic ability is rarely born, more often learned, but eminently achievable.

Acknowledging the theoretical uncertainties inherent in war, conflict and policy and strategy development is an important, if unsatisfying, step in understanding risk assessment. It allows a better framing of the strategic puzzle. It is simply a matter of knowing what is not known in order to make better use of what is known and, as von Moltke suggests, to guess what is not seen. Guessing well is an inherent part of the art of Grand Strategy.

THE ENDS, WAYS, MEANS CONUNDRUM IN RISK ASSESSMENT

The essence of the challenge of strategy in general and risk assessment in particular is the core problem of relating ends to ways and means. Compounding this basic conundrum is the fact that most often the ends will be abstract while the ways and means will be relatively well defined.[19] In addition, the real test of the master of strategic art is to translate obtuse, politically couched objectives into specific actions. This is likely to become more of a challenge as the nature, scope and direction of potential threats multiply. Articulating the political objective in the event of a Major Theater War is relatively easy; however, achieving significant clarity in political objectives in multiplying crises around the world, especially where vital U.S. interests are not at stake, will become increasingly problematic. One analyst notes in a critique of the U.S. foreign policy process:

> Any ambiguity in the ends-means relationship, any loss in the value roots of policy, or any failure to maintain a firm commitment to the achievement of the national purpose cannot help but deprive a foreign policy of essential meaning and effectiveness.[20]

A second related potential pitfall facing the grand strategist is the "tail wagging the dog" phenomenon. In the absence of clear political objectives or policy guidance, the means can in fact "deflect the direction of ends."[21] What gets done becomes what one has the capability of doing. The ways and means can develop a momentum of their own and the result is strategy by default, usually at the risk of desired political outcomes. The von Schlieffen Plan and America's experience in Vietnam are two stark historic examples of this effect.

This problem has been ascribed to the "triumph of technique" in American foreign policy. One critic specifically targets the militarization of foreign affairs during the Cold War and an emphasis on quantitative assessments based solely on capabilities.[22] In such cases, Clausewitz' "ephemeral factors" are discounted and "consideration of political subtleties tends to be shunted aside."[23] Ferdinand Foch, writing in 1903, complained of the same phenomenon but went further: "while the moral factors were depressed as *causes* [of war], they were also suppressed as *effects*." The unintended result is that strategy can become a function solely of material factors.[24] The dramatic changes of the last decade and the growing complexities and dimensions of current and future world problems make simplistic, capabilities-based approaches dangerous at their worst, or potentially ineffective at best. Getting ends, ways and means right has always been hard; it is becoming harder.

DETERMINING RISK

The simple definition of risk as an imbalance in ends, ways and/or means is straightforward but clearly incomplete. How does one measure the *degree* of risk in any particular strategic endeavor? This is the heart of the dilemma.

Neuchterlein and National Interests.

Risk assessment is inherent to the entire strategy formulation process. Donald Neuchterlein addresses risk in his discussion on identifying national interests and their intensities, a fundamental prerequisite to policy and strategy development. He posits sixteen criteria for assessing a particular issue as a vital interest.[25] These are divided into value and cost/risk factors[26*]:

Value Factors	Cost/Risk Factors
Proximity of the danger	Economic costs of hostilities
Nature of the threat	Estimated casualties
Economic stake	Risk of protracted conflict
Sentimental attachment	Risk of enlarged conflict
Type of government and human rights	Cost of defeat or stalemate
Effect on the balance of power	Cost of public opposition
National prestige at stake	Risk of UN opposition
Support of allies	Risk of congressional opposition
* Note there is no direct correlation between values and cost/risk factors; they are randomly listed.	

Figure 1. Value and Cost/Risk Factors.

Neuchterlein advocates using a simple valuation process by rating each factor high, medium or low or even assigning numerical scores to the factors. Likewise, for a particular issue, some factors may be more important than others and can be appropriately weighted or prioritized. The factor scores are then totaled. If the value totals of a particular issue are high compared to a low or medium cost/risk valuation, then the issue probably constitutes a vital interest. Neuchterlein does not claim a scientific basis for his methodology, only that "[i]t provides for systematic analysis of specific foreign policy issues; it should therefore lead to better judgments about levels of interest for the United States and its antagonists and, one would hope, to wiser policies than would otherwise be the case."[27] Thus, it provides a simple tool that assists in the discrimination of interests in relative terms. Having determined "vitalness," the policy maker/strategist is in a better position to articulate a balanced set of ends, ways and means in the strategy formulation process by accounting for degrees of risk up front.

Calculated Risk.

The noted naval theorist, Admiral J. C. Wylie, took a more rigorous approach to the problem in a tongue-in-cheek article published in 1953 entitled "The Calculation of Risk."[28] The impetus for the short article apparently arose from the 1953 budget hearings in which the Army representative answered difficult questions with the rejoinder "Mr. Congressman, that is a calculated risk." Of course no one knew what a calculated risk was or how to calculate it, so Wylie decided to try.[29] Although intended facetiously, Wylie's little paper does merit consideration in its own right. Using a series of variables and equations, he describes various strategic characteristics.[30]

P = Profit if successful
C_n = Cost if not attempted
C_f = Cost of attempt that fails
C_s = Cost of attempt that succeeds
S = Probability of success

Wylie defines risk as **P/C_f**, or the potential profit divided by the cost of a failed attempt. As long as this is greater than 1, the enterprise (or strategy) is "encouraged"; likewise, if less than 1, "discouraged." These machinations result in general determining equations:

If P x S < Cf (1-S) then "no go"
If P x S > Cf (1-S) then "go"

These equations describe what is already known instinctively: If the payoff times the probability of success is greater than the cost of failure times the probability of failure, the result is a winning strategy.

Risk is further defined by an equation: $Cf/Cs < S/(1-S)$

That is, the cost of a failed attempt over the cost of a successful attempt must be less than the probability of success divided by the probability of failure.

Having had his fun with the reader, Wylie further stipulates that "To insure success in its use, there is only one condition that must be met: the factors involved must never be expressed in arithmetic quantities. That would blunt the fine edge of judgment and obscure the true balance of intangibles." Wylie clearly subscribes to the Clausewitzian notions of uncertainty and unpredictability in war and he makes this clear in his important and short book, *Military Strategy: A General Theory of Power Control*. In it he further admonishes the reader to plan for a complete spectrum of strategies in order to have a "reserve" of strategies for the inevitable changes that will occur. He also warns that "the player who plans for only one strategy runs a great risk simply because his opponent soon detects the single strategy-and counters it . . . planning for certitude is the greatest of all military mistakes. . . ."[31] Wylie's reserve of strategies is essentially conceptual hedging for uncertainty with its inherent risk. This, to borrow from operational art, is planning for strategic branches and sequels or for potential developments requiring adjustments in ends, ways or means as a particular strategy is implemented

Although Wylie's formulations were intended to ridicule early whiz kids, he actually produced a relatively sophisticated approach to a difficult concept. For example, an examination of a recent study prepared by the CIA to address risk assessment and management of threats to security, uses an identical formulation.[32] Defining risk as the potential of damage or loss to an asset, the study assesses the level of risk as the impact of loss or damage to the asset and the likelihood (probability) that a specific vulnerability could be exploited by a particular threat.[33] The formulation is defensive in nature since it is addressing security protection issues. Nevertheless, it equates exactly to Wylie's **Cf (1-S)**, that is, the **Cost of Failure times the Probability of Failure.** Strategy and risk assessment are indeed eternal.[34]

RISK MANAGEMENT

The process of risk assessment is dynamic in nature over time and circumstance. That is, the variables are in constant flux. Risk assessment is simply the constant effort to identify and correct imbalances among the key variables. The first ability of the strategist is to recognize when variables change. The second is to adjust the remaining variables to account for the "delta" or, as it has been defined, the risk. This is known as risk management. In simplest terms, the strategist has several clear options:[35]

Modify Ends. When the price to achieve a particular objective is too high or the ability to affect a "center of gravity" is limited, it may become necessary to reduce the overall objective to more realistic terms. Examples include the decision to forego a cross-channel attack in 1942 in favor of North Africa, or accepting a lesser objective than the unification of the Korean peninsula after the Chinese intervention.

Modify Means. An increase or reallocation of resources may affect the ability to implement a strategy and achieve the objective. This is, however, not simply a quantitative solution. A definition of resources includes unpredictable and changeable elements as well. For example, public support of a particular policy/strategy is a key consideration in a democracy and must be accounted for even if difficult to measure. Vietnam is a classic example of not adequately modifying means by calling up the reserves and generating sufficient public support for the effort.

Modify Ways. Assuming that the objective is sound and resources are adequate, there will likely be multiple ways to achieve the desired end-state. Use of the various elements of power (political, military, economic, informational) in differing combinations with varying emphasis may enhance the ability to achieve the same overall objective. The recent Kosovo experience serves as a good case of modifying ways: The deployment of Task Force Hawk and increasing information about planning for possible ground options coupled with retargeting the air operation are thought to have contributed to Milosevic's decision to withdraw forces.

Reassess the Risk. Over time some of the going-in assumptions may be proven invalid. Additional information may become available or gaps in knowledge filled. The strategist needs to recognize the potential strategic effect of more or less information, recognizing that the 100 percent solution will always be elusive due to the "ephemeral factors." It is important to reemphasize that this process is dynamic and "at once abstract and rational, [and] must be capable of synthesizing both psychological and material data."[36] Indeed, one man's risk is another man's certitude and therefore grist for the continuously grinding strategic mill.

FIVE PATTERNS OF STRATEGY FOR RISK ASSESSMENT AND MANAGEMENT

Andre Beaufre addresses the "ends-means" conundrum in his classic book *Introduction to Strategy*. His intent is to provide a series of models, what he calls patterns of strategy, to assist in the process of strategic thinking.[37] The models are intended to show how various and fundamentally differing strategies can spring from the dynamic relationship between ends, ways and means. These five patterns are macro-descriptors and it is clear to see that countless variations are possible.

Ends Moderate, Means Large. This is described as a strategy of "direct threat"; nuclear deterrence strategy is given as example of this pattern.

Ends Moderate, Means Limited. Consisting of a pattern of "indirect pressure," this pattern is useful when freedom of action is limited. It emphasizes political, diplomatic, and economic elements of power at the expense of direct military action. It models the basis of Soviet strategy, that is, avoiding direct military confrontation with the United States.

Ends Important, Ways Limited (Low Freedom of Action), Means Limited. This pattern constitutes a combination of "direct threat" and "indirect pressure" applied in successive actions and reflects the strategy of indirect approach as described by Liddell Hart. It is most appropriate to nations strong defensively but with limited resources.

Ends Important, Ways Unlimited (High Freedom of Action), Means Inadequate. This reflects a strategy of protracted war but at a low level of military intensity. It is the theoretical basis for Mao Tse-Tung's theory of protracted struggle.

Ends Important, Means Unlimited. This traditional pattern is characterized by "violent conflict aiming at military victory." Beufre describes it as the classic strategy of the Napoleonic era with Clausewitz as its principal theorist.

With these five patterns of strategy as a basis, Collins addresses risk specifically with seven examples of how to balance the strategic equation:[38]

- Eliminate waste [modifying ways and/or means]
- Compress objectives [modifying ends]
- Adjust strategy [modifying ways]
- Augment assets [modifying means]
- Reduce ends and increase means [modifying ends and means]
- Bluff [adversary misinterprets your ends, ways, means]
- Give up on the objective [the ultimate modification of ends]

Intended as examples, achieving strategic balance and hence strategic effectiveness may require application of one, more or other creative elements to induce change in the strategic equation.

READINESS AND RISK

There does exist detailed and rigorously institutionalized processes for measuring risk within the U.S. defense establishment. The roots of these processes spring from the era of McNamara and the introduction of systems analysis to defense planning. In general, these methodologies represent an attempt to institutionally account for the unknown and help to "guess well." For example, the Joint Net Assessment (JNA) is the informal process that "provides a strategic level risk assessment and provides the basis for developing risk associated with alternative force structures and strategies."[39] The JNA draws on multiple sources of information and contributes to other strategic assessments and potentially to changes in the National Military Strategy. Normally a net assessment is developed every four years but dramatic changes in the geostrategic environment can result in more frequent assessments. One of the sources of information feeding the JNA process is the regularized readiness reporting system. Therefore, bureaucratically and institutionally, at least in the Department of Defense, strategic risk is related closely to readiness. That is the system. But as recent events in Kosovo have demonstrated, the reality of risk assessment can have as much to do with art as with science.

THE CHAIRMAN'S READINESS SYSTEM

The Chairman's Readiness System is the process by which the Chairman of the Joint Chiefs of Staff assesses the military's readiness to fulfill the requirements of the National Military Strategy (NMS). The vehicle for assessing and reporting readiness across the armed forces is the Joint Monthly Readiness Review (JMRR).[40]

The Chairman's overall strategic assessment draws on three sources of information: The individual services unit readiness reports, the Unified Combatant Commanders joint readiness assessments and the Combat Support Agencies reports on their ability to support the Combatant Commanders. A full JMRR takes place quarterly with an assessment of capabilities and risk currently and out to twelve months in the future.

The assessments are scenario driven and derive from the current National Military Strategy. The scenarios normally start with a real-world operation currently underway and include a Smaller Scale Contingency (SSC) or one or two Major Theater Wars (MTW) "in two distant theaters in overlapping timeframes"[41] Combatant Commanders are then required to address potential deficiencies in their ability to execute the scenario-based mission requirements. Deficiencies are identified and categorized. Fixes are suggested or they are forwarded for consideration and solution by other working bodies. Unresolved deficiencies are aggregated and considered collectively. These are then termed "key risk elements." Further aggregation may intensify into "overall strategic concerns";

these are potential risks to implementation of the National Military Strategy itself and constitute an overall strategic risk assessment.[42]

The system is largely score-based, that is, commanders at all levels are charged with assessing their own readiness and that of their subordinates and assigning a value to it. Scores are aggregated as assessments are forwarded upward. The process would appear at first glance to be relatively sound based as it is on seemingly quantitative assessments. However, the "granularity" of assessment becomes less clear as the reports are progressively aggregated. In fact, there are substantial opportunities for commanders to inject subjective assessments into the process.[43] It is here, as Clausewitz says, that "intellectual activity leaves the field of the exact sciences of logic and mathematics. It then becomes an art in the broadest meaning of the term."[44] Differing perceptions of readiness in turn drive differing perceptions of the degree of ultimate risk for the armed forces to implement the National Military Strategy, and by extension, elements of the National Security Strategy. This is the basis of the readiness debate within the services, the Joint Staff, the Department of Defense, and Congress today.[45]

Although the system would appear to guess well on the surface, there is growing concern that an ends-ways-means mismatch exists. Culturally, commanders are naturally reluctant to report their commands unready to execute their missions. Likewise, senior commanders are adverse to less than capable readiness assessments from their subordinates. Further clouding the process is the political scrutiny under which it takes place. The measure of risk may depend on how one interprets the current strategic mandate. For example, testifying to Congress in 2000, Chairman of the Joint Chiefs General Henry Shelton stated, "The United States [must be] able to deter and defeat large-scale cross-border aggression in two distant theaters in overlapping time frames. In short, we must be able to fight and win two major theater wars nearly simultaneously."[46] General Shelton assessed the risk factors for fighting and winning the first Major Theater War as "moderate," but the second as "high."[47] What does this mean in real terms, especially with the occasional Smaller Scale Contingency thrown in for good measure? One's point of view depends on where one sits. "Moderate" risk to the Department of Defense may be acceptable to the Senate Armed Services Committee, but as it is derived from an aggregated assessment, it may be considered downright dangerous by Central Command or Transportation Command.

THE CASE OF KOSOVO AND TWO MTW'S

The 1999 conflict in Kosovo provides a fitting vehicle for examining in more real terms the nature of risk in strategy formulation and implementation. It is not the intent to examine the strategy for the conflict itself although this has proven to be a rich field of discussion and debate, especially with regard to matching political ends to military objectives, courses of action and resources. More interesting is the impact the conflict had on the ability to execute, if need be, declared elements of the National Security and National Military Strategies and the risk thereby incurred as a result of the commitment to the Kosovo operation.

As established, the National Military Strategy (as well as the National Security and Defense Strategies) posit as a fundamental element the ability to "deter and defeat nearly simultaneous, large-scale, cross-border aggression in two distant theaters in overlapping time frames." Moreover, this obtains in an environment in which the United States is globally engaged and indeed, conducting "multiple concurrent smaller-scale contingency operations" at the same time.

The National Security Strategy addresses the possibility that in the event of one or two MTW's, of withdrawing from ongoing contingency operations. In doing so, the NSS acknowledges accepting a "degree of risk" since such a course is necessary to "reduce the greater risk incurred if we failed to respond adequately to major theater wars." What happens when a smaller scale contingency takes on the characteristics, at least in part, of a major theater war?

As outlined earlier, the Joint Monthly Readiness Report (JMRR) is the Chairman's snapshot of the U.S. Armed Forces ability to execute the National Military Strategy. The two JMRRs crafted during and immediately following the Kosovo conflict highlighted some of the risk entailed in the two-MTW component of the National Military Strategy.

The JMRR covering the April to June 1999 timeframe posited as a scenario an expanding Kosovo operation lasting until September with a simultaneous outbreak of war on the Korean peninsula.[48] It assessed the risk of not prevailing in the Korean MTW as "moderate" and the risk of successfully responding to a second, unstated MTW as "high." Moderate risk under the given scenario was defined in terms of time and potential casualties:

> This does not mean that U.S. forces would not prevail in either contingency [Kosovo and Korea], but rather, that potentially longer timelines required to initiate the counter-offensive increase the potential for higher casualties to forces in the interim and during the warfight.

As might be expected, the Air Force was particularly affected due to its significant commitment to Kosovo. In fact, the Air Force level of effort in Kosovo constituted an MTW in its own right.[49] The strategic concerns listed included mobility shortfalls, logistics/sustainment shortfalls, and C4 and ISR deficiencies. Since strategic concerns are "an aggregation of key risk elements that impact [on] readiness to execute the National Military Strategy," the JMRR in effect provides an overall and general articulation of risk.[50]

The overall strategic effect of this risk was well articulated in the Kosovo After Action Report to Congress:

> Without question, a situation in which the United States would have to prosecute two major theater wars nearly simultaneously would be extraordinarily demanding-well beyond that required for Operations DESERT SHIELD and DESERT STORM in 1990 and 1991. It would involve our complete commitment as a nation and would entail all elements of our total force . . . Consistent with our defense strategy, U.S. forces could not have continued the intense campaign in Kosovo and, at the same time, conducted two nearly simultaneous major theater wars.[51]

In fact, in the course of operations in Kosovo, higher levels of risk were reassessed and some measures were taken to bring the strategic variables into better balance. One assumption notes that the forces in and around Southwest Asia, coupled with elements enforcing the no-fly zone constituted an effective deterrent to Saddam. The air-bridge supporting the Kosovo operation was also considered to be a positive asset if operations had to be redirected to the Gulf. However, in Northeast Asia some units were repositioned and others put on a "tighter string" for a quicker response in the event of crisis. The objective was to "maintain a very visible defense capability to discourage leaders in Baghdad and Pyongyang. . . ."[52] In other words, some adjustments in ways and means were undertaken to reduce potential strategic risk in undertaking the Kosovo operation.

If all this language leaves readers slightly dissatisfied with the ability of the defense establishment to measure and articulate risk, then they are in good company. Both the Secretary of Defense and the Chairman of the Joint Chiefs also acknowledge a shortcoming in this particular strategic skill. The Kosovo experience brought home the potential impact that smaller scale contingencies could have on the execution of the National Military Strategy, especially the two-MTW capability.

> Risk analysis is important in judging force readiness where commitments are made to support important and necessary operations but do not involve our vital interests. Some smaller scale contingencies may be in this category.[53]

In fact, the statement of the Secretary and Chairman before Congress acknowledged that "managing these risks is a highly complicated endeavor that would benefit from a more structured and dynamic set of tools for assessing our ability to conduct major wars when we respond to contingencies."[54] The search for "the closest approximation of the truth," like strategy, is eternal.

CONCLUSION

Assessing and managing strategic risk is an inherently inexact process. It encompasses a combination of inputs, both material and moral, that defy empirical resolution. Weighing these inputs, identifying possible outcomes and planning for uncertainty should be done with the clear understanding that a complete solution is impossible to achieve but always striven for. Once a strategy is developed, the most important strategic skill and the true mark of strategic "genius" is accounting for potential change and recognizing actual change in a timely enough manner to adjust the strategic variables and thereby ensure a valid strategic equation oriented firmly on achieving the political objectives at hand. This is increasingly difficult to do in a dynamically changing strategic environment with myriad threats, challenges, actors and unclear potential effects. This is why the development and execution of strategy is primarily an art and why the requirement for developing masters of that art is so essential. In the end though, the essential elements of strategic risk are unchanged through the ages and consist in the proper balancing of ends, ways and means to achieve the desired strategic outcome. Understanding that fundamental relationship and "guessing well" through study, exercise and experience will ensure that assessing and managing strategic risk rises above simply "the comfort level of strategic planners." A gastro-intestinal assessment is not good enough. It never was.

ENDNOTES - CHAPTER 5

1. Carl von Clausewitz, *On War*, Michael Howard and Peter Paret, ed., Princeton, NJ: Princeton University Press, 1976, pp. 178-179.

2. Henry C. Bartlett, G. Paul Holman, Jr., and Timothy E. Somes, "The Art of Strategy and Force Planning," in *Strategy and Force Planning*, The Strategy and Force Planning Faculty, ed., U.S. Naval War College, Newport, RI: Naval War College Press, 1995, p. 20.

3. John M. Collins, *Grand Strategy: Principles and Practices*, Annapolis, MD: Naval Institute Press, 1973, p. 5.

4. Clausewitz, pp. 81, 92, 585.

5. B. H. Liddell Hart, *Strategy*, 2nd ed., New York: Meridian, 1991, pp. 322-323. Liddell Hart sounds here very much like Clausewitz. See Clausewitz, *On War*, p. 177: "A prince or general can best demonstrate his genius by managing a campaign exactly to suit his objectives and resources, doing neither too much nor too little."

6. See Clausewitz, pp. 92-95, for a discussion of "ways."

7. Arthur F. Lykke, "Defining Military Strategy," *Military Review*, Vol. 69, No. 5, May 1989, pp. 2-8.

8. Graham Allison and Philip Zelikow, *Essence of Decision: Explaining the Cuban Missile Crisis*, 2nd ed., New York: Longman, 1999, pp. 111-120.

9. David Jablonsky, *Why is Strategy Difficult?* Carlisle Barracks, PA: U.S. Army War College, Strategic Studies Institute, June 1992.

10. Andre Beufre, *An Introduction to Strategy*, New York: Praeger, 1965, p. 20.

11. Clausewitz, *On War*, pp. 178, 586.

12. *Ibid.*, p. 585.

13. *Ibid.*, pp. 112, 586. Attributed to Napoleon, it is interesting that Clausewitz uses it in support of two different discussions; one on Military Genius and the other on the Scale of the Objective and the Effort To Be Made.

14. Liddell Hart, p. 323.

15. *Ibid.*

16. Clausewitz, p. 102.

17. *Ibid.*, p. 103.

18. Von Moltke is quoted here in Ferdinand Foch, *The Principles of War*, New York: Holt, 1920, p. 17.

19. Roger S. Whitcomb, *The American Approach to Foreign Affairs: An Uncertain Tradition*, Westport, CT: Praeger, 1998, p. 71.

20. *Ibid.*

21. *Ibid.*

22. *Ibid.*, p. 72.

23. *Ibid.* See also M. Thomas Davis, "Size Military to Strategy, Not Vice Versa," *Government Executive*, Vol. 31, No. 12, December 1999, pp. 81-82.

24. Foch, *The Principles of War*, p. 3.

25. Donald E. Neuchterlein, *America Overcommitted: United States National Interests in the 1980s*, Lexington, Kentucky: University Press of Kentucky, 1985, pp. 18-28. Note that there is no direct correlation between value and cost/risk factors; they are randomly listed.

26. *Ibid.*, p. 28.

27. J. C. Wylie, "The Calculation of Risk," *United States Naval Institute Proceedings*, July 1953, p. 725.

28. See introduction by John B. Hattendorf in J. C. Wylie, *Military Strategy: A General Theory of Power Control*, Annapolis, MD: Naval Institute Press, 1989, p. xxvii.

29. I have modified the variables for greater ease of understanding.

30. Wylie, pp. 71-72.

31. Center for Central Intelligence Agency Security, *Analytical Risk Management*, December 1998.

32. *Ibid.*, p. 29.

33. A reference to Chapter 13 "Strategy Eternal" in Colin S. Gray, *Modern Strategy*, Oxford, U.K.: Oxford University Press, 1999.

34. Bartlett, Holman and Somes, "The Art of Strategy and Force Planning," *Strategy and Force Planning*, p. 19.

35. Beufre, p. 29.

36. *Ibid.*, pp. 26-29.

37. Collins, pp. 6-7.

38. CJSCI 3100.01A, *Joint Strategic Planning System*, September 1, 1999, p. E-5.

39. CJCSI 3401.01B, July 1, 1999, *Chairman's Readiness System*.

40. William J. Clinton, *A National Security Strategy for a New Century*, Washington, DC: The White House, December 1999, p. 19.

41. *The Chairman's Readiness System*, Enclosure E; see also Michael A. Pearson ed., *How the Army Runs*, Carlisle, PA: U.S. Army War College, April 1, 1999, pp. 8-6 – 8-10.

42. Admiral Joseph W. Prueher, "Measuring Readiness," *Armed Forces Journal International*, January 1999, p. 16.

43. Clausewitz, p. 585.

44. David Abel, "Two War Strategy is 'Unrealistic,' Senator Says," *Defense Week* , December 6, 1999, p. 1.

45. Congress, Senate Armed Services Committee, "Joint Statement of William S. Cohen and General Henry H. Shelton," *Hearing on Kosovo After-Action Review*, October 14,1999.

46. Henry H. Shelton, Chairman of the Joint Chiefs of Staff, *Posture Statement before the 106th Congress Committee on Armed Services, United States Senate*, February 8, 2000, p. 5.

47. JMRR information from Elaine M. Grossman, "U.S. Forces May Have Faced High Risk If Major War Erupted Last Spring," *Inside the Pentagon*, October 21, 1999, p. 1; and Elaine M. Grossman, "U.S. Forces Still Faced High Readiness Risk After Kosovo Air War," *Inside the Pentagon*, January 6, 2000, p. 1. See also Elaine M. Grossman, "DOD Finds Readiness Risks in 'One-And-A-Half' Overlapping Wars," *Inside the Pentagon*, May 25, 2000, p. 2.

48. William S. Cohen and Henry H. Shelton, *Report to Congress: Kosovo/Operation Allied Force After-Action Report*, January 31, 2000, p. 121.

49. The subsequent JMRR (July-September 1999) had an even more dire assessment. The scenario assumed all real-world ongoing commitments with an outbreak of war in Southwest Asia. The JMRR assessed "moderate to high risk factors for conducting this scenario." See Grossman, "U.S. Forces Still Faced High Risk After Kosovo Air War."

50. Cohen and Shelton, *Report to Congress*, p. 12.

51. "Joint Statement . . . ," *Hearing on Kosovo After-Action Review*, p. 7.

52. Cohen and Shelton, *Report to Congress*, p. 121

53. "Joint Statement . . . ," *Hearing on Kosovo After-Action Review*, p. 8.

CHAPTER 6

A THEORY OF VICTORY

J. Boone Bartholomees, Jr.

The United States is developing a reputation much like Germany had in the 20th century of being tactically and operationally superb but strategically inept. Often stated as a tendency to win the war but lose the peace, this problem has a huge theoretical component that the national security community has only recently begun to address. In fact, the concept of victory is the biggest theoretical challenge facing security professionals today. We simply do not really understand what victory is and how it happens. Worse, we do not have the necessary intellectual framework to think about the problem.

Doesn't everyone instinctively understand winning and losing—or at least hasn't everyone been taught since early childhood to understand those concepts? While there is truth in that assertion, it is not completely accurate in the field of warfare. What people understand as winning comes from the context with which they are most familiar—games and sports. In sports, winning is scoring more points or going faster than the other guy, usually within some pre-established parameters like time or distance. Card games, board games, and even computer games are similar in that there are clearly established conditions for winning—even if there might be multiple sets of potential outcomes that satisfy those conditions or multiple strategies for achieving them. The problem is that the concept of winning in sports and games is completely inadequate for understanding victory in war. Whatever war is, it is neither a sport nor a game, and analogies to either of those activities always fall short. In terms of a theory of victory, the first place a sports/game analogy falls short is specifically that there are no established or even universally accepted rules or conditions for winning in war. One might counter that soldiers and statesmen know—perhaps instinctively or perhaps as a result of training and study—that defeating the enemy's army produces victory. That may often be so, although it demonstrably does not work in every case, but our knowledge and understanding stops there. How does beating the enemy's army produce victory, and what can one do when that does not work?

The problem is that the security profession lacks a basic theoretical construct within which to think about winning wars. Because of this lack of theory, mankind has fought wars for at least 5000 years without systematically understanding why they are won or lost. In a sense, victory or defeat has always been a matter of serendipity or luck or intuition or genius or sheer hard fighting rather than the result of a well thought out and understood intellectual exercise. Gallons of ink have been expended over the centuries on how to win wars, but that effort has largely been uninformed by even a rudimentary theory of victory. Many existing theories of war skip over what victory is and why one theoretically wins or loses to directly address the seemingly more difficult issue of how one wins a war militarily. When theorists do address winning, it is usually in passing, as an assumption from which their analysis proceeds, or as a tangential excursion from their primary topic. Clausewitz is an exception to this broad assertion, but his musings on winning are scattered and incomplete. There is a school of thought that claims theory is not necessary for competent performance.[1] While that might explain how mankind has done without a theory of victory for so long, it does not negate the utility of theory. William C. Martel of the faculty of the Fletcher School at Tufts asserts that the theory of victory is and must be distinct from the theory of war.[2] Whether that is true or not, security professionals need to think systematically about winning. That is not to imply that military victory without luck or genius or hard fighting is either possible or desirable, or that existing theories of war are somehow wrong. They just might benefit from some supplemental thought specifically on winning and victory. Fortunately, the extant theoretical literature contains enough material that we can begin to construct a theory of victory.[3]

The author, unsurprisingly, is not alone in believing we need a theory of victory. In fact, the low-level debate that has been going on since at least the 1960's about both the meaning and possibility of victory has been substantially widened since the events of September 11, 2001. Theoretical discussions on victory and winning through the end of the Cold War tended to center around the possibility of victory in a nuclear exchange—could one really win such an exchange? Authors tended to assume both definition and understanding of victory. More recent scholarship has addressed the theory of winning more directly. Theorist Colin S. Gray wrote a monograph on the possibility of decisive victory that addresses the concept of winning, although his primary thrust is at the concept of decisiveness.[4] William Martel published a book on the theory of victory in 2007.[5] Martel acknowledges his is not a complete theory of victory, he calls it a pre-theory, but he offers an excellent start. I certainly cannot present a comprehensive theory of victory either, but I offer the following thoughts to continue the discussion and debate.

Webster's tells us a theory is simply a plausible or generally acceptable body of principles used to explain a phenomena. A theory should provide basic definitions, assumptions, and testable hypotheses. The first task, then, is to define winning or victory in war. To get at the definitions, we will explore some hypothesis on victory around the issues of what victory is, how victory works, who decides the winner, and based on what criteria. Finally, we will present some thoughts on how one wins a war. These will be at a theoretical level rather than the more common debate about attrition versus maneuver, direct versus indirect approaches, etc. Regrettably, this paper may pose more questions than hard, reliable answers. That reflects the nature of the topic and is perhaps inevitable at this stage of the discussion.

What Is Winning and Victory?

Victory in war is at the most basic level an assessment, not a fact or condition. It is someone's opinion—or an amalgamation of opinions. In sports terms, to use one of those bad analogies I warned against, it is taking score at the end of a game, but it is done by a combination of fans, sportswriters, players, coaches, and league officials voting, each with an indeterminate degree of impact on the final result and each able to review and alter his vote at any time. Victory in war may or may not have anything to do with objective criteria like respective casualties, territory taken or lost, tons of bombs dropped, or facilities destroyed. In winning a war, those things matter—at least at some level and always in terms of their effect on perception—but what matters most is the ultimate perception of the situation, not the facts. And the perception will be of the effects, not the effort—there is no credit for trying hard. Different people, depending on their perspective, can legitimately differ in their assessment. Initial assessments of victory are often merely gut feelings much like the Supreme Court's definition of pornography as something that depends on community values and you know when you see it. The assessment aspect complicates the issue of winning exponentially since it introduces the uncontrolled variables of whose assessment counts, for how much, and based on what criteria. More on that later.

Related to this idea is the hypothesis that the results of war can actually be different for the opposing sides. Obviously, results from any direct interaction of two bodies will be closely related and interdependent. This is especially true of a contest between them, but because winning is an assessment not a fact, the results of wars are independent for each side and may vary by participant. That is, the fact that one side won big does not necessarily mean its opponent lost big. It may not even mean that the other side lost at all, at least in terms of its own assessment.

Second, winning a war (as opposed to a battle or campaign) is a political condition. If war is a political act, victory at the highest levels must be defined in political terms. That is a fairly uncontroversial assertion today, but one with enormous implications. Misunderstanding or misapplying this simple concept is exactly why the United States gets criticized for winning the war but losing the peace, which is code for attaining decisive tactical and operational victories that do not produce similarly gratifying strategic results. The implication is that military victory (tactical or operational victory) without favorable political outcomes is sterile, and by any reasonable assessment that is true. But is knowing that victory is a political condition a sufficient understanding of winning? Actually, I believe it only serves to complicate or obscure the issue.

Next, and an aspect hinted at above, because it is a perception or assessment, victory or winning is heavily dependent on perspective. In a military sense, this translates into being sensitive to the level of war. It is possible to have a smashing tactical military victory that does not produce either operational or strategic results. Is that really a win? It certainly is from the point of view of the tactical commander—the view from the perspective of the operational or strategic commander might be quite different. It is this characteristic that allowed Saddam Hussein to claim victory after the First Gulf War. He suffered a huge tactical and operational loss, but his regime had survived (his strategic objective after the coalition intervened). The war was thus a strategic win for him—at least in his eyes and from his perspective. This again suggests the issue of who decides who wins and loses, which we will address later.

The characteristic of perspective allows us to think of victory in war as three tiered—tactical, operational, and strategic. Other authors have approached this categorization from different angles; for example, Martel calls his levels tactical, political-military, and grand strategic, and they do not correspond directly to the military levels.[6] While I believe coining language retards theoretical debate when accepted language exists, I do not believe Martel's categories can yet be considered widely accepted, and my terminology, based on common military usage, makes sense. The issue is not the names of the levels, but the recognition that winning differs conceptually depending on the perspective of the action and assessor. The levels correspond to increasingly complex conceptual (if not physical) tasks.

Because winning tactically is a fairly straightforward and almost exclusively military activity, we best understand it and can generally assess it through reasonably quantifiable criteria. Measures of effectiveness like comparative casualty ratios, ground taken or lost, sorties flown, tonnage sunk, prisoners captured, etc. all count and can actually produce a reasonable estimate of victory or defeat that is likely to be widely accepted. Again, however, the assessment is based on outcomes, not effort. There are complications inherent in fighting with allies or coalition partners, and fog and friction, chance and uncertainty mean the outcome is never guaranteed, but the measures of tactical success are well understood. Operational victory is similarly transparent at least in its purest form; the campaign succeeds or fails based on criteria that are usually well understood and quantifiable. However, strategic victory is a more complicated issue.

It is worth reemphasizing that the relationship on the subject of winning between the levels of war, although closely linked, is not linear. Tactical success does not necessarily lead to operational success, which likewise does not guarantee strategic victory. In fact, winning on one level may actually lead to or result from losing on another. In Algeria in the 1950's the brutal methods the French used to achieve a tactical victory were decidedly (perhaps decisively) counterproductive strategically. The art of war and strategy is largely making successes at each level contribute positively to successes at the higher levels.

Which level is most important? It is tempting to respond that all are equally important, but that would be incorrect. What counts in the end is the strategic outcome. The story comes to mind of

Colonel Harry Summers talking to a North Vietnamese officer about that war. Summers commented that the United States had won all the battles, and the North Vietnamese replied, "That may be so, but it is also irrelevant."[7] That is a vivid illustration of the point that strategy counts most. Tactical and/or operational success may set the stage for strategic victory—that is, they may be facilitators, and they certainly are huge contributors in any case—but they are not necessarily sufficient by themselves to achieve victory. The prudent strategist, however, knows full well that his brilliant strategy will be incredibly more difficult and risky without tactical and operational success. There are few examples like Nathanael Greene's southern campaign in the American Revolution where one can lose the battles and win the campaign and war.

Finally, as Gray and Martel both point out, victory occurs on a sliding scale—or actually multiple sliding scales. Victory and defeat, although polar opposites, are not binary. There are thousands of points along the scale that delineate degrees of success. And winning may or may not be decisive in the sense of settling the underlying political issues, again on a whole range of degrees. Martel actually uses four scales, although the one he calls "levels" is analogous to the levels of war categorization and his "change in status quo" scale is essentially a measure of decisiveness. The other two categories of "degree of mobilization for war" and "extent of post-conflict obligations" are interesting, but I am not convinced they really relate theoretically to victory as much as they relate practically to the strategist as a means test.[8] Gray uses two scales—one that might be called achievement running from strategic advantage through strategic success to decisive victory, and a second scale called decisiveness that is a measure of how well the victory or defeat decides the issue at question.[9] This is a useful concept. In some sense the two are so closely related that decisiveness might be considered part of the definition of winning. It is, however, a separate and important concept, especially since the significant interaction is the effect between levels (not to discount the fact that one might win on one level and still not produce decisive results even at that level). So, one might win a great battlefield victory that does not decide anything either militarily in terms of the campaign or politically in terms of the war. Gray's achievement scale looks only at the positive end of the spectrum. However, just as one can succeed to varying degrees, one can fail to varying degrees. Thus the achievement scale must be modified to add a negative component.

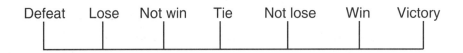

Figure 1. Scale of Success.

We hypothesize a scale of success that runs from defeat through losing, not winning, tying, not losing, and winning to victory with shades and gradations between each point. (See Figure 1.) Victory is completely fulfilling while defeat is catastrophic, but the other possible results contain aspects of both winning and losing to at least some extent. Note that this model draws distinctions between winning and victory and losing and defeat. While the words are commonly used interchangeably, they offer a unique opportunity to distinguish important gradations that exist in the condition of success in war. The assertion here is that victory will be essentially total and probably final; that it will resolve the underlying political issues. However, it is certainly possible to succeed in a war without achieving everything one sought or resolving all the extant issues. Winning implies achieving success on the battlefield and in securing political goals, but not, for whatever reason, reaching total political success (i.e., victory). Thus, to win one must accomplish one's immediate political goals, but not necessarily resolve all the underlying issues. Lesser levels of success reflect lesser degrees of battlefield achievement and/or lesser degrees of decisiveness in solving or resolving underlying issues. On the losing end, defeat is also a total concept. It implies failure to achieve battlefield success or to attain political goals and simultaneously not only not resolving underlying issues but actually exacerbating them. Thus, what we have is two components of success—or if you like, two measures of success—in war. They are portrayed here as the scales of achievement and decisiveness. These are related but independent variables.

Decisiveness reflects a wide range of potential outcomes. The decisiveness scale (Figure 2) shows potential outcomes varying from completely resolving the political issues at stake through various degrees of partial resolution to no effect (or status quo) through degrees of worsened or deteriorated political conditions to the final potential outcome that the war not only does not solve the problems for which it was fought, but actually exacerbates them. Decisiveness talks about the effect on the political issues.

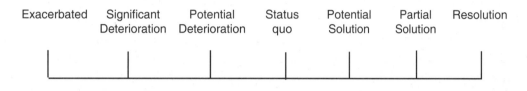

Figure 2. Scale of Decisiveness.

Achievement talks about how well one executes his strategy—in a sense, how well one did on the battlefield/campaign and in the immediate political realm. Achievement (Figure 3) can range from accomplishing nothing through increasing degrees of success until one is completely successful. The achievement scale is by far the primary scale in tactical and operational assessments of victory and is often confused with or used as synonymous with the success scale.

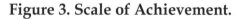

Figure 3. Scale of Achievement.

The two scales are closely related, particularly since at the operational and strategic levels the achievement scale considers political issues as well as military. The distinction is that one may accomplish one's political goals without necessarily resolving the political issues.

One might array the scales as axes and stack them by corresponding levels of war; however, I do not find that particularly useful or informative. All such manipulations really illustrate is that winning/victory requires separate definitions by level of war.

Characteristics of Winning.

How one defines the problem influences what you think you can or want to achieve, which influences what winning looks like. In a sense, this (a political job) is the most difficult task in initiating a war. It is a policy task—why are we fighting and what will winning look like? This is the concept we call defining the endstate, which the US military taught its political masters during the frustrating limited wars and peacekeeping of the 1980s and 90s. The problem is that endstates change. What the modern military derisively refers to as mission creep is actually a legitimate political process of continual evaluation and assessment of possibilities and risks in a changing strategic environment. As an altered situation presents new strategic possibilities or challenges, a statesman would be negligent to ignore them. The effect of changing endstates on winning is that every change in mission or endstate alters acceptable strategic outcomes; that is, changes the conditions for victory. That changing endstates should also cause the strategist to reevaluate ways and means is an important strategic problem that is not part of a theory of victory.

One author has postulated that winning is just achieving an outcome you like or at least prefer over other alternatives. The same author later writes, "*'Victory' is an all-purpose word used to describe imprecisely the concept of success in war* [italics in original]."[10] That has merit as far as it goes, but it is a fairly low bar, and I believe only a part of what winning really is. Achieving a preferred outcome or a success is perhaps the most basic element of conflict termination—theoretically one fights to achieve a favorable state of affairs or at least an outcome preferable to either the alternatives or a continuation of the war. It is not clear, however, how that equates to winning. It is fairly easy to postulate a desirable political and/or military condition that would be both better than losing yet less than victory—one example would be a tie or a stalemate. No widely accepted definition of victory considers a tie a win. As to victory being the concept of success in war, if we accept the sliding scale paradigm, success may just get one an outcome only slightly preferable to a tie—again not a condition most (including this paper) would accept as winning. Not losing is better than losing but not equivalent to victory just as not winning is better than losing but not defeat.

However, it is clear that fighting will not stop unless the combatants see peace as more desirable than a continuation of conflict. In Clauswitzian terms, if the effort required exceeds the value of the political objective, the fighting must stop.[11] Achieving a desired or acceptable outcome may be a precondition for conflict termination, but the end of fighting does not necessarily signify victory. In fact, victory and conflict termination are two distinct and sometimes mutually antagonistic concepts. It is possible and sometimes desirable to terminate conflicts without producing a winner. Conversely, it is also possible to continue a war unnecessarily in hopes of achieving victory or avoiding defeat. To win, one must achieve at least to some extent one's immediate political goals. If avoiding fighting altogether or stopping it immediately once begun (the typical pacifist stance) is the political goal, then any outcome that stops the shooting is a win. However, few governments, and I contend few individuals, would seriously consider that victory. Simply stopping the shooting is not winning except perhaps in the domestic partisan political sense.

Conversely, winning a war almost certainly implies that a state of peace exists even if the existence of peace does not necessarily imply victory. If one thinks of peace as the normal state and war as an aberration, then peace should follow victory. That is, victory should bring the situation back to a sustainable steady state. If war is the normal state interrupted occasionally by periods of temporary peace, this may not be the case. However, Americans tend to view the world as normally at peace with occasional interruptions of war. Thus, an American definition of winning would be closely linked to peace and security. The immediate peace at the conclusion of a war is generally a period when combat ceases (a military condition) because one side collapses and either stops fighting or surrenders, or because one or both sides decide stopping is in their best interest. But none of that has anything to do with winning. One cannot discern from a postwar state of peace who won or lost the war. In fact, one can cite cases of decisive military wins that do not result in perfect peace—low-grade insurgencies often follow crushing military victories without altering the overall assessment of winning and losing. This is particularly true at the tactical and operational levels.

Winning is no different if your goal is positive or negative, that is if you are trying to accomplish something or prevent something. The same is true for limited or total goals. It really makes no difference if the goal is something existential like continuing to exist as a nation or something less vital like "signaling". There is a difference, however, in the degree of difficulty. Total wars or wars for some concrete object like possession of territory are much more likely to be judged by concrete criteria—did you achieve or prevent the occupation of the territory; who was still standing at the end of a total war? There are also no absolute criteria that ensure victory. When President Bush announced the end of major combat operations after Operation Iraqi Freedom, he was proclaiming victory. He was (and remains) absolutely correct in his claim. At that moment and from an American perspective the United States and its coalition partners stood victorious over a badly beaten Iraqi military. The coalition had achieved all the classic measures of a tactical and operational victory— destroyed the enemy military and occupied his capital and country. However, because there are no absolute criteria, and winning is not fixed or permanent, that victory slipped away as other political forces exerted themselves. Going back to the sports analogy, some of the voters changed their vote— or as the game reached the final innings their votes suddenly became more significant. Perhaps it was a new game with new players and new rules. The point is that victory is an assessment, and assessments can change.

Can both sides win a war? If so, why fight? It would seem that reasonable men could discover the political solution that is likely to result from war without the unfortunate necessity of all the shooting and killing. That, however, has never been the case, and it is so because of both the nature of war and the nature of victory. War is a dynamic process. As it progresses the political objectives can change. Thus, the peace settlement upon which the assessment of victory and defeat will be made may have little relation to the initial political issues—although the most basic and loudly proclaimed are likely to get at least lip service in the final settlement. World War I is an excellent example of this phenomenon. The issues that provoked the war (at least the most immediate political issues) did not require four years of total war, so ends escalated as the effort expended escalated, and the final settlement had almost nothing to do with the original issues. Conversely, unexpectedly stiff resistance can force politicians to scale back on initial political objectives. The point is that it is impossible for all except the Monday morning quarterback to decipher the likely postwar political settlement. Additionally, if his political goals are very limited like demonstrating capability, showing resolve, or sending messages, the presumptive loser may be able to correctly claim he accomplished his objective and thus won. This is particularly true in cases of indecisive battlefield results, but it can occur after decisive tactical victories. The 1973 Arab-Israeli War provides an example. At the conclusion of hostilities the Egyptians had crossed the Suez, still had forces on the eastern side, and had stood up to the Israelis. Politically, they could overlook the fact that when the ceasefire went into effect the Israelis were conducting a counterattack, had isolated one of the two attacking Egyptian armies, and were in position to complete its destruction. The Egyptians were in a difficult military situation, but President Sadat was able to negotiate and accept the Camp David peace accord precisely because he was able to persuasively (at least to the Egyptian people) claim victory in the war. Thus, one side can win big without the other side necessarily losing big—or even at all.

It is equally possible for neither side to win, unless one postulates an unwritten rule that a tie go to the underdog for not losing. The theorist Sir Basil H. Liddell Hart wrote, "Peace through stalemate, based on a coincident recognition by each side of the opponent's strength, is at least preferable to peace through common exhaustion—and has often provided a better foundation for lasting peace."[12] Liddell Hart was implying that no victory is sometimes a win. Does that mean that not losing can be the same as winning? Why not if that is the political goal? If one begins a war militarily in an underdog or even a hopeless military position—a not uncommon state of events historically—then isn't surviving that war a form of victory? While ethicists might question a decision to undertake a war without true hope of victory, politicians have frequently found it necessary. Of course, since aggressors seldom attack without a distinct advantage, examples of nations at extreme disadvantage when attacked abound. In such cases, the attacked party can hope for little more than survival. If it achieves that, isn't it a victory despite whatever battlefield success or failure it may have experienced? It has become fashionable to refer to this survival goal as regime survival when pursued by an unpopular government, as though there was something illegitimate or unsavory about regime survival, but isn't it really indistinguishable from national survival as the objective of total wars? Saddam Hussein claimed victory after the first Gulf War precisely because he had stood up to the world and survived.

Is there a temporal aspect to winning a war either in terms of achieving it or in terms of sustaining the assessment over time? Obviously winning takes some amount of time, and equally obviously the amount of time and effort expended will influence assessments of the postwar political situation. A strategic victory must also have *some* temporal permanence—rational assessments of victory will never concede success to a condition that is only sustainable for a matter of weeks or months. However, because winning at the strategic level is an assessment of political results, it is subject to revision. Victory can be reevaluated either in terms of achievement or decisiveness, and is, therefore, not necessarily permanent. The degree of impermanence relates directly to the magnitude of the achievement and its decisiveness. World War I again provides an example. At the time, the outcome looked like an Anglo-French-American victory. Over time the degree of decisiveness has been reevaluated. Now the result is generally considered to be a military success that did not resolve and in some cases aggravated underlying issues. This *ex-post facto* reevaluation of the decisiveness scale has so radically altered the assessment of victory that some authors talk about World Wars I and II as one long war.

Tactical and operational victories, because of their firmer basis of judgment, tend to remain fixed. Only very marginal victories at those levels are subject to reinterpretation. That is also true of significant, very decisive strategic wins. It is much more difficult to reevaluate a total victory that decisively settles the political issues involved than to reevaluate a situation somewhere lower on the sliding scales. For example, It is unlikely that anyone will ever seriously claim Germany or Japan won World War II. In each of those cases one can look at subsequent history and say the long-term outcome was overall beneficial for all the countries involved; however, that does not change the assessment of winning and losing. The degree of impermanence also relates to the degree of consensus on the assessment. Results that are universally accepted are difficult to change.

Does or should the cost affect victory? Of course it does. Liddell Hart pointed out that a victory is useless if it breaks the winner's economy or military or society.[13] Cost will certainly factor in to the equation about winning or losing. Costs, real and perceived, cannot help but be parts of any postwar assessment. This goes back to the point that winning on one level of war can produce disastrous results on another. It is possible to win tactically at such an expense in men and materiel that it becomes a strategic defeat. The classic statement of this possibility was by King Pyrrhus of Epirus who was alleged to have replied to congratulations on a bloody victory over the Romans in 279 B.C. that one more such victory would undo him.[14]

One final question for this section is, what does winning give you? We might say peace, but that is not certain. Liddell Hart asserts that, "The object of war is a better state of peace—if only from your own point of view," so perhaps winning is just a better peace.[15] I believe we can state with conviction that winning gives one the ability to dictate peace or at least the terms of the political settlement. That might translate into political gains or territorial acquisitions or a better sense of security. Theoretically, it should avoid, mollify, or negate future problems, but given human fallibility, that is not certain. In the purest sense, a total victory should give the winner anything he wants, but it may come down in reality to just the ability to influence, if not dictate, the solution to the political issues.

Who Decides?

Because of the reasonably measurable victory conditions at the tactical and much of the operational levels, who decides who won or lost at those levels is not especially controversial. That is not true, however, at the strategic level, and the operational level also can get contentious as it merges with the strategic. If victory at the strategic level is an assessment of the postwar political conditions, then who does the assessment becomes a critical issue. Does the victor decide whether he won or lost? The vanquished? Both? Neither? What about a "disinterested" or uninvolved party? Can the decider be multiple people? If multiple people, must there be unanimity, a consensus, a majority, or a plurality? Of whom/what—public opinion, national opinion, world opinion? If the decider can be multiple, could one get several different (and equally valid) decisions? The issues here are endless, and that is just to decide who makes the assessment. There is a whole second set of issues around the question of what criteria should be used for the assessment. Is there an objective set of criteria? Are the criteria cultural? Are the criteria different for different kinds of war (total or limited)? Do the criteria vary over time? We must also keep in mind that everyone who makes an assessment uses his/her own scales and can place the degree of achievement and/or decisiveness wherever they want.

Despite its complexity the question has a simple answer. Because we have defined this as an assessment of the postwar political condition, it is a political issue and everyone gets an opinion. Then the problem becomes not who decides but whose opinion matters, and that is a much more manageable issue. As a general rule, opinion counts based on the political clout of the opinion holder. For Americans the opinions that matter in order of priority are: 1) the American people, 2) American political and military elites (1 and 2 together might be thought of as American public opinion on military issues), 3) the opinion of our friends and allies, and 4) world opinion—sort of everybody else. As the issue fades from the immediate political forum, the interested audience declines precipitously until eventually only historians will debate the issue. However, by then the base assessment of winning and losing will already have been established, and historical debates will be adjustments based on new evidence or consequences revealed by the passage of time.

Of course, the analogue of this process occurs in the enemy country or organization (if a nonstate actor). Who decides in the enemy camp and how is a critical but very situationally dependent fact. It must be considered in the strategic estimate process, but this paper cannot attempt to speculate on how it might work.

Returning to our own side, how does one determine American public opinion? Usually the mass media and polling agencies sense and report public opinion. Is polling accurate for a war? Absolutely not if accurate means does it reflect conditions on the ground; but it is generally accurate as a reflection of what the public believes. Is there ever a poll that asks, "Did we win such and such a war?" No, probably not. So, if the normal process does not function in this case, how do we determine who won and lost?

The determination results from the confluence of two other processes. First, political leaders try to convince the public. That is successful or not based on the facts of the particular circumstances, the persuasiveness of the message, and the perceived legitimacy and veracity of the messenger. Credible politicians backed by convincing evidence of military achievement and political profit can proclaim victory and simply establish the fact. The second process is more like the pornography test—people just recognize victory when they see it. They make up their own minds using whatever evidence they have. This is a much more subjective process that quickly escapes political control (or is controlled by atypical political forces). The consequence of this is that at the strategic level victory and defeat can be as much issues of public perception and even partisan politics as they are of battlefield achievement or diplomatic negotiations.

However, there is another key point to consider. Clausewitz said victory was tripartite. "If in conclusion we consider the total concept of a victory, we find it consists of three elements:

1. The enemy's greater loss of material strength.
2. His loss of morale.
3. His open admission of the above by giving up his intentions.[16]

This points out one significant fact about who decides—regardless of who makes the decision or on what criteria it is made, to stick, both sides have to acknowledge its correctness. Clausewitz was writing about tactical victory where his three points are usually apparent. At the strategic and even operational level the assessment is much more difficult and debatable. The admission of loss, however, is an important caveat for all levels, and at all levels it intertwines with the issue of who decides. This is particularly evident at the tactical level, but there are times when one side or the other for whatever reason (too dumb or too stubborn or too committed, etc. to accept defeat) continues the fight. Usually, this leads to disaster, but occasionally the stubborn individual who refuses to accept defeat can actually snatch victory. Ulysses Grant at Shiloh is an example at the tactical level. Although beaten and nearly driven off the field on the first day, Grant's refusal to admit defeat and his attack the next day produced a smashing tactical victory. Significantly, acceptance of defeat makes mute the issue of who decides who won—both sides acknowledge the outcome, and it is difficult for even the most radical reinterpretation to contest the decision.

Traditionally, governments indicate they are beaten by signing some form of peace accord or treaty, while armies acknowledge defeat by formally surrendering or perhaps agreeing to an armistice. Those are very important symbolic acts as an acknowledgement of victory and defeat— they are an integral and perhaps essential part of the political/social mythology of victory. They indicate to the other legs of the Clausewitzian trinity that the government and/or the army thinks itself beaten and that further resistance is futile. This is important even if parties not part of the process do not accept the verdict and try to continue the war. At a minimum, and disregarding for the moment all the impacts on legitimacy and logistics, formal governmental or military surrender will have a huge impact on the will of the remaining trinitarian elements. It is difficult for either the people or the military to continue fighting if the government has formally surrendered, and the government faces the huge challenge of recreating a military if its army has surrendered. Battleship Missouri-like ceremonies acknowledging victory and defeat are extremely important and significant. However, such ceremonies must be authentic to be useful. Contrived ceremonies for the sake of having a formal surrender do not convince the target audience. Unilaterally proclaiming victory from the deck of a U.S. aircraft carrier was better than conducting a trumped-up ceremony featuring "Bagdad Bob," but a formal surrender by Saddam Hussein or an acknowledged major subordinate legitimately representing the Iraqi government would have been better still.

The current thinking that there will not be such a ceremony at the conclusion of the War on Terrorism is probably correct; however, there should have been such a ceremony at the conclusion of the initial phases in both Afghanistan and Iraq. Especially in Iraq the people needed to see and believe that the Saddam government was actually defeated. The difference in the War on Terrorism is that the enemy is a nonstate actor. There are no internationally recognized procedures for accepting the surrender of nonstate actors, and if there were, no state could take lightly legitimizing such an actor even by formally accepting its surrender. If nonstate actors mirror/mimic in some ways the trinitarian characteristics of states, the impact of formal surrender might be similar, but the extent of such similarity is unclear. For example, it is not certain that the surrender of the leader of a nonstate actor (who is presumably analogous to the government in a state sense) would have the same impact as the surrender of the head of a government. This is the reasoning behind warnings that the capture or death of Osama Bin Laden will not end the war on terrorism.

So, what can we conclude about victory in warfare so far? It is an assessment of two variables—achievement and decisiveness—at three levels—tactical, operational, and strategic. At the tactical and in most cases the operational levels winning is a military condition and the assessment rests on reasonably well understood military criteria. At the strategic level (and the portions of the operational that directly overlap the strategic), public opinion decides who wins and loses and to what extent based on an assessment of the postwar political conditions. The military situation as the public understands or interprets it will, of course, play a huge role in the assessment, but the overriding criteria will be political. To be effective, a victory must be recognized and accepted by the opponent and sustainable over time. Thus, *strategic victory in war is a positive assessment of the postwar political situation in terms of achievement and decisiveness that is acknowledged, sustainable, and resolves underlying political issues.* Similarly, *Tactical victories are battlefield military outcomes that achieve their purpose and give one side a significant, acknowledged advantage over its opponent.* Substituting operational for tactical and eliminating battlefield in the above definition yields a satisfactory definition of operational victory.

How Does One Win?

Theoretically, how one wins a war is fairly straightforward—it is doing it that is difficult. Clausewitz pointed out that war is both a physical and moral struggle. His recipe for victory was simple: "If you want to overcome your enemy you must match your efforts against his power of resistance, which can be expressed as the product of two inseparable factors, viz. *the total means at his disposal* and *the strength of his will.*" (italics in original)[17] One can express that as a mathematical formula: $R = M \times W$. In the formula, R represents the power of resistance, M is the total means available, and W is the strength of will. Victory then, is achieved as R approaches zero; that is, as the power of resistance drops to an ineffective level. One can push R toward zero by reducing either M or W (or both). In some respects one might think of a strategy designed to attack the M aspect of the equation as a physical approach and a strategy designed to address the W aspect as psychological, although making such a distinction too starkly can be dangerous since both elements will appear in any strategy. We will examine briefly both approaches.

The traditional concept of winning a war is based on reducing the enemy's means of resistance. This is generally done physically. Typically, it involves destroying or neutralizing the enemy's military or at least attriting it to the point of ineffectiveness. The underlying purpose is to remove the enemy's capability to resist so you can impose your will on him directly. The theorist of deterrence Thomas Schelling wrote about the use of military power to hurt. His point was that one function of militaries is to inflict pain on the enemy. Inflicting pain is easiest when the enemy cannot resist—that is, after you have beaten him in battle.[18] Thus, the real significance of the loss of one's army is that it leaves you vulnerable to whatever pain the enemy wants to inflict. That is why nations surrender when their armies are defeated. The trick has always been how one goes about destroying or attriting the enemy. Another physical approach attempts to avoid the issues of destruction or attrition through paralysis. The concept is that one paralyzes vital enemy systems, especially command and control, to make their resistance ineffective. Postulated by advocates of the indirect approach and some airpower enthusiasts, the intent is to avoid hard fighting by maneuver or by precise attacks on specific targets.[19] However, the final mechanism for achieving victory is still placing the enemy is a situation where your armed forces can directly impose their will. In every case, winning by reducing the enemy's physical means of resistance comes down to an evaluation of whether you can hit and hurt the enemy, the cost to do so, and the effectiveness of the resulting damage. The underlying theoretical rational is always that removing the enemy's ability to resist allows one to directly impose his will without the possibility of effective resistance.

Attacking psychologically to reduce the enemy's will to resist works somewhat differently. The intent of all action is not to place oneself in position to impose one's will but to cause the enemy to lose his will and quit. All strategies designed with this intent share two major issues. First, is whose will should one attack. If we accept Clausewitz's description of the forces interacting in war as the people, the government, and the military, then we can ascribe a will to each.[20] Whose will counts most? The French general and theorist André Beaufre wrote,

> Whom do we wish to convince? Ultimately it must be the enemy government but in some cases it may be easier to work on leading personalities (e.g. Chamberlain at Bad Godesberg or Munich), choosing arguments to which they are most susceptible. Alternatively it may be best to work directly on a certain section of public opinion which has some hold over the government or an influential Allied Government or through UNO [the United Nations].[21]

Regardless of the route he followed, Beaufre was focused ultimately on breaking the will of the enemy government. That is a very state-centric appreciation of a means of winning that deserves reconsideration in a world where nonstate actors play increasingly significant roles, especially in war and warlike activities.

The recent rediscovery of counterinsurgency (COIN) theory provides other possibilities. COIN theory generally acknowledges the population as the objective—in terms of a theory of victory it is the population that decides what victory is and who prevails. Winning hearts and minds is how one wins COIN because the people's will counts most. That is not the case in all wars.

The examples imply whose will matters most may be largely an issue of the type of war one is fighting. This goes back to Clausewitz's famous dictum about the first and greatest act of a commander and statesman being to understand the nature of the war in which he is about to engage.[22] In a total war, one probably has to break at least the government's and the people's will. You may have to break both, and certainly must to achieve a lasting settlement that is viewed as just. In limited wars for limited objectives, one may only have to break the will of the government—assuming sufficient governmental control to prevent the people and/or the military from ignoring the government's decision and reinitiating the fight. As a caveat, there is no guarantee either that breaking the will of one of the trinitarian legs will produce victory or that both sides will be contesting over the same will. A second caveat is that the model may not fit nonstate actors well.

The second issue in reducing the enemy's will is understanding how to break will. There is a classic approach that is highly physical. One physically seizes, perhaps preemptively, what he wants or what is important. That is, he directly imposes his will on the enemy. In its purest form, the idea is that the enemy will concede the political point (i.e. his will breaks) without further contest. This is the most easily understood concept and makes postwar assessment simple—you either have or don't have what you said you wanted. Execution is also theoretically simple. It involves directly taking or doing what you want. If the enemy's will persists, you are still presumably in a better position for the fight that follows than you were before the opening of the gambit. There is nothing wrong with this concept of winning, and it is a very useful approach when the desired end is suitable. It is, of course, both most useful and common when there is a significant disparity between opposing forces, since the enemy will presumably try to counter your move.

In other will-oriented approaches, physical effects are also important and are typically a primary method. Remember that Clausewitz said physical means and will were inseparable.[23] The distinction is in intent. The desired result of a psychological approach is the collapse of will rather than rendering the enemy incapable of resistance as in the physical approach. Some examples may help clarify. Early strategic airpower theory as represented by the Italian theorist Gulio Douhet was based on the use of strategic bombing to directly attack the will of the enemy people and government. The bomber could fly over fielded forces and directly attack enemy cities. The intent was to break morale.[24] This theory, which is at the heart of all strategic bombing theory, has yet to work unambiguously. As with any attempt to produce psychological effect, the results are unpredictable. Similarly, John Warden's theory of directly attacking the will of the government or military (striking leadership) as manifested in spin-off concepts like "Shock and Awe" should work theoretically—if you convince the government that you have an invincible capability to overwhelm it and the will to use that capability, the government should surrender—it just never has worked exactly like that.[25] The only proven way to break will is to convince the enemy that resistance is futile—the cost of resistance exceeds the potential gain. That is the real point of overwhelming force and related concepts. It may make the physical job easier, but is also an important element in the psychological equation of will.

The only method currently available to directly attack will is information operations; all other options attack indirectly through some other aspect presumed to influence will. However, information operations are very blunt instruments whose impact is incredibly difficult to reliably predict or target. Second and third order effects are always present and may produce exactly the opposite of the intended result. Conversely, if victory is an assessment, information operations are strategically critical in deciding the winner. Our inability to come to grips intellectually, physically, or psychologically with this aspect of war in an age where control of information is impossible is a huge part of our current perceived inability to achieve positive strategic results.

What role does ethics play in winning? This is not the classic question of whether war is really a no-holds-barred fight to the finish, or whether there are or should be rules/ethical limitations. The ethical component of winning, if one exists, is limited to two aspects. First is how much weight, if any, the decider gives to the ethical conduct of the war. If the entity making the victory assessment uses ethics as a standard of measurement, ethics are significant in victory; if the decider ignores ethics in his analysis, ethics will play no role in victory. A second way ethics figures in the victory equation is that ethical (or unethical) conduct may have second or third order effects that influence durability. Thus, a war that initially looks like a victory may become something less as evidence of unethical conduct emerges. Like every other aspect of the victory assessment, the ethics standard does not necessarily apply equally to both sides, is a sliding scale rather than a binary ethical/ non-ethical assessment, and considers or ignores acts/issues serendipitously. The American people expect ethical conduct of war and might very easily assess a war conducted in an unethical manner as a loss regardless of battlefield outcomes. That appears to be at least a portion of the attitude behind the resistance to the Iraq war that rages as I write. Ethical considerations in the victory assessment are self-imposed and self-enforced, but they are real.

What is the bottom line? Victory in war is about breaking will. Eliminating means of resistance completely is impossible. Theoretically there will always be one enemy soldier armed with at least a knife who is willing to give her life to continue the fight. Destroying the enemy's means without breaking his will leaves you with a less capable but still hostile foe. Conversely, breaking the will to resist ends the war regardless of the enemy's remaining combat capability. The issue then becomes the much more practical one of how does one break an enemy's will? This is where we loop back on our argument. Will is a difficult concept to define much less attack directly, so militaries invariable attack the enemy military as a means not to reduce his power of resistance to zero and win, but as a means to destroy his will. Concepts like classic strategic airpower theory that attempts to bypass fielded forces to attack enemy will (either government or people) directly or John Warden's strategic rings that adds to the classic approach the idea of striking command and control and other vital systems to make resistance ineffective are tempting because theoretically they should work. They should not be ignored, but if one is looking for promising alternative approaches to victory, the field of information operations is the most fertile available. We just need to get out of the technological emphasis (or perhaps fixation) and approach it from the direction of understanding how one influences opinion, especially political will.

The Implications for War.

War is about winning. This is not a new concept. The general and theorist Raimondo Montecuccoli wrote in the seventeenth century: "War is an activity to inflict damage in every way; its aim is victory"—and the concept was already ancient by then.[26] Sun Tzu had expressed the same thought—"Victory is the main object in war"—a thousand years earlier.[27] Only an idiot would fight to lose—even fighting in an impossible cause is done in the hope of victory if only by miracle. In *The Mouse that Roared* from the series of satirical books by Leonard Wibberley made famous by the 1959 movie starring Peter Sellers in multiple roles, the fictional Duchy of Grand Fenwick fought to lose, but the goal was still to gain a better peace. The idea was to declare war on the United States, lose quickly, and then graciously accept the flood of foreign aid that would surely flow to a defeated foe. The fact that the Duchy's military stumbled into military victory was fortuitous, but totally unplanned and unexpected. Fighting in a hopeless or losing cause is valiant and sometimes necessary, but difficult to justify morally. Politically, it is not difficult to justify since one can always hope to achieve at least the survival objective. So, war is about winning.

However, the fact that war is about winning does not mean war is about victory. One can win a war, especially a limited war (a war that is consciously limited in either or all of ends, ways, or means), without achieving victory. Military force can legitimately be used to obtain goals short of the total victory where one's forces end up standing over a prostrate enemy with a bayonet at his throat dictating peace terms. It is also legitimate to use military force for immediate political advantage even understanding that one may not resolve the underlying issues.

This points out that war is also about politics, and consequently in the final analysis, strategic victory must be a political state. It is a perception by the people that matter that one side did better overall in a war than the other. The judgment is based on results, not effort. At the strategic level the scale of assessment is political, although physical or military aspects like casualties influence considerations, and some acts (like the capture or loss of specific territory) may have a decisive impact on the assessment when that issue is the basis of the political dispute. Liddell Hart was correct when he asserted that the object of war is a better peace if only from our point of view. Attaining that object is a primary prerequisite for victory. That may translate in political terms into a fairly innocuous set of less than optimal conditions that are more acceptable than the alternative, but the public must assess their attainment as a positive achievement worth the cost. The assessment must be shared by the people that matter. In America that is the general public and the political elites. The enemy must also accept the assessment if we expect the condition to last for any reasonable amount of time.

Winning is different at different levels of war, and winning at some levels can produce unintended results and even losses at other levels. Because winning is an assessment and subject to interpretation, it is sensitive to perspective. Tactical conditions that look like winning may be counterproductive strategically. This is particularly true when the goal is overtly political like winning the hearts and minds of the people.

War is a contest of wills conducted with physical means. This concept is absolutely critical to understanding the nature of war and the nature of victory. It leads directly to scales for weighing victory. One can assess any and every physical means employed against its probable outcome in terms of enemy and friendly will. If, despite how tactically effective it might be, the strategic result is likely to be minimal or unfavorable, its use must be very carefully considered. A great example is the 500 lb bomb in the counterinsurgency role. Regardless of how accurately targeted, 500 lb bombs inevitably produce collateral damage. In a COIN situation one might kill the targeted insurgents, perhaps in great numbers, but if the explosion also kills or injures bystanders (regardless of how innocent or complicit they might be) or even property, their use is inadvisable.

It is a characteristic of war that both sides try to dominate the opponent's will while protecting their own. The respective wills of the people, government, and military of both sides are potentially vulnerable. Protecting one's own will is as important as attacking that of the opponent. The military is responsible for its will—politicians are responsible for the wills of both the government and the people. While the will analysis works best for state-on-state contests, it is also applicable to wars with nonstate actors. In their case, some of the components may be atrophied or combined in the same person or element, but because Clausewitz's initial concept of the trinity dealt with basic characteristics of war that he then ascribed to the legs of the trinity, each of the trinitarian elements is still represented by some entity even in a nonstate actor where there may not be an identifiable people, military, or government. Targeting will in an enemy state is difficult enough; the same task against a nonstate actor is extremely tough.

Because war is a contest of wills, and victory is an assessment made by peoples or governments, information is critical, and being clumsy or too scrupulous in that arena unnecessarily ties one's hands. Being inept at information operations can be strategically fatal regardless of the power of one's military, the skill of his diplomats, or the size of his GDP.

Because war is about will and winning is an agreed upon assessment, formal ceremonies to acknowledge victory and defeat are important traditional psychological tools and political/social symbols that should be sought whenever possible. However, sham ceremonies featuring insignificant functionaries do not accomplish the same objective and may in fact be counterproductive.

Have we answered (or even asked) all the relevant questions? Certainly not. There is much work remaining in this arena. I hope, however, that these thoughts can advance the discussion. If not, we may end the 21st century still bemoaning our inability to turn spectacular tactical victories into decisive strategic results.

ENDNOTES - CHAPTER 6

1. See, for example, Donald Schon, *The Reflective Practitioner: How Professionals Think in Action*, New York: Basic Books, 1983.

2. William C. Martel, *Victory in War: Foundations of Modern Military Policy*, New York: Cambridge University Press, 2007, p. 3.

3. Bradford Lee at the Naval War College has been working on a concept he calls a theory of victory that is very interesting; however, it is more a theory of winning specific contests against specific enemies in the terms we will develop in this chapter.

4. Colin S. Gray, "Defining and Achieving Decisive Victory," Carlisle Barracks, PA: Strategic Studies Institute, U.S. Army War College, 2002.

5. Martel.

6. *Ibid.*, pp. 94-95.

7. Harry G. Summers, Jr., *On Strategy: The Vietnam War in Context*, Carlisle Barracks, PA: Strategic Studies Institute, U.S. Army War College, 1981, fifth printing 1989, p. 1.

8. Martel, pp. 94-5.

9. Gray, pp. 9-10; for Martel on sliding scales, see Figure 1 in Martel, pp. 95, 4.

10. Martel, pp. 2, 87.

11. Carl von Clausewitz, *On War*, Michael Howard and Peter Paret, eds., Princeton, NJ: Princeton University Press, 1989, p. 92.

12. Basil H. Liddell Hart, *Strategy*, New York: Frederick A. Praeger, 1954, reprint 1967, p. 370.

13. *Ibid.*, pp. 366-370.

14. Plutarch "Pyrrhus," John Dryden, trans., available at *classics.mit.edu/Plutarch/pyrrhus.html.*, accessed May 10, 2007.

15. Hart, p. 351.

16. Clausewitz, pp. 233-234.

17. *Ibid.*, p. 77.

18. Thomas C. Schelling, *Arms and Influence*, New Haven, CT: Yale University Press, 1966, pp. 4, 14.

19. Colonel John A. Warden III, "The Enemy as a System," *Airpower Journal*, Spring 1995, pp. 41-55.

20. Clausewitz, p. 89.

21. André Beaufre, *An Introduction to Strategy with Particular Reference to Problems of Defence, Politics, Economics and Diplomacy in the Nuclear Age*, R. H. Berry, trans., London, U.K.: Farber and Farber, 1965, p. 24.

22. Clausewitz, pp. 88-89.

23. *Ibid.*, p. 77.

24. David Jablonsky, ed., Roots *of Strategy, Book 4: 4 Military Classics*, Mechanicsburg, PA: Stackpole Books, 1999, p. 270-271; Azar Gat, *A History of Military Thought: From the Enlightenment to the Cold War*, New York: Oxford University Press, 2001, pp. 577-581.

25. Warden, pp. 41-55.

26. Gat, p. 24.

27. Sun Tzu, *The Art of War*, Samuel B. Griffith, trans., New York: Oxford University Press, 1963, 1973, p. 73.

CHAPTER 7

TOWARD A STRATEGIC THEORY OF TERRORISM: DEFINING BOUNDARIES IN THE ONGOING SEARCH FOR SECURITY

Frank L. Jones

"More, more, more . . . to destroy whole cities, provinces, an entire country, the whole world, this would be the greatest happiness."[1] These words conclude Polish author Stanislaw Przybyszewski's novel of terrorism, *Satan's Kinder* (*Children of Satan*) as the protagonists delight in torching a nameless city. At the time of its publication in Berlin in 1897, this German-language novel was a popular work of fiction. Critics of the time, citing the limited technical means for carrying out such enormous devastation, dismissed the story as a mere fantasy or just another apocalyptic vision of the sort fashionable at the turn of the century.[2] Today, the subject of this story would be equally popular, but it has also become the topic of serious deliberation and debate by government officials, scholars and citizens alike because the ability and implied intent of terrorists to wreck mass destruction is no longer far-fetched.

Nonetheless, despite volumes of books, articles and studies of terrorism, there has been scant investment made in developing a theory of terrorism. Instead, scholars and practitioners devote their efforts to writing about the history of terrorism, examining a variety of terrorist movements, discussing the influence of political ideologies and religious belief on terrorists' motives, dissecting their operational environments, or analyzing the psychological makeup of terrorists. This has resulted in a broken looking glass approach to understanding terrorism whereby each shard casts a portion of the image but not a complete likeness. As Richard Schultz points out, there has been intense study of terrorism, but the literature has been "primarily descriptive, prescriptive and very emotive in form."[3] This is still the case three decades after Schultz made that assertion, and such an approach continues to suggest why terrorism is often simply understood as a tactic.

This is an unfortunate state of affairs with serious repercussions, perhaps even disastrous results. It leads government officials to fixate on tactics, which, in turn, leads to the belief that there is a political, social, or economic antidote or vaccine—some combinatory "drug cocktail" that if used can eliminate terrorism. Tactics, as Carl von Clausewitz observed, are fighting techniques that can be addressed with prescriptive doctrine, that is, at a level where method and routine are useful and even essential. Strategy involves questions of broad purpose in which complexity, contingency and difficulty rule—doctrine is not only useless, it is unattainable.[4]

Therefore, this paper seeks to advance a strategic theory of terrorism as it relates to all orders of nonstate actors by using an interdisciplinary approach that integrates social science and the theory of war and strategy. In essence, the proposed theory argues that terrorists make choices to attain a future state or condition. Those choices concern how (concept or way) they will use the coercive or persuasive power (resources or means) available to exercise control over circumstances or a population to achieve objectives (ends) in accordance with their policy. This calculated relationship among ends, ways and means, which is a rational construct for strategy, forms the basis for this theoretical approach. Such a theoretical approach, like any theory, should specify essential terminology and definitions, explicate underlying assumptions and premises, present substantive propositions that can be translated into usable hypotheses, and lastly, provide or identify methods that can be used to test the hypotheses and modify the theory as appropriate. Ideally, it should also meet certain standards such as economy of language, applicability to the largest possible range of cases, and conformance to the facts.[5]

Defining Terrorism.

One of the reasons for a lack of focus on theoretical and conceptual issues, it is argued, stems from the definitional problems associated with the term "terrorism." Some scholars have become so discouraged by the lack of an accepted definition that they have abandoned any attempt to devise it. Walter Laqueur, a noted scholar of terrorism, contends, "A comprehensive definition of terrorism . . . does not exist nor will it be found in the foreseeable future."[6] However, sociologist Jack Gibbs suggested that it is impossible to pretend to study terrorism without some of form of definition, otherwise, discussion lapses into obscurantism. He also argues that one of the problems is definitional parsimony to the degree that oversimplification occurs: " . . . it is inconsistent to grant that human behavior is complex and then demand simple definitions of behavioral types."[7] As Martha Crenshaw remarked, clarity is often sacrificed for brevity.[8] In attempting to meet these challenges, Gibbs defines terrorism as "illegal violence or threatened violence directed against human or nonhuman objects" that has five characteristics: (1) the violence is undertaken to alter or maintain at least one putative norm in at least one population; (2) it has secret, furtive, and/or clandestine features so the participants can conceal their identity and location; (3) it is not undertaken to further the permanent defense of territory; (4) it is not conventional warfare and because of the participants concealed personal identity and concealment of their location, their threats, and/or their spatial mobility, the participants perceive themselves as less vulnerable to conventional military action; and (5) this violence is perceived by the participants as contributing to the normative goal previously described by inducing fear of violence in persons (perhaps an indefinite category of them) other than the immediate target of the actual or threatened violence and/or by publicizing some cause.[9] This definition lacks one essential aspect, which one of the earliest definitions of terrorism found in the 1948 edition of the *Encyclopedia of Social Sciences,* provides. This text defines terrorism as a "method or a theory behind the method whereby an organized group or party seeks to achieve its avowed aims chiefly through the systematic use of violence."[10]

The value of joining these two definitions is not only that it seeks to explain a complex subject in the manner it deserves, that is, the complexity associated with human motivation, where the admixture of political motives, as an example, cannot be readily distinct from personal motives. It also has another valuable feature: it recognizes terrorism as a theory with violence as the essential feature. Violence, collective violence to be precise, is the strategic concept, the way, used to advance a strategy consisting of a putative norm that the terrorists are attempting to alter and maintain using various tactics (e.g., bombing, assassination) in a strategic environment.

Premises.

For the purposes of this chapter, strategy is defined as a "synergy and symmetry of objectives, concepts and resources to increase the probability of policy success and the favorable consequences that follow from that success. . . . Strategy accomplishes this by expressing its logic in rational, linear terms — ends, ways and means."[11] In taking such an approach, several premises are critical to framing a strategic theory of terrorism.

The first premise is that "political purpose dominates all strategy."[12] Political as defined herein is an enunciation of policy, an expression of the preferred end state whether it is attainable or not. Ideally, this policy is clearly articulated by the terrorist leaders as it represents guidance for the employment of means, the instruments of coercive or persuasive power, toward the achievement of aims. However, policy can change as the strategic environment or circumstances change, for example, limitations imposed by others on the means available to the terrorists.

A second premise is the primacy of the strategic environment, which has a number of dimensions.[13] Terrorist leaders strive to attain a thorough understanding of the strategic situation and knowledge of the strategic environment. The strategic environment is physical and metaphysical, domestic and international, requiring an understanding of cultures, beliefs and worldviews of adversaries, allies (actual or potential), and neutralists. In implementing his strategy, the terrorist creates a security dilemma for other actors, he introduces change, and change upsets the status quo, the equilibrium of the strategic environment. The other actors are forced to do something.[14]

It is in the strategic environment that signaling occurs in order to have a psychological influence on politically behavior and attitudes.[15] The terrorist sends a signal that a target is vulnerable, that the perpetrators of violence exist, and that these perpetrators have the capability to strike numerous times. The signals are usually directed at three different audiences: the target or victims themselves, who may be killed and therefore can no longer be influenced; the group that identifies with the victim and therefore are affected by the implicit message that they are vulnerable as well; and all others, a "resonant mass." This group is composed of those who may react emotionally in a positive or negative manner, depending on which side they sympathize with in the conflict, as well as the government, the legitimate power, responsible for protecting the victims.[16]

The strategic environment should also be understood in terms of social geometry, which permits conspiratorial theories to flourish. David Black stresses, "Although a longstanding grievance usually underlies terrorism [and therefore justifies the resort to violence], the grievance alone does not explain the violence. It must have the right geometry—a particular location and direction in social space."[17] In other words, a condition of "social polarization" exists between society and the aggrieved. For the terrorist, society must be understood as having certain characteristics: it is sick and the illness cannot be cured, the state is violence itself and can be opposed only with violence, and the truth of the terrorist's espoused cause justifies any action that supports this stated objective.[18]

A third premise is that adaptation, that is, learning from experience, is required by all involved, and the key is who is adapting quicker—the terrorists or the government and its security forces. The terrorists and the governments with which they contend must recognize the magnitude of change required and strive for an improved fit between the organization and its external environment. The rate of change internal to the states, its leaders, institutions, and organizations must keep pace with the rate of change in the environment in order to cope with unfolding events and the terrorists' countermoves.[19] Thus, strategy is a "process, a constant adaptation to shifting conditions and circumstances in a world where chance, uncertainty, and ambiguity dominate."[20]

The fourth premise is that "strategy has a symbiotic relationship with time." Deciding when to execute the strategy is crucial to the terrorist leaders. If the historical timing is appropriate, then small actions can have large strategic effects. These effects can be cumulative and thus become part of the interplay between continuity and change. They also become part of the continuities of the strategic environment. If the timing is not propitious, then the results may be meager, require additional exertion, and cost more in terms of tangible and intangible resources. However, even in failure the strategic effects become part of the framework of change and interaction in the strategic environment and thereby influence future actions.[21]

A fifth premise is that for terrorists efficiency is subordinate to effectiveness. This is not to suggest that efficiency is not valued, but that the purpose of the strategy is to attain strategic effect. If strategic objectives are achieved, they in turn generate or contribute to the generation of the strategic effects that favor the realization of the desired end state.[22] The strategic effect in terrorism is to create a sense of vulnerability and intimidation. It is "intended to create a state of fear that is acute and long-lasting enough to influence behavior."[23]

The sixth premise is that the terrorists' strategy seeks a proper balance among the objectives wanted, the methods used to pursue the objectives, and the resources available for the effects desired. In formulating the strategy, the ends, ways, and means are interconnected, working synergistically to accomplish the strategic effect.[24] Terrorist leaders must be understood as rational calculators.

The seventh and final premise is that terrorists understand the importance of strategic risk; recognize the inherent existence of uncertainty, chance, and nonlinearity in the strategic environment; and attempt to produce a favorable balance in the ends-ways-means calculation to overcome or at least ameliorate the impact. Nonetheless, the risk of failure remains.[25] Since action is imperative, terrorist leaders must take risks in order to maintain the organization. Action also serves to address internal factors such as solidifying shared values and objectives though a sense of belonging and unity, generating excitement, elevating social status and acquiring interpersonal or material reward. It also promotes external objectives such as recruitment and material and popular support from sympathizers and constituencies. Therefore, the terrorist strategists and leaders must manage the friction between their need to preserve the organization (since action risks destruction by government forces) and the foot soldiers' demand for action. Inaction can breed internal power struggles and major disagreements on any number of subjects.[26]

To paraphrase Carl von Clausewitz, terrorism has a grammar of its own, changing from age to age and place to place, but its logic—the rationale for terrorism—remains durable. The violent act is designed to send a message to a wide audience, not just the immediate victim, generally, "to create, instill or perpetuate a perception of fear within that audience." Further, "no specific ideological, theological, or bases are assumed, since the intent is to create or foster a sense of fear beyond the immediate victim remains the principal *raison d'être* for the violent act or threat."[27] Thus, terror is the strategic effect and violence provides the strategic concept, which is why it must be discussed first.

The Strategic Concept of Terrorism and Its Means.

Violence is the principal way or strategic concept by which terrorists will achieve their espoused ends. The terrorist uses collective violence, that is, personal injury by a group, albeit a small one, as a form of protest, a quest for justice, the purposeful expression of concrete and identifiable grievances, which are precipitated by any number of social, economic, [cultural] or political issues.[28]

Terrorism is also an organized form of violence that includes the concept of collective liability. Collective liability means that a group or members of the offender's group or social category are held accountable for the offender's conduct. The population of the offending government is answerable for the government's actions, the source of oppression, and impediment to the terrorists' ideal state. Thus, any member of this population, including women, children and the elderly, may be vulnerable to attack.[29] In the words of the French anarchist Emile Henry, "*Il n'y a pas d'innocents*",[30] (There are no innocents); therefore, the violence is justified since all are complicit.

Moreover, violence, as Martha Crenshaw notes, is the "primary method of action," and terrorists are individuals who have a bias for action—are "impatient for action."[31] This preference for violent action is made explicit to the victim of terror in the hope it will be coercive: ". . . the power to hurt is often communicated by some performance of it. Whether it is sheer terroristic violence to induce an irrational response, or cool premeditated violence to persuade somebody that you mean it and may do it again, it is not the pain and damage itself but its influence on somebody's behavior that matters."[32] This approach bypasses the Clausewitzian formula that resistance is a product of two variables—means and will.[33] The terrorist has no interest in reducing the adversary's means because the terrorist is less powerful and less capable than the adversary is. The way must therefore focus almost exclusively on the will. The terrorist must determine "what an adversary treasures" and "what scares him;" while the adversary must comprehend what the terrorist wants in order to be compliant, to know how to avoid pain or loss. The threat of violence must be personalized so that the adversary's pain or loss is "so anguishing as to be unendurable" and makes surrender a relief.[34] It must also lead to political action on the part of the government.

There appear to be two factors that promote this aim of prompting governmental action. First, there is some evidence that if the terrorist tells the target how to find relief from the stress there is less chance of inaction. Second, sporadic violence, as opposed to sustained relentless violence, appears to be more psychologically and socially effective by creating fear, anxiety and a feeling of vulnerability as well as undermining society's networks of trust, solidarity, cooperation and interdependence.[35] If emotional terror and social anomie occur, with each individual only concerned about his or her personal survival, then the state has failed for this sense of insecurity signals the fact or at least provides the impression that the provision of security as a public good — the very purpose for the state — can no longer be guaranteed by the state.[36] The state becomes the locus of frustration, and people blame it for not protecting them. If, however, a certain level of violence can be tolerated psychologically, then the antidote to the violence lies in its management by the government with it offering prudent countermeasures to meet this objective.

Thus, for the terrorist, the threat of violence must combine with unpredictability in the mind of the potential victims. Violence becomes a form of "costly signaling." Terrorists employ costly signaling to signal their resolute and credible willingness to resort to violence, a costly action. The terrorists cannot afford to bluff or lie since to do so would only undermine their claims of strength and capability to impose costs on those who oppose them.[37]

By inflicting pain (accomplishing the aim), the feeling of vulnerability is heightened and violence serves a purpose. Strangely, this purpose is not only one of coercion or destruction but for the terrorist it can also be a redemptive act, symbolic in meaning. A terrorist act is a scene in a morality play within the theater of protest. The allusion to drama is strong: labeled by some social scientists as a form of symbolic action in a "complex performative field" and a "dramaturgical framework,"[38] or a "bloody drama played out before an audience."[39] As Georges Sorel notes, violence is a purifying act.[40] The terrorist is a moralist. A moral order must be returned to equilibrium.

The tactics of terrorism are simple. They are the visible and violent acts taken by the means or resources available, which include not only terrorist foot soldiers but also other resources such as finances, weapons, and other materiel. These tactics further the group's ends as well as provide inducements needed to recruit and maintain a membership. These acts consist of assassination, arson, bombings (including suicide bombings), armed robbery, and kidnapping for the purposes of extortion. They are used to destabilize society in three respects: political instability by killing government leaders and undermining the political process; social instability by disrupting various systems of exchange (social, economic) and by propagating such fear that distrust becomes normal and disorder results; and moral instability by provoking authorities to respond to these political and social threats with brutal actions that will delegitimate vital institutions in the society.[41]

Defining the Ends of Terrorism.

The late Philip Windsor argued that terrorists' objectives are rooted in the "conditions of an historical legacy that have created a cause that can no longer be defined in terms of political compromise but instead must be redefined in terms of a moral claim."[42] "The agenda is dominated by long-standing historical legacies that have created a universe of moral problems." Thus, terrorists understand themselves to be "inheritors dispossessed by history." It is this historical grievance of being cheated of their "rightful" inheritance and their "quest for legitimacy in an as-yet only imagined proper order that lends them moral justification." This is an important distinction for the tendency on the part of those who seek to counter terrorism is that only two options are available. The first is that terrorism must be wiped out because it hampers civilized political discourse. The other is the belief that a dialogue with the terrorists is critical to co-opt them into the political process. Both of these avenues may prove sterile. The extermination of terrorists tends to breed more terrorists and thus confirms the moral claims of the terrorists, while co-optation can prove futile because moral claims cannot always be solved by political resolution.[43]

The objectives of terrorist organizations are often grandiose and visionary, calling for sweeping and uncompromising change in the allocation of power in society or contesting the legitimacy of political and social elites.[44] Yet, the commitment of terrorist organizations to a specific ideology is often weak or inconsistent;[45] it certainly is not homogenous. Ideas are often borrowed loosely from a number of theoretical sources to define ends that have ranged from Marxist-Leninism to a variety of religious doctrines. Instead, the ideology should be understood more broadly, "in the sense of being based on beliefs that comprise a systematic, comprehensive rejection of the present political world and the promise of future replacement."[46] In appealing to diverse audiences to support the terrorists or to at least cooperate and support them, the terrorists' ends are syncretist.

More dangerously, the vast majority of terrorists cannot articulate the political stages or tasks necessary to achieve their objectives but instead offer only an end state. Further, terrorism may be considered, according to Jeffrey Alexander, "*postpolitical*," that is, "it reflects the end of political possibility." If that becomes the case, then it is an experience of overwhelming political impotence expressed through "drawing blood." Its tactics "deliver maiming and death; they serve a strategy of inflicting humiliation, chaos, and reciprocal despair."[47] In other words, terror becomes an end unto itself. This has led one scholar to conclude that the "cause is not the cause." The cause, as articulated by the group's ideology, becomes the rationale for the violent acts the terrorists commit.[48]

Terror as an End.

In this respect, terrorism is a deliberate political choice by a political actor to use the power to hurt.[49] This power to hurt is not incidental to the use of force, but is an object itself. The power to hurt, as Thomas Schelling argued, is the capacity to "influence somebody's behavior, to coerce his decision or choice."[50] It is a coarse form of behavior modification in which both the afflicter and the victim know that pain can be imposed, even anticipated, and there is equally, the understanding that it might be avoided under certain conditions. However, as Windsor suggested, the terrorist has no patience with the complexities involved in political matters. This is not the protracted armed struggle of the people's army in the process of revolutionary war, as an example, where the people's army is built progressively during the course of the war. Where time, patience, or ingenuity is in short supply, the terrorist will slash through this Gordian knot. He reverts to brute force where destruction is the strategic end.[51]

This should not be surprising because terrorism is a form of *social antimovement*, to use Michel Wieviorka's term. It is an "extreme, degenerate, and highly particularized variety of social antimovement."[52] Terrorist actors exhibit three defining principles of this phenomenon, principles that fuse or "feed on themselves." Terrorism "takes the form of a course of violence, which, possessed of a rationale all its own, propagates itself without its perpetrators having to verify their words or deeds with the people in whose name they claim to be acting."[53] Instead, the actor and the cause become indistinguishable. "In the most extreme of cases, and less often than one may think, he internalizes—sometimes to the point of nihilism and self-destruction—the inability of a social movement to assert itself." The enemy is objectified, a target to be assailed, a person to be eliminated, a system to be destroyed. Lastly, a radical disengagement occurs, a death struggle ensues and attainment of a utopian state, a new order or a just society is dismissed. "The ends become confused with their means, with all sense of vision being reduced to plans for the destruction of all that stands in the way of the actor's subjectivity."[54] In other words, the desire for annihilation—self, opponent, and the state—comes to fore. In some cases, the oppressor's values are such an abomination that annihilation is the only course if the enemy will not convert to the terrorists' view. This is not the destruction of the politico-military power of the bourgeoisie or oligarchic state as part of the armed struggle of Marxist-Leninist theory. Terrorists are not interested in the eradication of their adversaries' military power. Instead, they are interested in radical change to structures or conditions through violent means or the threat of violence. The terrorist is committed to planning and strategy. "These plans and strategies presume a situation of total war" that advocates unlimited violence and a standard of action that, carried to its furthest extremes, can result in martyrdom and self-destruction. However, terrorism as an end unto itself is an anomaly and is not the usual manner in which terrorist organizations end.

Ultimately, terrorism is an exceedingly rational strategy, calculated in terms of costs and benefits with the terrorist relying on the accuracy of those calculations.[55] For the vast majority of terrorists, the strategic environment is reduced to a power struggle between opposing forces wherein the terrorist assumes an ethic of total resistance. In the system in which the terrorist lives and moves, "this ethic can only take a martial—and thereby planned and strategic—form."[56]

Terrorism and War.

Terrorism operates in two dimensions simultaneously—as a theory of violence and as a strategy of violence perpetrated to achieve a putative end. Tying these two concepts together, which is the thrust of this essay, the strategic theory of terrorism is a theory of action, to paraphrase Bernard Brodie, with violence as the critical and defining element in both of these dimensions.[57] Thus, how should we understand the violence that terrorism uses, its "martial form"? The answer to this question is again hindered by the definitional debate highlighted previously since scholars hold a legion of differing views describing what it is not rather than what it is, but largely distinguishing it from other forms of collective violence (e.g., lynching, rioting, and vigilantism).[58]

There are some problems with this categorization with understanding it as solely another variety of collective violence. These other types of collective violence are not modes of political behavior nor do the people involved seek to challenge the authority of the state and to acquire political influence. Further, terrorist groups are not mobs, but organizations with "internally consistent values, beliefs, and images of the environment." They seek a logical means to advance a particular though not always clearly articulated end using rational decision-making calculations to attain short-term and long-term objectives.[59] Colin Gray, however, offers a way out of the definitional wilderness by questioning whether terrorism is war.

Gray answers the question by referring to two theorists: Clausewitz and Hedley Bull. Clausewitz defined war as "an act of force to compel our enemy to do our will."[60] Political scientist Hedley Bull followed Clausewitz's line of reasoning and wrote, "war is organized violence carried on by political units against each other."[61] Thus, terrorism meets this definition since terrorists apply this force, violence, for a political end. If it is not for this end, then it "may be sport, or crime, or banditry of a kind integral to local culture, but it is not war. War, its threat and actuality, is an instrument of policy."[62] As Gray notes, "war has many dimensions beyond the political, but its eternal essence is captured by Clausewitz and Bull." From his perspective, the political context is principal, though he admits that it is far from the "sole, driver of the incidence and character of war."[63] In other words, Gray is willing to concede that terrorists use force to achieve ends that are political as well as social or religious in nature.

Some thinkers suggest that terrorism is a form of "new war," and that Clausewitz overlooks unconventional and so-called non-Trinitarian war, thereby arguing that Clausewitz and his remarkable trinity is not relevant.[64] These critics define the concept of the trinity as the commander and his army, the people, and the government. In Gray's view, this is a serious misreading of Clausewitz and neglectful of the primary trinity, which still pertains. That primary trinity consists of passion (violence, hatred, and enmity), chance and probability, and subordination to reason, or policy.[65] In this context, policy can be understood as the decision to take an action and perform this act in a particular way, or it can be described as the activities and relationships that influence the formulation of policy. For Clausewitz, the formulation of policy was a matter of judgment and other qualities and could be undertaken by both states as well as nonstates (he uses the example of the Tartar tribes). Thus, Clausewitz thought not only in terms of the nationstate model.[66]

Nonetheless, terrorism contains all three elements of both trinities with the primary trinity's relationship to terrorism being self-evident. In the secondary trinity, the titles are changed, but the functions remain the same: the strategist; the operational commander of terrorist groups consisting of foot soldiers and members of the support network who execute the missions or provide the financial and logistical support; and the broader populace, "which provides expressive and instrumental support for the terrorists or sympathy to their cause."[67]

Thus, terrorism fully meets the definitions set out by Clausewitz and Bull. It is a form of war, irregular war, similar to insurgency but having its own characteristics. Nonetheless, it shares with insurgency and other forms of violent military conduct the capacity to generate a strategic effect. That effect can be produced upon the mind, the military or security forces of the opponent, or both, but regardless all have in common that they must have political consequences.[68] In truth, it matters not whether the character of the war has a regular or irregular feature—the qualifying adjectives are of no import. Clausewitz's general theory of war and strategy are equally valid to both. A general theory of war and strategy explains both regular and irregular [terrorism] warfare. While they are different forms of warfare, they are not different strategically.[69]

Conclusion.

T. S. Eliot concluded his 1925 poem "The Hollow Men" with the words: "This is the way the world ends/Not with a bang, but a whimper." These are words worth remembering. Some scholars point to the apocalyptic cast of contemporary terrorism, particularly its religious variant, suggesting that this form of terrorism is unlike its predecessors in that the actors are irrational, self-destructive, and are marching willingly to martyrdom, or that religious terrorism represents a new "wave," or it is a "cosmic war," significantly different from political terrorism.[70] Nonetheless, the continuities terrorism manifests over the past centuries make one skeptical of any explanation that puts the emphasis on uniqueness.[71] Further, in classifying and giving prominence to terrorism in this form and with this ideology, they propagate a new stereotype of terrorism that is not conducive to thinking about terrorism as a rational, calculated strategic mode of thinking. This perspective perhaps underscores a strategy deficit, a failure to perceive war and politics as a unity in which war is fused with political considerations that include social and religious dimensions.[72] For how else should we interpret the notion of a caliphate but as a theocratic understanding of the notion of the state.

While terrorists' ideology, regardless of its stripe, offers a criticism of the existing political system and a prophecy of a perfectly just and harmonious society that will last the ages, it is imperative as well to understand the strategic challenge that terrorism represents. As Colin Gray reminds us, it would be imprudent to believe that terrorists are isolated from the world of strategy any more than that can be said of other practitioners of small wars and savage violence, even professional soldiers.[73]

ENDNOTES - CHAPTER 7

1. Quoted in Walter Laqueur, *The New Terrorism*, New York: Oxford University Press, 1999, p. 103.

2. *Ibid.*

3. Richard Schultz, "Conceptualizing Political Terrorism: A Typology," *Journal of International Affairs* 32, No. 1, p. 7.

4. Jon Tetsuro Sumida, "The Relationship of History and Theory in *On War*: The Clausewitzian Ideal and Its Implications," *The Journal of Military History*, Vol. 65, April 2001, p. 336.

5. Gregory D. Foster, "A Conceptual Foundation for a Theory of Strategy," *The Washington Quarterly*, Vol. 13, No. 1, Winter 1990, p. 47; Roberta Senechal de la Roche, "Toward a Scientific Theory of Terrorism," *Sociological Theory*, Vol. 22, No. 1, March 2004, p. 3.

6. Walter Laqueur, *Terrorism*, London, U.K.: Weidenfeld and Nicolson, 1977, p. 5.

7. Jack P. Gibbs, "Conceptualization of Terrorism," *American Sociological Review*, Vol. 54, No. 3, June 1989, p. 329.

8. Martha Crenshaw Hutchinson, "The Concept of Revolutionary Terrorism," *The Journal of Conflict Resolution*, Vol. 16, No. 3, September 1972, p. 384.

9. Gibbs, p. 330.

10. Quoted in Hutchinson, p. 383.

11. Harry R. Yarger, *Strategic Theory for the 21st Century: The Little Book on Big Strategy*, Carlisle, PA: Strategic Studies Institute, U.S. Army War College, 2006, p. 1.

12. *Ibid.*, pp. 6-7; Martha Crenshaw, "An Organizational Approach to the Analysis of Political Terrorism," *Orbis*, Fall 1985, p. 472.

13. Yarger, p. 7.

14. *Ibid.*, pp. 7-8.

15. Hutchinson, p. 385.

16. Charles Tilly, "Terror, Terrorism, Terrorists," *Sociological Theory*, Vol. 22, No. 1, March 2004, p. 9; H. Edward Price, Jr., "The Strategy and Tactics of Revolutionary Terrorism," *Comparative Studies on Society and History*, Vol. 19, No. 1, January 1977, p. 52; and T. P. Thornton, "Terror as a Weapon of Political Agitation," in H. Eckstein, ed. *Internal War*, New York: Free Press, 1964, pp. 78-79.

17. Donald Black, "The Geometry of Terrorism," *Sociological Theory*, Vol. 22, No. 1, March 2004, p. 18.

18. Arthur H. Garrison, "Defining Terrorism: Philosophy of the Bomb, Propaganda by Deed and Change Through Fear and Violence, "*Criminal Justice Studies*, Vol. 17, No. 3, September 2004, p. 260.

19. Amy Zegart, "An Empirical Analysis of Failed Intelligence Reforms Before September 11," *Political Science Quarterly*, Vol. 121, No. 1, Spring 2006, pp. 35-36, 39.

20. Williamson Murray and Mark Grimsley, "Introduction: On Strategy," *The Making of Strategy, Rulers, States, and War*, Cambridge, U.K.: Cambridge University Press, 1994; 1997, p. 1.

21. Yarger, pp. 13-14.

22. *Ibid.*, p. 14.

23. Alison M. Jagger, "What Is Terrorism, Why Is It Wrong, and Could It Ever Be Morally Permissible?" *Journal of Social Philosophy*, Vol. 26, No. 2, Summer 2005, p. 208.

24. Yarger, p. 14.

25. *Ibid.*, pp. 15-16.

26. Crenshaw, pp. 472-482; Randy Borum, *Psychology of Terrorism*, Tampa, FL: University of South Florida, 2004, pp. 24, 52-56.

27. Daniel S. Gressang IV, "Terrorism in the 21st Century: Reassessing the Emerging Threat," in *Deterrence in the 21st Century*, Max Manwaring, ed., Portland, OR: Frank Cass, 2001, p. 73.

28. Roberta Senechal de la Roche, "Collective Violence as Social Control," *Sociological Forum*, Vol. 11, No. 1, March 1996, pp. 97-98; Martha Crenshaw, "The Causes of Terrorism," *Comparative Politics*, Vol. 13, No. 4, July 1981, pp. 381-384.

29. de la Roche, p. 103.

30. Quoted in Garrison, p. 268.

31. Crenshaw, "An Organizational Approach to the Analysis of Political Terrorism," p. 466.

32. Thomas C. Schelling, *Arms and Influence*, New Haven, CT: Yale University Press, 1966, p. 3.

33. Carl von Clausewitz, *On War*, ed. and trans. by Michael Howard and Peter Paret, Princeton, NJ: Princeton University Press, 1984, p. 77.

34. Schelling, pp. 3-4.

35. Hutchinson, pp. 387-389.

36. Philip G. Cerny, "Terrorism and the New Security Dilemma," *Naval War College Review*, Vol. 58, No. 1, Winter 2005, p. 16.

37. Andrew H. Kydd and Barbara F. Walter, "The Strategies of Terrorism," *International Security*, Vol. 31, No. 1, Summer 2006, pp. 58, 78.

38. Jeffrey C. Alexander, "From the Depths of Despair: Performance, Counterperformance, and 'September 11,'" *Sociological Theory*, Vol. 22, No. 1, March 2004, pp. 88, 90.

39. Anthony Oberschall, "Explaining Terrorism: The Contribution of Collective Action Theory," *Sociological Theory*, Vol. 22, No. 1, March 2004, p. 27.

40. H. Stuart Hughes, *Consciousness and Society: The Reorientation of Social Thought, 1890-1930*, New York: Vintage Books, 1958, p. 165.

41. Alexander, p. 89.

42. Philip Windsor, "Terrorism and International Order," in *Studies in International Relations: Essays by Philip Windsor*, Mats Berdal, ed., Portland, OR: Sussex Academic Press, 2002, pp. x, 195.

43. *Ibid.*, p. 195.

44. Crenshaw, p. 466; Alexander, p. 89.

45. Crenshaw, p. 471.

46. *Ibid.*, p. 481.

47. Alexander, p. 89.

48. Borum, p. 24.

49. Martha Crenshaw, "Theories of Terrorism: Instrumental and Organizational Approaches," in *Inside Terrorist Organizations*, ed. David C. Rapoport, Portland, OR: Frank Cass, 2001, p. 13.

50. Schelling, p. 4.

51. Windsor, p. 193.

52. Michel Wieviorka, *The Making of Terrorism*, David Gordon White, trans., Chicago: The University of Chicago Press, 1993, p. 9.

53. *Ibid.*, pp. 7-8.

54. *Ibid.*, p. 8.

55. Hutchinson, p. 394.

56. Wieviorka, pp. 11-12.

57. Brodie's exact words are: "strategy is nothing if not pragmatic. . . . Above, all, strategic theory is a theory for action." Quoted in Colin Gray, "What is War? A View from Strategic Studies," in *Strategy and History: Essays on Theory and Practice*, New York: Routledge, 2006, p. 185.

58. de la Roche, p. 102.

59. Crenshaw, The Causes of Terrorism, pp. 379-386.

60. Clausewitz, p. 75.

61. Quoted in Gray, p. 185.

62. *Ibid.*, p. 185.

63. *Ibid.*, p. 187.

64. *Ibid.*, p. 186.

65. Gray, p. 187; and Colin S. Gray, *Irregular Enemies and the Essence of Strategy: Can the American Way of War Adapt?* Carlisle, PA: Strategic Studies Institute, U.S. Army War College, 2006.

66. Antulio J. Echevarria II, "Clausewitz and the Nature of the War on Terror," in *Clausewitz in the Twenty-First Century*, Hew Strachan and Andreas Herberg-Rothe, eds., Oxford, U.K.: Oxford University Press, 2007, pp. 196-230.

67. Borum, p. 54.

68. Gray, *Modern Strategy*, pp. 295-296.

69. Gray, *Irregular Enemies and the Essence of Strategy*, pp. vi, 4-5.

70. See Mark Juergensmeyer, *Terror in the Mind of God: The Global Rise of Religious Violence*, Berkeley: University of California Press, 2000; and David C. Rapoport, "The Four Waves of Modern Terrorism," in Audrey Kurth Cronin and James Ludes, eds., *Attacking Terrorism: Elements of a Grand Strategy*, Washington, DC: Georgetown University Press, 2004, pp. 46-73.

71. Oberschall, "Explaining Terrorism," p. 27.

72. Gray, *Irregular Enemies and the Essence of Strategy*, p. vi.

73. Bernard Crick, *In Defence of Politics*, 4th ed., Chicago: The University of Chicago Press, 1992, pp. 34-35; Gray, *Modern Strategy*, p. 294.

CHAPTER 8

LANDPOWER IN TRADITIONAL THEORY AND CONTEMPORARY APPLICATION

G. K. Cunningham

Our distant ancestors, wise for all their Neolithic lack of elegant refinement, were quick to note that the world was divided into mediums, a model of thought so adequate for most human endeavors that it lasted for millennia. In this worldview, the universe seemed to consist of varying mixes of these elements: air, water, fire, earth, and void.[1] We moderns view ourselves as more knowledgeable and sophisticated, but the technological explosion of the last few centuries, while it has altered the hard sciences of chemistry and physics, has not had much impact on our strategic thinking. We still conceptualize military power in terms of the same basic mediums: airpower, seapower, landpower, and space power. (Firepower, it would seem, is common to all of them.)

In the 20th century, airpower dominated major conflict so much that each U.S. service now has its own air arm specifically adapted for its primary medium—sea for the Navy and Marine Corps and land for the Army. Of course, the Air Force reigns supreme in the air and has also concurrently (and reasonably) assumed primary responsibility for the realm of space. In fact, dominance of space may be an essential characteristic of the American way of war in the 21st century, as the medium of space is home to constellations of satellite systems used for position and location determination, communications, intelligence gathering, and targeting.[2] However, for all its usefulness, no one lives there. People live on the land (barring a few hardy seadogs), commerce takes place on land (and merely across seas), and ideas are acculturated on the land. As T. R. Fehrenbach so eloquently pointed out in his masterpiece history of the Korea War, *This Kind of War*:

> You may fly over a land forever; you may bomb it, atomize it, pulverize it, and wipe it clean of life--but if you desire to defend it, protect it, and keep it for civilization, you must do this on the ground, the way the Roman legions did, by putting your young men into the mud.[3]

Complementing Medium-based Visions of Strategic Warfighting Theory.

In 1904, when Sir Halford Mackinder postulated the first nascent modern version of what we now call "geopolitics," he did so in the context of the end of the colonial era. Mackinder claimed that during the preceding four centuries of expansion, the world had been divided up about as far as it was going to be, and that politics in the 20th century would be played out in a closed system of vying states. To Mackinder, the geography of the world was the stage on which such political, ideological, military, economic, and social affairs were carried out.[4] Hence, anyone wishing to know more about the drama of human interaction should start with a thorough study of stagecraft, as the foundation of the rest of the art.

His approach was not without merit. Alfred Thayer Mahan, the American proponent of seapower, had earlier published his seminal work, *The Influence of Sea Power upon History, 1660-1783*, in which he postulated that the then preeminent dominance of the maritime nation of Great Britain rested on its ability to control sea lines of communication to resource-rich colonies. Any nation, like the United States for instance, that desired to expand its power had best follow that model. Mahan was indeed innovative in this regard, for he was the principal author of the notion that the seas were not obstacles to be overcome, but avenues of approach for military forces and wide-open lanes of commerce for economic ventures.[5] Thus, far from being barriers to trade, transportation, and power projection, the seas provided the very means by which a nation might exert its national power and enlarge its influence. However, while Mackinder recognized the validity of Mahan's approach, he believed the land and not the sea was the key to national prosperity and power. The expansion of modern transportation across continents was fast shrinking nations to mere islands across which railroads, the sea lanes of the land, would carry commerce.

At the time Mackinder and Mahan were making these initial sweeping statements, World War I had not been fought, so the impact of air power had yet to be felt. Air power made dramatic advances during the war. One spectacular raid conducted late in the war hinted at the potential of air power. On 9 August 1918, Italian Major Gabriele D'Annunzio commanding the 87th fighter squadron, "La Serenissima," organized one of the great feats of the war. The flamboyant and dashing D'Annunzio was an accomplished novelist, poet, and dramatist, as well as a daring pilot. Leading a small squadron of nine SVA-5 two-seat warplanes, D'Annunzio flew a 700-mile round trip mission over Vienna, dropping thousands of leaflets, written in Italian and German and sporting the tricolors of Italy, urging the Viennese to surrender. This pioneer roundtrip flight of over 700 miles exemplified the potential of aviation to dominate both the air and sea mediums.[6]

It is no surprise, then, that the foremost proponent of airpower was an Italian, Giulio Douhet, who constructed a general theory of air power that has defined the parameters of discussion on warfare in this medium since the early 20th century. He was the first military theorist to grasp the impact of the airplane as an offensive weapon and translate it into a comprehensive mode of warfare in a new medium.[7] His insightful, visionary analysis would be championed by others, such as the British airpower advocate Hugh M. Trenchard and the American aviation enthusiast Billy Mitchell. While it would take the massive strategic bombing campaigns of World War II to provide practical evidence of the validity of their approach, the flight of the B-29 bomber Enola Gay was ample and definitive proof that control of the air was the fundamental prerequisite of modern warfare.[8]

All that said, the American approach to warfare is inherently joint, so much so that jointness is a fundamental precept of all national security planning:

> The campaign is the central organizing instrument for joint warfare. Campaigns, by their nature, are joint undertakings. They are planned and executed by applying operational art. The joint operational art encompasses the translation of national security and military strategies into operational design for the joint employment of forces at all levels of war. Combatant commands develop command and theater strategies to apply the joint operational art to their contemporary missions and situations.[9]

In the Department of Defense (DoD), the various services, organized by medium of action, are tasked by DoD Directive 5100.1, *Functions of the Department of Defense and Its Major Components*, among other things, "to recruit, organize, train, and equip interoperable force for assignments to combatant commands" and also "to conduct research; develop tactics, techniques and organization; and develop and procure weapons, equipment, and supplies essential to the fulfillment of the functions [so prescribed]."[10] While service cultures produce norms of behavior and institutionalized perspectives that are medium-dominated, the employment of United States armed forces takes place under the command and control of combatant commanders, organized by regional theater or global function.

Even though joint doctrine specifically defines all military planning and operations as joint campaigns under the combatant command of unified, joint commanders, the particularization of warfare into separate operations on land, sea, air, and space makes intuitive sense insofar as the actual manning, equipping and organizing of forces for employment is concerned. And in that context, landpower remains a foremost strategic consideration unlikely to be supplanted by control of the seas, supremacy in the air, or control of space and cyberspace. Colin Gray points out:

First, the land matters most. Whether or not land constitutes the principal geographical medium on which combat is waged, strategic effect ultimately must have its way in a territorial context. Most wars entail some fighting on the geography where the belligerents live, the land. Even if a war is dominated by the ebb and flow of combat at sea and in the air, still the whole object of the exercise is to influence the behavior on an enemy who needs to be controlled where he lives, on land.... Human beings do not live at sea, or in cyberspace.[11]

Mackinder and the Continental Theory of Landpower.

For Halford Mackinder, the abstract and somewhat emblematic debate over the relative worth of seapower or landpower (or subsequently, airpower) often overshadows his more important contribution to the military theory of landpower. While it is true that the prestige of Mahan was probably greater among Mackinder's fellow Britons than among Mahan's own American citizenry, Mackinder's work was not predominantly a refutation of that popular strategic theory. Rather it was a reminder that geopolitics is a subject that transcended single mediums of conflict. Geography was not a matter of static boundaries and coastlines, but an ever-transforming element of a global world organism that was subject to change and interpretation. Mackinder began his commentary on seapower by stating, "The influence of geographical conditions upon human activities has depended, however, not merely on the realities as we know them to be and to have been, but in even greater degree on what men imagine in regard to them."[12] To Mackinder, then, the geography was actually less important than the perceptions men had of it and the uses to which it was put. His own detailed charts and illustrations, as well as the detail in which he presented the seaman's and the landsman's points of view, often appear to overshadow his real intent, which was to explain to a complacent United Kingdom after the victory of World War I that continental powers were still a threat with which they must reckon.

Indeed, Mackinder's most widely regarded work, *Democratic Ideals and Reality*, was first published in 1919 and was routinely ignored until World War II proved it to be a foresighted and penetrating treatise. As the title suggests, the book was predominantly a work of social strategy, or geopolitics, not pure geography. Mackinder grasped as an absolute what other strategic theorists from Corbett to Mitchell overlooked: people live on land, and power projection alone cannot disrupt national culture and state ambition for long. "In this war," Mackinder wrote of World War I, "German anticipations have proven wrong in many regards, but that has been because we have made them so by a few wise principles of government, and by strenuous effort, notwithstanding our mistakes in policy." Prophetically he continued, "Our greatest test is yet to come."[13] The euphoria emerging from the defeat of Germany in World War I seemed to result from, in part, a conviction on the part of many of his countrymen that Britannia did indeed rule the waves, that democracy was a predestined condition for all mankind, and that a democratic seapower such as England could contain a continental power and was hence invulnerable.

But what Mackinder postulated was that such an interpretation was idealistic and not at all predictable. He based his premise not only on world geography, but also on an analysis of cultures and national intents. The central issue was not the absolute supremacy of either seapower or landpower, but that the two concepts represented rival nationalistic intentions that would inevitably come into competition and conflict. Great Britain was able to maintain a global empire because of its ability to quickly exert national elements of power over sea lines of communication around littoral parts of the world. In fact, its empire was largely a matter of access to littoral areas, and only extended inward in places such as the Indian subcontinent and central Africa, where land-based rivals could exert threatening influence outward into those littoral areas. From this condition, Mackinder extrapolated that a power acting from a geographical base somewhere in Eastern Europe—the Heartland of a Eurasian World Island—could indeed become a rival empire. Mackinder was never really specific in defining a precise location for the Heartland, but always referred to this in political terms as an area relative to German (that is, Prussian) and Russian interests. What was clear, though, was that this heartland was a split interest, and should it become a unified political entity, its power would become immense.

Again, this conclusion evolved from a conviction on Mackinder's part that the world stage was fixed. Even the poles had been explored and categorized. "In outline our geographical knowledge is now complete . . . claims to the political ownership of all the dry land [have] been pegged out. Whether we think of the physical, economic, military, or political interconnection of things on the surface of the globe, we are now for the first time presented with a closed system."[14]

Hence, any geopolitical considerations in the 20th century would involve rehashing of past conflicts, struggles over the same finite resources, and determinations of political control over the same regions as had characterized the past. If one analyzed that as a struggle of sea powers against land powers, the outcome in the 20th century was not guaranteed by past outcomes. The internal combustion engine and the extension of railroads throughout Eurasia created a different construct — one in which a landpower acting on interior lines of communication could marshal resources and employ manpower to effectively rule the world. Seen in this light, Mackinder was not prescriptive, but cautionary. Given state political ambition in a closed system, the reality was that conflict was quite a likely outcome in the times ahead. While the Great War to Save Democracy was won, and the optimistic hope for a successful and effective League of Nations was a fine ideal, those were Anglo-French perceptions not held by Germany, Russian, or the Chinese for that matter — not to mention a plethora of minor, outer rim states like Japan or the United States. The geopolitical reality was likely to prove that:

> Who rules East Europe commands the Heartland:
> Who rules the Heartland commands the World-Island:
> Who rules the World-Island commands the World.[15]

But just who *did* rule East Europe in 1919? The social and political fact was that it was a divided region, not one ruled by any particular nationality. Rather, it was an area torn by rivalry, as the past World War had demonstrated. Mackinder emphasized, "But it cannot be too often repeated that these events were the result of a fundamental antagonism between the Germans, who wished to be masters in East Europe, and the Slavs, who refused to submit to them."[16] With Germany soundly defeated, and Russia impeded by social turmoil following a disruptive revolution, this division was likely to be a standing condition for the immediate post-World War I period. However, that condition, for Mackinder, could in no way be interpreted as a certain future. Should either the Slavs or the Germans command the Heartland, freedom-loving and democratically organized states had best be prepared to defend themselves.

Mackinder's proffered solution was a good one, simple, reasonable, and politically attainable: divide the Heartland into more than two states, one Germanic and one Slavic. Since the Heartland was never definitely delineated, the extent of the division was rather a fluid concept, but it most certainly demanded an independent and economically viable Poland.

> In other words, we must settle this question between the Germans and the Slavs, and we must see to it that East Europe, like West Europe, is divided into self-contained nations.... If you do not now secure the full results of your victory and close this issue between the German and the Slav, you will leave ill-feeling which will not be based on the fading memory of a defeat, but on the daily irritation of millions of proud people.[17]

The central foundation of the geopolitical theory that Mackinder espoused was not the concept of Heartland, which in fact he periodically revised and redefined, but his pioneering assertion that in the post-World War I world rivalries would take place in a closed system.[18] He was more prescient than he may have realized, had he lived to see the division of the world between bipolar superpowers for much of the latter half of the 20th century. In that world the United States assumed the mantle of predominant seapower, and the Soviet Union became undisputed master of the Heartland of East Europe, a stable division that demonstrated the supremacy of neither seapower nor landpower alone, nor the ability of air- and space power to tilt the balance in any particular direction.

Interpretations of Landpower and Strategic Intent.

In retrospect, the varying comparison of maritime power with continental power should not be surprising, as it is, at least as far as geography is concerned, a repetition of the lines of operations maxims Jomini postulated in the 19th century on a global scale:

> Interior lines of operations are those adopted by one or two armies to oppose several hostile bodies, and having such a direction that the general can concentrate the masses and maneuver with a whole force in a shorter period of time than it would require the enemy to oppose to them a greater force. Exterior lines lead to the opposite result, and are those formed by an army which operates at the same time on both flanks of the enemy, or against several of his masses.[19]

Seapower as Mahan described it was not just a military theory, but encompassed the full range of elements of national power. But insofar as military operations go, seapower is operationally an approach working from exterior lines. The mobility of the sea enables a power to rapidly move forces around the periphery of a continental power, gaining and retaining initiative by exerting power at times and places of its choosing. In contrast, Mackinder accepted the Jominian principle that interior lines of operation were generally superior to exterior.[20] Hence, a power operating from the strategic center of a continent would have an advantage over a maritime power circumnavigating the littorals. It is a valid, if somewhat simplistic, point.

Jomini based his analysis predominately on the operations of the supreme commander of his era, Napoleon Bonaparte. It was fundamentally a historical approach that retains its validity, since the spectrum of human endeavor is the source of any conclusions regarding the theory of any subset of human endeavor like warfare. However, in any field of study so complex, conclusions and perspectives will differ, and historian-analysts and military theorists have often approached the fundamentals of armed conflict as a means to achieve national policy objectives from a variety of perspectives.

Even earlier commentators offer contrasts. Sun Tzu, a Chinese theorist writing about 500 BC, is perhaps the earliest landpower theorist who presented a coherent approach to land operations. His era was one of warring states, in which rival kingdoms and king-like warlords struggled for supremacy between the decline of the Zhou dynasty and the establishment of central order under the Qin and Han dynasties.[21] His observations took the Confucian mode of terse aphorisms, not always well organized, but consistently emphasizing what B. H. Liddell Hart would later famously label "the indirect approach."[22] Maneuver was highly valued, especially if it avoided actual battle until conditions were favorable. Sun Tzu encouraged indirect methods of action, exploiting intelligence, resource depletion, and subterfuge:

> For to win one hundred victories in one hundred battles is not the acme of skill. To subdue the enemy without fighting is the acme of skill. Thus, what is of extreme importance in war is to attack the enemy's strategy; next best is to disrupt his alliances; the next best is to attack his army. The worst policy is to attack cities. Attack cities only when there is no alternative.[23]

Such an outlook is consistent with the geopolitical exigencies of the use of landpower in Sun Tzu's era. In the case of warring principalities, prolonged conflict depleted resources, emptied treasuries, and sacrificed manpower. He pointed out that military power is only one element of state power and that its use is problematic: "When the army engages in protracted campaigns the resources of the state will not suffice."[24]

But the advent of firearms changed the balance considerably, and when military power was concentrated in the hands of two or three antagonists, as developed in feudal Japan, Sun Tzu's advocacy of skillful battlefield gymnastics was not as efficient a means to the end as a powerful, well-aimed thrust at the heart. After the death of the emperor Toyotomi Hideyoshi in 1598, rival feudal lords (daimyo) struggled for control. Tokugawa Ieyasu quickly surfaced as the dominant figure in an alliance of about half the diamyo and defeated his western rivals in the pivotal set-piece battle of Sekigahara in 1600, becoming the Shogun. During the great battle of Sekigahara, an estimated 60,000 matchlock firearms were used, a vast quantity compared, say, to the mere 3,000 matchlocks then employed in the French army. This technological advance in killing efficiency in terms of range and lethality was balanced by the inherent inaccuracies of the weaponry that mandated the massing of forces and direct action to achieve a culminating battle.[25] The outcome of this decisive battle was a shogunate that lasted until the arrival of Commodore Matthew Perry to Japan in 1853, and hence Japanese strategy emphasized directness and thoroughness as not only a means to military victory, but also to national security and prolonged peace.

Miyamoto Musashi, a samurai who survived the battle of Sekigahara (almost miraculously, as he was a part of the defeated alliance most of which was hunted down and slaughtered), became the strongest Asian proponent of directness in warfare. After a life of legendary proportions, in which he fought over 60 duels without a defeat, he retired to complete his notable work on strategy, Go Rin No Sho, that is, A Book of Five Rings. This work remains both enigmatic, as it is largely an extended allegory, and routinely ignored outside of Japan, as it was only translated into English in a readily available published version in 1974. But the work is clearly one with broad conceptual intent, designed as a strategic treatise rather than a fencing manual. As Musashi writes, "The principles of strategy are written down here in terms of single combat, but you must think broadly so that you attain an understanding for ten-thousand-a side battles."[26]

Key to Musashi's approach to strategy is directness. He advocates no flourishes, teaching instead that success depends on clear focus on the objective of defeating the enemy:

> The primary thing when you take a sword in your hands is your intention to cut the enemy, whatever the means. Whenever you parry, hit, spring, strike or touch the enemy's cutting sword, you must cut the enemy in the same movement. It is essential to attain this. If you think only of hitting, springing, striking or touching the enemy, you will not be able actually to cut him. More than anything, you must be thinking of carrying your movement through to cutting him. You must thoroughly research this.[27]

Whatever stance one takes, or whatever strategic ends, ways, and means one considers, Musashi advises a direct, no-nonsense attitude: "Think only of cutting."[28] It is ironic, perhaps, that the Japanese theorist's concepts were most represented in World War II, in use against his nation, by the bellicose American advocate of unrestrained strategic bombing Curtis LeMay.[29]

Another way of viewing the direct-indirect dichotomy is through the portal of technological or tactical advances and their impact on operational art. In his book, Breaking the Phalanx: A New Design for Landpower in the 21st Century, Douglas A. Macgregor takes exactly that approach, which is largely a contrast of mass versus maneuver. Macgregor postulates that the Roman legions, in order to counter the crushing weight and shock of massed spears that was the Macedonian phalanx, had to devise more flexible and maneuverable formations. By deploying legionaries in boxed, offset "checkerboard" formations, depending on the coordinated use of stabbing sword and shield rather than pikes, Roman commanders gained maneuverability at the expense of Macedonian mass. [30] In the crucial battle of Cynoscephalae in 197 BC, an alert tribune, acting on initiative, diverted 20 mandibles into an attack on the exposed rear of the Macedonian phalanx. The phalanx, like the modern battle tank, was designed to fight from the front. The Macedonians, unable to turn because of their powerful but unidirectional formation and unwieldy long pikes, were slaughtered. [31]

To Macgregor, this battle illustrates the swing of a long pendulum. He draws from it the conclusion that the U.S. Army of the 21st century must be light, agile, and rapidly deployable. In fact, historian Lynn Montross characterized much of military history as a cyclic interplay of mass versus maneuver. He pointed out that the very mobility of the Roman legions that Macgregor cited, when faced with increasingly active Gothic and Persian horsemen centuries after Cynoscephalae, shifted gradually into more stable, massed formations of phalangial density to counter the speed and tactical agility of light cavalry. [32]

The Macedonia phalanx was proof against both the Greek hoplites, who were typically organized in a less dense array, and the lightly armored Persian skirmishers that the Macedonians faced as Alexander conquered the Hellenic world—mass over maneuver. However, the flexible Roman mandibles countered the massed Macedonian pikemen, proving to be more adaptable in rugged terrain and faster to reorient in pitched battle—maneuver over mass. By the end of the Roman era, massed Frankish infantry would fight, again shoulder to shoulder, against barbarian horsemen in the form of Moors and Goths, degenerating into a simple human wall formation that repulsed the Moorish assault at Poitiers—mass over maneuver once again. This stubborn shoulder-to-shoulder human wall tactic succumbed to mail-armored cavalry at Hastings in 1066, when William defeated the massed housecarls of Harold Goodwinson. Such cavalry in turn fell before the increased range and penetrating power of English longbows and later firearms, until cavalry again countered by armoring themselves and their horses with thick plate armor. [33] Montross postulates that this mass-maneuver cycle typifies most land warfare, as when, in World War I, the massed firepower of entrenched machine guns and artillery, which had forced land battle into a stalemate on the Western front, was challenged once again by maneuverable forces in the form of the British technological advance of the tank, which proved decisive and dominant in 1917 at Cambrai. [34]

The lethality of firepower, whether first seen as a basic ball of rock propelled from a metal tube, as in a primitive harquebus, or the massive potential of contemporary improved conventional munitions, or cluster bombs, whether delivered by warplanes or ground-based artillery or missiles, has itself generated another way of viewing the historical transformation of land warfare as an element of landpower. As modern armies, over the past few centuries, have slugged it out in the pursuit of national policies, the focus has shifted from battles and campaigns to the ability of a nation-state to bear the costs of warfare at the strategic level. As described by Russell F. Weigley, one pole of the spectrum is attrition, a strategy based on the continuous, perhaps even gradual, wearing down of a nation's capability to resist. In this concept, the ultimate will of the people to replace lost manpower and to fund the interminable costs of the war effort become paramount.

In America, George Washington successfully practiced such an attrition strategy in the American Revolution—eventually the costs of continuing the conflict simply became more than the British king and parliament were willing to bear. Washington, according to Weigley, was foredoomed to a strategy of attrition out of the necessity of military poverty. The weak colonial states could not withstand the disciplined, well-armed, and well-led British forces on any contested field. Moreover, the mobility of the British Navy made it possible to maneuver the length of the colonial coastline virtually without interference. Washington's only hope for success lay in an erosion of British will to continue the conflict. Operationally, Washington had to become a master of disengagement, avoiding decisive battles and preserving his minimal fighting strength for as long as possible.[35]

The protracted 20th century Cold War between the United States and the Soviet Union similarly is an example of attrition strategy in a simmering conflict with occasional violent eruptions in Korea, Vietnam, and the Middle East. That long competition was finally won, at least in part, when the costs of countering a massive military build-up under President Ronald Reagan proved more than the Soviet Union could economically and socially support, resulting in the collapse and dismemberment of the Soviet empire. Of course, the very nature of attrition warfare postulates a protracted conflict—the Cold War lasted from the end of World War II until 1989. Inherent in that extended effort to attrite enemy resources and will power is the potential for one's own resources and willpower to erode in the process. Hence, a strategy of attrition warfare is not without risk. In regard to Weigley's example of the American Revolution, one might wonder, for example, what would have become of the rebellious colonies had not the French fleet fortuitously weighed in heavily on their side to counter the British domination of sea lines of operation.[36]

Hence, American history also includes periods in which Weigley's antipodal concept, annihilation, bears sway. The quintessential example of annihilation strategy at work, in an American context, is the American Civil War. In the dual strategy of General Ulysses S. Grant, the operative concept was the annihilation of the enemy's capability to resist, both in terms of military forces and also in terms of the will of the people to continue the struggle. Grant's experiences in the West had convinced him that the South simply did not have enough forces or resources to sustain a drawn-out conflict. His strategic vision was simple and hence all the more effective. In concert with the reliable General George G. Meade, he would put unrelenting pressure on General Robert E. Lee's Army of Northern Virginia, allowing him no chance to regroup and resupply his Confederate forces. Meanwhile, in the West, General William T. Sherman would slash the Confederacy to pieces, so that no forces, arms, or supplies could find their way to Lee. To Meade, he issued clear intent: "Lee's army will be your objective point. Wherever Lee goes, there you will go also."[37] To Sherman, he wrote: "You I propose to move against General Joseph E. Johnston's army, to break it up, and to get into the interior of the enemy's country as far as it is possible, inflicting all the damage you can against their war resources."[38]

Annihilation policy dominates Grant's prosecution of the war, in which the aim was the complete destruction of any enemy capability to continue, both by the defeat of armies in the field and by the terrorizing of the civilian population into political capitulation. Weigley writes:

> Sherman's war against the enemy's mind like Grant's war for the complete destruction of the enemy armies was a recipe for the achievement of total victory. The Northern generals were pulled toward both methods because their aim was the utter and complete conquest of the South. ...Considerations of the possible dangerous effects of military means upon the ultimate ends of postwar sectional understanding had to be sacrificed to the immediate quest for victory, because nothing less than total victory seemed to offer an prospects for reunification at all.[39]

The strategic approach of Grant, one of unrelenting pursuit of total victory, is repeated in the next century in the American demand for unconditional surrender of the Japanese and German nations during World War II. Indeed, one of Weigley's basic premises is that the American way of war is largely one of annihilation rather than attrition.

As callous and rough-handed as Sherman's destruction of Southern resources and intimidation of its population may seem, it pales before the determination of General Curtis Lemay to firebomb the Axis powers into submission. Hamburg, Dresden, and Kassel in Germany, and Tokyo and Kobe in Japan, were wiped off the map by incendiary munitions. LeMay's prosecution of a war of annihilation in the Pacific was particularly brutal. The aerial campaign against Japan may have killed more than one million Japanese civilians. Official estimates from the United States Strategic Bombing Survey suggest that the aerial campaign directed by LeMay between March and August, 1945, killed 330,000 people and injured another 476,000, with 8.5 million people made homeless. In that regard, nearly half the built-up areas of 64 cities were totally destroyed, an astonishing count of 2.5 million buildings. LeMay accepted the viciousness of the incendiary and nuclear attacks, and had America perchance lost the war, he fully expected retaliatory treatment as a war criminal. However, he never flinched from what he considered his patriotic professional duty in carrying out such destructive and, more importantly, demoralizing attacks.[40]

Annihilation remains the preferred method of joint warfare. Joint Publication 1, *Joint Warfare of the Armed Forces of the United States*, states that "the Armed Forces of the United States employ decisive force—powerful enough to unequivocally and rapidly defeat an opponent."[41] This declaration of doctrine is accompanied by a quotation from Lieutenant General Mike Short, U.S. Air Force, that clearly and colorfully extends the limits of the doctrine:

> We use force as a last resort...then we need to go in with overwhelming force, quite frankly, extraordinary violence that the speed of it, the lethality of it . . . the weight of it has to make an incredible impression on the adversary, to such a degree that he is stunned and shocked...you take the fight to the enemy. You go after the head of the snake, put a dagger in the heart of the adversary, and you bring to bear all the force that you have at your command.[42]

Short's emphasis on lethality as well as weight is significant, for American military muscle depends more on technological superiority than sheer weight of numbers. While emphasizing that "the design of future capabilities must avoid dependence on unique systems whose malfunction may cause mission failure,"[43] the capstone doctrine of Joint Publication 1 states that the foremost responsibility of joint and Service research and development programs is to "remain abreast of the leading edge of American and foreign science and technology so that new developments and their promise can be professionally incorporated into military statements of future requirements."[44] But Frederick W. Kagan points out that technological advantage requires continuous updating and advances to be effective, stating, "'asymmetrical advantages gained by one state do not normally last very long. Technology and technique inevitably spreads. Other states acquire either similar or counteracting capabilities."[45] Hence, technology alone is not likely to prove able to maintain supremacy without counterbalancing supremacies in conventional forces in terms of both concentrated mass and strategic maneuverability.

This cursory glance at the history of the application of landpower theory in terms of principles of war and operational perspectives suggests that Mackinder was, by and large, right. The exact location and extent of the Heartland, however, is not as critical as the understanding that landpower is more than a military construct. It is as Mackinder asserted a function of culture, resources, and social fabric. The military application of landpower is in practice both cyclical and evolutionary. Mass versus maneuver, attrition versus annihilation, or indirect versus direct approaches all demonstrate that the application of landpower is a contextual issue. The operational applications are heavily influenced by the technology available to the antagonists, whether better armor or better firepower, and change as opposing forces seek advantage on the battlefield. However, regardless of the angle from which a theorist may look at it or the historical context in which it is employed, the strategic importance of landpower remains a stable and enduring concept.

Landpower in the 21st Century.

What then is the situational context of landpower at the beginning of the 21st century, and what direction should the U.S. Army move in regard to it?

Certainly in the modern world, mass armies and industrialized military forces predominate. Even in irregular or partisan armies in far-flung and obscure hotspots in areas of crisis, the sources of munitions, weapons, supplies and equipment are the industrialized nations. What may be a break from the historical precedents on which a Baron Antoine Jomini or a Carl von Clausewitz[46] theorized is that today tactical supremacy alone is unlikely to achieve national strategic objectives except in the most particularized of cases.

One can only speculate about the state of affairs in the century ahead, and any prognostication assumes risk. However, there is a general consensus of opinion that guides the development of national security policy and the transformation of military preparedness in the decades ahead. Secretary of Defense Donald H. Rumsfeld sums up the central matter as one of ambiguity:

> We live in a time of unconventional challenges and strategic uncertainty. We are confronting challenges fundamentally different than those faced by the American defense establishment in the Cold War and previous eras. The strategy we adopt today will help influence the world's strategic environment, for the Untied States is an unusually powerful player in world affairs.[47]

This changing security environment is not a total departure from the past, but is an enlargement of it. *Traditional* challengers remain among states with strong military capabilities. While none challenge U.S. global dominance, many could become significant regional actors in historical modalities of confrontation and conflict. *Irregular* challengers will employ terrorism and guerilla methods to oppose and in some ways negate the immense technological advantages of American armed forces operating jointly. In fact, *disruptive* challenges may seek to employ widely available high technology breakthroughs to counter the technology-dependent American network-centric approach to warfare. And increasingly, both non-state actors and nations may seek to counter U.S. hegemony through the *catastrophic* use of weapons of mass destruction or effects.[48] Indeed, this particular scenario is among the most compelling drivers of national policy: "America is now threatened less by conquering states than we are by failing ones. We are menaced less by fleets and armies than by catastrophic technologies in the hands of an embittered few."[49]

Thus the potential sources of disorder and destruction are varied and great. The apparent lack of usefulness of conventional military force against the United States should not be taken as a guarantee that it will never be used. Particularly in terms of regional ambitions, even minor powers can marshal enough military might to give the United States pause for concern. The use of convention military force is not always a judicious decision made by rational actors. "Passion will always dominate reason. People will find reasons to fight even when they should not," points out Charles M. Maynes.[50] Indeed, the 1990 invasion of Kuwait by Saddam Hussein was based on exactly that premise, that a regional power could muster the local concentration of forces necessary to act against the national interests of the United States. That Saddam Hussein was wrong will not preclude others from making the same mistake.

In some respects, especially as regards weak multi-cultural, failed, or under-governed states, the current world system of states is likely to prove rather fragile. While in the past, industrially based economies favored the nation state, current high technologies contribute to the formation of non-state actors—both commercially and politically. In a globalized economic system many multinational corporations have assets and resources that exceed the gross domestic products of many nations, hence, they cannot avoid an increasing interest in political affairs.[51] While multinational businesses tend to favor stability, they make decisions based on profit and thus can produce, even if unintentionally, conditions conducive to political instability. Affordable, reliable, and globally accessible communications facilitate interactions not only of decentralized businesses but also of political groups. Ethnic nationalism, tribalism, and a resurgence of religious identification act centrifugally to pull multicultural nations apart, whether as large as the former Soviet Union or as small as Rwanda. As William G. Heyland suggested in 1993, "Those who argue that the purpose of American policy is to safeguard democracy and democratic practices, also have to confront its handmaiden—self-determination."[52] It is extremely unlikely that the United States as a nation with global interests will be immune to the disorders that state fragmentations will cause.

In this tumultuous state of instability, non-state actors are likely to proliferate and even thrive. The sanctuaries created by the chaotic conditions in ungoverned territories and failed states allow such menaces to operate with anonymity and lack of effective interference. Even in well-established states with intact governance, criminality and politics may prove to be synergistic as criminal elements find they can exert political power and political entities find they can profit from criminal activities. In the Western hemisphere, narcotraffickers assume just this position in many Latin American countries, and al-Qaeda and other terrorist cells depend on criminal activities for much of their revenue.[53]

In such chaotic and unpredictable geopolitical terrain, military responsibilities are not likely to be confined to decisive military operations. Landpower will perforce be expended in occupation duties and nation-building operations, a historical truism that many military planners and strategists overlook. The Defense Science Board pointed out that "Stabilization and reconstruction [S&R] operations are not a lesser included task of a combat mission, but a separate and distinct mission with unique requirements for equipping and training. Thus, S&R requirements should be a major driver for the future force."[54] Naturally, as this is a distinctly population-oriented activity, one can well expect it will take place just as Halford Mackinder stipulated—where the people are, to wit: the land. Landpower forces will play the predominant role in these operations, with the Army designated as the lead executive agent for stabilization and reconstruction.

Landpower, then, as an element of this 21st century geopolitical environment will extend beyond combat situations and encompass much more than land-oriented military forces, which leads to a wider definition of landpower as "the ability in peace, crisis, and war to exert prompt and sustained influence on or from land."[55] Landpower, so defined, must be employed in concert with other components of military power. Such joint orchestration will be essential at all stages of implementation of this national strategy, woven into a context of integrated application of all elements of national power: diplomatic, informational, military, and economic. This will require broader interagency cooperation and increasing joint military interdependence. However, landpower and land forces will be central to the process of transformation:

> Aggression flowing from internal instability thus demands the actual transformation of an unstable or aggressive state into one which is both stable and willing to adhere to the norms of the international community. . . . Landpower is crucial for this new grand strategy since it is the tool by which aggressive or conflict-ridden states can be transformed into stable ones.[56]

The challenge for the U.S. Army is to respond appropriately to all, some, or none of the potential threats deriving from this global geopolitical environment of ambiguity. It must become and remain a more ready, adaptable, and strategically deployable landpower force with a modular mix of flexible forces that can respond appropriately to any future challenges to U.S. interests.[57] Chief of Staff of the Army General Peter J. Schoomaker declared, "Whereas for most of our lives the default condition has been peace, now our default expectation must be conflict. This new strategic context is the logic for reshaping the Army to be an Army of campaign quality with joint and expeditionary capabilities."[58]

Landpower: Adding Versatility to National Security Strategy.

William T. Johnsen postulates that landpower's principal contribution to military strategy in the 21st century will stem in great measure from its inherent versatility. In analyzing the application of military power across the potential range of employment options, Johnsen concluded that landpower uniquely spans the widest portion of the spectrum. (See Figure 1.) He does not discount the importance of air-and seapower in an overall deterrence posture, particularly when the employment of nuclear options is concerned at the upper end of the spectrum, when national survival may well be at stake. But that eventuality, while a quintessential one from the standpoint of catastrophic danger, is an unlikely one in terms of probability. Hence, landpower offers the most options for practical employment of the military component of national power in pursuit of United States security policies:

> [Land power] offers significant contributions to the key roles of supporting the nation, shaping geostrategic conditions, and deterring or compelling adversaries. Land power also offers the greatest operational and strategic flexibility across the spectrum of conflict, throughout the full range of military operations, and in all roles that the Armed Forces of the United States can be expected to perform.[59]

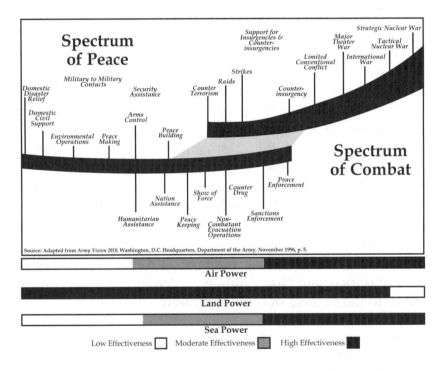

Figure 1. The Range of Effectiveness of Military Options.[60]

This conceptualization is important in implementing the kinds of decisions essential to prosecuting the National Defense Strategy in the context of an unstable and uncertain world order. In the broad range of smaller-scale contingencies such as civil support operations, counterinsurgency operations, peacekeeping missions, or counterterrorism operations that are essential to the promotion of peace and deterring war, land forces may have far greater utility than their more technology-oriented counterparts on the sea or in the air. Thus, from the standpoint of the variety of military operations that land forces can undertake, the ability of land forces to operate in direct proximity to other forces, host nations, and civilian populations, and the scalability of both kinetic and non-kinetic response capabilities, land forces represent a powerful arrow in the national military quiver.

Landpower, then, retains a preeminent role in national defense, as it represents the nation's ability to influence events and persons before challenges to national security and international stability degenerate to become more fractious, more volatile, and less manageable. In times of relative calm, when theater combatant commanders are charged with engagement strategies for bolstering relationship and reassuring potential partners, landpower is invaluable in developing the close personal relationships among regional nations that prepare later avenues for the employment of landpower in concert with coalition partners.

In the advent of crisis, land forces can act aggressively to intercede to deter continued aggression, dissuade potential adversaries from further hostile actions, and reassure multinational partners of United States' commitment to regional stability and a peaceful world order. In the unfortunate instance of natural disasters, land power can provide relief from suffering and establish the preconditions for a return to normalcy and a restoration of essential civil functions.

Should deterrence fail, land forces can exert decisive military force to defeat adversary combat forces or deny access to territory, resources, and supportive populations. The technological overmatch of U.S. conventional forces assures American dominance of global battlespace for the foreseeable future. Despite the theoretical advantages of asymmetric approaches for countering U.S. superiorities, it is unlikely that any state or non-state actors employing such tactics or techniques will seriously threaten U.S. national security. That said, the introduction of weapons of mass destruction or effects into this equation will, of course, change that potential. However, the persistent use of lower level asymmetric threats over extended periods can in fact act as an impediment to the furtherance of U.S. interests and can become a particularly virulent form of conflict. Thus, while large-scale traditional warfare may well become less prevalent in the 21st century, particularly compared to the last one, overall small scale violence may in fact increase in both frequency and intensity. As ethnic struggles, confrontations caused by competition in a globalized economic environment, and population pressures on scarce resources of petrochemicals, water, minerals, and arable land proliferate, violence may be seen as an increasingly viable course of action despite its inherent risks. Truly desperate or hopeless people may resort to violence simply because they believe they have nothing to lose. The ideologically extreme may not recognize or consider the risks. In any case, the widespread use of handheld communications technologies will act to facilitate small group connectivity and global networking, making coordination of such violence feasible on a worldwide scope.[61]

Once combat-intensive military operations cease, a full range of national effort will likely be needed to reestablish good governance, defeat pockets of organized resistance, and establish the kinds of security conditions incident to stability and reconstruction activities. It is clear that many reconstruction activities would be best performed by host nation agencies, nongovernmental and private sector organizations, or professionals from international agencies such as the United Nations. However, these kinds of organizations are generally ill-equipped to maintain their own security, and it will be incumbent on military forces to do so. In fact, U.S. military forces must be prepared to assist in rebuilding local institutions, encourage economic activity, and even establish representative government.[62] Such activities will necessitate increased attention to organizational design and manning issues, as they have prerequisite calls on foreign area officers, civil affairs units, military police, engineer units, and psychological operations specialists. The U.S. Army as the landpower service of the United States will, in large part, determine the direction of joint concept development, experimentation, acquisition, training, and capabilities expansion.

However, the global potential for violence, the wide spectrum of possible military force scenarios, and uncertainty of time and place will mandate sourcing of forces from a global pool of available forces, rather than the 20th century's regional perspective. To shorten response times and maximize use of available strategic lift assets, U.S. Army planners must coordinate very thoroughly on the positioning of Army formations. Heavier, more potent combat formations will likely be located in the United States, while more expeditionary airborne, infantry, and Stryker brigades are situated in forward deployed locations to shorten immediate response times.[63] Hence, even from a landpower focus, the capabilities of seapower and airpower remain an active part of the national strategic equation, and the old paradigm of the sequential duality of strategic movement and operational maneuver will become inseparably compressed into a single perspective of strategic dominant maneuver. Strategic dominant maneuver will not only require Army initiatives to enhance mobility improvements in terms of deployment infrastructure (railway and airfield improvements and container handling facilities), but also a joint approach to equipment prepositioning and sealift vessels and enhanced airlift capabilities, notably by the U.S. acquisition of C-17 cargo aircraft.[64] Moreover, the military capabilities of space and cyberspace will become increasingly central to command and control of combat forces operating from dispersed global locations.

The Army as a Joint Land Component: Applying Landpower in a Theater.

In the context of land forces employed by joint, regional combatant commanders, the role of large army formations in theater is complex and fluid. As part of joint and combined theater assets, the land force commander makes key contributions to the ability of a combatant commander to further national security objectives. First and foremost, in peace or war, forward deployed ground forces provide an on-site ability to continuously assess the theater's posture and potential threats to stability, since their very deployment forward provides physical presence and frequent interactive contact. Moreover, in terms of actual Title 10 responsibilities and apportionment of national resources, the U.S. Army has specific requirements in setting the theater for the joint use of military forces, either as unified United States action or as part of an international combined task force. In the areas of force protection, theater-level logistics, command and control, and in many other enabling capacities, only the Army has forces trained organized, and equipped to carry out essential theater-wide functions. For example, while strategic movement of forces into a theater of operations is most likely the purview of Air Force and Navy planners, intra-theater joint reception, staging, onward movement, and integration of these forces into a coherently organized land component of the joint force will usually be an Army-run function.

It is also typically the U.S. Army's lot to develop the joint and combined land operations plan that supports and augments the combatant commander's own campaign plans. Of course, in actual decisive combat operations, it will be the land component commander's role to actually command and control the land forces fight as well as integrate that action with the operational activities of the air component commander and the maritime component commander. Additionally, any land operation of major combat forces will need to be integrated with theater-wide special operations missions, as the likelihood of such actions taking place on contiguous or overlapping terrain is high.

But as operations in Iraq have illustrated most distinctly, it is landpower that assures long-term campaign success. The structures for reconstruction, stability operations, interagency and intergovernmental action, and sustainment of coalition resolve all take place on that element of geography where people actually work, farm, go to school, travel, and live—the land. Uniquely among the armed services, Army forces are trained, organized and equipped for three principal types of operations across a full spectrum of military action: offensive, defensive, and stability and reconstruction operations.[65] These operations may well be simultaneous and continuous, but stability and reconstruction operations tend to coalesce at the lower end of the range of military actions. These sorts of civil support operations, while neither glamorous nor effortless, are essential to the sustained application of landpower beyond decisive combat operations. They may lead to the kind of stable and secure national environment in which other elements of national power — diplomatic, economic, and informational — can generate more effective results in cooperation with legitimate and functional local self-government.[66]

To affect this broad range of landpower activities, Army Service Component Commands (ASCCs) support geographic unified commands and also some designated sub-unified commands. Commanders of ASCCs are normally the senior Army officer not assigned to specific and primary joint duties within a combatant command. However, this commander may well also have other joint and multinational titles, and may well be designated as the joint force land component commander. ASCC organizational structures are neither mandated nor uniform, but rather are modular and scaleable to provide a combatant commander with a range of army capabilities in accordance with anticipated missions. In peacetime, they may vary from less than 2,000 in a deferred theater such as U.S. Army South as an economy-of-force theater, to the some 65,000 in U.S. Army Europe. For a major theater war, U.S. Army Central Command would grow to over 300,000. Some selected ASCCs have the embedded capability to establish numbered armies, when augmented, as an operational-level headquarters for multi-corps operations.[67]

The ASCC commander need not be collocated in the theater of operations to which assigned, but regardless of actual physical location, must be able to perform essential functions for the combatant commander. As mentioned, this command constitutes the component headquarters necessary to accomplish joint planning tasks and also to act as a liaison headquarters for the U.S. Army, as the principal proponent Service for landpower. Of course, it also sources and supports those U.S. Army forces that may be assigned to the theater of operations, and it also, conducts joint and combined land operations if assigned that role by the combatant commander. If fact, when designated, this commander may act as the joint or combined land component commander.

Figure 2 depicts the varying and overlapping responsibilities of the Army Service Component Commanders. The block outlined by large dashes lists those functions an ASCC exercises in support of the combatant commander. These responsibilities have both joint (J) and Army (A) objectives. While not all-inclusive, they do serve to illustrate what functions an ASCC performs on an ongoing basis. However, an Army commander at any level can be designated as an Army forces commander in any joint task force formation. As an Army representative, this commander has the same service responsibilities for any Army element in the joint force. But he also assumes joint responsibilities, as depicted in the figure in the short dash-outlined block.

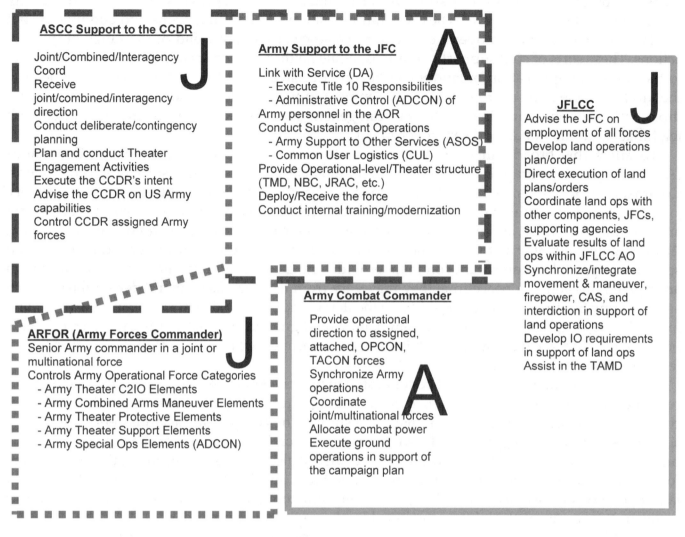

ASCC Support to the CCDR

Joint/Combined/Interagency Coord
Receive joint/combined/interagency direction
Conduct deliberate/contingency planning
Plan and conduct Theater Engagement Activities
Execute the CCDR's intent
Advise the CCDR on US Army capabilities
Control CCDR assigned Army forces

Army Support to the JFC

Link with Service (DA)
 - Execute Title 10 Responsibilities
 - Administrative Control (ADCON) of Army personnel in the AOR
Conduct Sustainment Operations
 - Army Support to Other Services (ASOS)
 - Common User Logistics (CUL)
Provide Operational-level/Theater structure (TMD, NBC, JRAC, etc.)
Deploy/Receive the force
Conduct internal training/modernization

JFLCC

Advise the JFC on employment of all forces
Develop land operations plan/order
Direct execution of land plans/orders
Coordinate land ops with other components, JFCs, supporting agencies
Evaluate results of land ops within JFLCC AO
Synchronize/integrate movement & maneuver, firepower, CAS, and interdiction in support of land operations
Develop IO requirements in support of land ops
Assist in the TAMD

ARFOR (Army Forces Commander)

Senior Army commander in a joint or multinational force
Controls Army Operational Force Categories
 - Army Theater C2IO Elements
 - Army Combined Arms Maneuver Elements
 - Army Theater Protective Elements
 - Army Theater Support Elements
 - Army Special Ops Elements (ADCON)

Army Combat Commander

Provide operational direction to assigned, attached, OPCON, TACON forces
Synchronize Army operations
Coordinate joint/multinational forces
Allocate combat power
Execute ground operations in support of the campaign plan

Figure 2. Responsibilities of a Theater Army in Joint and Combined Operations.[68]

Finally, the Army commander is also a combat commander who must accomplish warfighting missions, as depicted in the solid-outlined block. If he is designated as a joint or combined land component commander, his responsibilities increase relative to the overall joint and combined joint force organization. Again these functions pertain to both joint and Army functions. This requires that the ASCC and combatant commanders and their staffs must understand the roles, missions, and functions required of both headquarters for joint and Army-centric operations. To do this, the ASCC commander and his or her staff must organize for the mission and identify any critical augmentation requirements with regard to force posturing, sustainment capabilities, and command, control, and communications arrangements.

While this concept focuses on joint capabilities and processes, it is probable that 21st century conflicts will be multinational in character, and that any such architecture will be shifting and multi-polar in nature. Stable alliances will continue, but any joint force land component commander will need to deal with ad hoc security arrangements, necessitating imaginative approaches to dealing with the reception and employment of forces from coalition partners from a wide range of readiness postures, with regard to manning, equipping, and training.[69]

There are several options available for the designation of an Army forces commander or for the ground component commander in any size task force in a joint or combined operation. That is, in every joint or coalition organization that includes an Army force there must be a commander who is charged with the responsibilities of ensuring support and control of those Army forces. In every case where he is appointed as a joint commander, as the senior Army commander in the command, this Army forces commander retains his Army-specific responsibilities unless he in turn establishes a separate, subordinate army forces command. This delegation must be done by directive in order to avoid confusion with regard to who the joint Army forces commander actually is.

Thus, if the Army forces commander is in fact the senior Army commander in a joint or multinational force he may have several other hats. For example, he may be the actual Army Service Component Commander for a unified or subunified commander, as Commander, Army Forces Central Command was in Operation IRAQI FREEDOM. He may be a tactical-level commander in smaller contingencies, as was XVIII Corps in Operation ENDURING FREEDOM. The commander, Army forces may also be tasked to function as a joint land forces component commander, when forces outside the U.S. Army are committed to ground operations in the theater of operations as part of a larger joint or combined land force, as was Commander Army Forces Central Command when designated the Combined Force Land Component Commander in Operation Iraqi Freedom. He alternatively may be assigned as a joint task force commander in his own right, as was XVIII Corps as Commander Joint Task Force (CJTF)-180 for Operation JUST CAUSE. Regardless of designation, any such commander must still perform all the Title 10 responsibilities for all Army forces in the command unless another, separate commander is delegated those duties within a specific joint force.

Any Army Service Component Commander, then, functions not as a mere administrative headquarters, but as the combatant commander's chief soldier, the main headquarters for planning, conducting, and sustaining land-based campaigns. He or she must provide authoritative direction to any land forces assigned, attached, or otherwise under the operational or tactical control, especially if designated as a combined or joint force land component commander, as determined by the combatant commander. He or she must create synergies among land forces, as well as synchronization with other joint and multinational forces in peacetime operations and open warfare and in any type of conflict between those extremes. That includes providing the operational-level theater structure for the prosecution of a land campaign. Beyond operational responsibilities in theater, the Army Service Component Commander is the combatant commander's principal link with the Department of the Army in the execution of Title 10 responsibilities. Other mandated support operations include Army support to other services and common-user logistics mandates, which typically extend in practice to include coalition partner forces as well as U.S. joint formations.

Landpower, the Foundation of Pax Americana.

The steady tramp of the booted feet of thousands of legionaries over centuries ensured the crowning achievement of the Roman empire, the Pax Romana, which marked an era in which peaceful commerce and relative security was the dominant characteristic of the Western world. In sunny Hispania or the damp forests of Germania, the forts and patrols of the Roman legions represented the determination of the people of the Roman state to maintain their frontiers and fend off the inroads of barbarian hordes on the move. Behind the shields of the legionaries, commerce, engineering, arts, language, and social institutions took on distinctly Roman characteristics, so much so that much of what we today acknowledge as Western culture is Roman in origin. If the 21st century is to see a parallel state of affairs, a Pax Americana, it will surely rest on a similar foundation.

Landpower is more than military forces deployed to far-flung places. Rather, it is a conglomerate of elements, each interacting so that the whole is greater than the sum of its parts. Certainly military forces are the power projection element of landpower, but governments, commercial and financial corporations and industrial systems; nongovernmental organizations and institutions; science and technology; agriculture; social and political factors; and cultural norms all play a significant part in preparing and sustaining those forces in action. In concert with other mediums of military operations, landpower's major contribution to the national security objectives of the United States lies in its versatility and scalability. Land forces can be tailored precisely to address specific situations with many component variables. From the mere presence of soldiers on the ground to the lethal employment of a wide range of kinetic and non-kinetic weapons, the U.S. Army is uniquely postured to provide the military force necessary to influence human activity in the domain where human beings dwell, where their business is conducted, and where their values are maintained—the land.

Land forces provide the capability to sustain peace by proactively shaping the security environment of the theaters to which they are deployed. They provide visible, personal, face-to-face contact with other people and other governments, creating lasting relationships and enduring demonstrations of American commitment. Particularly at the lower, less kinetic ranges of the spectrum of conflict, land forces interact with people and provide unmatched flexibility in reassuring allies, persuading potential coalition partners, and deterring would-be aggressors. Land forces extend landpower in virtually countless ways for as far or fast or long a national policy dictates, limited only by the strategic reach of deployment means, and bounded only by the speed and clarity of policy formulation, the resoluteness of leadership decisions, and the national will to persevere.

It is landpower that interrupts the security environments of enemies of the nation, whether structured as political territories or as non-state organizations. Seapower, airpower, space power, and even cyberspace power have enabling roles to play and may even actually prove decisive in the outcome of a war, but they will only rarely prove definitive in determining a conclusive and persistent change for the course of the future. The final outcomes will always be relative to landpower. In this way landpower is uniquely the final arbiter of national defense policy, as it works synergistically with other elements of military power to curtail the flexibility and freedom of movement of adversaries, to deny them sustainment and support, to defeat their open challenges, and to squelch organized resistance and create the conditions for a secure peace.

After the decisive conclusion of major combat actions the duties and responsibilities of a combined or joint force land component commander are not likely to cease, but will merely take on new policy objectives and a more wide-reaching axis of advance. When the warship's missiles and the warplane's bombs no longer descend, the land warrior's work still remains, often as active and dangerous as combat operations were, for landpower is the essential enabler for the stability operations necessary to secure territory, for the creation of the conditions conducive to infrastructure reconstruction and renewal, and for the facilitation of an atmosphere of change so that interagency and intergovernmental objectives aimed at stabilization, economic progress, and political self-sufficiency can be attained.

So long as America is to remain the beacon of liberty, the protector of democratic principles, and the endorser of free enterprise, landpower offers the nation the versatile, sustained potential to accomplish national security objectives, demonstrate and defend the American way of life, and act as an agent of good for all humanity.

ENDNOTES - CHAPTER 8

1. Miyamoto Musashi, *The Book of Five Rings,* Victor Harris, trans., Woodstock, NY: Overlook Press, 1974.

2. U.S. Department of the Air Force, *Air Force Basic Doctrine,* Air Force Doctrine Document 1, Washington, DC: U.S. Department of the Army, November 17, 2003, p. 17. Indeed, airpower proponents say therein, "The prompt, continued, aggressive application of airpower may actually constitute the conflict's decisive phase."

3. T. R. Fehrenbach, *This Kind of War*, New York: Bantam Books, 1991, p. 408.

4. Halford J. Mackinder, "The Geographical Pivot of History," 1904, cited in Harold Sprout and Margaret Sprout, *Foundations of International Power,* New York: D. Van Nostrand Company, 1951, p. 98.

5. Alfred Taylor Mahan, "The Isthmus and Sea Power," 1893, cited in Harold Sprout and Margaret Sprout, p. 154.

6. *Gabriele D'Annunzio: Vita, Opere, Gesta e Amori del Vate,* available from *www. gabrieledannunzio.net,* Internet, accessed December 12, 2006.

7. Bernard Brodie, *Some Notes on the Evolution of Air Doctrine*, RAND Report P-527 rev., Santa Monica, CA: RAND Corporation, December 1954, p. 2.

8. Donaldson D. Frizzell, "Early Theories of Air Strategy," in *Military Strategy: Theory and Application*, Arthur F. Lykke, ed., Carlisle Barracks, PA: U.S. Army War College, 1989, pp. 147-169.

9. Chairman, U.S. Joint Chiefs of Staff, *Joint Warfare of the Armed Forces of the United States*, Joint Publication 1, Washington, DC: U.S. Joint Chiefs of Staff, November 14, 2000, p. ix.

10. Chairman, U.S. Joint Chiefs of Staff, *Unified Action Armed Forces, UNAAF, p.* Joint Publication 0-2, Washington, DC: U.S. Joint Chiefs of Staff, 10 July 2001, p. II-12 - II-13.

11. Colin Gray, *Modern Strategy*, Oxford, UK: Oxford University Press, p. 207.

12. Halford J. Mackinder, *Democratic Ideals and Reality*, Washington, DC: National Defense University Press, 1996, p. 21.

13. *Ibid.,* p. 6.

14. *Ibid.,* p. 22.

15. *Ibid.,* p. 106.

16. *Ibid.*

17. *Ibid.,* p. 111.

18. H. W. Weigert, "Critique of Mackinder," 1946, cited in Harold Sprout and Margaret Sprout, pp. 174-179.

19. Antoine Henri de Jomini, *The Art of War,* London, UK: Greenhill Books, p. 102.

20. *Ibid.,* p. 127.

21. Mark Borthwick, *Pacific Century: The Emergence of Modern Pacific Asia,* 4th ed., Boulder, CO: Westview Press, 1998, p. 20.

22. B. H. Liddell Hart, *Strategy,* 2nd rev. ed., New York, NY: Praeger Publishers, 1967, p. 5.

23. Sun Tzu, "Offensive Strategy, Maxims 3-7," *The Art of War*, Samuel B. Griffith, trans., Oxford, UK: University Press. 1963, pp. 77-78. With regard to attacking strategy, Lionel Giles translates this phrase as "to baulk the enemy's plans" in Thomas R. Phillips, *Roots of Strategy,* Mechanicsburg, PA: Stackpole Books, 1985, p. 26.

24. Sun Tzu, "Waging War, Maxim 3," p. 73.

25. Borthwick, pp. 58-51.

26. Musashi, p. 53.

27. *Ibid.,* p. 59.

28. *Ibid.,* p. 56.

29. Thomas M. Coffey, *Iron Eagle: The Turbulent Life of General Curtis LeMay*, New York: Random House, 1986.

30. Douglas A. Macgregor, *Breaking the Phalanx: A New Design for Landpower in the 21st Century*, Westport, CT: Praeger Publishers, 1997, p. 2.

31. Peter Connolly, *Greece and Rome at War,* London, UK: Greenhill Press, 1998, p. 206.

32. Lynn Montross, *War Through the Ages*, 3rd ed., New York: Harper & Brothers Publishers, 1960, p. 533.

33. George Cameron Stone, *A Glossary of the Construction, Decoration and Use of Arms and Armor in All Countries and in All Times*, New York: Jack Brussel, 1961, p. 515. In fact, the term "bulletproof" comes from the practice of firing a musket or pistol at the plate armor to prove it capable of withstanding the shot, after which it was "proof" and could be certified and stamped with the maker's mark.

34. Montross, pp. 735-739.

35. Russell F. Weigley, *The American Way of War: A History of United States Military Strategy and Policy*, Bloomington, IN: Indiana university Press, 1973, p. 17.

36. Robert Leckie, *George Washington's War*, New York: HarperCollins Publishers, 1992, pp. 637-639.

37. Ulysses S. Grant; quoted in Bruce Catton, *Grant Takes Command,* Boston, MA: Little, Brown & Co., 1969, p. 153.

38. Ulysses S. Grant; quoted in J. F. C. Fuller, *The Generalship of Ulysses S. Grant*, Reprint ed., New York: Da Capo Press, 1991, p. 221. Originally published: London, UK: J. Murray Publishers, 1929.

39. Weigley, p. 150.

40. "Curtis LeMay," *Wikipedia*, available from *en.wikipedia.org/wiki/Curtis_Lemay*; Internet, accessed January 2006.

41. Chairman, U.S. Joint Chiefs of Staff, *Joint Warfare of the Armed Forces of the United States,* p. IV-7.

42. *Ibid.*.

43. *Ibid.,* p. VIII-2.

44. *Ibid.*

45. Frederick W. Kagan, "The Art of War," *New Criterion Online*, November 2003, p. 15, available from *www.newcriterion.com*, Internet, accessed July 8, 2004.

46. Baron de Jomini, *The Art of War*, G. H. Mendell and W. P. Craighill, trans., Philadelphia, PA: J. P. Lippincott & Co., 1862, reprint Westport, CT: Greenwood Press; Carl von Clausewitz *On War*, Michael Howard and Peter Paret,

trans., Princeton, NJ: Princeton University Press, 1984. Jomini provides much of the operational level language for the U.S. armed forces. Clausewitz is perhaps the preeminent military theorist of all time, and his concepts and language permeate U.S. joint and Army doctrine. His omission from the general discussion is deliberate, because his concepts are definitive and often directly translated into modern doctrinal language. His monumental work is recommended for any serious student of landpower.

47. Donald H. Rumsfeld, *The National Defense Strategy of the United States of America*, Washington, DC: U.S. Department of Defense, March, 2005, p. iii.

48. *Ibid.*, pp. 2-3.

49. George W, Bush, "The National Security Strategy of the United States of America," Washington, DC: Office of the President of the United States, September 2004, p. 1.

50. Charles M. Maynes, "The World in the Year 2000: Prospects for Order or Disorder," in Charles M. Maynes and William G. Heyland, *The Nature of the Post-Cold War World*, Carlisle Barracks, PA: Strategic Studies Institute, U.S. Army War College, March 1993, p. 17.

51. Matthew Horseman and Andrew Marshall, *After the Nation-State: Citizens, Tribalism and the New World Disorder*, London, UK: Harper Collins Publishers, 1994, p. 213. The authors recount Machiavelli and state, "The head of a large transnational is a modern Prince, a strategist who must negotiate his way through a hostile world. . . . Most companies have seen an enlargement of their political functions with units devoted to 'public affairs' and 'embassies' in Brussels and Washington."

52. William G. Heyland, "Reexamining National Strategy," in Charles M. Maynes and William G. Heyland, *The Nature of the Post-Cold War World*, Carlisle Barracks, PA: Strategic Studies Institute, U.S. Army War College, March 1993, p. 27.

53. Susan Strange and Letizia Paoli, "The Retreat of the State," in *The Diffusion of Power in the World Economy*, Cambridge, UK: Cambridge University Press, 1996, pp. 110-121.

54. U.S. Defense Science Board, "Executive Summary," in *Transition to and from Hostilities*, Washington, DC: U.S. Department of Defense, December 2004, pp. vi-vii.

55. William T. Johnsen, *Redefining Landpower for the 21st Century*, Carlisle Barracks, PA: Strategic Studies Institute, May 7, 1998, p. 6.

56. Steven Metz and Raymond Millen, "Intervention, Stabilization, and Transformation Operations: The Role of Landpower in the New Strategic Environment," *Parameters*, Vol. 34, Spring 2005, p. 42.

57. Richard A. Cody, "Providing Relevant and Ready Dominant Landpower Forces." *Army*, Vol. 44, No. 10, October 2004, pp. 131-136.

58. Peter J. Schoomaker and R. L. Brownlee, *Serving a Nation at War: A Campaign Quality Army with Joint and Expeditionary Capabilities*, Washington, DC: Army Strategic Communications, 2005, p. i.

59. Johnsen, p. 15.

60. Johnsen, p. 14.

61. Steven Metz and Raymond Millen, *Future War/Future Battlespace: The Strategic Role of American Landpower*, Carlisle Barracks, PA: Strategic Studies Institute, U.S. Army War College, March 2005, pp. 9-11.

62. Gordon England, Acting Deputy Secretary of Defense, "Military Support for Stability, Security, Transition, and Reconstruction (SSTR) Operations," Department of Defense Directive Number 3000.05, Washington, DC, November 28, 2005, p. 2.

63. Rumsfeld, p. 20.

64. Bruce K. Scott and Robert M. Toguchi, "Strategic Dominant Maneuver," *Army*, Vol. 45, No. 1, February, 1995, pp. 20-26.

65. U.S. Department of the Army, *The Army*, Field Manual 1, Washington, DC: U.S. Department of the Army, June 2005, pp. 3-6.

66. *Ibid.*, pp. 3-7.

67. U.S. Department of the Army, *The Army in Theater Operations*, DRAG ed., FM 3-93, 100-7, Washington, DC: U.S. Department of the Army, February 2, 2005, Appendix B.

68. From David A. Brown, Carlisle Barracks, PA: Department of Military Strategy, Planning, and Operations, U.S. Army War College, 2005.

69. Huba Wass de Czege and Antulio J. Echevarria II, " Landpower and Future Strategy: Insights from the Army After Next," *Joint Forces Quarterly*, Vol. 21, Spring 1999, pp. 62-69.

CHAPTER 9

THUCYDIDES AND CONTEMPORARY STRATEGY

R. Craig Nation

A POSSESSION FOR ALL TIME

Nearly 2 1/2 millennia have passed since the Greek historian Thucydides composed his famous history of the Peloponnesian War (432-404 B.C.E.).[1] Although well known among scholars, the text was not translated from the Greek original until 1478.[2] Contemporary interest in Thucydides dates to the European renaissance and emergence of the modern state system, whose dynamic of armed competition between contending sovereignties his work is often presumed to represent. Ever since, Thucydides has been a source of inspiration for policymakers as well as scholars. In our time no armed conflict anywhere in the world is fought to a conclusion without some attempt to use his work as a vehicle for interpretation.[3]

Thucydides' influence has been manifest in modern American strategic thought. In 1947 U.S. Secretary of State George Marshall turned to Thucydides to fathom the emerging Cold War: "I doubt seriously," he proposed, "whether a man can think with full wisdom and with deep conviction regarding certain of the basic issues today who has not at least reviewed in his mind the period of the Peloponnesian War and the fall of Athens."[4] A latter U.S. Secretary of State and former general officer, Colin Powell, speaking upon his retirement as chairman of the Joint Chiefs of Staff in 1993, cited Thucydides to the effect that "of all manifestations of power, restraint impresses men most." Powell kept the passage posted at his desk for many years.[5] When Stanfield Turner set out to revamp instruction at the U.S. Naval War College in the 1970s he made Thucydides the focal point of the curriculum. Today Carl von Clausewitz, Sun Tzu, and Thucydides are the only strategic theorists whose work predates the twentieth century that are systematically studied at U.S. senior service schools.

In the past several decades, there has been an explosion of work devoted to Thucydides, no longer addressed primarily to an audience of classical scholars, but rather the larger community of security and strategic studies.[6] This attention rests on an appreciation of his work's multi-faceted relevance. Leo Strauss represents Thucydides' text as a commentary upon war itself: "The Peloponnesian war is that singular event which reveals fully, in an unsurpassable manner, for all times, the nature of war."[7] Clifford Orwin sees it as a political primer; "Of all writers on politics, none stays closer than Thucydides to the world of citizen and statesman," whose work belongs "to students of political life of whatever time and place."[8] Richard Ned Lebow concentrates on Thucydides' contributions to international relations theory, as "the first writer to analyze the origin of war, the role of power in international relations, the relationship between domestic and foreign politics, the process by which civil and international orders unravel and what might be done to restore them."[9] Such commendations can be multiplied many fold. Thucydides' *Peloponnesian War* is without question a seminal study of warfare and a "possession for all time" as the author aspired for it to be.[10]

Why is this so? What does *The Peloponnesian War* have to teach us about the problems of war and strategy? It is in fact generally easier to assert the text's importance than to discern the character of its insights. Like any great work, its message is ambiguous and has been read in different ways depending on the prevailing *Zeitgeist*. In the early modern centuries, Thucydides was viewed as a guide to the primacy of power and *raison d'état* in the Westphalian state system. The young Thomas Hobbes, who in 1624 authored one of the first English translations of *The Peloponnesian*

War, provides an example. Hobbes' philosophical work, which considered the urge to power to be integral to human nature and emphasized the insecurity that results from an anarchic state of nature, was deeply influenced by his classical predecessor.[11] The realist tradition in international relations theory has consistently claimed Thucydides as a progenitor—Joseph Nye calls him "the founding father of Realism."[12] For Marshall, the war between Athens and Sparta became a prototype for the bipolar confrontation of the emerging Cold War, and the clash of values between democracy and totalitarianism that informed it. Others see the work as a humane reflection on the human condition whose overarching theme is "the suffering of war."[13] Powell, from the perspective of the victorious U.S.A. of the post-Cold War, found a cautionary tale about the limits of power. Today, Thucydides' work is being applied as a vehicle for understanding the logic of terrorism in the world after 9/11.[14] This is as it should be. Classic works of strategic literature cannot be read as users manuals. They offer illuminations rather than answers—their status as "timeless" works in a sense demands that it be so.

Policy and strategy, defined as the craft of statesmanship and the use of military force in the pursuit of political aims, are practical undertakings. Many U.S. commanders carried copies of Antoine Jomini's work onto the battlefields of the American Civil War—the Swiss theorist made a conscious attempt to provide maxims that could be applied to tactical and operational problems. Alexander the Great is reported to have slept on campaign with a version of *The Iliad* prepared by his tutor Aristotle at his bedside (as modern commanders might carry a *Bible* or *Koran*)—cultural inspiration may also serve as a foundation for waging war. It is difficult to imagine Thucydides in a knapsack on campaign; his insights are too complex to serve as guides on the tactical level, and his conclusions too elusive to provide cultural inspiration. His work has a different kind of merit, however, that is perhaps no less relevant and profound.

What Thucydides provides is strategic insight. He offers invaluable points of orientation for statecraft and supreme command in the domain of national policy, as well as searing judgments about the factors that lead states to victory or defeat in protracted strategic competition. His subject is the institution of war in all its dimensions, and his text illustrates that although we no longer fight with shields and stabbing spears, on the strategic level warfare has remained remarkably constant over time. Those who read Thucydides for the first time are usually struck by his work's astonishing current relevance—not so much as an agenda for action as a guide to understanding.[15] As a reflection on war intended to help us to come to terms with the larger strategic environment, *The Peloponnesian War* remains unsurpassed.

A WAR LIKE ALL OTHERS

Much of the current literature concerning the Peloponnesian War is focused on the conflict itself, considered as an event in space and time that can be understood empirically. Victor David Hanson's recent study, *A War Like No Other*, emphasizes the distinctiveness of the struggle, which he portrays as an armed conflict virtually unique in history in its scope and complexity.[16] This is potentially misleading. Almost everything that we know about the Peloponnesian War is based on what Thucydides tells us, and despite the best efforts of archeologists and classical scholars that is not likely to change.

There is an ongoing debate about the accuracy of Thucydides' narrative, but it rests on distressingly few supplementary sources (essentially stone tablets containing state records and a very small number of fragmentary primary and secondary accounts). Basically, much of Thucydides' story must either be accepted on faith or rejected as improbable. Thucydides was in an excellent position to assemble an accurate record of events. His appreciation for the importance of the war gave him a strong motive to do so. And he went out of his way to demonstrate his objectivity, a trait for which his work has long been appreciated. David Hume, later echoed by Immanuel Kant, famously remarked that the first page of his text "was the commencement of real history," while even the skeptical George Cawkwell lauds his "monstrous passion for the truth."[17]

Up to the publication of Jacqueline de Romilly's seminal study of Athenian imperialism in 1947, the issue of chronology dominated Thucydides scholarship—when the work was composed, the stages of composition, and how much the author was in a position to know.[18] Today, scholars broadly accept that *The Peloponnesian War* was conceived and composed as a whole. Scholarship has shifted from issues of accuracy in narration toward an immanent reading of the text, viewed as an artful reconstruction used to convey the author's personal view of Greek political life.[19] This kind of research agenda may be exaggerated in its own right, but it is certainly true that Thucydides interprets as well as describes—his account is infused with the author's perspective. "Thucydides has imposed his will," notes the commentator Arnold Gomme, "as no other historian has ever done."[20] The Peloponnesian War was indeed a great armed conflict, but it was not the only one waged in classical antiquity. It may be perceived as a "war like no other" only because of the brilliance of Thucydides' rendition of events. And as a 19th century commentator warns, Thucydides' masterly text can lead us to neglect the fact that "history does not consist of events in and of themselves, but rather in the impact that they have upon others."[21] For the purposes of strategic studies, as distinct from classical studies and historiography, it is *Thucydides'* Peloponnesian War that matters.

What do we know about Thucydides? Three vitae survive from the Byzantine period, but they are contradictory and sometimes clearly erroneous. Most of what we can assert derives from what Thucydides himself tells us in four brief references to his personal circumstances in *The Peloponnesian War*, and perhaps more importantly from what we can infer about the author from reading his text.[22]

Thucydides was born in the 5th century, around 460. He was therefore 29 years old and in the prime of life in 431 when the Peloponnesian War began, and 55 in 404 when it ended with Athens' defeat. The date of his death is not known with certainty, but probably occurred around 400-397. The author records his full name as Thucydides son of Olorus from the deme of Halimous. This indicates Thracian origin and possible familial ties to the powerful and conservative Philaidea clan, which included the Athenian statesman Miltiades (550-489, the victor at Marathon in 490) and his son Cimon (510-450, ostracized from Athens in 461). Thucydides was clearly of high social standing, and a man of means. At one point he mentions that his family possesses the Athenian concession for gold mining in all of Thrace. In 424 the citizens of Athens elected him to the post of general, one of only ten individuals to hold that post annually and therefore a leading figure in the state. In the same year, ordered to come to the relief of the commercial center of Amphipolis in Thrace with a small fleet of seven triremes (warships), he arrived too late to prevent the city's fall to the Spartan general Brasidas. Returning to Athens, Thucydides was condemned as a sign of disfavor and exiled from the city for 20 years (a fairly common punishment in the era). For the remainder of the conflict, he was therefore able to observe, from the perspective of a not entirely disinterested onlooker, the war swirling around him. During the war, when he may have spent much of his time on his Thracian estate, and after his return to Athens on its conclusion he composed on a series of papyrus scrolls, what was in effect a contemporary history, recording in great detail the course of events from 431 to 411. Thucydides' history is left unfinished, and in fact breaks off abruptly in the midst of a paragraph.[23]

More important than the details of this modest biography is what it seems to indicate about the author's intellectual orientation. Thucydides' life ran parallel to the golden age of classical Hellenic civilization. He lived to see the triumph of Athenian material civilization with the raising of the great temples on the Acropolis, the construction of the long walls linking Athens to the port of Piraeus, and the constant expansion of an Athenian maritime empire. He was contemporary with the political leader Pericles (495-429), the historian Herodotus (484-425), the sculptor Phidias (490-430), the philosophers Gorgias (483-375) and Socrates (469-399), and the dramatists Sophocles (497-406), Euripides (480-406), and Aristophanes (448-380).[24] Thucydides was therefore a participant in one of the greatest cultural flowerings in all of history, and present at the creation of what we call Western Civilization. He also lived to see the defeat and ruin of his native city, an event whose cultural as well as strategic importance he fully appreciated. Thucydides begins his history by remarking that its subject is "the war between the Peloponnesians and the Athenians . . . believing that it would be a great war, and more worthy of relation than any that had preceded it."[25] He makes no attempt to justify this focus, and in fact none is required. "War is the father and king of all," wrote the pre-Socratic philosopher Heraclitus (535-475), in a passage that is not incongruous for a civilization whose founding text was Homer's *Iliad*.[26] It was a valuation that Thucydides shared. The sentiment was echoed from the other side of the world by Thucydides' approximate contemporary Sun Tzu, for whom: "Warfare is the greatest affair of state, the basis of life and death, the way to survival or extinction. It must be thoroughly pondered and analyzed."[27] Thucydides' experience with hegemonic warfare led him to validate these conclusions, and to perceive war as the essential focus for all political life. The political, social, and cultural implications of the great war between the Athenians and the Peloponnesians are the real subject of his history.

One might surmise that as a young man Thucydides turned away from the oligarchic political preferences that would come naturally to someone of his social standing, and embraced the idealism of Periclean Athens. The tribute to the civic culture of democratic Athens that he transcribes in Pericles' funeral oration in Book Two of *The Peloponnesian War,* where the Athenian leader honors the city's fallen soldiers by evoking the cause for which they offered their lives, is obviously sincere.[28] Thucydides also sees and describes in brutal detail the dark side of democratic governance, but his allegiance to Pericles as the embodiment of the ideal of an open society never wavers. In this sense his history takes on the contours of a tragedy—the account of the downfall, occasioned by its own hubris and tragic flaws, of a great civilization. W. Robert Connor notes a "recurring paradox" in Thucydides' history; "the intense emotional power of a work ostensibly so detached."[29] The paradox is only apparent. Thucydides' major themes, the harsh reality of warfare as a locus of political intercourse and the corruption of a civilized polity exposed to the pressures of total war, are passionately felt. It is the importance of these themes that leads him to insist on a dispassionate investigation of the questions of causation and responsibility. "The absence of romance in my history," he writes, "will, I fear, detract somewhat from its interest; but if it be judged useful by those inquirers who desire an exact knowledge of the past as an aid to the understanding of the future . . . I shall be content."[30] Thucydides' Peloponnesian War is important not primarily for what makes it unique, but for what it shares in common with and reveals about the nature of other hegemonic conflicts. It is a war like all others that poses themes of universal and enduring importance.

THE PELOPONNESIAN WAR

The war that Thucydides recounts certainly merits his judgment that in scope and importance it was "much greater than the wars which preceded it."[31] This is due to its length and extent, but also because of the cultural stakes. Thucydides begins his narrative with an account of the evolution of Hellenic civilization itself (known to modern students as the *Archaeology),* which demonstrates the development from the 7th to 5th centuries of a classic Greek civilization around the political unit of the city-state (*polis).* City states were engaged in constant feuding over agricultural land at the margin of their territories, waging a "Greek way of war" with armed citizens' militias deployed as heavy infantry (hoplites) fighting in close formation (the phalanx) in a strategic context heavily constrained by myth and ritual.[32] This relatively harmonious system, whose value system Homer depicted in his epics, was soon to be swept away — first by external shocks and then by war waged between its leading polities.

The Greek world drew together to repel the Persians in the *Persian Wars* (490-479) as recounted in the *Histories* of Herodotus, culminating with the famous battles of Marathon (490), Salamis (480), and Plataea (479).[33] What followed might be compared, with due allowance for changed circumstances, to the emergence of the Cold War after 1945, when disparate allies forced together to resist a common threat fell out when the threat was removed.[34] Athens and Sparta, the leading Greek powers, allies in the struggle against the Persians but possessed of radically different institutions and aspirations, were soon engaged in a struggle for dominion. Thucydides devotes a large section of his text (the *Pentecontaetia* or "50 years") to describe the rise of a revisionist Athens, bent upon replacing Sparta as the leading power in Hellas, in the decades following the Persian War.

Thucydides' analysis of the causes of war has a strong cultural dimension. The author repeatedly refers to the differences in style, attitude, and values that divide the major belligerents. Sparta represents a distinctive variant of the oligarchic tyranny, with an agricultural economy based on the labor of a massive population of enslaved helots, and defense provided by professional warriors or Spartiates organized in elite infantry units famed for their courage and discipline. Sparta's force as a land power is justly famed — no other power in the Greek world is presumed to be capable of standing before it. Sparta also heads a loose alliance based on bilateral agreements with like-minded allies known as the Peloponnesian League. As an agrarian based oligarchy committed to traditional values and an unchallengeable land power with a status-quo geopolitical orientation Sparta may be said to represent a conservative force in Greek life. By way of contrast, Thucydides portrays Athens as dynamic and innovative. Though like all Greek city-states its economy rests on slave labor, it is ground breaking in developing democratic institutions and offers a considerable degree of empowerment to its free citizens. Its international position rests on sea power, commerce, and an empire of subject states (city-states in the Aegean, Thrace, and Asia Minor) that originally ally with Athens to resist the Persians and are organized under Athenian leadership in the Delian League in 478. Athens is culturally innovative, economically dynamic, and strategically expansive. After the construction of the long walls linking Athens to Piraeus in 450, it is also virtually invulnerable. Periclean Athens is bent on extending its power, and brash and assertive in its dealings with others.

When the city-state of Megara withdrew from the Spartan alliance and joined with Athens in 460, a First Peloponnesian War that pitted Athens and Sparta against one another as primary belligerents ensued. The war ended in 446 with a compromise known as the Thirty Years Peace, including a pledge to submit future differences to binding arbitration. Between 433 and 431, however, a series of events on the periphery of the Greek world drove the two antagonists to war once again. Thucydides' Peloponnesian War was waged from 431-404, over a span of 27 years. For purposes of simplification (the distinction is not made by Thucydides), historians generally divide the war into three phases: the *Archidamian War* from 431-421, named for the Spartan King Archidamus, who ironically opposed a resort to arms and sought to contain hostilities once in progress; the *Peace of Nicias* from 421-412, named for the Athenian general Nicias who negotiated the truce in 421 and went on to meet a tragic fate as commander of the doomed Athenian expeditionary force on Sicily; and the *Ionian War* from 412-404 beginning with an Athenian revival but concluding with her final defeat.

The Archidamian War unfolded as a stalemate between Spartan land power and Athenian sea power. Each side was capable of hurting its opponent, but not overthrowing it. A turning point came when Athens established a base on the Peloponnesus at the isolated outpost of Pylos, capturing several hundred elite Spartiate warriors and threatening to inspire a helot revolt. The Peace of Nicias was the result, but it did not strike deep roots. By this point the war had taken on a momentum of its own, with allies and local commanders refusing to respect ceasefires, and a war party on each side committed to pursue the conflict *jusqu'au bout*. Thucydides goes to some length to argue that the Peace of Nicias, which he calls a "treacherous armistice," does not divide the Peloponnesian War into two distinct parts, but rather represents an integral part of an extended conflict with a consistent strategic logic.[35]

In 416, with rivalry between the two parties unabated, Athens, led by the flamboyant, ambitious, and unprincipled young Alcibiades, launched a great armada with the intention of shifting the balance of power decisively by conquering the island of Sicily.[36] The destruction of its expeditionary force at Syracuse weakened Athens substantially, but not decisively. An oligarchy overthrew the Athenian democracy in 411, but democratic forces quickly regained political control of the city. Athens eventually recouped its strength and launched a military comeback, carrying the war into the Aegean and the Hellespont. The Ionian War was essentially a naval contest waged in these regions, with the Athenian fleet successful at the outset but unable to force the issue to decisive conclusion. In the end it was the intervention in the Spartan cause of the former common enemy Persia that turned the tide. In 405 at the battle of Aegospotami, the Spartan admiral Lysander caught the Athenian fleet drawn up on shore and destroyed it. In 404, with its real center of gravity eliminated, Athens surrendered. The Spartan army occupied the Acropolis, tore down the long walls, and imposed an oligarchic tyranny under a kind of junta known to history as the Thirty Tyrants. As a competitive polity in the eastern Mediterranean Athens' authority would eventually be restored, but its Golden Age, inspired by the ideals of Pericles, would not return. Thucydides' account of the war ends at the year 411, but it is clear throughout the narrative that he is aware of its eventual outcome, and that this awareness importantly shapes the way in which he structures his text and develops its themes.

THUCYDIDES AND GRAND STRATEGY

Even in brief outline, the Peloponnesian War presents the observer with an extraordinarily wide variety of strategic gambits, military adventures, and political ploys. Thucydides' history includes detailed descriptions of major fleet actions, pitched battles, sieges, unconventional operations, plague, revolution, atrocity, and massacre, political confrontations, instances of decisive leadership, and in fact virtually every kind of circumstance that shapes the outcome of major wars. The story is engrossing, but as already argued, it is not unique. What is it that makes Thucydides' account the "classical and canonical work of Western culture" that it is universally considered to be?[37]

Part of the answer lies in the controlled emotion with which Thucydides infuses an account of a war that he firmly believes to be an unprecedented tragedy. Part lies in the author's methodological contributions. Thucydides sets out to chronicle a war, not to craft a general theory of warfare. But he clearly states the conviction that because human nature remains essentially the same, by examining the past we can identify recurrent patterns in social and political intercourse, learn from them, and on that basis develop strategies for more effective action in the future. The author's magisterial detachment, refusal to accept conventional explanations at face value, and unapologetic rationalism are nothing short of remarkable. Moses Finley calls Thucydides "the most careful and in the best sense the most skeptical historian the ancient world ever produced."[38] In this regard, his work provides a solid foundation for modern historiography and the discipline of political science. Most importantly, perhaps, *The Peloponnesian War* is timeless because it develops an appreciation of warfare in a larger strategic context and poses classic problems in strategic analysis in a particularly lucid way. We can illustrate the way in which this occurs with three examples: Thucydides' reflections on the causes of war, the strategic level of warfare, and ethical and moral concerns.

The Origins of War.

Identifying the causes and nature of war is a basic challenge that arguably has become more difficult in an era when declarations of war have become things of the past, when the state of war has lost much of its formal legal status, and when the U.S. finds itself engaged in an open-ended "war on terrorism and radical extremism" that may last for generations. Thucydides' account of the origins of the Peloponnesian War offers an interesting case study for working through these problems.

Thucydides devotes a great amount of attention to discussing the causes of the Peloponnesian War and makes a fundamental distinction, which he is sometimes said to have invented, between the immediate or short-term sources of the conflict and underlying or structural causes.[39] Simon Hornblower describes this aspect of his work as "a conscious, secular theory of causation in terms of deep and superficial political causes."[40] Perhaps the most famous sentence in Thucydides' history is the comment that however one might adjudicate immediate causes, ultimately "the growth of the power of Athens, and the alarm which this inspired in Sparta, made war inevitable."[41] The pessimistic fatalism that seems to be reflected here, the view of political life as an endless striving for power and dominion, has found great resonance in the realist camp of international relations theory. Hans Morgenthau quotes Thucydides to the effect that: "Of the gods we know, and of men we believe, that it is a necessary law of their nature that they rule whenever they can."[42] Athens' ambition, opines Raymond Aron, condemns it to brutality: "The servitudes of power are inescapable."[43]

In fact, Thucydides does not make any effort to develop a systematic theory of causation. He describes the origins of the Peloponnesian War in considerable detail, but leaves the reader to draw conclusions concerning the relative weight of the various factors on which he touches. Thucydides mentions Sparta's fear of growing Athenian power on several occasions.[44] Clearly, the security dilemma occasioned by the rise of a great power challenger, competitive bipolarity, and an impending power transition are powerful structural factors that contribute to systemic instability and increase the likelihood of war.[45] Much the larger part of Thucydides' description, however, is devoted to immediate causes. One set of variables that he discusses concerns economic motivation. The Spartans emphasized the Megarian Decrees that imposed a commercial embargo on Athens' rival Megara as a primary cause of war. In response, Pericles enjoined Athens to rigorously enforce the decrees. The origin of the war in an obscure dispute over a small settlement on the margin of the Greek world is not unrelated to the fact that the settlement in question is strategically poised along the trade route leading to Italy. Thucydides does not offer a reductionist explanation that locates the roots of war in an Athenian imperialism driven by the merchants of the Piraeus, but he is not insensitive to the weight of economic factors.[46]

Thucydides also probes the diplomatic interaction leading up to the war. Neither of the belligerents necessarily seeks to provoke war, but all become caught up in a maze of misperceptions, ambiguous communication, erroneous calculations, and policies of bluff and bluster. As in the July Crisis of 1914, there is a sense in which the Peloponnesian War becomes a "war by accident" as a result of the failure of diplomacy. Domestic politics and policy processes, including the critical role of charismatic leadership, also have their place. The Spartans decision for war results from the crude *va-t'en-guerre* rhetoric of the ephor Stenelaides, who declaims that he does "not pretend to understand" the long speeches of the Athenians, but nonetheless urges a "vote for war, as honor demands."[47] Pericles' personal authority and powers of persuasion are critical factors that turn Athens away from a policy of compromise that it might otherwise have preferred.

Thucydides' account does not resolve the issue of the relative importance of structural and immediate causes, nor does it seek to do so. What the text demonstrates is multiple causality.[48] Structural explanations alone do not suffice—the choice for war is an ambiguous action that is conditioned by numerous variables, "a confluence of causes at multiple levels of analysis."[49] While the calculus of power may be a necessary context for a decision for war it must be filtered through a screen of perception and misperception, threshed out in the domestic policy process, refined by diplomatic interaction, and implemented in practice. Nothing is fixed and inalterable. Wars are seldom clear cut, war aims and strategic calculations are subject to change, and the precise combination of factors that may have motivated a choice for war at one point in time will alter as the dynamic of conflict unfolds.

The Strategic Level of Warfare.

Thucydides' depiction of warfare is nearly unparalleled in its intensity and power. There is no more sophisticated rendering of the complementary roles of land and sea power, the burden of command, the consequences of defeat, the impact of political faction on strategic choice, or the role of chance and circumstance in effecting strategic outcomes. Despite the best efforts of responsible leaders, momentous events continue to turn on the unpredictable and unexpected—an eclipse of the moon and bolt of thunder, cloud cover during a night attack, unidentified terrain features, or the personal foibles of leaders under stress. The Peloponnesian War is one of the greatest books ever written about the theme of war itself. But Thucydides does not just depict the face of battle. He places warfare in a grand strategic context where a multiplicity of factors must be explored to account for the difference between victory and defeat. Thucydides' appreciation for the strategic level of warfare is one of the most important, and neglected, dimensions of his work.

Thucydides depicts grand strategy as *comprehensive*. In great wars, everything matters and nothing is superfluous. In *The Peloponnesian War* this includes such things as the *domestic political environment* (Sparta is chronically concerned with the possibility of a helot revolt, there is a constant struggle between oligarchic and democratic factions within individual city-states with serious strategic implications); *economic necessity* (control of commercial routes, access to strategic raw materials); *pride and reputation* (alliance defection becomes unacceptable because the hegemonic power will lose face); *military innovation* (the enhanced role of light infantry, including archers, slingers, and Thracian *peltasts*; as the war proceeds the new Corinthian ramming tactics that wreak havoc with the Athenian fleet in the Great Harbor of Syracuse); *geostrategy* (control of maritime choke points and lines of communication); *alliance stability* (much of Spartan strategy consists of attacking the integrity of the Athenian alliance system); and *decisive battle* (the encounters at Delium, Mantinea, or Syracuse where strategic outcomes hinge on a single day's fighting). Thucydides makes no attempt to identify a unique hub of power and movement capable of serving as a Clausewitzian Center of Gravity (even if his narrative provides plenty of material for making such an assessment retrospectively). What he depicts is an extraordinarily complex strategic environment where victory can be a consequence of many things, some of which are virtually impossible to predict.

In addition to being comprehensive, Thucydides' strategic environment is *dynamic*. At the outset of the Peloponnesian War, the two major belligerents have clearly outlined strategies for waging and winning the war. Sparta's intention is to invade Attica and force the Athenians to confront their army in order to prevent the ravaging of their lands and homes. Presumably the Spartans will defeat the Athenians in a major battle between opposing hoplite armies, leaving Sparta in a position to dictate the terms of peace. Athens, led by Pericles, intends to withdraw its population from exposed rural regions and concentrate it inside the city walls, refuse battle, subsist by importing vital commodities via sea, avoid adventures, and use naval power to raid and harass the Peloponnesus. Eventually, the Athenians presume, Spartan resolve will flag, and Athens will be in a position to impose an advantageous peace.[50] Each set of assumptions proves misguided, and what follows is an extraordinary set of strategic innovations.

Athenian resolve is weakened by the great plague that strikes the overcrowded city in the second year of the war—a completely unforeseen event with great strategic consequences.[51] The most prominent victim of the plague is Pericles himself. After his passing, Athens, led by the demagogue Cleon, becomes more aggressive, establishing the base at Pylos and using it as a means for placing pressure on its enemy. Sparta, inspired by the generalship of Brasidas, counters by attacking the Athenian alliance in Boeotia and Chalcidice. Both sides make partial gains but come no closer to ultimate victory. The Peace of Nicias represents an attempt to impose a strategic pause, but it does not address the underlying sources of hostility and fails to break the momentum of confrontation. Enduring resentment allows the talented adventurer Alcibiades to up the ante by creating an alliance with Argos, Mantinea, and Elis to challenge Spartan control of the Peloponnesus. He succeeds in provoking a decisive battle at Mantinea in 418, in which the Spartans are compelled "to stake their all upon the issue of a single day," but in the end it is Sparta that prevails.[52] Alcibiades' next gambit is the Sicilian Expedition, a strategic disaster but not yet a decisive defeat. Athens recovers from the setback, and it is only when Sparta enters into a closer association with the Great King of Persia, builds a battle fleet, and finds a ruthless commander in the person of Lysander that it is able to win decisively at Aegospotami in 405.

This brief overview calls attention to a great diversity of strategic initiatives. Thucydides' history demonstrates that in protracted conflicts strategy must be flexible and adaptive. Security, of course, is grounded in a capacity for self-defense. The author has composed the history of a war, and his image of strategy is firmly tied to "the part which is played by force, or the threat of force, in the international system."[53] Strategy, the domain of force, is not a synonym for policy. But the clear implication of Thucydides' study is that on the level of grand strategy all instruments of national power must be leveraged in conjunction with military means in pursuit of national goals. Events and local circumstances as they unfold and develop will determine what "mix" of factors will be most relevant at any given point in the conflict.

Ethical and Moral Context.

Thucydides' *History* is notable for its lack of illusion. War, he remarks, is a "rough master that brings most men's characters to a level with their fortunes."[54] The strategic environment that he depicts is filled with instrumental logic, cynicism, abuse of power, and brutal massacre. [55] It is a Hobbesian universe where the struggle of all against all is often the essence of strategic interaction and the limits of morality are defined by *Staatsraison*. Hugo Grotius used the remark of Thucydides' Athenian emissary Euphemius to the effect that "for a king or a free city nothing is wrong that is to their advantage" as a foil for his effort to assert a law of nations.[56] Finley argued that "nothing so marks Thucydides' work as the sense of living in a world where moral sensitiveness and inherited tradition were . . . a luxury, and the very survival of states hung on the skillful use of power and power alone."[57] The discourse of power that drives interstate relations leads inexorably toward the harsh doctrine of might makes right, as imparted by the Athenians to the Melians: "You know as well as we do that right, as the world goes, is only in question between equals in power, while the strong do what they can and the weak suffer what they must."[58]

In a recent attempt to update realist theory John Mearsheimer describes the above passage as "Thucydides' famous dictum," but it is no such thing. [59] The Melian Dialogue, in which Athens lays down the law to the representatives of the would-be neutral power of Melos, is perhaps not quite so clear in its implications as might appear at first glance. The Athenian representatives speak the words during their negotiations with the Melians; they do not necessarily express the opinions of the author. The views of the Athenians are far from being self-evident, and in fact they belie the larger spirit of Thucydides' work as a whole. In *The Peloponnesian War* breaches of the moral order are punished, and pride comes before the fall. Sparta comes to believe that its early military misfortunes are the consequence of its unethical breaching of the Thirty Years Peace. Pericles' glowing funeral oration is followed immediately by the terrifying description of the great plague. The doctrine of naked power defended at Melos is the prelude to Athens' descent into the heart of darkness in Sicily. The blustering and violent Cleon comes to no good end. The unbridled ambition of Alcibiades leads him, and the policy he represents, to ruin.

These contrapositions are not accidental. Thucydides is not a moralist—he rejects the gods, strives for neutrality in his explanation, and does not preach. Nonetheless, his work forcefully poses the moral and ethical dilemmas of protracted strategic rivalry. Alternatives to the realist interpretation of Thucydides emphasize the compassion and austere humanity with which he contemplates the disasters of his time. [60] The Melian Dialogue, often read out of context as a set piece and touted as a foundation for political realism, can also be viewed as a depiction of the moral decline of Athens that leads inexorably to her defeat. [61] Viewed through this lens the Athenian discourse at Melos is not prudent but pathological, and the crass exercise of overwhelming force that it embraces is intended to provoke revulsion rather than encourage emulation. The dialogue is in fact unique in Thucydides' text. Among the forty discourses cited verbatim it is the only one constructed as a real dialogue—a conversation between two parties with a theatrical structure and dramatic denouement. This gives it a unique intensity and centrality in the text that is clearly intended. In the dialogue it is the Athenians who are dogmatic and inflexible and the Melians who argue instrumentally. The Melians see the big picture, calculate the odds of defiance on a cost-risk basis (even if their calculations are faulty), and attempt to point out that by striking at the vulnerable without constraint Athens will place its long term interests at stake. And the Melians are right. Athens' harsh conduct reflects an overweening pride that eventually leads to disaster. Its policies and attitude offend allies, alienate neutrals, create new enemies, and encourage rivals to redouble resistance.

In *The Peloponnesian War*, power without principle does not prevail. Thucydides does not portray interest and justice as antithetic, they are rather "inextricably connected and mutually constitutive." [62] Thucydides does not shy from the carnage of war, but he also does not glory in it as some "blood and guts" realists suggest. [63] His gripping narration places the reader on the ground alongside leaders, soldiers, and citizens caught up in the midst of calculated violence and coping as best they can, but he laments the "general deterioration of character throughout the Greek world" that protracted war promotes. [64] War is indeed a violent teacher, and as such, in the words of Leo Strauss, "it teaches man not only to act violently but also about violence and therefore about the truth." [65] *The Peloponnesian War* is in large part a cautionary tale about the use and abuse of power with the implicit moral warning "to use it wisely or lose it woefully." [66] For much of the war and despite many setbacks, Athens sustains its great power status, but in the end it abandons the high ground of legitimate authority and is lost. In a harsh world, administering force effectively demands rigorous professionalism, including a strong sense of purpose and adherence to an elevated moral code. [67] Successful strategy, one may conclude, must be developed within a sound and stable ethical context.

CONCLUSION

The real subject of Thucydides' history is the decline and fall of a political civilization under the strains of hegemonic warfare. Thucydides built the narrative on careful observation and detailed accounting, but the story line inexorably directs the reader's attention to the big picture, the grand strategic environment within which the decisions are made that lead to victory and defeat. What are the dynamics that cause great power war? Can they be contained, and if so, how? What kinds of policies are most conducive to the pursuit of victory? How can the various instruments of national power be combined in a coherent grand strategy? How should strategy be sustained or adapted in the course of protracted armed conflicts? What are the attributes of effective strategic leadership? How can power be linked to purpose, and justice to interest, in a balanced national strategy that sustains legitimate authority? These are the kind of questions that emerge from a careful reading of *The Peloponnesian War*. Thucydides does not reach the end of this history, and his text does not include a formal summary or conclusion, but he clearly intended it as a guide to statecraft and a plea for caution and moderation that is as relevant in our time as on the day it was written.

ENDNOTES - CHAPTER 9

1. There are several excellent modern English translations. Rex Warner's version, completed in 1954, appears in Thucydides, *The Peloponnesian* War, Harmondsworth, UK: Penguin, 1986. The Richard Crawley translation, originally published in 1874 and rendered in eloquent Victorian prose appears in Richard B. Strassler, ed., *The Landmark Thucydides: A Comprehensive Guide to the Peloponnesian War*, New York: The Free Press, 1996. The Strassler compilation, with extensive reader aides including maps and explanatory notes, is an invaluable tool. Henceforward all dates cited will be B.C.E. unless otherwise noted.

2. The first English translation by Thomas Nicolls dates to 1550.

3. This is a long-standing tradition. See Gilbert Murray, *Our Great War and the Great War of the Ancient Greeks*, New York: Thomas Seltzer, 1920, for parallels with World War I, or Carlos Alonso Zaldívar, "Tucídides, en Kosovo," *El Pais*, May 17, 1999, for applications to the war in Kosovo during 1999.

4. Marshall made this remark in a public address at Princeton University on Washington' Birthday in February 1947. The articulation of the Truman Doctrine was several weeks away.

5. See George F. Will, "Powell's Intrusion," *The Washington Post*, November 25, 2001, p. B07.

6. The publication of *The Landmark Thucydides* in 1996 was both a reflection of and contribution to swelling interest. Some subsequent works (the list is long) include George Cawkwell, *Thucydides and the Peloponnesian* War, London, UK: Routledge, 1997, a sophisticated introduction; Gregory Crane, *Thucydides and the Ancient Simplicity: The Limits of Political Realism*, Berkeley: University of California Press, 1998; Simon Hornblower, *Thucydides*, Baltimore, MD: The Johns Hopkins University Press, 2000; Philip De Souza, *The Peloponnesian War, 431-404 B.C.*, New York: Routledge, 2002, a detailed general history; Donald Kagan, *The Peloponnesian War*, New York: Viking, 2003, a one-volume summation of Kagan's earlier four volume history; Richard New Lebow, *The Tragic Vision of Politics: Ethics, Interests and Orders*, Cambridge, UK: Cambridge University Press, 2003; John F. Lazenby, *The Peloponnesian War: A Military History*, New York: Routledge, 2004; the eloquent introduction by Perez Zagorin, *Thucydides: An Introduction for the Common Reader*, Princeton, NJ: Princeton University Press, 2005; and Victor Davis Hanson, *A War Like No Other: How the Athenians and Spartans Fought the Peloponnesian* War, New York: Random House, 2005, a series of essays that attempt to demonstrate the human dimension of the conflict.

7. Leo Strauss, *The City and Man*, Chicago: Rand McNally & Co., 1964, p. 155.

8. Clifford Orwin, *The Humanity of Thucydides*, Princeton, NJ: Princeton University Press, 1994, pp. 3, 4.

9. Lebow, p. 26.

10. *The Landmark Thucydides*, 1.22.4.

11. David Grene, ed., *The Peloponnesian War: The Complete Hobbes Translation*, Chicago: University of Chicago Press, 1959. Hobbes' work contains some technical errors in translation.

12. Joseph S. Nye, Jr., "Neorealism and Neoliberalism," *World Politics*, Vol. 40, 1988, p. 235.

13. W. Robert Connor, *Thucydides*, Princeton, NJ: Princeton University Press, 1984, p. 32.

14. Hanson, pp. 89-122.

15. The conclusion is based upon student reactions in a seminar devoted to reading and discussing *The Peloponnesian War* conducted by the author at the U.S. Army War College for the past 8 years.

16. Hanson.

17. Cited in Connor, *Thucydides*, p. 20; and from Cawkwell, p. 9. In the early 19th century, Thomas Macauley could declare Thucydides "the greatest historian who ever lived." Thomas Babington Macauley, *The Letters of Thomas Babinton Macauley*, Thomas Pinney, ed., 6 vols., Cambridge, UK: Cambridge University Press, 1976, Vol. 3, p. 138.

18. Eduard Schwartz, *Das Geschichtswerk des Thucydides*, 3rd ed., Hildesheim, GE: Georg Olms Verlagsbuchhandlung, 1960; and Finley, *Thucydides*, outline, respectively, the "stages of composition" and "unitarian" approaches to the Thucydides Question. See also Jacqueline de Romilly, *Thucydides and Athenian Imperialism*, Oxford, UK: Basil Blackwell, 1963.

19. Richard Ned Lebow, "Thucydides the Constructivist," *American Political Science Review*, Vol. 95, No. 3, September 2001, pp. 547-560.

20. Arnold W. Gomme, ed., *A Historical Commentary on Thucydides*, 5 vols. (vols. 4 and 5 co-edited with Anthony Andrewes and K. W. Dover), Oxford, UK: The Clarendon Press, 1945-1918, Vol. 1, p. 29.

21. Schwartz, *Das Geschichtswerk des Thucydides*, p. 19.

22. A survey of what we know of Thucydides' life appears in John H. Finley, Jr., *Thucydides*, Ann Arbor, MI: University of Michigan Press, 1967, pp. 1-35.

23. The history of the Peloponnesian War from 411 to its conclusion in 404 is taken up in a conscious attempt to complete Thucydides' account by Xenophon in his *Hellenica*. See the Rex Warner translation in Xenophon, *A History of My Time*, Harmondsworth, UK: Penguin Books, 1979.

24. Patrick translation from Heraclitus, *Fragments*.

25. *The Landmark Thucydides*, p. 1.1.

26. Patrick translation from Heraclitus, *Fragments*.

27. Sun-tzu, *The Art of War*, Ralph D. Sawyer, trans., Boulder, CO: Westview Press, 1994, p. 167.

28. *The Landmark Thucydides*, pp. 2.35-2.46.

29. Connor, p. 6.

30. *The Landmark Thucydides*, 1.22.4.

31. *Ibid.*, 1.21.2.

32. Victor Davis Hanson, *The Western Way of War: Infantry Battle in Classical Greece*, Berkeley: University of California Press, 2000.

33. Herodotus, *The Histories*, London, UK: Penguin Books, 2003.

34. Donald Kagan, *The Outbreak of the Peloponnesian War*, Ithaca, NY: Cornell University Press, 1969, p. 41, specifically compares the Delian League to the Cold War's North Atlantic Treaty Organization (NATO).

35. *The Landmark Thucydides*, , p. 5.26.

36. Steven Forde, *The Ambition to Rule: Alcibiades and the Politics of Imperialism in Thucydides*, Ithaca, NY: Cornell University Press, 1989, sees Alcibiades as the apotheosis of Athenian individualism and self-aggrandizement. His rise to prominence is not accidental—he embodies both the dynamism and self-destructive egoism of the polity he represents.

37. Zagorin, p. 8.

38. M. I. Finley, *The World of Odysseus*, New York: The Viking Press, 1965, p. 34.

39. Kagan, *The Outbreak of the Peloponnesian War*, p. 345, makes the assertion that Thucydides "invents" the distinction between immediate and underlying causes of war.

40. Hornblower, p. 191.

41. *The Landmark Thucydides*, 1.23.6.

42. Hans J. Morgenthau, *Politics Among Nations: The Struggle for Power and Peace*, 5th ed., New York: Alfred A. Knopf, 1978, p. 38. The passage is cited from the Melian Dialogue, *The Landmark Thucydides*, p. 5.105.2.

43. Raymond Aron, *Peace and War: A Theory of International Relations*, New York: Doubleday & Company, Inc., 1966, p. 137.

44. When the Spartan assembly votes in 432 that Athens has violated the Thirty Years Peace, Thucydides remarks that the decision was made because "they feared the growth of the power of the Athenians, seeing most of Hellas already subject to them." At the conclusion of the *Pentecontaetia*, he notes that Sparta has concluded that "the growth of the Athenian power could no longer be ignored" and "that they could endure it no longer." *The Landmark Thucydides*, pp. 1.88 and 1.118.2.

45. See the classic study by Geoffrey Blainey, *The Causes of War*, New York: The Free Press, 1973.

46. In his popular history of the Sicilian Expedition, Peter Green places particular emphasis upon Athens' economic motivation: "The constant foreign aggression, the search for *Lebensraum*, the high-handed treatment of the subject-allies—all these things had as their aim the securing of desperately needed raw materials." Peter Green, *Armada from Athens*, Garden City, NJ: Doubleday & Company, Inc., 1970, p. 46.

47. *The Landmark Thucydides*, p. 1.86.

48. Crane, p. 37, suggests that Thucydides' famous reference to the growth of Athenian power as the "real cause" of the war can be adapted to multiple causation with more refined translation. The best rendering of the passage, he suggests, refers to the "truest cause," that is one among many.

49. Lebow, p. 112.

50. German military historian Hans Delbrück interpreted Periclean strategy as a prototype for what he called strategies of "attrition." Hans Delbrück, *Die Strategie des Perikles: erläutet durch die Strategie Friedrich des Grossen mit einem Anhang über Thucydides und Kleon*, Berlin, GE: Reimer, 1890.

51. Thucydides' description of the plague is justly famed. See *The Landmark Thucydides*, pp. 2.47-2.54.

52. *The Landmark Thucydides* , p. 6.16.6.

53. Cited from "The Strategic Approach to International Relations," in Michael Howard, *The Causes of Wars*, 2nd ed., Cambridge, MA: Harvard University Press, 1984, p. 36. See also Hew Strachen, "The Lost Meaning of Strategy," *Survival*, Vol. 47, No. 3, Autumn 2005.

54. *The Landmark Thucydides*, p. 3.82.2.

55. Hanson, *A War Like No Other*, pp. 89-121.

56. Hugo Grotius, *The Law of War and Peace*, Roslyn, NY: Walter J. Black, Inc., 1949, p. 3. This passage is rendered in *The Landmark Thucydides*, p. 6.85, as "for tyrants and imperial cities nothing is unreasonable if expedient."

57. Finley, *Thucydides*, p. 29.

58. *The Landmark Thucydides*, 5.89.

59. John J. Mearsheimer, *The Tragedy of Great Power Politics*, New York: W. W. Norton & Company, 2001, p. 163.

60. See, in particular, Strauss; Lebow; Orwin, *The Humanity of Thucydides*; and Thomas L. Pangle and Peter J. Ahrensdorf, *Justice Among Nations: On the Moral Basis of Power and Peace*, Lawrence: University Press of Kansas, 1999, pp. 13-32.

61. Finley, *Thucydides*, pp. 208-212; and Peter J. Euben, *The Tragedy of Political Theory: The Road Not Taken*, Princeton, NJ: Princeton University Press, 1990, pp. 178, 197-198.

62. Lebow, p. 166.

63. See Michael W. Doyle, *Ways of War and Peace*, New York: Norton, 1997, pp. 49-92.

64. *The Landmark Thucydides*, pp. 3.82-85.

65. Strauss, p. 162.

66. Cawkwell, p. 19.

67. Note the uncompromising statement of this premise in the Antistrophe of Euripides' *Andromache*, composed during the Peloponnesian War: "It is better not to have a victory that sullies reputation than to overthrow justice by force and win hatred. Such gain brings men delight at first but in time it withers in their hands and voices of reproach beset their house. This is the way of life I approve, this the one I wish to make my own, to wield no power in my home or my city that transgresses justice." Euripides, *Andromache*, lines 779-784.

PART II

THE ELEMENTS OF POWER

CHAPTER 10

NATIONAL POWER

David Jablonsky

I put for a general inclination of all mankind, a perpetual and restless desire of power after power, that ceaseth only in death.[1]

Thomas Hobbes

Thomas Hobbes personifies the realist approach to international relations in a world of anarchy and self-help, in which individual man and men aggregated into states seek to maintain or to increase power. In the modern era, this approach is reflected quintessentially by Hans Morgenthau, who presents national power not only as an end in the Hobbesian sense that "power is always the immediate aim," but as a means to that end.[2] The study of strategy also deals with power primarily from the national security perspective, an acknowledgment that the nation-state is still the most important actor in the international arena.

Most scholars focus on power as a means, the strength or capacity that provides the "ability to influence the behavior of other actors in accordance with one's own objectives."[3] At the national level, this influence is based on relations between nation-state A and another actor (B) with A seeking to influence B to act in A's interest by doing x, by continuing to do x, or by not doing x. Some governments or statesmen may seek influence for its own sake. But for most, influence, like money, is instrumental, to be used primarily for achieving or defending other goals, which could include prestige, territory, raw material, or alliances. To achieve these ends, state A can use various techniques of influencing, ranging from persuasion or the offering of rewards to threats or the actual use of force.[4]

From this standpoint, the use of a nation's power in national security strategy is a simple relational exercise. But in dealing with the concept of national power, as Clausewitz remarked of war, "everything . . . is very simple, but the simplest thing is difficult."[5] To begin with, there are subtle characteristics of power that render its use in the national strategic formulation process more art than science. Moreover, relationships among the elements of national power as well as the context in which they are to be used to further a nation's interests are seldom clear-cut propositions. All this means that in the end, national power defies any attempts at rigorous, scientific assessment. The purpose of this chapter is to demonstrate why this is so and, more important, why, all the complexity notwithstanding, the concept of national power remains a key building block for understanding and developing national security strategy.

THE CONTEXT OF NATIONAL POWER

National power is contextual in that it can be evaluated only in terms of all the power elements and only in relation to another player or players and the situation in which power is being exercised. A nation may appear powerful because it possesses many military assets, but the assets may be inadequate against those of a potential enemy or inappropriate to the nature of the conflict. The question should always be: power over whom, and with respect to what?[6]

Multidimensional Interrelationship.

National power is historically linked with military capacity, a natural relationship since war in the international arena is the *ultima ratio* of power. Nevertheless, one element of power alone cannot determine national power. For instance, there is the huge size of Brazil, the large population of Pakistan, the industrial makeup of Belgium, and the first-class army of Switzerland. Yet none of these states is a first-rank power. Morgenthau calls the mistaken attempt to define national power in terms of one element of that power the "Fallacy of the Single Factor." Another aspect of this fallacy is the failure to distinguish between potential and actual power. Part of the problem stems from the fact that the term "power" has taken on the meaning of both the capacity to do something and the actual exercise of the capacity. And yet a nation's ability to convert potential power into operational power is based on many considerations, not the least of which is the political and psychological interrelationship of such factors as government effectiveness and national unity.[7]

In this context, the elements of national power, no matter how defined, can be separated only artificially. Together, they constitute the resources for the attainment of national objectives and goals. And while those goals may be judged as moral, immoral, or amoral, the elements of power are simply means to national strategic ends and as such are morally neutral. It is possible, in other words, to reject the cynic's belief that God is on the side of the largest number of battalions, as well as the assumption that the side with the smallest number always fights for the right.[8]

Relations and Dynamics.

National power is relative, not absolute. Simply put, a nation does not have abstract power in and of itself, but only power in relation to another actor or actors in the international arena. To say that the United States is the most powerful nation on earth is to compare American power with that of all nations as they currently exist. Nevertheless, leaders of a nation at the peak of its power can come to believe that such power has an absolute quality that can be lost only through stupidity or neglect. In reality the superior power of a nation is derived not only from its own qualities, but from that of other actors compared with its own. Many observers in the late 1930s, for example, perceived France as more than a match for Nazi Germany, since the French military of that era was superior in quality and quantity of troops and weaponry to the victorious French forces of 1919. But the French military power of 1919 was supreme only in the context of a defeated and disarmed Germany; that supremacy was not intrinsic to the French nation in the manner of its geographic location and natural resources. Thus, while the French military of 1939 was superior to that of 1919, a comparison of 1939 French military power to that of Germany in the same year would have shown a vastly different picture for many reasons, not the least of which was the German adoption of the military doctrine of blitzkrieg.[9]

Closely allied to all this is the fact that national power is dynamic, not permanent. No particular power factor or relationship is immune to change. In this century, in particular, rapid changes in military technologies have accelerated this dynamism. America's explosion of a nuclear device instantly transformed its power position, the nature of warfare, and the very conduct of international relations. A war or revolution can have an equally sudden effect on power. The two world wars devastated Europe, caused the rise of the flank powers, the United States and the Soviet Union, and set the developing world on a road to decolonization that in less than 50 years dismantled a system that had been in existence for over three centuries. Economic growth can also quickly change a nation's power position, as was the case with Japan and Germany after World War II. In addition, the discovery of new resources, or their depletion, can alter the balance of power. Certainly OPEC's control over a diminishing supply of oil, coupled with its effectiveness as a cartel, caused a dramatic shift in power relations after 1973.[10]

Such shifts are not always so immediately discernible. Power, as Hobbes long ago pointed out, is what people believe it is until it is exercised. Reputation for power, in other words, confers power on a nationstate regardless of whether that power is real or not. At the same time, there are examples throughout history of nations that continued to trade on past reputations, only to see them shattered by a single event. For France, the battles of Sedan produced just such effects in 1870 and again in 1940.[11]

This subjective characteristic of power also plays a key role in deterrence, the exercise of negative power as state A influences actor B *not* to do x. The influence is effectively exercised because B perceives that A not only has the capability to prevent B from doing x, but the willingness to use that capability as well. In other words, national credibility must be a concomitant of national capability for deterrence to work. When the combination doesn't occur, as Britain and France discovered when Hitler discounted their guarantee of Poland in the summer of 1939, the result can be war. "*The men of Munich will not take the risk,*" the Nazi leader explained to his commanders on August 14, 1939.[12]

Situational.

Some elements of national power or combinations of power cannot be applied to certain situations involving certain actors. The United States in 1979-80, for instance, was powerless to rescue American citizens held hostage in Teheran, and American nuclear power during the Cold War had little value in causing nonaligned countries to modify their policies; nor did it deter North Korea or North Vietnam in their attempts to unify their countries.

The Vietnam War also illustrates another contextual aspect of national power, that of cost-risk-benefit analysis, in which power can be exercised but the costs and risks are perceived to be disproportionate to the benefit achieved. Power, in other words, must be relevant in the existing circumstances for the particular situation. This explains why, during the 1973 Arab-Israeli War, the United States was not able to persuade its European allies to allow American planes to use North Atlantic Treaty Organization (NATO) bases for refueling and maintenance. The overall economic and military strength of the United States as well as the political bonds of alliance solidarity proved less influential on European decision makers than the possible economic loss of their access to oil. This type of American power was equally irrelevant in late 1994 when Britain and France, with troops involved in peace operations on the ground in Bosnia, turned down a U.S. plan for NATO air strikes to support Muslims in the besieged town of Bihac.[13]

This aspect of the contextual nature of national power introduces even more complications when the diversity of actors in the international arena is taken into account. In an increasingly multi-centric world, nationstates will increasingly deal with transnational actors in the exercise of national power. The European Union is just one example of international government organizations in which the confluence of political and economic trends has created a supra-national regional unit that transcends in many ways both the legal- territorial aspects of the state and the psychological unity of the nation. This type of challenge is abetted by international nongovernmental actors ranging from multinational corporations focused on self-interested profit and national liberation movements seeking to establish new governments within existing states, to organizations such as Amnesty International or Greenpeace, seeking to mobilize international public opinion in order to bring pressure on national governments to alter particular policies.[14]

Some of these actors respond more willingly to one aspect of national power than to another. Multinational corporations, for example, will generally react to economic factors more rapidly than the United Nations or a national liberation movement. Conversely, negotiations and appeals to human morality may prove to be more powerful at the United Nations than in the corporate boardroom or in the field. And the allegiance of an uneducated people in a newly independent country may help create a powerful national liberation movement, yet be meaningless for a multinational corporation or the United Nations. National power, then, is contextual not only in its application to other states, but to other global actors as well.[15]

THE ELEMENTS OF NATIONAL POWER

It is convenient to organize the study of national power by distinguishing between natural and social determinants of power. The natural determinants (geography, resources, and population) are concerned with the number of people in a nation and with their physical environment. Social determinants (economic, political, military, psychological, and, more recently, informational) concern the ways in which the people of a nation organize themselves and the manner in which they alter their environment. In practice, it is impossible to make a clear distinction between natural and social elements. For instance, resources are a natural factor, but the degree to which they are used is socially determined. Population factors, in particular, cut across the dividing line between both categories. The number of people of working age in the population affects the degree of industrialization of a nation, but the process of industrialization, in turn, can greatly alter the composition of the population.[16]

NATURAL DETERMINANTS OF POWER

Geography.

Geographical factors, whether they are location and climate or size and topography, influence a nation's outlook and capacity. Location, in particular, is closely tied to the foreign policy of a state. Vulnerable nations, like Poland caught geographically between Russia and Germany, have even had to deal with the loss of national existence. Conversely, Great Britain, the United States, and Japan have been protected by large bodies of water throughout their histories. Each, in turn, used the combination of a large navy and overseas trade to become a great power. With its oceanic moats, the United States was able to follow George Washington's advice to avoid entangling alliances and expand peacefully for almost a century, free of external interference. In addition, that expansion came about primarily without conquest, through the purchase of huge land tracts from European powers that found the location of the territories too remote to defend easily.

The connection between foreign policy and location is, in fact, so fundamental that it gave rise in this century to geopolitics as a field of study. At its most extreme, geopolitics can succumb to Morgenthau's "Fallacy of the Single Factor" or be distorted as it was at the hands of Karl Haushofer and his disciples into a kind of political metaphysics with a call for adequate national living space (*Lebensraum*) that was put into ideological service for Nazi Germany. At its best, geopolitics has many insights to offer. Consider, for instance, the connection between the British and American development of democracy and civil rights and the relatively secure strategic locations of both countries, as opposed to the authoritarian regimes of Germany and Russia, direct neighbors for much of history, lying exposed on the North European plain. Or consider the continuing Russian drive for warm-water ports and the continuing value of choke points, as was demonstrated when Egypt's closure of the Straits of Tiran in May 1967 led to war. The persistence of this field of study was reflected in the Cold War by Raymond Aaron, who described the forward deployment of U.S. troops as analogous in geographical terms to earlier British policy:

> In relation to the Eurasian land mass, the American continent occupied a position comparable to that of the British Isles in relation to Europe: the United States was continuing the tradition of the insular state by attempting to bar the dominant continental state's expansion in central Germany and in Korea.[17]

148

Location is also closely tied to climate, which in turn has a significant effect on national power. The poorest and weakest states in modern times have all been located outside the temperate climate zones in either the tropics or in the frigid zone. Even Russia has chronic agricultural problems because all but a small part of that country lies north of the latitude of the U.S.-Canadian border. Russia is also a good example of how geographical factors such as size and topography can have advantages and disadvantages for a nation. The Soviet Union, with its 11 time zones, was able to use its vast size during World War II to repeat the historical Russian military method of trading space for time when invaded. At the same time, that immense size certainly played a role in the complex ethnic and political centrifugal forces that eventually pulled apart the Union of Soviet Socialist Republics (USSR). In a similar manner, the predominantly north-south Russian rivers are great natural resources that would have been economically and politically more valuable had they run in an east-west direction. In the future, technology may mitigate some of these factors in the same way that intercontinental missiles affected the importance of insular locations. But here, as in other areas, there are many geographical obstacles to the acquisition of power that are costly or impossible to overcome.[18]

Population.

Demographics in the form of size, trends, and structure are an important aspect of national power. A large population is a key prerequisite, but not an automatic guarantee of strength. Thus, there is Canada, more powerful than the more populous but less industrialized Mexico. And Japan, with a small population marked by widespread technical skills, has been able to exercise national power far in excess of China for all its masses. At the same time, trends in population growth and decline can have significant effects on national power. The Prussian unification of the German-speaking peoples in 1870, for example, instantly created a great power with a population that grew by 27 million between then and 1940, even as that of France reflected the shift in European power, increasing by only four million in the same period. In another example, the historical increase in American power was partly due to the arrival of more than 100 million immigrants between 1824 and 1924. During the same century, Canada and Australia, comparable in territory and developmental level but with populations less than a tenth of America's, remained secondary powers. That such trends could have more complex causes dealing with other elements of power was illustrated by the Austro-Hungarian Empire, which had a large and growing population during most of that period, but also remained a secondary power because it was divided ethnically, weak politically, and at an extremely low level in terms of industrial development.[19]

In the future, global trends also will affect the structure and balance of national populations, particularly those of the poorest countries. In 1830, the global population reached one billion for the first time; it required 100 years to double. It took only 45 more years (1975) for the population to double again to four billion. In the next 21 years the population increased almost two billion, reflecting a growth rate of about 90 million a year. For the next several decades, 90 percent of this growth will occur in the lesser-developed countries, many already burdened by extreme overpopulation for which there is no remedy in the form of economic infrastructure, skills, and capital.[20]

Population structure and balance are also significant for developed nations. Important here is the percentage of the population in the most productive cohort, generally considered to be somewhere between the ages of 18 and 45, that can best meet the needs of the nation's military and industry as well as create the following generation. Comparing the numbers in this group to those in the younger cohort also provides a more accurate picture of population trends and the interaction of demographics with all power elements. Israel, for example, has to deal with its relatively small population and the fact that the military siphons off a significant segment of the civilian workforce in the middle cohort. One consequence is government emphasis on education across all age groups. Another is the government's military focus on sophisticated weaponry, mobility, air power, and the preemptive strike in order to avoid drawn-out land warfare that could be costly in manpower. Finally, a comparison of the middle population group to the older will provide a picture of trends that can have significant consequences for a nation's power. For example, any nation with an increasing cohort of retired people coupled with generous social welfare benefits will eventually have to face hard choices between guns and butter on the one hand, and possible limits to its national power as well as to its investment and economic growth potential on the other. These choices already face the United States as the "baby boomer" generation approaches retirement age against the backdrop of a staggering explosion in social entitlements.[21]

Natural Resources.

Large amounts of natural resources are essential for a modern nation to wage war, to operate an industrial base, and to reward other international actors through trade and aid, either in modern industrial products or in the raw materials themselves. But these resources, whether they be arable land and water or coal and oil, are unevenly distributed around the world and are becoming increasingly scarce. Moreover, as in the case of the geopolitical ownership of strategic places, the physical possession of natural resources is not necessarily a source of power unless a nation can also develop those resources and maintain political control over their disposition. In their raw state, for example, minerals and energy sources are generally useless. Thus, the Mesabi iron deposits had no value to the Indian tribes near Lake Superior, and Arabian oil a century ago was a matter of indifference to the nomads who roamed above it. Conversely, those nations with great industrial organizations and manufacturing infrastructures have traditionally been able to convert the potential power of natural resources into actual national power.

Very few nations, however, are self-sufficient. A country like the United States has a rich store of natural resources, and yet may be dependent on imports because of its voracious consumption. Japan, on the other hand, has few natural resources; it is dependent on imports for 100 percent of its petroleum, bauxite, wool, and cotton; 95 percent of its wheat; 90 percent of its copper; and 70 percent of its timber and grain.[22] Nations have traditionally made up for such difficulties in several ways. One time-honored method is to conquer the resources, a principal motivation for the Japanese expansion that led to World War II and the Iraqi invasion that led to the Gulf War. A second method is to develop resources in another country by means of concessions, political manipulation, and even a judicious use of force—all used earlier to considerable effect by the United States in Latin America. In an age of increasing interdependence, this type of economic penetration has long since lost its neocolonial identity, particularly since both of America's principal World War II adversaries now regularly exercise such penetration in the United States.

The third and most common method for obtaining natural resources is to buy them. In recent years, however, the combination of rapid industrial growth and decline of resources has changed the global economy into a seller's market, while providing considerable economic leverage to nations in control of vital commodities. The Organization of Petroleum Exporting Countries' (OPEC) control of oil, for example, provided its members influence all out of proportion to their economic and military power. A similar transformation may occur in the future with those nations that are major food producers as the so-called "Green Revolution" faces the prospect of more depleted lands and encroaching deserts. Finally, there is the short supply of strategic and often esoteric minerals so necessary for high technology and modern weapons. One consequence of this diminishment of raw materials has been the emergence of the sea bed, with its oil and manganese reserves, as a new venue of international competition, in which those nations with long coastlines and extensive territorial waters have the advantage. Such shortages are a reminder of how closely connected is the acquisition of natural resources to all the elements of power, particularly for a truly dependent nation like Japan, which can neither feed its people nor fuel its high-technology economy without access to overseas markets. Absent its alliance with the United States as a means to ensure its access to such resources as Persian Gulf oil, Japan would be forced to expand its "self-defense" military force, perhaps even becoming a declared nuclear power.[23]

SOCIAL DETERMINANTS OF POWER

Economic.

Economic capacity and development are key links to both natural and social determinants of power. In terms of natural resources, as we have seen, a nation may be well-endowed but lack the ability to convert those resources into military hardware, high-technology exports, and other manifestations of power. Ultimately, however, economic development in a nation flows from the social determinants of power, whether they be political modernization and widespread formal education, or geographic and social mobility and the ready acceptance of innovation. All this, of course, is worked out against the backdrop of balanced military investment. An excess of military spending can erode the underlying basis for a nation's power if it occurs at the expense of a larger economy and reduces the national ability to invest in future economic growth. For developing countries already short of economic investment capital, military spending represents a serious allocation of resources. But even advanced countries, especially since the end of the Cold War, have to make some choices between guns and butter. Because a nation's political stability as well as the legitimacy of its government are increasingly linked to domestic economic performance, excessive military spending, as the former Soviet Union discovered, can be dangerous for large and small countries alike.

Strong domestic economies also produce nonmilitary national power in the international arena. Leading industrial nations have available all the techniques for exercising power, including rewards or punishment by means of foreign trade, foreign aid, and investment and loans, as well as the mere consequences their domestic policies can have on the global economy. This type of power can be weakened, however, if a nation suffers from high inflation, a large foreign debt, or chronic balance-of-payment deficits. In short, the strength of a nation's economy has a direct effect on the variety, resiliency, and credibility of its international economic options. The size of the U.S. budget and trade deficits, for example, means that the Federal Reserve must maintain interest rates high enough for deficit financing, which limits its ability to stimulate the economy with lower rates. And American foreign aid is becoming less influential as an economic instrument of power as budgets decline. On the other hand, U.S. trade policy has become increasingly important to the U.S. economy, with American exports, as an example, expected to create 16 million jobs by the year 2000.[24] That such economic considerations are closely interrelated to other elements of power is demonstrated by the perennial question of whether most-favored-nation status, which is nothing more than normal access to U.S. markets, should be made conditional on progress in human rights by countries such as China.

Finally, increasing interdependence has caused major changes in the economic element of national power. National economies have become more dependent on international trade and on financial markets that have become truly global in scope. This in turn makes it more difficult for a nation to raise short-term interest rates or to coordinate monetary policy with other international actors. In a similar manner, the ability of nations to use exchange rates to further their national interests has declined as governments deal more and more with international capital flows that dwarf the resources available to any nation to defend its currency. From a security perspective, this type of economic interpenetration is reflected in the mutual vulnerability of national economies. Moreover, a nation's economic policy is now influenced by myriad international governmental organizations such as the International Monetary Fund (IMF) and the General Agreement on Tariffs and Trade (GATT), while multinational corporations stand ready to manipulate the domestic politics of nationstates to further their transnational interests.[25]

Military.

Military strength is historically the gauge for national power. Defeat in war has normally signaled the decline if not the end of a nation's power, while military victory has usually heralded the ascent of a new power. But military power is more than just the aggregation of personnel, equipment, and weaponry. Leadership, morale, and discipline also remain vital factors of military power. Despite rough quantitative parity between the Iraqi military and the allied coalition, the dismal Iraqi performance in the Gulf War demonstrated the enduring relevance of those intangibles. That performance also showed how political interference or the gradual infection of a nation or its military by incompetence, waste, and corruption can weaken a nation's armed forces. By contrast, there is the example of the U.S. military working over the years in tandem with political authorities to move from the hollow force of the immediate post-Vietnam period to the joint military machine of Operation DESERT STORM.[26]

The Gulf War also highlights how important power projection and sustainability are in the modern era for military effectiveness. For a global power like the United States, the focus on these factors produced not only the unique air and sea lift capability that provided transportation for a half million troops to the Persian Gulf in 1990-91, but incredible resupply feats in an environment in which a single division during the 100-hour ground offensive consumed 2.4 million gallons of fuel, brought forward in 475 5000-gallon tankers.[27] Allied to these factors, of course, are readiness considerations ranging from training and maneuver opportunities to the availability of fuel and repair parts. In a similar manner, a nation's potential for rapid mobilization may also play a key role. Israel, for example, has a permanent force of only 164,000 highly trained and ready soldiers. But that force can be augmented within 24 hours by almost three times that many combat-ready troops. And Sweden has the capability to mobilize a force almost overnight that can equal many European standing armies.[28]

The quality of arms technology also has become a vital military factor for all nations in a period marked by rapid and important scientific breakthroughs. Timely inventions ranging from the crossbow to the airplane have often been decisive when accompanied by appropriate changes in military organization and doctrine. When these two components lag technological change, however, as they did in the American Civil War and World War I, the results can be horrific diminishment and waste of military power. In addition, new technologies in the hands of rogue states or nonstate actors such as terrorist groups will continue to be an important consideration for nations in the exercise of military power. Weapons of mass destruction are and will probably continue to be of primary concern in this regard. But even relatively cheap, recently developed conventional weapons in the appropriate situation can be decisive, as was illustrated by the American-built, shoulder-fired *Stinger* anti-aircraft missiles that enabled the Afghan *mujahedeen* guerrillas to neutralize Soviet air power. Finally, technological advances are a useful reminder once again that military power, like all elements of national power, is contextual. Technology is not an automatic panacea for producing quick victories and low casualties, particularly absent clear political direction and coherent strategy. There comes a time, as Britain's thin red line discovered under the weight of the Zulu offensive at Isandhewana, when quantity has a quality all its own.[29]

Political.

This element of power addresses key questions, many of which are related to the psychological element: What is the form of government, what is the attitude of the population toward it, how strong do the people want it to be, and how strong and efficient is it? These questions cannot be answered with simple statistics, yet they may be paramount in any assessment of national power. If a government is inadequate and cannot bring the nation's potential power to bear on an issue, that power might as well not exist. Nor can an analysis turn on the type of government a state claims to have, for even the constitution of a state may be misleading. The 1936 Soviet Constitution, for example, was a democratic-sounding organic law that had little in common with the actual operation of the Soviet regime. And the German Weimar Constitution, a model of democratic devices, did not prevent Hitler from reaching power and from creating his own "constitutional law" as he proceeded.

What is clear is that the actual forms of government, each with its own strengths and weaknesses, play a role in the application of national power. An authoritarian system, for instance, restricts in varying degrees individual freedom and initiative, but permits formulation of a highly organized state strategy. Democratic systems, by comparison, require policy formation by consensus-building and persuasion in an open, pluralistic society. Consequently, it is extremely difficult for democracies to develop and implement a long-range state strategy or to change policy direction as abruptly as, for example, Nazi Germany and the USSR did in the ideological *volte-face* marked by the August 1939 nonaggression treaty. In addition, the level of political development within a state is also important. This development involves both the capability, and more particularly the efficiency and effectiveness, of a national government in using its human and material resources in pursuit of national interests. Thus, administrative and management skills are crucial if a nation is to realize its full power potential.

A government also takes the shape and operates the way it does for very complex reasons, many of which reflect the experience of a people and their attitude toward, and expectations of, what the government is to do and how strong, as a consequence, it should be. For example, a fear of too much state power caused the Founding Fathers deliberately to make the U.S. Government inefficient (in the sense of a quick, smooth operation) by means of "checks and balances." In a similar manner, the French fear of a "man on horseback" in the wake of their second experience with Bonapartism caused a curtailment of executive powers that resulted in the weakness of the French governments after the Franco-Prussian War. Under both the Third and Fourth French Republics, as a result, the French strengthened the legislative branch to a degree that made strong executive leadership almost impossible. The French preferred to suffer the executive weakness rather than run the risks entailed in a strong government. Consequently, while the United States had 14 administrations between 1875 and 1940, and the British 20, France had 102. After World War II, the Fourth French Republic averaged two regimes a year.[30]

Psychological.

The psychological element of power consists of national will and morale, national character, and degree of national integration. It is this most ephemeral of the social power determinants that has repeatedly caused nations with superior economic and military power to be defeated or have their policies frustrated by less capable actors. Thus there was Mao's defeat of Chiang Kai-shek when Chiang at least initially possessed most of China's wealth and military capability, the ability of Gandhi to drive the British from India, and that of Khomeni to undermine the Shah. And it is almost a cliché that any measurement of U.S. economic and military power vis-à-vis that of the North Vietnam-Vietcong combination during the late 1960s would have led to the conclusion that U.S. superiority in these two categories would result in an American victory. Colonel Harry Summers recounts a story, in this regard, that was circulating during the final days of the U.S. retreat from Vietnam:

> When the Nixon Administration took over in 1969 all the data on North Vietnam and on the United States was fed into a Pentagon computer — population, gross national product, manufacturing capability, number of tanks, ships, and aircraft, size of the armed forces, and the like. The computer was then asked, *"When will we win?"* It took only a moment to give the answer: *"You won in 1964!"*[31]

National will and morale are defined as the degree of determination that any actor manifests in the pursuit of its internal or external objectives. For a given international actor, however, will and morale need not be identical at all levels of society. During 1916 and early 1917, the Russian nobility continued to plan for new offensive action even as Russian troops were abandoning their weapons and their battlefield positions. National character has an equally complex relation to national power inasmuch as that character favors or proscribes certain policies and strategies. Americans, for example, like to justify their actions. Thus, the United States did not enter World War I until Wilsonian idealism had to confront the loss of American ships and American lives. The elevation of "moralism" in the conduct of foreign policy, in turn, diminishes the ability of the United States to initiate a truly preemptive action. In the Cuban missile crisis, for example, the choice of a blockade over an air strike was based in part on the argument that from the standpoint of both morality and tradition, the United States could not perpetate a "Pearl Harbor in reverse."[32] In all such cases, as with will and morale, it is extremely difficult to identify the constituent parts of and sources behind national character. Historical experiences and traditional values undoubtedly are important, as are such factors as geographic location and environment. Russian mistrust of the external world, for instance, is historically verifiable as part of the national character, whether it is because of the centuries of Tartar rule, three invasions from Western Europe in little more than a century, or something else. And Russian stoicism is a character trait, whether the cause is Russian Orthodox Christianity, communism, or the long Russian winters.[33]

Finally, there is the degree of integration, which refers simply to the sense of belonging and identification of a nation's people. In many ways, this contributes to both national will and morale as well as character. In most cases there is a direct correlation between the degree of perceived integration and the extent of ethnic, religious, linguistic, and cultural homogeneity, all of which contribute to a sense of belonging, manifested in a sense of citizenship. On the other hand, despite examples to the contrary (Belgium, Canada, and the states of the former Yugoslavia), a lack of integration need not necessarily cause a lack of identity. Swiss unity has continued across the centuries despite low degrees of integration in ethnicity, language, and religion.[34]

Informational.

The communications revolution, which began over a century ago with the advent of global transmission of information, has taken on new momentum in recent decades with the development of fax machines, television satellites, and computer linkages. As the revolutions in Central and Eastern Europe demonstrated in the fall of 1989, a new fact of life in the international arena is that it is no longer possible for any nationstate to deny its citizens knowledge of what is taking place elsewhere. Ideas, in other words, move more freely around the world than at any other time in the past. This has had particularly fortunate results for the United States. Even as some other aspects of power have gone into relative decline, America's influence as a source of ideas and as a shaper of culture has increased. This "soft power," in Joseph Nye's words, has been a major factor in formulating the U.S. national security strategic objective of "enlargement."[35] So in one sense, information has contributed to the concept of the world as a global village.

This combination of enhanced communication and dissemination of information, however, is a two-edged sword that cuts across all the social determinants of power in national strategy. In the economic realm, for instance, global interdependence has been enhanced by information-communication improvements. On the other hand, near instantaneous downturns of major economies are always a possibility with the immediate transmission of adverse economic news concerning any nation-state or transnational economic actor. Politically, instantaneous and pervasive communication can enhance the ability of governmental elites to lead the people in a democracy or to act as a national consoler in times of tragedy, such as the *Challenger* explosion or the Oklahoma City bombing. At the same time, these developments can also aid the demagogues, the great simplifiers always waiting in the wings to stir fundamental discontents and the dark side of nationalism. In terms of psychological power, Winston Churchill demonstrated repeatedly that the pervasive distribution of targeted information can have momentous effects on intangibles such as national will. Conversely, however, this type of ubiquity has the pernicious potential of altering in a matter of years basic values and cultural beliefs that take generations to create.

Nowhere is the effect of developments in communications and access to information more far-reaching than on warfare. In the purely military realm, information dominance can create operational synergies by allowing those systems that provide battlespace awareness, enhance command and control, and create precision force to be integrated into the so-called "system of systems." One result of all this is to compress the strategic, operational, and tactical levels of war, previously considered as separate and distinct loci of command and functional responsibilities. The commander will be faced in the future with the much more complex job of recognizing those events occurring simultaneously at all three levels and integrating them into the calculation that results from the traditional consideration at the operational level of which tactical battles and engagements to join and which to avoid. Equally important, shorter time for decisions—occasioned by both the compressed continuum of war and electronically gathered information—means less time to discover ambiguities or to analyze those ambiguities that are already apparent.

At the higher level of cyberwar, the two-edged potential of communications and information is even more evident. In the future, nations will wage offensive information warfare on another state's computer systems, targeting assets ranging from telecommunications and power to safety and banking. Such an onslaught could undermine the more advanced aspects of an adversary's economy, interrupt its mobilization of military power, and by affecting the integrity of highly visible services to the population, create almost immediate pressure on government at all levels. As activities rely increasingly on information systems rather than manual processes and procedures, information infrastructures of the most developed nations, such as the United States, become progressively more vulnerable to state and nonstate actors. Even as there are advances in information security technologies, hacker tools are becoming more sophisticated and easier to obtain and use. One analyst concludes in this regard that, for the United States, "the possibility of a digital Pearl Harbor cannot be dismissed out of hand."[36]

EVALUATION

Evaluation of national power is difficult. The basic problem, as we have seen, is that all elements of power are interrelated. Where people live will influence what they possess; how many they are will influence how much they possess; what their historical experience has been will affect how they look at life; how they look at life will influence how they organize and govern themselves; and all these elements weighed in relation to the problem of national security will influence the nature, size, and effectiveness of the armed forces. As a consequence, not only must each separate element be analyzed, but the effects of those elements on one another must be considered. These complexities are compounded because national power is both dynamic and relative. Nationstates and other international actors change each day in potential and realized power, although the rate of change may vary from one actor to another. And because these changes go on continually, an estimate of a state's national power vis-à-vis the power of another actor is obsolescent even as the estimate is made. The greater the rate of change in the actors being compared, the greater the obsolescence of the estimate.

In other words, like all strategic endeavors, more art than science is involved in the evaluation of where one nationstate stands in relation to the power of other regional and global actors. This has not deterred one former government official from creating a formula to develop a rough estimate of "perceived" national power—focused primarily on a state's capacity to wage war:[37]

$Pp = (C + E + M) \times (S + W)$ in which:

Pp = Perceived power
C = Critical mass: population and territory
E = Economic capability
M = Military capability
S = Strategic purpose
W = Will to pursue national strategy.

Regardless of its prospective contribution in calculating a Pp value, this formula has some important lessons. The more tangible elements (C, E, M) that can be objectively quantified also involve varying degrees of subjective qualifications: territory that is vast but covered with mountain ranges and has few navigable rivers; a population that is large but unskilled and uneducated; or cases in which, despite qualitative military superiority in technology and weapons on one side, the opponent is able to prevail through superior intangibles ranging from leadership to morale. Most important, by demonstrating that national power is a product—not a sum—of its components, the formula is a reminder of how important the relational and contextual aspects are. The United States discovered in Vietnam that no matter how large the sum of the more tangible economic and military capabilities in relation to an adversary, their utility is determined by the intangibles of strategic purpose(S) and national will(W). Zero times any number, no matter how large, is still zero.

These considerations are particularly important in evaluating what some might consider to be irrational acts by states that use force to alter the status quo. In fact, these states may simply differ from others in the perception of low risks where others perceive high ones, rather than in the willingness to take risks. There is growing evidence that the 1990 Iraqi invasion of Kuwait falls into this category. In another era, many of Hitler's "Saturday surprises" in the 1930s were considered reckless by those who would eventually have to redress their consequences. These incidents came about, however, not because the Nazi leader willingly tolerated a high probability of conflict, but because he was certain that the other side would back down. When the German military opposed such policies as the Rhineland coup and the *Anschluss* with Austin on the basis that they were too dangerous, Hitler did not argue that the risks were worth the prizes, but that instead, taking the social determinants of power in Germany and the other countries into consideration, the risks were negligible. In terms of the concept of gain and risk assessment displayed in Figure 1 below, Hitler's analysis of potential opposition came to rest at the MAXIMIN approach of Quadrant 2, not that of MAXIMAX in Quadrant 1.[38]

		Risk	
		High (MAX)	Low (MIN)
Gain	High (MAX)	1 (MAXIMAX)	2 (MAXIMIN)
	Low (MIN)	3 (MINIMAX)	4 (MINIMIN)

Figure 1. Gain and Risk Assessment.

In the Rhineland episode of 7 March 1936, for example, the military correlation of forces was quantifiably against Germany, as Hitler was well aware. "We had no army worth mentioning," he reflected later; "at that time it would not even have had the fighting strength to maintain itself against the Poles."[39] But unlike his military advisors, who were focused firmly on French military capabilities, the Nazi leader considered other elements of power, particularly the lack of political integration and coherency in the French Popular Front government and the connection to the psychological component of French national will. As a result, he concluded that France had no intention of responding militarily to the German military incursion. On March 9, the Wehrmacht commander received warning of impending French military countermoves and asked to withdraw troops from major cities in the Rhineland. Hitler, however, was still taking an essentially MAXIMIN (Quadrant 2) approach and correctly discounted the possibility of intervention by a French government vacillating between two incorrect positions: MAXIMAX (Quadrant 1) and MINIMAX (Quadrant 3).[40]

THINKING IN THE BOX

A great deal of lip service has been paid of late to the need for students of strategy to "think outside the box." The "box" in this case presumably contains the traditional approaches to those issues that affect America's national security. It is natural, of course, in a time of great change to search for a "Philosopher's Stone," or to look for the sword that can, in one clean stroke, preclude the tedious unraveling of the Gordian knot of post-Cold War strategy. And perhaps this will all be possible in an extra-box environment of the future. But such explorations cannot and should not be made until the student of national security has learned to think inside the box, and that begins with an understanding of concepts like national power.

The concept of national power helps to provide an initial organizational focus as students deal with the deceptively simple thought process that links strategic ends, ways, and means. National elements of power, however they are described, provide the conceptual foundation for this process at the national strategic level. An understanding of the characteristics and the interrelationships of these elements allows the student to expand the process to comprehend how derivative instruments of power can be combined most effectively as policy options to achieve national strategic objectives. This is a key step in strategic maturation that will play an increasingly larger role in the future for military and civilian professionals concerned with national security strategy.

Military planners already deal with Flexible Deterrent Options, in which military instruments of power are matched with instruments derived from other elements of power. Military options in response to a challenge could include an increase in specific reconnaissance activities, the exercise of certain pre-positioned equipment, or the deployment of small units. Politically, this could mean consultation by executive branch elites with congressional leaders or initiation of a specific diplomatic demarche. At the same time, economic options might include, alone or in combination, the enactment of trade sanctions, the freezing of assets, and the restriction of corporate transactions. In all this, the effectiveness of small discrete response options depends on how well the instruments of power are wielded together. And that will depend to a great deal on how well military strategists and their civilian counterparts understand the elements of national power from which those instruments are derived.[41]

The focus on these elements of national power as means to national strategic ends also serves as an organizational link to the overall strategic formulation process. That process begins by demonstrating how national strategic objectives are derived from national interests, which in turn owe their articulation and degree of intensity to national values. This linkage is also a useful reminder that power, the "means" in the strategic equation, ultimately takes its meaning from the values it serves. Absent the legitimation provided by this connection to national values, national power may come to be perceived as a resource or means that invites suspicion and challenge; at worst it could be associated with tyranny and aggrandizement. Without the bond of popular support and the justification that comes from an overarching purpose, national power can be quick to erode and ephemeral as a source of national security.

What takes place within the box in dealing with concepts like national power is an educational process, a not inconsiderable achievement in an era mesmerized by techno-chic innovations which tend to confuse training with that process and data collection with knowledge.

In the final analysis, the study of national power is a valuable educational objective because it is so difficult. Aspiring national security strategists must grapple with concepts that overlap, that are subjective in many cases, that are relative and situational, and that defy scientific measurement. All this teaches flexible thinking—the *sine qua non* for a strategist. In short, it is this very complexity that causes students to mature intellectually, to understand that within the box there is no such thing as a free strategic lunch. Equally important, students learn that they cannot escape these limitations by moving outside the box, a lesson that many futurists need to absorb.

ENDNOTES - CHAPTER 10

1. Thomas Hobbes, *Leviathan*, Indianapolis: Bobbs-Merrill, 1958, p. 86.

2. Hans J. Morgenthau, *Politics Among Nations: The Struggle for Power and Peace*, 4th ed., New York: Knopf, 1968, p. 25. Although Morgenthau sees the concept of national interest defined in terms of power, much of this discussion is under a subheading that treats political power "As Means to the Nation's Ends." *Ibid.*

3. John Spanier and Robert L. Wendzel, *Games Nations Play*, 9th ed., Washington, DC: CQ Press, 1996, p. 128. See also Theodore A. Couloumbis and James H. Wolfe, *Introduction to International Relations: Power and Justice*, 2d ed., Englewood Cliffs, NJ: Prentice Hall, 1982, p. 64. Many scholars use this broad interpretation of influence in their definition of power: "the ability to influence the behavior of others in accordance with one's own ends." A. F. K. Organski, World Politics, 2d ed., New York: Knopf, 1968, p. 104, and "the ability of an actor to influence the outcomes of international events to its

own satisfaction." Walter S. Jones, *The Logic of International Relations*, Boston: Little, Brown, 1985, p. 245. For arguments against mixing power and influence, see Robert A. Dahl, *Modern Political Analysis*, Englewood Cliffs, NJ: Prentice Hall, 1976, p. 29; Daniel S. Papp, *Contemporary International Relations: Frameworks for Understanding*, New York: Macmillan, 1984, p. 308; and Michael P. Sullivan, *Power in Contemporary Politics*, Columbia: University of South Carolina Press, 1990, p. 98.

4. K. J. Holsti, *International Politics: A Framework for Analysis*, 5th ed., Englewood Cliffs, NJ: Prentice Hall, 1988, pp. 142, 152-53. On patterns of influence, see *Ibid.*, pp. 154-56. On similar methods or techniques of exercising power, see Organski, pp. 112-15. Realists, in general, treat power as the "currency of politics." Just as economists focus on the definition and variety of currency types, students of international relations define and distinguish the types of power. See, for example, Klaus Knorr, *The Power of Nations: The Political Economy of International Relations*, New York: Basic Books, 1975.

5. Carl von Clausewitz, *On War*, Michael Howard and Peter Paret, trans., Princeton, NJ: Princeton University Press, 1976, p. 119.

6. On the context of power, see Spanier and Wendzel, pp. 144-45; Papp, pp. 309-11; and Gordon C. Schloming, *Power and Principle in International Affairs*, New York: Harcourt Bruce Jovanovich: 1991, p. 528.

7. Morgenthau, p. 153; Spanier and Wendzel, pp. 128, 131; and Organski, p. 102. In English and German, Macht, for example, "power" indicates both capacity and the exercise of that capacity. In French, however, there are two words: puissance, indicating potential or capacity, and pouvoir, indicating the act or the exercise of power. Dennis H. Wrong, *Power: Its Forms, Bases and Uses*, New York: Harper & Row, 1979, pp. 9-10. Frederich Hartmann deals with the distinction between potential and real in his definition of national power as "the strength or capacity that a sovereign nationstate can use to achieve its national interests." Emphasis in original. Frederick H. Hartmann, *The Relations of Nations*, 5th ed., New York: Macmillan, 1978, p. 43.

8. Organski, pp. 101-102.

9. *Ibid.*, p. 121; Morgenthau, pp. 149-51; Spanier and Wendzel, p. 128; and Eugene J. Kolb, *A Framework for Political Analysis*, Englewood Cliffs, NJ: Prentice Hall, 1978, pp. 50-52.

10. Organski, p. 110; Kolb, pp. 50-52; Morgenthau, pp. 151-53; and Schloming, p. 527. For the declinist approach to the dynamic nature of national power, see Paul M. Kennedy, *The Rise and Fall of the Great Powers: Economic Change and Military Conflict from 1500-2000*, New York: Random House, 1987; Mancur Olsen, *The Rise and Decline of Nations: Economic Growth, Stagflation, and Social Rigidities*, New Haven, CT: Yale University Press, 1982; Aaron L. Friedberg, *The Weary Titan: Great Britain and the Experience of Relative Decline*, Princeton, NJ: Princeton University Press, 1988.

11. Organski, pp. 108-09; Spanier, p. 128; and Hobbes, p. 106.

12. Emphasis in original. Franz Halder, *The Halder Diaries: The Private War Journals of Colonel General Franz Halder*, ed. Arnold Lissance, Boulder, CO, and Dunn Loring, VA: Westview Press and T. N. Dupuy Associates, 1976, pp. I, 8. After the Munich Conference, Mussolini appraised the British leaders as "the tired sons of a long line of rich men." Winston S. Churchill, *The Second World War*, Vol. I, *The Gathering Storm*, Boston: Houghton Mifflin, 1948, p. 341. On the concept of negative power as used in this context, see Holsti, p. 144, and Dahl, p. 43. On a different view of negative as well as positive power, see Organski, pp. 118-19. See also Robert Jervis, Richard Ned Lebow, and Janice Gross Stein, *Psychology and Deterrence*, Baltimore: Johns Hopkins University Press, 1985.

13. Papp, p. 311; Spanier and Wendzel, pp. 144-45; Kolb, pp. 49-50.

14. Sullivan, pp. 21-24; and Papp, p. 12.

15. Barry O'Neill, "Power and Satisfaction in the United Nations Security Council," *Journal of Conflict Resolution*, Vol. 40, June 1996, 219-37; and Papp, p. 311.

16. For the distinction between natural and social determinants of power, see Organski, chaps. 7, 8. Morgenthau, p. 106, breaks the elements down into "those which are relatively stable and those which are subject to constant change." See

also Couloumbis and Wolfe, pp. 65, 73-78, who break national power into two categories: tangible, population, territory, natural resources, industrial capacity, agricultural capacity, military strength and mobility; and intangible, leadership and personality, bureaucratic-organizational efficiency, type of government, societal cohesiveness, reputation, foreign support and diplomacy, accidents.

17. Raymond Aron, *Peace and War*, New York: Praeger, 1966, p. 1. See also Derwent Whittlesey, "Haushofer: The Geopoliticians," *Makers of Modern Strategy*, Edward Mead Earle, ed., Princeton, NJ: Princeton University Press, 1973, pp. 388-414; Colin S. Gray, *The Geopolitics of the Nuclear Era: Heartlands, Runlands, and the Technological Revolution*, New York: Crane, Russak, 1977; Hartmann, pp. 49-52; Morgenthau, pp. 106-08, 153; Spanier and Wendzel, p. 132; and Organski, pp. 126-38, who believes that geography's effect on national power has been exaggerated.

18. Schloming, p. 530. Hartmann, p. 49, believes climate is the most important geographical factor. Life magazine listed the air conditioner as one of the most important inventions in world history because it would enable tropical areas to begin industrialization. The shape of a nation is also important, as witness Israel's difficulty in returning to its pre-1967 configuration of long frontiers and very little depth. Spanier and Wendzel, p. 132. See also Isaiah Berlin, *Against the Current: Essays in the History of Ideas*, New York: Viking Press, 1980, p. 258, who attributes the aggressive nationalism of such leaders as Napoleon, Hitler, and Stalin to their geographical origins on the borderlands of the empires they will later rule.

19. Schloming, p. 531; and Julian L. Simon, *Population Matters: People, Resources, Environment, and Immigration*, New Brunswick, NJ: Transaction Publishers, 1990.

20. Nafis Sadik, "World Population Continues to Rise," *The Brown and Benchmark Reader in International Relations, 1992*, ed. Jeffrey Elliott, Dubuque, IA.: Wm. C. Brown, 1992, pp. 291-96. See also Spanier and Wendzel, pp. 135-36; Hartmann, pp. 46-49; Schloming, p. 531; Organski, pp. 153-54, and George D. Moffett, *Global Population Growth: 21st Century Challenges*, Ithaca, NY: Foreign Policy Association, 1994.

21. Hartmann, p. 47; Schloming, p. 532; and Peter G. Peterson, "Will America Grow Up Before It Grows Old?" *The Atlantic Monthly*, May 1996, pp. 55-92.

22. Spanier and Wendzel, p. 139. See also Schloming, p. 531, and Organski, pp. 138-141.

23. On problems with the most basic of all resources, see Miriam R. Lowi, *Water and Power: The Politics of a Scarce Resource in the Jordan River Basin*, New York: Cambridge University Press, 1995. See also Organski, p. 142; Schloming, pp. 533-534; and Morgenthau, pp. 109-112.

24. National Defense University, Institute for National Strategic Studies, *Strategic Assessment 96*, Washington, DC: U.S. Government Printing Office, 1996, p. 49. See also Organski, p. 169. Hartmann, pp. 52-56, includes natural resources in the economic element of power.

25. Strategic Assessment 96, p. 51; and Schloming, p. 158.

26. For questions concerning the jointness of Operation DESERT STORM, see Michael R. Gordon and Bernard E. Trainor, *The General's War: The Inside Story of the Conflict in the Gulf*, Boston: Little, Brown, 1994. Stalin's great purges of the 1930s are an extreme example of political interference. In addition to the roughly 800,000 party members who were killed, about half of the army officer corps, some 35,000 in all, were eliminated despite the weakness it imposed on the USSR in a time of growing foreign danger. Gordon A. Craig, *Europe Since 1815*, New York: Dryden Press, 1974, p. 383.

27. U.S. Department of the Army, Field Manual (FM) 100-5, *Operations*, Washington, DC: U.S. Government Printing Office, June 1993, p. 12-21. See also Spanier and Wendzel, p. 143.

28. Switzerland is another prime example with the capability of mobilizing in excess of a half million troops in less than 2 days. Schloming, p. 543.

29. In the subsequent battle of Rourke's Drift, of course, technology plus an inspired combination of all the intangibles ranging from leadership to unit cohesion produced a British victory in which 11 Victoria Crosses were earned. On revolutions in military affairs, see the Strategic Studies Institute monographs from the fifth annual U.S. Army War College Strategy Conference, April 1994. See also Schloming, p. 540.

30. Papp, p. 316; Hartmann, pp. 59-60; and Morgenthau, pp. 133-35.

31. Emphasis in original. Harry G. Summers, *On Strategy: The Vietnam War in Context*, Carlisle, PA: U.S. Army War College, Strategic Studies Institute, 1983, p. 11. See also Papp, p. 378.

32. Graham T. Allison, *Essence of a Decision: Explaining the Cuban Missiles Crisis*, Boston: Little, Brown, 1971, pp. 123-124. See also Papp, pp. 382-384, and Morgenthau, pp. 122-134.

33. On the Russian national character, see Morgenthau, pp. 125-127, and Papp, p. 383. On the American character, see Spanier and Wendzel, pp. 186-192.

34. Papp, pp. 386-387.

35. Joseph S. Nye, Jr., *Bound to Lead: The Changing Nature of American Power*, New York: Basic Books, 1990; and "Understanding U.S. Strength," *Foreign Policy*, No. 72, Fall 1988, 105-129.

36. *Strategic Assessment 96*, p. 197. See also *Ibid.*, pp. 195-196, and chap. 15; Joseph S. Nye, Jr., and William A. Owens, "America's Information Edge," *Foreign Affairs*, Vol. 75, March-April 1996; and Roger C. Molander, Andrew S. Riddle, and Peter A. Wilson, *Strategic Information Warfare: A New Face of War*, Santa Monica, CA: RAND, 1996. A recent Defense Science Board report on information warfare repeated this warning. Thomas E. Ricks, "Information Warfare Defense is Urged: Pentagon Panel Warns of `Electronic Pearl Harbor'," *The Wall Street Journal*, January 6, 1997, p. B2.

37. Ray S. Cline, *World Power Trends and U.S. Foreign Policy for the 1980s*, Boulder, CO: Westview Press, 1980, p. 13. See also Papp, pp. 308-309; Hartmann, p. 67; and Couloumbis and Wolfe, pp. 66-67. For another approach to quantifying and ranking the actual and projected capabilities of states, see Karl Deutsch, *The Analysis of International Relations*, Englewood Cliffs, NJ: Prentice Hall, 1968, pp. 21-39.

38. Robert Jervis, *Perceptions and Misperceptions in International Politics*, Princeton, NJ: Princeton University Press, 1976, p. 52.

39. Albert Speer, *Inside the Third Reich*, Richard and Clara Winston, trans., New York: Macmillan, 1970, p. 72. General von Blomberg pointed out after the war that if the French had resisted, the Germans would "have to have beat a hasty retreat." And General Keitel confided that "he wouldn't have been a bit surprised" if three battalions of French troops had flicked the German forces right off the map. G. M. Gilbert, *The Psychology of Dictatorship*, New York: Ronald Press, 1950, p. 211.

40. This did not mean that Hitler was not nervous. "The 48 hours after the march," he stated, "were the most nerve-wracking in my life." Allan Bullock, *Hitler: A Study in Tyranny*, New York: Harper & Row, 1962, p. 345. For additional measures Hitler took to make the operation as unprovocative as possible, see John Thomas Emmerson, *The Rhineland Crises*, Ames: Iowa University Press, 1977, p. 101.

41. For the flexible deterrent options, see *The Joint Staff Officer's Guide 1993*, AFCC Pub 1, Washington, DC: U.S. Government Printing Office, 1993, pp. 6-11 - 6-16. For some reason, JCS currently defines national security strategy in terms of instruments of power (diplomatic, economic, military, and information) as the means "to achieve objectives that contribute to national security." JCS Pub 1-02, pp. 254-255. The same publication, however, defines elements of national power as "the means that are available for employment in the pursuit of national objectives," *Ibid.*, p. 130. The use of power elements as the "means" in the definition of national strategy (*Ibid.*, p. 255) is in keeping with the Goldwater-Nichols terminology concerning power and strategy. Professor Michael Morin, U.S. Army War College, November 21, 1996. See also note 4.

CHAPTER 11

NATIONAL POWER

R. Craig Nation

Power is an essential concept in international theory but also an essentially contested and chronically ambiguous one.[1] The word itself, derived from the Old French *povoir* (to be able) connotes capacity. As a concept power can be usefully defined as the capacity to impose a desired outcome in the face of resistance. In the words of Robert Dahl, "A has power over B to the extent that he can get B to do something that B would not otherwise do."[2] This makes power both a dispositional concept and a function of coercive behavior—the purposeful exercise of capacity in order to arrive at a determined end in a context of conflict or goal incompatibility. Power can also be defined more broadly, as the ability to shape the operational environment in such a way as to encourage certain kinds of behavior and discourage or place beyond the pale various alternatives. The scope of what is considered legitimate behavior is thereby reduced—what does not happen is as important as what does. In this framework power implies securing compliance by leveraging influence and authority.[3] Desired outcomes can be imposed coercively (power to), but also assured by the consensually grounded institutionalization of authority and a corresponding code of values (power over).[4]

Much of the formal literature addressing the concept of power focuses on social systems and domestic political order, where the institutionalization of authority is placed front and center. Writing in this context, Hannah Arendt anchors the concept of power to popular will: "All political institutions are manifestations and materializations of power; they petrify and decay as soon as the living power of the people ceases to uphold them."[5] Thomas Hobbes' famous evocation of mankind's "perpetual and restless desire for power after power, that ceaseth only in death," describes a proclivity to dominate others grounded in human nature that must be constrained by the power of the state, presumably sanctioned by some kind of hypothetical social contract.[6] On the level of domestic governance, coercive capacity and legitimate authority combine to allow the effective application of political power as an alternative to the unregulated struggle of all against all.

On the international level different priorities prevail. The classic realist vision of international order rests on the assertion that the modern state system (the so-called Westphalian state system) is defined first of all by the *absence* of any effective supranational authority. It is an anarchic, self-help system where sovereign states must act without recourse to institutions of world governance to confront "the conflicts of interests that inevitably arise among similar units in a condition of anarchy."[7] Morgenthau accepts Hobbes' tragic vision of the human conditions. He quotes Thucydides' Athenians address to the Melians to the effect that: "Of the gods we know, and of men we believe, that it is a necessary law of their nature that they rule wherever they can."[8] The domestic analogy does not apply—international law and associated norms of state behavior will be ignored when vital interests are at stake, or at best evoked hypocritically as rhetorical justification for the pursuit of selfish goals. No international civil society of sovereign states is possible. In the words of Hobbes' great contemporary Baruch de Spinoza, in interstate competition the strong are bound to "devour" the weak.[9] Power, unmitigated by systemic constraint, becomes the currency of relations between states and the driving force of statecraft, famously capsulated by Morgenthau as "interest defined as power."[10] The strategic image of statecraft that came to dominate both the theory and practice of international relations in the post-World War II era makes the pursuit of power its most basic premise. Speaking on behalf of the realist camp, Donald Kagan defines power austerely as "the capacity to bring about desired ends," and asserts that "in the world in which we all live, it is essential, and the struggle for it is inevitable."[11]

STRUCTURAL MODELS OF POWER

Power is the measure of a relationship. It has no objective stature in and of itself and can be manifested in many ways. It is not a fungible commodity. The combination of power resources required to accomplish Task A, can be completely different from the combination required to address Task B. Physical strength, for example, will be a useful facilitator for positive outcomes in some contingencies (a wrestling match) but altogether irrelevant in others (a chess contest). Morgenthau defines power as "man's control over the minds and actions of other men" and "a psychological relation between those who exercise it and those over whom it is exercised,"[12] thus adding a subjective dimension to the calculus of power grounded in personal and cultural considerations. National power is also a dynamic concept, whose components have changed considerably through the modern centuries, and which continues to evolve.

Modern policy analysis has been predisposed to emphasize the primacy of national security as a motive for state behavior and the essential role of military power as the guarantor of national survival and state interests. There is no doubt that in the modern centuries military power has been the most important arbiter in relations between states. But superior military capacity has never been a sufficient condition for achieving successful outcomes in international competition. Military strength is only one dimension of what are sometimes referred to as *hard power* assets: the capacity to coerce including both the threat of and resort to armed force, economic pressure including fiscal and commercial sanctions, subversive techniques, and various other forms of intimidation. Moreover, the capacity of states to develop and sustain military capacity rests on a more complex combination of power attributes, including economic, organizational and motivational assets.

Military power has always been employed as one of several tools of statecraft. Edward Gullick notes that in the age of the classic European balance of power, the calculus of power rested on the diverse mechanisms of alliance, coalition, and compensation, with resort to arms or warfare as a popular but also last resort.[13] Immanuel Wallerstein describes the constituents of power in the early modern European state system complexly as: (1) *mercantilism* implying the use of state capacity to promote economic strength; (2) *military power*; (3) *public finance*; (4) *effective bureaucracy*; and (5) the *hegemonic bloc*, defined as the capacity of dominant social groups to impose their own vision of national priorities.[14] The 19th century Concert of Europe used consultation between the great powers to prevent systemic conflict on the scale of the Napoleonic era, relying on a series of "rules of the game" defined by Paul Schroeder as "compensation; indemnities; alliances as instruments for accruing power and capability; *raison d'état*; honour and prestige; Europe as a family of states; and finally, the principle or goal of balance of power itself."[15] Among the classic realists, Morgenthau's emphasis on the subtleties of diplomacy and Raymond Aron's identification of prudence as the foundation for statecraft make clear that their image of the role of force in interstate relations is a nuanced one.[16]

During the Cold War, confronting what was consensually identified as the real and present danger of aggressive Soviet power, the United States and its allies made the quest for security their most important national priority. This demanded the cultivation of military power as a balance to the considerable Soviet arsenal. The Cold War was a militarized interstate rivalry, but it was also something more. Military containment was accompanied by a successful diplomacy of alliance, the purposeful use of economic power, and, critically, the moral force provided by the example of the open society and Free World when contrasted with Soviet totalitarianism. In the end it was the non-material dimensions of power that were decisive. The vulgar realist image of military power as all important has never been reflected in sophisticated political theory or real world state practice.

Beginning with the publication of Robert Keohane and Joseph Nye's *Power and Interdependence* in 1977 there has been an ongoing effort by international relations scholars to develop a more nuanced view of the concept of power in international relations that breaks with some of the core assumptions of the realist paradigm. In the interdependent world of the late 20th century, Keohane and Nye argued, the relative importance of military power as an instrument of statecraft is in decline. Survival remains the primordial national goal, and force is still the ultimate guarantor of security. But in a more interdependent world, relationships of mutual dependence bind countries more closely together, and "in most of them force is irrelevant or unimportant as an instrument of policy."[17] In his subsequent work Nye has championed the concept of *soft power*, including cultural and ideological assets, transformational diplomacy, information strategies, the power of example, and the like, as an alternative that leverages the power of attraction in place of the coercive strategies of traditional statecraft.[18]

Many analysts have developed variations on this theme. Alvin Toffler's *Powershift* identifies three main sources of power, defined as violence, wealth, and knowledge. The role of violence is exclusively punitive and negative, wealth can be used both to punish and reward, but only the leveraging of knowledge has the potential to be transformational under 21st century conditions— for Toffler the knowledge sector will be the key to national power looking into the future.[19] In her *States and Markets* Susan Strange develops a "structural model of power" with four sectors: productive, fiscal, military, and informational. Strange asks how the United States has been able to expand its global influence despite the relative contraction of its productive and fiscal sectors. She finds the answer, in part, in military dominance, but also, and perhaps more importantly, in the attraction of America's open society and "way of life," the unparalleled prestige of U.S. institutions of higher education, cutting edge scientific and technological innovation, the status of the English language as the *lingua franca* of international communication, effective public diplomacy, and in general the capacity to mobilize cultural power in service of U.S. interests.[20] The United States has embraced this kind of more complex image of national power, and a series of formal policy documents have introduced contrasting models of power intended to convey the conclusion that viewed comprehensively national power has multiple and overlapping sources. These models are expressed by the increasingly ambitious acronyms DIME (Diplomatic, Informational, Military, and Economic power); DIMEFIL (Diplomatic, Information, Military, Economic, Financial, Intelligence, and Law Enforcement); and MIDLIFE (Military, Intelligence, Diplomacy, Legal, Information, Financial, and Economic power). [21]

The nuances of any one of these models and the degree of appropriateness of this or that particular term being attached to the power equation are less important than what the models share in common. That includes the conclusion that in the globalized world of the 21st century, conventional military power has indeed lost at least some of its salience as the *ultima ratio* of statecraft. Global interdependence and the democratic peace dynamic have arguably made conventional armed conflict between great powers less likely.[22] Nuclear weapons have made all out war between nuclear armed states virtually unthinkable. International Law places formal constraints on the institution of war that can and do impact on states' prerogative to opt for a resort to force.[23] Economic competition, on the other hand, has become more important as a driver of international competition. Analysts like Edward Luttwak have coined the notion of "geo-economics" to characterize a world order where competition between nations will be based more on economic rivalry than an older vision of geopolitics built on contention by force.[24] Power has become more diffused and a more diverse palette of instruments of power is required to pursue national interests effectively.

THE FOUNDATIONS OF NATIONAL POWER

National power is constituted on a number of distinct levels: (1) physical resources and attributes (latent power); (2) the effectiveness of national institutions in mobilizing, sustaining, and applying the instruments of power (applied power); and (3) the structural context (facilitators or constraints on the application of power derived from the international environment). The ultimate measure of effective national power should be outcomes or performance. Measuring outcomes, however, depends on the strategic setting—the ends toward which national power is being directed, or "power over whom, and with respect to what?"[25]

Latent Power.

The physical attributes of national power include human resources (population), agricultural potential and the endowment of strategic resources, productive capacity, and geostrategic characteristics.

From the military revolution of the early modern centuries to the present, powerful states have required a population base sufficient to raise and sustain strategically competitive mass armies. Large populations also contribute to greater productive power and a larger gross domestic product (GDP), a basic measure of economic strength. Indeed it is virtually impossible to imagine a state rising into the ranks of the great world powers without a significant population base. The U.S. ability to attract and assimilate large immigrant populations, and to sustain demographic growth, has been a meaningful source of national power. Demographic decline in the European Union (EU) and Russian Federation threaten their capacity to function as great powers in the long term. But large impoverished populations can also place constraints on development and the mobilization of strategic power. Contemporary China presents the example of a rising power that is committed to what some consider a draconian policy of limiting population growth. Size matters, but there is no direct correlation between the size of a country's population and its underlying national strength.

Agricultural potential and the endowment of strategic raw materials can also be critical facilitators of national power. All things being equal, nations with the capacity to feed themselves have a strategic advantage over competitors who are dependent on imports. Historically, its great agricultural potential has been a significant source of U.S. strength. Strategic raw materials can also provide a foundation for economic and military power. Oil rich states such as Saudi Arabia carry weight beyond their inherent capacity specifically because of the degree to which they control access to a vital strategic resource. The dramatic revival of the Russian Federation over the past decade, driven by a ten fold increase in the price of oil and natural gas on world markets between 1998 and 2008, is a clear example of how a raw material endowment can be translated into strategic power. Conversely, dependence on foreign sources of supply for vital resources can place states at a competitive disadvantage unless compensated for by special diplomatic or commercial arrangements. Like other potential pillars of national power, however, control of vital raw materials does not translate directly into strategic leverage. A raw material endowment can also be squandered due to lack of technological expertise, corruption and disreputable political direction, or insufficient social discipline—the modern world offers many examples. The nature of strategic resources also changes over time in tandem with technological development. Salt and ship timbers were once considered to be strategic raw materials on a par with hydrocarbon reserves today. In the near future environmental pressures may make access to fresh water resources a vital national interest as well—with considerable implications for the global balance of power.

Industrial capacity was once considered to be the bed rock of national power. It was the foundation of Britain's preeminence as a European great power and global empire all through the 19th century. The stage was set for the First World War by the power transition implicit in the relative decline of France as an industrial power and the rise of Germany as the continent's leading center of industrial production. The U.S. assumed the mantle of leadership in the productive sector at the same time that it was supplanting the United Kingdom as the leading world power, and its stature as the "arsenal of democracy" was a key to victory in the 20th century's most destructive industrial war.[26] In the wake of the Second World War the idea of European unification came to life as the European Coal and Steel Community in an effort to promote functional cooperation in key productive sectors as a basis for a lasting peace. Today, however, development has become associated with the rise of post-industrial economies based on the service sector where informational assets have become more important than productive power. The extent to which the nature of power itself remains contested is revealed by continuing controversy over whether this trend is salutary and should be encouraged. There is no lack of voices to argue that in allowing its industrial capacity to degrade, the United States is sacrificing a vital pillar of national power, and to call for a state directed "industrial policy" to revive domestic production.[27]

A state's geostrategic situation can also either facilitate or retard its ability to mobilize national power. Access to the world's oceans, serviceable harbors, and control over maritime choke points and strategic lines of communication are essential to maritime capacity. Even in the space age, the U.S. continues to derive benefit from the extent to which it is shielded from strategic threats by the great oceans that flank it east and west, and the absence of predatory neighbors in North America. Russia's strategic situation in the heartland of the Eurasian land mass has always been a source of national strength, but the lack of naturally defensible frontiers has also left it exposed to a series of catastrophic invasions. Strategic exposure can also contribute to state power by reinforcing national will and the commitment to survive—the case of Israel is an excellent illustration. Cultural geography also matters. Ethnic, linguistic, and confessional diversity can be culturally enriching, but also create strategic vulnerabilities. The relative homogeneity of American culture, extended over a vast continental expanse, is commonly and correctly cited as an important source of unity and national strength (which some see as endangered by uncontrolled immigration and increasing cultural diversity). China's powerful and integral cultural legacy, combined with overwhelming Han dominance on the Chinese mainland, is also a facilitator of national power. On the other hand, the Soviet federation fractured along ethnic fault lines and collapsed despite its immense military potential. Europe's rich linguistic and cultural diversity places barriers in the way of efforts to create a more united Europe capable of functioning as a strategic actor in world affairs under the aegis of the EU.

Applied Power.

Resources are the raw material of national power. They must be translated into applied power to be relevant to the pursuit of national goals. The degree of efficiency that states bring to the task of converting latent power into applied power is determined by political, social, and organizational interactions. The stability and effectiveness of governing institutions, economic performance, aptitude for innovation, educational standards, social structure, organizational proficiency, and reputation are more difficult to quantify than the resource endowment, but arguably no less important as foundations for national policy.

Military strength is the classic foundation of national power. It can be quantified rather handily using national defense budgets and militarily related expenditures as a comparative measure. Currently the U.S. defense budget represents 46 percent of global military spending—larger than the next 168 countries combined and approximately ten times greater than the nearest competitors (China, Japan, Russia, France, and the United Kingdom, each with between 4 and 5 percent of the global total).[28] At 3.7 percent of GDP the U.S. budget represents a lesser military burden than that borne by some other states (in Saudi Arabia, for example, defense spending represents over 10 percent of GDP), but globally the U.S. quantitative advantage is overwhelming.[29]

Unfortunately, bean-counting has never been a reliable measure of real military capacity. From the campaigns of Alexander the Great to the present, history provides many examples of smaller but more highly motivated, effectively led, and technically proficient armed forces defeating larger rivals. Militaries are social institutions whose performance rests upon a number of criteria outside the control of the uniformed services, including societal levels of educational achievement and standards of physical conditioning, technological capacity, social disciple and motivation, and strategic leadership. Effectiveness will also be a function of the kinds of tasks that military organizations are called on to perform. Traditionally, the U.S. armed forces have been configured to engage in conventional and nuclear warfare with major peer competitors. At present and for the foreseeable future the need to counter various kinds of asymmetric threats will arguably require a very different configuration of forces and new approaches to strategic competition. High levels of military spending that exceed the capacity of the national economy can undermine national power in the long run—the fate of the Soviet Union, armed to the teeth but collapsed of its own weight without a shot fired in anger, is a salutary example.

Globalization, understood as a process of enhanced international interdependence and space/time compression driven by technological change, has changed the nature of economic power. GDP and GDP per capita remain valid measures of overall economic strength. The World Bank's categorization of low, middle, and high income countries (representing 60 percent, 25 percent, and 15 percent of the world population respectively) provides a fair global index of relative economic power.[30] The U.S. continues to lead the global economy in terms of overall GDP and remains the world's largest national market and most powerful national economy. But raw numbers can also obscure important variables. Is economic performance based on extractive industry, declining manufacturing sectors, or advanced, technologically driven sectors? Are growth models sustainable in the face of resource, environmental, and competitive constraints? Is growth balanced and equitable? In fact the pressures of globalization seem to have provoked an increase in inequality even in the best performing national economies, a trend with unsettling political implications—societal and class division can undermine national purpose and reduce a state's capacity to leverage national power.[31] In the new world economy the familiar distinction between domestic and global markets has been obscured if not obliterated. Economic volatility has increased and the challenge of leadership has become more acute. Market power will be built on different kinds of assets than in the past—efficiency and productivity, educational attainment and the quality of human capital, the ability to adapt, technological creativity, environmental sensitivity, and social stability among them.[32] Education is critical, and the purposeful developmental of the tertiary educational sector has become a conscious strategy for some emerging states. China now produces more than twice as many university graduates as the U.S., which was for many years the world leader. The nineteen countries associated with UNESCO's World Educational Indicators Project (Argentina, Brazil, Chile, China, Egypt, India, Indonesia, Jamaica, Jordan, Malaysia. Paraguay, Peru, Philippines, Russian Federation, Sri Lanka, Thailand, Tunisia, Uruguay, and Zimbabwe) graduate more students from university than the 30 Organization for Economic Co-operation and Development (OECD) countries combined, and devote 53 percent of GDP to support tertiary education compared to 40 percent in the OECD.[33] Such trends could culminate in significant shifts in the global balance of power. In the future, qualitative factors may have as much or more to say about overall economic performance than many traditional quantitative indicators.

The strength of governing institutions and effectiveness of the policy process can also enhance or inhibit the application of national power. Different kinds of governments can accomplish these tasks in various ways. Authoritarian regimes usually lack popular legitimacy, but can be adept at imposing coherent national strategies and pursuing them consistently over time. But authoritarian leaders can also become isolated by in-groups of sycophantic courtiers and denied the kind of realistic appraisals that are required for intelligent strategic choices — as seems to have been the case, for example, with Iraq's Saddam Hussein. Democratic polities must construct policy by consensus building and persuasion, and vet it through a complex decision making process, with a certain degree of incoherence an almost inevitable result. It is usually more difficult for democratic states to build and sustain a national consensus on strategic options and to shift course rapidly in the face of changed international circumstances. Nonetheless, a state with respected and legitimate institutions grounded in popular consensus, and capable of mobilizing its population to accept sacrifices in the face of real threats to national well being, will be inherently stronger, often in subtle ways, than an authoritarian polity imposed and sustained by force.

The policy process itself can become an independent variable. Improved strategic education and professional development for civil servants working in the national security sector, better coordination between government agencies, and more adept management can arguably lead toward more effective strategic choices. Coordinating the varied instruments of national power, including diplomatic, intelligence, informational, and legal tools, demands professional insight and an efficient decision-making environment within which ideas can be exchanged freely and alternative courses of action considered on their merits.

The ability to apply power effectively also depends on social cohesion and the degree to which a country is regarded as an honorable and trustworthy member of the community of nations. National values, political stability, an active and engaged citizenry and dynamic civil society, and international reputation can all be meaningful sources of national power. If states are convinced that the ideals and priorities of a potential rival are sincere and worthy of respect, they are more likely to opt for policies of accommodation that acknowledge mutual interests. This is the case along a continuum stretching from bilateral relations to systemic competition. Hegemonic powers cannot sustain their position on the basis of coercive strategies alone — they must construct a framework of authority and system of values to which subordinate states accord voluntary acquiescence — the "power over" accorded by non-material sources of national power. Dysfunctional or rogue states that fail to cultivate this kind of cohesion or flout the normative context within which interstate relations are conducted will inevitably pay a price.

In the classic statement of the philosophy that might makes right, Thucydides' Athenians tell their Melian interlocutors that "right, as the world goes, is only in question between equals in power, while the strong do what they can and the weak suffer what they must."[34] Moses Finley remarks that "nothing so marks Thucydides' work as the sense of living in a world where moral sensitiveness and the inherited tradition were ... a luxury, and that the very survival of states hung on the skillful use of power and power alone."[35] And yet the Athenian polity that Thucydides so admires was ultimately destroyed by a war in the course of which it gradually abandoned the values and progressive spirit that originally made it great. The Pope may have no divisions (to paraphrase Joseph Stalin), but moral force and reputation are critical enablers of national power that states ignore at their peril. Faith and morale, remarks Niall Ferguson, are "perhaps as important a component of power as material resources."[36]

International Context.

National power is contextual and relational in the sense that it can only be measured in the context of a particular pattern of interstate relations and against the capacities of other national and nonstate actors. The constantly evolving nature of threats to national well-being must also be taken into account. These are dynamic variables—the power equation in international relations is never stable and the substance of national power is constantly changing. What are the most salient characteristics of the current international system, and the most significant trends working to transform it? How is systemic transformation affecting the structure of threats against which states are required to maneuver? These kinds of dynamic factors, embedded in the mechanisms of international society, will affect the ways in which national power is configured, conceptualized, and realized.

Globalization pushes toward the diminution of de facto state sovereignty. The diffusion of technology has made the effort to maintain an effective nonproliferation regime appear increasingly quixotic. As access to weapons of mass destruction becomes more widespread, including potentially to terrorist and extremist organizations, even the most comprehensively armed states will find themselves increasingly exposed. The phenomenon of global migration has strained the ability of states to maintain physical control over their borders, once considered the most basic attribute of sovereignty. The revolution in information technology has shattered the state's monopoly over certain kinds of information, and created new and powerful channels of communication across borders. It has also enabled the global market, which can now react to economic stimuli with a speed and flexibility that states cannot rival or control. A variety of nonstate actors (multinational corporations, nongovernmental organizations [NGO] such as Amnesty International or Oxfam International, multilateral forums such as the International Monetary Fund [IMF], the North Atlantic Treaty Organization [NATO], or the Shanghai Cooperation Organization [SCO], regional economic associations such as the EU or Association of Southeast Asian Nations [ASEAN]) now rival states in an effort to "set the agenda" and impose priorities in world politics. Some argue that the most critical challenges confronting the international community—the proliferation of weapons of mass destruction and effects; environmental disintegration; impoverishment and economic marginalization; the threat of pandemic disease; trans-boundary crime including drug and human trafficking; terrorism, low intensity conflict sometimes extending to the level of genocidal violence produced by dysfunctional regional orders and failing states; traditional, mass casualty, and cyber terrorism—can no longer be confronted by nation states acting in isolation. Global threats that transcend the capacity of individual states, no matter how powerful, have become more important.[37] What is needed, champions of a pluralist image of international relations will argue, is more effective instruments of global governance that look beyond the anarchic and archaic character of the Westphalian state system.[38]

The case for the decline of the state can easily be overstated. States are no doubt more subject to transnational forces than they were in the past, but they remain the building blocks of international society and by far the most significant repositories of the kind of power resources that will have to be mobilized to confront new global challenges. States are the only effective guarantors of popular empowerment and basic social security, and there is no one to replace them. International cooperation is still overwhelmingly generated on the interstate level, whether bilaterally, in the legal and normative framework of international regimes, or in international organizations. Nor have traditional threats to national well being altogether disappeared. The United States, as the world's predominant power, confronts the emergence of potential new peer competitors in the EU and the rising economic challengers of the so-called BRIC group (Brazil, Russia, India, and China).

Regional security complexes are still preoccupied by competitive interaction between states and the very traditional threat of armed aggression. The effort to increase national power, and the security dilemmas to which that effort gives rise, remains a driver of international political competition. But the dynamic of enhanced sensitivity and vulnerability born of globalization cannot be ignored, and the way that we understand national power must be adjusted to take it into account.

THE CHANGING NATURE OF POWER

How does globalization impact on the configuration of national power? On the international level, power has become more diffused, and states are no longer its unique proprietor. The leverage available to various kinds of nonstate actors and their ability to shape and affect the power of states has become more significant. In discrete areas such as human rights and international humanitarian law, environmental policy, and humanitarian assistance, NGOs have been successful in imposing frameworks for international action that on some level states are obliged to respect. The Ottawa Treaty and Kyoto Protocol are only two examples. The diffusion of information through the world wide net and a proliferation of "virtual networks" tying people together across borders in what some have called a nascent "international civil society" have eroded states' capacity to dominate the dissemination of ideas and sustain control through compliance.

The nature of national security, the fundamental challenge of traditional statecraft, is also changing. The physical attributes of national power, including territory, population, and resources, remain salient. But in an age of increased international interconnectedness and interdependence the Westphalian premise of territoriality has lost some of its force—control over terrain is no longer the kind of driver in international political competition that it once was. Even the largest and inherently most powerful states confront new and unfamiliar kinds of vulnerabilities for which the traditional instruments of national security policy are not always well-suited.

Conventional military power has lost at least some of its centrality. Traditional conceptions of the role of military power emphasize the forceful defense of borders and the containment of threats to national integrity posed by "Napoleonic neighbors" and armed adversaries. But traditional military priorities are less well adapted to confront the new threat structure emerging in an age of sacred terror and new kinds of existential concerns. The security problem has become more complex and multidimensional. In his seminal *People, States, and War*, first published in 1983, Barry Buzan spoke of military, political, economic, societal, and ecological security as diverse facets of a broader security equation.[39] The so-called Copenhagen School has explored the "securitization" of non-military challenges, with particular emphasis on societal security and identity issues.[40] Other analysts argue for a deepening of the security agenda in a Kantian sense, with the referent for security displaced from the sovereign state to the autonomous human subject. In its 1994 *Human Development Report* the United Nations Development Programme introduced the concept of *human security* manifested in seven issue areas (economic, food, health, environmental, personal, community, and political) and six threats (unchecked population growth, disparities in economic opportunity, migration pressures, environmental degradation, drug trafficking, and international terrorism).[41] Such arguments take us some distance away from the traditional priorities of defense policy, but they point to emerging vulnerabilities that may become increasingly relevant to the calculus of national power under 21st century conditions.

It is still possible to draw up an approximate index of national power using quantitative measures such as population, territory, resource base, GDP, defense spending, average educational attainment, per capita expenditure on research and development, and the like. A recent study sponsored by the National Security Research Division of the RAND Corporation uses a basket of such metrics to calculate that the U.S. holds about 20 percent of total global power, compared to 14 percent each for the EU and China, and 9 percent for India.[42] This is an interesting exercise that may have some relevance as a rough measure of overall capacity. It does not effectively address what is ultimately the most basic issue of shaping outcomes by translating latent power into applied power and using it judiciously to promote national interests. This remains the domain of strategy and the art of statecraft, where the instruments of national power must be applied in a dynamic and uncertain international environment and in a context of mutual vulnerabilities that demands careful calculation, prudence, and a healthy dose of strategic restraint.

ENDNOTES - CHAPTER 11

1. For the notion of "essentially contested concepts," which "inevitably involve endless disputes about their proper uses," see W. B. Gallie, "Essentially Contested Concepts," *Proceedings of the Aristotelian Society,* Vol. 56, 1955-56, pp. 167-198.

2. R. A. Dahl, "The Concept of Power," *Behavioral Science,* No. 2, 1957, pp. 201-215.

3. P. Bachrach and M. S. Baratz, *Power and Poverty: Theory and Practice,* Oxford: Oxford University Press, 1970.

4. These categories correspond to the "two dimensions" of power defined in the seminal work of Steven Lukes, *Power: A Radical View,* Houndsmills, Basingstoke: Palgrave Macmillan, 2005, pp. 14-29. Lukes goes on to elaborate a "three dimensional" image of power built on the Gramscian notion of hegemony.

5. Hannah Arendt, *On Violence*, New York: Allen Lane, 1970, p. 41.

6. Thomas Hobbes, *Leviathan*, Harmondsworth: Penguin Books, 1968, p. 161.

7. Kenneth Waltz, *Man, the State and War*, New York: Columbia University Press, 1959, p. 238.

8. Hans J. Morgenthau, *Politics among Nations: The Struggle for Power and Peace,* 5th ed., New York: Alfred A. Knopf, 1978, p. 38.

9. See Ian Clark, *Reform and Resistance in the International Order,* Cambridge: Cambridge University Press, 1980, pp. 55-77.

10. Morgenthau, *Politics among Nations*, pp. 5-6.

11. Donald Kagan, *On the Origins of War and the Preservation of Peace,* New York: Doubleday, 1995, p. 7.

12. Morgenthau, *Politics among Nations*, p. 30.

13. Edward Vose Gullick, *Europe's Classical Balance of Power: A Case History of the Theory and Practice of one of the Great Concepts of European Statecraft,* Westport, CT: Greenwood Press, 1982, p. 39.

14. Immanuel Wallerstein, *The Modern World System II: Mercantilism and the Consolidation of the European World Economy, 1600-1750,* New York: Academic Press, 1980, pp. 113-114.

15. Paul W. Schroeder, *The Transformation of European Politics, 1763-1848,* Oxford: Clarendon Press, 1994, p. 6.

16. Raymond Aron, *Peace and War: A Theory of International Relations,* New York: Doubleday & Company, Inc., 1966, pp. 591-600.

17. Robert O. Keohane and Joseph S. Nye, *Power and Interdependence: World Politics in Transition,* Boston: Little, Brown and Company, 1977, p. 27.

18. Joseph S. Nye, Jr., *Soft Power: The Means to Success in World Politics,* New York: Public Affairs, 2004.

19. Alvin Toffler, *Powershift: Knowledge, Wealth, and Violence at the Edge of the 21st Century,* New York: Bantam Books, 1990.

20. Susan Strange, *States and Markets,* 2nd ed., London: Pinter Publishers, 1994.

21. For these designations see The White House, *National Strategy for Combating Terrorism,* Washington, DC: U.S. Government Printing Office, September 2006; Chairman of the Joint Chiefs of Staff, *National Military Strategic Plan for the War on Terrorism,* Washington, DC: The Pentagon, February 1, 2006; and Homeland Security Council, *National Strategy for Homeland Security,* Washington, DC: U.S. Government Printing Office, October 2007.

22. John M. Owen, "Give Democratic Peace a Chance: How Liberalism Produces Democratic Peace," *International Security,* Vol. 19, No. 2, Autumn 1994, pp. 87-125.

23. Ingrid Detter, *The Law of War,* 2nd ed., Cambridge: Cambridge University Press, 2000, pp. 62-81.

24. Edward Luttwak, *The Endangered American Dream: How to Stop the United States from Becoming a Third World Country,* New York: Simon & Schuster, 1993.

25. David Jablonsky, "National Power," in J. Boone Bartholomees, ed., *U.S. Army War College Guide to National Security Policy and Strategy,* 2nd ed., Carlisle Barracks, PA: U.S. Army War College, June 2006, p. 127.

26. R. J. Overy, *Why the Allies Won,* New York: W. W. Norton. 1996.

27. Dani Rodrik, John F. Kennedy School of Government, Harvard University, "Industrial Policies for the 21st Century," September 2004, accessed at *ksghome.harvard.edu/~drodrik/UNIDOSep.pdf.*

28. Statistics from Chapter Eight, "Military Expenditures," *SIPRI Yearbook 2007: Armaments, Disarmament, and International Security*, Stockholm: Stockholm International Peace Research Institute, 2007.

29. *Ibid.*

30. *World Development Indicators, 2007*, Washington, DC: The World Bank, 2007.

31. *World Economic Outlook: Globalization and Inequality*, Washington, DC: International Monetary Fund, October 2007.

32. Thomas L. Friedman, *The World is Flat: A Short History of the 21st Century,* New York: Farrar, Straus and Giroux, 2005.

33. UNESCO Global Education Digest 2007, accessed at *www.uis.unesco.org/ev.*

34. Cited from Richard B. Strassler, ed., *The Landmark Thucydides: A Comprehensive Guide to the Peloponnesian War,* New York: The Free Press, 1996, Vol. 5, p. 89.

35. Moses I. Finley, *The World of Odysseus,* New York: The Viking Press, 1965, p. 29.

36. Niall Ferguson, "What Is Power?" *Hoover Digest,* No. 2, 2003.

37. See, for example, Joseph S. Nye, *The Paradox of American Power: Why the World's Only Superpower Can't Go It Alone,* Oxford: Oxford University Press, 2002.

38. James P. Muldoon, Jr., *The Architecture of Global Governance: An Introduction to the Study of International Organizations,* Boulder: Westview Press, 2004.

39. Barry Buzan, *People, States, and Fear: The National Security Problem in International Relations,* Chapel Hill: University of North Carolina Press, 1983.

40. Ole Wæver, "Securitization and Desecuritization," in Ronnie Lipschutz, ed., *On Security,* New York: Columbia University Press, 1995, pp. 45-86.

41. United Nations Development Programme, *Human Development Report 1994,* Oxford: Oxford University Press, 1994. See also the subsequent Commission on Human Security, *Human Security Now,* New York: United Nations, 2003.

42. Gregory F. Treverton and Seth G. Jones, *Measuring National Power,* Santa Monica, CA: RAND, 2005. The study sees the relative U.S. power position in decline, and demotes the United States from "hegemonic" status in the first post-Cold War decade to the status of "preponderant" power in the first decade of the 21st century.

CHAPTER 12

STRATEGIC COMMUNICATION:
WIELDING THE INFORMATION ELEMENT OF POWER

Dennis M. Murphy

It is generally accepted in the United States government today that information is an element of national power along with diplomatic, military and economic power and that information is woven through the other elements since their activities will have an informational impact.[1] Interestingly, however, one needs to go back to the Reagan administration to find the most succinct and pointed mention of information as an element of power in formal government documents.[2] Subsequent national security documents allude to different aspects of information but without a specific strategy or definition. Given this dearth of official documentation, Drs. Dan Kuehl and Bob Nielson proffered the following definition of the information element: "Use of information content and technology as strategic instruments to shape fundamental political, economic, military and cultural forces on a long-term basis to affect the global behavior of governments, supra-governmental organizations, and societies to support national security."[3] Information as power is wielded in an increasingly complex environment consisting of physical, information, and cognitive dimensions. This chapter will focus on strategic communication and how the U.S. Government wields power in the cognitive dimension of the information environment. Specifically it will consider how information is used to engage, inform, educate, persuade and influence perceptions and attitudes of target audiences in order to ultimately change behavior.

Before addressing strategic communication as a U.S. Government process, it is important to consider the complex environment in which that process occurs. Consequently, the information environment is initially covered in some detail, including a description of "new media" capabilities and their impact. Information as power is both colored and informed in the psyche of Americans through the historical lens of "propaganda," and so it is also addressed in this section. With this foundational knowledge established, strategic communication is then considered from historical and current perspectives. Finally, recognizing both challenges and opportunities, a way-ahead is offered for future U.S. Government efforts to effectively wield information as power.

THE CHALLENGES OF TODAY'S INFORMATION ENVIRONMENT

The current information environment has leveled the playing field for not only nation states, but nonstate actors, multinational corporations and even individuals to affect strategic outcomes with minimal information infrastructure and little capital expenditure. Anyone with a camera cell phone and personal digital device with internet capability understands this. On the other hand, the U.S. military has increasingly leveraged advances in information infrastructure and technology to gain advantages on the modern battlefield. One example from Operation IRAQI FREEDOM is the significant increase in situational awareness from network centric operations that enabled coalition forces to swiftly defeat Iraqi forces in major combat operations.[4] Another includes the more prevalent use of visual information to record operations in order to proactively tell an accurate story or effectively refute enemy "dis-information."

Even a cursory look at advances in technology confirms what most people recognize as a result of their daily routine. The ability to access, collect, and transmit information is clearly decentralized to the lowest level (the individual). The technology is increasingly smaller, faster, and cheaper.

Consequently, the ability to control and verify information is much more limited than in the recent past. Nor will it get any easier.

> In 1965, the physical chemist Gordon Moore, co-founder of Intel, predicted that the number of transistors on an integrated chip would double every 18 months. Moore predicted that this trend would continue for the foreseeable future. Moore and most other experts expect Moore's Law to remain valid for at least another two decades.[5]

So, if you're into control (as nationstates, bureaucracies and the military tend to be) the future may appear bleak since not only is the ability to access, collect and transmit information decentralized, the capacity to do the same continues to increase exponentially. These challenges are readily apparent in the examination of many current information capabilities collectively referred to as "new media."

The Internet.

The internet is the obvious start point for any discussion of the impact of today's new media. It is important to note that the World Wide Web is essentially ungoverned, providing obvious freedoms and cautions. The web gives the individual a voice, often an anonymous voice . . . and a potentially vast audience. Websites are easily established, dismantled, and reestablished, making them valuable to extremist movements. Islamic extremist websites have grown from 20 to over 4,000 in only 5 years.[6]

Web logs (blogs) are another example of the power that the internet provides to individuals along with the dilemma they pose for nationstates. There were 35.3 million blogs as of April 2006 reflecting a doubling of size every 6 months of the previous 3 years.[7] Most of these, of course, have little effect on the conduct of nationstates or their militaries, but those that gain a following in the national security arena, can have a huge impact. President George W. Bush recently cited Iraqi bloggers to point to progress being made in Iraq,[8] having apparently learned both the importance and value of blogs in 2004 when investigative bloggers cleared his name in the infamous CBS airing that questioned his military service.[9] The U.S. Central Command actively engages dissident voices by participating in blogs that are critical of the war on terror noting "with the proliferation of information today, if you're not speaking to this forum, you're not being heard by it."[10]

Video use and dissemination has skyrocketed as the capabilities of the Internet have increased. The YouTube phenomenon's power and access is evidenced by its purchase for $1.6 Billion by Google only 20 months after its founding. Like blogs, YouTube serves a variety of purposes to include entertainment. But, also like blogs, YouTube can empower individuals to achieve strategic political and military effects where easy upload of their videos (without editorial oversight) allows access to a nearly unlimited audience. Thus, the use of the improvised explosive device (IED) by insurgents shifts from a military tactical weapon to a strategic information weapon when the IED detonator is accompanied by a videographer. And, again like blogs, the U.S. military has recognized the importance of competing in the video medium, using YouTube to show ongoing images of U.S. operations in Iraq.[11]

While websites, bloggers and video proliferate in today's internet ("web 2.0") the "over the horizon" technology of "web 3.0" while in its infancy, is rapidly increasing in popularity." Web 3.0 is generally about being inside a 3D virtual world that is low-cost and emotive. This is the "metaverse" or virtual universe of applications like Second Life and others. Second Life is attractive as an opportunity to socialize where there is no need to compete and can be exploited as a tool for learning. Multinational corporations see a movement where they will plan and execute business plans in the 3D internet world.[12] But, like the other internet based applications, web 3.0 provides opportunities for darker undertakings. The virtual universes show initial signs of providing training grounds for terrorist organizations and anonymous locations for criminal money-laundering.[13]

Mobile Technologies.

The internet clearly is part of the new media phenomenon, but the internet has not penetrated large areas of the world, especially in the poorest areas of underdeveloped countries. The cell phone, however, as a means of mobile technology, is increasingly available worldwide and deserves discussion as a potentially potent capability to affect national security and military issues; arguably even more so than the internet.

There are numerous examples of cell phone Short Message Service (SMS text) messaging shaping political campaigns by mobilizing and revolutionizing politics. It is used both to call people to popular protests as well as used by governments to provide misinformation in order to quell such protests. Text messaging is the medium of choice in overseas countries. It bypasses mass media and mobilizes an already persuaded populace as a means of lightweight engagement. Cell phones currently contain the technology to text, provide news, video, sound, voice, radio, and internet. Mobile is pervasive in the third world. Ninety-seven percent of Tanzanians have access to mobile phones. Mobile coverage exists throughout Uganda. There are 100 million handsets in sub-Saharan Africa. Radio is the only media device more prevalent than mobile.[14]

Like any other new media capability cell phone technology provides opportunities and challenges. Many young Iranians are turning to cell phones as a means for political protest . . . an opportunity that can be exploited.[15] On the other hand, criminals and terrorists can use cell phones to quickly organize an operation, execute it and disperse using phone cards to provide cover from being traced. On an international scale, the challenge is often in the same laws that provide individual protections in democratic societies. Witness recent court battles in the United States regarding eavesdropping on foreign conversations without a court order when those conversations may be routed through a U.S. cell phone service provider.[16]

Mainstream Media in the Age of New Media.

Mainstream media certainly takes advantage of technological advances in order to remain competitive. Marvin Kalb, in the Harvard report on the Israeli-Hezbollah War notes that:

> To do their jobs, journalists employed both the camera and the computer, and, with the help of portable satellite dishes and video phones "streamed" or broadcast their reports . . . , as they covered the movement of troops and the rocketing of villages—often, (unintentionally, one assumes) revealing sensitive information to the enemy. Once upon a time, such information was the stuff of military intelligence acquired with considerable effort and risk; now it has become the stuff of everyday journalism. The camera and the computer have become weapons of war.[17]

This real time reporting from the field has obvious impacts on the warfighter, but competition with new media for the first and fastest story also means that today's mainstream media is not your father's mainstream media. Because of the plethora of information available today, newspapers, which once competed for knowledge as a scarce resource, today compete for a new scarce resource: the readers' (or listeners' in the case of broadcast media) attention.[18] Perhaps that is why increasing numbers of young adults turn to Jon Stewart's "The Daily Show" for their news.[19] It should come as no great shock, then, that "good news" stories about military operations do not appear with regularity in mainstream print and broadcast journalism.[20] Good news doesn't sell . . . because it doesn't grab the reader's (or viewer's) attention.

Of course in an environment where the speed of breaking news means viewership and thus advertising dollars, accuracy is sometimes sacrificed as well. In a strange twist, mainstream media now turns increasingly to bloggers for their stories, and the most respected bloggers require multiple sources to verify accuracy.[21] Consequently, the distinction between new and mainstream media sources becomes blurred, leaving it to the reader, already bombarded with information, to distinguish fact from fiction (or perhaps more accurately "spin" from context).

Propaganda and American Attitudes toward Information as Power.

Propaganda is "any form of communication in support of national objectives designed to influence the opinions, emotions, attitudes, or behavior of any group in order to benefit the sponsor, either directly or indirectly."[22] Certainly propaganda has been used from time immemorial as a tool in warfare. But it is only since the U.S. experience of World War I that this rather innocuously defined term has become pejorative in our national psyche. That historical context included not only the obvious abhorrence of Hitler's propaganda machine, but also an introspective reflection of the way the United States used information as power in both World Wars. The resulting perspective may likely be the reason that information as an element of power remained mostly absent from recent official government strategy documents until the May, 2007 publication of a *National Strategy for Public Diplomacy and Strategic Communication*, well over 6 years after September 9, 2001 (9/11). That's not to say the U.S. Government does not recognize the value and importance of information to wield power—but it appears that term "propaganda" keeps getting in the way.[23]

In 2005, the Lincoln Group, a government contractor, paid Iraqi newspapers to print unattributed pro-U.S. stories in an effort to win the war of ideas and counter negative images of the U.S.-led coalition. Their actions were immediately and loudly condemned as "propaganda" by the mainstream U.S. press, members of Congress, and other government leaders, and so contrary to the democratic ideals of a free press.[24] The subsequent Pentagon investigation, however, found that no laws were broken or policies ignored. But even prior to this the Department of Defense (DoD) showed both its need to use information as power and its squeamishness toward accusations of propaganda use. The Pentagon established the Office of Strategic Influence (OSI) within weeks of 9/11. Its stated purpose was simple: to flood targeted areas with information. It didn't take long for the mainstream media to pick up on the office and posit that "disinformation" was being planted abroad and would leak back to the U.S. public. These claims of propaganda were all it took to doom OSI, which was shut down soon thereafter, even though subsequent investigations proved that information they provided was, in all cases, truthful.[25]

This conundrum, where the United States must fight using propaganda but faces internal criticism and backlash whenever it does, produces an information environment that favors an adversary bent on exploiting it with his own strategic propaganda. Propaganda is the weapon of the insurgent franchised cell. In a broad sense, terrorist organizations have learned the lessons of propaganda well. Hezbollah integrated an aggressive strategic propaganda effort into all phases of its recent conflict with Israel. "Made in the USA" signs sprung up on Lebanese rubble immediately after the war, courtesy of an advertising firm hired by the insurgents. There was no doubt who the intended audience was since the banners were in English only.[26]

It is in this challenging environment of both new media capabilities and a cautionary American attitude toward propaganda, that the United States finds itself attempting to compete and win. Given these challenges it may become increasingly difficult to gain and maintain information superiority or even information dominance; however, the U.S. Government should be expected to manage that environment effectively. It does that through the use of strategic communication.

STRATEGIC COMMUNICATION: AN OVERVIEW

The executive branch of the U.S. Government has the responsibility to develop and sustain an information strategy that ensures themes and messages are promulgated consistent with policy. This strategy should guide and direct activities across the information environment. Strategic Communication can be described as the proactive and continuous process that supports the national security strategy by identifying and responding to strategic threats and opportunities with information related activities. It is "focused United States Government processes and efforts to understand and engage key audiences in order to create, strengthen, or preserve conditions favorable to advance national interests and objectives through the use of coordinated information, themes, plans, programs, and actions synchronized with other elements of national power" whose primary supporting capabilities are Public Affairs; military Information Operations; and Public Diplomacy.[27]

Public Affairs within the DoD is defined as "those public information, command information, and community relations activities directed toward both the external and internal publics with interest in the Department. . . ."[28] The definition of Public Affairs in the State Department more broadly discusses providing information on the goals, policies and activities of the U.S. Government. While State sees a role for public affairs with both domestic and international audiences, the thrust of its effort is to inform the domestic audience.[29]

Information Operations (IO) are "the integrated employment of electronic warfare, computer network operations, psychological operations, military deception, and operations security . . . to influence, disrupt, corrupt or usurp adversarial human and automated decision making while protecting our own."[30] DoD recognizes that the primary IO capability in support of Strategic Communication is psychological operations.[31]

Public diplomacy is primarily practiced by the Department of State (DOS). It is defined as "those overt international public information activities of the U.S. Government designed to promote U.S. foreign policy objectives by seeking to understand, inform, and influence foreign audiences and opinion makers, and by broadening the dialogue between American citizens and institutions and their counterparts abroad."[32]

Some definitions cite international broadcasting services as strategic communication means. Under the supervision of the Broadcasting Board of Governors (BBG), the International Broadcasting Bureau (IBB) provides the administrative and engineering support for U.S. Government-funded, nonmilitary, international broadcast services. Broadcast elements are the Voice of America (VOA) and Radio and TV Martí (Office of Cuba Broadcasting). In addition, the IBB provides engineering and program support to Radio Free Europe/Radio Liberty, Radio Free Asia, the Middle East Broadcasting Networks (Radio Sawa and Alhurra Television), and Radio Farda, a joint Persian-language project between VOA and Radio Free Europe.[33]

Unfortunately, this list limits the perceived means available to *communications* (emphasis intentionally added) based activities and so reinforces the lexicon of the term (strategic "communication")itself. And therein lies a rub with current interpretations of strategic communication by leaders. Considering strategic communication as a menu of self-limiting communications capabilities will significantly limit its impact. Instead, interpretation of the definition itself must serve as the basis of understanding by practitioners who plan and implement it.

Strategists use a model of "ends, ways and means" to describe all aspects of a national or military strategy. Strategy is about how (the way) leaders will use the capabilities (means) available to achieve objectives (ends).[34] Understanding and engaging key audiences is meant to change perceptions, attitudes, and ultimately behaviors to help achieve military (and in turn national) objectives. Thus, parsing the definition it is apparent that strategic communication is a "way" to achieve an information effect on the cognitive dimension of the information environment (the required "end").[35] Strategic communication employs multiple "means," and these means should be restricted only by the requirement to achieve the desired information effect on the target audience.

Messages are certainly sent by verbal and visual communications means, but they are also sent by actions. (Note that the definition specifically includes "actions"). In fact, senior officials point out that strategic communication is "80% actions and 20% words."[36] Specifically, how policies are implemented and supporting military operations are conducted affects the information environment by impacting perceptions and attitudes. Recent examples include use of U.S. Navy hospital ships in regional engagement and Pakistani earthquake relief efforts in permissive environments.[37] But operations in hostile environments like the Iraq and Afghanistan theaters also provide opportunities to positively shape the information environment. This clarification and expanded understanding of the definition is critical in order to fully exploit strategic communication to support U.S. Government policy and military operations. Fully integrated words, images, *and actions* are necessary. Key to success is an organizational culture that values, understands, and thus considers strategic communication means as important capabilities to be integrated within established development and planning processes. Strategic communication must be considered at the beginning of the planning process and not as a reactive crisis response when something goes wrong.

THE HISTORY OF STRATEGIC COMMUNICATION

While "strategic communication" is a fairly new term in the U.S. Government lexicon, the concept, theory, and practice behind it is not. Winfield Scott recognized the importance of strategic communication at the theater level in Veracruz in 1847. Realizing the influence of the Catholic Church on Mexican society, Scott attended Mass with his staff at the Veracruz Cathedral to display the respect of U.S. forces. He further ordered U.S. soldiers to salute Mexican priests in the streets. Each of these measures was "part of a calculated campaign to win the friendship of the Mexicans."[38]

The more recent history of national strategic communication shows concerted efforts to positively portray the U.S. story in order to persuade and influence. The Committee on Public Information (CPI) (1917), also known as the Creel Committee after its chief newspaperman George Creel, sought to rally U.S. public opinion behind World War I on behalf of the Wilson administration. Its focus was the domestic audience and it used public speakers, advertising, pamphlets, periodicals, and the burgeoning American motion picture industry.

CPI's domestic efforts during the war met with high success: draft registration—the first since the tumultuous call-up of the Civil War—occurred peacefully, bond drives were over-subscribed, and the American population was generally behind the war effort. CPI operations in foreign capitals enabled Wilson to relate his war ideals and aims to the world audience. Indeed, Wilson was taken aback by this effective dissemination of his peace aims and the world's reaction to it. He remarked to George Creel in December 1918, "I am wondering whether you have not unconsciously spun a net for me from which there is no escape."[39]

The post-war appraisal of CPI was darker. George Creel compiled his official report on the Committee's activities in June 1919, and soon after authored his public account, *How We Advertised America*, in 1920. But at home and overseas, the reality of the peace lagged behind Wilsonian aspirations. The allies forged a treaty that many Americans and others believed unfair and incomplete. Americans also started to reflect on an ugly side to the war enthusiasm in the United States. Germans and German culture had been vilified. Sauerkraut had become liberty cabbage, hamburger was Salisbury Steak, but more seriously, teaching the German language and subject matter in schools became viewed as disloyal, and authorities banned it in some states. There were incidents of physical attacks and even lynching's of suspected German sympathizers and war dissenters. The attorney general enlisted volunteer "loyalty enforcers" who carried official looking badges and who were encouraged to report those of their neighbors who spoke out against the war.[40]

World War II saw the establishment of The Office of War Information (OWI), which focused both domestically and overseas, with broadcasts sent in German to Nazi Germany. The Voice of America (VOA) began its first broadcast with the statement, "Here speaks a voice from America. Everyday at this time we will bring you the news of the war. The news may be good. The news may be bad. We shall tell you the truth."

There were several significant differences between the OWI and its CPI predecessor of 23 years earlier. Some of these were by design, but others reflected the style of the President. Franklin Delano Roosevelt (FDR) was highly adept at communicating to the public doing so directly over radio via his addresses and "Fire Side Chats." In 1941, 60 million radio receivers reached 90 percent of the population in their homes.[41] Roosevelt was, however, not entirely comfortable with a formal propaganda apparatus, and the leadership of OWI, unlike Creel, did not have direct access to the President. Unlike Wilson, Roosevelt, preferring to be ambiguous regarding policy guidance, provided little political cover for OWI in its skirmishes with the Congress.

Operating in the absence of such policy guidance the OWI staff, particularly in the Foreign Branch, sometimes got out ahead of stated government pronouncements, or it responded with what its members thought American policy should be. Some OWI techniques came under very pointed criticism. The use of pseudonyms by some OWI authors in their articles was denounced by prominent newspapermen, such as Arthur Krock of the *New York Times*. The *New York World Telegram* said the same incident, "smells of dishonesty."[42] President Truman disbanded OWI in 1945.

The Smith-Mundt Act (1948) (formally, "The U.S. Information and Educational Exchange Act [Public Law 402; 80th Congress]"), established a statutory information agency for the first time in a period of peace with a mission to "promote a better understanding of the United States in other countries, and to increase mutual understanding" between Americans and foreigners. The act also forbade the Voice of America to transmit to an American audience (based on the experiences of the World Wars). It is worth noting that Smith-Mundt is often cited today as the basis to limit the use of government information activities since they may result in "propagandizing" the American public. This, of course, is complicated by the inevitable "blowback" or "bleedover" of foreign influence activities based on the global information environment as previously described.[43]

The United States Information Agency (USIA) (1953) was established by President Dwight Eisenhower as authorized by the Smith-Mundt Act. It encompassed all the information programs, including VOA (its largest element), that were previously in the DOS, except for the educational exchange programs, which remained at State. The USIA Director reported to the President through the National Security Council and received complete, day-to-day guidance on U.S. foreign policy from the Secretary of State.

A 1998 State Department reorganization occurred in response to calls by some to reduce the size of the U.S. foreign affairs establishment. (This is considered the State Department's "peace dividend" following the Cold War). The act folded the USIA into the DOS. It pulled the Broadcasting Board of Governors out of USIA and made it a separate organization. The USIA slots were distributed throughout the State Department and its mission was given to the Bureau of International Information Programs.

CURRENT STRATEGIC COMMUNICATION PROCESSES

The demise of USIA is generally regarded (in retrospect) as diluting the U.S. ability to effectively promulgate a national communication strategy, coordinate and integrate strategic themes and messages, and support public diplomacy efforts worldwide.[44] Additionally, organizations and processes have experienced great flux in recent years. The George W. Bush administration retained Presidential Decision Directive (PDD) 68 that was issued in 1999 by the Clinton administration. PDD 68 addressed those problems when no single U.S. agency was empowered to coordinate US efforts to sell its policies and counteract bad press abroad. It directed top officials from the Defense, State, Justice, Commerce and Treasury departments as well as those from the Central Intelligence Agency and FBI to establish an International Public Information (IPI) Core Group chaired by the Under Secretary for Public Diplomacy and Public Affairs at the DOS.[45] It is evident, however that this core group is currently inactive. Other recent initiatives to coordinate and integrate national strategic communication efforts have also faltered. The White House Office of Global Communication was disbanded in 2003. A Strategic Communication Policy Coordinating Committee (PCC) met on several occasions, but then went dormant. A Muslim Outreach Policy Coordinating Committee was more active and in fact, developed a draft national communication strategy that did not make it out of the White House.[46] On the other hand, an Interagency Strategic Communication Fusion Team has remained an active, albeit informal, coordinating body at the action officer level. The team coordinates and deconflicts the production and the dissemination of information products but does not task. Instead, team members reach across office, bureau, and agency boundaries to offer or to seek support for their strategic communication plans and activities.[47]

Despite the failures in the recent past, currently ongoing actions at the national level are encouraging. Ambassador Karen Hughes assumed duties as the Under Secretary of State for Public Diplomacy and Public Affairs in the early fall of 2005 (Note: Ambassador Hughes announced her resignation effective December 2007). The Under Secretary helps ensure that public diplomacy (which she describes as engaging, informing, and influencing key international audiences) is practiced in harmony with public affairs (outreach to Americans) and traditional diplomacy to advance U.S. interests and security and to provide the moral basis for U.S. leadership in the world.[48] Ambassador Hughes had taken positive steps while in her job. She had provided specific guidance to public affairs officers at embassies throughout the world that shortcuts (and eliminates in many cases) bureaucratic clearances to speak to the international press. She had established a rapid response unit in the State Department to monitor and respond to world and domestic events. She had reinvigorated the Strategic Communication PCC and established communication plans for key pilot countries. And she had established processes to disseminate coordinated U.S. themes and messages laterally and horizontally in the government. Finally and perhaps most importantly, a long awaited *National Strategy for Public Diplomacy and Strategic Communication* was published under her leadership in May 2007.

The Defense Department recognizes the problems as well. The Quadrennial Defense Review (QDR) conducted a spin off study on Strategic Communication that resulted in a roadmap addressing planning, resources, and coordination. Perhaps the most important aspect of the roadmap is the stated objective of developing strategic communication plans in conjunction with policy development, thus fulfilling Edward R. Murrow's desire to be brought in on the takeoff, not the crash landing.[49]

Despite these recent positive initiatives, it remains to be seen whether Ambassador Hughes' efforts or those of DOD will result in adequate resourcing or processes and organizations that endure after she departed and beyond the current administration.

THE WAY AHEAD

The current information environment, the American attitude toward propaganda, bureaucratic processes that are, by their very nature, cumbersome and slow, all combine to make effective strategic communication difficult indeed—but not impossible. Along with the challenges are opportunities. Overcoming the challenges while exploiting the opportunities, however, requires procedural and cultural change and the leadership necessary to force that change.

Procedurally, the United States must approach strategic communication as an integral part of policy development. To do otherwise will doom the it to always remain on the defensive in the war of ideas—and that certainly has not worked well to date. Incorporation of such a plan in the policy development process allows for both cautions to policy developers regarding potentially negative foreign reactions and the proactive ability to explain the policy with messages to all audiences. On the other hand, understand that poor policy will not be salvaged by any messages or themes that attempt to explain it. ("You can put a lot of lipstick on a pig, but it's still a pig").[50]

Failure to quickly and accurately react to adversary propaganda cedes the international information environment to the enemy. "Quickly" here is often measured in minutes, not hours, days, or weeks. The reality of instant communications means that individuals on the ground at the lowest tactical levels must be empowered to respond to enemy propaganda to the best of their ability. This requires a cultural change on the part of both individual "messengers" and their leaders. Training and education can provide the baseline competencies to equip American officials (be they soldiers, diplomats, or others) to appropriately respond to propaganda. But the driving force in allowing the freedom to do so will come from leaders who are willing to delegate the authority to communicate publicly. This comes with an understanding that "information fratricide" may occur, but also comes with an acceptance that to do otherwise takes the United States out of the information fight. A culture of information empowerment to the lowest levels must be inculcated among U.S. Government officials with clear guidance provided to subordinates, risk mitigation procedures established and, perhaps most importantly, acceptance that this will not be a zero defect undertaking.

Winning hearts, minds, trust, and credibility, in the end, requires a local approach. Consider a major U.S. metropolitan area. Neighborhoods take on their own personalities driven by socio-economic factors and ethnic and racial identity, among other considerations. Value sets are different among the diversity of communities that make up the melting pot that is a large U.S. city. It should not be difficult then to understand how it is nearly impossible to influence perceptions among audiences in a foreign nation with a "one size fits all" set of messages and actions. Long-term U.S. presence and engagement on the ground in foreign nations allows for a deep understanding of cultural differences within communities. These cultural underpinnings combined with the hard work of relationship building allow for effective tailoring of messages and successful identification of key influencers. Engagement is the key whether it is by U.S. soldiers in their area of operations,[51] diplomats in Provincial Reconstruction Teams, U.S. Agency for International Aid workers, or Nongovernmental Organizations. Where no U.S. presence exists, efforts must include recruiting key influencers for U.S. exchange programs such that they will tell the story for the nation upon their return home.

The National Strategy for Public Diplomacy and Strategic Communication discusses the "diplomacy of deeds." The U.S. hospital ship *Mercy* completed a 5-month humanitarian mission to South and Southeast Asia late last year, resulting in improved public opinion of the United States in those predominately Muslim nations where the missions took place. Similar increases in favorability ratings occurred following the U.S. response to the Indonesian tsunami and Pakistani earthquake.[52] These low-cost, high visibility efforts pay significant dividends in improving the U.S. image. Leaders need to understand that strategic communication is more than programs, themes, and messages; it is, perhaps most importantly, actions as well.

Countering the inherent national aversion to the inflammatory term "propaganda" again lies in both process and culture driven by leadership. A U.S. Government organization paying to have articles printed (under Iraqi pseudonyms) in Iraqi newspapers, regardless of whether it is ultimately found to be legal, is simply asking for trouble in today's information environment. Supporting the government of Iraq to tell its own story is a better way to go. Leading from the rear in the information war still gets the message told while avoiding direct confrontations with democratic ideals. On the other hand, an "Office of Strategic Influence" had the potential to provide focus, resources and potentially significant results in the information war, but a few misguided articles in the mainstream press was all it took to bring about its quick demise. And so, ultimately countering American angst over the effective use of propaganda requires strong national leadership. National leaders must admit that the United States actually does want to (truthfully) influence foreign audiences. To do anything less abrogates the information battlespace to our adversaries. Attempts to influence foreign audiences, however, will almost certainly produce some bleedover to American audiences. That must be accepted and, with knowledge of forethought, preparations must be made to both proactively educate the media regarding information efforts and to respond to any potential media backlash. The recent initiatives to incorporate strategic communication into the policy development process as previously described are encouraging in this regard.

CONCLUSION

The National Strategy for Public Diplomacy and Strategic Communication is a large step in the right direction to allow the United States to compete in the information environment and proactively tell its story. Defeating an enemy whose center of gravity is extremist ideology requires nothing less than an all out effort in this regard. But changing perceptions, attitudes, and ultimately behavior is a generational endeavor. It remains to be seen whether processes can be adopted that endure beyond political cycles and national leadership can step forward to lead a charge to change the current culture of reticence to apply information as power while competing in an increasingly challenging information environment. Only then can the information battlefield be leveled, and the battle of ideas won.

ENDNOTES - CHAPTER 12

1. Emergent NATO doctrine on Information Operations cites Diplomatic, Military, and Economic activities as "Instruments of Power." It further states that Information, while not an instrument of power, forms a foundation as all activity has an informational backdrop.

2. Ronald Reagan, National Security Decision Directive 130, Washington, DC: The White House, March 6, 1984, available from *www.fas.org/irp/offdocs/*nsdd/nsdd-130.htm, Internet, accessed October 18, 2007.

3. Daniel T. Kuehl and Robert E. Neilson, "Evolutionary Change in Revolutionary Times: A Case for a New National Security Education Program," *National Security Strategy Quarterly*, Autumn 1999, p. 40.

4. Jeffrey L. Groh and Dennis M. Murphy, "Landpower and Network Centric Operations: How Information in Today's Battlespace Can be Exploited," *NECWORKS Journal*, Issue 1, March 2006.

5. Kevin J. Cogan and Raymond G. Delucio, "Network Centric Warfare Case Study, Volume II," Carlisle Barracks,

PA: U.S. Army War College, 2006, p. 4.

6. Timothy L. Thomas, "Cyber Mobilization: A Growing Counterinsurgency Campaign," *IOSphere*, Summer 2006, p. 23.

7. James B. Kinniburgh and Dorothy E. Denning, "Blogs and Military Information Strategy," *IOSphere*, Summer 2006, p. 6.

8. Sheryl Gay Stolberg, "Troop Rise Aids Iraqis, Bush Says, Citing Bloggers," *New York Times*, March 29, 2007, p. 17.

9. Kinniburgh and Denning, p. 5.

10. William R. Levesque, "Blogs are CentCom's New Target," *St. Petersburg Times*, February 12, 2007, p. 1.

11. Carmen L. Gleason, "Coalition Servicemembers Reach out to America via YouTube," *American Forces Press Service*, March 14, 2007.

12. The author attended a conference on "new media" sponsored by the Open Source Center at the Meridian House in Washington, DC, in April 2007. The referenced comments reflect panelists' presentations. IBM already has a presence in Second Life with over 7,000 associates meeting and conducting business there. The conference was held under Chatham House rules, allowing free and open dialog while ensuring the anonymity of speakers.

13. Natalie O'Brien, "Virtual Terrorists," *The Australian*, July 31, 2007, available from *www.theaustralian.news.com.au/ story/0,25197,22161037-28737,00.html*, Internet, accessed September 25, 2007.

14. New Media Conference, Meridian House.

15. John Moody, "A 'Celler's' Market for Information in Iran," *FoxNews*, June 14, 2007, available from *www.foxnews. com/story/0,2933,282456,00.html*, Internet, accessed September 25, 2007.

16. Richard Willing, "Growing Cell Phone Use a Problem for Spy Agencies," *USA Today*, August 2, 2007, p. 2.

17. Marvin Kalb and Carol Saivetz, "The Israeli-Hezbollah War of 2006: The Media as a Weapon in Asymmetrical Conflict," John F. Kennedy School of Government Research Working Papers Series, February 2007, p. 4.

18. Phillip Meyer, "The Proper Role of the News Media in a Democratic Society," *Media, Profit, and Politics*, Kent, OH: The Kent State University Press, 2003, p. 12.

19. Page Kollock and Suzanne Presto, "US Youth Use High-Tech Media for Political Communication," *VOAnews. com*, November 16, 2005, available from *www.voanews.com/english/archive/2005-11/2005-11-16-voa5.cfm*, Internet, accessed August 24, 2007.

20. J. D. Johannes, "How Al Qaeda is Winning Even as it is Losing," *TCS Daily*, July 11, 2007. The author provides a statistical analysis using "gross rating points" to convey that 65 percent of coverage of the Iraqi war is pessimistic.

21. Roxie Merritt, Director of Internal Communications and New Media, Armed Forces Information Service, interview with the author, February 22, 2007.

22. *DOD Dictionary of Military Terms*, Washington, DC, Department of Defense, March 22, 2007, p. 430. While there are numerous definitions found in any number of publications, this one is chosen because it reflects the accepted U.S. Government definition.

23. Interestingly, the U.S. Government avoids using the term "propaganda" in any of its official publications, (short of the DoD definition). Instead, the use the terms "psychological operations," "information operations," "public diplomacy," and "strategic communication" is found, apparently as an ironic twist to change American perceptions favorably toward the use of information to influence foreign audiences.

24. Lynne Duke, "The Word at War; Propaganda? Nah, Here's the Scoop, Say the Guys Who Planted Stories in Iraqi Papers," *The Washington Post*, March 26, 2001, p. D1.

25. David E. Kaplan, "How Rocket Scientists Got Into the Hearts and Minds Game," *U.S. News and World Report*, April 25, 2005, pp. 30-31.

26. Kevin Peraino, "Winning Hearts and Minds," *Newsweek International*, October 2, 2006.

27. Various definitions of strategic communication exist. There is no overarching U.S. Government definition. As of this writing, DoD is still debating the definition. The one shown here is taken from Department of Defense, *QDR Execution Roadmap for Strategic Communication*, Washington, DC: U.S. Department of Defense, September 25, 2006, p. 3.

28. U.S. Department of Defense. *DoD Dictionary*, available from *www.dtic.mil/doctrine/jel/doddict/data/p/04372.html*, Internet, accessed November 30, 2007.

29. U.S. Department of State, available from *www.state.gov/r/pa/*, Internet, accessed November 30, 2007.

30. Chairman of the Joint Chiefs of Staff, "Joint Publication 3-13, Information Operations," February 13, 2006, pp. I-1.

31. *QDR Execution Roadmap for Strategic Communication*, p. 2.

32. U.S. Department of Defense. *DOD Dictionary*, available from *www.dtic.mil/doctrine/jel/doddict/data/p/04372.html*, Internet, accessed October 18, 2007.

33. *The U.S. Government's International Broadcasting Bureau*, available from *www.ibb.gov*, Internet, accessed October 18, 2007.

34. Harry R. Yarger, "Toward a Theory of Strategy: Art Lykke and the Army War College Strategy Model," *U.S. Army War College Guide to National Strategy and Policy*, June 2006, p. 107.

35. Chairman of the Joint Chiefs of Staff, "Joint Publication 3-13, Information Operations," February 13, 2006, pp. I-1. This publication indicated the information environment consists of three interrelated dimensions: physical, informational, and cognitive.

36. The author has attended numerous briefings by the Deputy Assistant Secretary of Defense for Joint Communication (DASD, JC)) and his staff where this has been stated. Note: the DASD, JC is responsible for the *DoD Strategic Communication Roadmap*.

37. Anju S. Bawa, "U.S. Aid Ship Cures Public Opinion," *Washington Times*, November 17, 2006, p. 15.

38. John S. D. Eisenhower, *Agent of Destiny: The Life and Times of General Winfield Scott*, New York: The Free Press, 1997, pp. 245-246.

39. Margaret McMillan, *Paris 1919: Six Months That Changed the World*, New York: Random House, 2002, p.15.

40. David M. Kennedy, *Over Here: The First World War and American Society*, New York, Oxford University Press: 1980, p. 81.

41. Allan Winkler, *The Politics of Propaganda: The Office of War Information, 1942-1945*, New Haven: Yale University Press, 1978, p. 60.

42. *Ibid.*, p. 97.

43. The Smith-Mundt Act is still in effect to include the requirement not to "target" U.S. audiences. The current information environment with ubiquitous, world-wide media outlets, satellite communications, and real-time reporting makes it difficult to target foreign audiences without exposing U.S. audiences to the message, however . . . a fact not

envisioned in 1948 when the act became effective, and one that continues to cause friction between the military and media.

44. David E. Kaplan, "Hearts, Minds, and Dollars" *U.S. News and World Report*, April 25, 2005, pp,. 25, 27.

45. Federation of American Scientists, Intelligence Resource Program, *U.S. International Public Information (IPI)*, Presidential Decision Directive PDD 68, April 30, 1999, available from *www.fas.org/irp/offdocs/pdd/pdd-68.htm*, Internet, accessed October 18, 2007.

46. U.S. General Accounting Office, *U.S. Public Diplomacy*, Washington, DC: U.S. General Accounting Office, April 2005, pp. 10-13.

47. Interagency Strategic Communication Fusion Team, Meeting summary, October 27, 2006, p. 4.

48. U.S. Department of State, *Senior Officials: Under Secretary for Public Diplomacy and Public Affairs- Karen Hughes*, available from *www.state.gov/misc/19232.htm*, Internet, accessed October 18, 2007.

49. *QDR Execution Roadmap for Strategic Communication*, p. 3.

50. Torie Clark, *Lipstick on a Pig*, New York: Free Press, 2006, p. 1. Ms. Clark was the chief spokesperson for the Pentagon during the first George W. Bush administration. The quote is the title of the first chapter of her book.

51. An excellent overview of the effectiveness of a local military approach can be found in an article written by Colonel Ralph Baker, U.S. Army, on his application of information operations as a brigade commander in Baghdad. The article appears in the May-June 2006 issue of *Military Review*.

52. Bawa, p. 15.

CHAPTER 13

DIPLOMACY AS AN INSTRUMENT OF NATIONAL POWER

Reed J. Fendrick

A diplomat is an honest man sent abroad to lie for his country.

Apocryphal

The patriotic art of lying for one's country.

Ambrose Bierce[1]

The media and intellectual elites, the State Department (as an institution), and the Foreign Service (as a culture) clearly favor the process, politeness, and accommodation position.

Newt Gingrich[2]

Ordinary Americans have often been uncomfortable about the art and practice of diplomacy. Frequently, they associate diplomacy and American diplomats either with elitist, pseudo-aristocratic bowing and scraping before supercilious foreigners whose aim is to impinge on our sovereignty and partake of our largesse; or as naïve country bumpkins whose gullibility allows them to forsake key American goals and objectives; or as ruthless, cynical practitioners of Bismarckian realpolitiek whose aims and practices fall far short of our Founders' noble aspirations; or as liberal, one-worldists whose collective ideology is far from the American mainstream and who seek to undermine the political aims of elected Administrations. These stereotypes go back to our country's origins and have been reinforced by such traumatic events as Wilson's perceived failure at Versailles, the Yalta Conference near the end of World War II, Henry Kissinger's role as architect of the opening to China, and the failure to obtain a United Nations (UN) Security Council resolution endorsing the use of force in Iraq.

Is any of this true? True or not, does it matter? What is diplomacy supposed to do? Does the U.S. wield diplomacy effectively? Can democracy and diplomacy function harmoniously? How does diplomacy fit in with the protection and furtherance of national security?

First, diplomacy is one instrument among many that a government utilizes in its pursuit of the national interest. Among others are: military power, actual or potential; economic power; intelligence-gathering and operations; cultural and information or "soft power"; relative degrees of national unity and probably others. Diplomacy never functions in isolation from the other instruments of power but may at times be emphasized as the situation warrants. In its simplest, most original form diplomacy is the official means by which one state formally relates to other states. Although ambassadors have existed since antiquity representing one sovereign to another, the earliest diplomats often functioned more as de facto hostages to ensure peace or compliance with some agreement than in the modern understanding of an ambassador's role. Since nation-states were more or less legitimized by the Treaty of Westphalia in 1648, a whole series of codes and protocols have been established to create a framework for the practice of diplomacy. These include such seeming anomalies (and irritants to common citizens) as diplomatic immunity; creation of embassies; establishing and breaking diplomatic relations; sending and receiving diplomatic notes, demarches, non-papers and other forms of communication; holding international conferences and many other means of interstate communication and relations.

Diplomats are agents of the State. In theory, they act on instruction. Until the advent of modern communications, their instructions necessarily had to be general and they required a nearly innate understanding of the national interest of the country they represented. Both because of the nondemocratic nature of nearly all States before the American and French Revolutions, and due to the need for confidentiality to protect state secrets and national security, diplomatic exchanges and even treaties or agreements were often undertaken in secret or with quiet discretion. When Woodrow Wilson's Fourteen Points called for "open covenants openly arrived at" (a reference to Allied agreements for post-World War I division of spoils from the Central Powers that appeared to make a mockery of claims the War was meant to make the "world safe for democracy"), he was publicly challenging the entire edifice of traditional diplomacy that had, however, begun to be modified with the rise of the mass media and popular participation in the nineteenth century. Increasingly, mounting scrutiny from democratic media and academics and ever-increasing intrusive clandestine intelligence-gathering make formal secret agreements less and less palatable.

One prism through which to view diplomacy is to think of it as an element on the spectrum of national security devices. In the "normal" course of events, most nations most of the time while competing for influence, markets, relative perceived power and other markers of strength, relate to one another the way competitors do in seeking market-share—not as gangs fighting over turf. In other words, the assumption is that peaceful approaches, use of agreements and treaties, and normal intercourse will prevail. In this scenario, diplomacy provides the lubricant for acceptable relations, seeks to remove irritants, and strives for mutual understanding. However, even in the relations between traditionally peaceful entities, in the semi-Hobbesian universe of contemporary international relations, diplomacy holds in its quiver the potential threat of force. In the cases where rivalry becomes equated with threats to vital national interests (a determination that is difficult to objectively define but that governments make drawing on their specific cultural, historical, and political traditions and bringing to bear whatever institutions or individuals wield predominant influence on this subject), diplomacy becomes an adjunct to overt or masked displays or use of armed force. In this situation, diplomacy becomes the main instrument to build coalitions, influence publics and elites in other countries of the justice of the cause, and work closely with the military establishment to make available critical spaces in non-national territory for the possible deployment of armed force (i.e. aircraft overflight rights, port visits, shipment of men and materiel). Finally, if armed conflict does erupt, diplomacy continues during that period (albeit with a lower emphasis) focusing on post-war planning, cost and burden-sharing, and international organization endorsement (or at least non-condemnation) of the military actions.

Diplomacy fundamentally consists of a constant assessment of other countries' power potential, perceived vital interests, and relationship with other states, in an attempt to maximize one's own country's freedom of action with the ultimate purpose of assuring the achievement of the nation's vital interests, the core of which is survival. Diplomacy traditionally and currently utilizes a variety of practices or maneuvers to obtain the protection or furtherance of the national goals or interests. Essentially all these practices are elements of diplomatic strategy that seek advantage for the state short of war (although war always remains the ultimate recourse). From the realist perspective, all strategies, while perhaps amoral in themselves, have as the ultimate goal the moral aim of the survival of the state and its core values. Thus, leaders must take account of the particular circumstance of the place in the international order of their state to determine what would be an effective strategy and tactics or maneuvers to enable its success. Thus, from the British and French perspective in 1938, the decision to appease Germany over the Sudetenland may have been a misperception of the relative power of each state but was not, a priori, an invalid tactic. The constant politically-charged accusation of "Munich" or "Yalta" in quite different circumstances is meaningless. Sometimes appeasement is good or unavoidable. In the case of Nazi Germany, in hindsight, it was a bad tactic because Hitler could not be appeased, and the Allies simply postponed the inevitable clash to a moment when they yielded military advantage to Hitler. Détente (especially the series of arms control and human rights agreements) as practiced by Nixon and Kissinger was an effort to reach accommodation with the Soviet Union at a time when it appeared a balance of power in nuclear weapons had been struck and neither side could expect to gain a decisive advantage. The effort by President George H. W. Bush to create a coalition in the First Gulf War was not so much to increase U.S. military advantage over Iraq as it was to demonstrate—especially in the Arab and Islamic worlds—the broad support to repel Iraqi aggression in Kuwait. In the recent Gulf War, the relative absence of a significant coalition was largely a function of the Administration's desire to not be constrained in tactics, operations (targeting), and strategy in the way it believed NATO operations in Kosovo had been hampered.

Diplomatic Instruments.

The main instrument of diplomacy is negotiation, whether in a formal or informal setting. In a sense all diplomacy is a constant adjustment of relations among states pursued simultaneously through multiple, overlapping dialogues: bilateral, multilateral (e.g., UN); special conferences and other venues. The goal is usually, but not always, to reach an agreement that could range from those containing significant enforcement mechanisms for implementation (e.g., the Non-Proliferation Treaty) to hortatory proclamations such as the Kellogg-Briand pact that purported to outlaw war. One of the special advantages diplomats as a profession may have is that they should possess significant knowledge of the personalities and national cultural styles of their interlocutors. Since much diplomatic maneuvering by states consist of bluffs and feints as well as subtle signals either of accommodation or willingness to risk war, a capable diplomacy can discern and characterize the meaning of a given action. Misinterpretation, ignorance, lack of knowledge, or arrogance can lead to unforeseeable consequences (e.g., ignoring India's warning during the Korean War that China would intervene if U.S. forces approached the Yalu River).

Diplomatic relations among countries have long followed a common set of practices. The necessity to maintain contact as a means to facilitate dialogue between states leads to diplomatic recognition that can be of the state but not the government (e.g., North Korea by the U.S.); or of the government as well. Normally, such recognition is not a moral stamp of approval but a reflection that a regime controls the preponderance of national territory, and that it is in the interest of the other country to have formal channels of communication. Breaking relations can be a prelude to war; more often it is a mark of extreme disapproval. But if the regime survives, non-recognition can be a cause of great inconvenience since maintaining a dialogue usually involves talking either through third parties or in multilateral institutions. There are also anomalous situations such as is currently the case with Cuba where the U.S. maintains a large Interests Section under the technical protection of the Swiss embassy in order to pursue business with the Castro regime without compromising its disapproval. Sometimes a decision is made to withdraw the ambassador, temporarily or for longer periods, to deliver a significant rebuke for some policy or action of the host government. The downside to such an action is that dialogue between the states may become more rigid and is certainly conducted at a lower level of authority. In normal practice, the ambassador heads an embassy that is usually divided into numerous sections each specializing in a particular subject area. The number of persons granted diplomatic status, which under the Vienna Convention imparts immunity to certain host government laws, is negotiated between the two states.

An American embassy is normally organized in the following manner: at the apex is the Ambassador, appointed by the President as his personal representative and confirmed by the U.S. Senate. He may be a career Foreign Service Officer from the Department of State or he may be chosen form other agencies or the private sector. His/her alter ego is the Deputy Chief of Mission (DCM) who serves under the Ambassador to assure the timely, efficient and correct carrying out of instructions and to assure good management practices in the embassy (i.e. avoidance of waste, fraud and mismanagement). There are usually several functional State Department Sections (i.e. Political, Economic, Consular and Administrative) that handle the reporting, management and protection of U.S. citizens and issuance of visas to foreign nationals. Many Embassies also maintain a Defense Attaché Office with representatives from one or more of the armed services; a Defense Cooperation Office that manages foreign military sales and transfers; often a Foreign Commercial Service that promotes U.S. exports; a Foreign Agricultural Service that does the same for agricultural commodities; a Legal Attaché (normally FBI) that liaises with host country police authorities; Drug Enforcement Agency that does the same on narcotics issues; and a representative from Customs, possibly the Immigration and Naturalization Service. Depending on the country, many other Federal agencies may be represented. Similarly, the receiving country may have similar sections in its embassy in Washington.

How, in the real, contemporary world, does modern American diplomacy work? With or without the publication of the National Security Strategy, which is an explicit annual overview of an Administration's top priorities often together with a general roadmap on how to achieve the objectives, the Department of State, usually in conjunction and coordination with the other foreign affairs agencies under the auspices of the National Security Council, will send telegraphic (or sometimes e-mail or telephone) instructions to an embassy in a given country or international organization. It might be a request for information on a matter that has risen to the attention of at least the Country Director in a regional or functional bureau of the Department of State (perhaps due to media attention, pressure from a lobbyist, or a request from a member of Congress). Or the department could instruct the Ambassador to raise with the host country a matter of concern such as the arrest of an American citizen, a report of human rights abuse by a military unit, allegations of unfair commercial practice harmful to an American firm, sale of military weapons, a request for port visit of a U.S. warship, surveillance of a suspected terrorist or many other possible items. In what becomes a continuous conversation, the appropriate section in the embassy (Political, Economic, Consular, Defense Attaché, Commercial Service or others) would be tasked to take the necessary action. Sometimes the embassy itself reports on a matter and offers a recommendation. In rare cases where immediate action is vital, the embassy might report what it did and implicitly request endorsement of the action. Often, in parallel fashion, especially on important issues, the Department would convoke the Ambassador or an appropriate official from the relevant embassy in Washington or its Mission to the United Nations to make similar points. Because embassies and foreign ministries are organized on highly hierarchical principles, it is often possible to adjust the tone and content of the message to a particular rank, thus making clear the relative importance of the message. Depending on response, the message's content, deliverer and recipient can be ratcheted up or down accordingly.

Diplomatic Roles.

What are the principal roles of a diplomat? First, he is an agent of his government ordered to carry out instructions from authorized superiors. In the American case, there is often a vigorous internal debate throughout the foreign affairs agencies of the government on a given policy, as well as on the tactics of its proposed execution, a dialogue in which both Department of State and embassies continuously engage. However, once a decision is made, the action is carried out. Whatever an individual diplomat's private feelings on a given issue may be, he is duty-bound to carry out the instructions. If his conscience does not so allow, he may request a transfer to another assignment or region or offer to resign. In effect, the diplomat in this role functions as a lawyer with the U.S. Government as his client. Just as a lawyer's ethical responsibility is to make the most vigorous possible advocacy for his client regardless of his personal opinions of the client's innocence, so is a diplomat in public or in conversation with foreign interlocutors expected to make the best possible presentation on behalf of his government.

The diplomat is also an information-gatherer and analyst. Although not expected to compete in real-time with the media organizations such as CNN or the *New York Times* on basic facts, due to his presumed experience and familiarity with a country, its culture, institutions, and key personalities, the diplomat should be able to bring added value by analyzing and putting in context what to harried Washington senior leaders can seem like isolated, meaningless events. So, for the diplomat to be well-informed, he ideally should speak, read and understand the local language, extract from the mass media key nuggets of important information, develop a string of well-informed contacts covering a wide spectrum, and attend major events such as political party congresses. As a message-drafter, the diplomatic drafter needs to be succinct, clear, and pungent enough to both hold busy readers' attention and to answer the "so-what" question. The analysis needs to be substantiated by fact and interpretation, each clearly labeled as such. While never writing with the intent to provoke, when necessary, the drafter may have to call attention respectfully but clearly to actual or potential situations that may be unpleasant or resented by policymakers. At the same time, national leaders must be careful not to shoot the messenger even if they disagree with the analysis or recommendations. Sometimes, this requires courage from the drafter and restraint from the recipient. It is always the policymakers' prerogative to choose other courses. But retaliation against unwanted advice or analysis can lead to self-censorship and ultimate harm to the national interest through failure to realistically assess events.

In Washington, the middle-level diplomat is not as concerned with interpreting events in a foreign country as he is with assisting in defining his agency's position on a given issue (usually a whole host of them) while interacting with other elements of the foreign affairs agencies in order to glean their positions to better support their own agency's position.

A diplomat is also a negotiator. Depending on the issue, a diplomat may have more or less freedom to adjust from basic instructions, tactics and goals. In order for a negotiation to succeed, which may not always be desirable or the preferred outcome, the astute diplomat will have a good general understanding of his counterpart's baseline requirement, some sense of the national cultural manner of negotiating, and a willingness to bargain—but not to bargain away essential or vital objectives. This propensity for negotiation, also an inherent part of a lawyer's toolkit, is what sometimes infuriates ideological or idealistic individuals since they believe it immoral to negotiate with either blatantly evil states or leaders or they believe it puts the U.S. in a position of appearing to make compromises on what can be construed as vital interests. Unless there is no longer a need to negotiate at all because of acknowledged overwhelming power of one country, or because diplomacy has yielded to open war, such compromises are an inherent property of having to deal with a Hobbesian world of sovereign states. Even criminal prosecutors make plea-bargains with criminals to achieve a balance of justice, resource use, and likelihood of conviction on the most serious charges.

In a slightly different key, a diplomat facilitates and maintains dialogue with his counterparts, hopefully with a view to arriving at complementary assessments of threats, benefits, and actions to take to maximize their respective national interests. If the dialogue goes far enough, it can lead to commitments usually expressed in the form of treaties or agreements. They can range from reciprocal reduction of tariffs to willingness to go to war on behalf of another country.

Diplomats also act as spokesman and sounding board for the country. A good diplomat will be effective in public and private gatherings at furthering his country's interests and refuting criticism of it by couching his advocacy in a manner best suited to the culture where he is stationed. Because of the ubiquity of media outlets, a good diplomat learns how to access the host country media, key decision-makers, and most relevant institutions (parliament, military, chambers of commerce, labor union federations etc.), and gets his point across over the blare of "white noise" emanating in the modern media.

At the more senior level, diplomats serve as counselors to national leaders, few of whom are regional or global experts. While diplomats rarely have the final say in the most solemn decision a nation can make — the decision to go to war — they can serve to make clear the potential costs as well as benefits of such acts and the likely prospects of coalitions in favor (or opposed) to their country. While certainly not pacifists, diplomats are temperamentally and professionally inclined to seek non-violent solutions partly because that is what they do, and partly because they frequently can foresee second and third order consequences that can lead to a worse situation than the status quo ante bellum. It is at this juncture that politicians and the media sometimes confuse reporting and analysis that may be at odd with national leadership goals with disloyalty. It is not a desire for the status quo, let alone a preference for dealing with dictators, that may drive diplomats as some have charged. Rather it is a realization that in the absence of comprehensive universally-acknowledged supremacy, negotiation with other regimes, no matter how unpalatable, may be necessary. The obvious classic quote is that of Winston Churchill who, despite being before and after World War II an adamant anti-Communist, said upon Hitler's attack on the Soviet Union in 1941, "If Hitler invaded hell, I would make at least a favorable reference to the devil in the House of Commons." [3]

Conclusion.

To sum up, diplomacy is a mechanism — one among many — used in furtherance of the national interest and in protection of the national security. While styles of diplomacy may differ by national cultures, personal idiosyncrasies, and historical memories, they all have a common purpose. As long as there are states and they hold differing assessments of their national interests, there will be diplomacy. While technology is making certain traditional means of conducting diplomacy obsolete, the core functions of diplomacy will remain. In the past, the airplane and telegraph made clipper ships and quill pen instructions redundant. New information technology is already making reporting far more focused on analysis than simple newsgathering that is done better by CNN, and e-mail and cell-phone are replacing cabled instructions. Such advances occasionally produce serious suggestions to eliminate some or many embassies, but only because of a perceived more efficient manner of performing their functions. Diplomacy is still a vital element of national power.

ENDNOTES - CHAPTER 13

1. Ambrose Bierce, *The Devil's Dictionary*, Sioux Falls, SD: NuVision Publications, LLC, 1906, available at *www.alcyone.com/max/lit/devils/d.html*, accessed August 7, 2003.

2. Newt Gingrich, "Rogue State Department," *Foreign Policy*, July-August 2003, available at *www.foreignpolicy.com/story/story.php?storyID=13742&PHPSESSID=7580b0d87d9d1e0995f9bc68fbeab56d*, accessed August 7, 2003.

3. Winston Churchill, *The Grand Alliance*, New York: Houghton Mifflin Company, 1950, p. 370.

CHAPTER 14

THEORY AND PRACTICE OF MODERN DIPLOMACY: ORIGINS AND DEVELOPMENT TO 1914

Louis J. Nigro, Jr.

Diplomacy, broadly defined as the peaceful dialogue and interaction between political units, is as old as civilization itself. The first known peace treaty was signed about 2300 BC between a king of Ebla, in what is today Syria, and the king of Assyria. The Amarna tablets record the diplomatic correspondence between Egypt and Syrian rulers more than 1,400 years ago, while *Genesis* 14 talks of Abram's "treaty of alliance" with Amorite kings. From the eighth to the third century BC, China was divided among several "warring states" that conducted diplomacy as well as made war on each other in order to survive and succeed, as Sun Tzu's writings indicate. Other early civilizations offer similar examples of diplomatic activity.

This chapter, concerning the development of modern diplomacy from its origins in 15th-century Europe until the 20th century, seeks to accomplish five things. First, the chapter describes the origins of the modern state in Renaissance Italy and shows how that new type of political organization developed a new kind of diplomacy that met its needs. Second, it examines the role of Florentine political thinker Niccolò Machiavelli in providing a theoretical basis for the new state and for the new diplomacy used to accomplish its goals. The chapter stresses that Machiavelli gave directions to rulers of the new states—whether monarchies, principalities, or republics—on how to be successful in an international system characterized by constant interaction among geographically sovereign units for power, influence, and security. Third, it describes the parallel development of the modern sovereign or Westphalian state and the modern diplomacy that serves it. Fourth, it looks at the application of modern diplomacy to the classic European age of grand strategy and the balance of power from 1648 to the First World War. Finally, the chapter serves as background and introduction to other essays in this volume that deal with the characteristics of the state, the nature of the international system, and the role of diplomacy as an element of national power in the contemporary world.

FROM MEDIEVAL TO MODERN

Europe created modern diplomacy because Europe created the modern, geographically sovereign state—the so-called Westphalian state after the Peace of Westphalia in 1648. The new form of international actor that has characterized the modern international system required a new kind of diplomacy, matched to its needs and consonant with its nature.

The modern, geographically sovereign state (or, nation-state) began to emerge in Europe during the 16th century as the old structures of European international order began to break down. The international order that Europe had inherited from the Middle Ages was composed of structures of power that were different from the nation-states that compose our contemporary international system. There were structures that existed above and beyond today's nation-state, structures that we can call *supra-statal* and structures existing below and within today's nation-state that we can call *infra-statal*.

The chief supra-statal institutions were the Papacy and the Holy Roman Empire, both rooted in the spiritual domain and both reflecting the glory of the ancient Roman Empire. Both Popes and Emperors claimed to be the heirs of Rome. Popes and Emperors claimed wide and broad powers over other rulers and over the subjects of other rulers that gave them legal, religious, financial, and other authorities. The primary infra-statal institutions were a bewildering (to us, not to contemporaries) assortment of thousands of autonomous jurisdictions, starting from "national" kingdoms like England, France, and Aragon, and continuing down a long hierarchical chain of political organizations through principalities, duchies, free counties, bishoprics, free cities, commercial alliances (like the Hanseatic League), baronies, petty lordships of all types and sizes, to corporate bodies like guilds, military orders, and religious orders. All of them exercised what we would call political power in various ways. The jurisdictions, rights, powers, and responsibilities of both the supra-statal and the infra-statal institutions often conflicted and overlapped.

Together these supra-national and infra-national institutions made up what contemporaries called Christendom. Christendom's institutions drew their strength and legitimacy from feudal traditional practices that mixed public office and public functions with private property and hereditary rights; from religious and spiritual sanctions; and from social and cultural habits a thousand years in the making. Political order in Christendom was characterized by interlocking networks of rights and responsibilities fragmented into many small, autonomous parts. The focus of political authority was personal, feudal, and local. The idea that political rule was strictly linked to control of territory rather than to other sources of authority was largely absent, so that rulers were not geographically sovereign in the sense of exerting supreme and monopolistic authority over and within a given territory and population. Christendom as a political system appears to us to have been ambiguous, complicated, messy, and illogical, but it worked as long as people believed in it.

The medieval order of Christendom started to break down under pressure from rising political units that drew their strength and legitimacy from new territorial and demographic realities; that were sanctioned more by the possession and use of practical power than by religion and tradition; and that were evolving behind borders that were more definite and more restrictive than the old porous, overlapping medieval political units. The growth of vernacular languages and the concomitant beginnings of national consciousness aided the process of the development of the new political units, which would eventually become the legally equal, sovereign states. This would intensify into the process of state formation at the expense of both the old supra-national institutions and the old infra-national institutions.

THE ITALIAN RENAISSANCE ORIGINS OF MODERN DIPLOMACY: 1450-1500

Italy was the birthplace of the Renaissance and also of the first prototypes of the modern, geographically sovereign state. The reason for this was Renaissance Italy's vanguard status in most areas of European endeavor—art, literature, science, jurisprudence, philosophy, economics, and finance—but also in political development. Jacob Burckhardt's classic 1860 interpretive essay, *The Civilization of the Renaissance in Italy*, had as its central theme the problem of politics and of political anthropology. Burckhardt believed that it was the unique political environment of Renaissance Italy that led to the development of the Renaissance mind with its more liberated ideas, ideals, morals and attitudes. The two overarching organizing institutions of the pre-Renaissance West, of what people thought of, not as Europe, but as Christendom—the universal Papacy and the universalistic Holy Roman Empire—had been effectively absent from Italy and had therefore exerted little or no influence in Italian political life for over a century and a half. That absence, Burckhardt wrote, "left Italy in a political condition which differed essentially from that of other countries of the West" and explained why "in them we detect for the first time the modern political spirit of Europe." [1]

The Italian Microcosm.

Because the foundations of the medieval international order crumbled in Italy around 1300, the Italians began to create a new political institution to fill the void left by that collapse. This new institution was called in Italian the stato, transforming a word that until then had been used to describe the legal classes into which people fell within a political unit. Now *stato*—and all its cognates, such as *state* in English, *état* in French, *estado* in Spanish, *Staat* in German, and so on— would become the term used to describe the basic political unit of the new international order. The Italian microcosm was an anarchic political space. The new states that the Italians evolved to fill that space were the prototypes of the future Westphalian state. They were, in contemporary eyes, illegitimate, existing outside the medieval and feudal hierarchies of political authority. They had to create their own legitimacy by defending their existence. They were, therefore, warlike and aggressive. They were geographically discrete—separate and distinct from other states or any other authorities and were nearly "sovereign" in the modern sense of the term, jealously guarding a monopoly of political authority within their borders and recognizing no other authority higher than themselves.

The power vacuum created by the absence of higher authority in Renaissance Italy resulted in the growth of several Italian city-states into territorial states that absorbed smaller and weaker neighbors. This Darwinian process of political consolidation by conquest resulted eventually in the creation of a miniature state system in Italy, an enclosed political space with five "great" powers contending among themselves for hegemony and influence over smaller, weaker city-states. By 1450, the five principal territorial states of Florence, Venice, Milan, Naples, and the Papal State (based on Rome) dominated the Italian peninsula. As they maneuvered against one another for power and advantage, making and breaking alliances among themselves, the Italian peninsula came to constitute an enclosed system of interacting states—a state system—that was a microcosm of the European state system to follow. In 1454, a series of wars to resist Milanese hegemonic aggression resulted in the general Peace of Lodi. In 1455, most of the five powers and other smaller ones signed a mutual security agreement, the Italic League, which guaranteed the existence of signatory states and called for common action against outsiders. These arrangements led to nearly 50 years of peace on the peninsula. Managing the peace was largely the work of Lorenzo "the Magnificent," the Medici ruler of Florence who believed that maintaining a balance among the five powers was better policy than trying to eliminate enemies. This was the first conscious balance of power policy in a post-medieval state system.

The State as a Work of Art.

The 15th century Italian states were prototypes of the modern state in the sense that they interacted as equals with the other states of their microcosmic systems and in the way they interacted with the other powers and lesser political units of Italy. The new territorial states existed because of the absence in Italy of the great, overarching, hierarchy-anchoring, legitimacy-conferring institutions of Papacy and Empire. As such, the new, legitimacy-challenged Italian states had to struggle to survive, and they knew it. The Italian state was "a new fact appearing in history—the state as the outcome of reflection and calculation, the state as a work of art," according to Burckardt.[2] The Italian states, lacking the luxury of traditional legitimacy, were on their own. To survive, they adopted an approach to statecraft that responded more to necessity than to the traditional approach that enjoined Christian moral standards on rulers and the diplomats that served them. They acted if not in an *immoral* way then at least in an *amoral* way, according to the medieval canons of princely comportment. The end—the survival of the state—justified the means—whatever efforts the state was capable of—regardless of the established standards of international conduct. This is the argument that makes *raison d'état* (reason of state) the ultimate justification for action by states vis-à-vis other states.

As the Italian states became more self-conscious of their circumstances, they began to recognize that the medieval way of diplomacy was no longer adequate to their needs. Medieval diplomacy was based on the occasional dispatch and receipt of very prestigious but often untrained individuals as envoys on specific, short-term missions. Occasionally, diplomats were as much hostages as negotiators. The diplomat usually viewed himself as serving as an emissary for the higher needs of Christendom, not the political ruler who sent or received him. But the new Italian territorial states needed diplomatic institutions and mechanisms more effective, more durable, and more permanent than the old medieval ones. They needed both continuous dialogue with their neighbors and continuous intelligence regarding their neighbors' designs. The Renaissance ruler needed a mechanism to gather and report intelligence and to sustain diplomatic dialogue. They invented therefore the key institution of modern diplomacy—the resident ambassador endowed with diplomatic immunity—to conduct the relations between the five states of the system continuously and seamlessly. During the second half of the 15th century, all five of the major Italian states and many smaller ones established permanent accredited diplomatic missions headed by ambassadors in each of the five major capitals. [3]

In summary, the Italian Renaissance produced the basic elements of the future European state system. It created the geographically sovereign international actor called the state. It posited an anarchical international environment in which states struggled ceaselessly for power and rulers deployed statecraft, diplomacy, and military force according to calculations, not of right or wrong, but of political expediency. It developed the notion of *raison d'état*; that what was good for the state was the right thing to do, because in politics the end justified the means. It created the mechanism for continuous, sustained diplomacy to manage the state's engagement with the world. Finally, Renaissance Italy developed the idea of the balance of power as a goal of the state system.

At the end of the 15th century, the days of the Italian microcosm of an enclosed and protected peninsular state system were numbered. The world beyond the Alps, with political units much more militarily powerful than the Italian states, began to influence Italian affairs. In 1494, the French invaded successfully, drawing other non-Italian powers, especially Spain and the revived Holy Roman Empire, into a struggle for control of the peninsula that made Italy a battle field for 60 years. The Italian microcosm was destroyed, but not before its transalpine destroyers adopted the diplomatic methods and diplomatic institutions that the Italian states had developed and deployed to meet the needs of their prototypical modern state system. The Italian Renaissance way of diplomacy became the basis of the European way of diplomacy for the future. [4]

MACHIAVELLI AND THE THEORY OF MODERN DIPLOMACY

Concepts like the amorality of politics, the ends justify the means, and *raison d'état* are usually labeled "Machiavellian," referring to the ideas of the Florentine statesman, diplomat, and political thinker Niccolò Machiavelli (1465-1527). His works have come to epitomize the difference between the pre-modern, medieval international system, and the modern, geographically sovereign one that first appeared in the Italian state system of the 15th century.

Machiavelli received a typical Italian Renaissance education based on the ancient Greek and Roman classics. That was the essence of the Renaissance, which means rebirth—the Italians and others believed that they were presiding over a rebirth of learning, art, and philosophy based on the recovery of ancient examples of those pursuits. The Renaissance was obsessed with ancient Greek and Roman culture as the Reformation would latter be obsessed with ancient Jewish and Christian culture. Renaissance humanism was a preference for those areas of ancient Greek and Roman culture that were oriented toward empowering human beings in this world rather than preparing them for another, better world. The Renaissance humanist curriculum stressed rhetoric, history, and ethics, because these were tools men could use to pursue secular, and especially political, economic, and social objectives.

Machiavelli put those tools to work as a bureaucrat in the government of the Florentine Republic. From 1498 to 1512, he worked in the equivalents of its war and foreign ministries and went on many diplomatic missions to the other courts of Italy and those of France and the Empire. He was a participant in the political and diplomatic life of Italy in the last years of the existence of the Italian microcosm as well as the first years of the spread of the new state structure and the new diplomacy to the rest of Europe. In 1512, the republic he served underwent a revolution and the autocratic Medici family returned to power. Machiavelli was forced into exile in a hamlet near Florence. There he wrote his principal works, especially *The Prince, The Discourses,* and *The Art of War,* all classics of political realism. *The Prince* gives advice to monarchical regimes, especially to princes newly raised to power, on how to retain and extend their power and influence. *The Discourses* does much the same thing for republican regimes. *The Art of War* analyzes the military element of national power in terms of its relationship to the political and social bases of the state.

Machiavelli's contribution to political thought was instantly, inevitably, and lastingly controversial. Most of his readership was confined to *The Prince,* a short, enigmatic, epigrammatic, and elusive work that lent itself to misinterpretation. (Machiavelli's other more straightforward works, including *The Art of War* and *The Discourses,* were less often read.) In *The Prince,* Machiavelli gave practical advice to an Italian prince trying to create a new state. His advice was blunt: In order to be successful the new prince had to use every tool available to him, including violence, deceit, treachery, and dissimulation. The desired end was to increase his own and his state's power. The means were politically expedient actions, without reference to justice or traditional morality. The standard of a ruler's conduct was *raison d'état*, not Christian ethics.

Contemporaries and later writers interpreted *The Prince* as the bible of the doctrine of political expediency that justified immoral conduct if it produced the desired result, that elevated power over principle, and that denied that Christian morality applied to politics. He was accused of justifying any means to accomplish political goals, especially the retention of and extension of state power. He was denounced for advising rulers to use cunning, duplicity, and bad faith to enhance their own power and undermine their enemies. Criticism of Machiavelli's ideas developed into a genre of writing on political theory, as thinker after thinker wrote an "anti-Machiavelli" attack on his doctrines. Shakespeare called him "the murderous Machiavel." The Catholic Church condemned all Machiavelli's writings and placed them on its Index of Prohibited Books. Later, Machiavelli was praised for the very same doctrines, now seen as *Realpolitik*—the "politics of reality" or "power politics"—based on practical and material factors rather than theoretical or ethical objectives. Proponents hailed *The Prince* as an attempt to "liberate" politics from morality and ethical concerns and to see politics "as it really is." Louis XIV called *The Prince* his "favorite nightcap;" Napoleon annotated his copy of it heavily; Benito Mussolini extolled it as a "handbook for statesmen;" and Adolf Hitler said he kept a copy of it by his bedside.[5]

Machiavelli's Message.

Machiavelli's ideas went much further and deeper than such readers of *The Prince* realized. In fact, when one takes into account his ideas as expressed in his more substantial political works, Machiavelli emerges as the first and still the preeminent theorist of the new geographically sovereign state. He was also the first theorist of the new diplomacy that the new states required in order to survive and prosper. Machiavelli's political theory is a reflection of the rise of the state system in Italy and the new diplomacy that kept them running. As such, they are both descriptive and prescriptive. Machiavelli's political theory constitutes the "user's manual" for rulers and servants of the new state—statesmen, diplomats, and military leaders alike—in the new international environment. They instruct those who ruled the new state and directed its engagement with the world how to succeed at statecraft under the new conditions.

Machiavelli's world-view is a primer for the realist theory of international affairs. In all his major works, Machiavelli assumed a Westphalian international order long before the Peace of Westphalia gave its name to such an order—one composed of geographically sovereign states with durable boundaries, equal in legal standing and legitimacy, in which the ruler monopolized the lawful use of force. He assumed an anarchic international order, with no higher court of justice or authority than the state itself in defending and advancing its interests. He assumed that recourse to war will be frequent and that the new state must be organized for war to be successful. And he assumed that the state's engagement with the world would be constant; the state must also be organized for continuous, professional diplomacy, in order to be successful. If we read Machiavelli broadly—not just *The Prince*, but *The Discourses* and *The Art of War* as well—with these assumptions in mind, we take away a coherent theoretical structure that reflects the Italian microcosm's political realities that were already on their way to becoming the future international political realities of Europe as a whole.

Machiavelli's lessons for statecraft, war, and diplomacy were generally valid for monarchies and republics. Rulers were responsible for the good of their state, for its survival and stability, in a word, for its security. Rulers were judged by their success in defending and advancing the interests of the state, not by any other standards, moral or political. The more legitimate the government, that is, the more recognized its use of state power by constitutions, laws, tradition, custom, and religious sanction, the stronger it would be, and the less the ruler would need recourse to extreme measures. The less legitimate the government, the more likely its ruler would need to use extreme measures to enforce the government's rule. Republics and monarchies could possess strong legitimacy. But republics were by virtue of their representative nature stronger and more stable than monarchies. Republics owed their strength and stability to their ability to mobilize the loyalty and power of the people better than monarchies, because the will of the people lent powerful reinforcement and legitimacy to any state that represented their interests rather than those of the monarch. Well-constituted republics were internally stable and externally strong because they were better able to promote and exploit the economic prosperity, military potential, and patriotism of their people. But the rulers of a republic had the same responsibility for the security of the state as monarchs and they were judged by the same standard—reason of state. Machiavelli advocated a return to ancient Roman republican values, especially replacement of decadent Christian religious values with a Roman-style "civic religion" that worshiped service to the state as the highest value, in order to reform the Italian states of his day and prepare them for success in the anarchic international order in which he lived.

One of Machiavelli's key legacies was the concept that the state's primary role was external, to deal with other states through diplomacy and war—the primacy of external policy. Another was that all states, including republics, needed a strong executive power in their constitutions to facilitate action against external threats. The state that Machiavelli designed in his major works would be able to fulfill its mission of active and successful participation in an anarchic international system. That state could contend with other sovereign states for power, influence, and security and would justify its actions by their success according to the measure of reason of state.[6]

THE SPREAD OF MODERN DIPLOMACY TO EUROPE: 1500-1650

The French King Louis XI led his army into Italy, took and occupied cities from the border to Naples, and then successfully retreated despite suffering tactical defeat by Italian forces. This revealed the stark power differential between the small Italian states and their European counterparts, especially the strong monarchies of France and Spain. Italy became a battleground for foreign powers for the next 60 years. The invasions of Italy helped spread the Renaissance to all of Europe, including the new Italian political institutions. The idea of the new state with its exclusive territorial basis and its concentration of power in the ruler's hands was attractive to Western European rulers. And the European rulers had one thing that the Italian Renaissance new states lacked — legitimacy. Their rule, whether over kingdoms, principalities, duchies or other jurisdictions, was sanctioned and supported by the soft power of legitimacy based on religion, tradition, or custom. When these rulers adopted the ways of the Italians in concentrating power within defined territorial limits, they became more and more powerful at the expense of the old medieval system. Diffused authority and fragmented rights and responsibilities among nobility and church, cities and social orders, and all the other atomized institutions that claimed a share of political power on traditional and feudal grounds could not withstand the new state system.

The northern rulers also adopted the diplomacy that the Italians had developed to serve their new states. More and more, diplomacy was restricted to political units that had pretensions to sovereignty — a monopoly of legitimate force within the borders of the territory they controlled. The Italian system of permanent, resident ambassadors, duly accredited and endowed with diplomatic immunity rapidly became the standard for Europe. The resident ambassadorial system gave rulers ways to influence other states by representing policies and views to other rulers, by providing timely and accurate political intelligence back to the capital, and by concerting actions with allied and friendly governments; it soon became the norm throughout Europe.

The Reformation.

The invasions of Italy and the spread of the Renaissance Italian state system to the rest of Europe in the early 16th century coincided with the beginnings of the Protestant Reformation. The Reformation had great influence on the development of the modern state system and modern diplomacy because it discredited the two great supra-statal political institutions of Christendom, the Papacy and the Empire. The Reformation radically reduced those institutions' ability to influence the international system, and at the same time greatly strengthened the power of the rulers of the new states. The Reformation strengthened the hand of Protestant rulers by transferring to them the effective leadership of the reformed churches. The Reformation therefore intersected with the rise of territorial states in ways that powerfully accelerated the process of state formation that the Renaissance had begun. The Reformation harnessed the immense power of religion to the *raison d'être* of the state and added religious differences to the already long menu of reasons for states to conflict with other states. In the short run, the expansion and development of diplomacy suffered as states of different religions downgraded or interrupted normal diplomatic relations for a time.

In the long run, however, the development of diplomacy resumed its previous trajectory, keeping pace with the development of state power and self-awareness, as well as with the extension of a state system that required continuous and consequential diplomatic activity in order to function effectively.

The Reformation led to a long series of religious struggles, first in Germany and Central Europe, and later in France, the Low Countries, and elsewhere. It led, too, to the Catholic Counter-Reformation, which reorganized the Church in Catholic lands as the Reformation reorganized the churches in Protestant lands. In both Catholic and Protestant Europe, however, the religious breakdown of the unity of Christendom resulted in a tremendous source of political influence for the new states—religious uniformity under the control of the state and its ruler became the norm. Everywhere, the sanction of guardian of the faith was added to the secular ruler's authority, vastly increasing the concentration of his power. This fact was recognized in international law and practice by the Peace of Augsburg of 1555 between the Catholic Emperor Charles V and the rebellious Protestant states of his Empire. The question of which religion people would be allowed to practice—in this case, either Catholicism or Lutheranism—was to be decided by the local ruler. This arrangement was expressed as the principle of *cujus regio, ejus religio*—the ruler's religion is the religion of the ruler's people. At the state level, no toleration of religious minorities was foreseen. At the macro level, the result was greater toleration for religious diversity in the international system of sovereign states.

Balance-of-Power Diplomacy and the Wars of Religion.

As the modern state system developed, its characteristic dynamics developed as well. In an anarchic system, hegemonic threats appeared as one state grew stronger than others. The system began to respond to hegemonic threats through the mechanism of the balance of power, in which coalitions developed to resist, restrain, and reduce the would-be hegemon's power and influence to manageable proportions. This happened even during the wars of religion. The attempts of Habsburg Emperor (and King of Spain) Charles V to restore and extend the power of the Holy Roman Empire from the 1530s until his abdication in 1556 led to the formation of coalitions against him on both religious and purely political grounds (although the distinction was losing its edge). This was the last serious attempt by a Holy Roman Emperor to achieve European hegemony and Christian unity, another indication that the modern state was succeeding in crowding out pre-modern political forms. The development of the major European states into absolute monarchies was another. The balance of power mechanism was extended beyond Europe when France signed a treaty with the Turkish Sultan in 1536 to bring the Ottoman Empire into play diplomatically in its resistance to Charles's hegemonic effort.

Habsburg dynasts made two more attempts to assert hegemony over Europe using religion as a justification. Charles V's son, King Philip II (1556-1598) of Spain, tried to leverage the power of his realm and its wealthy overseas empire to achieve European hegemony, but met the opposition of coalitions that linked his Dutch and Belgian Protestant subjects with England and France. Between 1618 and 1648, the Habsburg rulers of Spain and the Empire again grasped for hegemony, trying to exploit the Counter-Reformation's partial successes to once again impose a Habsburg-controlled order on Europe. The Thirty Years War that prevented that from happening was the result of the resistance of a wide coalition of German Protestant states backed by Catholic France and Lutheran Sweden. The leading anti-hegemonic statesman of the first half of the 17th century was France's Cardinal Richelieu, who knitted together the anti-Habsburg coalition that won the Thirty Years War by blocking the Spanish and Austrian branches of that family's bid for mastery of the continent.

THE ABSOLUTE MONARCHIES AND BALANCE-OF-POWER DIPLOMACY: 1650-1815

The Westphalia settlement of 1648 ended the period of religious wars and ushered in one in which the Great Powers engaged in episodic struggles to extend their power and influence in order to achieve hegemony for themselves, or in order to prevent the achievement of hegemony by others. The settlement itself is generally considered to have established definitively the sovereign state as the basic international actor and to have christened the European state system as one composed of distinct and juridically equal, sovereign states. These Westphalian sovereign states monopolized the legitimate use of force within well-defined borders and struggled for power in an anarchical international environment. The reality was not quite so advanced, but the idea of the modern Westphalian state would gradually become accepted as the norm. A constant search for equilibrium governed the system through diplomacy that sought to restore the balance of power among competing states. The universalist idea was no longer seriously considered outside the Papal Apartments in the Vatican.

Adam Watson describes how the period from Westphalia to Vienna contributed to the development of modern diplomacy. First, there was the propagation of the concept of the professional career diplomat, who cultivated specific skills that ensured effective performance of his duties. Second, there arose the idea that these professional diplomats belonged to informal but useful groups of accredited diplomats at various courts of Europe who shared a common outlook and common goals. These included a common need to protect their status and privileges; mutual advantage in exchanging information and evaluations, especially among representatives of allied and friendly states; and reciprocal advantage in maintaining good working relations, even as their governments quarreled. The diplomatic corps had taken shape and would become permanent, although its members came and went. Third, diplomatic congresses began to play an increasingly important role in ending and regulating conflict, and began to be seen not as isolated events, but as "climaxes in dialogue."[7]

Diplomacy was becoming continuous and general, as war was becoming occasional and limited to certain principals, while some neutrals normally stood aside. Negotiation was increasingly regarded as valuable in and of itself, as Cardinal Richelieu stated in his *Political Testament*. Richelieu also sought to remain in constant diplomatic contact with the enemies of France, including during war, in order to be better placed to influence their policies even as their respective armies fought. Fourth, diplomacy was increasingly conceived of as the management mechanism for the balance of power, which ensured the continued existence of all international actors by adjusting and readjusting the alignment of states to compensate for changes in the level of power of individual states. Diplomacy was needed to negotiate these adjustments. Finally, institutions to manage the conduct of diplomacy in capitals coalesced into regular ministries of foreign affairs, as a "logical complement of resident envoys."[8]

The balance of power could ensure the survival of most states, but it could not preserve the peace entirely. First France under Louis XIV (1640-1715) threatened to become the European hegemon, especially by unifying France and Spain into one grand-dynastic empire that would include Spain's far-flung international holdings. This brought coalitions led by the Netherlands, the Holy Roman Empire, and Britain into play in order to deny French ambitions. Such coalitions fought the French and their allies four times between 1667 and 1713, exhausting France and Spain. The last of these wars, the War of the Spanish Succession (Queen Anne's War in America) (1702-1713), was very nearly a world war, because it involved operations and alliances with local rulers on several continents.

Through the rest of the 18th century, French attempts to reassert itself and English efforts to prevent France from dominating Europe while extending its own colonial and commercial empire were played out in a series of wars based on shifting alliances—the War of the Polish Succession

(1733-1738), the War of the Austrian Succession or King George's War in America (1740-1748), the Seven Years War (1756-1763) called the French and Indian War in America (1754-1763), and the War of the American Revolution (1775-1783). The war in America became a Great Power struggle as skillful diplomacy and astute use of intelligence by the colonists intersected with French desire for revenge on Britain. That produced an American-Franco-Spanish alliance that fought the British militarily and a pro-American, Russian-led League of Armed Neutrality served to isolate Britain diplomatically and economically.

The French Revolution and the Napoleonic period brought a renewed French drive for continental hegemony as well as British resolve to prevent it, involving coalitions on both sides. Napoleon, in fact, realized albeit briefly (1807-1811) the general European hegemony about which Charles V and Louis XIV had dreamed. In Europe in 1811, only Britain was outside the French orbit. The French Empire was surrounded by satellite states and allies of dubious loyalty but unwilling to oppose Napoleon's dictates openly. Napoleon's political overreach in Spain and military defeat in Russia in 1812 revived British efforts to create an anti-French coalition. British diplomacy was ultimately successful in exploiting the state system's inherent unwillingness to tolerate an aggressive hegemon by constructing and maintaining a Grand Coalition of all the other Great Powers to defeat Napoleon and finally to impose regime change on the French.

BALANCE-OF-POWER DIPLOMACY AND EUROPEAN EQUILIBRIUM: 1815-1914

The post-Napoleonic settlement began an unprecedented period of comity in the European state system. After the Congress of Vienna that codified the post-Napoleonic settlement, no general wars lasting more than a few months or involving all of the Great Powers were fought for nearly a century. The statesmen and diplomats gathered at Vienna were intent on restoring the 18th-century balance of power in the European state system as the best way of ensuring peace. The territorial changes they made and the institutional initiatives they took were successful in providing the basis for a durable peace among the Great Powers for nearly a hundred years. No shock to the international system as great as that produced by the French Revolution and the Napoleonic Hegemony has yet been followed by such a sustained period of peace.

Sir Harold Nicolson described the chief characteristics of the diplomacy of the period from Vienna to the First World War, when grand strategy was implemented on the basis of the balance of power, first in Europe and then in the rest of the world, as the European powers spread their influence internationally. First, diplomacy was Eurocentric. Europe was regarded as the most important area of the world and the other continents of secondary importance. Second, diplomacy was Great-Power-centric. The smaller and weaker powers were drawn into the orbits of one of the Great Powers in order to play their supporting roles in the unending maneuver to maintain, restore, or overthrow the existing balance of power. Third, the Great Powers possessed a "common responsibility for the conduct of the Small Powers and the preservation of peace between them." This implied a right of intervention by the Great Powers in crises and conflicts involving the smaller and weaker powers. Fourth, there was the establishment in every European country of a "professional diplomatic service on a more or less identical model." These professional diplomats developed a kind of corporate identity based on a common belief, notwithstanding the policies of their various governments, "that the purpose of diplomacy was the preservation of peace." Finally, diplomacy was conducted on "the rule that sound negotiation must be continuous and confidential." [9]

From 1815 to 1848, Britain followed its successful war-time diplomatic leadership with an ambitious attempt at peace-time coalition diplomacy. The British aimed to create a system of collective security based on dynastic legitimacy and participation in periodic international congresses to regulate the balance of power diplomatically. British foreign secretary Lord Castlereagh was the architect and inspiration both of the anti-Napoleonic coalitions and of the post-war settlement. Charles de Talleyrand, who served in leading political and diplomatic roles for every French government from the Old Regime before 1789 to Napoleon's Empire, deserted Napoleon to lead the French diplomatic effort to preserve key territorial gains since 1789 and win a seat at the table of European congress-diplomacy after 1815, thereby rescuing and restoring France's Great Power status. In 1818, the victorious powers—Britain, Austria, Russia, and Prussia—welcomed the same France they had defeated into a quintuple alliance that would exert a kind of collective supervision over the European state system. Five-power congresses authorized French intervention in Spain and Austrian interventions in Italy to put down revolutions there in the 1820s. The collective security arrangements of the Congress System did not last long, but the idea of a less institutionalized but still effective Concert of Europe, with the Great Powers acting as a kind of continental directorate, ensured general peace among themselves while permitting minor adjustments to the prevailing order for 30 years. Austrian Prince Clemens von Metternich, called "the coachman of Europe", guided the concert-system on the continent through the second quarter of the century, successfully pursuing peace and stability through the Concert of Europe and the conservative Holy Alliance of Russia, Austria, and Prussia to defend dynastic legitimacy against the threat from the most dangerous non-state actors, the nascent national movements. Even so, the system peacefully absorbed the effects of revolutions in France, Belgium and Poland in 1830.

During the period 1848-1871, the wave of nationalistic political and social revolutions that swept over Europe in 1848-1849 strongly challenged the system, and the gradual breakup of the Ottoman Empire in Europe, which led to the Crimean War of 1856, further taxed it. The processes of Italian and then German national unification were severe tests for the state system and deeply affected the balance of power, but even these events involved short, limited wars that were not allowed to become general European conflicts. The forces of nationalism were managed without recourse to general war. Italy was united under the Kingdom of Piedmont-Savoy through the diplomatic virtuosity of Prime Minister Camillo di Cavour, who joined the Franco-British alliance against Russia in the Crimean War (1854-1856). This gained him the British diplomatic support and the French military assistance he needed to defeat the Austrians (1859) who ruled northern Italy and to begin the unification process completed by his successors in 1870. Prussian Chancellor Otto von Bismarck united Germany by isolating France diplomatically while constructing an anti-French coalition among the smaller German states to defeat France in 1870 and proclaim the creation of the German Empire in 1871 with the Prussian king as Kaiser. Lord Palmerston put British naval and financial might to work to influence the balance of power on the continent to London's advantage. The American Civil War did not tempt the European powers, especially Britain and France, to serious intervention, either militarily or diplomatically. U.S. diplomacy, aimed at keeping the Europeans out of the issue, bested Confederate diplomacy, which sought European intervention and eventual recognition of the Confederacy as a legitimate, sovereign state. Even under the difficult conditions created by a rising tide of nationalism and political and social revolutionary sentiments the European powers managed to regulate their state system without recourse to general war or war between certain powers for more than a few months.

During the years 1871-1914, European diplomacy was concentrated on the peaceful management of two intense contests among the European powers, the competition for the remnants of the dissolving Ottoman Empire, especially in Europe, and the competition for colonial expansion in Africa and Asia. Bismarck's political foresight and diplomatic skill were demonstrated in both spheres, first as he assembled the Powers in Berlin in 1878 to craft a general settlement to the Russo-Turkish War of 1877-1878 that involved multiple changes of boundaries and prevented war from spreading. He called them together again in 1885 to submit a number of African colonial disputes to general arbitration and international decision. The United States under Theodore Roosevelt played a leading diplomatic role in ending the Russo-Japanese War of 1904-05 through mediation at Portsmouth, New Hampshire.

The 19th century produced advances in diplomatic institutions in response to developments in military affairs, economic expansion, nationalist ambitions, and the rise of public opinion. From the 1830s, military attachés were added to embassy staffs, reflecting the growing complexity of the military element of national power. Soon after, commercial attachés made a similar appearance in the diplomatic world, reflecting the growing importance of the economic element of national power. Governments also began to engage in cultural diplomacy by supporting missionaries they saw as spreading their languages and cultures as well as the faith, and by promoting cultural associations like the French *Alliance Française* and the Italian *Società Dante Alighieri* to encourage familiarity with and respect for their respective languages and cultures. Finally, Governments started to exploit the possibilities of influencing foreign public opinion, usually by trying to influence the popular press to report and comment favorably on their policies and actions.[10]

The ability of the European powers to continue to manage their diplomatic relations without recourse to general war ended in the cataclysm of 1914-1918. Historians would later see the First World War, and especially the inability of the powers to reach a durable settlement after it in Paris in 1919, as the end of the European state system and the beginning of the global state system of the 20th and 21st centuries. Diplomacy would, nevertheless, continue as a crucial element of power. [11]

ENDNOTES - CHAPTER 14

1. Jacob Burckhardt, *The Civilization of the Renaissance in Italy*, Oxford: Paaidon, 1944, p. 2. A long struggle for preeminence between the Popes of Rome and the Holy Roman Emperors resulted in the defeat of the German emperors and their expulsion from the Italian peninsula from 1250-1275. The Popes had called on French arms to do so and soon thereafter fell under French influence. From 1307-1378, most Popes were French and resided in Avignon in Southern France rather than Rome. That period of "Babylonian Captivity" in France was followed by nearly 50 years of deep division in the Church government, the Great Schism, when two or three different popes, each one of them considering the others "antipopes," elected by different factions and residing in different places inside and outside Italy, contended for the papal authority. The schism was only fully healed when Pope Martin V won general recognition as the only legitimate pope and returned to reside regularly in Rome in 1420.

2. Burckhardt, *Civilization*, p. 2.

3. Several Italian states had long experience with intelligence systems based on agents resident in foreign capitals. The Papacy had clerical envoys in every Christian court, and the repository of their reports in the Cancelleria palace in Rome was the prototype for the foreign ministries of later times; some governments still refer to foreign ministers as chancellors. The Venetian Republic also had its commercial agents all over Europe and the Middle East who were tasked with providing topical information to the city's rulers. In the 15th century, the Medici family that ruled Florence started to require the managers of the foreign branches of the family banking house to submit similar reports.

4. A superb introduction to Renaissance diplomatic history, theory, and practice is Garrett Mattingly's *Renaissance Diplomacy*, London: Jonathan Cape, 1955. The same author's *Catherine of Aragon*, London: Jonathan Cape, 1955, captures the political transformation of medieval *Christendom* into pre-modern *Europe* during the 16th century.

5. Good introductions to Machiavelli and his influence on political theory and practice are J. R. Hale, *Machiavelli and Renaissance Italy*, New York: Collier, 1960; Maurizio Viroli, *Machiavelli's Smile: A Biography*, New York: Farrar, Strauss and Giroux, 2000; Bernard Crick, "Introduction to Niccolò Machiavelli," *The Discourses*, London: Penguin, 1970, pp. 13-69; and Torbjörn L. Knutsen, *A History of International Relations Theory: An Introduction*, Manchester: Manchester University Press,1992, pp. 25-40.

6. Machiavelli was a major influence on Clausewitz, who read the Italian's main works and admired his approach to war and politics: "No book on earth is more necessary to the statesman than Machiavelli's; those who affect disgust at his principles are idealistic dilettantes . . . The twenty-first chapter of Machiavelli's *Prince* is the basic code for all diplomacy – and woe to those that fail to heed it!" Carl von Clausewitz, *Historical and Political Writings*, Peter Paret and Daniel Moran, eds., and trans., Princeton: Princeton University Press, 1992, pp. 268-269.

7. Adam Watson, *Diplomacy: The Dialogue Between States*, New York: McGraw-Hill, 1983, p. 103. Adam Watson served in the British Diplomatic Service from 1937 to 1974, including as ambassador in West Africa and to Cuba. He later taught at the University of Virginia. He is the author of many books on history, diplomacy, and international relations, including *The Evolution of International Society: A Comparative Historical Analysis*, London and New York: Routledge, 1992; and *The War of the Goldsmith's Daughter*, London: Chatto and Windus, 1964. He is considered one of the leading figures in the English school of international relations theory.

8. Watson, *Diplomacy*, p. 107.

9. Harold Nicolson, *The Evolution of Diplomacy*, Oxford and New York: Oxford University Press, 1966, pp. 100-105. Sir Harold Nicolson was a distinguished British diplomat and historian. From 1909-1929, he represented the British government in various parts of the world. He was an active participant in the Paris Peace Conference of 1919, which he described in the study *Peacemaking, 1919*, Boston: Houghton Mifflin, 1933. He served in the House of Commons from 1935 to 1945 and was knighted in 1953. See also his *Diplomacy*, Oxford and New York: Oxford University Press, 3rd edition, 1963; and *The Congress of Vienna: A Study in Allied Unity, 1812-1822*, New York: Viking, 1964.

10. M. S. Anderson, *The Rise of Modern Diplomacy, 1450-1919*, New York: Longman, 1993, pp. 128-141.

11. Besides the references cited elsewhere, I consulted the following in preparing this chapter: G. R. Berridge, Maurice Keens-Soper, and T. G. Otte, *Diplomatic Theory from Machiavelli to Kissinger*, New York: Palgrave, 2001; Keith Hamilton and Richard Langhorne, *The Practice of Diplomacy: Its Evolution, Theory, and Administration*, London and New York: Routledge, 1995; David Jablonsky, *Paradigm Lost? Transitions and the Search for a New World Order*, Carlisle, PA: Strategic Studies Institute, U.S. Army War College, 1993; Henry A. Kissinger, *Diplomacy*, New York: Simon and Schuster, 1994; Paul W. Schroeder, *The Transformation of European Politics, 1763-1848*, Oxford: Oxford University Press, 1994; and A. J. P. Taylor, *The Struggle for Mastery in Europe, 1848-1918*, Oxford: Oxford University Press, 1954. I recommend them for further study.

CHAPTER 15

MILITARY POWER AND THE USE OF FORCE[1]

John F. Troxell

Force without wisdom falls of its own weight.

Horace

International politics is a struggle for power. Power, in the international arena, is used to protect a nation's interests by influencing potential competitors or partners. The most important instrument of power available to a nationstate is military power. "In international politics in particular," according to Hans Morgenthau, "armed strength as a threat or a potentiality is the most important material factor making for the political power of a nation."[2] The other elements of power are certainly important and can contribute to the furtherance of national interests; however, as long as states continue to exist in a condition of anarchy, military power will continue to play a crucial role in international politics. As Kenneth Waltz aptly put it, "In politics force is said to be the ultima ratio. In international politics force serves, not only as the ultima ratio, but indeed as the first and constant one."[3]

The current world situation once again focuses the international community's attention on the role of military power, due in part to the absolute and relative dominance of the world's sole superpower, the United States. According to recent figures, U.S. defense expenditures account for 39 percent of the world's total spending on defense. The United States spends more than eight times the combined defense budgets of China and Russia, and more than 25 times the combined defense spending of the remaining six "rogue nations" (Cuba, Iran, Libya, Sudan, Syria, and North Korea). These comparisons do not reflect the defense contributions of the closest allies of the United States, nor do they include the impact of the Pentagon's fiscal 2005 budget request of $400 billion, a cumulative increase of 24 percent over the past 3 years.[4] The resultant gap in military capabilities is huge, and may even be greater than that reflected in a comparison of defense budgets, due to the technological lead and the high quality professional armed forces of the United States. Recent conventional operations in Kosovo, Afghanistan, and Iraq, only confirm this dominance.

As important as military power is to the functioning of the international system, it is a very expensive and dangerous tool of statecraft—one, as Robert Art recently pointed out, that should not be exercised without a great deal of wisdom:

> Using military power correctly does not ensure that a state will protect all of its interests, but using it incorrectly would put a great burden on these other instruments and could make it impossible for a state to achieve its goals. Decisions about whether and how to use military power may therefore be the most fateful a state makes.[5]

Art's caution is clearly evident in the emerging security environment of the 21st century. Despite undisputed U.S. military supremacy, the United States and its allies sense a greater vulnerability to their basic freedoms and way of life than at any time since the height of the nuclear standoff with the Soviet Union. Military supremacy has yet to find an answer to the combined threats of proliferation of weapons of mass destruction (WMD) and international terrorism. Failed states and rogue states continue to present security concerns and the resultant demand for military forces to contain conflicts and rebuild nations. The United States faces two strategic challenges—one of ends and the other of means. The most prominent declinist of the last decade, Paul Kennedy, argued that great powers succumb to "imperial overstretch" because their global interests and obligations outpace their ability to defend them all simultaneously. James Fallows recently echoed this concern in claiming that "America is over-extended" because the U.S. has so many troops tied down in so many places that we can no longer respond to emerging crises. Beyond the concern with over-ambitious ends, Fallows also claims that the United States is in danger of actually breaking the military instrument of power through overuse and thus returning to the days of the post-Vietnam "Hollow Army."[6]

The purpose of this chapter is to examine the role of military power in the international arena in an effort to address challenges, highlighted above, associated with its use. There are two major parts to this discussion. The first concerns the political purposes of military power, and the second concerns the actual use of military force. The use of force discussion will include a brief consideration of employment options (the Range of Military Operations), a presentation of various guidelines for the use of force, and a look at the issue of legitimacy.

POLITICAL PURPOSES OF MILITARY POWER

Despite all of the changes that have occurred in world politics since the end of the Cold War, there is in many respects an underlying continuity with earlier eras. The recent conflicts in Bosnia, Kosovo, Afghanistan, Iraq, and mass-casualty terrorism are evidence that the use of military power as an instrument of political purpose remains as relevant today as in the past. Clausewitz' famous dictum continues to ring true, "that war [the application of military power] should never be thought of as something autonomous but always as an instrument of policy," and that "war is simply a continuation of political intercourse, with the addition of other means." While still serving as the Chairman of the Joint Chiefs of Staff, Colin Powell analyzed the military successes that the United States had experienced through most of the 1990's. The principal reason for these achievements, he concluded, "is that in every instance we have matched the use of military force to our political objectives."[7]

From a modern day American perspective, the U.S. Constitution establishes the political context in which military power is applied and the framework for civilian authority over the Armed Forces. An earlier version of the capstone publication for the U.S. Armed Forces, Joint Publication 1 (JP 1), *Joint Warfare of the Armed Forces of the United States*, which addressed the employment of the U.S. military as an instrument of national power, was very explicit on this point: "Under the Constitution's framework, American military power operates for and under conditions determined by the people through their elected representatives. This political context establishes the objectives and the limits of legitimate military action in peace, crisis, and conflict in the United States and abroad."[8]

Military power can be matched to several different categories of broadly defined political objectives. The traditional categories that were developed and articulated during the Cold War, in the context of the U.S./USSR nuclear rivalry, included deterrence, compellence, and defense.[9] Since the threat of large-scale nuclear war between competing nationstates has largely receded, it seems more appropriate to focus on the political purposes behind the use of conventional forces. In this context the categories can be modified, as shown in Figure 1.

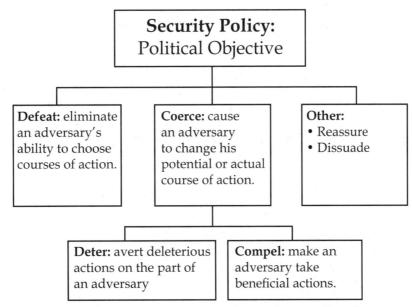

Figure 1. Components of Security Policy.[10]

Defeat.

Military power can be used in its purest sense to physically defeat an adversary. United States military doctrine clearly articulates this objective as the fundamental purpose of military power—to fight and win the nation's wars. Although recognizing other, potential non-combat objectives, U.S. doctrine argues that "success in combat in defense of national sovereignty, territorial integrity, societal values, and national interests is the essential goal and measure of the profession of arms in American society."[11] Thomas Schelling, in the classic *Arms and Influence*, used the phrase brute force, and referred to a country's ability, assuming it had enough military power, to forcibly seize, disarm or disable, or repel, deny, and defend against an opponent.[12] Schelling's discussion clearly recognizes both offensive and defensive uses of force. Robert Art, on the other hand, focuses on the defensive use of force as the deployment of military power to either ward off an attack or to minimize damage if actually attacked. Despite this focus, Art also argues that a state can use its forces to strike first if it believes that an attack is imminent or inevitable. This leads to the distinction between a preemptive attack—in response to an imminent threat, and a preventive attack—in response to an inevitable attack. A preventive attack can be undertaken if a state believes that others will attack it when the balance of forces shift in their favor, or perhaps after key military capabilities are developed. In the case of either preemptive or preventive actions, Art concludes that "it is better to strike first than to be struck first," and supports the maxim that "the best defense is a good offense." The defeat aspect of military force seeks to eliminate the adversary's ability or opportunity to do anything other than what is demanded of it.[13]

Coercion.

Because of the high cost and uncertainty associated with combat operations, a nation's primary strategic objective is usually an attempt to cause an adversary to accede to one's demands short of war or actual combat operations. As such, most states attempt to achieve their goals through coercion. Successful coercion is not war-fighting, but is the use of threatened force, including the limited use of actual force to back up that threat, to induce an adversary to behave differently than it otherwise would. Coercion relies on the threat of future military force to influence an adversary's decisionmaking.[14] As opposed to brute force, coercion is the "threat of damage, or of more damage to come, that can make someone yield or comply."[15] From this perspective, it is withheld violence that can influence an adversary's choice. It is this perception of withheld consequences that causes a nation to acquiesce to a coercer's demands. Those consequences can take the broad form of anticipated punishment in response to an action, or anticipated denial or failure of an opponent's chosen course of action. Punitive coercion seeks to influence an opponent through fear, and coercion by denial through hopelessness. Finally, just as it is important to recognize the dynamic nature of the strategy formulation process, strategists should also view coercion as a dynamic, two (or more) player contest. Each side acts, not only based on anticipation of the other side's moves, but also based on other changes in the security environment. The adversary can react to alter the perceived costs and benefits and certainly has a vote in assessing the credibility of the coercer's threat.[16] Coercion has two subcategories: deterrence and compellence.

Deterrence. Deterrence, in its broadest sense, means persuading an opponent *not to initiate* a specific action because the perceived benefits do not justify the estimated costs and risks. Deterrence can be based on punishment, which involves a threat to destroy what the adversary values, or on denial, which requires convincing an opponent that he will not achieve his goals on the battlefield. In either case, the adversary is assumed to be willing and able to engage in well-informed cost-benefit calculations and respond rationally on the basis of those calculations. An irrational (or ill-informed) opponent that will accept destruction or disproportionate loss may not be deterrable.[17] Deterrence theory became almost synonymous with strategy during the Cold War as both superpowers sought to ensure their survival through mutual threats of massive nuclear retaliation.[18] Nevertheless, there are certain important distinctions concerning the term: [19]

- General (strategic) or immediate (tactical) deterrence (the former refers to a diffuse deterrent effect deriving from one's capabilities and reputation; the later to efforts to discourage specific behavior in times of crises). An example of tactical deterrence was the evidently successful threat conveyed to Saddam Hussein during the first Gulf War to dissuade Iraq from using WMD against coalition forces. An unsuccessful example was the U.S.-UAE tanker exercise that failed to dissuade Iraq from invading Kuwait.
- Extended and central deterrence (the former alludes to endeavors to extend deterrent coverage over friends and allies; the latter to the deterrence of attack upon one's homeland). Examples continue to abound concerning extended deterrence — one particularly difficult issue concerns the U.S. security guarantees extended to Taiwan.

There are two challenges to the future deterrent posture of U.S. forces. The first is the on-going issue of trying to evaluate the effectiveness of a deterrent policy. The willingness of a legislative body to allocate resources to various elements of military power is normally contingent on recognition of beneficial results. Henry Kissinger aptly describes the problem:

> Since deterrence can only be tested negatively, by events that do not take place, and since it is never possible to demonstrate why something has not occurred, it became especially difficult to assess whether existing policy was the best possible policy or a just barely effective one. Perhaps deterrence was unnecessary because it was impossible to prove whether the adversary ever intended to attack in the first place.[20]

The second challenge deals with the changing nature of the threat. During the Cold War deterrence was based on a known enemy operating from a known location and under the assumed direction of a rational leader. The emergence of rogue states and transnational terrorist networks that could gain access to weapons of mass destruction has created what Colin Gray defines as the current crisis of deterrence. These new actors do not necessarily share the long-standing and highly developed theory of deterrence that emerged from the Cold War, and the cost-benefit calculus that underpins deterrence may be clouded by cultural differences and varying attitudes towards risk. In fact, as Gray observes, "…some of the more implacable of our contemporary adversaries appear to be undeterrable. Not only are their motivations apparently unreachable by the standard kind of menaces, but they lack fixed physical assets for us to threaten."[21] The current U.S. *National Security Strategy* is in full accord with these views: "Traditional concepts of deterrence will not work against a terrorist enemy whose avowed tactics are wanton destruction and the targeting of innocents; whose so-called soldiers seek martyrdom in death and whose most potent protection is statelessness."[22]

Compellence. Compellence is the use of military power to change an adversary's behavior. It attempts to reverse an action that has already occurred or to otherwise overturn the status quo. Examples include evicting an aggressor from territory it has just conquered or convincing a proliferating state to abandon its nuclear weapons program. According to Thomas Schelling, who initially coined the term, "Compellence… usually involves initiating action that can cease, or become harmless, only if the opponent responds."[23] Physical force is often employed to harm another state until the later abides by the coercer's demands. It is important to recognize the difference between compellence and deterrence. The distinction, according to Robert Art, "is one between the active and passive use of force. The success of a deterrent threat is measured by its not having been used. The success of a compellent action is measured by how closely and quickly the adversary conforms to one's stipulated wishes."[24]

Compellence may be easier to demonstrate than deterrence, because of the observable change in behavior; but it tends to be harder to achieve. It is usually easier to make a potential aggressor decide not to attack in the first place than to cause the same aggressor to call off the attack once it is underway. A state that is deterred from taking a particular action can always claim that it never intended to act in such a way, and thus publicly ignore the deterrent threat. However, if a state succumbs to compellent actions, it is much harder to change behavior without an associated loss of prestige and possible national humiliation. Consequently, compellent threats should be accompanied by a complementary set of concessions or face-saving measures to make it politically acceptable for a state to comply. Success can also be driven by the perceived or actual imbalance of interests at stake. As the American experience in Vietnam demonstrated, compellence tends to fail when the issue is of vital importance to the adversary but possibly only represents an important or peripheral interest to the coercing state.[25]

In the post-Cold War era, three broad conditions have emerged that facilitate the effective use of military threats. These relationships are expressed in Figure 2. Together, the credibility of the threat and the degree of difficulty of the demands shape the targeted leader's evaluation of the likely cost of complying or of not complying with U.S. demands. If the threat is perceived to be wholly incredible, the anticipated cost of noncompliance will be low. The balance between the cost of compliance and the cost of defiance represents the potency of the threat. In the post-Cold War period, despite overwhelming U.S. military supremacy, it has been extremely difficult for the United States to achieve its objectives without actually conducting sustained military operations. A principal reason for this difficulty is the existence of a generation of political leaders throughout the world whose basic perception of U.S. military power and political will is one of weakness. They enter any situation with a fundamental belief that the United States can be defeated or driven away.[26]

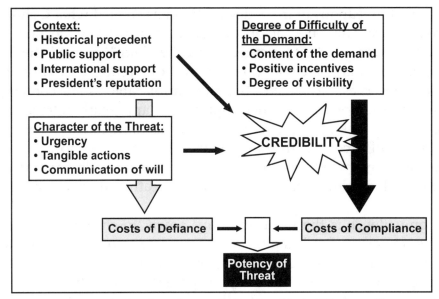

Figure 2. Evaluations of Compellent Threats.[27]

Echoing Colin Gray's crisis of deterrence, perhaps there is a similar crisis of compellence. According to Blechman and Wittes:

> American presidents have been reluctant to step as close to the plate as had been required to achieve U.S. objectives in many post-cold war conflicts. They have made threats only reluctantly and usually have not made as clear or potent a threat as was called for by the situation. They have understood the need to act in the situation but have been unwilling or perceived themselves as being unable to lead the American people into the potential sacrifice necessary to secure the proper goal. As a result, they have attempted to satisfice, taking some action but not the most effective possible action to challenge the foreign leader threatening U.S. interests. They have sought to curtail the extent and potential cost of the confrontation by avoiding the most serious type of threat and therefore the most costly type of war if the threat were challenged.[28]

This conclusion was written prior to the tragic events of 9/11 and the subsequent operations in Afghanistan and Iraq. Time will tell if Americans will sustain their support for two very challenging and increasingly costly nation-building projects.

Reassurance.

Finally, there are two other political objectives listed on Figure 1. The first of these is reassurance, a term that began as a key element of U.S. nuclear strategy. In particular, reassurance was closely associated with the notion of extended deterrence in that its objective was to extend security guarantees to friends and allies. As a consequence, reassurance played a crucial role in the Cold War if for no other reason that the concept helped to prevent the proliferation of nuclear weapons to states like Germany and Japan. In a similar manner, the current U.S. defense policy includes, as its first objective, the goal of assuring friends and allies. This assurance is gained through the forward presence of U.S. forces and ensures allies and friends that the U.S. will honor its security commitments and continue to be a reliable security partner. In addition to the stationing of large numbers of U.S. military personnel overseas, the political objective of reassurance/assurance is achieved through numerous security cooperation activities and agreements. Security cooperation serves U.S. national interests by advancing U.S. values and beliefs, promoting regional stability, and improving cooperation among allies, partners and friends.[29] From this perspective, security is this country's most influential public-sector export. "We are the only nation on earth," one analyst observes, "capable of exporting security in a sustained fashion, and we have a very good track record of doing it."[30] A primary consequence of a more secure environment is the promotion of global economic growth. With this focus on both security and economic interests, the ultimate purpose of U.S. military engagement, according to some analysts, is to maintain international order, thereby allowing the American people to continue to reap the benefits of globalization.[31]

Dissuasion.

The final political objective is dissuasion, sometimes presented as the ultimate purpose of both defense and deterrence, that is, persuading others not to take actions harmful to oneself. The notion here, however, is more in keeping with that of the *National Security Strategy*, which describes building U.S. military forces strong enough "to dissuade potential adversaries from pursuing a military build-up in hopes of surpassing, or equaling the power of the United States."[32] The QDR elaborates on this objective: "Well targeted strategy and policy can therefore dissuade other countries from initiating future military competitions. The United States can exert such influence through the conduct of research and development, test, and demonstration programs. It can do so by maintaining or enhancing advantages in key areas of military capability."[33] The goal is clearly to maintain, if not grow, the tremendous capability gap that U.S. military forces enjoy over virtually all other militaries. The origin of this objective dates back to the formerly discredited draft 1992 Defense Planning Guidance. When initially leaked to the press, this document included a call to preserve American global military supremacy, to discourage others from challenging our leadership, and to maintain a military dominance capable of "deterring potential competitors from even aspiring to a larger regional or global role."[34] More recently, Secretary of Defense, Donald Rumsfeld has been equally explicit: "Just as the existence of the U.S. Navy dissuades others from investing in competing navies—because it would cost them a fortune and would not provide them a margin of military advantage—we must develop new assets, the mere possession of which discourages adversaries from competing."[35]

The concept, however, need not be so rough edged; dissuasion can also apply to countries that are not full-fledged adversaries, but those with which the U.S. has a mixed relationship—mutual suspicions and common incentives to avoid violence. The term goes to the heart of the new geo-strategic era. "In short, dissuasion aims at urging potential geopolitical rivals not to become real rivals by making clear that any sustained malevolent conduct will be checkmated by the United States. It involves military pressure applied with a velvet glove, not crude threats of war and destruction."[36] The key relationship for U.S. dissuasion is that with China in terms of preventing the People's Republic from developing assertive, and menacing geo-political policies. Colin Gray is much more sanguine about this policy's prospects, noting "we should expect state-centric enemies to attempt to organize to resist the American hegemony, and in particular to work hard in search of strategic means and methods that might negate much of our dissuasive strength."[37]

In all this, it is important to recognize that military power alone is not sufficient to conduct a successful foreign policy. Military power must be properly integrated with the other elements of statecraft—political, economic, diplomatic, and information. Even for the greatest of nations, as Joseph Nye argues, military power is always in short supply and consequently must be rationed among competing goals: "The paradox of American power is that world politics is changing in a way that makes it impossible for the strongest world power since Rome to achieve some of its most crucial international goals alone."[38]

RANGE OF MILITARY OPERATIONS

The broad political purposes for the use of military power clearly encompass many different employment options for military force. These operations vary in size, purpose, and combat intensity in what the Joint Staff calls the "Range of Military Operations (ROMO)" that extends from military engagement, security cooperation, and deterrence activities to crisis response and limited contingency operations, and if necessary, major operations and campaigns (Figure 3).[39] The dividing lines between various categories of military operations have become much less distinct over the years.

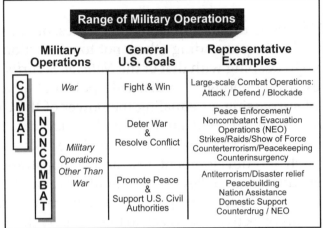

Source: Joint Publication 3-0, Doctrine for Joint Operations, September 10, 2001, I-2

Figure 3. Range of Military Operations.

Major operations and campaigns generally involve large-scale combat, placing the United States in a wartime state. Crisis response and limited contingency operations can be a small-scale, limited duration operation not involving combat or a significant part of an extended duration major operation involving combat. The level of complexity, duration, and resources depends on the circumstances. These operations may include humanitarian assistance, civil support, noncombatant evacuation, peace operations, strikes, raids or recovery operations.

Peace operations can be considered as either peace enforcement or peacekeeping operations. Peace enforcement operations are also referred to as Chapter VII operations referring to Chapter VII of the UN Charter, which addresses enforcement actions "with respect to threats to the peace, breaches of the peace, and acts of aggression." A closely related category is peace-making, which assumes that one of the protagonists opposes the status quo. These operations take place in a non-consensual environment. Peacekeeping is often referred to as a Chapter VI operation under the UN Charter, which addresses "pacific settlement of disputes." Peacekeepers are impartial and relatively passive, called upon to monitor or verify troop withdrawals, separation of forces, or provide security during elections. These operations take place in a consensual environment.

Using military forces for military engagement, security cooperation, and deterrence represent on-going operations that shape the environment and maintain cooperative relations with other nations. In general these missions are below the threshold of armed conflict and are designed to build trust and confidence, develop partner capacity and in the case of deterrence to present a credible threat of counteraction.

In any event, all of these different classifications of military operations can be viewed as fulfilling one of the three principal political purposes: defensive, compellent or deterrent. For example, the political goal of humanitarian interventions and peacekeeping operations is to save lives; this is defense of parties under attack. The political goal of nation-assistance is to construct a viable government; this can be viewed as compelling armed groups or other elements of the society to obey the new central government. As a final example, the political goal of any collective security arrangement is to prevent aggression; which is deterrence.[40]

There is one important type of military operation that is not explicitly cited in the "Range of Military Operations" chart—covert action. These actions are a specialty of the U.S. Special Operations Forces (SOF) community, which is currently enjoying an unprecedented prominence within the U.S. military. Covert action is defined by U.S. law as activity meant "to influence political, economic or military conditions abroad, where it is intended that the role of the United States Government will not be apparent or acknowledged."[41] According to the Special Operations Command posture statement, "SOF are specifically organized, trained, and equipped to conduct covert, clandestine, or discreet counterterrorism missions in hostile, denied, or politically sensitive environments."[42] The current definition of covert operations was adopted as part of the effort to fill gaps in oversight that led to the Iran-Contra scandal. According to the law, covert actions must first be authorized by a written presidential finding, and the House and Senate intelligence committees must be notified before the operation has begun.[43]

In the past, SOF missions were viewed as "traditional military activities" in support of on-going or anticipated military campaigns and were thus not subject to the covert action oversights just mentioned. However, in the on-going, and broadly defined campaign against global terrorism—a campaign in which the Special Operations Command directly plans and executes its own missions—there is some concern that this type of use of force will be completely removed from congressional oversight. On the one hand, the U.S. government should be able to use every tool available in the fight against terrorism. However, such broad-brush authority, combined with an increasing propensity to use SOF in covert operations in support of an aggressive preemption strategy, may lead to abuse and risks to U.S. foreign policy.[44]

One final point concerning the current nature of military operations is the increasingly cluttered battlefield from the standpoint of other coalition partners, interagency elements, and even non-governmental organizations. The Joint Staff describes the nature of these operations as *unified action*. The concept of unified action highlights the synergistic application of all of the instruments of national and multinational power and includes the actions of nonmilitary organizations as well as military forces.[45]

GUIDELINES FOR THE USE OF FORCE

> War cannot be divorced from political life; whenever this occurs in our thinking about war, the many links that connect the two elements are destroyed and we are left with something pointless and devoid of sense.
>
> Clausewitz

> If not in the interests of the state, do not act. If you cannot succeed, do not use troops.
>
> Sun Tzu

> Madeleine Albright asked me in frustration, "What's the point of having this superb military that you're always talking about if we can't use it?" I thought I would have an aneurysm.
>
> Colin Powell[46]

These quotations emphasize the importance of linking political objectives to the use of military force. One of the best ways to ensure this is to use military force only in support of the national interest and when success is assured. The difficulty with such a straight forward prescription is reconciling the various degrees of interests, to include valid concerns about furthering important national and international values. In addition, the resort to war or conflict always unleashes the forces of chance and friction, creating in one analyst's description, "a fearful lottery."[47] Creating the conditions for success, let alone guaranteeing success is much easier said than done. Decisions concerning the use of force are the most important that any nation can make. Given that the post-Cold War experience supports the necessity of resorting to force and the threats of force, but also emphasizes the risks of doing so, national security decision-makers are left with a critical issue in the theory and practice of foreign policy: under what conditions and how can military force and threats of force be used effectively to accomplish different types of policy objectives. In the final analysis, political leaders should come up with convincing answers to these questions before sending soldiers in harms way.[48]

Debates in the United States about appropriate guidelines for the use of force normally revolve around the Weinberger Doctrine—which is habitually viewed as an outgrowth of the lessons from the Vietnam War[49]. However, the origins of the current debate actually go back to the Korean War. Two schools of strategic thought developed from an assessment of that limited and inconclusive war. The first was the never-again, or all-or-nothing school, which advocated that either the United States should do everything necessary to win a decisive military victory or it should not intervene at all.[50] At the other extreme was the limited-war school. Proponents of this view held that the United States could expect to become involved in regional conflicts demanding intervention in support of less than vital interests. Colin Powell, although normally associated with the all-or-nothing school, has argued that all wars are limited; either by territory on which they are fought, the means used, or the objectives for which they are fought.[51]

Secretary of Defense Casper Weinberger articulated his six criteria for the use of force in response to two major issues—the lessons of the Vietnam War and an on-going policy debate in the Reagan administration about the appropriate response to terrorism. Both issues are clearly relevant as the debate on the use of force enters the 21st Century. Lessons from Vietnam included the recognition that military victory does not always result in political victory and that sustaining public and political support throughout a prolonged war can be difficult. Both of these issues continue to resonate in the debate about U.S. operations in Iraq. Senator Kennedy, for instance, recently charged that "Iraq has developed into a quagmire," and has become George Bush's Vietnam.[52]

Concerning terrorism, when the Weinberger doctrine was unveiled in 1984, the national security elites were in a heated debate about this issue, particularly as it related to the failure of U.S. policy in Lebanon. Weinberger was reluctant to commit troops to such an indeterminate and chaotic situation. Secretary of State George Shultz, on the other hand, argued that the Weinberger doctrine counseled inaction bordering on paralysis, and that "diplomacy could work these problems most effectively when force—of the threat of force—was a credible part of the equation." The *Wall Street Journal* referred to "Mr. Shultz's sensible anti-terrorist policy of 'active-prevention, pre-emption and retaliation'."[53] Shultz was on the losing end of this debate in the 1980's, but twenty years later his approach seems to have carried the day, at least in the Bush administration. Figure 4 shows the Weinberger doctrine and several more recent versions of guidelines for the use of force.

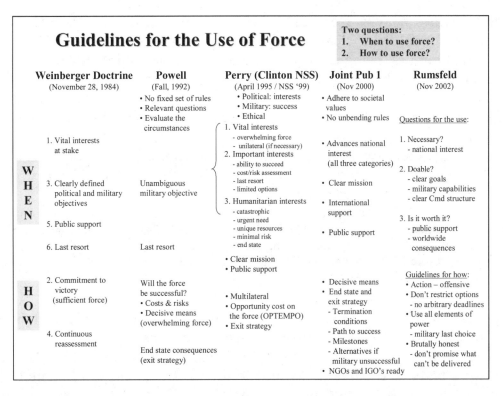

Figure 4. Guidelines for the Use of Force.[54]

When to use force is the first critical question. The linkage of such use in support of vital national interests harkens back to the Napoleonic notion of fighting wars for grand purposes. Samuel Huntington defined national interest as a public good of concern to all or most Americans; and a vital national interest as one that Americans are willing to expend blood and treasure to defend. The 2000 *National Security Strategy* defined vital interests as those directly connected to the survival, safety, and vitality of the nation. There are two problems with this very straight forward proposition. The first is the difficulty in determining what those vital interests are. The domestic consensus that supported U.S. foreign policy during the Cold War has been shattered, resulting in a lack of agreement on the nature and importance of U.S. national interests.[55] The recent focus on commercial and ethnic interests exacerbates the lack of widespread agreement on national interests. "The institutions and capabilities created to serve a grand national purpose in the Cold War," according to Huntington, "are now being suborned and redirected to serve narrow subnational, transnational, and even nonnational purpose."[56] Conversely, the attacks of 9/11 have undoubtedly contributed to a recognition of grand purposes and vital national interests, at least as associated with the war on terrorism.

The second concern is that states often use force in support of secondary and even tertiary interests. They do this either to protect vital interests, or to support important national values. Secretary of Defense William J. Perry supported the selective use of force and thus distinguished between three categories of interests—vital, important, and humanitarian. He argued that different uses of limited force, and not necessarily applied in an overwhelming manner, were appropriate to protect these interests in the pursuit of limited objectives.[57] Perry's Chairman of the Joint Chiefs, General Shalikashvili, also desired more flexibility in the use of force. He reportedly claimed that he did not have the right to put a sign on his door saying, "I'm sorry—we only do the big ones." The United States has clearly continued to use force in support of non-vital interests or important national values. And wars waged in the name of values invariably turn out to be more controversial than wars waged for interests.[58]

Weinberger borrows heavily from Clausewitz for his third, and relatively uncontroversial criteria, the importance of having clearly established objectives. According to Clausewitz, "No one starts a war . . . without first being clear in his own mind what he intends to achieve by that war and how he intends to conduct it."[59] This criteria is common across all of the sets of guidelines. Recognizing the need for clear objectives, however, does not necessarily remove all debate on the issue. The objectives chosen, just as the articulation of the national interests at stake, may not reflect broad agreement.

There are two other points worth considering on this criterion. First, once a war begins, chance, friction, and uncertainty take effect and original political objectives and force requirements, as Michael Handel has observed, can change.

> Weinberger's assumptions are more correct for military interventions/operations that can be carried out swiftly and decisively, . . . than they are for prolonged interventions and wars. The problem, of course, is that it is often very difficult to tell in advance which interventions will be short and decisive, and which will be costly and long.[60]

The second point is that it is always difficult to determine in advance if a certain compellent or deterrent action will have the desired effect, or result in an unanticipated counter-reaction by an adversary. As Richard Haass so aptly puts it, "It is as simple—and as basic—as the difference between winning a battle and winning a war. It only takes one party to initiate hostilities, but it takes everyone involved to bring hostilities to an end."[61]

The next two criteria: public support and last resort, are also common across all of the sets of guidelines. The need to maintain public and political support is common sense but not completely without debate, and certainly not without potentially great difficulty in execution. In the original argument over the Weinberger doctrine, Secretary Shultz took issue with the need for public support prior to initiating action. In his view, the duties of leadership could require action before mobilization of public support.

> My view is that democratically elected and accountable individuals have been placed in positions where they can and must make decisions to defend our national security. The risk and burden of leadership is that those decisions will receive, or not receive, the support of the people on their merits. The democratic process will deal with leaders who fail to measure up to the standards imposed by the American people. . . .[62]

There is a great deal of historical validity to the "rally-around-the-flag" and "support-the-troops" effect. That approach can be particularly effective for short and decisive campaigns. In prolonged wars, however, the difficulty does not lie so much in obtaining initial public and political support as it does in sustaining it for the duration.[63] Leaders must lead and mobilize public support. That can most easily be done by appeals to moral values or national interests. In any event,

> the inertia of the governed can not be disentangled from the indifference of the government. American leaders have both a circular and a deliberate relationship to public opinion. It is circular because their constituencies are rarely if ever aroused by foreign crises, even genocidal ones, in the absence of political leadership, and yet at the same time U.S. officials continually cite the absence of public support as grounds for inaction.[64]

Last resort is an important component of the just war theory of *jus ad bellum*, or just resort in going to war. Americans have traditionally been very reluctant to resort to force unless they have been directly attacked. There is always a strong desire to give diplomacy a chance, or obtain sufficient results through the application of economic sanctions or other pressures. Time is also needed to mobilize domestic and international support. However, it may not always be wise to delay military action. Once again, George Shultz challenged this point, "The idea that force should be used 'only as a last resort' means that, by the time of use, force is the only resort and likely a much more costly one than if used earlier."[65] General Wesley Clark, in his examination of the Kosovo campaign, concluded that the key lesson must be that "nations and alliances should move early to deal with crises while they are still ambiguous and can be dealt with more easily, for delay raises both the costs and the risks. Early action is the objective to which statesmen and military leaders should aspire."[66] All of this has direct relevance for the threat of catastrophic terrorism. Countering undeterrable terrorist organizations armed with weapons of mass destruction places the other instruments of statecraft at a huge disadvantage. "To consider force as a last resort is appropriate when trying to settle inter-state conflict," according to Ivo Daalder, "but when it comes to . . . preventing the proliferation of weapons of mass destruction, or defeating terrorism waiting too long to employ force can both enhance the cost and reduce the effectiveness of its use."[67]

The last two items on Weinberger's list concern how force should be used. The first of these addresses the importance of committing sufficient forces to accomplish the objectives. The goal is to avoid a long, drawn-out gradual employment of force that may not accomplish the objectives in a swift and decisive manner. This is the essence of the Vietnam syndrome. The U.S. military wants to avoid a half-hearted approach that results in higher casualties, a prolonged war, and a decision to quit before the mission is accomplished. One significant deterrent to U.S. action in Bosnia was the estimated steep cost of intervening in terms of troops required. For instance, the Joint Staff estimated in 1992 that it would take 50,000 U.S. ground troops to secure the Sarajevo airport for humanitarian relief operations. The airlift was eventually conducted under the watchful care of only 1,000 Canadian and French forces.[68]

On the other hand, it is normally better to go into a hostile environment with too much rather than too little force. General Powell used the phrase decisive force and indicated that decisive means and results are always preferred, and that if force is used "we should not be equivocal: we should win and win decisively."[69] Decisive means eventually evolved into overwhelming force, and related concepts, such as shock and awe. The controversy about U.S. end strength in Iraq, in both the initial combat phase and the subsequent stabilization and reconstruction phase, will only contribute to renewed military reluctance to undertake operations with less than overwhelming or decisive force. General Wesley Clark has argued in this regard that Operation Iraqi Freedom took "unnecessary risk because it skimped on the forces made available to the commanders," during the combat phase, and he claimed the existence of excessive risk during the post-combat phase. "The result was a U.S. force at the operation's end that was incapable of providing security, stopping the looting and sabotage, or establishing a credible presence throughout the country."[70] The all-or-nothing versus limited objective (limited war) debate continues.

Michael Handel refers to the final item, the need for continuous reassessment, as the escape clause. Circumstances may change, or the enemy may respond in an unexpected manner, all necessitating a reassessment of objectives (ends), concepts (ways), and forces (means). That criteria also implies that if the costs become too high or if the objectives do not justify a greater commitment of resources, it may be prudent to terminate the conflict.[71]

Figure 4 clearly shows that several of the Weinberger guidelines have evolved and been modified over the years. One of the most important and far-reaching evolutions is the expansion of applicable interests categories and the recognition that limited options for the use of force may be appropriate in the pursuit of less than vital interests. Another is the inclusion of the concern about multilateral or international support. That guideline was added in the Clinton administration's national security strategies and reflected a growing interest in ensuring multilateral responses to security issues. Multilateralism obviously included deliberations and support from NATO, but also recognized an enhanced role for the United Nations. America's alliances were one of the keystones of Clinton's selective engagement strategy, and the administration saw the UN as an important actor in the new world order. Having partners when it comes to using force also contributes to gaining and sustaining public support. As Charles Krauthammer argued at the close of the Gulf War, "Americans insist on the multilateral pretense. A large segment of American opinion doubts the legitimacy of unilateral American action, but accepts action taken under the rubric of the 'world community.'" He went on to say that the ultimate problem with "multilateralism is that if you take it seriously you gratuitously forfeit American freedom of action."[72]

Finally, in terms of the evolution of the Weinberger guidelines, there is the inclusion of end state and exit strategy concerns. The desire to establish an exit strategy is principally associated with interventions that do not involve vital interests. If vital interests are at stake, national security experts generally assume that politicians will apply overwhelming force, unilaterally if necessary, until the conflict is resolved. For interventions in support of important or humanitarian issues, there is much more of a premium placed on quickly reaching an agreed upon end-state, getting U.S. forces out, and reconstituting them for the next "big one." Some analysts have argued that this criteria should be expanded to include specific termination conditions, paths to success, and milestones along those paths. Rumsfeld's guidelines, however, seem to challenge this point by specifically cautioning against arbitrary deadlines. He is supported in this view by Richard Haass who argues that it is important to "avoid a specific end point or certain date for ending the commitment regardless of local developments. Artificial boundaries on a U.S. intervention run the risk of emboldening adversaries, who need only to wait until the deadline has passed, and unnerving allies."[73] End states can also be very ambiguous and constrained, since they rarely include unconditional surrender, regime change or destruction of the war-making capability of the other side.[74]

Michael Handel's analysis of the Weinberger doctrine concluded that it represented a utilitarian, realistic yardstick not much concerned with moral and ethical questions, although it does in fact provide useful insights for moral and ethical decisions about the use of force.[75] The proliferation of intra-state conflicts in the post-Cold War world, and the growing threat posed by nonstate actors, will continue to place pressure on decision-makers to decide when and how to use force. Figure 5 represents a score card of sorts to portray a subjective assessment of the application of the Weinberger doctrine to recent U.S. military operations.

Weinberger Doctrine from Vietnam to Iraq

Criterion	Vietnam	Grenada	Lebanon	Panama	Persian Gulf War	Somalia	Haiti (1994)	Bosnia	Kosovo	Iraq (2003)
1. Vital interests at stake	NO	NO	NO	NO	YES	YES	NO	NO	NO	YES
2. Commitment to victory	NO	YES	NO	YES	YES	NO	YES – for regime change NO – nation bldg	NO	NO	YES – for regime change ? – nation bldg
3. Clearly defined pol/mil objectives	NO	YES	NO	YES	YES	YES then NO	NO	?	YES – short term ?- long term	YES
4. Continuous reassessment	YES	YES	YES	YES	YES	YES	YES	YES	YES	YES
5. Public support (mobilized by the gov't)	NO	NO	NO	NO	YES	YES (at first)	YES	YES (?)	YES	YES
6. Last resort	NO	NO	NO	NO	NO	NO	YES	NO	NO	YES/NO
Success or Failure	FAILURE	SUCCESS	FAILURE	SUCCESS	SUCCESS	FAILURE	FAILURE	?	?	?

Figure 5. Weinberger Doctrine from Vietnam to Iraq.[76]

LEGITIMACY

One of the main tenets of the Weinberger doctrine was the need to garner public and congressional support—"some reasonable assurance we will have the support of the American people and their elected representatives in Congress."[77] Public support represents the will of the people, and as Harry Summers concluded, the failure to invoke that national will was one of the principal strategic failures of the Vietnam War, producing a strategic vulnerability that the North Vietnamese were able to exploit.[78] Public support and national will are both a reflection of the legitimacy with which the use of force is viewed. Legitimacy is fostered and sustained through many channels, including the steadfast application of Weinberger doctrine-like guidelines, Congressional resolutions and legislation, Presidential leadership, and actions of the international community. Legitimacy is thus grounded in both domestic processes and international or multilateral organizations and processes.

The President and the Congress.

Constitutional provisions represent the foundation of legitimacy in the United States. Under the constitution, the president and Congress share the war powers. The president is commander in chief (Article II, Section 2), but Congress has the power to declare war and raise and support the armed forces (Article I, Section 8). Congress, however, has only declared war on five occasions, the last being World War II. Despite having considerable constitutional authority over decisions about the use of force, Congress has largely deferred to the president as commander in chief, in general recognition that this role makes him responsible for leading the armed forces and gives him the power to repel attacks against the United States. Consequently, the executive branch has executed most military interventions.[79]

In an effort to regain some control over decisions on the use of force, and as a backlash to the Vietnam War, Congress passed the War Powers Resolution (WPR) over President Nixon's veto in 1973. The purpose of the War Powers Resolution was to ensure that Congress and the President share in making decisions about the use of force. Compliance becomes an issue when the president introduces forces abroad in situations that might be construed as hostilities or imminent hostilities. The law included a broad set of triggers for executive consultations and explanations of the rationale for, and the scope and duration of military operations. If Congress does not grant authorization in a certain period, the law does not permit the action to continue. Presidents have never acknowledged the constitutionality of the War Powers Resolution; however, they have made modest efforts to comply with its reporting requirements, submitting 104 reports to Congress concerning troop deployments abroad.[80] Some deployments were not reported because of the brevity of the operation or the perceived lack of hostilities or imminent hostilities. Most of the reports submitted to Congress are done "consistent with the War Powers Resolution," and not in "compliance" with the WPR.

Despite this record on reporting, a longer-term issue concerns the degree to which Congress is actually participating in the decisions to employ force. The WPR requires the president to consult with Congress prior to introducing U.S. forces into hostilities and to continue consultations as long as the armed forces remain. The conclusion of one Congressional Research study is that there has been very little executive consultation with Congress, "when consultation is defined to mean seeking advice prior to a decision to introduce troops."[81] It is certainly in the country's best interest to garner Congressional support, and thus the two branches of government need to work out useful political processes that debate, inform, and support the country's engagement in conflict. From this perspective, a major purpose behind the WPR was not necessarily to constrain the president, but to force the Congress to meet its obligations to share in decisions on the use of force, "compelling members to face within a predictable period and under specified procedures the fundamental question regarding military action by the United States: Does the Congress endorse or oppose the commitment of American blood and treasure to a particular mission?"[82] The question is appropriate for Congress. As confirmed by Secretary Weinberger, U.S. military personnel want to know that they have the backing of the public—a commitment affirmed through a constitutional political process.[83]

The WPR played an important role in the Persian Gulf War of 1991. In response to the Iraqi invasion of Kuwait in 1990, President Bush notified Congress that he had deployed forces to the region. Although he had not consulted with Congress before acting, both houses later adopted resolutions supporting the deployment. Throughout the fall of 1990 there was intense debate within Congress concerning the use of force. Urged by congressional leaders, President Bush later asked for a resolution supporting the use of all necessary means to implement the UN decrees on Iraq. On January 12, 1991, both houses, by narrow margins, approved a joint resolution authorizing the use of force pursuant to UN resolution 678, which had been passed on November 29, 1990.[84]

In the crisis in Bosnia, on the other hand, the United States participated without congressional authorization in humanitarian airlifts into Sarajevo, naval monitoring and sanctions, and aerial enforcement of no-fly zones and safe havens. In late 1995, after President Clinton committed over 20,000 combat troops as part of the NATO-led peacekeeping force, Congress considered several bills and resolutions authorizing this deployment, but failed to reach a consensus. In 1999, President Clinton ordered U.S. military forces to participate in the NATO-led military operation in Kosovo, without specific authorization from the Congress, a state of affairs that one analyst has termed. "virtual consent," in which the public is consulted but the formal institutions of democracy are bypassed: "The decay of institutional checks and balances on the war-making power of the executive has received almost no attention in the debate over the Kosovo conflict. This suggests that citizens no longer even care whether their elected politicians exercise their constitutional responsibilities. We have allowed ourselves to accept virtual consent in the most important political matter of all: war and peace."[85]

The catastrophic events of 9/11 initially created a united sense of purpose between the executive and Congress. Only three days after the terrorist attacks, Congress passed a Joint Resolution authorizing the president "to use all necessary and appropriate force against those nations, organizations, or persons he determines planned, authorized, committed, or aided the terrorist attacks." Three weeks later, "consistent with the War Powers Resolution," President Bush reported to Congress the use of force against Afghanistan.[86] In a similar manner, Congress passed the Joint Resolution, "Authorization for the Use of Military Force Against Iraq," in October 2002. This resolution authorized the President to use the armed forces of the United States "as he determines to be necessary and appropriate," to defend the United States against the threat posed by Iraq and to enforce all relevant UN Security Council Resolutions regarding Iraq. The President, in turn, dutifully reported to the Congress on March 21, 2003, "consistent with the War Powers Resolution" and pursuant to his authority as Commander-in-Chief, that he had "directed U.S. Armed Forces operating with other coalition forces, to commence operations on March 19, 2003, against Iraq."[87]

The political storm gathering around the 9/11 Commission and the on-going struggle in Iraq will constitute a severe test of the nation's willingness to support a prolonged and deadly conflict. The legitimacy of these actions will largely be dependent on the President's ability to mobilize public opinion, and the willingness of Congress to continue to provide support. According to Alton Frye, "unless there is continuing consultation in good faith between Congress and the Executive, the unity that marks the beginning of the campaign against terrorism could degenerate into the profound disunity that scarred American politics thirty years ago."[88] But the harsh reality is that Congress rallies around victory and piles on in defeat. Success matters more than procedure in the politics of making war.[89]

The United Nations.

The founding of the United Nations substantially narrowed the legitimacy of the use of force by individual nationstates. The UN Charter indicates in its Preamble that the UN is established "to save succeeding generations from the scourge of war," and its substantive provisions obligate the member states to "settle their international disputes by peaceful means" (Article 2(3)) and to "refrain . . . from the threat of use of force against the territorial integrity or political independence of any state. . . ." (Article 2(4)). In place of the traditional right of states to resort to force, the charter creates a system of collective security in which the Security Council is authorized to "determine the existence of any threat to the peace" and to "decide what measures shall be taken. . .to maintain international peace and security" (Article 39).[90]

The UN security apparatus, created in 1945, was a hybrid, combining a universal quality with a great power concert. The system did not work well during the Cold War because the UN was kept on the sidelines by U.S.-Soviet bipolar rivalry. With few exceptions, UN involvement in use of force decisions began in the 1990's. The evolving nature of global threats, however, has caused a reexamination of the collective security apparatus. UN Secretary General, Kofi Annan helped set the stage for this process: "The United Nations Charter declares that 'armed force shall not be used, save in the common interest.' But what is the common interest? Who shall define it? Who shall defend it? Under whose authority?"[91]

Article 51 of the UN Charter recognizes the inherent right of self-defense: "Nothing in the present Charter shall impair the inherent right of individual or collective self-defense if an armed attack occurs against a member of the United Nations, until the Security Council has taken measures necessary to maintain international peace and security." Some authorities interpret Article 51 to permit anticipatory self-defense in response to an imminent attack. Such an interpretation allows action, either unilaterally or collectively in self-defense, or preemptively based on an interpretation of imminent threat. The threat of catastrophic terrorism argues for a requirement to establish intelligible and transparent criteria of imminent threat that could provide for legitimate unilateral, coalition of the willing, or hopefully UN Security Council action.[92] Even Kofi Annan has suggested that UN members should consider developing "criteria for an early authorization of coercive measures to address certain types of threats—for instance, terrorists groups armed with weapons of mass destruction."[93] Article 106 of the charter can be interpreted to allow coalitions of states to take action to maintain international peace and security pending UN Security Council action. This article was originally added to accommodate regional alliances such as the RIO Pact and NATO. By modifying certain aspects of the charter, to include article 106, a better understanding may be developed for the legitimate requirements for multilateral response to threats outside the confines of the Security Council.

Based on the use of force in the last decade, some analysts have argued that the UN Security Council must be reformed: enlarged to become more representative, and restructured to replace the veto system. One rationale for the elimination of the veto power of the permanent five is based on the need for legitimacy:

> All modern military operations need international legitimacy if they are going to succeed. Consequently, the great powers, especially America, face a difficult choice: they can either maintain the veto, and embark on unsanctioned military adventures with their partners only to see these fail because of lack of international

approval; or they can surrender veto power in return for the increased likelihood of securing majority approval for the use of military power.[94]

As this argument relates to the debate in the UN about Iraq, France, or any other country on the Security Council, should be in a position to adopt and support a particular view, but it should not be in a position to block pursuit of a vital interest and put at risk the entire UN enterprise. "What do you do if, at the end of the day, the Security Council refuses to back you?" asks Charles Krauthammer, "Do you allow yourself to be dictated to on issues of vital national — and international security?"[95] Thomas Friedman answered the question, "The French and others know that . . . their refusal to present Saddam with a threat only guarantees U.S. unilateralism and undermines the very UN structure that is the best vehicle for their managing of U.S. power."[96]

This debate also touches on the concept of multilateralism. Americans define multilateralism as a policy that actively seeks to gain the support of allies. As such, Security Council authorization is a means to an end — gaining more allies — not an end in itself. The Europeans, on the other hand, view multilateralism much more narrowly as a legitimate sanction from a duly constituted international body — the Security Council. Despite the fact that the United States enjoyed the support of dozens of nations for the war in Iraq, and is supported by 33 troop-contributing coalition partners as I write, many critics continue to charge that the United States is acting unilaterally. The current debate "over multilateralism and legitimacy is thus not only about the principles of law, or even about the supreme authority of the UN; it is also about the transatlantic struggle for influence. It is Europe's response to the unipolar predicament."[97] In any event, it is clear that any new arrangements to exercise collective security need to be developed and given legitimacy by the international community.

CONCLUSION

War between nationstates endures because human interests, values and commitments are often irreconcilable. In addition, because of the existence of a much more insidious kind of violence - catastrophic terrorism - military power remains the ultimate defender of common human values, and the ultimate arbiter of human disagreements:

> The efficacy of force endures. For in anarchy, force and politics are connected. By itself, military power guarantees neither survival nor prosperity. But it is almost always the essential ingredient for both. Because resort to force is the ultimate card of all states, the seriousness of a state's intentions is conveyed fundamentally by its having a credible military posture. Without it, a state's diplomacy generally lacks effectiveness.[98]

Strategists must be able to answer the classic charge from Clausewitz, "No one starts a war . . . without first being clear in his own mind what he intends to achieve by that war and how he intends to conduct it." The political objectives for the use of force must be continually reassessed in light of the changing nature of warfare and the proliferation of non-traditional threats. Likewise, remembering the caution raised by President George H.W. Bush that there can be no single or simple set of fixed rules for the use of force, the prudent strategist needs to keep in mind relevant questions and issues he should evaluate in each particular circumstance that might require military force. Finally, democracies have the unique challenge of dealing with the elusive and malleable concept of legitimacy. "Discovering where legitimacy lies," according to Robert Kagan, "at any given moment in history is an art, not a science reducible to the reading of international legal documents."[99] Still there are immutable principles such as that of Horace who cautioned that "force without wisdom falls of its own weight." Today, more than ever, the key question concerning the use of force is not whether it is lawful, but whether it is wise.[100]

ENDNOTES - CHAPTER 15

1 . The author would like to acknowledge the grateful assistance of Dr. Charles Krupnick and Dr. David Jablonsky in reviewing and making valuable suggestions for this chapter.

2. Han J. Morgenthau, *Politics Among Nations*, 5th Edition, New York: Alfred A. Knopf, 1973, p. 29.

3. Anarchy refers to the absence of government, but should not be confused with chaos. International politics exhibits a great deal of order, regularity, and cooperation, but also includes much coercion, unpredictability, and bloodshed. Robert J. Art, *A Grand Strategy for America*, Ithaca, NY: Cornell University Press, 2003, p. 4. Kenneth Waltz is quoted in Robert J. Art, "The Fungibility of Force," in Robert J. Art and Kenneth N. Waltz, eds., *The Use of Force: Military Power and International Politics*, 5th ed., New York: Rowman & Littlefield Publishers, Inc., 1999, pp. 5-6.

4. *The Military Balance: 2003-2004*, London: The International Institute for Strategic Studies, 2003. Also refer to Anup Shah, "High Military Expenditures in Some Places," *www.globalissues.org/Geopolitics/ArmsTrade/Spending.asp*, accessed March 23, 2004.

5. Art, "The Fungibility of Force," p. 4.

6. Paul Kennedy, *The Rise and Fall of the Great Powers*, New York: Vintage Books, 1989, p. 515. Kennedy posits two challenges for the longevity of every major power: "whether, in the military/strategical realm, it can preserve a reasonable balance between the nation's perceived defense requirements and the means it possesses to maintain those commitments; and whether, it can preserve the technological and economic bases of power." P. 514. His basic declinist argument is that if a "nation overextends itself geographically and strategically" and chooses "to devote a large proportion of its total income to 'protection,' leaving less for 'productive investment,' it is likely to find its economic output slowing down, with dire implications for its long-term capacity to maintain both its citizens' consumption demands and its international position." P. 539. The United States was able to harness the economic vitality of the information age and thus avoid the predictions of decline at the end of the 20th century. Perhaps it will not be as fortunate in this new century. James Fallows, "The Hollow Army," *The Atlantic Monthly*, March 2004.

7. John Baylis and James J. Wirtz, "Introduction," in John Baylis, James Wirtz, Eliot Cohen, and Colin Gray, eds. *Strategy in the Contemporary World: An Introduction to Strategic Studies,* Oxford: Oxford University Press, 2002, p. 12; Carl Von Clausewitz, *On War*, Michael Howard and Peter Paret, eds. and trans., Princeton, NJ: Princeton University Press, 1976, pp. 88, 605. As famous as this dictum is, it is not fully accepted without some debate. Colin Gray goes into some depth on this issue in his book, *Modern Strategy*. He goes so far as to say, "Although Clausewitz was more wise than foolish in this dictum, the wisdom in the formula is hostage to the folly." He concludes his initial review of this topic by stating that "the idea of force as an agent of political purpose is generally persuasive," but should be viewed as the product of not only political purpose, but also of an on-going political process. Colin S. Gray, *Modern Strategy*, Oxford: Oxford University Press, 1999, p. 30; and Chapter 2, "Strategy, Politics, Ethics," pp. 48-74; Colin L. Powell, "US Forces: Challenges Ahead," *Foreign Affairs*, Vol. 71, No. 5, Winter, 1992/93, p. 39. General Powell contrasted the success of military operations in the 90's with the failed mission to Lebanon in 1983. Concerning Lebanon, he stated that we, "inserted those proud warriors into the middle of a five-faction civil war complete with terrorists, hostage-takers, and a dozen spies in every camp." Perhaps the successes of the 90's resulted from simpler problems or an avoidance of the very complex, a prescription that the West may not be able to follow in the new century.

8. Joint Publication JP, p. 1, *Joint Warfare of the Armed Forces of the United States*, Washington, DC: The Joint staff, November 14, 2000, p. I-4.

9. Robert J. Art, "To What Ends Military Power?" *International Security*, Vol. 4, No. 4, Spring 1980, pp. 3-35.

10. Figure is a modified version from David E. Johnson, Karl P. Mueller, and William H. Taft V, *Conventional Coercion Across the Spectrum of Operations: The Utility of U.S. Military Forces in the Emerging Security Environment*, Santa Monica, CA: Rand, 2002, p. 9. Several noted analysts, including Art and Gray, are more inclined to classify compellence as the sole coercive component. Colin Gray, in *Maintaining Effective Deterrence*, Carlisle, PA: Strategic Studies Institute, U.S. Army War College, August 2003, p. 13, refers to compellence as coercion or coercive diplomacy. But he later recognizes that deterrence is "executed as a coercive strategy intended to control unfriendly behavior." P. 17. Thomas Schelling, who coined the term compellence, also concluded that, "'Coercion' . . . includes 'deterrent' as well as 'compellent' intentions." *Arms and Influence*, New Haven: Yale University Press, 1966, p. 71.

11. JP 1, p. III-1.

12. Schelling, pp. 1-2.

13. Art, "To What Ends Military Power," pp. 5-6. Richard Haass includes preventive attacks and punitive attacks, along with deterrence and compellence as the principle uses of military power. See Richard N. Haass, *Intervention: The Use of American Military Force in the Post-Cold War World,* Washington, DC: The Carnegie Endowment for International Peace, 1994, pp. 50-56. For another interesting discussion of preventive war and preemption as strategic choices, refer to Richard K. Betts, *Surprise Attack*, Washington, DC: The Brookings Institution, 1982, pp. 141-149.

14. Daniel Byman and Matthew Waxman, *Confronting Iraq: U.S. Policy and the Use of Force Since the Gulf War,* Santa Monica, CA: Rand, 2000, p. 6.

15. Schelling, p. 3.

16. Johnson *et al.,* pp. 15-17; Byman and Waxman, pp. 8-9.

17. John J. Mearsheimer, *Conventional Deterrence,* Ithaca, NY: Cornell University Press, 1983, p. 14; Amos A. Jordan, William J. Taylor, Jr., and Michael J. Mazar, *American National Security,* Baltimore, MD: The John Hopkins University Press, 1999, p. 38. A fundamental debate concerning U.S. grand strategy involves the continued deterrability of U.S. opponents. Failed and rogue states may not be viewed as rational, particularly from a western perspective. Nevertheless, as David Jablonsky argues, even crazy states can be deterred: ". . . a state may behave rationally in an instrumental sense of effectively achieving its ends or goals which in themselves may be 'crazy'." He emphasizes that there must be at least a modicum of instrumental rationality on the part of a nation to be deterred. David Jablonsky, *Strategic Rationality is not Enough: Hitler and the Concept of Crazy States,* Carlisle, PA: Strategic Studies Institute, U.S. Army War College, 1991. Unfortunately, the current list of opponents includes highly lethal nonstate organizations, such as the al Qaeda terrorist network. As Paul Davis and Brian Jenkins argue, this class of terrorist, driven by extremely strong, messianic, religious views, lacks instrumental rationality, and therefore cannot be deterred and must be eradicated. Paul K. Davis and Brian Michael Jenkins, *Deterrence & Influence in Counterterrorism*, Santa Monica, CA: Rand, 2002.

18. Henry Kissinger, *Diplomacy,* New York: Simon & Schuster, 1994, p. 608. There is a vast literature on the evolution of nuclear strategy during the Cold War. One source for a systematic and comprehensive treatment of the major themes of nuclear strategy is Lawrence Freedman, *The Evolution of Nuclear Strategy,* New York: St. Martin's Press, 1983. Despite using the word "evolution" in the title, he claims that it is somewhat misleading. In the introduction, he mentions the cyclical character of the debates and states that "much of what is offered today as a profound and new insight was said yesterday; and usually in a more concise and literate manner." The utility of military power during the Cold War, particularly concerning great power competition, was constrained by the logic of nuclear deterrence. As Bernard Brodie declared, "Thus far the chief purpose of our military establishment has been to win wars. From now on its chief purpose must be to avert them." Bernard Brodie, "Implications for Military Policy," in *The Absolute Weapon: Atomic Power and World Order*, New York: Harcourt Brace, 1946, p. 76.

19. Gray, *Maintaining Effective Deterrence,* p. 13. See also Johnson *et. al.,* pp. 10-12; Haass, pp. 50-51; Philip Bobbitt, *The Shield of Achilles: War, Peace, and the Course of History,* New York: Alfred A. Knopf, 2002, pp. 14-15, 328-329. Bobbitt makes the argument that extended deterrence has driven U.S. nuclear strategy, not central deterrence. Concerning a more contemporary issue—missile defense—Bobbitt reiterates the on-going importance of extended deterrence: "Extended deterrence is the single most effective instrument the United States has to prevent major-state proliferation because it permits these states to develop their economies without diverting vast resources to the nuclear arms competition, and yet remain relatively safe from nuclear attack." Although the United States has vastly reduced and restructured its nuclear force posture, nuclear deterrence retains its relevancy even after the end of the Cold War.

20. Kissinger, p. 608.

21. Gray, *Maintaining Effective Deterrence,* p. vii. See also William T. Johnsen, *The Future Roles of U.S. Military Power and their Implications,* Carlisle, PA: Strategic Studies institute, April 17, 1997, p. 7; and Bobbitt, p. 12. Colin Gray points out that the current concern is not about irrational leaders—those leaders that cannot connect means purposefully with ends. "The problem is not the irrational adversary, instead it is the perfectly rational foe who seeks purposefully, and rationally, to achieve goals that appear wholly unreasonable to us." He goes on to argue that he believes Al Qaeda is

deterrable. "Al Qaeda has many would-be martyrs in its ranks, but the organization is most careful of the lives of its key officers, and it functions strategically. It can be deterred by the fact and expectation of strategic failure." Gray, *Maintaining Effective Deterrence*, pp.vii, viii, 21-22. He also recommends several practical measures to enhance the role of deterrence under the current circumstances and recognizes the synergy achieved through combining elements of both deterrent and defensive preventive-preemptive postures. "A little prevention-preemption would do wonders for the subsequent effectiveness of deterrence in the minds of those whose motives were primarily worldly and pragmatic." *Ibid.*, pp. v, 29. Gray's bottom line is that deterrence, though diminished in significance, remains absolutely essential as an element of U.S. grand strategy.

22. *The National Security Strategy of the United States of America*, Washington, DC: The White House, September 2002, p. 15. Also, see John Lewis Gaddis, *Surprise, Security, and the American Experience*, Cambridge, MA: Harvard University Press, 2004, pp. 69-70.

23. Byman and Waxman, p. 6; See also, Art, *Grand Strategy*, p. 5; Schelling, p. 72.

24. Art, "To What Ends Military Power?" p. 8. See also, Schelling, pp. 69-91. Byman and Waxman argue that it is often difficult to distinguish compellence and deterrence. "Classifying cases as compellence as opposed to deterrence is always speculative to some degree, given the inherent opacity of enemy intentions. And, ultimately, general deterrence and compellence are codependent, as success or failure in coercion affects the coercing power's general reputation to some degree and thus its overall ability to deter." P. 7.

25. Art, "To What Ends..." pp. 8-10; and Haass, pp. 53-54.

26. Barry M. Blechman and Tamara Cofman Wittes, "Defining Moment: The Threat and Use of Force in American Foreign Policy," *Political Science Quarterly*, Vol. 114, No. 1, Spring 1999, pp. 5-11. This point was explicitly expressed by Mohamed Farad Aideed to Ambassador Oakley concerning the disastrous U.S. involvement in Somalia: "We have studied Vietnam and Lebanon and know how to get rid of Americans, by killing them so public opinion will put an end to things."

27. A slightly modified version of a chart found in *Ibid.*, p. 7.

28. Ibid., p. 27.

29. Bobbitt, p. 14; *The Quadrennial Defense Review Report*, Washington, DC: The Department of Defense, September 30, 2001, p. 11. For a good discussion of the benefits of forward presence, see Art, *A Grand Strategy for America*, pp. 139-145; Johnsen, p. 11.

30. Thomas P. M. Barnett, "The Pentagon's New Map," *Esquire*, March 2003, p. 228.

31. Andrew Bacevich, *American Empire: The Realities & Consequences of U.S. Diplomacy*, Cambridge, MA: Harvard University Press, 2002, p. 128. Bacevich argues that the United States has been pursuing a grand strategy of "openness" since the days of Woodrow Wilson. This strategy seeks economic expansion and aims to foster an open and integrated international order, thereby perpetuating the undisputed primacy of the world's sole remaining super power.

32. *National Security Strategy*, 2002, p. 30.

33. *QDR*, 2001, p. 12.

34. Barton Gellman, "Keeping the U.S. First: Pentagon Would Preclude a Rival Superpower," *The Washington Post*, March 11, 1992, p. 1. The principal author of the document was then Under Secretary of Defense for Policy, Paul Wolfowitz. When the draft DPG was leaked it was roundly criticized and, consequently, dramatically toned down in the final version. It seems that the Secretary meant what he said 10 years ago, in that it is now an accepted tenet of the U.S. defense strategy.

35. Donald H. Rumsfeld, "Transforming the Military," *Foreign Affairs*, Vol. 81, No. 3, May/June 2002, p. 27. He goes on to site several specific examples: deployment of effective missile defenses to dissuade ballistic missile programs; hardening U.S. space systems to dissuade the development of killer satellites; new earth-penetrating weapons that would make deep-underground facilities obsolete as hiding places for terrorists or WMD capabilities.

36. Richard Kugler, "Dissuasion as a Strategic Concept," *Strategic Forum*, Institute for National Strategic Studies, NDU, No. 196, December 2002, pp. 1-2.

37. Gray, "Maintaining Effective Deterrence," p. 14.

38. Joseph S. Nye, Jr., "U.S. Power and Strategy After Iraq," *Foreign Affairs*, Vol. 82, No. 4, July/August 2003, p. 72.

39. This list is taken from JP 1 *Doctrine for the Armed Forces of the United States*, 14 May 2007, pp. I-15−I-17; and Haass, pp. 51-65.

40. Art, *A Grand Strategy for America*, pp. 5-6.

41. Jennifer D. Kibbe, "The Rise of the Shadow Warriors," *Foreign Affairs*, Vol. 83, No. 2, March/April 2004, p. 104. Covert actions are distinct from clandestine missions. The term "clandestine" refers to the secrecy of the operation itself, "covert" refers to the secrecy of its sponsor.

42. United States Special Operations Command, *Posture Statement 2003-2004*, p. 36.

43. Kibbe, p. 105. The definition and oversight requirements were contained in the Intelligence Authorization Act for fiscal year 1991.

44. Donald Rumsfeld, *2003 Secretary of Defense Annual Report to the President and the Congress*, Washington, DC: The Pentagon, 2003, p. 2. This report highlights the historic change in the charter of the SOCCOM, from supporting missions of the other regional combatant commanders, to planning and executing its own missions in the global war on terrorism. Kibbe, p. 109.

45. Joint Publication 3-0, *Doctrine for Joint Operations*, September 10, 2001, pp. II-3-II-4.

46. Clausewitz, *On War*, p. 605; Sun Tzu, *The Art of War*, Samuel B. Griffith, trans., New York: Oxford University Press, 1963, p. 142; and Colin Powell, *My American Journey*, New York: Ballantine Books, 1995.

47. Michael Ignatieff, *Virtual War: Kosovo and Beyond*, New York: Picador USA, 2000, p. 179.

48. The discussion in this section is related to the discussion on just war theory, as presented in Vol. II, Chapter 14, "Ethical Issues in War: An Overview," by Martin L. Cook. This section will focus on political and military considerations, as opposed to the international legal framework associated with just war theory. However, it should be clear that many of the issues overlap.

49. Michael I. Handel, *Masters of War: Classical Strategic Thought*, 3rd ed., London: Frank Cass, 2001, pp. 10-11.

50. Edward Luttwark refers to this as "Napoleonic" warfare—wars fought for grand purposes, implying the decisive employment of large forces. Edward N. Luttwark, "Toward Post-Heroic Warfare: The Obsolescence of Total War," *Foreign Affairs*, Vol. 74, No. 3, May/June 1995, pp. 113-114.

51. Alexander L. George, "The Role of Force in Diplomacy: Continuing Dilemma for U.S. Foreign Policy," talk at CSIS Security Strategy Symposium, June 25, 1998; Available from *www.pbs.org/wgbh/pages/frontline/shows/military/force/article.html*, accessed March 2, 2004; Colin Powell, "U.S. Forces: Challenges Ahead," *Foreign Affairs*, Vol. 71, No. 5, Winter 1992/93, p. 36. Also see Les Aspin, "The Use and Usefulness of Military Forces in the Post-Cold War, Post-Soviet World," from an address to the Jewish Institute for National Security Affairs, Washington, DC, September 21, 1992, excerpted in Haass, pp. 183-190.

52. Handel, p. 10; Evan Thomas, "The Vietnam Question," *Newsweek*, April 19, 2004.

53. George P. Shultz, *Turmoil and Triumph: My Years as Secretary of State*, New York: Charles Scribner's Sons, 1993, p. 650.

54. The Weinberger doctrine was first presented in a speech before the National Press Club, November 28, 1984. Its rendition for the figure is from Handel, pp. 310-311. The criteria are numbered in accordance with the sequence in which they were originally presented. However, that sequence is broken on the chart to help categorize criteria as either addressing the "when" or "how" of using force. Colin Powell's list is taken from Aspen as excerpted in Haass, pp. 184-185. The best first person account is from Powell's *Foreign Affairs* article which was previously cited. Secretary William Perry's list is from "The Ethical Use of Military Force," the Forrestal Lecture, Foreign Affairs Conference, U.S. Naval Academy, Annapolis, MD, April 18, 1995. These points were largely incorporated in all subsequent National Security Strategies issued by the Clinton Administration. The final set, from Secretary Donald Rumsfeld, is taken from his remarks before the Fortune Magazine Global Forum, November 11, 2002.

55. Samuel Huntington, "The Erosion of American National Interests," *Foreign Affairs*, Vol. 76, No. 5, September/October 1997, p. 35. Huntington goes on to state that "national interests usually combine security and material concerns, on the one hand, and moral and ethical concerns, on the other." *A National Security Strategy for A Global Age*, Washington, DC: The White House, December 2000, p. 4; George, p. 3.

56. Huntington, p. 37.

57. Handel, p. 312; Bobbitt, p. 298. Perry was initially responding to the on-going debate about committing U.S. forces to help solve the crisis in Bosnia. The National Security Advisor for Bush (p. 41), Brent Scowcroft, clearly reflected the opposite view that helped keep U.S. forces out of Bosnia for years. "We could never satisfy ourselves that the amount of involvement we thought it would take was justified in terms of U.S. interests involved . . . We were heavily national interest oriented . . . If it [war] stayed in Bosnia, it might be horrible, but it did not affect us." Quoted in Samantha Power, *"A Problem From Hell": America and the Age of Genocide*, New York: New Republic Book, 2002, p. 288.

58. David Halberstam, *War in a Time of Peace: Bush, Clinton, and the Generals*, New York: Scribner, 2001, pp. 390-391; Ignatieff, p. 72.

59. Clausewitz, p. 579.

60. Handel, p. 316.

61. Haass, p. 74.

62. Shultz, p. 650.

63. Handel, p. 318.

64. Power, p. 509. Public support can be very fickle, based on the latest news from the battlefield, and is particularly problematic in prolonged and costly military operations. Handel, p. 319.

65. Haass, pp. 88-89; Shultz, p. 650.

66. Wesley K. Clark, *Waging Modern War: Bosnia, Kosovo and the Future of Combat*, New York: Public Affairs, 2001, p. 423.

67. Ivo H. Daalder, "The Use of Force in a Changing World—U.S. and European Perspectives," The Brookings Institution, November 25, 2002, p. 12.

68. Handel, p. 314; Power, p. 283. Another example cited is the claim, once again in 1992, by LTG Barry McCaffrey, to Congress, that 400,000 troops would be needed to enforce a cease-fire. Scowcroft conceded that the military's analysis was probably inflated.

69. Powell, "U.S. Forces: Challenges Ahead," p. 40.

70. Wesley K. Clark, *Winning Modern Wars: Iraq, Terrorism, and the American Empire*, New York: Public Affairs, 2003, pp. 86-87. Clark went on to conclude, that the "ensuing disorder vitiated some of the boost in U.S. credibility won on the battlefield, and it opened the door for deeper and more organized resistance during the following weeks."

71. Handel, p. 317.

72. Quoted in Harry G. Summers, Jr., *On Strategy II: A Critical Analysis of the Gulf War*, New York: Dell Publishing, 1992, p. 252.

73. Haass, pp. 76-77.

74. Ignatieff, p. 208. As an example of an ambiguous end state, he cites the military technical agreement that concluded the conflict between NATO and Serbia. It specified the terms and timing of Serbian withdrawal and the entry of NATO troops, but left entirely undefined the juridical status of the territory over which the war was fought.

75. Handel, p. 324.

76. This chart has been modified from one that appears in Handel, p. 326. Handel's chart did not include Haiti (1994) and Iraq (2003). Handel had also included a column for Central America, which has been omitted. As mentioned in the body of the chapter, these ratings should be viewed as subject to open debate and discussion. In fact a useful exercise would be to determine your own ratings for particular interventions. As one example of the subjectiveness of these ratings, concerning Kosovo, Handel concluded that the public supported the operation. Ignatieff, on the other hand, stated that "the public did not sign up to 78 days' worth of bombing, and had they been asked, most would have said no." P. 183.

77. Handel, p. 311.

78. Summers, *On Strategy*, p. 43.

79. Roger H. Davidson and Walter J. Oleszek, *Congress and Its Members*, 9th edition, Washington DC: Congressional Quarterly, Inc., 2004, p. 439.

80. Richard F. Grimmett, "War Powers Resolution: Presidential Compliance," *Issue Brief for Congress*, Congressional Research Service, updated March 24, 2003, CRS; Robert B. Zoellick, "Congress and the Making of US Foreign Policy," *Survival*, Vol. 41, No. 4, Winter 1999-2000, p. 33. Of the 104 reports, Ford submitted 4, Carter 1, Reagan 14, George H. W. Bush 7, Clinton 60, and George W. Bush 18; Grimmett, p. CRS-11.

81. Grimmett, p. CRS-13.

82. Alton Frye, "Applying the War Powers Resolution to the War on Terrorism," testimony before the Senate Judiciary Committee, April 17, 2002.

83. Zoellick, p. 34.

84. George Bush and Brent Scowcroft, *A World Transformed*, New York: Vintage Books, 1998, p. 446. For a superb discussion of the intricacies of gaining both domestic and international support for the use of force refer to pp. 355-449. Concerning this debate, Brent Scowcroft had this to say: "We were confident that the Constitution was on our side when it came to the president's discretion to use force if necessary: If we sought congressional involvement, it would not be authority we were after, but support." p. 398. And President Bush added; ". . . even had Congress not passed the resolutions, I would have acted and ordered our troops into combat. I know it would have caused an outcry, but it was the right thing to do. I was comfortable in my own mind that I had the constitutional authority." P. 446.

85. Grimmett, pp. CRS-3 — CRS-4; Ignatieff, pp. 180-181.

86. Davidson and Oleszek, p. 440.

87. "Congressional Joint resolution to Authorize Use of Force Against Iraq," *Washington Post*, October 11, 2002, p. A12; Grimmett, p. CRS-12.

88. Frye, Congressional testimony.

89. John Lindsay, cited in Zoellick, p. 34.

90. David M. Ackerman, "International Law and the Preemptive Use of force Against Iraq," *CRS Report for Congress*, Congressional Research Service, updated march 17, 2003, p. CRS-3.

91. Kofi Annan, "The Legitimacy to Intervene," *Financial Times,* December 31, 1999, available from *www.globalpolicy. org/secgen/interven.htm.*

92. John Burroughs *et. al.*, "The United Nations Charter and the Use of Force Against Iraq," October 2, 2002, p. 2; Robert S. Litwak, "The New Calculus of Pre-emption," *Survival*, Vol. 44, No. 4, Winter 2003-03, p. 73.

93. Quoted in Robert Kagan, "America's Crisis of Legitimacy," *Foreign Affairs*, Vol. 83, No. 2, March/April 2004, p. 81.

94. Ignatieff, p. 182.

95. Charles Krauthammer, "The Unipolar Moment Revisited," *The National Interest*, Number 70, Winter 2002/03, p. 17.

96. Thomas Friedman, "Present At . . . What?" *New York Times,* February 12, 2003.

97. Kagan, pp. 82-83.

98. Art, "To What Ends Military Power?," p. 35; The United States Commission on National Secuirty/21st Century, *New World Coming: American Security in the 21st Century*, September 15, 1999, pp. 3-5.

99. Kagan, p. 77.

100. Michael J. Glennon, "Why the Security Council Failed," *Foreign Affairs*, Vol. 82, No. 3, May/June 2003, p. 16.

CHAPTER 16

POLITICAL ECONOMY AND NATIONAL SECURITY:
A PRIMER

Janeen M. Klinger

Economics and politics are quite different realms. Each obeys a dynamic of its own with the logic of one realm often conflicting with the other. Economics obeys the logic of the market, which tends to jump or circumvent national boundaries in order to escape political control. In contrast, the temptation of all political systems is to restrict, regulate and shape economic activity to the requisites of the national interest. Ultimately, politics involves contests over power frequently conceptualized as zero-sum interactions with clear winners and losers—elections are a quintessential case in point. Since the time of Adam Smith, economics views competitive interactions like trade as mutually beneficial. The world of national security and military policy more closely resembles conditions found in the realm of politics. It is no wonder then, that military officers with clear notions of victory and defeat as a frame of reference find politics intelligible but may be completely confounded by the paradox of economics where contests yield outcomes beneficial to both parties. To be sure, the military view recognizes the possibility of a tie in the form of stalemate or armistice, however, such an outcome is viewed as quite undesirable and therefore alien to the economist's conviction that competition renders outcomes beneficial to both parties.

There is an irony in the fact that military leaders and economists approach each other's disciplines with some degree of suspicion. Each holds expertise in one of two subject areas that traditionally lie at the core of state sovereignty: (1) command over the legitimate (legal) use of force, and (2) the ability to coin money and determine its value. That states hold the former as a pillar that defines sovereignty is self-evident. After all, the international community recoils at terrorist acts, not because the fatalities are as great as in war, but because the violence is perpetrated by actors not authorized to use it. The importance states attach to their ability to maintain the value of currency is sometimes obscured by the arcane technical practice of monetary matters. Yet the importance attached to money as a constituent element of sovereignty can be illustrated by the fact that when Margaret Thatcher remained unenthused about European integration, she expressed her concern in terms of protection and preservation of the powers of the Bank of England to control money supplies and set British interest rates. She asserted that losing these powers would be, "the greatest abdication of national and parliamentary sovereignty in our history."[1]

What follows is an examination of the global economy from the standpoint of its impact on national security. A sound place to begin this examination is with a discussion of the historic debate between mercantilists and economic liberals over their contradictory views concerning the advantages and disadvantages of an open global economy because national security concerns are at the heart of the disagreement between these two schools of thought. Because mercantilist views are gradually eclipsed by liberal ones, we will explore factors that contributed to the acceptance of economic liberalism. In particular, we will contrast the British experience and policy in the 19th century with that of the United States in the 20th. For each country sought to champion economic liberalism once its hegemony was well established. We will conclude with a brief review of the history of the Bretton Woods system which was the instrument used by the United States to create the open economy that ultimately provided the foundation for globalization.

Protectionism Versus Free Trade: The Mercantilists and Their Challengers.

Current public policy debates about the impact of interdependence and "globalization" were foreshadowed by the earlier debates between mercantilists and economic liberals. Both mercantilists and liberals believed that states pursued two kinds of goals. The first goal, most closely associated with national security, includes the pursuit of power and prestige. The second one involves the pursuit of prosperity and wealth. Though mercantilists and liberals might agree that the pursuit of power must take precedence over the pursuit of prosperity, each would configure domestic and international arrangements in a different way to achieve prosperity. Although the debate between the two schools began in the 18th century with the first articulation of an alternative to mercantilism, neither set of ideas succeeded in eliminating the other. Consequently, elements of each school can be found in contemporary debates like that concerning the ratification of the North American Free Trade Agreement or the impact that outsourcing has on domestic employment and wage levels.

The mercantilists were a diverse group of thinkers working from the sixteenth through the eighteenth centuries, but all shared the view that they were coming to grips with the inefficiencies inherent in the decentralized feudal economic structure. This decentralization meant, among other things, that every town might have its own currency system. Consequently, the mercantilists were interested in promoting something that we take for granted today: unified national economies. At the time that mercantilists were writing autocratic monarchs were intent on state-building to overcome the centrifugal pull of feudal institutions and became a receptive audience for mercantilist ideas.

What then were the ideas of mercantilism that Europe's early modernizing monarchs found so attractive? Mercantilism begins with two assumptions that strike a 21st century observer as fundamentally non-economic. First, the economy was thought to be static or a zero-sum game. Hence, the only way for one to increase his share (to gain wealth) was to take it from someone else. In this way, competition was expected to lead automatically to conflict as the struggle over finite supply became endemic within the national economy. At the international level, the no-growth assumption meant that territorial expansion looked like the best means for assuring prosperity. The assumption of limited supply in turn, meant that conquest would appear to be a paying proposition and war an effective instrument for achieving prosperity. The expectation that war was a commonplace activity for states led to a related mercantilist conclusion: states needed to minimize economic ties to others so as to be less vulnerable to potential disruption in the event of war.

The second assumption that the mercantilists make is to measure wealth not by individual income, but by gold sitting in the national treasury. In the most extreme mercantilist formulation then, one would argue that a country with a full treasury could be viewed as rich even if the vast majority of its inhabitants were poor and living at a subsistence level. With stores of gold in the national treasury as the measure of wealth, it was incumbent on the monarch to do anything to accumulate more stores of precious metal while preventing the export of gold to other countries.

Both assumptions point to certain logical policy prescriptions concerning external economic ties. Each country would strive to export as much as possible as a means of accumulating gold (and sometimes silver). Conversely, imports should be held to a minimum to prevent the loss of gold and thereby contribute to a balance of payments surplus. Acquisition of colonies was closely linked to mercantilist policies because colonies provided another means for governments to acquire resources without expenditures of gold. Thomas Mun, a prominent 17th century mercantilist, summarized the view this way:

Although a Kingdome may be enriched by gifts received, or, by purchases taken from some other Nations, yet these things are uncertain and of small consideration when they happen. The ordinary means therefore to encrease our wealth and treasure is by Forraign Trade, *where wee must ever observe this rule; to sell more to strangers yearly than wee consume of theirs in value.*[2] (emphasis added)

In short, mercantilists posited fundamental disharmony among competing economic interests domestically and internationally. The disharmony was so acute that governments needed to regulate and control all aspects of economic life. Two concrete examples illustrate typical mercantilist policies. Navigation acts required all trade to be carried in ships of the regulating country. In this way a country could collect income from all trade conducted between it and other countries regardless of the origin of the goods traded. (British use of such navigation acts provided American colonists one irritant in their relations with the mother country that would eventually lead to the Declaration of Independence.) A second example of mercantilist policy was the chartering of trading companies granted monopoly privileges by the government. The British East India Company established in 1600 is the classic example of such an arrangement.[3]

One of the earliest challenges to mercantilist ideas was provided by Adam Smith's Wealth of Nations published in 1776. His school subsequently labeled economic liberalism or laissez-faire, sought to explain why mercantilist regulation was unnecessary and indeed might be positively harmful to the economy. Underlying the ideas of economic liberalism are two assumptions that provide a stark contrast to those made by mercantilists. First, economic growth does occur which means that economic competition is not zero-sum and conflict over finite supply is muted if not eliminated. For Smith, the division of labor is the most important factor that generates economic growth. Further, because of economic growth, the need for government regulation to reconcile conflict is minimized.

The second assumption made by economic liberals relates to the fact that the wealth of nations is not measured by gold stores in the national treasury but instead by individual income providing a taxable resource base. Unlike the mercantilists who saw the sole purpose of economic activity to enhance state power, liberals believe the very *raison d'etre* of the economy is to serve individuals. Smith justified this view by emphasizing the fact that all value derives ultimately from the labor that went into production. Since labor determines value, labor should garner rewards commensurate to its contribution to value. Smith's assumptions lead to a simple policy admonition to governments: Do not interfere in economic activity.[4]

Nowhere is the difference between mercantilism and economic liberalism sharper than over the issue of trade policy. Economic liberalism urges governments to allow free and open trade with other countries as the best means for improving everyone's prosperity. Moreover, liberals are not at all concerned that such openness might leave a country vulnerable in the event of war because the more open the trading system is, the more likely that countries will have diverse sources of supply and not be dependent on any single trading partner.

Although Smith asserts there are benefits to free trade, it took the work of David Ricardo (*Principles of Political Economy and Taxation,* 1817) to elaborate a theoretical justification with his concept of comparative advantage. The benefits of trade are easy to demonstrate in the case of a country that is less efficient in the production of a commodity than another country. For example, one can easily see that the United States is better off importing coffee than trying to grow its own. However, Ricardo's contribution of comparative advantage shows why trade results in mutual advantages even if one country can produce two goods more efficiently than another country. Ricardo's classic example used production of wine and cloth for two countries, Portugal and England. He demonstrated that even though Portugal might produce each item with less labor than England, the Portuguese would enhance their prosperity by transferring labor resources to the good they produce comparatively more efficiently (wine). With greater production of one commodity in which they have comparative advantage, they could purchase more cloth from England than they could produce themselves.[5] Once Ricardo had shown free trade to be mutually beneficial, the economic rationale for colonization fell away.

Although comparative advantage provides a theoretical refutation of mercantilist doctrine, it does so by making two simplifying assumptions that intrude in the real world of practical policy. Comparative advantage assumes there are no costs to adjustment and that workers can painlessly be shifted from one economic activity to another. In practice, of course, labor is not so mobile as theory suggests. Second, comparative advantage assumes that the production of all goods has equal and similar consequences for the national economy overall. In fact, production of the two goods in Ricardo's own example have quite different effects and producing an agricultural good like wine has a less dynamic effect than producing cloth. The production of cloth on the other hand, leads to an accumulation of mechanization and experience which, in the case of Britain, facilitated the ripple effects (positive and negative) of the industrial revolution. And the greater prosperity generated through the industrial revolution gave the British a firm and superior foundation for building both its economic strength and its military capability. Given economic liberalism's two simplifying assumptions, it is not surprising that its conception of free trade never completely succeeded in eliminating mercantilist ones and that historically free trade has been the exception rather than the rule.

Despite the fact that liberal conceptions of trade begin to take root after the appearance of Wealth of Nations in 1776, they were incorporated into public policy very gradually. For instance, Britain did not begin to dismantle its mercantilist policies until the middle of the 19th century with the repeal of the tariffs known as the Corn Laws and abolition of its Navigation Acts. The East India Company, too, was dissolved in 1858. The reasons for the time lag between the emergence of liberal ideas and their implementation in policy are both technical and political. Until steam power was adapted to ocean transport, the cost of moving goods long distances was sufficiently high that it dampened free trade. Given the limitations of sailing vessels compared with steam ships, the only goods worth shipping great distances were those of extremely high value relative to their bulk — like rare spices, silk or gold. The second technical reason that governments were slow to implement free trade in practice derived from the fact that in an era before income taxes, governments relied on customs and import duties as the primary source of revenue for the state. Free trade, to the extent it requires the elimination of such duties, forces governments to devise alternative sources of revenue.

Politically, free trade doctrines faced another obstacle to implementation. Free trade proponents had to overcome the opposition of the landed aristocracy who tended to support prohibitions on grain imports (Corn Laws) as a way to protect their income. Manufacturing interests on the other hand tended to oppose the protectionism embodied in the Corn Laws because tariffs raised the price of food, which placed upward pressure on wages. In economies that were only beginning to industrialize and that remained primarily agricultural, landed interests were bound to dominate and carry the day on trade policy. As the industrial revolution gained momentum, the manufacturing sector became more predominant, and its influence on policy increased so that political pressure on behalf of open trade grew.

Although much in mercantilist doctrine was made obsolete by economic liberalism — mercantilist sentiments enjoy periodic resurgence. Two near contemporaries who wrote in a mercantilist vein despite the appearance of Adam Smith were Alexander Hamilton and Friedrich List.[6] Both men disputed the claim that all countries achieve mutual benefits from trade. In particular, they recognized that trade between countries at different stages of economic development might work to the detriment of less developed countries. In their day they saw a real difference between countries exporting only agricultural goods and those exporting manufactures. Both men appreciated the kind of dynamic economic gains to be made in a manufacturing economy that we noted in our discussion of comparative advantage. Furthermore, manufacturing generates innovation leading to productivity gains that are indispensable for creating an economic base capable of supporting military might. Therefore, in any exchange between a manufacturing economy and an agricultural one, the manufacturing economy would fare better.[7] List's analysis illustrates the problem with an example drawn from the U.S. experience. In 1816, the United States exported 81 million pounds of cotton to earn 24 million dollars. In 1826, the American cotton exports grew to 204 million pounds but earned only 25 million dollars. List pointed out that from the standpoint of national prosperity, the U.S. would have been better served by destroying part of its cotton crop so that the reduced supply translate into higher prices.

List and Hamilton arrived at a conclusion obscured by the notions of free trade and comparative advantage—what might be good from the standpoint of global economic efficiency might not be good for a particular national economy. In short, tension between international and national prosperity compels governments to choose policies for their own benefit, sacrificing global economic efficiency. So acute was the tension between national and international prosperity that List used a military analogy to capture the conflictual nature of trade. List suggested tariff protection for national industry could be likened to fortifications that provide military security.

List and Hamilton had different motives for opposing free trade than the more traditional mercantilists of the 16th and 17th centuries, and their motives contain a more modern economic understanding. Classic mercantilists saw protectionism as an end in itself, whereas List and Hamilton saw it as a means to the end of a stronger economy. Nevertheless, the policy implication of their views are similar to the mercantilists in the extent they recognized the national security implications of open trade.

How thoroughly a country accepts and implements policies drawn from economic liberalism depends in part on the strength of its national economy and the extent of its vulnerability to others—a vulnerability that might be defined in various ways. Vulnerability might grow from excessive dependence on agricultural exports for foreign exchange earnings or grow from excessive reliance on the import of raw materials. Two countries in particular have historically been the most vehement champions of free trade: Great Britain in the 19th century and the United States in the 20th. It is to the experience and policies of these countries that we now turn.

The Political-Economy of Hegemony.

Whether a country supports free trade and implements policies designed to facilitate openness depends on whether it views foreign economic competition as positive or negative. Receptiveness to openness, in turn, depends on whether a country sees itself as weak or vulnerable to external economic competition. Thus, when it comes to a country's policy preference concerning free trade, weak economies tend to oppose it and strong economies support it. Given the link between economic success and the preference for free trade, it is not surprising then that the greatest champions of free trade were Britain in the 19th century during the heyday of Pax Britannica and the United States after 1945 during an era often labeled as Pax Americana. Yet one should note that each country pursued protectionist (mercantilist) policies at earlier stages of their respective histories.

British commitment to free trade was symbolized by repeal of the Corn Laws and abolition of the Navigation Acts in the mid-19th century. So committed were the British to laissez-faire policies at that time that the government did not interfere with the Russians when they floated a loan on the London money market even though Britain was at war with them in Crimea. Such overwhelming confidence that a transfer of resources across borders poses no national security threat is certainly the luxury of a hegemonic country. Similarly the United States signaled its commitment to free trade when it dismantled its favorite protectionist policy — the high tariff wall — after World War II. But U.S. foreign economic policy after the war was quite a contrast to its policy in the 19th century when the U.S. was aptly described as the "mother country of protectionism."

For each of these champions of free trade, the trade policy reflected more than merely economic rationality. Each country also enjoyed considerable geographic security that made it fairly immune to the threat of military invasion. Freedom from invasion meant that economic activity was unlikely to be disrupted by war and that neither country would have to squander resources to support standing armies to repel invasion. Thus, the fundamental national security that each enjoyed due to its geography helped re-enforce the economic pre-eminence they enjoyed. The economic pre-eminence that translated into a policy preference for free trade is graphically depicted in Figure 1.

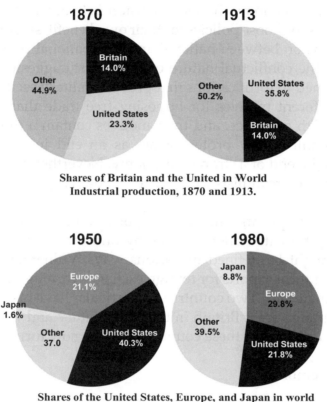

Shares of Britain and the United in World
Industrial production, 1870 and 1913.

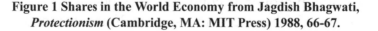

Shares of the United States, Europe, and Japan in world
gross domestic product, 1950 and 1980.

Figure 1 Shares in the World Economy from Jagdish Bhagwati,
Protectionism **(Cambridge, MA: MIT Press) 1988, 66-67.**

How do the economic policy preferences of hegemonic countries compare with those of other states? Countries with greater vulnerability to outside economic forces try to shield their economies as much as they can. Historically the tendency toward protection is especially pronounced in countries that experienced the industrial revolution later. Britain, as the pioneer of the industrial revolution had the luxury of minimizing the role of the state in fostering domestic development because it faced no serious competitors. In contrast, the more difficult task of industrialization for late developers required a stronger governmental role.[8]

Besides protectionism, another way to compensate for late economic development is through close government and business cooperation. Such cooperation might involve finance where state-directed banks loan money at negative interest rates to enable "strategic" industries to grow and thrive. Government financial support enhances the ability of industries to export, and such arrangements are often viewed as the secret behind the phenomenal economic success of contemporary East Asia. One negative consequence of a symbiotic government/business relationship is that it makes a political system prone to corruption. Indeed, the Asian economic crisis that began in 1997 has been attributed to precisely that kind of close government involvement in the private sector.

If national commitment to free trade relates to economic strength, one would expect declining economic strength (also depicted in Figure 1) to erode that commitment. As the British economy receded in size relative to others, the country gradually reverted to more protectionist trade policies. Some British politicians began agitation for "fair" trade by the 1880s and 1890s in response to growing American and German competition. Likewise, the commitment to openness of the United States weakened as the size of its economy as a portion of the world total declined from nearly 50 percent in 1950 to less than 25 percent in 1990. Indeed, one reason the NAFTA debate took on such a histrionic tone in the rhetoric of presidential candidate Ross Perot ("the giant sucking sound" of jobs going to Mexico) was because the United States began to see itself as less able to withstand economic competition.

Despite the success of the two national champions of openness, two controversies concerning the advantage of free trade remain unresolved today. The first controversy is whether free trade is the ultimate source for economic growth, or whether economic growth is the necessary precondition for free trade. On this point the evidence is mixed. In the 19th century economic growth led to free trade, although after World War II the causal link was reversed with free trade providing an impetus to phenomenal growth.

The second controversy relates to the impact of open trade on national prosperity. Here again there is no absolute rule about the inherent virtues of free trade. For example, when Britain introduced free trade, its per capita level of industrialization was more than twice as great as that of its closest competitors. British persistence in maintaining a free trade system made less sense, however, when its industrial lead was declining to the point where, on the eve of World War I, it stood at a level of only thirty or forty percent of its rivals.

Despite the ambiguity concerning which policy is universally best, one lesson from the recent Soviet collapse seems clear. The pursuit of complete self-sufficiency through a policy of autarky is an illusion likely to result in an economic dead end. The Soviet experience demonstrates that autarky can ruin even a country that is rich in natural resources and can have debilitating economic consequences over the long term. The only successful sector in the Soviet economy was the military sector, which was the only portion subject to discipline because it was not shielded from external competition, that is, Soviet weapons had to be able to match American weapons.

Analysts frequently draw parallels between the experience of British decline in the 19th century and American decline in the 20th to suggest that the United States is likely to abandon its support for free trade. Fundamental differences between the two cases exist that caution against taking the historical comparison too literally. Though each country claimed a certain economic hegemony, that position rested on quite different foundations. British economic pre-eminence rested on two characteristics: colonial possessions (because it never had the resource base of a continental sized economy); and (2) the historic coincidence that it pioneered the industrial revolution. In "fair" trade agitation in the late 19th century, one solution suggested as a logical response to British economic decline was to consolidate the empire into one large free trade area. In that way, Britain might be able to meet competition from a continental sized competitor like the United States. While the productivity gains the British enjoyed from being the first country to experience the industrial revolution enabled it to grow more rapidly than others and race ahead of them, the advantage was bound to disappear as the industrial revolution spread to other countries.

American economic hegemony rested, in a sense, on a firmer foundation: a command of a continental size resource base able to support a large population. Given the very favorable circumstances and resource endowment of the United States, it is likely to remain the world's largest economy for the foreseeable future, and claims of American decline exaggerated. Japan, the world's second largest economy still trails the United States and is less than one-half as large. The latest figures from the World Bank calculate that Japan's gross domestic product (GDP) stands at 4.3 trillion dollars while the U.S. GDP is 13.2 trillion dollars. China's GDP, although increasing dramatically in recent years, still lags well behind both at 2.7 trillion dollars.[9] If the U.S. decline depicted in Figure 1 looks so dramatic, it is because the destruction of World War II artificially magnified the relative size of the U.S. economy in 1950. What appears to be a drastic fall is really the recuperation of the rest of the world and a diminishing of the impact of World War II. Moreover, that world recovery was deliberately fostered by the United States as an integral part of its national security strategy. The U.S. intended, and in fact orchestrated, its own relative decline through its economic policies to foster the reconstruction of its World War II adversaries and allies. Surely, American decline must reflect, then, a success story from the standpoint of U.S. policy!

The other important difference between British and American economic hegemony is the instrument chosen by each to pursue open/free trade. Britain unilaterally pursued free trade policies, regardless of actions by other countries. Britain allowed fairly free access to its market and acted as a lender of last resort for those countries experiencing financial difficulties. Unilateral policies to pursue openness were bound to become untenable once economic decline began to set in. Furthermore, given the basis of British economic hegemony noted above, it was a decline the British were almost powerless to halt. In contrast, America preferred to pursue its preference for openness via the creation of multilateral institutions like the International Monetary Fund (IMF) and the General Agreement on Tariffs and Trade (GATT). By creating legitimacy for open trade such a multilateral institutional framework generated widespread commitment to openness throughout the world. Such an institutional network means that open trade is less dependent on the will or ability of a single country to maintain it. The continued viability of open trade in the post cold war will depend on those international institutions known collectively as the Bretton Woods system.

The Evolution of the Bretton Woods System of Multilateral Management.

American foreign policy after World War II was quite a deviation from previous practice, in both the political and economic spheres. Politically, the United States abandoned its preference for unilateralism to form an unprecedented peacetime alliance—NATO.[10] Unilateralism combined with protectionism characterized American foreign economic policy as well. The American predilection on this score was viewed as especially destructive in the 1920s and 1930s when as the world's largest economy and largest creditor nation, the U.S. refused to assume a leadership role in economic reconstruction and stabilization. So serious was this oversight that some scholars see American policy as the single most important factor aggravating and prolonging the crisis of the Great Depression.[11] Specifically, the Smoot-Hawley tariff passed in 1930 prompted retaliation by other countries as each tried to shore up domestic employment levels at the expense of foreigners through the elimination of import competition. The inter-war years witnessed a wave of economic nationalism reflected in such "beggar thy neighbor" trading policies. The absence of economic recovery in the 1930's poisoned international diplomacy, ultimately providing fertile soil for fascist movements to take root.

The international repercussions of Smoot-Hawley and the rise of fascism in Europe had a chastening effect on the U.S. Congress. Congress began to conclude that the original constitutional division of responsibility that gave it authority to "regulate commerce with foreign nations" made trade policy especially vulnerable to sectional economic interests at the expense of an overarching national one. Consequently, Congress acquiesced to a gradual shift of power over trade matters to the executive branch by granting authority to negotiate bilateral agreements through passage of the Reciprocal Trade Agreement Act (RTA) of 1934.

As the second world war drew to a close, the United States continued to build on the promise of the RTA in order to avoid the errors of its inter-war economic diplomacy. Thus, in July 1944, 44 nations met in Bretton Woods, New Hampshire, to work out an agreement to create multilateral institutions that would facilitate post-war economic recovery. The Soviet Union attended this meeting but would not join any of the economic institutions created there.[12] Thus, the post war economic order would come to resemble the political order as lines between East and West solidified. The two institutions created in New Hampshire, known collectively as the Bretton Woods system, are the IMF and the International Bank for Reconstruction and Development (the World Bank). Discussions began for forming a third institution, the International Trade Organization (ITO) but disagreement over the scope of authority for such an organization proved to be too serious an obstacle for finalizing an agreement. A temporary solution was found by negotiating the General Agreement on Tariffs and Trade which governed international trade until it was finally replaced by the World Trade Organization (WTO) in July 1995.

In a sense, all three institutions acted as concrete manifestations of the triumph of Adam Smith's ideas about the virtue of openness in the international economy and established the preconditions necessary for current globalization in the international economy. The overarching purpose of the institutions was to promote the free flow of goods, services, and capital among nations with a minimum of tariff restrictions and a maximum of monetary stability. The IMF and the GATT worked in tandem to achieve these purposes. Expansion of trade requires as a precondition some sort of international monetary system to smooth transactions. In the absence of an international monetary system, trade can only be conducted on a barter basis that is, at best, cumbersome. For comparisons of value—like how much wine is worth how much cloth—are more easily calculated on the basis of some common denominator or currency.

The IMF supported an international monetary system in two of its functions. First, the IMF administered the rules affecting exchange rates and currency convertibility. At the outset, the creators of the IMF presumed (based on the experience with floating rates in the 1930s) that fixed exchange rates, to the extent they created stable expectations about value, must be the centerpiece for the international monetary system. Member nations pegged their currency at a fixed rate and pledged to maintain its value at that level. Member nations also pledged to make their currencies readily convertible to others at that pegged rate. Despite fixed rates, some flexibility in exchange rates was possible and governments could let their currencies float within one percent over or under the pegged rate. Larger devaluations of a currency were still possible but had to occur under the auspices of IMF consultation.

Undergirding confidence in the entire system was the pledge by the United States to redeem dollars for gold at the rate of $35.00 an ounce. Thus any country concerned about the value of paper currency retained the option of exchanging any currency for dollars, and exchanging those dollars for gold. (Historically gold has been viewed as intrinsically a better store of value than paper currency because its supply is not susceptible to government manipulation.) This anchor to gold gave private investors and governments alike confidence in the international monetary system as long as the U.S. pledge to convert dollars to gold remained credible. In the immediate post World War II era, the U.S. pledge was credible because the U.S. owned three-quarters of the world's supply of monetary gold. However, as post war economic recovery proceeded and U.S.

dollar liabilities overseas came to exceed its gold supply, the promise to convert dollars into gold at the promised rate became untenable. Economists identified the danger of the "dollar overhang" as early as 1958. Members of the Western Alliance, notably Charles DeGaulle (President of France, 1958-1969), chafed at the fact that the use of the dollar as an international reserve asset gave the United States an "exorbitant privilege" to run balance of payments deficits. Eventually the problem became so acute that President Nixon was forced to suspend dollar convertibility in 1971.[13]

After 1971, the rules for exchange rate conversion changed from a fixed system to a floating one, and that alteration turned out not to have the debilitating impact on trade that Bretton Woods founders had assumed. Although floating rates had little impact on trade, the change did introduce a measure of instability in the financial system and presented an invitation to private investors to speculate in currencies. There is no universal agreement about whether such speculation may ultimately undermine the integrity of the international financial system.[14] Because the IMF was concerned that the international monetary system had become excessively reliant on the U.S. dollar, the Fund attempted to create a new source of liquidity for the international community called Special Drawing Rights (SDRs). Despite the creation of the new reserve asset, governments and businesses still continued to prefer holding dollars (and other strong national currencies) as reserves.

The second role that the IMF plays in the international monetary system is as a source of liquidity for members. Although operating not quite like a central bank for the international economy, the IMF does act as a lender of last resort. From time to time, all countries may need access to foreign currency to settle outstanding accounts when domestic foreign currency reserves are low or depleted. The IMF can provide needed financing through resources obtained from members. In order to join the Fund, all countries must pay a quota subscription (25 percent paid in gold or dollars; and 75 percent paid in local currency) and it is from this pool of financing that countries are able to draw. These loans tend to be of short duration (3- to 5-year repayment schedule) and must be used for balance of payments emergencies only, with long term financing for development projects funded by the World Bank.

With the IMF providing a foundation for an international monetary system, the open trade objectives of GATT were easier to achieve. The main mechanism GATT used to achieve its purpose was to convene periodic multilateral conferences where trading partners negotiated bilateral agreements to reduce tariffs. Once established, these tariff levels are then automatically applied to all members of GATT—the famous most-favored-nation dictum of the organization. Reductions take place in a manner that is reciprocal and non-discriminatory leading to ever increasing openness in the trading system so that today tariffs are 75 percent lower than they were prior to World War II.

GATT's definition of free trade was not absolute, and the system always allowed states to retain a number of escape or "safeguard" clauses. First, countries could shield agriculture as a guarantee that they could continue to feed their own populations. Second, members could protect industries (temporarily) that were threatened with extinction because of import competition. Third, states had the right to defend against predatory trade practices (known as dumping) when exporters sell goods below the costs of production. Finally, in 1964 GATT amended its rules in recognition of the idea dating back to Hamilton and List, that developing countries may be at a disadvantage in trading relations with developed ones. Therefore, in trade between countries at different stages of development, the less developed country were allowed to waive the reciprocity rule without violating the spirit of free trade principles.

Besides allowing exceptions on tariffs, there is another sense in which free trade is not absolute. GATT was less able to deal effectively with non-tariff barriers to trade. Tariffs are fairly easy to regulate because they are easy to recognize and standardize. Non-tariff barriers have neither characteristic. Non-tariff barriers include a wide variety of practices from government procurement policies to customs procedures and import licensing. Any of these practices can make it difficult for foreign companies to easily enter another's market.[15] Another example of non-tariff barrier can be found in health and sanitary regulations like FDA approval for foreign pharmaceutical companies that may indeed prevent foreigners from competing in the U.S. market. However, the intent of such safety regulation is to serve domestic policy objectives of consumer protection and GATT cannot easily reconcile various national standards because doing so requires establishing a single global standard that would impinge on the authority of domestic legislatures.

Since inception of the GATT, the United States has shouldered a greater burden for openness, and its role has sometimes been characterized as providing "the market of last resort." Whenever the global economy slowed or entered a recession, the United States used fiscal [taxing] and monetary [interest rates] policies to stimulate demand. Such policies were conducive to increasing foreign exports into the U.S. and enabled foreigners to use their earnings to buy more goods from the United States. In this way the American economy acted as a locomotive to pull the world out of recession.

As the size of the American economy declined relative to that of others, the American locomotive became too small to pull the rest of the world and the United States became burdened with permanent trade deficits.[16] During the Cold War the United States had a national security incentive for playing the role described. American military and security interests required that its allies recover from the war and remain prosperous as a hedge against Soviet influence. As John Lewis Gaddis notes, ". . . the idea was to reconstitute independent centers of power that would balance the Soviet Union; but the price willingly if not always wisely paid was to create future economic competitors."[17] Given the declining threat from a peer competitor and a decline in the American share of the global economy, Americans began to see the trading system as "unfair" leading to public debate over a return to a "level playing field" in the trade arena.

Recent American insistence on "fair" (rather than free) trade, echoing 19th century British debates, grows from a concern that economic arrangements that served U.S. interests well during the Cold War may now be working to American disadvantage. Ironically, the very arrangements that western allies saw as exploiting them, are now viewed in a negative light by American leaders concerned with maintaining U.S. competitiveness. With a weakening commitment to free trade coming from the US, many observers believe the Bretton Woods trading system is itself threatened. Concrete evidence to support the view of decreasing openness to free trade is mixed. Some experts view the intensification and spread of regional trade agreements (EU and NAFTA) as portending a gradual closure in the global economy. Moreover, some see countries as increasingly relying on managed trade arrangements like voluntary export restraints as evidence that global commitment to free trade is on the wane. However, on a positive note, the newly created World Trade Organization (WTO) is more independent than GATT and gives states less leeway to circumvent free trade principles. For example, whereas in GATT a single member could obstruct resolution of a trade dispute with a veto, the WTO requires a consensus of all members to stop the dispute mechanism at any stage. The key for maintaining commitment to open trade in the future will be whether the U.S. as the world's largest economy, will continue to support the actions of the WTO—an organization the U.S. helped to create.

Conclusion.

If the historic debate between mercantilists and economic liberals holds a lesson, it is a caution against simplistic assertions about the future evolution of the international economy. For one cannot easily discern whether a trend is a temporary aberration or an emerging permanent feature of international economic life. Three examples illustrate just how easy it is to make erroneous judgments about the direction of the global economy. First, in the heyday of colonialism, governments viewed colonies as an integral element to a prosperous economy. Indeed, the renewed scramble for colonies that followed German unification (1870) was indicative of the high value placed on possession of colonial real estate. In fact, colonies were never that profitable for the metropolitan countries, and any contributions they made to prosperity was more mythical than real once the costs of imperial policing were calculated.

Second, in 1969, Jean-Jacques Servan-Schreiber wrote a book called The American Challenge in which he argued that Europe faced a real threat as it moved toward a more integrated common market. He predicted that European integration would benefit American business to the point that it would come to dominate the common market. By the year 2000 he warned, the third largest economy would not be a united Europe, but rather American business in Europe. In fact, of course, the Europeans have been the primary beneficiaries of closer European union.

Finally, in the wake of the quadrupling of oil prices in 1973-1974 a fear emerged that shortages in other commodities would enable producers to form similar cartels capable of raising prices in a like manner. Indeed, an article in Foreign Policy written in 1974 raised the specter by asking the question in a title: "One, Two, Many OPECs?" Other commodity producers never achieved the sort of leverage predicted, and even the OPEC cartel lost the kind of power it once commanded.[18]

Given the difficulty of extrapolating current conditions into the future and the even greater uncertainty when formulating policy in response to them, only one projection seems a safe bet. Governments will continue to have an imperative to foster innovation because innovation is crucial for stemming economic stagnation and decline. What is much less certain is the best means or policy for governments to adopt to reach that objective. Conventional wisdom is ever shifting concerning the best domestic institutional arrangements to meet changing economic conditions. A few years ago, the Japanese "miracle" was so unchallenged that many scholars began to study the way it structured government/business relations in an effort to replicate Japanese success. Today the bloom is off the rose of the Japanese miracle because slower growth in Japan has combined with their worries that they too might be losing their competitive edge to emerging economies like South Korea.[19]

In the final analysis, the United States is better positioned than other countries to meet whatever uncertainties lie ahead for the global economy: the U.S. remains the world's largest economy creating jobs faster than any other; it has a large market that all countries desire to access; it prints the currency that most governments and businesses still prefer to hold as reserves; and it leads a multilateral system that gives legitimacy to core values of free competition and openness. Within the context of all these advantages an American retreat into a mercantilist stance with its zero-sum conception of trade makes little sense. The 20th century has been called the American century — given all the advantages the U.S. retains, the 21st century might also be known in that way.

ENDNOTES - CHAPTER 16

1. "She Makes Her Stand," *The Economist*, June 29, 1991, 27.

2. Robert Lekachman, *A History of Economic Ideas*, New York: McGraw-Hill Book Co., 1959, 33.

3. Mercantilist monopolies are quite different from publicly owned enterprises in centrally planned economies. A mercantilist monopoly relied on private capital with profits going to private individuals. In a centrally planned economy all proceeds from state enterprises accrue to the state directly.

4. Of course, Smith recognized that governments played some role in smoothing the functioning of the national economy. Governments were to maintain a military to insure against foreign invasion, and to maintain police and court

systems for domestic security. Finally, Smith recommended that all governments needed to create and sustain "public works." Although in Smith's day the last item included things like roads and bridges, today it can be broadened to include any of the functions associated with the modern welfare state.

5. The logic of comparative advantage can be illustrated using an often cited non-economic example. President Woodrow Wilson led the U.S. delegation to the Paris Peace talks that concluded World War I. He could also type faster than his secretary. Nevertheless, rather than perform both functions, it makes more sense for him to allow his secretary to do the typing, enabling Wilson to be more efficient at the task he is comparatively better at: diplomacy.

6. Alexander Hamilton's views are contained in his Report on Manufactures prepared while he was Secretary of the Treasury for George Washington. List makes his points in a book called *The National System of Political Economy* published in 1841. The works of both men are described in Edward Mead Earle, "Adam Smith, Alexander Hamilton, Friedrich List: The Foundations of Military Power," in *Makers of Modern Strategy*, Peter Paret, ed., Princeton, Princeton University Press, 1986.

7. In Hamilton's day the United States was primarily an agricultural economy. and it remained so until 1869 the last year that the value of farm output exceeded the value of manufacturing output. Hamilton's arguments concerning the disadvantages faced by an agricultural economy would be recognized by leaders in the Third World today that subscribe to dependency theory.

8. The classic discussion of this point can be found in Alexander Gerschernkron, *Economic Backwardness in Historical Perspective*, Cambridge, MA: Harvard University Press, 1962. Gerschenkron goes so far as to suggest the acute economic backwardness of Russia in 1917 prompted the institutional response of central planning and communist ideology as the most effective means for overcoming backwardness.

9. See *geo.worldbank.org/*, accessed December 10, 2007.

10. The U.S. formed only one other formal alliance, with France during the American Revolution. The U.S. even fought World War I as an "associated" power and not an allied one.

11. See, for example, Charles P. Kindleberger, *The World in Depression, 1929-1939*, London: Penguin Press, 1973.

12. As late as December 1945, Soviet foreign ministry officials showed every indication of ratifying the Bretton Woods arrangements. However, Stalin vetoed the move because he believed that joining the institutions would amount to an admission of weakness. See John Lewis Gaddis, *We Now Know: Rethinking Cold War History*, Oxford: Clarendon Press, 1997, 193.

13. The end of the dollar's convertibility into gold is often described as "the collapse of the Bretton Woods system." However, such a description defines the Bretton Woods system too narrowly. For the system was predicated on much more than gold/dollar exchange, it also involved a commitment to open trade and multilateral oversight of the international economy. Both elements remained in place after the U.S. stopped exchanging dollars for gold.

14. In 1995 a young currency trader stationed in Singapore caused the bankruptcy of Barings PLC Merchant Bank. Some observers draw a negative lesson to suggest that the entire international financial system might be in jeopardy. Others draw a reverse lesson to conclude that despite integrated financial markets the Barings bankruptcy stayed fairly contained and did not spill over in other countries. For a discussion of some of the issues involved with today's volatile exchange rates, see Susan Strange, *Casino Capitalism*, New York: Basil Blackwell, 1986.

15. The use of non-tariff barriers by Japan has been a primary source of trade friction with the U.S. Japanese companies are known for their "keiretsu" behavior where they retain a preference for doing business with other Japanese companies. Such behavior provides an insurmountable barrier to American firms.

16. C. Roe Goddard, John T. Passe-Smith, and John G. Coklin, eds., *International Political Economy: State Market Relations in the Changing Global Order*, Boulder: Lynne Rienner Publishers, 1996.

17. Gaddis, 197.

18. The economic collusion embodied in cartels is problematic at best and the oil industry had several unique features that allowed for the relative success of the cartel. Two stand out as particularly important. First, oil production is concentrated in relatively few producers, and seven of these were Arab countries that had a high degree of political cohesion for manipulating supplies in a manner that harmed Western supporters of Israel. Second, oil is characterized by price inelasticity which means large price increases will not cause consumers to switch to other products because there is no substitute for oil—an indispensable commodity for an industrial economy. No other commodity has these features conducive to forming a successful cartel.

19. See Martin Fackler, "The Japanese Fret that Quality Is in Decline," *The New York Times*, September 21, 2006.

CHAPTER 17

ECONOMICS:
A KEY ELEMENT OF NATIONAL POWER

Clayton K. S. Chun

Modern conflict, from conventional warfare to diplomatic disputes, has increasingly involved economics in some form. Nations use economic tools to pursue objectives, seek economic resources as national goals, or are affected by economic events that influence their national security. Both state and non-state actors use economic power to wage war and to influence events regionally or globally. Economic considerations range from simple access to resources like water or raw materials through transforming resources into finished products or services to providing financial resources. The ability to gather, transform, and use resources is a key component to national security. Many human activities, including those involving national security, can be either severely limited or dramatically enhanced by economic factors. Military operations and other national security actions frequently depend on the results of economic capability. Without the capacity to produce, finance, or support key national security activities, a nation would have a limited ability to protect its domestic and international interests.

Economic power has spread widely and gained importance in recent years. Globalization, the reliance on economics, and the diffusion of economic power from a few industrial states to many developing ones has radically changed the world. Global economic success has also conferred power on a large group of sovereign governments and even corporations. The threat or actual action by a government can create enormous economic impact. Markets are extremely sensitive to news that would affect potential financial or economic activity. Oil prices can rise rapidly if tensions increase in the Persian Gulf or if a natural disaster occurs. Single events with little obvious international significance could ignite a sell off by investors in overseas and domestic stock markets. Global communications can spread panic and exacerbate the condition.

The changing environment has altered the emphasis on national elements of power so that military power is not necessarily the primary coercive tool in international relations, and economic power has gained increased importance. During the age of total war that spanned World Wars I and II, military power was the coin of the realm in foreign affairs. Economic power played a role in those wars, but the fight for national survival overrode the impact of domestic and international macroeconomic stability or growth. Economics served primarily as a provider of resources to the military element of power. In an era of increased consumer demand, technological growth, changes in society, and the evolving nature of conflict, the importance of economic considerations rose. During the Cold War, national survival was still at stake, but even then economic considerations became just as important as nuclear parity with the Soviet Union. President Dwight D. Eisenhower warned of military expenditures impeding future economic growth the net result of which would degrade security for the nation. The Kennedy administration raised questions regarding how much defense spending was sufficient to ensure national security. The U.S. engaged the Soviet Union in a nuclear arms race while it fought a war in Vietnam, but Washington tempered its strategy to constrain defense spending. Nuclear sufficiency became acceptable rather than superiority with the associated costly numbers of intercontinental ballistic missiles, strategic bombers, and submarines. "Guns versus butter" questions also arose as the challenges of an undeclared Cold War against Moscow pitted social spending against defense resources.

Today, economic issues play a pivotal role in conflict. Advanced technology, contractors on the battlefield, volunteer militaries (that tend to be more expensive than conscript armies), reconstruction of battle ravaged nations, and other considerations make war and conflict expensive. Countries do not have inexhaustible resources to conduct long wars even if there is a direct and desperate threat to national survival. Questions of national treasury, consumer demand, labor constraints, finance, and other economic considerations can sway public sentiment against a conflict. If one nation wages war or takes other actions to isolate another state, investors around the world become nervous. Stock and commodity markets could affect financial conditions and create unforeseen reactions. These reactions may create adverse conditions that could force a change in strategy by the nation trying to influence a rival's behavior.

As economic issues affect national security capabilities and activities, so might efforts that involve national security create global economic impacts. War or political disruption in an oil producing region will initiate tremors in the international energy sector. Although a nation might not be directly affected by the initial problem, the populace can suffer from increased prices from petroleum products that could result in greater unemployment or inflationary economic conditions. Demands for added military expenditures could translate to increased taxes that discourage consumer spending and business investment or reductions in other governmental activities that can directly shape the economic landscape. Competition for limited resources to meet national security policy objectives could also hamper private or other governmental activities. Nations can increase borrowing, raise taxes, spend surpluses, confiscate resources, or monetize debt. All of these options have unique economic effects on a nation.

Economics is an element of national power. Normally, one of a nation's key national interests is maintaining a viable economy to ensure a certain standard of living for its citizenry. States can use economic power to deter, compel, coerce, fight, and even rebuild a former opponent to meet a particular need. Economics becomes a vital component of the ends, ways, and means of security. Perhaps uniquely among the traditional elements of national power, economics might be any of the three aspects of strategy—the objective of a nation's strategy might be economic; economics might provide the means to achieve the end; or a nation might pursue its ends using economics as the primary way to exert power. Whether economics is a way or a means to achieve a national interest or if it is a cause or motivation to take an action, national leaders must play attention to this increasingly significant security factor.

Economics as an Objective or an End to a National Interest.

States and non-state actors have historically fought over economic issues. Wars about open access to resources, trade routes, competition, profit, and other economic issues are common in military and diplomatic history. A keen competition for resources among governments, individuals, corporations, and other actors has created a complex web of economic dependencies and rivalries that was not as important in the past. Similarly, economic conditions can create an environment that fosters demands for change that could create a civil war, a fight for access to markets or resources, or other forms of economic competition. Countries with weak or failing economies may resort to actions that they might not have considered had their economies been stronger.

One specific area that deserves a brief discussion is oil as a cause or objective of war. Reliable access to oil at reasonable rates is a vital national security interest for every developed and many of the more developing nations. Governments or international organizations that control oil production or pricing can effectively disrupt global economic conditions—whether purposefully or accidentally. A monopoly or oligopoly that controls a strategic asset has great potential to disrupt economies and create political instability, although few commodities have the same potential impact as oil. Major perceived or actual disruptions in the oil market are serious events that easily can trigger hostile responses from concerned governments. Today, oil is the best example of a resource that is both scarce and vital; however, other resources like water are also likely sources of conflict. We can expect economic issues — particularly access to raw materials and resources — to remain one of the significant objectives of international relations and causes of conflict.

Economics as Ways or Means to achieve a National Interest.

Differentiating whether economics is being used as the ways or means of strategy or policymaking can be difficult. The distinction is often in the eye of the beholder. Fortunately, making a fine distinction between ways and means is not necessary for the purposes of this article. Thus, we will discuss the two together — fully recognizing they are distinctly different functions in the strategy and policy process.

One prerequisite for maintaining long term government activities is a strong and vibrant economy. The economy serves as the source of government revenue. In the short term, assuming a nation has a relatively resilient economy, a government can spend money fairly freely without serious consequences. However, that is not true in the long term. Government actions like high taxes, irresponsible borrowing, or spending surpluses under a failing or substandard economy will ultimately create political and economic conditions that will create significant future problems. In a national emergency, a government can take a number of actions to raise vital capital. During World War II, the U.S. Government spent massive amounts of funds to fight the war. Despite lingering effects from the global 1929 depression, the Treasury Department started to raise revenues for military and foreign aid expenditures before the U.S. entry into the war. Congress passed two key tax increases in 1940 and 1941 on individual and corporate taxes. Tax rates and the requirements on who must file income taxes expanded to fund the war. Simultaneously, War and Navy Department demands for weapons and personnel injected a fiscal stimulus into the economy that allowed some of the sustained tax increases. In 1940, Washington collected about $5.4 billion from individual and corporate taxpayers; by 1945, collections rose to $46.5 billion.[1] Although the government could set price controls on products, limit military pay due to conscription, and appeal to the public and corporations to make financial sacrifices, the efforts could only make limited reductions in expenditures. The Treasury Department recouped some of the government expenditures through increased taxation, but that too was insufficient to fund the war. War Department expenditures skyrocketed from $695 million in 1940 to $50.1 billion by 1945. World War II costs amounted to more than $90 billion for 1945. Tax revenues alone could not sustain the war effort.

The U.S. Government could raise custom duties on imported goods, but during World War II the market for consumer imports was small. Most of the imported goods and raw materials went to the war effort; raising prices on those was counterproductive.

Another major way to pay for military and other national security related expenditures was through public debt. During the Great Depression, Washington used a number of public works projects to employ people who had lost their jobs. By 1940, the public debt was about $3.7 billion; it ballooned to $53.9 billion at the end of the war. The federal government conducted a series of massive bond drives to fund World War II. The public was encouraged to lend excess cash to the government. Repayment would be made later with interest, so bond sales placed the burden of war expenditures on future taxpayers, unlike raising taxes during the conflict. Additionally, the government reissued bonds that reached maturity rather than paying them off. These policies would limit future discretionary government spending, but the war took precedence. During the Vietnam War, the Johnson administration was unwilling to initially raise taxes to pay for military operations in Southeast Asia and new domestic social programs. Raising taxes to fight an unpopular war would be difficult. Instead, the Federal Reserve System used its ability to sell Treasury securities to finance government debt; an action it had not taken since 1951. It acquiesced to the Johnson administration to fund the war through massive bond sales.[2] Inflation, a general rise in prices, rose greatly and Johnson was forced to raise taxes temporarily with a 10 percent surcharge on income taxes. He later repealed investment tax credits, revoked certain tax-exempt claims among organizations, and widened the eligibility of workers who had to pay taxes.

Countries could monetize their government budget deficits. The government could simply print or coin more money for its expenditures. Unless the money is backed by some standard, like gold, this action only cheapens its currency and may produce undesirable effects like inflation. These negative impacts can be severely injurious to an economy. In many respects, one could argue the selling of Treasury securities acts to monetize government deficits.

Related to deficit spending is supporting another nation's debt. Global open trading of official government securities allows a state to use its economic power to assist a friend by underwriting his debt. Buying another nation's securities can transfer resources to that nation immediately. Additionally, the aid provided must be repaid, which eliminates some of the stigma of a grant or aid and often makes the strategy more politically palatable at home. The only "cost" to the securities purchaser is the upfront expense and time to recover repayment. However, the purchaser also bears a risk of default if the government seller of the securities falls, losses a war, or suffers some other catastrophic collapse. Short of such drastic events that make repayment impossible, the risk of default may be manageable. Debtor countries may not be able to make payments on schedule, but they generally attempt to repay debt in the long run. Reneging on debt repayment might provide short term benefits to a debtor nation strapped for cash, but default devastates future credibility in the security market. Conversely, if a sovereign power purchases securities, it acquires some influence, at least theoretically, over the debtor country. The power resides in the lender's ability to demand or withhold demands for repayment or to hold or sell the securities on the international market. Threats to sell the debtor nation's securities could weaken its currency, cause a drop in the value of the securities, or drain resources from the government depending on the conditions of the bond. However, exercising the power inherent in holding the debt of another nation is not a costless tactic. As the lending country starts to sell, the price of the securities will begin to fall. The amount of the decline will vary with the magnitude and timing of the sales. At some point, the sell-off becomes economically counterproductive as the value the seller receives falls below what he paid for the securities. In the case of a massive sell-off, the targeted country could actually benefit since it can repurchase its debt at discounted prices—assuming it can generate the necessary funds to purchase the securities.

Economic intervention in or withdrawal from the economy of a foreign nation—as opposed to supporting its debt—can have tremendous impact on the financial well being of a region or country. Governments do not usually participate directly in the economy of another nation. However, direct participation in the economy of another nation through private companies is widespread. Depending on the business and political climate of firm's home state, such participation may provide some degree of power for that home state. Regardless of the degree of external governmental control, decisions by private firms and multinational corporations to invest or do business in a country can influence national policies. Such decisions are independent and can be contrary to a host nation's interests. In an age of globalized financial markets, almost any corporation, organization, or individual can transfer capital into a country or take it out. This transfer generally can occur by using national or international stock, bond, commodity markets, or through direct investment into business ventures. Rapid inflow of capital can provide a needed boost to growth while rapid outflow can sink a nation into recession.

Governments can use their economic power through other means. For example, rather than lending money by bond purchases, they can provide direct support to another nation through a variety of programs that essentially provide money or services. Foreign aid, loan guarantees, technical aid and services, and other assistance can provide a number of flexible tools to support national interests. The State Department distributes foreign aid in support of national policy objectives that include sustaining and strengthening key allies. Another use of the economic tool is to fight one of the major causes of global strife today, failed states. The United States Agency for International Development (USAID) provides help to nations to fight poverty. Poor economic health frequently breeds political conflict and potential civil war in a state. Economically poor regions often become breeding grounds for terrorists. USAID promotes economic development through humanitarian relief, food and commodity aid, training, construction, technical support, small-enterprise or micro-loans, credit guarantees, human health aid, and fostering economic growth to a market economy. This aid can strengthen fragile states, support transformational development, support geostrategic interests, address global and regional issues, and provide humanitarian relief.[3] Along with diplomatic and military capability, development aid gives national leaders another tool to help prevent conditions that could lead to civil and eventually military unrest.

The transfer of wealth from developed to developing countries that sell raw materials or manufacture low-cost products can create economic problems. Governments worried about the outflow of capital, goods, services, industries, and jobs might erect barriers to restrict or stop trade. Such actions rarely go unchallenged, and a counter tariff barrier or legal challenge is a likely response. Conversely, governments willing to accept what are hopefully temporary trade imbalances for potential future benefits may allow the transfer of wealth and even industries and jobs to continue. Such is the political and economic theory behind the whole free trade movement — the North Atlantic Free Trade Agreement being an outstanding example. Transfer of key technologies, processes, equipment, or skills can also enable foreign governments and private firms — granting in some cases access to capabilities that would have taken years and many resources to acquire independently.

Economic power normally involves the trade of finished goods or raw materials. Few countries can claim to produce all of the goods and services that their citizens use. Many nations require energy imports to subsist. Conversely, nations that may have oil, natural gas, or other energy sources might need food imports or other foreign services like skilled labor. Nations can work within international trade agreements, or they may take unilateral action to expand or restrict trade. A country might try to limit trade to hurt a rival. A government may impose import or export quotas, limit certain business activities, set requirements for strict "quality" standards for imports, designate excessive administrative requirements to import the items, enact tariffs or taxes on selective foreign goods, subsidize domestic competition to make the imports appear more expensive, dump or sell large quantities of goods at a much lower price than a foreign opponent to destroy competition, enact laws to force citizens to purchase only domestic products, and other measures. A major concern about enacting such measures is retaliation by the injured state, other nations, and organizations like the World Trade Organization. Trade imbalances and currency fluctuations can also have adverse impact on domestic and global markets.

Economic power could also prevent or limit actions taken by a rival. Suppose a country requires a scarce raw material. If an adversary has sufficient funds, influence, or credit, it could purchase and withhold that raw material from its foe. The nation could also coerce sellers to prevent sale of that raw material to the opponent. States could put pressure indirectly on an opponent's allies to force a nation to take certain actions. After the 1973 Yom Kippur War, Arab oil-producing countries refused to sell oil to the United States and other nations that supported Israel. This embargo boosted oil prices and shifted international power from the developed nations to ones that relied primarily on oil extraction. Political and economic power was redistributed when these actions were combined with the nationalization of private, foreign-owned petroleum companies in these oil exporting nations.[4] Although in most cases, expropriating foreign assets endangers future investment or business, oil is different. Oil is the lifeblood of the world economy. Oil companies risk future confiscation of infrastructure, equipment, and capital to get this vital raw material.

The classic uses of economic power as coercive tools are embargoes, blockades, and sanctions. All of these are aggressive, hostile actions intended to restrict the target's economic access to the global economy. While often the first tool thought of, none of these are without disadvantage. Blockade, for example, is an act of war—not even considering the legal and practical necessity to make it effective by positioning naval forces to enforce the declaration. Sanctions work best when they are multilateral, massive, immediate, and used to achieve relatively minor policy changes from countries that value world opinion. Economic sanctions work poorly as a tool to coerce significant policy shifts, and they work best when used against countries where the common people, who are most immediately and directly affected by any sanction, have some political power. The imposing countries always suffer some economic cost, since cutting off trade to a nation means you lose the value of that trade as well as the target. Also, there are usually nations that for political or economic reasons are willing to trade with sanctioned nations; they reap a benefit while undermining the effectiveness of the sanction.

The Private Sector as a Strategic Tool.

Although not generally controlled by governments, disregarding currency manipulations designed to offset them, commercial balance of payments are another form of debt that can have foreign policy implications. The United States has been a major recipient of surplus foreign savings that has allowed the nation to purchase imports and pay for its current account deficit. From 1999 to 2006, foreign sources have lent America $4.4 trillion, about 85 percent of foreign surplus savings.[5] Fears of a pending financial disaster could cause lenders to pull capital out of the market and further exacerbate the situation. Unfortunately, globalized communications can now spread fears among global investors almost instantaneously. The result is that economic issues that might have been localized events only decades ago can now turn into global issues. Additionally, since private investors may act contrary to government desires, governmental and even international efforts to stem economic crises may be ineffective. Some nations fear excessive foreign investment due to a perceived influence or concern over precipitous withdrawal; others accept the risk and welcome foreign investment as a reasonably available source of funds. Although some nations find these actions helpful, critics argue that this capability can also be used to stifle competition, protect national interests, or create "geopolitical troublemaking."[6] Foreign funds do provide a needed economic boast, but they can also disappear quickly should confidence fail.

Multinational corporations and firms typically have the resources and ability to get access to once closed markets. Governments might offer subsidies or grant special benefits to attract business to their country. Once established, the multinational corporation could exert a powerful influence on the government since its affairs affect the nation's economy. Similarly, in highly contested markets, a multinational corporation could offer restricted technologies, move production of key subcomponents, offer bribes, expand production beyond the initial plan, or provide other incentives to gain access to the market. Companies can lobby their home country's government (assuming it favors the move into the other nation's market) for help lifting trade restrictions or access to technology or influencing the host nation's foreign policy.

Economics as a Source of Other Instruments of Power.

In the most basic sense, economic power is an entity's ability to acquire, produce, and use raw materials, goods, and services. A nation cannot engage in conflict over an extended period without an adjustment to its economy. In many cases, countries must devote goods or services to prepare for or fight a war or even to conduct other activities that affect the national interest. Humanitarian aid, defense expenditures, diplomacy, alliance membership, and other vital actions depend on a country's ability to raise and spend tax revenues, borrow funds, use surpluses, or finance these measures. Economic power allows players to conduct actions by providing the personnel, equipment, operating materials, infrastructure, and short or long term sustainment of that capability. Governments purchase commodities and equipment like a business, obtain labor (military, government civilian, and contractor), maintain physical capital, conduct research and development, and in some cases also produce unique goods and services peculiar to national security. The government funds these capabilities by extracting resources from the public and businesses that must sacrifice their own economic well being. Within the government, the competition for resources is very tough, especially in times when the domestic economy has a downturn that may limit funding of large or new initiatives. Skeptical lawmakers and the executive branch that must choose between these requirements and other programs of national interest must be convinced that military or diplomatic programs are the best use of scarce resources.

Resource decisions mold the creation of force structure to include investments in weapons, recruitment and retention of military and civilian personnel, decisions to fund military or non-military government programs, and a host of other concerns that affect national security policy. Further, economic conditions, once the exclusive concern of financial institutions, investors, and businesses, now affect military decisions that range from recruitment to government borrowing that directly influences a power's ability to provide military capability. Arms sales, transfers of key military technologies or technologies related to weapons of mass destruction, contracting for goods and services by individuals and firms, and other economic activities can influence the national security environment.

Nations that have sufficient resources can upgrade their military forces with more and better capabilities. Military forces that lack personnel or equipment could rely on contracted services or purchase advanced weaponry from other nations. If the state has limited forces, it can change the composition of its military forces by hiring specialized services that would have taken years to develop or that they only need for a limited time. Contractors on the battlefield are not new phenomena. The U.S. Government has used contractors in several wars. Other nations have hired military pilots and aircraft, logistics, and combat forces to expand and enhance their limited capabilities. Today, governments can lease satellite communications, photographic imagery, multi-spectral analysis, and navigational systems that were once the province of superpowers that had exclusive use of space systems. Individuals, firms, and governments can use these functions—for a price. This capability can change a balance of power at critical times during a conflict.

Economic success empowers nations with new capital, technology, or raw materials. This can be translated into military power and allow a formerly impoverished nation to complicate another state's security. For example, after the end of the Cold War the Russian Federation could not compete economically with free nations. A culture of economic inefficiency based on state owned enterprises and centrally planned economies destroyed entrepreneurship, investment, and innovation. The Russian economy was barely alive. Russia turned to raw materials exploitation to include natural gas and oil. Demand for energy has expanded, and with problems in the Middle East, oil prices have risen greatly. Russia's Gross Domestic Product (GDP), a measure of the country's total value of consumption, government, investment, and foreign trade, rose 380 percent from 2000 to 2006.

Oil profits have allowed the Russian government to finance a larger military budget that has given Moscow the ability to build a new intercontinental ballistic missile, aircraft, and other weapons to revitalize its national security and foreign policies. Nations building advanced technology consumer goods like information systems could use similar technologies to improve their military forces.

While national leaders consider and adapt economics as an element of national power, these same leaders are also affected by economic events that may limit their policies options. Economic considerations can have very influential impacts on the conduct of military operations and diplomatic actions. Globalization has allowed nations to conduct business with allies, former enemies, and potential rivals. New relationships between citizens and governments that highlight cost reductions, profits, and long range business activities can impact national security measures in a host of ways.

Government expenditures, borrowing, taxes, and other direct financial effects on a nation's public, financial markets, and business can skew short term consumption and longer term investment. The challenges government faces in the economic realm are not limited to these direct effects. A wider scope of national economic health is involved. The ability to pay for national security or the influence of foreign policies on business may strongly shape operations. Conversely, certain international events that affect a country's economic health may heighten support for aggressive national security policies. For example, policies that advocate the use of naval forces to arrest criminals or stop piracy would be hailed by a number of individuals from international shippers, insurers, consumers of goods transiting the area, and producers of exported and imported goods and raw materials.

Current economic conditions also have a large impact on military operations. Inflation contributes to reduced purchasing power by a government. This includes activities from purchasing fuel, paying for contracted work, demands for greater pay for military and civilian workers, and other acquisition activities. Similarly, a recession — a sustained downturn in economic activities — reduces tax revenues and encourages moves by politicians to stimulate the economy or support the unemployed or struggling citizens. These policies can significantly reduce the amount of defense spending for a nation. However, some of these conditions might provide relief to the government. Unemployment may ease recruitment and retention problems in the military. Increased competition for fewer government contracts might reduce the cost of operations. Tools to fight economic problems may also create unforeseen issues. A central bank could raise or lower interest rates. These actions can affect the availability of investors to purchase government debt and the cost of borrowing for contractors to build the latest fighter aircraft.

Economic crises can, if left unchecked, create an environment that leads to political upheaval and disintegration. A victorious British and French Allied delegation demanded economic reparations from Imperial Germany at Versailles after World War I. That move was partly a punishment and partly a way to repair the financial and economic problems caused in France and Britain during the war. A defeated Germany now faced the loss of Alsace-Lorraine, coal mining rights in the Saar for 15 years, territory in eastern Germany, and the payment of financial reparations. The German government was willing to pay damages to civilians and civilian property due to the war. Britain and France wanted Germany to admit guilt for the war and pay damages for the entire cost of the conflict, to include their loans from the United States. There was no fixed sum for the war debt during the surrender negotiations, and Germany was unable to start payment immediately. Instead, the Allies demanded that payments of $5 billion per year be made until 1921. The Allies would later issue a final accounting of war costs, and Germany would pay the remainder for another 30 years.[7] These demands limited Germany's ability to rebuild and ensured that Berlin was incapable of becoming a military threat to France. In 1929, a global depression created great, universal economic hardship. Unemployment increased, and governments tried a series of moves to fix problems within their borders. Most of these moves failed since many of the actions were uncoordinated and sometimes inappropriate in the global context of the depression. Germany was hit hard with reparations, the Great Depression, unemployment, and hyperinflation that made its currency worthless. German citizens demanded a change in government to fix economic problems; a democratically elected Adolph Hitler replaced the Weimar Republic.

Other Economic Security Considerations.

Expanding trade can provide several benefits to nations. It can create better efficiencies in production by seeking the lowest cost, most effective producers. This situation could lead to greater economic growth and improved standards of living around the world. However, not all nations find an economic niche that allows economic growth. Cheaper outsourced services and imported goods may destroy domestic industries. Large numbers of unemployed workers could create domestic problems for a government. Further, reliance on foreign imports could impoverish the state and complicate its financial and credit situation. If nations rely on foreign goods, then any problem that hinders trade could cause issues globally. A natural disaster, potential conflict, trade dispute, or other problem could restrict the flow of needed products.

Modern economic crises have had greater impact on nations than they might have in the past. Global investment and business have tied disparate business partners to global ventures as diverse as manufacturing computers and call center services. What used to threaten domestic economies can now become the basis for a worldwide economic crisis. In mid-1997, the Thai currency, the baht, collapsed due to a number of reasons to include overvaluation of the baht, poor financial systems, over-extended credit, and a construction and real estate "bubble." Banks, financial institutions, investors, and citizens started to panic and pull their money out of Thailand. They demanded payment in American dollars. Riots ensued in Bangkok and throughout Thailand. The World Bank and the International Monetary Fund took action. The Thai government almost collapsed. Investors lost millions of dollars, and the panic spread to South Korea and then throughout Asia. The contagion jumped as far as Latin America and Russia. Today, a quick glance at any copy of a financial newspaper will reveal issues from oil production problems, credit concerns, or other local problems that have the potential to create another global crisis and instability in almost any region of the world.

Government financial or policy changes actions can also shape the domestic markets in the short and long terms in ways run that can affect a state's health and security. The attacks on New York, Washington, and plane crash in Pennsylvania on September 11, 2001, shook global financial markets. Investors and firms were concerned about global market panic. The terrorist attacks on New York were partly intended to target Wall Street, which meant there were global financial implications. Immediately, the Federal Reserve and the Treasury Department stepped in to assure financial markets. Some of their actions included expanded bank borrowing opportunities to increase consumption among firms and individuals, assuring the bond market that adequate Treasury securities were available for trading to compensate for bond trading offices that had been destroyed, and injecting funds into the economy by purchasing Treasury securities through open market operations.[8] These steps served to settle domestic and global markets and ensured that a catastrophic failure of the United States economy with the attendant effects on the global economy did not occur.

Similarly, a government could take a number of domestic economic actions to settle cyclic downturns and uncontrolled growth. Injection of funds into an economy like tax rate reductions, increased aid from extended unemployment benefits, entitlement and other income supplements, tax rebates, greater federal programs aimed at expanding employment, and other programs could provide stimuli to help turn a struggling economy toward recovery. Federal programs that target certain industries could provide areas of new growth or repair damaged ones. Investment in energy programs, advanced technology, and other programs could in time provide solutions to some key economic problems. Although expensive, these programs could head off massive unemployment and social disruption that may create political issues and unrest. Legislation to reduce prices, like petroleum and other limited products, is an oft mentioned option. Price and wage controls normally do not work. These are temporary measures that lapse and leave the underlying reasons for the crisis unresolved.

War and conflict has always been an expensive proposition. Spending national treasure to fight for sovereignty or survival is normally an unquestioned policy choice. Debate about participating in smaller, limited wars that do not involve a vital national interest is another matter. Limited budgets create competition among government agencies, the public, and other interested parties that can result in bitter debates between guns and butter priorities. A public accustomed to receiving generous social, health, or income redistribution programs would object to greater demands to spend on national defense, foreign aid, or other activities that absorb discretionary funds that might otherwise be added to social spending. National leaders might be forced to curtail or end funding for a conflict. In extreme situations, such considerations may radically affect foreign policy.

Defense spending in the United States is the largest single expense for national security purposes. Budgetary pressure has mounted to reduce defense spending to pursue other types of federal programs. During the height of the Cold War, defense spending consumed approximately 6 percent of the nation's GDP. In 2000, the amount of defense spending had fallen to 2.1 percent of GDP. After September 11, 2001, the defense budget increased greatly to fund operations in Iraq, Afghanistan, and homeland defense. The defense budget's share of GDP more than doubled to 4.7 percent. In 2007, Washington spent $622 billion on defense that included $173 billion for operations in Iraq and Afghanistan.[9] The Congressional Budget Office estimates that defense spending will approach $671 billion for 2008. Defense spending is not without limits. Concerns about acquiring new and replacement equipment, increased military and civilian pay and benefits for existing and expanded forces, and operating costs may cause major adjustments to future defense budgets. Funding these budgets will force tough prioritization decisions.

National leaders can take several paths. If all government programs are fully funded, leaders must find new sources of federal revenue. Increased taxes are an obvious source of resources, but may come at the expense of future economic growth since individual and business investment and consumption may react negatively to tax increases. Borrowing the funds may damage future business investment due to interest rate hikes to attract capital to purchase securities. Large federal budget deficits can strangle the economy by siphoning investment funds from individuals and firms. Additionally, corporations compete for the same investment funds, so the interest rates they pay will rise. In 2000, the federal debt amounted to $5.6 trillion; by 2008 the estimated debt is poised to jump to $9.5 trillion.[10] These debt levels may slowly squeeze out discretionary funding, like defense, and limit federal spending to mandatory expenditures. Non-discretionary spending like interest payments and pensions is mandated by law and must be funded. The popularity of health, welfare, and other programs makes drastic social program cuts politically infeasible. The most likely scenario is that no federal program will receive all of its requested funding.

Economics and Future National Security Issues.

There are only a few nations that can possibly pose a military challenge to the United States in a conventional conflict. There are fewer still that possess nuclear weapons with the appropriate delivery systems to threaten major American cities. In the future, security conflict among nations may change from predominately military contests to ones primarily featuring other elements of national power. That option is also open to non-state actors. While there has always been economic competition, the conscious, planned, coercive use of economic power as the main tool to achieve national security objectives has been largely uncommon in American history. Moving to the use of non-military instruments of power to accomplish national security goals will take greater integration, coordination, planning, vision, time, and patience.

Using economics as an element of power will require consideration of a host of issues and unintended effects. National leaders will find numerous challenges from domestic and international camps that will complicate and constrain policy options. In the past, the American public has been largely spared from sustained, large scale military actions inside the national borders. That may not be the case with economic conflicts. If the nation uses a trade sanction to force another country to change its behavior, it may be targeted with its own set of countersanctions. Suppose the Washington applies trade restrictions against a country. That country could seize assets of American-owned firms, organize a boycott of American-made goods and services, ban the sale of critical raw materials, or undertake other retaliatory acts. That does not even consider the opportunity cost of lost potential trade with the target country. Many or most American citizens could suffer from higher prices, less choice, unemployment, or other economic disruption. The resulting political pressure could influence national decision making.

National security issues involving economics will only expand in the future. Global economic growth has introduced new powerhouses like China and India that complicate American national security and foreign policy decisions. Economic tools, once the province of a few developed countries, are now available to many developing and smaller powers. If these states can cause economic disruption, they can influence the behavior of not only regional rivals but of nations around the world. Small states, non-state actors, or even super-empowered individuals that have the economic ability to turn a local action into a global one must be expected to use that power to their advantage. In the past, such actors might have constrained their foreign policy due to a lack of military power or in the case of non-state and individual actors been incapable of exerting effective influence. Today, economic power or leverage could allow those entities to become more proactive and willing to flex their muscles in the belief their economic power will deter an opponent's military power. Conflict by pocket book could spread from a localized disagreement to a global one. Globalized markets and the dependence of nations on one another have made them vulnerable to many new threats; economic ones will find a greater place on the world stage in the future.

ENDNOTES - CHAPTER 17

1. U.S. Department of Commerce, *Statistical Abstract of the United States 1946,* Washington, DC: U.S. Department of Commerce, 1946, p. 312.

2. Paul Poast, *The Economics of War*, New York: McGraw-Hill, 2006, p. 33.

3. U.S. Agency for International Development, *USAID Primer: What We Do and How We Do It*, Washington, DC: U.S. Agency for International Development, January 2006, p. 3.

4. Daniel Yergin and Joseph Stanislaw, *The Commanding Heights: The Battle for the World Economy,* New York: Touchstone, 2002, p. 71.

5. Matthew Higgins and Thomas Klitgaard, "Financial Globalization and the U.S. Current Account Deficit," *Current Issues in Economics and Finance*, Vol. 13, No. 11, December 2007.

6. "The Invasion of the Sovereign-wealth Funds," *The Economist*, January 18, 2008, p. 11.

7. Donald Kagan, *On the Origins of War and the Preservation of Peace*, New York: Anchor Books, 1996, p. 288.

8. James J. McAndrews and Simon M. Potter, "Liquidity Effects of the Events of September 11, 2001," *Economic Policy Review*, November 2002, p. 69.

9. Congressional Budget Office, *Long-Term Implications of Current Defense Plans: Summary Update for Fiscal Year 2008*, Washington, DC: Congressional Budget Office, December 2007, p. 2-3.

10. Council of Economic Advisers, *Economic Indicators*, Washington, DC: Government Printing Office, December 2007, p. 32.

PART III

STRATEGIC ISSUES AND CONSIDERATIONS

PART III

DEVELOPMENT AND CURRENT OPERATIONS

CHAPTER 18

AIR POWER THEORY:
AN ANALYTICAL NARRATIVE FROM THE FIRST WORLD WAR TO THE PRESENT

Tami Davis Biddle

The role that airplanes should play in war has been, arguably, the most consistently controversial of all the issues pertaining to modern warfare over the last century.[1] This essay will explore the ideas and the theories that have served as the foundation for the use of aircraft in war. What was expected of the airplane as an element of the military instrument of power, and what has it brought to the conduct of warfare? How do we assess its record over the last 100 years? While my remarks apply in a general way to most of the industrialized nations that have built air forces, I shall focus principally on the United States and Britain through the end of World War II, and the U.S. after World War II. And while I shall address tactical aviation in a general way, I shall devote most of my attention to independent air power and the question at the heart of its theory: Is air power an effective coercive tool, and under what conditions can it be used to extract concessions from an enemy and force him to comply with the political terms being sought by the use of force?

Air power can be used in support roles for ground and sea warfare, and indeed it has proven itself extremely effective — and essential — in these applications. In addition it can be used as the primary arm in warfare, with the other services providing support and follow-on capabilities and resources. Most of the major theorists of air warfare have been proponents of the latter role for aircraft, advocating a primary emphasis on aerial bombing as a means of directly influencing an enemy's ability and will to fight a war. But if one believes that bombing can bring an enemy to terms, what assumptions does one make, implicitly, about the enemy? And what assumptions does one make about the ability of aerial bombing to so disrupt and disorient the enemy's economy and society that its war-making capacity (and will to war) must cease? The century-long experience of air warfare has shown, above all, that one must know a great deal about an enemy (in terms of politics, economics, culture, and social organization) to understand where its weak points are and how they may be exploited by bombing. It has revealed, too, that effective aerial bombing is a difficult, demanding, and technology-dependent enterprise.

A Long History of Speculation.

The dawn of the 20th century was accompanied by great speculation about the prospects for heavier-than-air flight. Such speculation had captured the human imagination for a long time, and late 19th century advances in science, technology, and engineering had created an environment pregnant with expectation and anticipation. Those who pondered human flight imagined it in a wide array of roles, including transportation, travel, and warfighting.

As scientific progress continued, notions of air war were modernized and infused with the hopes, concerns, and fears of the day. In the Victorian era, a common and recurring theme was that air warfare would be terrible, thus prompting enemies to mitigate their behavior, or even abolish war altogether — fostering a better, more peaceful world. In 1862 Victor Hugo speculated that aircraft would bring about the universal abolition of borders, leading to the end of wars and a great "peaceful revolution."[2] Jules Verne's widely-read novel *Clipper of the Clouds* (1886) asserted that the future belonged to aerial warfare machines.[3] In 1893 Major J. D. Fullerton of the British Royal Engineers theorized about an aerial "revolution in the art of war." A year later inventor

Octave Chanute argued that because no territory would be immune from the horrors of air war, "the ultimate effect will be to diminish greatly the frequency of wars and to substitute more rational methods of settling international misunderstandings."[4] In a 1911 essay for *Collier's* magazine, noted military inventor Sir Hiram Maxim argued that there would be no defense against the airplane, the most potent machine of destruction ever invented.[5]

This kind of speculation should not, perhaps, be surprising. After all, human flight opened up the prospect of warfare raining down from the skies, making all those below vulnerable in ways they had never been before. No longer would armies and navies act as the shield for polities, defending the weaker citizens behind the frontlines of battle. And this prospect was surely unsettling to political leaders, policymakers, and military planners alike. Political elites worried that those on the homefront were alienated, already, due to the crowded conditions, long work hours, and heavy stresses of the industrialized, urbanized environment that increasingly defined life in the western world. How would these citizens hold up to the increased stresses of aerial bombardment?

On the Eve of World War I.

In 1905 the British War Office's *Manual of Military Ballooning* argued that the balloons dropping gun cotton charges might have a "moral effect" on the enemy that "should not be lost sight of" in estimating their combat value. The "moral effect" (pronounced "morale" but spelled without the "e," as in the French) reflected a particularly potent and widespread fixation in the European military of the day. It revealed in part the influence of the Prussian Carl von Clausewitz, whose writings had become particularly popular after the Franco-Prussian war when Field Marshal von Moltke claimed they had influenced him. Clausewitz's *On War* (1832) had been translated into English by the end of the century, and was studied at the Army Staff College in Britain.[6] The work of French military theorists du Picq, Foch, Langlois, and de Grandmaison added to a trend emphasizing the role of "will" and moral factors in warfare.[7] The emphasis on "moral effects" in warfare highlighted the qualities valued by upper middle class Victorian and Edwardian era societies—courage, initiative, resourcefulness, tenacity, and willpower—but it also resonated with prejudices and darker trends therein, including Social Darwinism, anti-intellectualism, a strong emphasis on virility and aggressiveness, and a strict class system.[8]

Speculation was widespread not only about how competing states would stack up against one another, but also about how different races and classes within a state might affect its overall strength, virility, cohesion, and steadfastness under stress. How would the urban working classes hold up under the stresses of modern, industrialized war? Would they be steadfast or brittle? In 1908 the flight tests of Count Ferdinand von Zeppelin's airships were watched closely and anxiously by the British. Lt. Gen. Baden-Powell (noted for fostering the Boy Scout movement) made a vigorous call to arms in the *Daily Mail* on 13 July.[9] Concern over England's perceived inability to defend itself was at the center of a flurry of invasion literature, peaking between 1906 and 1909.

In both the United States and Britain, civil strife and industrial crises became endemic as laborers struggled for more humane working conditions; the problem was particularly acute on the eve of the World War I. In Britain frequent, bitter strikes—especially by miners and railwaymen—were marked by unusual assertiveness.[10] Naturally, this atmosphere fueled speculation about how workers would behave in wartime. Commentators and observers worried that the subhuman conditions present in the nation's congested industrial cities created weaknesses in the national population that might cause fatal vulnerabilities in wartime. In two lectures to the Royal United Services Institution in 1909, T. Miller Maguire associated what he called "the flotsam and jetsam of decaying British humanity" with the perversions of the "factory system."[11]

World War I.

These concerns over public robustness formed the context and backdrop for military debate and planning over the role of aircraft in war. But there was no overarching consensus on what aircraft might accomplish in the near term, or how they ought to be assessed against other military resources. Enthusiasts clashed with traditionalists who doubted that a new machine—and a highly unreliable one at that—would change the entire nature of warfare. The only genuine point of agreement concerned reconnaissance: even the most conservative military thinkers were willing to concede that a mobile, aerial perspective would change the nature of warfighting to some degree. When war came in 1914, most of the combatant states were still in the throes of working out how to integrate aerial weapons into their force structures. Inter-service conflicts and rivalries slowed progress in most states, including Britain, where aerial resources were initially divided between the Royal Naval Air Service and the Army's Royal Flying Corps. The role of aerial defense remained a red-headed stepchild in Britain, unwanted by either service.

The value of aerial reconnaissance, and thus the value of air space—both the enemy's and one's own—became immediately apparent; indeed, this reality was made obvious right away at the battles of Tannenberg and the Marne in 1914. Recognition of the value of an aerial perspective set in train the development and rapid evolution of purpose-built "fighter" aircraft; these quickly became fast, agile, and well-armed. Other roles for aircraft evolved throughout the war, including communication, battlefield attack and assault, and battlefield interdiction. The relatively primitive state of communications technology in 1914 meant that air/ground and air/air contact was sketchy at best, but it improved generally over the course of the war, thus enhancing the battlefield role of the airplane. All of these roles for aircraft were in full development—indeed in rapid, telescoped development—during the course of the war. And the tactics for the employment of aircraft were worked out just as ground combat tactics were worked out, through intensive trial and error. By the end of the war a fairly sophisticated body of doctrine existed for the battlefield uses of aircraft.

If this were the whole of the story, then the history of air power theory would be much simpler than it is. It was, not, of course, the whole of the story since there was another powerful, compelling, and intensely controversial role for aircraft: the use of long-range or "strategic" bombers to produce a coercive effect on the enemy homefront. Most states possessing aircraft had shown some interest in this prospect, but the development of bombers and bombing doctrine varied. The French, who were in relatively easy reach of some German industry, began attacking elements of that industry as a way of eroding the German ability to make war. This was part of an integrated campaign, and was not seen as truly separate from the Army effort. As the French found themselves increasingly overwhelmed by the demands of the ground war in 1916, they had fewer resources to devote to the air war; they increasingly concentrated their aerial efforts on the battlefront, where their fighter pilots won acclaim and honor in what was, contrary to popular memory, a brutal, exhausting, and very deadly struggle with Germany's equally determined fighter pilots.

In Germany the Kaiser gave in to public pressure to use Zeppelins (airships) in an aerial offensive designed to undermine the warmaking capacity and will of their British enemy. Germany's great strategic problem in the west was the strength of the Anglo-French alliance, and they sought a means to break the will of one or the other of those allied states. The airships had been, for the German people, a symbol of power and pride: they were viewed as a manifestation of German technical and aerial prowess. Throughout 1915 and into 1916 the Germans expanded the range of targets in Britain open to airship attack. At first, the British were vulnerable to the onslaughts. Air defenses were poorly organized and under-funded, and early British fighters did not have the engine thrust to intercept the high-flying airships before they could get in and out of striking range. Over time, though, the trends shifted as British defenses improved rapidly. Better fighters, special incendiary bullets, and much more efficient signals and defensive communications made flying zeppelins over England a very risky task by late 1916. In addition, the Royal Naval Air Service launched an aerial offensive against zeppelin sheds on the European coast.[12]

In 1917 the Germans made another attempt to use strategic bombing to break the will of the British. That spring and summer "Gotha," and later four-engined "Giant" bombers (*Riesenflugzeuge*), began menacing British cities, including London. Two small daylight raids on London (13 June and 7 July) managed to cause significant casualties and to raise the indignation and anger of the British, especially in response to bombs that hit a kindergarten. The British public demanded better air defenses, and retaliation in kind against the Germans. This public outcry—the very fact of the public's demand for a voice in the prosecution of the war—was unsettling to British elites, who were already on the lookout for signs of domestic unrest. Coming in a year when strikes and industrial actions had become commonplace once again, and when the Russian Revolution was in full gear, the public agitation was worrying. Field Marshal Douglas Haig found himself forced, against his will, to send fighter squadrons from the western front back to England. And a commission established by Prime Minister David Lloyd George concluded that Britain's aerial performance in the war could be improved most effectively by the creation of a separate service. Indeed, the commission, under South African general and statesman Jan Christian Smuts, came to some radical conclusions: "As far as can at present be foreseen there is absolutely no limit to the scale of its future independent war use. And the day may not be far off when aerial operations . . . on a vast scale may become the principal operations of war, to which the older forms of military and naval operations may become secondary and subordinate."[13]

It is no small thing to change one's defense structure in the midst of a major war, and yet the British did it during World War I. It reflected their anxiety about the domestic front, and the perceived need to respond to public pressure. The internal politics of the newly-independent Royal Air Force (RAF) were bumpy at first since neither Haig nor Maj. Gen. Sir Hugh Trenchard, then commanding the Army's air offensive on the western front, was the slightest bit interested in creating a new service. But Trenchard found himself, in May 1918, in command of a long range bombing force referred to as the "Independent Force" (IF). France's Marshal Ferdinand Foch queried indignantly, "Independent of what, God?"[14]

Though promised a sizable force, Trenchard never received it; indeed, the aircraft he had were hardly up to the task they were given. After making requests for more and better aircraft (especially fighter escorts), Trenchard decided to make do with what he had. For the most part, he stayed with what he knew, attacking targets selected to affect the ground war. He was well aware, though, that the eyes of the public were upon him, and he was expected to achieve results. Thus, he directed attacks on cities and industry when such opportunities presented themselves. Trenchard's rather haphazard approach to the strategic campaign caused no end of exasperation among the newly-formed Air Staff planners back in London. They had devoted considerable effort to analyzing German war industry and identifying strategic targets of consequence. One analyst in particular, Lord Tiverton, authored a theory of strategic air war that sought to identify "bottlenecks" in the German war economy. A sophisticated plan, it was a precursor to the "industrial fabric" theory of bombing that would be stressed in the United States during the interwar years.

But Trenchard felt no obligation to heed his own staff, and carried on as he pleased. Because he could produce little in the way of physical results in Germany, he stressed instead the indirect results and the psychological impact of his air campaign. He argued that his bombers produced strain on workers and citizens, and lowered factory production due to ongoing air raids and alarms.

He argued that the "moral effect" of bombing was 20 times the physical effect. Though his math was haphazard, the language of the "moral effect" was resonant at the time. Needing to justify his operations, Trenchard waged a rhetorical offensive designed to achieve what his actual air offensive could not.[15]

From the time of their entry into the war, the Americans had shown a strong interest in the prospects for air warfare and long-range bombing. But they were not able to produce the aerial armada they had envisioned early on; indeed, they discovered that in the industrial era one could not simply create a fighting force overnight. While Gen. Billy Mitchell oversaw the air offensive at the St. Mihiel and Meuse-Argonne campaigns, the Americans engaged in no long range bombardment (or "strategical bombardment" as they called it at the time). They did, however, keep a keen eye on the bombing efforts of their allies, and they produced a plan—based entirely on one drawn up by Tiverton—to wage an aerial offensive on German industry. Though it was never implemented, the Americans did engage in an evaluation—a bombing survey—of the British and French efforts. The Americans were attentive to the critiques of Trenchard by the British Air Staff, and they too criticized his unsystematic application of air power; while they appreciated the "moral effect" of bombing, they did not feel it achieved all Trenchard had claimed for it. Instinctively, they preferred a more analytical approach.[16]

The experience of long range bombing in World War I was rushed, imperfect, and marginal: air warfare remained a side-show, ancillary to the tremendous effort taking place on the ground. The most impressive result was the body of ideas that emerged quickly from those analysts, like Tiverton, who devoted energy and effort to the key questions. But the ideas were well ahead of the actual weapons required to implement them. While the Germans managed to produce an impressive, four-engine long range bomber by the end of the war, and while the British were working on a plane capable of reaching Berlin, most of the World War I bombers were limited in size and lift capacity, had primitive navigation tools, and were prone to unreliability. All this meant that there was no full test of long range bombardment and its effects on the enemy. There was, however, just enough experience to allow interested parties to make claims—and to stake out positions—with respect to it.

For the Germans, the experience of bombing England had been largely disappointing. While they stirred up anger and indignation among the British, that unrest did not translate into military or political gain. While the British were forced to bring fighters back from the front and invest more heavily in air defenses, the timing was such that the entry of the Americans into the war made good the shortages that would otherwise have been felt more keenly. And the Germans found themselves frustrated by the improvements in British air defenses (against both airships and bombers), and by the difficulty of flying and bombing accurately in cloudy, rainy north European weather. By the spring of 1918 the Germans had largely abandoned the strategic air campaign against England, and had refocused all their aircraft on the ground war.[17]

The English interpretation of their experience was quite different, however. As noted, British elites were unsettled by the public demand for a voice in the war, by the need to bring fighters back to the homefront, and by the indirect effects—mainly production losses—from overflight and air raid alarms. Indeed, so grave were Lloyd George's concerns about the stability of the homefront that in the spring of 1918 a scheme was drawn up to provide for marshal law in the event of full-scale domestic unrest.[18] After the war RAF officials argued that in exchange for a limited offensive effort, the Germans were able to tie up considerable resources in the U.K. Indeed, the first commandant of the RAF Staff College pointed out in 1924 that in response to 452 German aeroplane flights over England, the British put up 1,882 defensive sorties.[19] In this environment Trenchard, who had become the postwar Chief of Air Staff, was able to make a persuasive case that Britain must be in a position, should war come, to wage a prompt and incessant air campaign against the enemy, designed to push him on to the defensive before that enemy could do the same to Britain. The argument was useful to Trenchard because it enabled him to argue that the RAF deserved to maintain its institutional autonomy after the war.

The Interwar Years.

Trenchard proved himself a master of the bureaucratic arts: he fended off claims on RAF resources, and he continually built the case—to military planners and policymakers—that the RAF was essential for deterrence and future warfighting. During the interwar years public views on warfare tended to embody extremes—either a determination to avoid the topic altogether, or a tendency to articulate it in the most apocalyptic terms. Perhaps this should be unsurprising in the aftermath of the unremittingly grim experience of the World War I, but its effect was to leave little room for rigorous or considered analysis. Dark forebodings in the realm of popular culture resulted in a flurry of books addressing the apocalyptic side of the spectrum: *The Poison War, The Black Death, Menace, Empty Victory, Invasion from the Air, War Upon Women, Chaos, Air Reprisal,* and *What Happened to the Corbetts.*[20] The impact of these was augmented not only by the futurist scenarios being played in the (increasingly popular) cinemas, but also by the ominous and troubling events of the 1930s, including the Japanese attack on Manchuria, the Italian attack on Abyssinia, and the Spanish Civil War.

By this time as well, the ideas of the Italian air enthusiast, Gen. Giulio Douhet, were becoming more widely known in English-speaking countries. Douhet's 1921 book, *The Command of the Air,* had painted a graphic vision of societal collapse in the face of air attack. Indeed, it was the futurist drama he conveyed rather than the analytical rigor of his ideas that gave Douhet a lasting place in the canon of air warfare.[21] A poet, painter, playwright and amateur novelist, Douhet brought to bear on his work "the intense modernist fascination with the latest advances in science and technology—with the automobile, with electricity, with gas and finally with the aeroplane—prevalent in prewar Italian protofascist *avant-garde* culture."[22] Though both British and American airmen had developed indigenous theories of air warfare that did not depend on Douhet—and though there is no evidence that Douhet was widely read in Britain or the U.S. before the 1930s—his ideas were cited thereafter and used to support apocalyptic visions of air warfare. His prose seemed to capture an important element of the mood in the West, and it seemed to capture, as well, a kind of archetypal image of the airplane as weapon.

Douhet's vision stressed the offensive, indeed he referred to aircraft as the offensive weapon "par excellence." Postulating that vast destruction could be wrought by 50 squadrons of bombers, he asked his readers, "How could a country go on living and working under this constant threat, oppressed by the nightmare of imminent destruction and death?" Douhet was impressed by the possibilities of attack against those of "least moral resistance" such as factory workers.[23] His vision was one of technological determinism: "The brutal but inescapable conclusion we must draw is this: in the face of the technical developments of aviation today, in case of war the strongest army we can deploy . . . and the strongest navy we can dispose . . . will provide no effective defense against determined efforts . . . to bomb our cities."[24]

Though Douhet believed that technology had given the defensive a permanent pride of place in ground warfare, he argued just the opposite with respect to air war. Douhet believed that the vastness of the sky made defense against the airplane virtually impossible: defender's inability to know the exact position and timing of air attack gave the attacker a tremendous edge. Douhet also largely dismissed the potential of ground defenses. As historian Phillip Meilinger has noted, "Douhet sarcastically concluded that ground fire might down some aircraft, much like muskets shot in the air might occasionally hit a swallow, but it was not a serious deterrent to air attack."[25] Douhet noted several target categories of primary significance: industry, transport, infrastructure, communication, seats of government, and the will of the people. Douhet emphasized the latter in particular, since he argued that wars in the future would see no distinction between combatants and noncombatants, and that urban targeting would do the most to collapse enemy will.

Because he saw airplanes as strategic rather than tactical weapons, Douhet did not advocate the use of aircraft in support of armies or navies. He did not believe, either, that ground forces would be required to occupy enemy territory. While he admitted that a strong and wealthy nation might opt to build both tactical and strategic air forces, his still believed that the utility of the latter vastly outweighed the former.[26]

But Douhet's perspective was narrow, and he saw only the evidence that supported his view. As historian Michael Sherry has pointed out, his idea of the future rested on crude extrapolation, and like many other interwar prophets of air power, he failed to see how it "might evolve unpredictably, strengthening the defense as well as the offense, creating its own futile charges and bloody stalemates."[27]

Much of the power of Douhet's vision came from his linkage of airplanes and chemical warfare. Gas weapons, though not terribly effective on the battlefield, had nonetheless brought to the surface a sense of dread in the public mind that was felt throughout Europe. Much earlier, the poet Alfred Lord Tennyson had tapped into this foreboding when he, in his poem *Locksley Hall* (1842), "dipt into the future, far as human eye could see," and postulated a "ghastly dew" raining from the heavens as "the nations' airy navies" grappled in "the central blue."[28]

Douhet's intense focus on the aerial offensive was also emblematic of the interwar years. In Britain the popular memory of the air war focused on the early raids, when defenses were disjointed and ineffective. By contrast, recollections of the later—and far more effective—defensive efforts seemed to fade. A full and rigorous analysis of the wartime experience would have supported conclusions quite different than those in the public mind, but such an analysis was never undertaken. Thus, in 1932, when once and future Prime Minister Stanley Baldwin declared, "the bomber will always get through," it was taken rather as an article of faith. To be fair, bomber speeds had run well ahead of fighter speeds in the early interwar years, and it seemed that bombers—which would be able to take advantage of the vastness of the air—might always have the advantage. But changes in fighter speeds, and, especially, developments in defensive technology (radar) should have caused the entire issue of bomber penetration to be entirely re-thought in the mid-1930s. It never was, however, setting up the first of many World War II clashes between expectation and reality in air warfare.[29]

When Trenchard handed the RAF off to his successors in 1929, it was secure in its autonomy. It was not, however, in a position to carry out the offensive policy it had touted so consistently. Trenchard did not give center stage to the questions and issues that should have dominated the service agenda: Can the bomber always get through? Under what circumstances? How do bombers find and hit targets accurately and reliably? What kinds of bombs are most effective under what conditions, and against which targets? How well can bombers fare in poor weather? But Trenchard's interwar traction rested on two elements besides his skill at bureaucracy. The first was a postwar environment that was still traumatized by the horrific experience of the stalemated ground war on the Western Front. So disturbing had been that episode that anyone who seemed to offer an alternative to it was given a hearing, at the least. The second was a claim that he, like other airmen of the day, truly understood the future of war. Setting themselves up as visionaries and men of the future, the air power enthusiasts could cast a certain disdain upon the stubborn, Luddite visions of those in the traditional services. Indeed, Billy Mitchell frequently referred to his Army colleagues as "the longbowmen."[30]

While Hitler set about renouncing the terms of the Versailles agreement and rearming the Luftwaffe, the RAF found itself increasingly insecure about its own capabilities. Indeed, the new head of Bomber Command, Sir Edgar Ludlow-Hewitt, discovered, to his disquiet in 1937, that Bomber Command was, "entirely unprepared for war, unable to operate except in fair weather, and extremely vulnerable both in the air and on the ground."[31] A year later, during the Munich Crisis, Prime Minister Neville Chamberlain would facilitate the handing over of a piece of Czechoslovakia to Hitler in a desperate act that stemmed from an overwhelming desire to head off war — and the terrible aerial bombardment it was expected to entail. Whatever effect it had on the enemy, the RAF's interwar rhetoric surely had been a deterrent to British statesmen as well.

Without any actual experience in long-range bombing, and with a parent service that was hostile to notions of independent air power, the U.S. Army Air Service/Air Corps made only incremental inter-war progress toward autonomy. If mavericks — led by Billy Mitchell — championed the cause, they did not win the day. Without an immediate threat to menace their nation, the American people saw no need to restructure the national defenses after World War I. But even in the absence of rapid institutional progress, American airmen began to define and hone a doctrine of aerial bombing. It rested on assumptions like those that Tiverton had used as the building blocks of his own air theory.

By 1926 William C. Sherman, who had gone from the Air Service Tactical School (later the Air Corps Tactical School [ACTS]) to instructor in air tactics at the Army's Command and General Staff School at Fort Leavenworth, Kansas, had taken the lead in articulating American air doctrine in his book, *Air Warfare*.[32] Explaining the future of the bomber, he pronounced enthusiastically: "The bomber now stands forth as the supreme air arm of destruction. . . . When nations of today look with apprehension on the air policy of a neighbor, it is the bomber they dread."[33]

Building on a traditional interpretation of the importance of interdiction in war, Sherman asserted that "the military objective of bombardment aviation, par excellence, is the hostile system of supply." Therefore, "The long range of the bomber should be utilized to the full, and every sensitive point and nerve center of the [supply] system put under pressure, in an effort to paralyze the whole." Sherman cogently articulated a set of ideas that would shortly thereafter take on a central doctrinal role at ACTS as the "industrial fabric" or "key-node" theory of targeting:

> Industry consists . . . of a complex system of interlocking factories, each of which makes only its allotted part of the whole. . . . Accordingly, in the majority of industries, it is necessary to destroy certain elements of the industry only, in order to cripple the whole. These elements may be called the key plants. These will be carefully determined, usually before the outbreak of war. . . . On the declaration of war, these key plants should be made the objective of a systematic bombardment, both by day and by night, until their destruction has been assured, or at least until they have been sufficiently crippled.[34]

Sherman's theory rested on a more rigorous and analytical foundation than Trenchardian doctrine, but it depended upon two important and ultimately problematical assumptions: that intelligence work would be able to identify the "key plants," and that bombers would be able to find and strike them without suffering prohibitive losses. In general, the Americans were not so inclined as the British to assume that an aerial *guerre de course* might be possible, and they devoted a considerable amount of time to considering bomber escorts. Upon failing to find their way to a solution, they opted instead to give bombers self-protection by arming them heavily. The long range escort problem was a hard one to crack: how do you build a fighter that can keep pace with a bomber, deep into enemy territory, and then, on arrival at the target, fight on equal terms with fast, agile, enemy defenders? The Americans side-stepped this technological challenge, for a time at least, by arguing that the interlocking fields of fire created by bombers flying in groups would facilitate a reasonably safe entry into (and return from) enemy airspace.

270

The Americans also focused their energy, from the outset, on the accurate bombing of specific targets. The authorization of the B-17 bomber had been based on a coastal defense mission, the B-17 would intercept ships at sea. And the Norden bombsight, the brainchild of the Navy's in-house designer/engineer, Carl Norden, would give the Americans the tool they would need to make the bomber a precise instrument. The Americans' lean toward a bombing doctrine that was oriented to the identification of specific, significant targets in the enemy war industry was driven, as well, by the prevailing cultural and intellectual climate, in particular: the influence of the industrial efficiency movement and Taylorism; a rational/economic approach to military problems facilitated by the nation's distance from immediate enemies; and the impact of the Great Depression, which hit the U.S. particularly hard and seemed to underscore the idea that complex economies are fragile and subject to ready disruption. Through the 1930s the industrial fabric theory would be refined at the Air Corps Tactical School, by then based at Maxwell Field in Alabama. Careful not to overstep their bounds and raise the suspicions of Army officials in Washington, ACTS instructors and students nonetheless worked quietly on a doctrine that was ready for implementation when President Franklin D. Roosevelt and General George C. Marshall began to turn their attention to air power as a means of warfighting.[35]

World War II.

By the time that the *Wehrmacht* and *Luftwaffe* launched their war, they had taken the doctrinal lessons of modern combined arms — worked out slowly and painfully between 1914 and 1918 — and refined them into a mode of warfighting that looked, for a time at least, unstoppable. The "Blitzkrieg" of 1939-40 was nothing more than the intelligent application of armor and air power to the ground war breakthroughs of 1918. But, for states that had not concentrated so effectively on tactical and operational integration, it seemed daunting to say the least. In Britain, where the RAF had focused nearly all of its energies on strategic bombing and home defense, air-ground cooperation had fallen by the wayside. Indeed, as historian Sir Maurice Dean has argued, "between 1918 and 1939 the RAF forgot how to support the Army."[36] The fault belonged to both services — but fault it was, nonetheless, and it revealed itself glaringly during the Battle of France. Air-ground cooperation on the battlefield would be re-learned by the Allies in the deserts of North Africa. Though much doctrinal ground had been lost, it was made up for relatively quickly by talented airmen like "Maori" Coningham of New Zealand, Sir Arthur Tedder of Britain, and Carl Spaatz of the United States. With their survival at stake, the Russians too learned the methods of effective air-ground interoperation.[37]

The problems of air-ground cooperation are relatively easy to grasp, but not always easy to solve. Because it requires cooperation between two different organizations operating in two different realms, communication is an on-going issue. Air and ground must be able to communicate effectively without jeopardizing their own indigenous operations. In addition, the structure of air support to the ground is tricky. Overcentralization of resources leads to a lack of responsiveness. But too much decentralization means that there is little ability to concentrate at a point. It means, as well, that many airplanes are likely to be left in locations where they can do little good at all. Finding just the right balance is crucial — and yet it is difficult to achieve.

Luftwaffe commander Hermann Goering launched his pilots into the Battle of Britain with an optimism unsubstantiated by the reality of the situation. While some Germans air theorists had shown interwar interest in long range bombing, their ability to translate it into something robust fell victim to the early death of a leading theorist, Walter Wever, and the tendency of Third Reich bureaucracy towards overweening insularities and inefficiencies. The Luftwaffe was controlled largely by the fighter pilots, to the detriment of bomber doctrine.[38]

In the meantime the British had developed an effective communications net into which radar, when ready, could be successfully inserted. A late-in-the-day push to build adequate numbers of fighters—and very good ones—enabled the British to hold out against the aerial onslaught of an overconfident enemy. But the failure of the Germans in the Battle of Britain did nothing to dissuade the British from trying their own air offensive against Germany. The decision reflected the desperate straits the British found themselves in by 1940-41. Without allies, and with only one potential offensive tool against Hitler, the British could not afford to countenance the possibility that bombing might not work. After all, in May 1940 Churchill had made bombing a main pillar of his argument that the British ought not to seek terms with Hitler, and ought, instead, to follow an economic and peripheral strategy against the enemy.

But the interwar lacunae in analysis and training all came painfully to the surface in the early years of the war. Bomber Command's initial missions—dropping propaganda leaflets—pointed out just how woefully unprepared the organization was for full-scale war. The long sorties told of the difficulties of finding distant cities, of the constant battles with weather, and of the physical discomforts crews would encounter in such operations. The effectiveness of German defenses pushed operations increasingly into the nighttime hours, when darkness could afford some protection. Crews were sent out with maps, astro-sextants, and directional radio. With these means, which required a high degree of skill to use effectively, they were expected to find their way about; in essence, crews were expected to navigate at night by observation—an all but impossible task under the weather conditions so frequently prevailing.[39]

Having been pressed into serious thinking about targeting, the RAF's Air Staff came up with a list that identified critical nodes in the German war economy: transport and oil figured prominently. If German defenses had forced the British to fly under cover of night, this, in turn, only exacerbated the navigational and target-finding problems. The first vigorous analysis of British accuracy, undertaken in the summer of 1941, produced results that the leaders of the RAF could barely believe: only one in five bombers was getting within five miles of its target. The Chief of Air Staff, Sir Charles Portal, saw the handwriting on the wall. There was little choice but to turn to the only targets that crews could find and hit reliably in darkness, cities. In mid-February 1942, Bomber Command came under a new directive calling for an attack on area targets; the objective was to undermine "the morale of the enemy civil population and in particular, of the industrial workers." This step, an expedient, removed any doctrinal underpinning that counted on precise targeting of specified industries or resources. While it did not abandon an economic rationale entirely, it shifted the emphasis back to Trenchard's point of focus, the morale of the enemy.

One week after the new directive was issued, Sir Arthur Harris became the head of Bomber Command. While the directive for city bombing predated him, he was an adherent of the strategy— and would remain so, stubbornly, until the end of the war. Harris believed that cities contained, and concentrated within them, everything important to modern industrial nations. Harris's own view of city bombing hinged on the idea that he could simply overwhelm the Germans by smashing their infrastructure, eroding their confidence in their leadership, and demoralizing them. The theoretical underpinning rested in part on "brute force"—the destruction of infrastructure and thus the erosion of the war economy—and in part on "coercion." Harris assumed that when the Germans began to believe they could not stop Bomber Command's overwhelming offensive, the prospect of seeing their entire nation in ruins would cause them to seek terms.

Harris set about making his crews technically proficient, skilled, and consistent in their new task. His was an immense job—both the public and the bomber crews themselves had begun to wonder if the investment in bombing had been sound—but Harris brought great energy and dogged determination to Bomber Command Headquarters. By 1944 he had under him an air force that was the most powerful and proficient of the war, able not only to devastate cities, but to find and destroy specific targets such as marshaling yards and synthetic oil plants.[40] Whatever Harris's flaws and blind spots, his proficiency as a field commander and a problem-solver was matched only by that of the young American general, Curtis Emerson LeMay.

In 1942 the American entry into the air war had been, as in 1917, painfully and frustratingly slow. While Harris waged thousand-bomber raids on British cities, the Americans flew 12-bomber raids to the coastal edges of France. Fearful that the American determination to employ "precision bombing" would fall victim to the same nemeses the British had faced, Prime Minister Churchill tried to intervene, imploring the Americans to join the nighttime area offensive. But the Americans would have none of it. They were, for a variety of reasons, committed to attacks on the German industrial fabric by groups of self-defending bombers flying in daylight.[41] The heady, unshakeable American faith in their bomber doctrine finally came a cropper in the late summer and autumn of 1943, however, when raids into Germany proved so costly as to be unsustainable. In four raids carried out over 6 days in October, 148 American bombers failed to return to their bases.[42] These raids were aimed in part at the supply of German ball bearings—an element of the enemy war economy the Americans assessed as pivotal.

At this point the Americans, too, were forced to reevaluate. But instead of changing targets like the British had done, they changed tactics. They embraced the long-range escort fighter, now usefully equipped with dropable, self-sealing auxiliary fuel tanks, and sped them into production. During the winter of 1944, the Americans fought a sustained, force-on-force battle for air superiority in Europe. Taking bombers to targets the Germans felt compelled to defend, they set up duels between American escorts and German short-range defenders. Backed by a powerful industrial base in full swing, and a steady supply of pilots, the Americans began to chip away steadily at *Luftwaffe* dominance. This was not what interwar theory had predicted: the Americans figured that they would win air superiority by attacks on the German aircraft industry on the ground. But the operational changes were effective, and by placing heavy pressure on the supply of German pilots, they relieved much of the strain on Bomber Command too.

In the spring of 1944 the Anglo-American bombers came under the control of General Dwight Eisenhower and his deputy, Tedder, who used the strategic bombers operationally—to great effect—to pave the way for the Normandy invasion. Heavy attacks on railways and bridges in France considerably reduced Germany's ability to move men and supplies to the new front as the amphibious assault gained a foothold. Though both Harris and Spaatz (by then the head of the U.S. Strategic Air Forces, or USSTAF) had hoped that the invasion would be unnecessary and considered the tactical preparation a diversion from their main task of bombing the heart of the enemy, both men complied proficiently with their orders. This work, along with the attrition of the *Luftwaffe* carried out by the Americans, did as much as anything else to insure the success of D-day and the Anglo-American ground war that followed it. After D-day, full exploitation of tactical air greatly aided the fortunes of the Anglo-American ground forces.[43]

Convinced that his city raids would bring about a German collapse, Harris sought to recommence them once he was out from under the demands of the Normandy campaign. But the Air Staff was now increasingly unconvinced that Harris's campaign made the best possible use of British bombers. Instead, they supported Gen. Spaatz's prioritization of Germany's remaining (and dwindling) oil supply. This led to an intense debate between Portal and Harris in the winter of 1944-45. Portal, who suspected that the lure of cities drew Harris to them even when weather conditions would support an attack on oil, encouraged Harris to embrace a new bombing directive designed to exploit Germany's Achilles' heel. Harris countered that he went to oil targets every time it was feasible to do so. There could be no victor in the debate since it all depended on differing interpretations of weather data. As it was, Harris and Portal were debating only the close calls—those nights when the weather conditions might support an attack on a specific target. But these were the minority; much of the time area bombing was the only real choice. Such was the technology of the mid-twentieth century.

In order to maintain American operations at something approaching a consistent tempo, head of the U.S. Army Air Forces Gen. "Hap"Arnold had authorized, by late 1943, bombing "on instrument" through cloud cover. Though he eschewed the term "blind bombing," Arnold was prepared for his crews to abandon the visual sighting and aiming of "precision bombing" when weather conditions did not support it, and to rely instead on imperfect navigational aids. Since they identified themselves as a visual force and had trained that way, the Americans did not adapt easily to the change. Indeed, in the winter of 1944-45, 42 percent of American bombs dropped through cloud fell more than 5 miles from the target. In order to increase the collateral impact of these poor weather raids, the Americans began adding incendiary bombs into their ordnance mix. Aimed typically at railway marshaling yards (big targets that can often be spotted through even a brief break in cloud cover), these raids did not differ much in their practical effects from British area bombing. Marshaling yards were attacked by the American air forces more frequently than any other target in Europe.[44]

The bombing theories motivating the British and the Americans remained distinct: the latter went to specific targets whenever weather would support it, and they did not ever embrace, in Europe, a focus on the fire-bombing of cities. But the constraints and limitations of the technology of the 1940s had pushed the two air forces in a similar direction. Bombing in Europe was a blunt instrument that pounded the body of the enemy; it was not a rapier that impaled central organs. By the end of the war the Americans—perhaps frustrated by the limited impact of their "precision" bombing—became more amenable to targeting for psychological effect, and targeting to hasten the progress of the ground war.

At the end of the day, two targets did provide an important payoff: by the end of the war, Germany's dwindling oil supply badly compromised her ability to continue to fight a war of maneuver dependent on tanks and aircraft. And attacks on German transport hubs increasingly compromised Germany's ability to distribute the fuel central to her war industry, coal. The American quest for a silver bullet—for the key card in the house of cards—did not yield a payoff until the very end of the war, when, in conjunction with the high-tempo ground war and the westward movement of the Red Army (which denied Germany the oil of southeastern Europe), it finally found a degree of vindication in the oil campaign. And Harris, by forcing the dispersal of German industry, had helped set the conditions that would make the late-war attacks on German railways quite devastating to the enemy. These achievements, however important and significant, came late in the war and did not follow the pattern of claims made by the most assertive interwar air theorists.

Though the Americans would make much of the oil campaign in their postwar survey (United States Strategic Bombing Survey [USSBS]), it was not a truly "independent" victory for air since its effectiveness rested on the enemy's cooperation in continuing to fight an intense, resource-demanding ground war. But if the industrial fabric theory of bombing had not worked out in quite the way that its proponents had expected, the Air Force and its supporters could—and did—claim that this was not an indictment of the theory itself. If, they argued, a bigger and better air offensive had commenced sooner, independent air power might have won the day. Harris's defense of Bomber Command was similar in tone if somewhat different in detail. Harris argued that if only he had been able to fight his war on cities—focused solely on the air and free of "diversions" like the Normandy campaign—he could have proved the war-winning capability of bombers. He never accepted what the evidence had revealed by the end: that, in a police state, it was hard to translate popular dissent into political pressure. The German people fought under and successfully endured the impact of a weight of bombs that any inter-war air theorist would have predicted as paralyzing to an enemy state. And German leaders were not so convulsed by the thought of their cities in ruins as to seek terms.

Much of the prewar speculation about the fragility of civilians and the frangibility of economies was simply wrong: both were more robust than the interwar writing had anticipated. Prior to the war the British had expected 30,000 casualties per day; in 1939 authorities handed out one million burial forms to local authorities. But these figures were way wide of the mark, having been based on a faulty interpretation of the World War I experience, and combined with the impact of apocalyptic interwar rhetoric. During the Blitz against London in the winter of 1940-41, the British population revealed stability and robustness instead of the flightiness and panic that many specialists had predicted. Hospital admissions for neurosis declined, suicide rates fell, and incidents of drunkenness declined by half.[45] To their credit, the psychologists admitted they had been wrong during the inter-war years. Writing in the *Lancet* in 1941, Dr Felix Brown explained: "The incidence of genuine psychiatric air-raid casualties has been much lower than might have been expected; the average previously healthy civilian has proved remarkably adjustable." He added that women had not been a "weakening element" in the general population, as they had been expected to be.[46]

There was certainly disruption after some raids, but this was almost always related to perceived inadequacies in relief efforts: people generally behaved well when they believed the government was making concerted efforts on their behalf. In response to a Gallup poll asking what had made them most depressed that winter, Londoners early in 1941 ranked the weather over aerial bombing.[47]

Even at the end of the war, when the bomb tonnage dropped in one month could equal the tonnage dropped previously in an entire year, popular pressure did not cause the Germans to sue for peace. To some extent this represented commitment to the cause, and to some extent it reflected the fact that people feared retribution for protest even more than they feared bombing. The former was more certain and swift than the latter. And propaganda indicating that the enemy would have no mercy in unconditional surrender surely was an element in the starch that kept the Germans fighting till the last. Culture mattered too. In Japan, for instance, Hirohito was able to turn his entire nation into a kind of human shield. The Emperor was perceived by the people as divine, and they felt it their obligation to protect him — to the last — with their lives. This enabled them to endure the fire-bombing of over 60 of their cities without losing their commitment to fight on.[48]

Speculation about popular reaction to bombing rested partly on faulty assumptions about the likely behavior of the masses — especially the working classes — under the fall of bombs. And it rested partly on extrapolation from experience with the bombing of troops in the field. Heavily bombed troops often reacted with panic and flight. This same behavior — and worse — was expected of civilians; after all, the civilian population had no formal training, and (according to elites) little self-discipline. But attempts to predict the homefront on the basis of the battlefront were erroneous. After all, troops under fire are pinned in place. Exposed, or sheltered in shallow trenches at best, they have little to protect them from the full brunt of aerial attacks. Civilian populations, however, are not like fish in a barrel; they are generally not "trapped" since they continue to have some say in their actions — some ability to avoid potentially dangerous places or to take shelter if they are caught under attack. Thus, their psychological state does not parallel the psychological state of the soldier who must endure a bombing raid on the battlefield.

Many of the economic assumptions underpinning the theories of World War II bombing also proved wide of the mark. Substitution and stockpiling (the latter explaining an ongoing ball bearing supply) could make up for many of the shortages caused by bombing; slack in the Germany economy meant that increased production could occur through expansions of the workforce and work hours;

and dispersal of industry could reduce vulnerability to bombardment. The German economy was nowhere near full stretch at the outset of the war (as intelligence analysts thought it was).

The experience of the Anglo-American bombing campaign pointed to one lesson above all: it is necessary to have highly accurate and highly detailed intelligence information about the enemy — and about the enemy's ability to adapt — in order to have any hope of using aerial bombardment as an effective tool of war.

Some of the lessons of the war came to the surface in the United States Strategic Bombing Survey, but the Survey was so vast and unwieldy (consisting of well over 300 separate reports) that the "Summary" reports were the only ones that garnered very much attention in the end. Committee products that ended up largely defending the big investment in strategic bombing, they did not contain the rigor or subtlety to guide future policy in an effective way. In Britain, Churchill's nervousness about the potential backlash against area bombing caused him to prevent any full-scale survey from taking place.[49]

The record of World War II strategic bombing has been intensely controversial, in part because of the ethical ramifications of the late-war raids (the American firebombing of Tokyo on 9-10 March 1945 killed over 100,000 persons), and in part because there is no way to satisfactorily calculate the cost and effectiveness of the bombing versus the military alternatives that might have been pursued. Many of the most recent histories have tended to give credit to strategic bombing for keeping at least some cap on German economic and military might during the course of the war. Historian Richard Overy has pointed out, for instance: "By the middle of the war, with the whole of continental Europe at her disposal, Germany was fast becoming and economic superpower. The harvest of destruction and disruption reaped by bomb attack, random and poorly planned as it often was, was sufficient to blunt German economic ambitions."[50] Bombing, he added, allowed the Allies to rely on their preference for bringing economic and scientific power (as opposed to large armies) to bear on their enemies, resulting in lower Allied casualties.[51]

What is clear is that neither the British nor the Americans were prepared to hazard a repeat of the World War I's Western Front. They were powerfully inclined, therefore, to turn to air power as a warfighting tool. Once they had done this, and had made the investment, they surely foreclosed other options: the investment in long range bombing meant that the United States would never build a 200-division ground force. And the same was true, albeit on a different scale, for the British. Indeed, the U.S. manpower crisis on the autumn of 1944 saw all sorts of specialist soldiers — including airmen — transferred unceremoniously into the infantry.

In addition to keeping a ceiling on German production, and aiding greatly in the collapse of the German war effort in 1945, the strategic bombing campaign provided the air superiority that made the Normandy invasion feasible. The actual process had not cleaved very closely to pre-war doctrinal expectations, but the Americans showed themselves adaptable (and blessed by a vast productive capacity well behind the front lines); their willingness to learn and change in real time proved crucial to a victorious outcome.

The Early Post-War Years, and the Korean War.

For the United States and its allies in Western Europe, the only threat on the horizon was the former Eurasian ally, the Soviet Union. Though there had been no lack of tension between the Anglo-Americans and the Soviets during the war, postwar conflict was by no means foreordained; indeed, it took several years before the hostility and mistrust became intolerable and laden with policy consequences. In the years between 1945 and 1950, the American military was largely preoccupied with demobilization, re-structuring, and the working out of postwar roles and missions. The Air

Force, in particular, had invested a great deal of energy in finally winning its autonomy from the Army—an event formalized as part of the National Security Act of 1947.

Aside from reorganizing and fighting for its independence, the new U.S. Air Force (USAF) focused on being able to help halt a possible Soviet advance across Europe. This meant that its doctrinal energy was shifted largely to the problem of delivering the small number of nuclear weapons the U.S. had available at the time. In eschewing a large standing army (and universal military training for its young men) the American people opted to rely on air power as their deterrent to war and their main tool against the enemy should war come. Gen. Curtis LeMay, who had run the devastating air campaign in Japan that culminated in two atomic attacks, became the head of the USAF's Strategic Air Command (SAC) in 1948 following his orchestration of the Berlin airlift. SAC became the dominant institution within the USAF, and it held its position for many years.

Naturally enough, the airmen's case for autonomy rested on the argument that the Air Force was best qualified to undertake a mission central to future warfare: long range bombing. This meant defending the wartime record, and asserting—as the British had in the aftermath of WWI—that a powerful strategic bombing force would be essential to deterring wars and to fighting them if they came. The advent of nuclear weapons, and the role of the USAF as the only service able to deliver them, only reinforced the tendency to focus on long range bombing to the exclusion of other missions. But this meant that the USAF was under-prepared for other contingencies. In the 1950s and 60s, as Americans found themselves fighting limited wars in Asia, the ideas underpinning Anglo-American WWII strategic bombing had little relevance to the circumstances at hand.

At the outset of the Korean War in 1950, SAC bombers were moved overseas to supplement the existing assets of the Far Eastern Air Force (FEAF), under the overall control of Gen. Douglas MacArthur, commander-in-chief in the Far East. The commander of SAC's Fifteenth Air Force, Maj. Gen. Emmett O'Donnell, became the commander in chief of FEAF Bomber Command (Provisional). In consultation with SAC chief, Gen. Curtis LeMay, he quickly requested MacArthur's permission "to do a fire job on the five industrial centers of northern Korea." He thought MacArthur should announce that the communists had forced him, against his wishes, to use "the means which brought Japan to its knees."[52]

In the early stages of the war, though, MacArthur was unwilling to escalate so dramatically. O'Donnell chafed under orders that saw his big bombers "diverted" to tactical support missions on behalf of the hard-pressed United Nations ground troops. In the late summer bomber missions were expanded to include broader scale interdiction and attacks on industry in North Korea. Following Chinese entry into the war in November, MacArthur permitted attacks on a wide range of targets—including fire raids on North Korean cities—in order to do everything possible to stem the tide of Chinese advance. He held back on striking North Korean hydro-electric plants, though, hoping they might prove useful bargaining chips in the negotiating process. Incendiary attacks on Pyongyang in early January 1951 burned out 35 percent of the city. Training for atomic missions went forward, but authority for actual use of A-bombs was withheld.[53] The wider use of bombers, however, did not translate into discernable progress toward victory, and, as time passed, American B-29s became increasingly vulnerable to North Korean air defenses: by the end of 1951 they were forced to fly almost exclusively at night.[54]

Airmen were frustrated by the politics of the limited war, which insured that enemy supply sources outside of North Korea remained permanently off the target lists, and that, therefore, the industrial fabric theory would remain a poor fit with the reality of the situation. Gen. LeMay would later say about the war, "We never did hit a strategic target."[55]

After Gen. MacArthur was fired in April 1951, Gen. Matthew B. Ridgway assumed command of UN Forces. Though he generally restrained the use of bombers, he continued to use them to maintain pressure on Chinese troops. Such pressure included interdiction-oriented attacks on Pyongyang (on 30 July and 14 August). But little headway was made in diplomatic negotiations, and, in the meantime, overworked air crews began to suffer morale problems and high abort rates.[56] In May 1952 Ridgway was replaced by Gen. Mark Clark, who was interested in using aircraft to compel movement in the negotiations. Clark authorized a FEAF-designed "air pressure" campaign designed to destroy military targets so situated as to have a "deleterious effect upon the morale of the civilian population actively engaged in the logistic support of enemy forces."[57] Pressure would now be applied to civilians as well as to combat troops. The rhetoric attempted to frame it carefully and to identify it under the rubric of a logistics campaign, but the emergence of the "air pressure" campaign signaled a familiar pattern of an air force, in frustration, turning to an increased emphasis on civilian morale.

The first targets were the previously off-limits North Korean hydro-electric power plants. The attacks saw FEAF destroy ninety percent of all North Korea's hydro-electric power potential in less than a week. The air pressure campaign also renewed full-scale attacks on Pyongyang and other North Korean cities, beginning in July. The 29 August attack on Pyongyang was designed to "punish the enemy with air power," yielding a psychological payoff during the Moscow Conference between the Chinese and the Russians.[58] Following a course similar to the one the USAAF had followed in World War II, FEAF's Bomber Command was, by early 1953, attacking small cities and towns deemed important to the communist supply and distribution system. Still, however, negotiations dragged on with little apparent change in the enemy's determination to hold out against UN pressure.

The last phase of the air pressure campaign manifested itself in a particularly dramatic way. In March 1953 FEAF planners began to study the North Korean irrigation system. Out of patience, Gen. Clark told the Joint Chiefs that he was prepared to breach 20 dams, which would flood areas producing approximately 250,000 tons of rice. In the event, the campaign went forward a bit more modestly, with mid-May attacks on three dams situated near railway lines. (Officially, the attacks could be designated "interdiction" attacks against those railway lines—although neither FEAF planners nor the communists perceived them in that way.) The raids produced dramatic effects, flooding nearby villages and rice fields. The North Koreans engaged in vigorous repair efforts at the Toksan dam site in particular: thirteen days later they had repaired the dam and the railway lines around it, and had placed anti-aircraft artillery all around the dam itself. Two more dams were struck in June and planning went forward for further strikes. These, however, were delayed pending the outcome of armistice negotiations. Those talks resulted, shortly thereafter, in a truce.[59]

There has been no consensus on the impact of the dams raids. Historians recently have tended to argue that they probably had some effect on the negotiations, even though that impact is difficult to specify and separate from other factors bearing on the outcome, including, in particular, the death of Stalin. Conrad Crane's recent conclusion is representative: "The resort by the UN to such extreme measures as the dam attacks might have alarmed the enemy enough to influence their negotiating position to some degree, though there were many other factors involved in their decision to sign the armistice."[60] If the exact impact of the raids was hard to specify, however, its effect on Korean civilians was not. In 1954 Brig. Gen. Don Z. Zimmerman, FEAF Deputy for Intelligence, argued that, "The degree of destruction suffered by North Korea, in relation to its resources, was greater than that which the Japanese islands suffered in World War II." He believed that "[T]hese pressures brought the enemy to terms." Many others in the USAF came to share his view, and the Air Force interpretation cast events in a positive light.[61]

By 1954 the USAF was anxious to put the Korean experience behind it. FEAF's 1954 final *Report on the Korean War* repeated a conclusion that Gen. Stratemeyer had already drawn in 1950: the Korean conflict contained so many unusual factors as to make it a poor model for future planning.

In particular, the USAF wished to distance itself from the successful close air support operations that had been a main a feature of the war. The final report stated: "Because FEAF provided UNC ground forces lavish close air support in Korea is no reason to assume this condition will exist in future wars."[62]

Air Force leaders were instead anxious to re-assert their priority: preparing for a strategic bombing campaign against the Soviet Union. The funding allotted to the services as a result of the Korean War had greatly increased the size and strength of SAC; now, more than ever, the SAC mission reigned supreme in the USAF. Gen. LeMay was appointed Vice Chief of Staff in 1957 and Chief of Staff in 1961; in 1964 three quarters of the high ranking officers on the Air Staff came from SAC. Between 1954 and 1962 the United States' total nuclear arsenal grew from 1,750 weapons to 26,500 weapons. SAC, which controlled the majority of them, planned to deliver them in a "massive pre-emptive bomber assault." Planning for other contingencies received little attention. Despite the political upheaval in Southeast Asia in the 1950s, the *Air University Quarterly Review* published (in the whole of the decade) only two articles relating air power to insurgency movements in that region.[63]

Vietnam.

When President Lyndon Johnson and his advisors dramatically increased the U.S. commitment to South Vietnam, they hoped that air power might facilitate a relatively quick and painless campaign that would not divert too many resources from the broader national agenda. They hoped that air strikes would demonstrate U.S. resolve, bolster morale in the South, erode the morale of Viet Cong cadres, and generally intimidate the leadership of the insurgency—convincing them that they could not win.[64]

In April 1964 the Joint Chiefs had compiled a list of 94 bombing targets in North Vietnam. The Air Force wished to see these targets attacked immediately and heavily, so as to impose psychological shock as well as physical damage. But the administration instead chose a more graduated approach that would punish by reprisal acts of terror committed by the Viet Cong, and would hold enemy targets (of presumed value) at risk. After Viet Cong guerillas struck a U.S. Special Forces camp at Pleiku in February of 1965, American policymakers implemented Operation ROLLING THUNDER, an aerial interdiction campaign that would, eventually, run for 4 years and would be characterized by increasing pressure on the enemy. In August 1965 Secretary of Defense Robert McNamara rejected a JCS recommendation for attacks on North Vietnam's strategic oil facilities and electric power plants. The Hanoi government began to disperse the nation's limited industry, and to erect passive and active air defenses; their efforts were aided by supplies and workers from the Soviet Union and China. In light of this, the JCS called for an expanded bombing program late in 1965. The Johnson administration did in fact expand the air campaign in 1966 and 1967: in June 1966 North Vietnam's oil storage facilities were bombed for the first time; in May 1967 Hanoi's main power station was attacked.[65]

Unsurprisingly, the Air Force chafed at the early restrictions: both during and after the war the Air Force claimed that the ROLLING THUNDER campaign had been undermined by the intervention of civilian planners and analysts who interfered with both the timing and the nature of the bombing sorties flown. While it is true that the destruction of all major targets was not completed until 1967 (whereas the Air Force would have preferred an all-out assault in 1965), the civilian intervention may not have been so consequential as it has been made out to be. The JCS list grew from 94 targets to 242 targets shortly after ROLLING THUNDER began, and the latter number changed little through the rest of the campaign. In 1965, 158 of these targets were destroyed (nearly all of them military targets below the 20th parallel); in 1966 22 more were destroyed. The President released nearly all the remaining targets for attack in 1967, and by December almost all of North Vietnam's industrial war capacity had been destroyed. The Air Force had the air campaign it wanted, but did not achieve the end it sought. There was, by the end of the war, virtually no target left unattacked that might have been bombed. Indeed, during the course of the war the USAF dropped some 6,162,000 tons of bombs—vastly more tonnage than had been dropped by the Allied powers in all of World War II.[66]

The insurgents required little in the way of supplies, and they could often move what they needed through territory that was off limits to the bombers. In addition, the insurgents could fight the war at their own pace, backing off when their losses became costly, and recommencing when they had recovered. The slow pace—and the inability of the Americans to either drain the enemy's will or to build an effective government in the south—eroded American public support for the war.

Robert Pape has argued that there is "no evidence that executing the sharp knock in 1965, instead of 1967, would have produced better results."[67] Structural factors (including the economy and geography of Vietnam) and the nature of the war itself helped insulate the North Vietnamese and Viet Cong against the effects of interdiction and coercive air power. Finally, even if an earlier all-out air assault had convinced the North to stop supporting the Viet Cong insurgency, this is no guarantee that the Viet Cong would not have continued the war on their own, and at their own pace.[68]

President Richard Nixon instituted a program of "Vietnamization"—a means of reducing the increasingly unpopular American commitment to the war by placing the main responsibility for the ground war back into the hands of the South Vietnamese. Along with this, he allowed the JCS to give more freedom to U.S. air commanders in Vietnam. Operation LINEBACKER, designed to halt Hanoi's 1972 spring ground offensive, largely achieved its purpose and appeared to put a settlement within reach. But North Vietnamese negotiators stalled late in the day, prompting LINEBACKER II, an 11-day campaign (18 December to 29 December) to bring enemy negotiators back to the table to sign a final accord. The latter concentrated on military assets in and around Hanoi. On the 29th, communist leaders indicated willingness to resume serious negotiations. This outcome reflected the impact of both LINEBACKER campaigns, which were—by that point in the war—oriented to fundamentally different circumstances and goals than the ROLLING THUNDER campaign had been.[69]

Many observers, both civilian and military, argued that if a LINEBACKER-style campaign had gone forward from the outset the war would have been brought to a successful conclusion promptly. Frustrated over the political constraints placed upon them, airmen argued—in the tradition of Harris—that they might have won had they been free to prosecute the war as they saw fit. Writing in the June 1975 edition of *Air Force Magazine*, Gen. T. R. Milton, USAF (Ret.) argued that LINEBACKER II was "an object lesson in how the war might have been won, and won long ago, if only there had not been such political inhibition."[70] But this perspective overlooked the crucial differences between 1965 and 1972. The success of the LINEBACKER I campaign was facilitated by the fact that, when it took place, Hanoi had shifted to a conventional war strategy that was far more vulnerable to the effects of strategic air power than the earlier guerilla war had been. And when LINEBACKER II commenced, the Hanoi leadership had already achieved most of its political goals, and was prepared to sign an accord that would put it, ultimately, within easy grasp of the final aims it was seeking. These important distinctions often were glossed over or ignored, however, and this had the effect of vindicating broad claims about the decisiveness of bombing and reinforcing proclamations about its future application in war.[71]

The Air Force's response to criticism implying that it had not lived up to public expectations was not to try to modify those expectations but rather to insist that bombing could be decisive—if only it could be freed from political restraints affecting the timing and targeting of air strikes.

Those air leaders who had held important positions during World War II particularly resented the constraints placed on them later. But two observations are worthy of mention here. First, there were few important targets in Korea or Vietnam that were not hit hard by bombers (often multiple times). And second, World War II was the exception rather than the rule: most wars in history have been fought within distinct political parameters—not to mention legal and ethical ones. For political reasons it will very rarely, if ever, be possible to carry out what air forces have traditionally believed to be the most effective form of a bomber campaign: an immediate, all-out strike on those assets most valuable to the enemy. Even in World War II—the most "total" of all modern wars—limits on Anglo-American bombers were lifted only slowly, over a period of years. And, even though the war was later considered a "good war" fought for the right reasons, the Anglo-American public has sometimes shown uneasiness with the unconstrained bombing undertaken at the end of the war.

After Vietnam, defensiveness inhibited USAF dialogues, and, for time at least, proscribed a thorough and searching analysis of doctrine (and the applicability of that doctrine to differing circumstances). There was still no satisfactory understanding of the crucial relationship between bomber raids and desired political outcomes. In the conclusion to his 1989 book, *The Limits of Air Power*, Mark Clodfelter wrote: "The tremendous rush of technology—which has produced gargantuan B-52s and sleek B-1s capable of carrying 30 tons of ordnance, and supersonic fighters capable of directing laser-guided bombs into a single warehouse in the heart of a densely-populated city—has not guaranteed military success. What it has done, however, is to create a modern vision of air power that focuses on the lethality of its weaponry rather than on that weaponry's effectiveness as a political instrument."[72] His critique was notable not only because it was perceptive, but because it was delivered by a serving USAF officer.

Air Power in Operation DESERT STORM.

The "Persian Gulf War," as it came to be called, saw the first extensive use of post-Vietnam era U.S. troops and equipment. U.S. Army General Norman Schwarzkopf, who led the military operation, envisioned it in four phases:

a strategic air campaign against Iraq
an air campaign against Iraqi forces in Kuwait
an attrition phase to neutralize the Republican Guard forces and isolate the Kuwaiti battlefield
a ground attack to drive Iraqi forces out of Kuwait

The first three of these would be carried out by coalition air forces, and the final phase would be conducted by ground forces.

The air campaign in the Kuwaiti theater of operations had three primary objectives: suppression of Iraqi air defenses, preparation of the battlefield for coalition ground attack, and support of the ground attack.[73] The strategic air campaign over Iraq was designed to support the war aim by directly pressuring Saddam's regime on a number of levels. A primary intellectual influence on the strategic air campaign was Col. John A. Warden III, USAF, who had been in charge of the Deputy Directorate for Warfighting Concepts within the Air Staff Directorate of Plans. A strong advocate of independent air operations, Warden had conceived of a targeting theory based on five principal categories, envisioned as five concentric rings (like the rings in a bull's eye) that increase in value as they approach the center. The focal point—his designated "center of gravity"—was the enemy leadership. Just outside of that, in the position of second priority, was the enemy state's energy sources, advanced research facilities, and key war-supporting industries. Beyond that, in the third ring, was enemy infrastructure, such as transportation systems. The fourth ring was comprised of the enemy's population, and the fifth ring designated the enemy's fielded military forces. Warden's ideas, which he promulgated effectively and energetically, brought back to the surface some heated service debates over the primacy that should be accorded to independent air operations.[74]

Warden was counting on developments in precision targeting to herald a new kind of air war. He went beyond the idea of targeting government buildings and communications nodes, instead, he thought in terms of cutting the enemy leaders off from the people. His was a targeting theory resting on assumptions about an enemy leader's control of his polity. Warden's book *The Air Campaign* (begun when he was a student at the National Defense University) argued that air power allows for strikes against the full spectrum of enemy capabilities, with leadership first and foremost. The five rings model was an extension of the operational concepts he had first explored in his book. "Decapitation" might or might not be possible, but it was only one of several approaches to largely the same end: targeting leadership directly to seek "strategic paralysis" of the enemy. It was not entirely clear, however, how this paralysis would translate into surrender.[75]

Only days after Saddam's invasion of Kuwait, American military aircraft began landing in Saudi Arabia. Schwarzkopf sent Air Force Lt. Gen. Charles A. Horner into the theater to receive incoming American air forces. The plan that Warden and his staff developed for the crisis in the Middle East, called "INSTANT THUNDER," focused on strategic air attacks on Iraqi centers of gravity; it was designed to pit American strengths against Iraqi weaknesses while minimizing U.S. casualties, collateral damage, and civilian deaths. Warden sought to target the heart of Saddam's regime—the key structures, institutions, and resources that facilitated his control of the state. INSTANT THUNDER aimed, ultimately, at regime change. It rested on a body of assumptions about the nature of the enemy—and on confidence that U.S. intelligence could support an intricate air campaign with ambitious goals. It was designed to place intense pressure on Iraqi leadership in a period of 6 to 9 days.

INSTANT THUNDER won Schwarzkopf's endorsement, and Warden went to Riyadh, Saudi Arabia, to brief Horner. Uneasy with the plan's failure to fully consider the offensive capabilities of the Iraqi army, Horner modified it somewhat, changed its name, and appropriated several members of Warden's staff to comprise a secret, elite "Central Air Forces Special Planning Group": the "Black Hole." As historian Richard G. Davis has pointed out, "If Lieutenant General Horner rejected the form, he kept the substance of INSTANT THUNDER." The main objectives of Warden's plan remained, and these "continued to emphasize leadership; electrical, nuclear, biological, and chemical facilities; and the other target sets derived from the five rings."[76]

Following in the tradition of some of the World War II air power advocates who believed that strategic bombing might preclude the need for a ground campaign, Warden believed that his plan could stand alone. The 700 aircraft that were ready on the eve of war, would, Warden hoped, achieve Coalition political aims. Schwarzkopf, following in the tradition of World War II ground commanders, saw the air plan as the first phase of a larger, integrated air-ground liberation of Kuwait.

Even though the aircraft coming into the theater comprised the vast majority of the USAF's precision delivery capability at the time, the force was not ideally suited to the task Warden had set for it. Technological evolution throughout the Vietnam War had yielded some promising results in highly precise, guided-bomb technology. But the USAF had been leisurely in appropriating it and integrating it into doctrine and mission statements: most of the combat aircraft procured between 1972 and 1990 (the F-15C, F-16, and A-10 series) did not include guided bomb unit-delivery capability.[77] Still, the USAF had the capacity to employ air-delivered, precision-guided munitions with hard- target penetrating capability, and this would become a centerpiece of its war effort. A dramatic new delivery system in the U.S. arsenal was the F-117A "Stealth" fighter, introduced to the public in late 1988.

The Black Hole planners, led by Lt. Col. David Deptula, updated the air war plan right through the opening hours of the war on 17 January 1991; they emphasized simultaneous attacks on target sets that would have overlapping and linking effects. Weeks before the kick-off of the war, Gen. Horner combined the Special Planning Group with CENTAF's tactical air planners in a newly-formed Directorate of Campaign Plans. The Black Hole planners became the Iraqi Target Cell, and the tactical planners became the Kuwaiti Theater of Operations (KTO) planners. The latter, departing from the practice of identifying individual targets, prepared to send packages of strike and support aircraft (guided by an airborne controller) to hit all targets of opportunity within its allocated "kill box."

Many hours before bombs began falling over Baghdad, seven hulking B-52Gs took off from Barksdale Air Force Base, LA, to begin a 14,000 mile round-trip delivery of air-launched cruise missiles into Iraq.[78] The Air Force, anxious to prove its "Global Reach," did not wish to be overshadowed by the Navy's ship-based Tomahawk missiles about to launch from the Persian Gulf and the Red Sea. Even though Baghdad was a heavily-armed city with plenty of time to prepare for combat, the massed Coalition air attacks largely overwhelmed the defenders. Throughout Iraq, Coalition forces struck command and control targets (including Baath Party headquarters), electrical facilities, and Scud missile launchers. Anti-radiation missiles homed in on radar facilities and anti-aircraft defenses while both British and American planes cratered the runways on Iraqi airfields. Iraqi oil refineries and storage facilities came under attack as well. At the end of only 2 nights, Coalition aircraft had struck nearly half of 298 identified strategic targets. They had won air superiority, and had cut off Iraqi electricity. The stealth fighter-bombers proved their worth early on; indeed, one F-117A with two bombs could do the same work as more than 100 World War II-era B-17 bombers carrying nearly 650 bombs.[79]

The great abundance of Coalition air power facilitated parallel attacks on arrays of targets. Rather than attacking targets in sequenced priority order, Coalition air forces were able to carry out simultaneous counter-air, interdiction, close air support, and strategic missions into Iraq. By mid-February Coalition bombers had struck the Iraqi Ministry of Defense, the Baghdad Conference Center, TV and press buildings, and the Military Intelligence Headquarters. As the month went on, strategic attacks were waged against airfields, nuclear and chemical targets, communication facilities, and mobile Scud launchers. Fearing that Iraqi Scud missile attacks into Israel would prompt Israeli entry into the war and thus fracture the carefully-constructed Coalition, the Bush Administration placed a high priority on targeting Scuds. No less than 15 percent of CENTAF's strategic effort went into attacks on Scuds, including launchers, as well as manufacturing, assembly and storage centers.[80]

The ground campaign, which had been planned all along as the final phase of major combat operations, finally kicked off on 23 February. Simultaneously, coalition aircraft struck Iraqi airfields, aircraft, and bridges near the front. Strategic raids continued to target leadership, and industrial facilities in Iraq. Newly-developed GBU-28 penetrator bombs were used against high priority targets including the Al Taji command bunker.

In an interesting inversion of roles, B-52 bombers — so long associated with strategic missions — were employed almost exclusively in ground support missions inside Kuwait. In postwar debriefings, Iraqi soldiers readily attested to the unnerving effect of the B-52 strikes. Indeed, Gen. Schwarzkopf so valued the B-52 strikes inside Kuwait that he resisted their use elsewhere. In the end, only a handful of B-52s operated outside Kuwait against targets that the Black Hole planners designated as "strategic."[81] But the attacks on troops proved responsible for the profound weakening of the morale and cohesion of segments of the Iraqi Army, thus contributing directly to a shorter ground war.[82]

The B-52s required 40 percent of the USAF's tanker force, as well as large packages of support aircraft. By contrast, the F-117 fighter bombers, which were the only planes authorized to strike targets in downtown Baghdad, required no support aircraft. One F-117 with two laser-guided bombs could achieve the same level of destruction as 108 World War II B-17s with 648 bombs.[83] Other fighter bombers, including the F-111F and the F-15E, helped carry the bulk of the strategic missions, with air-to-air refueling facilitating their range and effectiveness. This efficiency impressed the Air Force, prompting high and sustained attention to precision systems through the 1990s.

Attacks on Iraqi communication targets had a corrosive effect on the speed and efficiency with which Saddam could conduct his war. Rarely, however, were communications cut totally since the regime resorted to more primitive means such as message delivery by bicycle or motorcycle. And fiber optic nets were more redundant and elusive than the Black Hole planners had anticipated. The precise military and political impact of raids on leadership targets—the focus of Warden's theory—has been difficult to discern. As Richard Davis concluded, "little solid data is available to connect the bombing of leadership or command and control facilities with specific consequences."[84] And air planners who had hoped to integrate and implement a program of psychological warfare found themselves stymied by concerns over the sensitivities of Coalition partners, and by interagency conflict over the program.[85]

Strikes on Iraqi oil saw the collapse of refinery capacity by the end of the war. But the very fact that the war was so short in duration meant that Iraq was able to rely on stored supplies for military operations. Thus, in the end the oil campaign had no impact on the outcome of the war itself. Pressure placed on the Iraqi population due to strikes on the electrical net and fuel more generally may have contributed to the postwar uprisings by the Kurds and the Shi'ites, but did not lead to a weakening of the Sunni commitment to Saddam's regime.[86] This failure of pressure to create political effects was of course assisted by the strength of the Iraqi internal security forces; this paralleled, to some degree, the situation in Germany during World War II, when air planners in England and the U.S. hoped that deprivations might turn the population against an already unpopular leader.

The 5 months between the invasion of Kuwait and the commencement of Operation DESERT STORM gave Saddam time to further disperse and hide his weapons of mass destruction (WMD) capability—a set of resources already dispersed in reaction to the Israeli strike in 1981. The targets proved to be elusive, and postwar inspections revealed that many facilities had been missed by target planners (who had operated with limited and out-of-date intelligence). Attacks on mobile Scud mobile launchers failed to destroy any more than a handful of them, and while attacks on known production sites achieved some effect, the Iraqis had removed the bulk of it prior to the war. Thus, the considerable effort dedicated to Scuds yielded results that were less fruitful than planners hoped or expected.[87] As Richard Davis has pointed out, Scuds present air force planners with many of the same sorts of challenges Army officers face in counterinsurgency warfare.[88]

The Coalition achieved its main aims, including the withdrawal of all Iraqi forces from Kuwait, and the right of the U.N. to install peacekeepers on the border, and to inspect and eliminate any WMD in Iraq. The speed and apparent ease of the victory prompted many commentators to proclaim that a "Revolution in Military Affairs" (RMA) had occurred, based on the sophisticated technology employed by American forces. Indeed, the one-sided outcome had resulted from the *interaction* of American proficiency and Iraqi incompetence. Poor skills and training insured that Iraqi armies would be punished disproportionately by the enemy's modern military toolkit.[89] Perceptive analysts warned against reading too much into the victory, and called for more nuanced interpretations of the war and its outcome.[90]

At the end of the day, the political result of the war was mixed: Saddam Hussein remained in power and worked to quickly re-assert and consolidate his authority within his borders.

Air War in the Balkans.

Out from under the thumb of communism, the ethnically-mixed regions of what had been the state of Yugoslavia began to pull away from their center. Slovakia and Croatia escaped to independence in the summer of 1991, quickly winning recognition from European states. But the Serbians sought a halt to the disintegration, and took up arms to hold on to a new Federal Republic of Yugoslavia. Strife followed, heightened and inflamed by extremist rhetoric. President George H. W. Bush was not anxious to wade into the complex ethnic entanglement that was post-Cold War Yugoslavia, but the situation continued to fray badly.

In 1992 the Serbs began to shell Sarajevo, the capital of the new state of Bosnia-Herzegovina; Bosnian Serbs sought to displace the Muslim population and claim land for themselves. By the end of the year some 150,000 were dead from the bloody fights. During his campaign Bill Clinton criticized the Bush team for not doing enough about the humanitarian crisis in Bosnia. Many analysts in the U.S. feared the entrenched nature of the ethnic strife, and worried about how the U.S. might get out of the Balkans once it got in. They also believed that the Europeans ought to take a leading role in settling a fight taking place in their own backyard. After a particularly bloody Serb attack on a marketplace in Sarajevo in early 1994, American planes flew in to evacuate the wounded; thereafter the U.S. began to take on more a more aggressive role, helping to enforce the limits and constraints that the international community tried to impose on the Serbs.

In 1995, in the Muslim town of Srebnica, Serbs massacred thousands of Bosnian men and boys. Bosnian Serbs routinely raped Muslim women and girls. Later in the summer the U.S. and its NATO allies commenced air strikes against the Serbs while the Croats turned on their former Serb ally and began a ground campaign to help drive them out of Bosnia. Fearing a possible loss of power and a Serb collapse, Milosevic agreed to seek terms. The peace, arranged during an extended conference in Dayton, Ohio, included the establishment of an International Implementation Force (IFOR) to keep the peace in Bosnia; U.S. forces took a leading role in what eventually proved to be a worthwhile operation. The U.S. public, however, remained largely unmoved by the intervention, and the House at one point toyed with cutting off the funds for U.S. troops in Bosnia.[91]

The 1995 Dayton accords did not, however, persuade Milosevic to confine himself to acceptable standards of international behavior. In 1999, NATO went to war, in an air-only operation, to try to halt the Serbian annexation of the province of Kosovo. Ethnic Serbs formed a small part (about 10 percent) of the population of the province, which consisted mainly of Albanian Muslims, or Kosovars. The Serbian minority had long dominated the politics of the province, spurring a movement for independence led by the Kosovo Liberation Army (KLA). The failure to bring the opposed parties together at the Rambouillet conference in early 1999 led to a NATO decision to try to coerce Milosevic and the Serbs into accepting terms. Perhaps relying overmuch on a faulty interpretation of why Milosevic signed the Dayton accords when he did, the Clinton administration expected him to cave in under air strikes in a few days. Quite to the contrary, however, he encouraged his forces to run amok in Kosovo. Muslims poured out of the province and into refugee camps in neighboring states. Air strikes, waged from high altitude so as to minimize the risk to NATO pilots, could not halt events on the ground, and the strikes seemed only to unify the defiant Serbs behind Milosevic. NATO was cautious in all regards and there was considerable anxiety about whether the alliance would hang together long enough to solve the problem. Clinton, who could hardly escape recent memories of the American public's ambivalence about Bosnia, would not agree to the use of ground troops, even as the situation worsened and Milosevic carried out ethnic cleansing. In May an increasingly alarmed NATO took advantage of improving weather and intensified the bombing—attacking rail lines and bridges in Kosovo and Serbia, and striking the electrical net inside Serbia. Significantly, NATO began to discuss the use of ground troops. This put the Russians—old allies of the Serbs—in a particularly awkward situation since they had no intention of ending up in a shooting war with NATO. Pressure from the Russians surely helped convince Milosevic that he had to accept defeat. The bombing ceased in June, and the U.S. and NATO sent a force of 60,000 troops (Kosovo Force, or KFOR) into Kosovo. Milosevic, who in the meantime had been indicted as a war criminal by the International Criminal Tribunal, was ousted from power in the autumn of 2000.

The air war over Kosovo led to a rekindling of the debate over whether or not airplanes can coerce successfully enough to win wars on their own. Clearly, air strikes had not been able to halt the ethnic cleansing, and indeed hastened it. But the relationship between the intensification of NATO strikes in May and the acceptance of terms by Milosevic in June suggested that the strikes on Serbia proper had a role in the outcome. RAND analyst Benjamin Lambeth stated, appropriately, that "We may never know for sure what mix of pressures and inducements ultimately led Milosevic to admit defeat."[92] Any historical outcome is driven by a particular interweaving of events and perceptions of events, and those seeking to explain it must identify the contributing elements and arrange them into a structure that is logically coherent and robust relative to other possible explanations. But fitting together all the puzzle pieces is a complex process that tends to develop slowly, as additional bits of evidence are brought to light over time, and as the perspectives of all the key actors are brought to bear on the story.

The very fact that NATO managed to sustain a 78-day campaign that—Milosevic believed—might have continued indefinitely must have convinced the Serb leader that his opponents were committed to the cause. As another RAND analyst, Stephen Hosmer, has pointed out, Milosevic and others in his circle seemed to fear that there might be no limit to the level of destruction NATO might be willing to impose; indeed NATO, led by the U.S. and Britain, might continue escalating to the point of "carpet bombing" Serbia.[93] As much tension, political wrangling, and inefficiency as there was within NATO, the members of the Alliance held together in a campaign that grew more intense over time. (Milosevic himself contributed immensely to NATO's level of commitment through behavior that was reprehensible and deeply offensive to the international community.) Clear evidence that NATO was preparing to authorize the use of ground troops was an unmistakable sign of this continued commitment. Not only did it spur the Russians to pressure Milosevic into accepting terms, but it signaled to the Serb leader that his political and personal fortunes were more at risk from a continuation of the war than from a cessation of it. In addition, the playing out of the campaign revealed, as well, that Milosevic had miscalculated on virtually every important strategic issue concerning the war.[94]

The escalation of the air campaign was driven by frustrated policymakers who increasingly reached the conclusion that the only way to influence Milosevic via an air campaign would be to place pressure directly on the leader himself, in part by bringing hardship down upon Serbian citizens within Serbia. A main feature of the latter was the inclusion of attacks designed to damage the electrical power net in Serbia and to turn the lights out in Belgrade. The pattern of commitment and intensification seems likely to have been more significant to the outcome than the total level of physical damage and disruption suffered by the Serbs in the air campaign. The pressure placed by the 1999 air war on Serb civilians came nowhere close to the levels of pressure imposed on them by the earlier economic sanctions resulting from the Bosnia crisis. Those economic sanctions had essentially destroyed the Serbian economy in the early 1990s: Serbia's industrial output and retail sales fell by 40 percent and 70 percent respectively, and inflation reached the almost unfathomable level of 116 trillion percent. Sixty percent of Serbia's labor force was laid off, and by December 1993 80 percent of the population had fallen below the poverty level. None of this had budged Milosevic. By the time of Dayton, the Serbian economy was actually in recovery.[95]

The suffering imposed by the 1999 air campaign at no time approached this level of intensity. Neither the overall level of pain imposed nor the striking of any specific target is likely, therefore, to have more explanatory power in this case than the fact that Milosevic saw all the trends aligning against him, and that the Russians made it clear that they would not continue to support him. It would therefore be risky to attempt to draw specific targeting lessons from the Kosovo case—a case entailing a range of idiosyncratic characteristics that, in the end, came together in a unique way. Still, in the years after the Kosovo war, some in the USAF suggested that the laws of war regarding aerial targeting be revisited to allow more expeditious clearance of targets in the enemy's civilian infrastructure, in particular, to allow "tremendous destructive power to be applied discretely and efficiently against a wide range of objects that opportunistic, materialistic societies like Yugoslavia value."[96] Aside from the thorny ethical issues raised by loosening constraints on targeting civilian infrastructure (especially since even the most precise targeting of civilian infrastructure does not preclude the deaths of innocents), it rests on assumptions that not only tend to mirror American society in problematical ways, but also may not hold up across different cases. Under some circumstances air pressure on civilian infrastructure may produce a desired political effect; in other cases, however, it may have no effect at all other than to bolster enemy cohesion, or to erode international support for the attacking force. More recent literature has been more judicious. One USAF author recently argued: "The danger of Allied Force's success is that politicians could now view airpower as a panacea and substitute for jointness. . . . An actual invasion was obviously not necessary, but Milosevic may have complied sooner had he faced NATO's *joint* military might."[97]

OEF and OIF.

In an attempt to go after the perpetrators of the September 11, 2001, attacks on the World Trade Center and the Pentagon, President George W. Bush sent U.S. forces to Afghanistan in the autumn of 2001. Because of the nature of al-Qaeda, targeting information with respect to leadership was slim. The Air Force struck such infrastructure as there was in Afghanistan. When this did not coerce the various elements of the Taliban (including al-Qaeda), the USAF joined the effort to use U.S. Special Operations Forces (SOF)—working in conjunction with indigenous friendly forces in Afghanistan—to attack elements of the enemy dispersed through various regions of the country. In addition to flying some battlefield interdiction, the USAF flew lots of close support missions on behalf of soldiers on the ground. This inverted the Air Force's traditional mission preference, but pilots and aircraft proved up to the task, despite some occasional problems centering on the Air Force's strong preference for having its own forward controllers direct fires (as opposed to Army controllers).[98]

During the invasion of Iraq in March 2003, the USAF flew against its traditional set of targets in the opening phases of the war. Enemy air defenses were crippled, and communications were degraded. Due to American strength and preponderance, the USAF was able to attack a wide range of targets simultaneously, including an attack on the Dora Farms complex when intelligence indicated that Saddam Hussein might be located there. The USAF quickly won air supremacy, clearing the path for the ground forces that moved quickly into the battle. The Americans encouraged Iraqi troops to stay in their garrisons and decline to fight. If they did attempt to maneuver, they came under prompt air attack. When the ground war slowed due to a blinding sandstorm, USAF aircraft—with all-weather capability—were able to pound Republican Guard units located mainly in the Karbala Gap region. This facilitated an easier move into Baghdad by the Third Infantry Division, and a rapid capture of the capital city.[99] Possessed of far more precision-guided munitions (PGMs) than it had had during the first Gulf War, and with improved target acquisition technology, the USAF was able to engage in an overwhelming offensive that, once again, included effective support of ground troops. With excellent air-ground communication and ever-improving responsiveness, the USAF has proved itself highly capable of doing a mission that it traditionally would not prioritize. Indeed, so proficient is the Air Force in close air support (CAS) at the moment that a new defense debate centers on weather USAF CAS ought to largely substitute, in the future, for ground-based indigenous fire support. The question is a difficult and emotional one, and part of the question to be answered is whether OIF, with its highly-permissive environment for aircraft, is a reliable model for future conflict. If the air defense threat were greater, would the USAF still be willing to fly aggressive CAS? The Army is not convinced on this point, and the debate is likely to continue.

Currently, the USAF is engaged in many internal and external doctrinal debates. Some of these continue long-standing conversations about the effective identification and exploitation of enemy weaknesses. Others however, relate to space power theory (including the protection of vital military assets in space), and to the effective use of air power in counterinsurgency campaigns. One of the major debates at the moment pits proponents of the Warden systems approach (with its heavy emphasis on leadership) against proponents of battlefield effects. In his recent book, *Air Power*, Stephen Budiansky has argued that operations in Afghanistan, and in Iraq (2003) have largely discredited the Warden theory, or any "shock and awe" approach, and have instead validated the idea that air power's greatest contribution is to be made on the battlefield against fielded forces. He asserts: "despite the howls of protest heard from Army partisans, who claimed that Defense Secretary Donald Rumsfeld had taken inordinate risks by launching Gulf War II with only two heavy armored divisions . . . the effect of air power on Iraqi tanks, surface-to-surface missiles, artillery, and troops left little doubt that Rumsfeld was right: far smaller, lighter, and more agile ground forces could now do jobs that once required huge armies." Budiansky's argument has hardly gone uncontested, not least because its sweeping language oversimplifies a set of complex issues that require more analytical discernment than he gives them. But he has identified the direction of the debate, and, in the final paragraph of his book, introduces one more challenge: "The great historical joke on airmen was that having struggled for a century to escape the battlefield in their quest for equal status and independence—having fought so many bitter battles to free themselves from the indignity of providing 'mere support' to ground forces—it was on the battlefield where air power finally achieved not merely equality, but its claim to ascendancy."[100]

Issues of air power are vital to all military services, and should be a subject of sustained attention among professional officers. This is true for many reasons, not the least of these being the strong political appeal of air power. National political leaders who are in possession of air forces are likely to continue to look upon them as a relatively clean and cheap means of wielding force—a means of using the military instrument of power without the level of commitment (and potential entanglement) involved in deploying ground forces. Thus, they are likely to be used first—and increasingly, perhaps, alone—when conflicts arise and lead to military interaction.

Conclusion.

Organizational cultures, the impact and memory of the World War I, public fears and pressures, assumptions about technology, bureaucratic politics, and service rivalries all have major roles in this story. In general, the expectations of the major air power theorists ran well ahead of what could be achieved in wartime, and many who lobbied for independent air power were guilty of over-claiming and over-promising. They tended to assume that enemy states had weak points that could be readily exploited. Their reasons for holding these views were, in many respects, understandable. But advocacy often got in the way of critical thinking, and the theorists were disinclined to examine—or even countenance—those arguments that might challenge their underlying assumptions.

The complexity of modern societies and economies does not make them inherently fragile, as many air theorists assumed they must be. Human beings are adaptable creatures capable of adjusting to and accommodating new circumstances—even very stressful ones—if necessary. It is therefore often the case that what planners and analysts identify as readily exploitable weaknesses turn out to be much less exploitable than expected. And, because the *process* of exploitation is itself difficult, often, it becomes rather more iterative and protracted than planners assumed it would be. In the meantime, the enemy can continue to learn, to adapt, and to adjust to the pressures imposed. Under these circumstances, the attacking air force will often be tempted to broaden or intensify the campaign in some way.

There is an inherent tendency among planners to mirror-image the enemy: to assume that he is like us, that he values what we value, and that he will respond to threats and punishments as we assume we would respond. But this tendency has proven, again and again, to be a misleading and dangerous one. Precisely because societies are complex, we are prone to misinterpret and misjudge them. The relationship between dropping bombs and producing a desired political outcome (a relationship that one perceptive observer has recently called the "exchange mechanism" in air power theory) is still inadequately understood.[101] There is much to be learned, yet, about how and when different enemies will respond to aerial threats, punishment, and coercion. As they move into their second century, air forces—while more technically skilled and capable all the time—still have much to learn about the use of violence to achieve political aims.

ENDNOTES - CHAPTER 18

1. My thanks to Boone Bartholomees and Conrad Crane for their helpful comments on earlier drafts of this chapter.

2. Hugo quoted in I. F. Clarke, *Voices Prophesying War 1763-1984*, Oxford: Oxford University Press, 1966, p. 3.

3. On Warner and Coxwell, see C. F. Snowden Gamble, *The Air Weapon*, Vol. I, Oxford: Oxford University Press, 1931, 39, 45; on Verne, see Michael Paris, *Winged Warfare*, Manchester: Manchester University Press, 1992, pp. 22-23.

4. On Fullerton and Chanute, see David MacIsaac, "Voices from the Central Blue: The Air Power Theorists," in *Makers of Modern Strategy from Machiavelli to the Nuclear Age*, Peter Paret, ed., Princeton: Princeton University Press, 1986, pp. 625-627. Chanute is quoted on p. 626.

5. See H. Bruce Franklin, *War Stars: The Superbomb and the American Imagination*, New York: Oxford University Press, 1988, p. 84.

6. Moltke's statement is noted in an essay by Bernard Brodie titled, "The Continuing Relevance of On War" in M. Howard and P. Paret, eds. and trans., of Clausewitz's *On War*, Princeton: Princeton Univ. Press, 1984, 53. On Clausewitz, see also M. Howard's essay, "The Influence of Clausewitz" in the Howard and Paret Volume, 39; Howard, *Clausewitz*, Oxford: Oxford Univ. Press, 1983; Azar Gat, *The Development of Military Thought: The Nineteenth Century*, Oxford: Clarendon Press, 1992, and Christopher Bassford, *Clausewitz in English*, Oxford: Oxford University Press, 1994, 104-112.

7. Tim Travers, *The Killing Ground: The British Army, the Western Front and the Emergence of Modern Warfare, 1900-1918*, London: Unwin Hyman, 1987, pp. 37-97; the Gold Medal Prize Essay of the *Journal of the Royal United Services Institution* for 1913, reprinted in Vol. LVIII, No. 434, April 1914, titled: "How Can Moral Qualities Best Be Developed During the Preparation of the Officer and the Man for the Duties Each Will Carry Out in the War" by Maj. A. Lawson. On similar ideas in Germany at the time, see Antulio J. Echevarria II, "On the Brink of the Abyss: The Warrior Identity and German Military Thought before the Great War," in *War and Society*, Vol. 13, No. 2, October 1995, 23-40.

8. Travers, pp. 37-38, and chap. 2 generally).

9. Alfred Gollin, *No Longer an Island: Britain and the Wright Brothers, 1902-1909*, Stanford: Stanford University Press, 1984, 345 and 351. On Baden-Powell, see Travers, p. 39.

10. There were 399 industrial disputes in Britain in 1908; by 1911 there were 903. In the months before the outbreak of World War I, there were approximately 150 strikes per month. See Allen Hutt, *The Postwar History of the British Working Class*, NY: Coward-McCann, 1938, p. 3. See also Paul Addison, "Winston Churchill and the Working Class, 1900-1914," in Jay Winter, ed., *The Working Class in Modern British History*, Cambridge: Cambridge University Press, 1983, pp. 43-64; David Lloyd George, *War Memoirs*, Vol. IV, London: Ivor Nicholson and Watson, 1934, pp. 1926-1927.

11. See two lectures by T. Miller Maguire to the Royal United Services Institution, published in the Institution's journal as "Readiness or Ruin," in Vol. LIII No. 382, December 1909; and "National Recuperation," in Vol. LIV, No. 385, March 1910.

12. See, for instance, Douglas Robinson, *The Zeppelin in Combat, 1912-1918*, London: G.T. Foulis, 1962.

13. Tami Davis Biddle, *Rhetoric and Reality in Air Warfare: British and American Ideas about Strategic Bombing, 1914-1945*, Princeton: Princeton University Press, 2002, pp. 29-35. The report is quoted on 33.

14. See Malcolm Cooper, *The Birth of Independent Air Power*, London: Allen and Unwin, 1986.

15. Biddle, *Rhetoric and Reality*, pp. 35-48.

16. *Ibid.*, pp. 49-68.

17. *Ibid.*, pp. 74-75.

18. See Brock Millman, "British Home Defence Planning and Civil Dissent, 1917-1918," *War in History*, 5, No. 2, April 1998, pp. 204-232.

19. Commandant's lecture, "Air Warfare," RAF Staff College, 1924, in AIR 1/2385/228/10, Public Record Office, UK.

20. I. F. Clarke, pp. 169-170.

21. For some overviews of Douhet in English from this period, see "The Air Doctrine of General Douhet," no author given, in *The Royal Air Force Quarterly*, Volume IV, No. 2, April 1933, pp. 164-167; "General Giulio Douhet—An Italian Apostle of Air Power," and "Air Warfare—The Principles of Air Warfare by General Giulio Douhet," in *The Royal Air Force Quarterly*, Vol. VII, No. 2, April 1936, pp. 148-151, 152-168. For a recent authoritative account of Douhet's thought, see Azar Gat, "Futurism, Proto-fascist Italian Culture and the Sources of Douhetism," in *War and Society*, Vol. 15, No. 1, May 1997, pp. 31-51.

22. Gat, "Futurism" p. 39.

23. He asserted that "when the working personnel of a factory sees one of its machine shops destroyed, even with a minimum loss of life, it quickly breaks up and the plant ceases to function." See Giulio Douhet, *Command of the Air*, Washington, DC: Office of Air Force History, 1983, pp. 22-23., This is a reprint of the 1942 edition translated by Dino Ferrari and published by Coward-McCann Inc.

24. Douhet, p.10.

25. Phillip Meilinger, "Guilio Douhet and the Origins of Air Power Theory," in *The Paths of Heaven: The Evolution of Air Power Theory*, Meilinger, ed., Maxwell AFB: Air University Press, 1997, pp. 9-10.

26. See Meilinger, "Guilio Douhet," pp. 12-13.

27. Michael S. Sherry, *The Rise of American Air Power*, New Haven: Yale University Press, 1987, 27. In a perceptive critique of the interwar air prophets, he has written: "They could not really imagine a future except one crudely

extrapolated from contemporary experience. Dismissing most of the war's record, they simplistically assumed that bomb damage . . . would be a simple multiple of previous experience: a tenfold increase in bomb tonnage yielding 10 times the panic and dislocation."

28. Alfred, Lord Tennyson, *Works: With Notes by the Author*, Hallam, Lord Tennyson, ed., New York: Macmillan, 1935, 98.

29. Biddle, pp. 99-127, 164-175.

30. See , for instance, Walter Millis, *Arms and Men*, 3rd edition, New Brunswick: Rutgers University Press, 1986, pp. 254-258.

31. Quoted in John Terraine, *A Time for Courage*, New York: Macmillan, 1985, p. 82.

32. William C. Sherman, *Air Warfare*, New York: The Ronald Press Co., 1926, p. 6.

33. Sherman, *Air Warfare*, 197. Sherman also recognized that gas bombs might be a feature of any future air war. See pp. 203-205.

34. Sherman, p. 218.

35. Biddle, pp. 153-164.

36. Dean quoted in John Terraine, "Theory and Practice of Air War: The Royal Air Force" in *The Conduct of the Air War in the Second World War: An International Comparison*, Providence, RI: Berg, 1992, p. 469.

37. See B. F. Cooling, ed., *Case Studies in the Development of Close Air Support*, Washington, DC, Office of Air Force History, 1990.

38. See, for instance, Williamson Murray, *Luftwaffe*, Annapolis: Nautical and Aviation Publishing Company, 1985; James S. Corum, *The Luftwaffe: Creating the Operational Air War, 1918-1940*, Lawrence: University Press of Kansas, 1997.

39. Sir Charles Webster and Noble Frankland, *The Strategic Air Offensive Against Germany*, London: HMSO, 1961, Vol. I, pp. 105-106; Brereton Greenhous, *et al.*, *The Crucible of War, 1939-1945*, Vol. III, Toronto: University of Toronto Press, 1994, pp. 530-534.

40. Tami Davis Biddle, "Bombing by the Square Yard: Sir Arthur Harris at War, 1942-1945," *The International History Review*, XXI, No. 3, September 1999, pp. 626-664.

41. Biddle, *Rhetoric and Reality*, pp. 211-213.

42. Webster and Frankland, Vol. II, p. 39.

43. See, for instance, W. W. Rostow, *Pre-Invasion Bombing Strategy*, Austin: University of Texas Press, 1981.

44. Biddle, *Rhetoric and Reality in Air Warfare*, pp. 228-229, 243-244.

45. *Ibid.*, pp. 109-110, 190-191.

46. Brown, Civilian Psychiatric Air Raid Casualties" *The Lancet*, May 31, 1941, p. 691.

47. R.J. Overy, *Why the Allies Won*, London: Jonathan Cape, 1995, p. 109.

48. On the air campaign in the Far East, see generally Sherry, *The Rise of American Air Power*; and Conrad C. Crane, *Bombs, Cities, and Civilians*, Lawrence: University of Kansas Press, 1993.

49. Biddle, *Rhetoric and Reality*, pp. 270-288.

50. Overy, pp. 130-133.

51. Anglo-American losses, he points out, were far lower than those of the other fighting powers. Overy, pp. 127-128. In the conclusion to his comprehensive history of Gen. Spaatz and the World War II strategic air war, American historian Richard G. Davis credited strategic bombing for ending the war months earlier than otherwise might have been the case—and thereby saving the lives not only of Allied soldiers but also of those suffering at the hands of the Third Reich. See Davis, *Carl A. Spaatz*, 596.

52. O'Donnell quoted in Conrad C. Crane, "Raiding the Beggar's Pantry: The Search for Air Power Strategy in the Korean War," in *The Journal of Military History*, Vol. 63, No. 4, October 1999, 889. On the air war in Korea generally, see Conrad C. Crane's seminal book, *American Air Power Strategy in Korea, 1950-1953*, Lawrence: University Press of Kansas, 1999.

53. See Crane, pp. 893-903.

54. Mark Clodfelter, *The Limits of Air Power*, New York: The Free Press, 1989, p. 21.

55. LeMay quoted in Thomas Hone, "Strategic Bombardment Constrained: Korea and Vietnam" in R. Cargill Hall, ed., *Case Studies in Strategic Bombardment*, Washington, DC: Air Force History and Museums Program, 1998, p. 517.

56. Crane, p. 905.

57. Quoted in Crane, p. 912.

58. On the 29 August raid, see Crane, p. 914.

59. Crane, p. 918; Clodfelter, pp.18-20.

60. Crane, p. 918. Clodfelter argues: "While the May attacks against the dams did not directly produce the Communist's about-face, the raids did, in combination with other factors, contribute to their desire to negotiate seriously." See p. 23.

61. In February 1954, Maj. Gen. Otto Weyland stated that "We are pretty sure now that the communists wanted peace, not because of a 2-year stalemate on the ground, but to get air power off their back." See Zimmerman and Weyland quoted in Futrell, *Ideas, Concepts, Doctrine*, 177.

62. Futrell, 177, 180-181.

63. See Crane, p. 920; Greenwood, p. 236; Clodfelter, p. 27; and generally, Dennis M. Drew, "Air Theory, Air Force, and Low Intensity Conflict: A Short Journey to Confusion" in Meilinger, ed., *The Paths of Heaven*, pp. 321-355.

64. Clodfelter, pp. 39-56.

65. Hone, pp. 495-496.

66. The figure is from Earl Tilford, "Setup: Why and How the U.S. Air Force Lost in Vietnam" in *Armed Forces and Society*, Vol. 17, No. 3, 1991, 327. On Vietnam, see generally Clodfelter; and Pape, pp. 174-210.

67. Robert A. Pape, Jr. "Coercive Air Power in the Vietnam War" in *International Security*, Vol. 15, No. 2, Fall 1990, 123-124. See also Pape, *Bombing to Win: Air Power and Coercion in War*, Ithaca: Cornell University Press, 1996, pp. 174-210.

68. Clodfelter makes this argument on p. 205.

69. A perceptive analysis of the air war in Vietnam can be found in Robert Pape, *Bombing to Win*, Ithaca: Cornell University Press, 1997; see also Pape, "Coercive Air Power in the Vietnam War" in *International Security*, Vol. 15, No. 2, Fall 1990, pp. 103-146.

70. Milton quoted in Tilford, p. 335; see also Clodfelter, pp. 206-208.

71. Clodfelter, pp. 201-202; Tilford, pp. 334-336, 338.

72. Clodfelter, p. 203.

73. Richard G. Davis, *Decisive Force: Strategic Bombing in the Gulf War*, Washington, DC: Air Force Museums and History Program, 1996, p. 20.

74. *Ibid.*, pp. 9-12.

75. See Lt. Col. David S. Fadok, "John Boyd and John Warden: Airpower's Quest for Strategic Paralysis," in Meilinger, ed., *The Paths of Heaven*, pp. 357-399; and John Andreas Olson, "Col. John A. Warden III: Smasher of Paradigms?" in *Air Power Leadership: Theory and Practice*, London: The Stationery Office, 2002, pp. 129-159.

76. Davis, *Decisive Force*, p. 19.

77. *Ibid.*, p. 2.

78. Michael Gordon and Bernard Trainor, *The Generals' War*, Boston: Little, Brown, 1995, pp. 205-207, 223.

79. Richard G. Davis, "Strategic Bombardment in the Gulf War," in R. Cargill Hall, ed., *Case Studies in Strategic Bombardment*, Washington, DC: Air Force History and Museums Program, 1998, pp. 573-575; and Davis, *Decisive Force*, pp. 42-43.

80. Davis, *Decisive Force*, p. 44; Barry Schneider, "Counterforce Targeting: Capabilities and Challenges" USAF Counterproliferation Papers, No. 22, Air University, Maxwell AFB, AL: 2004, pp. 13-15.

81. Davis, *Decisive Force*, p. 40.

82. Gordon and Trainor, p. 474.

83. The figure is from Davis, *Decisive Force*, p. 41.

84. Davis, *Decisive Force*, p. 53; Gordon and Trainor, p. 474.

85. Davis, *Decisive Force*, pp. 53-54.

86. *Ibid.*, pp. 54-55.

87. Barry Schneider has concluded: "The best that could be said about the intensive Allied Scud Hunt of DESERT STORM, even if it resulted in few or zero kills, is that the operation at least kept the Iraqi Scud-launch teams continually moving, hiding, and taking evasive actions." "Counterforce Targeting," p. 14; Gordon and Trainor, pp. 245-246.

88. Davis, *Decisive Force*, p. 61.

89. Stephen Biddle, "Victory Misunderstood: What the Gulf War Tells Us about the Future of Conflict," in *International Security*, 21, No. 2, Fall 1997, pp. 139-179.

90. See, for instance, Andrew Bacevich, "A Less Than Splendid Little War," in *The Wilson Quarterly*, Winter 2001, pp. 83-94.

91. See, for instance, Robert Schulzinger, *U.S. Diplomacy Since 1900*, New York: Oxford University Press, 2002, p. 370.

92. Benjamin Lambeth, *NATO's Air War for Kosovo*, Santa Monica, CA: RAND, 2001, p. xiv.

93. Stephen T. Hosmer, *Why Milosevic Decided to Settle When He Did*, Santa Monica, CA: RAND, 2001, p. 94.

94. These included the following fallacious assumptions: (1) that the ethnic cleansing campaign might cause NATO to rethink the bombing; (2) that the elimination of the KLA would be swift and simple; (3) that the fallout from civilian casualties might break NATO; and (4) that Russia would provide steadfast support to the Serbs. See Hosmer, pp. 24-34.

95. American University Trade and Environment Data Bast, Serbia Sanctions Case: *gurukul.ucc.american.edu/TED/SERBSANC.htm*.

96. Col. Charles J. Dunlap, USAF, "The End of Innocence: Rethinking Noncombatancy in the Post-Kosovo Era," *Strategic Review*, Summer 2000, p. 14; Major Jeanne M. Meyer, "Tearing Down the Façade: a Critical Look at the Will of the Enemy and Air Force Doctrine, *Air Force Law Review*, Vol. 51, 2001, pp. 143-182.

97. See Maj. R. A. Renner, USAF, "America's Asymmetric Advantage: The Utility of Airpower in the New Strategic Environment, *Defence Studies*, Vol. 4, No. 1, Spring 2004, p. 105.

98. On Afghanistan, see Stephen Biddle, *Afghanistan and the Future of Warfare: Implications for Army and Defense Policy*, Carlisle, PA: Strategic Studies Institute, U.S. Army War College, 2002.

99. See for instance, Williamson Murray and Robert Scales, *The Iraq War*, Cambridge: Harvard University Press, 2003.

100. Stephen Budiansky, *Air Power*, New York: Viking, 2004, p. 441.

101. See Group Captain Neville Parton, "Strategic Air Power Theory in the 21st Century," *RAF Air Power Journal*, 2004.

CHAPTER 19

JOHN WARDEN'S FIVE RING MODEL AND THE INDIRECT APPROACH TO WAR

Clayton K. S. Chun

Military strategists and practitioners develop and execute campaign plans based on a host of factors. Experience, intelligence, force structure, technology, legal, the threat, and environmental factors are only a few elements that affect these decisions. Another key factor is theory. Theory attempts to explain and get a reader to understand the occurrence of an event or state of nature. Theory can provide a framework to consider how to approach a problem. It can help one consider issues or questions to solve before making detailed approaches toward developing a theater strategy or campaign plan. If a theory is sound, then one could use it to solve problems by predicting possible outcomes, identifying potential problems, and finding options to get an opponent to take certain actions or modify his behavior. Theory can provide a foundation to help military strategists contemplate or evaluate potential courses of actions.

Military theory is often criticized, not without justification, for being unrealistic or static. Theory may not seem relevant because it lacks details or does not adequately represent a situation. Additionally, a theorist may have created an appropriate theory for his age or historic context that does not seem to fit the contemporary environment. Societies, militaries, weapons, and political situations may evolve such that the theory may not be relevant. A theorist may have worked during a particular period with certain international conditions or technology available to fight a war. Over time, political relationships change, engineers replace technology, and the character of warfare evolves.

Although compared to other weapons like small arms, aircraft are relatively new weapons; they have changed significantly since the first Italian aircraft appeared in combat over Libya in 1911.[1] Aerial warfare has evolved from simple biplanes that dropped very limited bomb loads, which pilots hoped would land within miles of their targets. Today, aircraft using satellite navigation systems can place precision guided munitions within a few feet of the intended target. Airpower theory has also evolved. Early air power theorists like Giulio Douhet developed ideas about aerial bombardment and predictions about its impact on the battlefield with particular technologies in mind. In hindsight, Douhet's theories on breaking the will of people through bombardment of cities lacked credibility. Douhet argued that the most humane way to end war was a swift attack on the most vulnerable element of society: the populace. Perhaps more of vision than a theory, critics challenged his concept on moral, military, political, and technical grounds. For example, Douhet advocated that air forces could use poison gas against cities that "paralyzed all life" by killing civilians.[2] Still, Douhet's ideas had a great impact on future concepts and ideas during the interwar period and World War II. Many air forces developed bomber fleets with the thought that strategic bombardment would help destroy a foe's ability to fight a war. World War II demonstrated that breaking the will of individuals, let alone a society, by bombing was difficult. The United Kingdom, Germany, and Japan each suffered from massive bombing campaigns, but in each case strategic bombing alone proved inconclusive. Lack of information about targets, bombing effects, and the use of massive, indiscriminate attacks may have contributed to problems attacking the specific industrial and political centers of Germany and Japan.

Since the end of World War II, technology has changed significantly to include jet aircraft, radar, surface-to-air missiles, nuclear weapons, instant communications, improved reconnaissance and surveillance, improved bomb damage assessment, and precision guided munitions. Ideas that were once discounted as unrealistic might now find validity due to improvements in fighting capability, increased urbanization, enhanced intelligence abilities to pinpoint key targets, and other changes. One recent airpower theorist, John A. Warden III, believed that a state would collapse if sufficient pressure was placed on certain key elements of its government, economy, society, and military. Many World War II U.S. Army Air Forces (AAF) and British Royal Air Force (RAF) officers agonized over what targets would accomplish this same goal. Eighth Air Force B-17 and B-24 bomber crews smashed industrial targets, while losing thousands of crewmembers and creating massive collateral damage, in search of a way to force Germany to capitulate. Warden built many of his ideas on concepts developed during the interwar period before World War II.

Warden believed that advances in technology—precision guided munitions and stealth had made revolutionary changes to the nature of warfare. Instead of using masses of bombers like World War II, a single stealthy plane today, armed with precision guided munitions, could destroy a target. This fundamental change in aerial operations increased the options a commander had available in battle. Aircraft could attack several targets simultaneously with surprise. Precision guided munitions gave aircrews the ability to destroy or disable a target with a single mission instead of returning repeatedly to a target. Modern technology allowed air forces to avoid having to go to battle against the strength of most nation-states, their military. Attacks on several centers of gravity created more chaos and damage to an enemy than a single, direct clash between opposing militaries. Centers of gravity are targets that if destroyed or disabled have a significant impact on a nation's war making capability. Warden thought that technology freed campaign planners to consider more options to strike an enemy. A main concern involved not how many aircraft or systems could attack a target, but what type of target should military forces damage or destroy? Commanders needed to consider what effects that strikes on the targets would have on the enemy. They also had to question whether a particular sequence of attacks made sense.

John Warden was able to employ his ideas directly in a campaign plan without the concern of interpretation or potential misapplication of his ideas. Unlike some theorists, Warden was able to translate his ideas into actual combat planning for operations in the 1991 Persian Gulf War. The use of his ideas and concepts for that situation is a prime example of how a military theory guided campaign planning and how to think about what targets to destroy or disable. Although geared toward a state-on-state confrontation, one might ponder how much of his theory may or may not be relevant to the rise of conflict with non-state actors or states that do not have discernable centers of gravity.

The Enemy as a System.

Colonel John Warden believed that nation-states operate like biological organisms composed of discrete systems. In a perfect world these systems function in harmony and the organisms survive and flourish. However, certain systems controlled other systems and were thus significant, while other elements might appear to be vital, they were actually not important for sustaining the organism. Warden believed that like a biological organism a nation could be stunned. Military action could produce strategic paralysis. Strategic paralysis in Warden's terms would make an enemy incapable of taking any physical action to conduct operations.[3] The key was to think of the enemy as a related set of systems. By using this rationale, a strategist could distinguish the important systems and avoid wasting effort on less critical targets. How one can attack an enemy depends on the objectives being sought, the enemy's defensive capability and intensity of resistance, environmental conditions, and the effort and resources the attacker is willing to exert to attain his goals. But in every case Warden believed a systematic approach would produce the most efficient use of airpower. For example, striking targets essential to a nation's leadership or command and control functions might completely negate or at least inhibit the ability of an enemy to defend its cities or other locations. If a country could disable or destroy particular centers of gravity in an enemy nation, then it could stop that enemy from directing its political, economic, informational, and military elements of power. Victory was thus assured. Successful attacks on a particular hierarchy of systems might lead to a target country's downfall.

Warden believed that organizations from nation-states to terrorist organizations have a common critical feature: some type of leadership. An individual or a command group with control capability provides guidance and direction to that organization. Without this system, the organization would flounder and particular functions cease to exist or become severely limited. This leadership function has become a vital "center" of action against which an attacker should focus its military actions. Once an attacker neutralizes the "leadership" function, other systems become vulnerable for further assault or become neutralized. Ultimately, the goal of striking leadership targets was to destroy the psyche of the enemy's top command. Determining the level of success against the enemy's psyche is difficult, if not impossible. Warden reasoned that an attacker could only view the physical manifestations of the enemy that would help identify targets that would comply with this scheme.[4] A prioritized scheme of attacking leadership targets first, then others could provide a blueprint for a campaign plan.

Instead of attacking the "muscle" of the system, Warden advocated striking an enemy through a more indirect approach and creating a similar effect. A military force could clash directly in a conventional battle that could result in an attritional battle or a decisive encounter. However, if the leadership of the state was either disabled or unable to provide guidance to its forces, it might be possible to render those military assets useless much faster. Warden became an advocate for an indirect approach to warfare. This emphasis was developed while Warden was a graduate student at Texas Tech University where he developed an affinity to British military theorist, Basil H. Liddell Hart.[5]

Liddell Hart, a land power theorist, focused on an indirect approach to warfare. A veteran of World War I, Liddell Hart saw the horror of trench warfare and the folly of direct attacks against entrenched positions. Instead of concentrating on an enemy's strengths, a nation's land power should focus on a foe's weakness and then exploit it. If a military force could find an unlikely avenue to approach and defeat a foe's military, then a country might achieve its objectives with less casualties quicker. Liddell Hart contradicted post-World War I conventional wisdom concerning a direct approach to warfare. His ideas clashed with existing approaches like Carl von Clausewitz's focus on trying to defeat an opposition's military forces first. Supporters of the "false doctrine of war" from Napoleon and Clausewitz that saw enemy armies as the primary objective in war created the vast carnage from World War I.[6] Liddell Hart believed a nation's will was subject to exploitation by attacking elements of the society where they were vulnerable. If the elements that created the country's peace and security were threatened, then the state could collapse.

Warden, a career Air Force fighter pilot, predicted that airpower could play a pivotal role in conducting operations through an indirect approach. Given the nature of modern aircraft, support capabilities, and precision guided munitions, airpower could destroy or disable systems that range from leadership to economic capabilities. Unlike the World War I and II aircraft that required a mass of inaccurate munitions to destroy a command and control center or other target, technology had improved that allowed a single aircraft to deliver munitions within a few feet of its intended target quickly. Aircraft, if a country attained air superiority, were free to attack several different types of targets simultaneously. This ability to strike many targets would confuse an enemy by not letting a foe determine the direction and focus of an attack. This approach allowed aircrews to conduct parallel warfare and a commander could strike fast over a wide range of objectives. Other forces might need to attack in a slower, more linear manner. For example, ground forces would have to defeat a similar military force first, before proceeding to other targets like the rival's transportation networks or leadership. Aircraft could bypass the enemy's ground forces and strike directly against the capital, industrial centers, or other targets.

Although airplanes could attack most nation-states independently, Warden was careful to note that airpower alone might not be sufficient or efficient enough to use exclusively to attack an enemy.[7] Warden is an airpower advocate and stresses the value of using that means to achieve military and national objectives. However, commanders can use airpower to support land and naval forces as part of a joint operation. Other military forces could also act as a supporting force for airpower. Whether a commander uses airpower in a supported or supporting role, Warden believed that one essential element is the attainment of air superiority. Air superiority allows control of the skies that lets a military force attack from the skies while being protected from attack from the air by the enemy. An air force needs the ability to destroy enemy aircraft and support infrastructure, while protecting itself from similar enemy operations. Once a nation controls the air, it can conduct air and other operations without significant opposition.

Warden's theoretical blueprint for using airpower would combine non-physical (or in his term "morale") and physical effects on warfare. Non-physical factors include the impact of fog, friction, and other psychological affects on national leadership, military, and civilian populations. Physical targets included military forces and means to fight war. Warden believed that the relationship between the two was defined by the equation Morale X Physical = Outcome. He realized that attacking morale was difficult. Modern technology could do much to reduce the impact of friction and fog through better communications and the availability of information; however, a military force could not completely negate friction, fog, or morale issues. A nation could not guarantee its ability to predict perfectly an enemy's intentions and actions. Unexpected enemy actions could also affect any outcome.

Physical damage to enemy forces or economic targets is easier to accomplish. If an attack could significantly reduce the enemy through physical damage, then morale considerations might be moot. This approach assumes that the nation can identify correctly the appropriate physical targets. Alternatively, "morale factors" could change the physical dimension of warfare. Leadership could exhort workers to produce more munitions or the populace to better support the war effort. Conversely, the attacks on physical targets could alter the morale of population and affect the ability of a rival to discern an attacker's intention; this may create the fog of war. Pressure on enemy leadership or the adversary's population, based on physical attacks, could affect morale and may change enemy behavior. For example, the relentless bombing of economic targets could cause significant disruptions in everyday lives of workers. If conditions were bad enough, prominent members of the population might confront the national leadership with demands to negotiate or submit to the enemy. Short of such radical steps, opinion leaders and the general public might begin to openly question national policy.

John Warden's Five Ring Model.

John Warden selected five general areas or systems that he believed were key centers of gravity to exploit against any foe. This model provided a framework to analyze how to disable an enemy using strategic paralysis. The systems Warden picked were: leadership, organic essentials, infrastructure, population, and fielded military forces. One could envision this model as a series of five concentric rings with the most important element in the center and progressively less important ones moving outward. A way to think about defeating an enemy was to attack the concentric circles from "inside out." That is, disable the most important center of gravity first and work outward to less important rings. (See Figure 1.)

Leadership was at the center of Warden's ring model. In his biological system analogy, leadership equated to the brain of a living organism. The most important leadership in a state was the government because it could ultimately decide to concede in a conflict to another state. Leadership, above all else, was the primary center of gravity in a state. If the national leadership was isolated, disabled, or destroyed, then the country could not function. Leadership requires an ability to gather, process, and act on information—all functions that an adversary might strike and affect the functioning of a nation-state. Direct attacks against enemy leaders, command and control structures, or headquarters could affect an opponent's ability to continue a conflict. The Linebacker II bombing campaign in December 1972 impressed Warden. In his opinion, the campaign forced the North Vietnamese government to return to peace negotiations with the United States.[8] Hanoi had broken off diplomatic efforts in the Paris Peace talks until Linebacker II. Air campaign planners directed these bombing attacks at Hanoi. Similarly, the combined Air Force and Navy attacks on Libya during Operation El Dorado Canyon in April 1986 on Muammar al Qadhafi, who supported terrorist attacks on Americans, also impressed Warden. Neither attack destroyed enemy leadership. However, actual destruction of leadership targets might not be possible since political leaders might be highly mobile, operate in areas that are not conducive to military action, or are too diverse to effectively damage. Instead of direct attacks on leadership, Warden thought attacking other targets might produce enough internal pressure to force the leadership to capitulate.[9] Indirect attacks or effects against the leadership might produce the desired effect on the enemy.

Leadership targets can include executive, legislative, judicial, and other functions. Campaign planners could target physical governmental facilities. Attacking the means these targets use to coordinate or control activities within the nation requires a Herculean effort. Additionally, striking leadership targets of non-state actors that do not have established facilities or locations can create problems. Conversely, foes with a loose confederation of leadership, such as a cartel or combined revolutionary movements, who are highly mobile, may not lend themselves to a rapid attack.

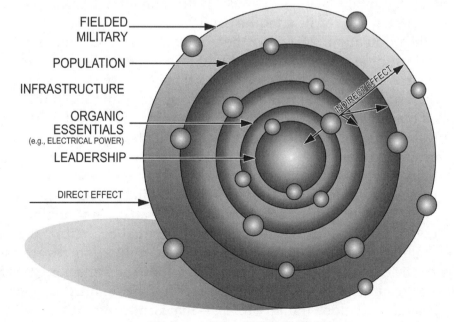

Figure 1. Five Ring Model.

299

Living organisms do not exist on their brains alone. An organism needs certain raw materials to live. Organic essentials provide elements to function, grow, and replace damaged tissues. Similarly, a state cannot exist on leadership alone. It needs raw materials that include sources of energy, food, and financial resources to maintain its existence. These raw materials provide energy to the entire state. Attacking such targets, especially food sources, needs careful consideration because of ethical issues and other strategic implications like the national and international opinion. However, industrial countries require oil to fuel industry and transportation that, if effectively interdicted, could slow industrial and military operations to a crawl. The lack of energy can influence national leadership's behavior and limit severely actions by subordinate actors in the state. Warden believed that successive degradation of a state's organic essentials could lead to the collapse of the entire system; create conditions for a state that make it physically difficult or impossible for the state to continue a policy or fight; and force significant political and economic impacts due to damage to the ring.[10] He thought that destruction of key targets in the energy field, like petroleum refining stations or electric production facilities, could paralyze a modern state. Industrial production, transportation, economic activities, and people's lives would be altered suddenly with massive disruptions rippling throughout the state. Pressure on national leadership to respond or mitigate the damages could force policy changes.

Warden's next ring is infrastructure. Infrastructure is like the vessels, bones, and muscles in the human body that allows an organism to move and take action. Society's infrastructure includes among other things road and rail networks, airports, power grids and factories. Potential infrastructure targets include a long list of activities—some of which are more valuable than others. Attacking rail lines may take months or years to destroy hundreds of thousands of miles of track. Destroying or disabling key infrastructure requires a careful analysis to find vital elements that, if struck, could disrupt operations. For example, instead of trying to bomb rail lines, a single bombing of a key bridge, tunnel, or rail junction might accomplish the same purpose. Commanders may need to consider the post-conflict impact of infrastructure attacks. Reconstruction of needed roads, rail lines, and other targets after the conflict may add time and cost to returning the nation to a normal state after the war. It might be wise to avoid destroying infrastructure you might need for your own purposes or will have to repair after the conflict.

The fourth ring is the population. Attacking the population does not focus solely on bombing civilians, but could also include using psychological warfare or other activities to reduce a populace's morale. Like an organism composed of millions of cells that can survive the loss of many of those cells, a nation can endure some loss of population. However, economic and military support might falter under air attack if the public perceives its losses are too high. The effect of bombing population is extremely unpredictable. Examples of increased morale under bombardment are numerous. Also, if organic essentials are limited, then a reduction in unessential parts of the population may actually improve the state's ability to operate by relieving pressure on limited resources.

The last ring comprises fielded military forces. Fielded military forces represent the "fighting mechanism" that protects the state from attack. Warden makes an organic analogy to leukocytes or white blood cells that ward off viruses.[11] If states lived in perpetual peace they would not require a protective force like a military or even police. Although fielded military forces are a formidable foe, they depend heavily on the other rings for support. Instead of directly attacking this ring, strikes on the supporting rings could sufficiently weaken these forces to the point that they were incapable of resistance. Fighting through the fielded military forces—that is, making a direct military on military effort—could take much time and cause many casualties before breaking through to the other more important rings. Unhampered, the enemy leadership could operate normally and replenish fielded military forces with which to continue the fight.

Commanders should take a systems approach to warfare. Instead of destroying an entire foe, attacks on key system components could render a strategic effect. This type of approach forces one to consider how to derive a specific end — paralysis — using specific ways — attacks on subsystems or rings. John Warden's theory of identifying and creating a priority of subsystems allowed strategic planners the ability to attack in a specific order. However, Warden also stressed that a combination of varying size and scope of attacks could create certain vulnerabilities to the rings themselves. For example, attacking infrastructure, like transportation networks, could alter the ability of fielded military forces to move and engage against another military force. Likewise, striking industrial targets that manufacture weapons or munitions could also delay or affect the fielded military forces. Thus, selecting the correct targets and assessing the probable effect of their destruction on the system becomes a prime concern.

Many of Warden's ideas had surfaced earlier. Early airpower theories and concepts in the United States were developed as a part of the Air Corps Tactical School (ACTS) at Maxwell Field in Alabama. ACTS writers had advocated the use of precision bombing to strike economic targets to undermine the ability of a nation to sustain itself in war. Writing during the interwar period, the ACTS faculty was influenced by the brutality of trench warfare and the destruction during World War I. Perhaps by using strategic bombers that could hit and destroy specific targets, the nation could avoid another replay of a World War I type of conflict. Although ACTS writers also contended with issues concerning service independence and the tactical use of airpower, the long-range, heavy bomber rose to prominence as a means to influence events in a strategic manner. Army Air Corps bombers would selectively attack targets like transportation, steel plants, ball-bearing manufacture, food sources, energy supplies, and especially, electrical production facilities.[12]

ACTS concepts focused on modern states. As a nation became more industrialized it generated complex economic interactions and increased degrees of specialization. Thus, modern nations became more susceptible to disruption by attacks on key nodes. A state could disrupt a foe more quickly, efficiently, and effectively through the air than by trying to conquer its fielded forces. Unfortunately, "precision" attack had not come of age. Low altitude bombing risked the aircraft and crews to air defenses. High altitude bombing forced crews to deliver their ordnance with great inaccuracy that would create collateral damage and cause massive casualties, a result ACTS faculty tried to avoid. Additionally, Air Corps pilots needed current target information. Given the lack of intelligence capabilities during the period, finding exact locations, functions, interrelationships, and impacts of destroyed targets may have overwhelmed the Army Air Corps' ability to accomplish actions ACTS had advocated. Technology was not available to either find the proper targets or to deliver munitions with "precision." However, today's aircrews have access to a host of precision guided munitions, navigational systems, weather reports, intelligence sources for targeting and bomb damage assessment, and other capabilities beyond the wildest imagination of the ACTS faculty.

Warden shared some of the ideas from the ACTS faculty. A common theme was the attack on targets using an indirect approach. Warden and ACTS concentrated on subduing an enemy through a particular center of gravity. Striking economic targets was the primary focus of the ACTS concepts. Warden used a series of targets to affect the will of national leadership. The ACTS approach of assaulting enemy targets by strategic bombardment alone created doubt in many minds throughout the 1930's and into World War II. Warden advocated the use of airpower too, but also recognized the value of other military instruments.

Airpower's Value.

To Warden, airpower offered many characteristics that could hasten the downfall of an adversary, especially if it were susceptible to his five ring model. Airpower offered a number of characteristics that could serve a nation. Aircraft, by their very nature, could provide a very fast, long-range and flexible tool for commanders.[13] Given these characteristics, airpower can conduct parallel attacks against an enemy that can hit simultaneously segments of all five rings. These multiple strikes can cause all types of second and third order effects and create pressures between rings. The leadership ring is especially susceptible to such pressures.

Airpower allows a nation to conduct parallel attacks since airpower transcends geography. Aircraft can simply fly over enemy fielded forces and avoid marching through an enemy. Like other military forces, airpower can mass against particular targets and is flexible enough to change targeting within minutes. The advent of stealth aircraft, improved battle management systems, precision guided munitions, instant information, and the growing capacity to integrate and use a combination of joint forces in combat operations simply enhanced this capability. Attacking in a parallel manner allows a nation to place demands on the enemy that can overwhelm an enemy's defenses. These missions create confusion and doubt for the enemy's leadership. Military force, airpower especially, can operate on several levels: strategic, operational, or tactical. Although these attacks could deal a direct blow against a foe, Warden recommended concentrated effort aimed squarely at a specific end—coercing the leadership to change its behavior.

For Warden, destruction of key targets had secondary importance to the effects such destruction would have on the adversary's leadership. Since the United States can achieve almost unfettered air superiority and can deliver munitions accurately, the use of airpower seemed logical. Countries around the globe did not have the capacity to challenge the United States' ability to conduct air and space operations. Although Warden developed many of his ideas while the Soviet Union was a viable nation, his ideas about airpower may have taken on more credence after 1991 when his concepts were tested in Desert Storm. In some respects, the focus on measuring the impact on a function instead of the physical destruction of a target forced a change in the way commanders viewed combat operations.

Effects-based operations became a key concern. Assessing particular targets for their impact on a larger scheme is not new. During the Combined Bomber Offensive in World War II, AAF pilots attacked ball-bearing plants to stop the manufacture of German industrial and military products. American officers believed that ball-bearings were a crucial center of gravity in German industrial production. Reducing ball-bearing production would severely affect engine production that could limit aircraft and tank inventories. Unfortunately, German industrial production in some cases did not cease, but actually increased. For example, BMW 801 aero-engines manufacture jumped from 5,540 motors in 1943 to 7,395 units in 1944.[14] Perhaps due to a shift to full mobilization or use of methods to ameliorate ball-bearing shortages through alternative production or substitution, the predicted outcome did not occur despite its apparent plausibility. Still, strategic bombardment did disrupt the German economy and reduce production. By January 1945, German Ministry of Armaments officials claimed that strategic bombardment reduced aircraft production by 31 percent, tanks by 35 percent, and trucks a further 42 percent.[15] The Allies attacked targets such as oil, transportation ncts, and other activities, but the selection of targets was difficult. Faulty intelligence, limited understanding of the German economy, and the changing nature of that economy made the feasibility of successful economic warfare questionable.[16] Although impressive in size and scope, the AAF bombing attacks could not stop German economic activities. The German juggernaut continued until its dying days of May 1945.

What has changed since World War II is vast improvements in technology that allow one to strike and make pre- and post-attack assessments against targets in a more effective and efficient manner than in the past. Could advances in aviation and other support systems today identify, find, and destroy targets that could cripple decisively an economy or national leadership? The dream of ending the war-making capability of an enemy, much like the hopes of AAF officers during the Combined Bomber Offensive during World War II, might come to fruition with these advances. Effects based operations require a commander to predict accurately the impact of the destruction of specific targets and their eventual influence on an adversary. Economic activities today are even more complex than those in World War II. Suppose a country wanted to disable an economy. What targets should the nation bomb? With complexity and increased specialization from globalization, this task might actually be easier today than in the past. Many nations today require outside resources and components to take advantage of global markets and comparative advantages in prices, wages, and capital. Weakening key transportation nodes, energy sources, or assembly plants that focus on a few industries might shock a nation's economy. Especially in countries that have found their niche in the world economy due to globalization, John Warden's concepts might still work. However, issues still abound. Does the nation have alternative sources of products and services that can substitute for the target? Due to specialization of industrial products, would attacks on the economy create hardship on allies who trade with or produce products within the targeted areas? What amount of collateral damage will result from these actions? Suppose a country wanted to disable an economy, what targets should the nation bomb? Reducing electricity could force a slowdown in industrial production, but this could affect hospitals and other services that cause innocent lives to be lost. What if the country has few, if any, visible targets, like non-state actors?

Warden's theory assumes that airpower has almost unlimited access to attack enemy targets. To gain maximum efficiency and effectiveness, a nation must have the ability to gain air superiority. Warden takes great pains to ensure readers understand that air superiority is a "necessity" that allows air forces to conduct operations and allows them to conduct attacks on the centers of gravity that he believes would cripple a foe.[17] Given this assumption, Warden proceeds with his theory, but what if the nation cannot achieve air superiority. That condition may not be a problem for the United States in the near future, but it might not be the case for other states or in a particular region. Additionally, much of Warden's theory assumes a fairly static enemy. A rival can react and might modify its behavior to compensate for attacks on the ring structure. For example, instead of maintaining a strict chain of command leadership, what if a terrorist organization or state fragments its leadership or it dissolves into a loose confederation of leaders? Disabling one specific leadership center of gravity may not halt significant operations in the terrorist cell or a particular country.

Timing is also a concern. Warden assumed that a country's air force could strike the enemy at the onset of any hostilities.[18] Attacking an enemy at the very beginning of a conflict could produce significant shock value to an adversary. A tremendous level of parallel attacks could cause the foe's leadership to snap. Contrast this situation with one where an air force has a gradual build-up of attacks, as it shifts forces or tries to wrest air superiority from an enemy. A foe could attempt to disperse its economic centers of production (admittedly difficult), build redundant capabilities, or find alternative sources of production. Targeting information, like the flow of activities, could change and cause the air force to bomb unnecessary or counterproductive targets.

Warden's ideas were tested in 1990-1991. During Operation DESERT STORM, the United States executed a strategic air campaign plan that reflected much of Warden's theory. The uncontested use of American airpower resulted in an asymmetric advantage over the Iraqi forces that pitted U.S. and coalition strength against Iraqi weakness. Iraq could not prevent the U.S.-led coalition from gaining air superiority. Strategic bombers, land-based tactical aircraft, cruise missiles, naval aviation, and multinational partners contributed to a massive attack on Iraq.

Planning an Air Campaign.

During the 1991 Persian Gulf War, John Warden served in the Pentagon in the Air Staff's directorate of plans where he was deputy director for warfighting concepts. This position allowed him to experiment with many creative concepts of airpower employment. During the opening days of the August 1990 during the Iraqi invasion of Kuwait, General Norman H. Schwarzkopf, commander of U.S. Central Command (CENTCOM) initiated planning activities that ranged from stopping a possible invasion of Saudi Arabia to immediately pushing Iraqi forces back into their own country. One area that Schwarzkopf found lacking in CENTCOM was the ability to conduct a strategic air campaign.[19] Schwarzkopf sought out the Air Staff. His request allowed Warden to work on a strategic air campaign against Saddam Hussein's government. The Five Ring model would be subjected to the test of action.

Warden proposed a number of approaches within the Air Staff. His final concept was presented as an Iraqi air campaign entitled INSTANT THUNDER. The intent of INSTANT THUNDER was to conduct a very short, six day, intensive bombardment that would "incapacitate" the Iraqi leadership and destroy vital Iraqi military capability. It would not touch "basic" infrastructure that would create undue civilian hardship.[20] Warden cautioned that this action was not designed to be a long term plan that would turn into an attritional campaign. INSTANT THUNDER would last days instead of the years of air operations by the Navy and Air Force over North Vietnam. The campaign plan seemed like a great opportunity to demonstrate his ideas. A rapid campaign could allow American air forces to isolate Hussein and attack systematically the centers of gravity of Iraq.

The five ring model capitalized on the strength of American airpower. The United States could launch such an attack immediately as ground forces were building up in Saudi Arabia. If Schwarzkopf conducted the campaign as written, Warden predicted it would minimize United States and allied losses and could reduce Iraqi civilian casualties and collateral damage. This campaign, more importantly, could eliminate Iraqi military capability for an extended period.

Warden developed a set of specific targets that closely resembled his model. The first targets were designed to gain air superiority by destroying air defenses, airfields, and the Iraqi air force. After the coalition achieved air superiority, its air forces would concentrate on leadership, command and control, key internal production and distribution centers, weapons of mass destruction (WMD) production and storage facilities, and offensive air and ballistic missile capability. Warden did not include Iraqi fielded land power in the INSTANT THUNDER proposal. Instead, Warden proposed to incapacitate the Hussein regime and tie up its telecommunications, civil and military, in an effort to reduce national leadership effectiveness. The organic essentials ring had several potential targets to include electricity, petroleum and oil distribution and storage for domestic Iraqi use. Warden did not want to destroy the export capacity or damage Iraqi's long term economic health. Aircraft would attack infrastructure targets that involved railroads and some bridges. Air forces would also use psychological warfare against the Iraqi population, foreign workers, and any forces in Kuwait to reduce Saddam Hussein and his Ba'ath Party's influence. The elements of the last ring, fielded military forces, which Warden addressed, were strategic air defenses and delivery systems like bombers and ballistic missiles that could use WMD or conduct strategic operations. The attacks would occur in parallel across all five rings from strategic air defenses to Saddam Hussein's palaces.

The key center of gravity was Saddam Hussein's ability to lead and control his nation.[21] Each target attacked by Coalition air forces would support this aim. The destruction of telecommunications and command and control capabilities would disrupt any connection between Hussein, his people, and Iraqi military forces. Striking at Iraqi strategic delivery capability would reduce any regional threat posed by Iraq at the time and into the future. Hussein had demonstrated his ability to use SCUD and modified ballistic missiles to hit targets in Tehran in the War of the Cities during his conflict with Iran in the 1980s. Hussein could use the same systems to attack south to Saudi Arabia or west to Israel. Eliminating Iraqi strategic air defenses would open Iraq to continual attacks and reduce a large threat to American air crews. A massive assault on electrical grids would cripple any industrial production and allow chaos to reign among the population. The lack of refined petroleum products could hamper transportation and paralyze civilian and military movements. These targets would underscore Hussein's weaknesses to his people and the world.

CENTCOM campaign planners modified Warden's original six-day INSTANT THUNDER campaign plan. Warden had used the idea of a six-day campaign as a device to sell the concept to Schwarzkopf.[22] When Warden was asked to develop a campaign plan, the Iraqis had just invaded Kuwait in August 1990. The original plan was an option to strike back at Baghdad. Fortunately, the United States and other powers had sufficient time to conduct an unmolested build-up of air, land, and maritime forces to eject Iraqi forces from Kuwait. The Coalition air forces did conduct a strategic air campaign, but planners dismissed the belief that airpower alone could defeat Iraq. Top military leadership and CENTCOM planners did not believe Warden's idea that a weeklong campaign that concentrated against 84 strategic level targets was credible. Instead, the Coalition conducted a four-phase campaign, after attaining air superiority, which included a longer strategic air campaign plan, followed by operations against Iraqi air defenses in Kuwait. The third phase featured air support of ground forces to attrite Iraqi forces and isolate enemy forces in Kuwait. The last phase used air and ground forces to push all Iraqi forces out of occupied Kuwait. The first two phases lasted 39 days. The Iraqi government did not capitulate nor did the will of the people erode significantly enough to affect Hussein.

John Warden's theories had a major impact on Operation DESERT STORM and the air campaign. Warden's ideas on precision guided munitions, stealth, parallel attack, and other airpower features did create some strategic paralysis within the Iraqi government. Although Hussein's government did not collapse, it was affected significantly during the strategic bombardment campaign. For example, air strikes disabled communications. In a centrally controlled state like Iraq, unimpeded communications was vital if Hussein expected to control every action in the country. Destruction and disruption of the center "ring" aided the Coalition efforts to reduce Baghdad's military capability and effectiveness. The destruction of key national leadership, command and control, communications, industrial sites, and other sites helped support Warden's ideas. However, Iraq was a nation-state that had these types of targets, and American air superiority was not really challenged. In the future, enemy nations or non-state actors may not present as lucrative a target to air forces as Iraq did in 1991.

John Warden's Impact.

John Warden focused his ideas on getting commanders to consider attacking the enemy by measuring the impact on those strikes on the enemy's ability to wage war. His five ring model gave campaign planners the ability to focus on a framework to paralyze a foe. Warden linked his ring attack to a plausible scheme against a modern nation-state. The advent of advanced munitions and delivery systems created conditions where these types of attacks might achieve what earlier air power theorist could only dream about.

Warden's ideas led to greater reflection among airpower advocates not only on the planning and actual attack on targets, but also on the more complex factor of the effect of an attack on the enemy. Commanders needed to consider not only the primary, but secondary and tertiary effects on the destruction or temporary disruption of these targets. Commanders through the ages have planned campaigns to meet objectives that require a study of the effects and assessment of target destruction. The advent of greater precision, speed, and lethality has allowed unprecedented opportunities to strike targets that can cripple a nation. Calls to limit damage and reduce human suffering have forced commanders to operate under increased constraints as they seek ways to accomplish their aims. Careful consideration of targets becomes a prime concern. Additionally, the ability to conduct parallel attacks forces commanders to consider how to paralyze a foe arrayed as a network or a complex of indistinct relationships. All these considerations need detailed study as commanders plan operations.

In the future, can national and military leadership gather and analyze sufficient information to implement Warden's concepts on the battlefield? Adaptive foes, lack of understanding about complex economic relationships, and other factors can limit the ability of militaries to conduct set-piece operations. Adversaries that gather information and disseminate it quickly via the Internet or cell phones can thwart efforts to conduct parallel attack schemes even if the strikes occur almost simultaneously and are separated by vast distances. Technologies that enable air and space operations to make John Warden's ideas come true are also available for an enemy to exploit as he develops countermeasures. Similarly, foes that do not operate or react like a nation-state or mirror how this country might respond could make Warden's theories difficult to implement. Still, the focus on what factors make an enemy operate as a system is a valuable way to think about an adversary. Military commanders might not overlook targets or weaknesses that they could now exploit. Warden helped integrate technology and strategic concepts that supported a major change in how nations use airpower in war.

ENDNOTES - CHAPTER 19

1. Bernard Brodie and M. Fawn, *From Crossbow to H-Bomb*, Bloomington: Indiana University Press, 1973, p. 177.

2. Giulio Douhet, *The Command of the Air*, Washington, DC: Center for Air Force History, 1983, p. 58.

3. John A. Warden III, "The Enemy as a System." *Airpower Journal* 9, Spring 1995, p. 43.

4. Phillip S. Meilinger, "Air Targeting Strategies: An Overview" in Richard P. Hallion, ed., *Airpower Confronts an Unstable World*, London: Brassey's, 1997, p. 61.

5. Diane T. Putney, *Airpower Advantage Planning the Gulf War Air Campaign 1989-1991*, Washington, DC: Air Force History and Museums Program, 2004, p. 36.

6. Thomas Greer, *The Development of Air Doctrine in the Army Air Arm 1917-1941*, Washington, DC: Office of Air Force History, 1985, p. 19.

7. David R. Mets, *The Air Campaign John Warden and the Classical Airpower Theorists*, Maxwell AFB, AL: Air University Press, 1999, p. 59.

8. Putney, p. 40.

9. *Ibid.*, p. 39.

10. Warden, p. 50.

11. *Ibid.*, p. 45.

12. Michael S. Sherry, *The Rise of American Air Power*, New Haven, CT: Yale University Press, 1987, p. 54.

13. David S. Fadok, "John Boyd and John Warden: Airpower's Quest for Strategic Paralysis," in Phillip S. Meilinger, ed., *The Paths of Heaven The Evolution of Airpower Theory*, Maxwell AFB, AL: Air University Press, 1997, p. 371.

14. R. J. Overy, *War and Economy in the Third Reich*, New York: Oxford Press, 1994, p. 372.

15. *Ibid.*, pp. 373-374.

16. Alan S. Milward, *War, Economy and Society 1939-1945*, Berkeley: University of California Press, 1977, p. 301.

17. John A. Warden, III, *The Air Campaign*, Washington, DC: Pergamon-Brassey's, 1989, p. 10.

18. Richard T. Reynolds, *Heart of the Storm*, Maxwell AFB, AL: Air University Press, 1995, p. 17.

19. *Ibid.*, p. 24.

20. John A. Warden, III, ""Iraqi Air Campaign Instant Thunder" briefing, undated, slide 2.

21. Thomas A. Keaney and Eliot A. Cohen, *Revolution in Warfare?* Annapolis, MD: Naval Institute Press, 1995, p. 30.

22. Putney, p. 360.

SPACEPOWER:
A STRATEGIC ASSESSMENT AND WAY FORWARD

Jeffrey A. Farnsworth

Space capabilities will probably provide the greatest added value to national power, wealth, and military lethality in the 21st century.[1] It is a virtual certainty that like the land, sea, and air domains before it, the space domain's exploitation will lead to power struggles and perhaps armed conflict as nations and transnational entities pursue their interests.[2] The United States has exploited space for various national purposes within the bounds of a bipolar nuclear deterrent, limited legal and policy regime, and a divisive political environment.[3] Despite noble attempts at strategy development, the U.S. does not have a valid National Security Space Strategy to orchestrate the elements of national power in a unified approach to achievement of National Space Policy goals. In the absence of strategy the U.S. has largely followed its technological prowess to exploit an uncontested space medium.[4] Meanwhile, the number of government, commercial, and nonstate entities engaged in space activities has multiplied. This growth of space activity comes at a time when cultural differences, information, and globalization have ushered in a more diverse set of security challenges including the real prospect of a contested space operating environment. The strategic environment is increasingly influenced by spacepower, which is defined here as the space medium's exploitation for military, political, economic, and other purposes.[5] In this age of "astropolitics," failure to understand the nature of spacepower and how to wield it could lead to serious miscalculations by strategic leaders.[6] From a national security perspective, failure to proactively address tough spacepower issues may erode the domestic and international conditions necessary to achieve and sustain a peaceful and prosperous future. From a military perspective, decisions regarding spacepower may inadvertently create unacceptable risks and vulnerabilities for land, sea, and air forces and impede transformation efforts. Such miscalculations could precipitate catastrophic consequences for national security and global stability in the 21st Century. Hence, a National Security Space Strategy is needed to better shape a favorable future.

Strategic Theory and the Army War College's Strategy Formulation Model provide a framework for this chapter to examine spacepower and space strategy formulation. Initially, the chapter examines the strategic environment's most pressing global and domestic factors influencing the development and employment of spacepower. Next, it considers the national purpose, national interests in space and current space policy followed by a survey of strategic thinking that has influenced defense space policy, programs, and doctrine. Finally, the chapter will assess major issues and offer specific recommendations to guide formulation of a valid National Security Space Strategy that can give substance to policy, influence the strategic environment, and shape a favorable future.

The Strategic Spacepower Environment.

Global and domestic trends are changing the strategic value of spacepower and are affecting the calculus of nations and nonstate entities alike. Historically, the 1957 launch of Sputnik and the specter of Soviet nuclear-armed spacecraft orbiting overhead were catalysts that rapidly ushered in the space age.[7] The ensuing space race to the moon was a brazen demonstration of competing ideologies, technical prowess and military power. In response to the space race and the threat of nuclear war, the U.S. and Soviets promulgated various treaties, declarations, and agreements that comprise the international legal regime governing space activities.[8] This space regime has mass appeal, since it extols idealist notions of peaceful coexistence in space, celestial bodies free from claims of sovereignty, and space as a sanctuary free from weapons of mass destruction. These notions were really peaceful cloaks that served as leverage points in a realist grand bargain between the Soviet Union and the U.S. The space regime's elements governing non-interference with national technical means, banning orbital weapons of mass destruction, and prohibiting anti-ballistic missile (ABM) systems effectively mitigated the risk of nuclear war. The space regime also prevented military domination of space by either the U.S or the Soviet Union, but its ambiguity on certain issues did permit space's militarization.[9] As a result, the U.S. now enjoys the world's most technically advanced military and intelligence space capabilities. Over time, the bi-polar system of the Cold War has broken up, but the world has not become a less dangerous place, and emerging threats are not confined to rational nation states. To deal with these new realities, the U.S. withdrew from the space regime's ABM treaty with Russia in order to build a national missile defense system against North Korean and Iranian threats. Similarly, other aspects of Cold War era space thought may warrant adaptation to meet the challenges of globalization and transnational threats in the 21st Century.

The principal value of satellites is their extensive view of earth, which enables effective and efficient gathering and dissemination of information.[10] Recognizing the value of satellites, many entities are engaged in commercial, civil, and scientific satellite applications that increase the quality of life for societies and individuals. Profitable international space consortia are growing, many businesses are engaged in space services, and where trade goes the flag follows. Russia, Europe, Japan, Canada, India, and China continue to develop space launch and satellite capabilities.[11] Next to the U.S., Russia has the largest number of national satellites. Russia is also pioneering space tourism and is an important contributor to international scientific space endeavors. France intends to increase its space budget by 50 percent, and other European countries are following suit to develop multinational space defense systems.[12] China is expanding its constellation of civil-military satellites and intends to conduct a manned mission to the moon. This fantastic growth and exploitation of space has evolved in a relatively benign political and military environment, and the result is many countries, militaries, and individuals have become dependent on space-based systems. Despite these dependencies, most players continue to respect peaceful space principals and do not interfere with national and commercial space systems. However, there are some concerns.

While the high vantage point of satellites may provide their principal value, this same attribute makes them easily observed and lucrative targets.[13] Therefore satellites are vulnerable to attack, and as the strategic environment becomes more volatile, hostile entities are more likely to exploit this weakness. Cases of state and nonstate actors developing anti-satellite capabilities or purposefully interfering with satellites are on the rise.[14] Iran recently launched a medium range ballistic missile to sub-orbital altitude, purportedly to develop its own peaceful space capabilities for communications.[15] Terrorist and drug trafficking organizations have demonstrated an adept ability to exploit satellite services to facilitate their planning, communications, and operations.[16] China kinetically destroyed one of its own satellites, illuminated a U.S. satellite with a laser, and has advocated space warfare in military publications.[17] While provocative, China's actions could be in response to a line already crossed by the U.S. with its own laser test on a satellite, kinetic interceptor tests on ballistic missiles in mid-course space transit, and a plethora of military publications exhorting the need to assure U.S. space superiority. These trends are likely to continue, and spacepower dynamics may dominate the behavior of nations and nonstate actors in the near future.

Meanwhile, international scientific endeavors and space exploration continue to inspire large cross-cultural segments of the global population. The International Space Station, robotic Mars explorations, and other space projects continue to foster international partnerships and provide benefits from spin-off technologies. The recent discovery of massive amounts of frozen water on Mars will undoubtedly inspire human exploration.[18] Rising concerns over global climate change, natural disasters, stressed food and energy sources, and the very real threat of asteroids devastating civilizations are making survival imperatives more prevalent in international political dialogue. Civil and scientific space projects help in understanding these natural phenomena and shaping responses, but unfortunately they languish as governments divert resources to address more immediate pressures.[19] Private capital is a potential source to invigorate space research and exploration, but the space regime's prohibition against sovereign rights on celestial bodies removes traditional financial incentives for private entities to explore and exploit such resources.[20] Earth sensing satellites, deep space sensors, and space projects that expand human presence elsewhere in the galaxy are more important to societies than ever before. The importance of spacepower is growing and changing the political calculus of governments.

In addition to these global trends, domestic factors are also changing spacepower's dynamics and influence on the strategic environment. The technological advantage and global market share of various U.S. space industries are eroding as globalization and proliferation foster new foreign space competitors. Maintaining a competitive edge is driving U.S. space service companies to innovate and seek relief from government licensing restrictions on technology exports.[21] The space launch industry has long suffered from high costs that make space-based solutions to various government and military needs unattractive and inhibit commercial exploitation of space. Smaller, netted satellites and launch projects like Falcon 1 and the X-Prize offer the prospect of reducing launch costs to very affordable levels.[22] Mass production of standard satellite buses that can host a variety of sensor and relay payloads are likely to mature in the near future. Laser communications technologies will migrate to space and expand the pool of available bandwidth, increasing data throughput, and reducing the latency of long range communications.[23] These technological advances will dramatically increase the pace of space exploitation.

National Aeronautics and Space Administration (NASA) projects continue to impress, but the media and the public have grown relatively complacent about space activities unless tragedy strikes. Conversely, Congress is anything but complacent. Emerging threats to space systems, growing defense and intelligence space budgets, satellite program failures, and Nunn-McCurdy breaches have caused Congress to exert pressure on the national security sector. As a result, defense and intelligence space acquisition policies were modified, the space roles and functions of the Services were clarified, and the DoD established the Air Force as the Executive Agent for Space, among other reforms.[24] Apparently these actions have not gone far enough. Congress again indicated that further change is needed by requiring the Secretary of Defense to conduct another independent review and assessment.[25] The resulting June 2007 report is expected to address defense space needs and efforts to fulfill those needs, ways to improve space organization and management, and the ability of DoD to execute future space missions.[26] In combination, these domestic and global space factors are having significant effects on the volatility, uncertainty, complexity, and ambiguity of the strategic environment and bringing the importance of spacepower to the forefront.

National Purpose, Space Interests, and Current Policy.

The U.S. national space purpose finds its roots in the ideals, pioneering spirit, and conflicts that forged the nation.[27] Fundamental beliefs are apparent in U.S. advocacy for an international plan to mutually control space in a way that incorporates the tenets of peaceful cooperation. Extending human presence into the virtually unexplored frontier of space invokes romantic notions of national destiny and inspires the collective U.S. technological genius.[28] The U.S. constitutional commitment to a common defense and preference for collective security arrangements includes protecting vital space interests.[29] The global spread of individual freedoms and democracy, international legal and trade regimes, reliance on cooperative international security arrangements, and a globalized economy have transformed parts of the American national purpose into values and beliefs that drive many of the world's societies.

U.S. national space interests center on free enterprise and national security. The U.S. has derived great wealth and technological benefit from its government and commercial space activities. The space domain's exploitation for national security broadened the array of remote sensing, communications, missile warning, and other satellite functions upon which U.S. military and national power depend.[30] Globalization of space enterprise has created an international space market of nearly one hundred billion dollars in annual revenues accounting for over one million jobs worldwide. One third of global space revenue and employment is attributable to the U.S. commercial space sector.[31] The U.S. Space Enterprise Council estimates that additional multi-billion dollar space business opportunities now exist in launch, metals, pharmaceutical and other sectors. Properly nurtured by government and unimpeded by law or policy, the U.S. commercial sector could maintain a technological and competitive edge and simultaneously enable advanced national security capabilities. Affordable and responsive launch, mass satellite production, applied materials and technology research, and development of pharmaceuticals are just some of the near future commercial developments with military application.[32] Wild card developments like neutrino detection satellites to detect and locate every nuclear device on the planet are also possible and would dramatically alter the strategic environment.[33] Less urgent, but no less important is a national interest in space projects motivated by survival imperatives to meet environmental challenges and expand human presence in the galaxy. Thus, American national interests in fostering a secure environment to conduct space exploration, space commerce, and enable national security are vital and shared interests with many nations.[34]

The purpose and vital space interests of the U.S. are reflected in the 2006 National Space Policy. The space policy provides a clear vision, if not initiating a grand strategy, in its declaration of guiding *principles* and *goals*.[35] The policy recommits the U.S. to ensuring freedom of access and use of space for peaceful purposes by all nations and maintains the long held rejection of sovereignty claims over outer space or celestial bodies. The policy asserts these principles to cooperatively extend space benefits to all humanity, enhance space exploration, and to protect and promote worldwide freedom. Peaceful purposes by all nations includes the right of *free passage* through space, the right to *operate in and acquire data from space . . . without interference*, and the right to conduct *defense and intelligence . . . activities in pursuit of national interests*.[36]

Consistent with these principles, the National Space Policy considers all components of space systems *vital* national interests and purposeful interference with space systems as an infringement on national rights. Therefore, the U.S. *will preserve its rights, capabilities, and freedom of action in space*. Possible actions the U.S. might take include the use of dissuasion and flexible deterrent options to counter others from impeding those rights or developing capabilities intended to do so. The U.S. will also take actions to *protect its space capabilities, respond to interference; and deny, if necessary, adversaries the use of space capabilities hostile to . . . national interests*.[37] Further, the U.S. will oppose new legal regimes, arms control agreements, or other restrictions that seek to impair its rights and prohibit or limit access to or use of space.

Based on the policy's principles, fundamental goals emerge that cut across the national security, diplomatic, civil, scientific and commercial space sectors. Focusing on national security, the goals are to *strengthen the nation's space leadership, . . . ensure that space capabilities are available in time to further . . . policy objectives*, and *enable unhindered U.S. operations in and through space to defend [national] interests.*

Goals to defend national space interests include encouraging *international cooperation*, and *use of U.S. space capabilities by friends and allies* in order to advance national security, homeland security, and foreign policy objectives. In keeping with the policy's principles and goals, the Secretary of Defense and Director of National Intelligence (DNI), in conjunction with the Secretary of State, are directed to *develop capabilities, plans, and options* and pursue *diplomacy* in order to achieve the policy's objectives.[38]

Past presidential space policies relied on ambiguous, evasive, and even contradictory language.[39] The new space policy is less timid in its clear assertion of long held principles, but judging by news dispatches registering official complaints from Moscow, Chinese anti-satellite demonstrations, and the tenor of media commentaries, the policy is widely misinterpreted. There is even a degree of contrived disinformation asserting that the space policy is clearing the way for deployment of space weapons and a unilateralist push toward U.S. domination of space.[40] The administration sought to clarify that the U.S. will continue to abide scrupulously by the outer space treaty, but the policy reflects the new realities of emerging space threats, recognizing that not all countries can be relied on to pursue exclusively peaceful space goals.[41] Despite these strategic communications, the policy is likely to remain controversial until an acceptable national security space strategy gives it substance.

Strategic Concepts and Schools of Thought.

Despite the absence of official national security space strategy, four schools of thought have dominated the shaping of policy and tenor of public discourse since the advent of spacepower.[42] They are the *Sanctuary, Survivability, High-Ground*, and *Control* schools.[43] Sanctuary stems from the premise of early nuclear deterrent strategy that defense against nuclear missiles is futile, and space, as an enabler of missile warning and arms control verification, should remain weapons-free by treaty and international law. Survivability contends that satellites are inherently vulnerable and shouldn't be depended upon for critical military functions. High-Ground rejects the mutually assured destruction nuclear deterrent strategy and asserts that space-based missile defense weapons should be used to defend against nuclear attack. Control uses sea and air power analogies oriented on allowing free passage of satellites in peacetime, but seizing control of space and achieving space superiority in time of war. Defense policy, doctrine, and culture widely trends toward versions the Control school.[44]

Two strategic concepts add a fresh perspective and alternative to the mix of strategic thought. In the book *Neither Star Wars Nor Sanctuary*, Michael O'Hanlon advocates a *Hedging* concept where the U.S. would continue to respect the current outer space regime, while simultaneously developing the capabilities needed to engage in space warfare, without being the first to deploy such weapons. If another entity crosses the space weapons line and violates the sanctuary premise, the U.S. could quickly gain control with its own deployment of space weapons.[45] Additionally, Everett Dolman in the book *Astropolitik: Classical Geopolitics in the Space Age* promotes a strategic concept called *Astropolitik* where the U.S. would withdraw from the space legal regime, replace it with a free market form of celestial sovereignty, and seize military control of low earth orbit with space weapons. These actions would establish a police blockade to control international access to space and efficiently destroy anti-satellite capabilities. Thus the U.S., as the most benign national power, could quickly create and maintain a safe operating environment, assure free access to space, and usher in a new age of space exploration replete with economic incentives for private enterprise.[46]

Given the schools and concepts above, a clearly suitable and acceptable choice for space strategy is not evident. These strategic concepts, together with defense policy and doctrine advocating space control and space force application, fuel assertions that the new space policy is clearing the way for the U.S. to weaponize and dominate space.[47] Such perceptions about U.S. spacepower exacerbate domestic and global factors that increase the strategic environment's uncertainty and volatility. Formulating valid space strategy may provide a way forward that yields a positive outcome.

Toward Valid Space Strategy and Effective Spacepower.

Formulating valid space strategy provides a vehicle to give the national space policy substance and dispel myths about U.S. intentions. Strategy formulation, by its nature, evaluates and validates the appropriateness, practicality, and consequences of policy. The formulation process informs decisionmakers of what spacepower can and cannot achieve, its associated costs and benefits, and areas of dissonance that require adjustment of either national policy, defense policy or strategy.[48] Valid space strategy must justify its objectives, the methods used to obtain them, and costs in blood and treasure when considering second and third order effects on the strategic environment. The chosen ends, ways and means must be suitable, acceptable, and feasible. Further, the level of risk must be acceptable after examining the entire logic and assessing whether the consequences of its failure or success result in a more or less favorable strategic environment.[49]

The earlier examination of space strategy's elements provides a basis to identify and assess the areas of dissonance that, if resolved, could yield valid space strategy. In the formulation of space strategy six concerns come to the fore. First, the lack of comprehensive spacepower theory contributes to the ineffective development and wielding of spacepower. Second, desired changes in the operating environment are not well understood and require better articulation. Third, selected objectives are typically improper and inappropriate. Fourth, supporting concepts and capabilities are usually unsuitable or infeasible. Fifth, typical strategic concepts and their supporting means would create effects in the operating environment that are undesirable and the associated risk is unacceptable. Finally, a tendency toward space-centric logic results in a general failure to demonstrate value and relevance to other forms of power and the outcome of events on land.

The first concern is fundamental since good strategic theory is a precursor to good strategy. Spacepower suffers from an acute malady since it lacks a theoretical foundation comparable to that of land, sea, and air power. While some have tried their hand at the theoretical foundations of spacepower and partially succeeded, the Clausewitz, Douhet, or Mahan of spacepower has yet to step forward. Consequently there is a vacuum of comprehension about the nature, structure and dynamics of spacepower, its interdependencies with other forms of national and military power, and its effects on the strategic environment across the spectrum of conflict.[50] As a result, policy is directed, doctrine promulgated, and programs resourced based on a variety of views, parochial interests, and a presumed need for space superiority and space weapons.[51] Recognizing this shortcoming, the Under Secretary of Defense (Preparation and Warning) requested that the National Defense University craft a comprehensive spacepower theory.[52] That effort is eminently needed to provide a basis for valid and enduring space strategy.

The second concern is to understand desired changes in the strategic environment that advance favorable outcomes and preclude unfavorable ones. The strategic environment exhibits complex, self organizing behavior and continuously seeks to find an acceptable order or relative balance.[53] Understanding the interdependent dynamics between spacepower and the strategic environment provides the insight and parameters to see the limitations and possibilities of space strategy and a path or multiple paths toward policy's goals. Thus space strategy must change, leverage, or overcome both global and domestic factors examined earlier and modify the strategic environment's equilibrium in a way that creates a favorable outcome.

Updating the space regime's security mechanisms to reflect the contemporary strategic environment could result in desired changes that enhance national security and stabilize international spacepower dynamics. With time, diplomacy, and objective analysis by other nations, the U.S. space policy's principles could gain universal appeal. Codifying and agreeing on these principles with Russia, China, and others might yield a needed degree of certainty and trust between spacepowers in order to reduce volatility. Treaties to ban all manner of space weapons may be naïve and ineffective over the long term, but they have mass appeal. Harnessing that popular support could provide negotiation leverage for other beneficial security agreements. For example, agreeing to a carefully defined orbital weapons ban seems plausible if certain anti-satellite and protection capabilities are not prohibited in order to defend against potential treaty violators and maintain the principle of sovereign rights. Incorporating the orbital weapons ban in a broader international space security agreement could enable a wider range of intelligence, law enforcement, economic, diplomatic, and military options to deal with purposeful interference and other hostile space acts. Such reforms and new international organizations could result in greater visibility into the operations of satellite service providers in order to detect, locate, and monitor terrorist and criminal activity or more responsively deny service and respond to purposeful interference. Other aspects of an agreement could establish conditions that justify the use of conventional military force to counter hostile space acts. These types of changes or variants of them may remove uncertainty about U.S. intentions, reduce the likelihood of a space weapons race or space warfare, facilitate national space policy objectives, and precipitate more cooperation and stability in other international affairs.

Changes in the domestic environment are also required. The national security sector organizes and manages space largely as an adjunct capability to other organizations, despite the need for specialized capacities unique to the space medium. Dedicated space professionals in military and other organizations are surely needed to fully integrate space capabilities. However, the rising importance of spacepower suggests the time may have come to execute bold leadership, visioning, and organizational change processes in order to develop people who will more effectively shape and execute America's spacepower in the 21st Century.

The third concern is ensuring space strategy objectives are properly selected, appropriate to the desired policy, and create the desired strategic effect.[54] Identifying correct objectives requires careful deliberation and should result in a marked departure from old paradigms. Attaining space superiority, unilateral space control, and applying force from space have long dominated strategic thought and defense policy.[55] However, as strategic objectives these notions may be fundamentally flawed for several important reasons.

First, they rely too heavily on analogies from other domains. These analogies do not comprehensively account for the unique medium of space with its different spatial and temporal scales, orbital physics, and operational characteristics. Space is as different from land, sea, and air as the latter are from each other.[56] Unlike the other domains, there are no territorial or international spatial distinctions to delimit space. Similarly, satellites cannot stop or maneuver around denied sovereign territory. Satellites, by their nature, inherently violate traditional notions of sovereignty and spatial control. The unique physics of the space domain and operational characteristics of satellites create multiple security dilemmas that are not easily explained away by earthly analogies.

Second, spacepower's brief history shows that the notion of space dominance invokes undesirable international actions and consequences. Pursued as an objective, space dominance or its variants are likely to create a deleterious if not catastrophic effect. Nations have grown accustomed to surrendering a small degree of sovereignty to relatively benign orbital sensors and relays given their positive effect on security and wealth. However, the specter of space weapons orbiting overhead and in the control of any single entity is a degree of sovereignty no nation is likely to surrender peacefully, no matter how benign the controlling power might be. Such coercive orbital military capabilities, particular if used to apply force to earth, probably rise to the level of a disproportionate and unprecedented military instrument.

Taken together, these considerations pose a moral challenge in adhering to the just cause, right intent, proportionality and legitimacy considerations of the Just War tradition.[57] Just as the specter of space weapons and Soviet space domination sparked the space race and the strong U.S. response in the Cold War, the same or worse reaction against U.S. space hegemony should be expected. Pursuit of unilateral U.S. space superiority would likely exacerbate perceptions of American imperialism, could permanently fracture important international relationships, and result in undesirable if not irreparable consequences. Further, the U.S. constitutional formula that separates and balances power to protect liberty and tranquility from tyranny, suggests that space dominance by any nation is antithetical to fundamental national beliefs and values.[58] Proper space strategy objectives must be congruent with these notions of peaceful international coexistence under the rule of law, balance and separation of power, and reflect the preference for collective security arrangements to protect common space interests while adhering to the *Just War* tradition.

Thus, while the new space policy does not advocate space superiority as an objective, its inculcation of defense policy and doctrine language, which does, is problematic.[59] DoD policy and doctrine advocating U.S. space control, space superiority, and force application should be expected, but these notions are advocated without a full theoretical foundation to rationalize the need for and consequences of space preeminence. This is not to say that objectives to establish some form of a controlled and stable space operating environment or the capacity to protect and defend space interests are not needed. It is to say that adopting current language from defense policy and doctrine into space strategy is probably not acceptable. Different paradigms are needed to formulate more appropriate objectives and temper cultural tendencies toward unilateralist space dominance objectives.

The fourth concern is to formulate strategy that relies on strategic concepts and capabilities that are suitable and feasible.[60] Following the pattern of the land, sea, and air domains, conflict is likely to spill over into space.[61] The history of warfare explains the predominant defense establishment view that space warfare is inevitable, and space control is the linchpin for military spacepower. However, enabling higher strategy and defending our space interests does not necessarily lead to selection of space warfare with orbital space weapons as the ways and means of choice for space strategy, even if a *casus beli* arises to justify space warfare.[62] As discussed earlier, while the high vantage of satellites for sensor and relay functions gives them their value, the same high vantage is also a vulnerability making them easily targeted and engaged. The same vulnerability holds true for orbital space weapons. Orbital satellite weapons, whether intended for space to space engagements or application of force to earth, are readily negated by earth based attack. Additionally, launch facilities, ground control sites, and communication links also present points of vulnerability to defeat an orbital weapon system. Modifying land, sea, and air capabilities for anti-satellite purposes or orchestrating the employment of joint forces against other segments of a space weapon system provide effective alternatives to orbital space weapons at less operational risk and cost. This basic argument makes the pursuit of orbital space weapon systems unsuitable for space strategy.

However, defending and protecting space systems from lethal or non-lethal attacks requires timely and precise information to discriminate purposeful interference from unintentional actions, quickly assess the impacts for operational commanders, identify and locate the offender, and orchestrate a rapid and effective response. This makes space situational awareness capabilities the prime concern for military spacepower's means. It is technically and fiscally feasible to field distributed and networked sensor and relay constellations hosted on small satellites to serve as unarmed space sentries, scouts, or target designators. The right combination of human, technical, and electronic intelligence along with netted orbital sensors and relays could provide timely, quality information to orchestrate rapid defensive and offensive responses to hostile acts.

In the event an adversary decides to employ orbital weapons or ground-based anti-satellite capabilities, operational risk posed by the loss of key satellite capabilities is readily mitigated by means other than space weapons. Affordable and responsive launch vehicles, mass production of satellite buses for a variety of standard payloads, networked arrays of small satellite sensors and relays, and balancing the space layer with interdependent high altitude and aerial layers are just a few of the ways to mitigate satellite dependence without resorting to space weapons. Therefore, barring some other compelling consideration or a wild card, it is hard to rationalize and justify the development and deployment of orbital space weapons as acceptable, suitable, and feasible means of valid space strategy.

The final issue is formulating a space strategy that is integrated with and valuable to the application of other elements of military and national power across the spectrum of terrestrial conflict. Space strategic concepts often suffer from space-centric logic or sea and air power analogies that devolve into the realm of space warfare tactics. People live on land and belong to politically organized terrestrial security communities, so military power has strategic meaning only to the extent its effects are relevant to the outcome of conflict on and with respect to land.[63] While conflict might precipitate from activities in space, spacepower alone is insufficient to determine outcomes across the spectrum of human conflict.[64] This strategy logic is geographically universal and temporally eternal.[65] Thus space strategy must not only be valid, it must influence the outcome of events on land. This requires space strategy that demonstrates value to the prosecution of higher strategy and broader policy, and development of interdependent spacepower capabilities that add synergy to the application of other military and national power.

Recommendations and Conclusion.

Given this examination and assessment, there are six broad recommendations that encompass theory and strategy, DoD processes, and international cooperation. These recommendations should be considered in total since they holistically build on one another. The first two recommendations deal with higher level theory and strategy. First, the DoD should complete current spacepower theory development efforts and promulgate the results for joint education, defense culture assimilation, and further refinement. Second, building on spacepower theory and considering the arguments of this assessment, the Secretary of Defense, in collaboration with the DNI and Secretary of State, should propose an interagency effort to develop several space strategy options and promulgate a National Security Space Strategy under the auspices of the National Security Council's Space Policy Coordination Committee (PCC). The Space PCC should ensure the strategy effort is carefully unveiled through a thoughtful strategic communications and foreign diplomacy plan in order to minimize adverse reaction from external actors. The formulation process should identify and resolve areas of dissonance between the National Space Policy, defense policy, doctrine, and the chosen strategy. Based on the selected strategy, the State Department should begin international deliberations aimed at modifying the current space regime.

The next two recommendations deal with defense processes. First, the Chairman of the Joint Chiefs of Staff should introduce the National Security Space Strategy into defense's Joint Strategic Planning System in order to drive a National Military Space Strategy, assist in formulating the Chairman's strategic guidance and assessments, inform the Chairman's planning and programming advice, and guide the activities of the Functional Capability Boards and Joint Requirements Oversight Council. The space strategies should also cause alignment of corresponding activities in defense planning and resourcing, capabilities integration and development, and joint concept development processes. Second, the Chairman needs to ensure the joint concept development process specifically produces a Joint Integrating Concept for Space that complements the space strategies in order to synchronize Service concept development and related force generation activities.

The last two recommendations focus on complementary interagency and global efforts that can be done in parallel or subsequent to the strategy effort. First, after reaching agreement with Russia and China, the State Department and NASA should secure the support of all space faring nations and establish an International Space Exploitation and Settlement Agency (ISESA). The ISESA should develop a bold shared vision that will inspire the world with aggressive cooperative space exploitation projects. Projects considered might include ways to mitigate global warming, divert threatening asteroids, or conduct a manned exploration of mars. The ISESA should also create licensing and revenue sharing schemes to foster exploitation of celestial bodies by private enterprise and public-private partnerships while still maintaining celestial sovereignty prohibitions. The ISESA and its projects would build confidence and trust between the U.S., Russia, and China. The agency could lay the groundwork for a new outer space regime built on economic interests and financial incentives rather than military concerns. Second, building on other international security cooperation efforts, the DoD and State Department should take the necessary actions to establish an International Space Security Organization (ISSO). The security cooperation effort should focus on combined space situational awareness operations with supporting reconnaissance and surveillance efforts. ISSO activities could involve collaborative development and employment of affordable and responsive launch, mass produced satellite buses and payloads, netted small satellite constellations, and a globally networked support infrastructure. Future efforts could include complementary legislative reforms, intelligence sharing, development of law enforcement mechanisms, and formation of other partnerships to strengthen international consequences for purposeful interference and hostile space acts. To the extent Russia and China are included, the ISSO could enable transparency into space activities, ameliorate space related political tensions, and reduce the likelihood of space conflict.

In conclusion, this chapter has shown that spacepower remains misunderstood, underdeveloped and underexploited despite the dramatic advances realized since the launch of Sputnik in 1957 and the race to the moon. Spacepower offers the prospect of tremendous benefits to peace, prosperity and stability in the 21st Century. However, spacepower introduces new challenges and dynamics that, left unattended, increase the volatility of the strategic environment and are likely to precipitate armed conflict on earth or in space. Failure to understand the nature of spacepower and how to wield it productively could lead to serious miscalculations and tragic consequences. Some aspects of this paper's assessment and recommendations may, with time and closer scrutiny, require reexamination. Nonetheless, the intentional thrust in a new direction is needed. Formulation of valid space strategy provides the mechanism to find the right path through the strategic environment and marshal the forces of the DoD, nation and the world toward a positive outcome.

ENDNOTES - CHAPTER 20

1. Colin S. Gray, "The Grammar Of Strategy, II: Altitude And Electrons," in *Modern Strategy*, Oxford: University Press, 1999, p. 258.

2. *Ibid.*, p. 257.

3. Everett C. Dolman, "Shaping the Outer Space Regime: Then And Now," in *Astropolitik: Classical Geopolitics in the Space Age*, Portland, OR: Frank Cass, 2002, pp. 113-141; Gray, pp. 254-256.

4. Gray, pp. 254-256.

5. James E. Oberg, *Space Power Theory*, Colorado Springs: U.S. Air Force Academy, 1999, p. 2.; Gray, pp. 255-256.

6. Dolman, pp. 12-16.

7. Walter A. McDougall, "A New Era of History and a Media Riot" and "A Space Strategy For The United States" in *The Heavens And The Earth: A Political History of the Space Age*, Baltimore: Johns Hopkins University Press, 1985, pp. 141-209.

8. *Ibid.*

9. Dolman, pp. 113-141.

10. Oberg, p. 124.

11. *Ibid.*, pp. 60-64.

12. Peter B. De Selding, "French Minister Urges 50% Hike in Space Spending," *Defense News*, March 5, 2007.

13. Oberg, pp. 124-125.

14. Bill Gertz, "Moscow, Beijing Eye Space Weapons," *Washington Times*, January 17, 2007; James Oberg, "The Dozen Space Weapons Myths," *Space Review*, March 12, 2007; P. R. Chari, "Wars in Space," *The Times of India*, March 9, 2007; Dale Anderson, "China ASAT: Space Preservation or Space Destruction," *Space Review*, March 12, 2007.

15. The Associated Press, "Iran's Space Program Raises Fears of Missiles," *AIM Points*, March 2007 (journal on-line), available from *http://aimpoints.hq.af.mil*, Internet, accessed March 20, 2007.

16. Raphael Perl, *Narco-Terrorism: International Drug Trafficking and Terrorism – A Dangerous Mix*, Testimony presented to the U.S. Congress, Senate, Committee on the Judiciary, Washington, DC: Congressional Research Service, May 20, 2003.

17. Bill Gertz, "Officials Fear War in Space by China," *Washington Times*, January 24, 2007; Times Wire Reports, "Official Confirms Anti-Satellite Test," *Los Angeles Times*, January 23, 2007; Peter N. Spotts, "Alarm Over China's Arms Pursuit – In Space," *Christian Science Monitor*, November 20, 2006.

18. Guy Webster, "Mars' South Pole Ice Deep and Wide," March 15, 2007, linked from the *National Aeronautics and Space Administration Home Page* at "Mission News," available from *http://www.nasa.gov/mission_pages/mars/new/mars-20070315_prt.htm*, Internet, accessed March 20, 2007.

19. Dolman, pp. 137-138.

20. *Ibid.*

21. *International Traffic in Arms Regulation*, vol. 22, sec. 38, 1993; John W. Vinter, "Meeting Minutes," Commercial Space Transportation Advisory Committee, Washington DC, October 25, 2006.

22. Vinter, pp. 1-9.; Jeremy Singer, "Responsive Space: Making space launch faster, easier, and cheaper sounds simple. It's not.," *Air Force Magazine*, March 2006 (journal on-line), available from *http://integrator.hanscom.af.mil/2006/March/03022006/03022006-18.htm*, Internet, accessed March 23, 2007.

23. Tony Ruggiero, "Laser Zaps Communication Bottleneck," *Science and Technology Review*, December 2002 (journal on-line), available from *www.llnl.gov/str/December02/Ruggiero.html*, Internet, accessed March 23, 2007.

24. Commission Members, *Report of the Commission to Assess United States National Security Space Management and Organization, Executive Summary*, Library of Congress, January 2001, i – E1; Donald Rumsfeld, *Letter to The Honorable John Warner, Chairman, Committee on Armed Services*, Washington, DC: U.S. Department of Defense, May 2001, pp. 1-3.

25. National Defense Authorization Act for Fiscal Year 2004, sec 913, 2006.

26. *Ibid.*

27. Steven Lambakis, *On the Edge of Earth: The Future Of American Space Power*, Lexington, KY: University Press, 2001, pp. 5-7, 73-75.

28. *Ibid.*, pp. 211-216.

29. Williamson Murray, MacGregor Knox, and Alvin Bernstein, *The Making of Strategy*, Cambridge: University Press, 1994, pp. 208-216.

30. Frank G. Klotz, "Space, Commerce, and National Security," *Council on Foreign Relations Paper*, 1998, pp. 1-15.

31. U.S. Census Bureau, "The 2007 Statistical Abstract, The National Data Book," available from *www.census.gov/compendia/satab/science_technology/space/*, Internet, accessed March 20, 2007.

32. Phillip J. Bond, *Market Opportunities in Space: The Near-Term Roadmap*, Speech presented at the Commercial Space Workshop, U.S. Chamber of Commerce, Washington, DC: Under Secretary of Commerce for Technology, November 7, 2001.

33. Oberg, *Space Power Theory*, p.131.

34. The new National Space Policy defines all Space Capabilities and their supporting infrastructure as "vital" and describes them as comprised of national security, commercial, and scientific sector space capabilities.

35. George W. Bush, *U.S. National Space Policy*, Washington, DC: The White House, August 2006, pp. 1-2.

36. *Ibid.*

37. *Ibid.*

38. *Ibid.*, pp. 2-7.

39. Dolman, p. 155.

40. Bill Gertz, "Moscow, Beijing Eye Space Weapons"; James Oberg, "The Dozen Space Weapons Myths" ; P. R. Chari, "Wars in Space."

41. Agence France-Presse, "U.S. Opposes Ban on Weapons in Space," *Defense News*, December 13, 2006.

42. John J. Klein, *Space Warfare: Strategy, Principles and Policy*, New York: Rutledge, 2006, pp. 16-18; David E. Lupton, *On Space Warfare: A Space Power Doctrine*, Maxwell Air Force Base, AL: Air University Press, 1988, pp. 51-121.

43. Lupton, pp. 51-121.

44. Examples of this trend are found in Klein; Larry J. Schaefer, "Sustained Space Superiority: A National Strategy for the United States," Occasional Paper No. 30, Air War College, August 2002.

45. Michael E. O'Hanlon, *Neither Star Wars nor Sanctuary: Constraining the Military Uses of Space*, Washington, DC: Brookings Institution Press, 2004, pp. 133-147.

46. Dolman, pp. 12-54, 156-165.

47. The Joint Staff, *Joint Doctrine for Space Operations,* Joint Publication 3-14, Washington, DC: U.S. Department of Defense, August 9, 2002, pp. ix-x.

48. *Ibid*, pp. 6-7.

49. Harry R. Yarger, "Strategic Theory for the 21st Century: The Little Book On Big Strategy," *The Letort Papers*, February 2006, pp. 65-71.

50. Gray, pp. 258, 254-256.

51. This is the author's assessment from many years of working various DoD and Army space policy, programs, doctrine, and operational issues.

52. Deputy Under Secretary of Defense, Preparation, and Warning Thomas Behling, "Space Power Theory," memorandum for President, National Defense University, Washington, DC, February 13, 2006.

53. Yarger, pp. 17-48.

54. *Ibid.*, pp. 48-55.

55. Multiple DoD Instructions, Joint and Service publications establish *space superiority, space control, and space force application* as the key terms and definitions in the policy, doctrine and conceptual lexicon of the department to describe space programs, functions, and purpose.

56. Gray, p. 260.

57. Anthony E. Hartle, *Moral Issues In Military Decision Making*, Kansas City: University Press, 2004, pp. 96-97.

58. Murray *et al.*, p. 211.

59. The national space policy uses "Space Control" and "Force Application" language in its specific guidance to DoD. This is a lift from defense policy and doctrine which presumes a military need to achieve space superiority and control of space.

60. Yarger, pp. 66-71.

61. Gray, pp. 258-259.

62. Hartle, pp. 96-97.

63. *Ibid.*, pp. 256, 258-259.

64. Oberg, *Space Power Theory*, p. 127.

65. Gray, p. 259.

CHAPTER 21

NETWORK-CENTRIC WARFARE:
LEVERAGING THE POWER OF INFORMATION

Jeffrey L. Groh

> . . . the general unreliability of all information presents a special problem in war: All action takes place, so to speak, in a kind of twilight, which like fog or moonlight, often tends to make things seem grotesque and larger than they really are.
>
> Whatever is hidden from full view in this feeble light has to be guessed at by talent, or simply left to chance. So once again for lack of objective knowledge one has to trust to talent or to luck.
>
> Clausewitz[1]

What is all this fuss about network-centric organizations? Is Network-Centric Warfare an "emerging theory of war" or just about technology? Is it possible to harness the power of information to gain a significant advantage in the operational environment? Scholars, politicians, appointed government officials and warfighters are lining up to take sides on the utility of information sharing and networking U.S. military forces.[2] The business community continues to grapple with knowledge management, business process management, information technology (IT), and enterprise networking to gain a competitive advantage in the market place.[3] There is a plethora of literature documenting how IT is enabling innovation in business as well as the military.[4] It is time to continue the dialogue and raise the awareness of the benefits of network-centric operations as an enabler to gain a competitive advantage over current and potential adversaries in the 21st century. If we agree that Clausewitz is correct about the unreliability of battlefield information, could Network-Centric Warfare concepts and capabilities improve this situation? The Department of Defense (DoD) has decided to pursue an aggressive policy to develop network centric warfare (NCW) capabilities as a "source of warfighting advantage."

This chapter argues that DoD is on the right track to pursue advanced integrated information technology to enable warfighting in the future. This chapter does not argue that information systems and technology are the panacea to solve all the complex issues associated with warfare in the 21st century. This chapter begins with a brief discussion of the fundamental concept of network-centric warfare and the current Department of Defense policy for networking the force. Then, the chapter will investigate the potential of information and knowledge sharing on the battlefield to provide a competitive advantage against potential adversaries. There are tactical, operational, and strategic implications[5] to sharing information and networking the force within the operational environment. This chapter would not be complete without addressing a few of the most prevalent arguments by those who caution against relying on information technology and networking. The final section will outline a few recommendations to proceed with the implementation of network-centric warfare.

Network Centric Warfare (NCW): Developing a Concept.

It should not be a secret that the world is squarely in the age of information. One only needs to view the nightly news, scan the newspapers, or pick up the latest technology books and trade journals to understand the magnitude of corporate investments in information systems. "Worldwide, businesses spend nearly $1 trillion a year on IT gear, software, and services—more than $2 trillion if telecommunications services are included."[6] The enormity of the spending by corporations around the world on new ways to capture, store, and share information inside and outside of organizations continues to increase since the turn of the century. The Department of Defense is well aware of the potential benefits of sharing information and knowledge to generate competitive advantage.

There is a significant body of literature that addresses the benefit of sharing information on the battlefield to develop a common operating picture. It is not possible to conduct an exhaustive review of the literature related to NCW in this short article. However, it is important to review some of the seminal works that establish the fundamental underpinnings of this emerging and dynamic concept. The Office of Force Transformation, Office of Secretary of Defense, as well as the DoD Command and Control Research Program are two of the conceptual leaders developing the theory of Network-Centric Warfare. The publication from the Office of Force Transformation, *Implementation of Network-Centric Warfare*, released in January 2005, establishes the current thinking on NCW, by providing "answers to some of the fundamental questions regarding NCW as emerging theory of war in the information age."[7]

There is a significant body of knowledge published by the Command and Control Research Program that provides the theoretical development of the concepts of Network-Centric Warfare for the Office of the Secretary of Defense.[8] One should begin the journey to examine the potential of NCW by closely reading the book authored by Dr. David Alberts, Mr. John Garstka, and Mr. Fred Stein titled, *Network Centric Warfare: Developing and Leveraging Information Superiority*. A careful reading of the book will explain the purpose and concept of NCW, how NCW has the potential to leverage information age technologies, and a methodology to implement the concept over time.[9] The authors proposed this early concept of NCW as a point of departure:

> NCW is about human and organizational behavior. NCW is based on adopting a new way of thinking—network-centric thinking—and applying it to military operations. NCW focuses on the combat power that can be generated from the effective linking or networking of the warfighting enterprise. It is characterized by the ability of geographically dispersed forces (consisting of entities) to create a high level of shared battlespace awareness that can be exploited via self-synchronization and other network-centric operations to achieve commanders' intent.[10]

The publications in 1998 set the stage for the intellectual debate on the potential of NCW as a new way to examine the conduct of war in the 21st century with networked forces and enhanced situational awareness.

NCW is about warfighting in the 21st century. It is about warfare in the information age. There are significant new information technologies that enable commanders to know more about the enemy, plan faster, make decisions faster, and synchronize sensors and shooters to create desired effects on the battlefield. David Alberts, in *Information Age Transformation*, conducts a thorough analysis of what warfare will entail in the 21st century; he postulates the challenges with warfare in the information domain. "As the global society enters the information age, military operations are inevitably impacted and transformed. Satellite communications, video teleconferencing, battlefield facsimile machines, digital communications systems, personal computers, the Global Positioning System, and dozens of other transforming tools are already commonplace."[11] The question then becomes how to transform a military force with the appropriate capabilities to operate in this new environment. The author proposes that the following NCW tenets should guide the adoption of information technologies and transformation:

- A robustly networked force improves information sharing.
- Information sharing and collaboration enhance the quality of information and shared awareness.
- Shared situational awareness enables self-synchronization.
- These, in turn, dramatically increase mission effectiveness.[12]

Alberts presents these tenets espousing the potential benefits of information sharing, networking, and enhanced situational awareness as organizing functions to transform the force in the information age. These tenets provide a series of research questions to analyze case studies to investigate the potential benefits of a networked force.[13]

Alberts and Hayes continued to expand the idea of the inherent benefits of sharing information in a networked environment in their next book titled, *Power to the Edge: Command, Control in the Information Age*. The book argues that current command and control relationships, organizations, and systems are just not up to the task of executing warfare in the information age.[14] It is critical to push essential decision-making information out to the "edges" of the organization. "*Power to the Edge* is about changing the way individuals, organizations, and systems relate to one another and work. 'Power to the Edge' involves the empowerment of individuals at the edge of an organization (where the organization interacts with its operating environment to have an impact or effect on that environment) or, in the case of systems, edge devices."[15] The ubiquitous nature of IT makes the vision of achieving "Power to the Edge" possible. The transition from strictly hierarchical organizational structures is already underway. The Army's restructuring to smaller more lethal Brigade Combat Teams and Stryker Brigades takes advantage of more powerful networks to push information and thus greater situational awareness out to the edges of organizations.

The power of the network has provided new and innovative approaches to command and control organizations. One needs only to review the legendary actions of small Special Forces Teams on horseback during Operation Enduring Freedom to see the power of interdependent edge organizations networked to accomplish desired effects on the battlefield.[16] Small Special Forces Teams operating with satellite communications equipment (data and voice) synchronized joint fires to attack targets. Special Forces Teams adroitly coordinated and laser designated targets for Joint Direct Attack Munitions from F-14, F-15E, B-1, and B-2 airframes during Operation ENDURING FREEDOM (OEF) with devastating results and accuracy.[17] The relationship between sensors (Special Operating Forces, Predator, and Global Hawk) and shooters (AC 130, B-1, armed *Predators*, numerous USAF fighter assets) linked through a network to command and control demonstrates the potential benefits of the concept. This is but one example of the future potential of a networked force that pushes critical information to those that need it when they need to accomplish tasks in the operational environment. The U.S. military is in the early stages of understanding the full potential of network-centric warfare and sharing knowledge out to the edges of an organization i.e., *Power to the Edge* becoming a reality.

This brief NCW literature review would not be complete without mentioning the Network Centric Operations Conceptual Framework Version 2.0. There are numerous critics of NCW calling for academic rigor to be applied to this emerging concept. There is a need to develop a framework to produce metrics that can empirically measure the efficiency and effectiveness of NCW. It is important to validate where to spend finite defense dollars to achieve the greatest possible return on investment.

As a consequence, OFT [the Office of Force Transformation] and OASD-NII [Office of the Assistant Secretary of Defense, Networks & Information Integration] began collaborating on an effort to develop metrics to test hypotheses in the NCW value chain. The primary objective was to develop a rich and comprehensive set of

NCW-related metrics that could be used in experimentation and other research endeavors to gather evidence. This evidence then could be used in experimentation and other research endeavors across the DOTML-PF [doctrine, organization, training, materiel, leadership and education, personnel and facilities] spectrum. This effort resulted in the development of a Conceptual Framework for Network Centric Operations and a variety of other NCO-related research, outreach and publications.[18]

This document begins to address a more rigorous approach to measure the efficiency and effectiveness of NCW. This framework may provide measures of effectiveness and performance to truly measure the benefits of NCW in the future.

The Network Centric Operations Conceptual Framework (NCO-CF) proposes a series of concept definitions, attributes and metrics to measure numerous elements of NCW based on the NCO-CF:

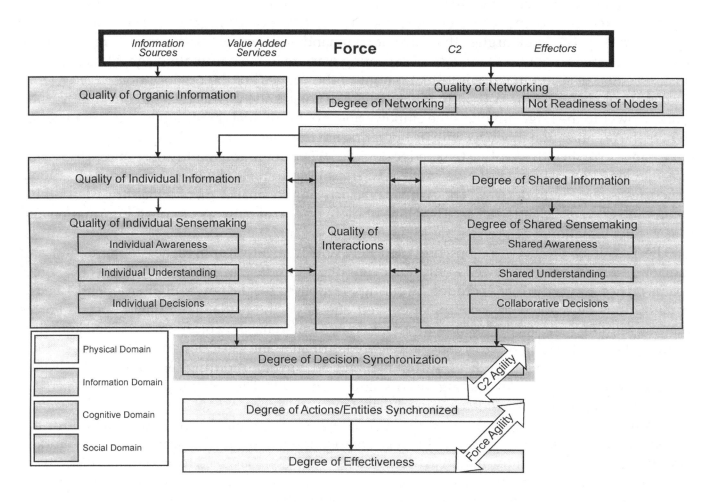

Figure 1. The Network Centric Operations Conceptual Framework.[19]

The NCO-CF defines each concept and attribute and recommends a quantifiable metric for each. The draft schema presented in the NCO-CF is complex and untested. It is however, a step in the right direction. This framework goes well beyond the general assertions of efficiency and effectiveness outlined in the NCW Tenets. The NCO-CF "provides basis for quantitative exploration and/or assessment of NCW hypotheses; and investment strategies and other DOTML-PF related issues."[20]

It will take a substantial effort to validate the attributes and metrics proposed in the NCO-CF. The metrics for many of the attributes are based on a Likert scale i.e., a scale of 1-5. There is a degree of subjectivity involved with assigning a value to the attribute. How does one truly measure quality, consistency, currency, precision, completeness, accuracy, relevance and timeliness of information? These attributes begin to investigate, experiment, and test metrics. However, the next step must be to gather a committee of experts to further define the attributes and metrics based on more objective criteria. Another approach is to begin gathering data using the proposed attributes and metrics to determine the validity of the framework. This work has already begun with the publication of the *Network-Centric Operations Case Study: the Stryker Brigade Combat Team.*[21] This report along with the NCW Operation Iraqi Freedom case, *A Network-Centric Operations Case Study: US/UK Coalition Combat Operations during Operation Iraqi Freedom,* as well as other cases published in 2007, points out the difficulties of applying the attributes and metrics of the NCO-CF in an empirical study. [22]

The latest publication to explain the potential of NCW and NCO as an emerging theory of war is the Office of Force Transformation (OFT) publication *The Implementation of Network-Centric Warfare.* This publication by the OFT touts NCW as an "emerging theory of warfare in the information age." The authors bring the numerous concepts associated with NCW, outlined in this compressed literature review, into a concise framework. The purpose of the framework is to begin to work the fundamental hypothesis of Network-Centric Warfare. "The working hypothesis of network-centric warfare (NCW) as an emerging theory of war, simply stated, is that the behavior of forces, i.e., their choices of organization relationships and processes, when in the networked condition, will outperform forces that are not." [23] It is important to review this work in order to have a meaningful dialogue about the potential of Network-Centric Warfare as an emerging theory of warfare.

The hypothesis stated above focuses on several critical variables prior to discussing the issue of a "networked force." Many critics of NCW focus mainly on the technology aspect of NCW.[24] However, NCW is much more than the information technology. First, NCW entails examining organizational relationships and processes. Then, highly effective and efficient organizations are networked to leverage shared knowledge and information in the operational environment. A balanced and holistic assessment of NCW is called for to determine the potential of this concept on the modern battlefield.

The human behavior variable remains a crucial aspect of NCW. "The implementation of NCW is first and foremost about human behavior as opposed to information technology. While "network" is a noun, "to network" is a verb. Thus, when we examine the degree to which a particular military organization, or the Department as a whole, is exploiting the power of NCW, our focus should be on human behavior in the networked environment."[25] This publication goes into considerable detail outlining the numerous benefits of networking humans to share information and knowledge. NCW is all about connecting individuals across the operational environment to leverage information age technologies to reduce the "fog and friction of war." There is no attempt to imply that all of the fog and friction of war can be eliminated through networking forces. "This will not be the case. Rather, the issue is how one creates and exploits an information advantage within the context of the fog and friction of war."[26] However, there is a case to be examined that linking warfighters together on the battlefield may increase speed of command and synchronize dispersed forces to more efficiently and effectively accomplish objectives. Therefore, although the reliance on technology is apparent when discussing the potential of NCW, it is important to examine the literature as it relates to the human dimension of the concept.

The OFT publication *Implementation of Network-Centric Warfare* goes further to outline the importance of human behavior in NCW by investigating the tenets of NCW. Figure 2 demonstrates the important relationship between the information domain, the cognitive and social domains, and the physical domains. The essence of the concept can be realized by understanding these relationships. The information domain is where data, information, and knowledge are created, manipulated and shared among warfighters. The cognitive domain is where the data, information, and knowledge are manipulated in the mind of the warfighter. The all important social domain is where the interaction between humans occurs. "This is also the domain of culture, the set of values, aptitudes, and beliefs held and conveyed by leaders to the society, whether military or civil."[27] An understanding of the relationship between the information, cognitive and social domains begins to address the core principles of NCW as they relate to the physical domain i.e., mission accomplishment.

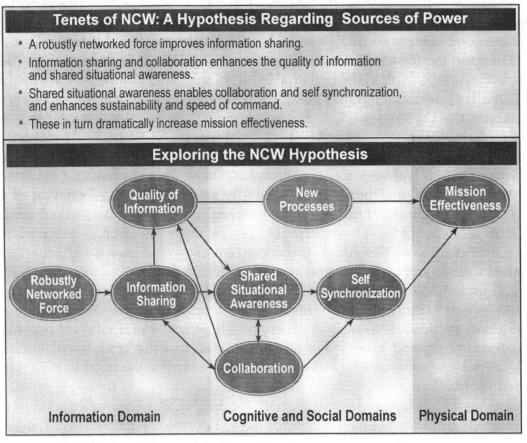

Figure 2. Tenets of NCW and the Value.

The human behavior aspect of this schema is central to understanding NCW as a "source of Warfighting advantage." The networked force enables information sharing, shared awareness, and self synchronization within the information domain. The real warfighting and decision-making functions remain in the cognitive and social domains. Is there any evidence that units are actually operating within this framework?

The Office of Force Transformation has set out to document the fact that units are already operating in a network centric operational framework. OFT is developing numerous NCO case studies that apply the NCO-CF, gather data, and analyze evidence. It is beyond the scope of this paper to review all of the case studies. However, the results of Ground Operations (Stryker Bridge Combat Team) will illustrate the potential benefits of NCW. The case study explored the hypothesis that "the NCO capabilities of the Stryker Brigade Combat Team (SBCT) would enable information and decision superiority and increase force effectiveness."[29] The conditions for the test were an operational environment (Small Scale Contingency) at the Joint Readiness and Training Center (JRTC) conducted in May 2003. The baseline for this study was to compare the SBCT against a non-digitized light infantry brigade. The study measured the quality of effectiveness of command and control based on the degree of situational awareness, speed of command, quality of decisions, and force self-synchronization.[30]

The results of the study are impressive. It is important to note that 75 percent of the SBCT had networked battle command systems. A few of the most interesting findings are the following:

- Friendly vs. enemy casualty ratio decreased from a normal JRTC rotation with a light infantry brigade from 10:1 to 1:1;
- Acceleration of speed of command from 24 to three hours in engagements;
- Increase in individual/shared information quality from 10% to 80%.[31]

The results only begin to scratch the surface of potential benefits of fully networked forces. One can argue the rigor, conditions, standards, and data gathering methods for this study. However, these results should stimulate additional rigorous experiments to validate the return on investment of maneuvering a networked force. The Army has yet to fully determine the actual benefits and effectiveness of the networked SBCTs serving in Operation IRAQI FREEDOM. It will be interesting to compare the results from this JRTC study, quantitative and qualitative, to the data collected in Iraq in ongoing counterinsurgency operations. It should then be possible to acquire a better understanding of the effectiveness of a networked force in an actual combat environment. Also, there is much more work to be done to analyze the potential benefits of networked forces at the operational and strategic levels of war.

Network-Centric Warfare: The Silver Bullet?

Now that the literature review is complete, it is possible to investigate the potential of NCW. This author has not found any proponents of NCW touting that this concept is the "Silver Bullet" to solve all the problems of future warfare. Many of the same problems that have plagued warfighters in the past exist today and will exist in the future: fog and friction, competing advances in technologies, the unpredictable nature of human behavior on the battlefield, and asymmetric warfare to name only a few. The issue isn't the existence of these challenges to modern warfare but how one exploits the advantages of information to mitigate risk and take advantage of strengths in the force to achieve objectives.[32] Are the potential benefits of NCW worth the opportunity costs associated with aggressively moving forward with the implementation of this new concept?

The concept of Network Centric Warfare has already moved beyond the "bumper sticker" stage. NCW is not a fad that will go quietly into the night. There is little doubt that significant finite resources are being expended to pursue NCW capabilities. DoD spending in the area of communications and electronics is approaching the $65 Billion level for 2007.[33] There may be changes to terminology, shifts in policy, and alterations in implementation plans. However, the core concepts that relate to leveraging the power of information will remain. DoD and senior military leaders have been consistent in their support of a networked force. Former Secretary of Defense Donald Rumsfeld concisely stated the importance a fully networked force in the *Transformation Planning Guidance*. "We must achieve: fundamentally joint, network-centric, distributed forces capable of rapid decision superiority and massed effects across the operational environment. Realizing these capabilities will require transforming our people, processes, and military forces."[34] ADM Giambastiani, USN, (Retired) and former Commander U.S. Joint Forces Command stated, "A fully collaborative and networked force is an imperative, not a luxury."[35] The Commandant of the U.S. Marine Corps, General Michael Haggee said, "The capability to connect disparate units spread over the battlefield will help to provide intelligence, surveillance and reconnaissance to commanders who can then call in fire support. . . . Information Technology (IT) will also be critical to Sea Basing, a key component of the Navy's Sea Power 21 Concept."[36] The Army's Training and Doctrine commander, General William S. Wallace, stated that,

The advantages of using a network in military operations are numerous and should be recognized. First, the network allows greater and faster collaboration among commanders and staffs at all levels, empowering them to exercise greater initiative in accordance with commander's intent. Second, the commander can receive better displays of the situation without having to send multiple requests for information to subordinates, thus allowing warfighters to focus on accomplishing their missions. Additionally, the commander can share the basis for his or her situational understanding with subordinates and staff. Finally, the network can give commanders unprecedented freedom to circulate on the battlefield among subordinate commanders and soldiers without losing essential connectivity to the information and analysis necessary for command.[37]

General Wallace goes on to caution that "despite the enormous benefits of using a network, it would be folly to lose sight of the fact that it is still merely a tool to aid the commander in understanding and decision-making."[38] The question is not if DoD will proceed with NCW, but how.

The NCW Way Ahead.

The DoD has a plan for the implementation of NCW. The plan calls for a holistic approach to the implementation of NCW that investigates the potential of NCO in joint, multinational, and interagency operations. As previously discussed in this paper, there has been a significant effort to establish the theoretical underpinnings of the concept. The most recent publication, *Implementation of Network-Centric Warfare,* establishes the outline of the plan to move forward with NCW. The next part of the process was to begin to study the tenets of NCW through case studies. Additionally, the Services are working to integrate information systems, sensors, and decision-making processes and technology to leverage the capabilities of a fully networked joint force. The Air Force Command and Control Constellation network is an example of the integration of C2; ISR; tankers; space, ground, and sea-based systems; and strike platforms to achieve shared awareness in the operational environment to maximize effects.[39] Constellation works with FORCEnet (U.S. Navy), and LandWarNet (U.S. Army) to achieve synergy on the battlefield.

It is not in the scope of this paper to examine all of the specific sub-elements of the implementation plan for NCW. However, there are several key pieces that provide a flavor for the journey ahead. It is important to remember that NCW is in fact a journey and not a particular destination. This is a dynamic process. Theories will be tested, concepts will be modified, technology will continue to advance, and budgeting priorities will shift over time. The overall path leads to a convergence of disparate sensor and command and control systems to create synergy among the numerous joint information systems. Many of the critics of NCW focus solely on the technology aspect of the concept. This is a short sited approach to a complex transformation in thinking about warfare to leverage technology to gain a competitive advantage over potential adversaries. "Progress in implementing network-centric warfare cannot be measured solely by focusing on one dimension, such as technology or doctrine. Rather, progress must be assessed in terms of the maturity of mission capabilities, that integrate key elements of DOTMLPF (Doctrine, Organization, Training, Materiel [technology], Leadership and Education, Personnel, and Facilities)."[40]

A program that highlights the potential advantages of NCW is the Force XXI Battle Command Brigade and Below (FBCB2/BFT) Blue Force Tracking systems. FBCB2/BFT was used extensively during Operation Iraqi Freedom to monitor the maneuver of U.S. Army, U.S. Marine, U.S. Special Forces, and British ground forces during the conflict. FBCB2/BFT uses the global positioning system and numerous sensors to pinpoint units on the battlefield. This capability provided unprecedented situational awareness to commanders at all levels on the battlefield. The qualitative data acquired from interviews with those on the ground validates the utility of acquiring better situational awareness. Leaders from General Tommy Franks, U.S.A. (Ret) down to battalion and company commanders marveled at the ability to track unit progress during major combat operations.[41] The data available through FBCB2/BFT allowed commanders to quickly adjust to changing operational conditions and manage complex logistical situations.[42]

The Global Information Grid-Bandwidth Expansion (GIG-BE) program will provide the backbone to facilitate NCO in the future. It is difficult to discuss NCW without touching on the importance of the GIG-BE. GIG-BE is the technology that will facilitate numerous NCW initiatives in the years ahead. MG Marilyn Quaglotti, former Vice Director of the Defense Information Agency (DISA), described the vision for the GIG as a single secure grid providing seamless end-to-end capabilities to all warfighting, national security and support users.[43] DISA achieved full operational capability of the GIG-BE in December 2005.[44]

It is essential to continue the development of the GIG-BE to realize the potential benefits of NCW. GIG-BE provides the necessary technology to facilitate the interaction of sensors, linked to command and control, to effectively engage shooter platforms to achieve desired effects on the battlefield. GIG-BE will provide necessary bandwidth to support requirements at all levels of war. The warfighters' ability to have access to necessary bandwidth with the appropriate integrated information systems across the services, DoD, joint, and interagency communities has the potential to truly stimulate innovative approaches to solving complex tasks across the spectrum of conflict. DoD is far from achieving this lofty goal at this time. Also, there is no guarantee that as the pieces fall into place the expectations of NCW will be achieved. However, the early indications of the potential synergy afforded by networked forces continue to form a powerful augment to continue down this path.[45] This is not to say that there is not room for caution as DoD and the Services invest large portions of their budgets in technology.

The Genie and NCW.

Let us postulate for a moment that this chapter convinced you that the Genie representing the power of knowledge through collaboration enabled by a robust network (information system) characterized by the latest information technology is outside the bottle. The challenge is to ask for the correct wishes that would facilitate achieving the principles and tenets outlined in the NCO-CF. There are numerous potential disadvantages to NCW. One could easily ask the Genie for a worthless wish. There is a fairly substantial list of those who point out the shortcomings of NCW.[46] These authors provide a valuable service in highlighting the potential deficiencies in the theoretical underpinnings of NCW as well as outlining the opportunity costs associated with pursuing this extremely expensive transformation of the defense information architecture. The naysayers stimulate dialogue and debate and assist proponents and decision makers to better allocate scarce resources in pursuit of NCW capabilities.

The disadvantages of NCW are well documented in the literature. Numerous scholars and warfighters have taken the time to thoughtfully outline the potential pitfalls in the pursuit of NCW capabilities. It would be impossible to enumerate all of the explicit and implicit disadvantages outlined by the critics. However, it is useful to highlight a few of the major concerns that deserve further attention and study in the years ahead:

- NCW places too much emphasis on tactics and the tactical nature of war.
- U.S. advances in information technology will outpace our allies and potential coalition partners ability to operate together on the battlefield.
- More information and superior information technologies do not translate into information dominance.

- Situational awareness is not going to eliminate the fog and friction of war.
- Too much speed of command can lead to unsound decisions.[47]
- NCW ignores the human dimension of warfare.
- Technology is dictating strategy. "[NCW is] driven by its self-centered concern with technology for technology sake."[48]
- NCW and its reliance on information technology fails to address the emergence of the current and future threat posed by insurgency, terrorists, Netwars, and 4th Generation Warfare. [49]

The articulated disadvantages help to focus research, funding, and execution of NCW in the years ahead. Also, many of these possible negative aspects will be addressed as DoD publishes empirical evidence to refute these concerns.

The proponents of NCW recognize these potential negative aspects of NCW. DoD, headed by the Office of Force Transformation, is working to harness the power of industry, academia, and the military community at large to thoughtfully address each of these concerns with rigorous conceptual and empirical study. COL Douglas Macgregor, USA (Ret.), a well known critic of numerous aspects of Army transformation, understands the potential benefits of technology and acquiring information on the battlefield. "In the pursuit of knowledge, the U.S. Navy has broken new ground in context of network-centric warfare with its cooperative engagement capability (CEC). This system distributes raw sensor and weapons data among warfighting units, enabling them to combine and share composite data in a coordinated joint defense."[50] This is why it is critical to proceed with the study and focused conceptualization of how technology can enable and facilitate warfighting in the 21st century.

Moving Forward: Course of Action Missouri.

It should be apparent by now that this author is an advocate of NCW. This should not imply total agreement with the concept. This author supports the continued study of how the principles of NCW will leverage information and knowledge on the battlefield. It is understandable that the academic community and even warfighters want to see solid evidence supporting the need to make large investments of scarce funding to pursue NCW capabilities. Thus, there is a requirement to develop a strategy and course of action that clearly demonstrates the return on investment to stakeholders, i.e., *Course of Action (COA) Missouri*. The designation of COA Missouri was selected based on the state of Missouri's nickname of the "show me state." NCW will need to clearly demonstrate value added to the warfighter. Elements of this proposed course of action are already beginning to take shape in the Office of Force Transformation. The empirical evidence and future studies begin to outline the potential of aligning the appropriate technology to support joint warfighting in a collaborative information environment. So what are the key elements of COA Missouri?

The Human Dimension of Warfare.

As previously discussed, many of the critics state that NCW does not appropriately address human behavior in warfare. The NCW literature does address the importance of the interaction of the cognitive, social, and information domains as an essential element of NCW. To address this concern, the Office of Force Transformation should focus future research and publications on the human dimension and leadership issues associated with information age warfare. There is adequate coverage in the current literature to indicate that the warfighter on the battlefield is and will remain the key to success and not the technology. However, the current case studies focus mainly on the enabling technology related to organizational effectiveness. Future studies should examine the effects of technology on human behavior in a combat environment at the tactical, operational, and strategic levels of warfare. Academic scholars in the fields of anthropology, sociology, and psychology should work with the developers of the NCO-CF to investigate the potential benefits as well as the negative aspects of NCW in the human behavior domain. The Office of Force Transformation has established transformation chairs at all of the Senior Service Colleges and Service Academies. These scholars would be a good place to begin studies investigating human behavior and leadership challenges to warfare in the information age. The results of this work should be published and disseminated for scholarly examination, critique, and additional study.

NCO-CF Attributes and Metrics.

There is little doubt the developers of the NCO-CF are in the early stages of defining rigorous attributes and associated metrics to conduct empirical studies of the model. Two of the NCW published case studies have stated that attributes and metrics must be further defined.[51] The US/UK case study on NCO highlighted several insightful observations and recommendations about the NCO-CF:

- The language of the NCO-CF be changed so it is better understood by combat units and non-U.S. forces.
- Quantifying metrics related to combat operations—as was done for this case study—can be very difficult. Beyond this report, it is recommended that a focused effort be made to incorporate into the NCO-CF recommendations for improvement and lessons learned from the application of NCO-CF within various case studies.
- Certain definitions and corresponding metrics are difficult to translate into meaningful interview questions.
- Many attributes definitions and metrics are liable to variations in interpretation.
- Difficult to identify data sources.
- Weakness in consistency and completeness in descriptions, explanations, measures and metrics for each of the attributes.[52]
- The Stryker BCT NCW Case Study called for the development of additional metrics:
  - Develop metrics that reflect the degree to which the development, maintenance, and sharing of the Common Operational Picture critically depends on the interaction of technology, training and personnel experience.
  - Current metrics don't measure the synergy between net-centric current operations and improved planning in land warfare.
  - Metrics don't exist that reflect the degree to which the Military Decision Making Process (MDMP) has been properly reengineered to exploit the potential advantages of information networks.
  - Metrics are required to reflect the degree to which process design, technology, business rules, training, personnel experience and other factors combine to either enhance or impede effective and efficient collaboration.[53]

These observations highlight the requirement to conduct focused research to develop appropriate new attributes and metrics based on lessons learned in previous studies. This study could provide new insights and directions to develop the appropriate NCW capabilities.

Convergence of Services' Information Systems.

A further defined NCO-CF with appropriate attributes and metrics will assist in selecting the correct enabling technologies. Information technology and systems will remain the cornerstone of the enabling technologies to create the competitive advantage against U.S. adversaries in the future. Currently, there is a proliferation of waveforms, software, and hardware dispersed throughout the current DoD information system. There should be little doubt that the "to be" DoD information system supporting NCW was based on the convergence and interoperability of the enterprise architecture. Voice, video, and data communications must be seamlessly shared between the services in an interoperable information system. This is the essence of transformational communications.[54]

The GIG-BE became fully operational in December 2005 providing the backbone for a DoD information system to support Joint communications and enable NCW. The services must continue to fund initiatives to integrate and upgrade their information systems. FORCEnet (U.S. Navy), Constellation C2 (U.S. Air Force), and LandWarNet (U.S. Army) have the potential to move toward an interoperable Joint communications network supported by the GIG-BE. "Operationally, the foundation of transformational communications rests on four primary supports: the Transformational Satellite Communications System, or TSAT; the Global Information Grid Bandwidth Expansion, or GIG-BE; and the Warfighter Information Network Tactical system, or WIN-T; and the Joint Tactical Radio System, or JTRS."[55] The JTRS initiative provides the promise of a joint communications system that will support information sharing between the Services. The integration and convergence of Services' information systems and the abundance of disparate waveforms must remain a high priority.

Network-Centric Warfare: Proceed with Caution.

This chapter has demonstrated that NCW is much more than developing an integrated DoD information system on steroids. NCW is more than just technology. NCW is about harnessing the power of information in the operational environment. In order to argue the merits of NCW as more than just information technology it is essential to review the body of literature that supports the fundamental underpinnings of the concept. This paper has provided a brief literature review of the key documents to bring the dialogue on the merits of NCW up to date. NCW is still an emerging concept yet to be fully developed and validated. The recently published Office of Force Transformation NCW case studies begin to illustrate the potential of leveraging information and knowledge on the battlefield. However, there is still much work to be done to demonstrate benefits of NCW at the operational and strategic levels of war.

DoD should continue to aggressively pursue case studies that investigate the relationships in the NCO-CF that deal with the human dimension of warfare. The interaction between the information, cognitive, and physical domains enabled by appropriate technologies should be a priority. There should be collaboration between scholars in the fields of psychology, sociology, and anthropology to examine the implications of NCO on human behavior and leadership. Next, this essay has provided ample evidence that it is time to reexamine the attributes and metrics associated with the NCO-CF. Finally, the Services and DoD must continue to work the "network" in terms of interoperability and convergence of unique applications, waveforms, and information technologies. A clearly articulated action plan for NCW that includes these recommendations will continue to move NCW in the right direction to harness the power of information on the battlefield to support the warfighter.

ENDNOTES - CHAPTER 21

1. Carl Von Clausewitz, *On War*, Michael Howard and Peter Paret, eds., and trans., Princeton: Princeton University Press, 1984, p. 140.

2. David S. Alberts, John Garstka, J., and Frederick P. Stein, *Network Centric Warfare: Developing and Leveraging Information Superiority*, Washington, DC: DoD Command and Control Research Program, 2002; Thomas P. M. Barnett, "The Seven Deadly Sins of Network-Centric Warfare," *Proceedings: U.S. Naval Institute* 125, 1999; Arthur K. Cebrowski, *Transformation and the Changing Character of War*, Office of the Secretary of Defense, Office of Force Transformation, 2004 [accessed September 7, 2004], available from *www.afei.org/transformation/documents/TransformationTrends-17June2004Issue.pdf*; Milan Vego, "Net-Centric Is Not Decisive," *Naval Institute Proceedings* 129, No. 1, 2003.

3. Thomas Stewart, *The Wealth of Knowledge*, New York, NY: Currency, 2001.

4. See Leslie C. Eliason and Emily O. Goldman, "Introduction: Theoretical and Comparative Perspectives on Innovation and Diffusion," in *The Diffusion of Military Technology and Ideas*, Leslie C. Eliason and Emily O. Goldman, eds., Stanford, CA: Stanford University Press, 2003.

5. See Jeffrey L. Groh, and Dennis Murphy, "Landpower and Network-Centric Operations: How Information in Today's Battlespace Can Be Exploited," *Network Enabled Capabilities/Network-centric Warfare Journal*, 2006; and Jay B. Tisserand, "U.S. V Corps and 3rd Infantry Division (Mechanized) During Operation Iraqi Freedom Combat Operations, Mar-Apr 2003, Volume III: Network Centric Warfare Insights." Carlisle Barracks, PA: Center for Strategic Leadership and Office of Force Transformation, Office of the Secretary of Defense, 2006.

6. Nicholas G. Carr, *Does IT Matter?*, Boston, MA: Harvard Business School Press, 2004; Gartner Dataquest, *Update: IT Spending*, 2003 [accessed August 13, 2003); available from *www.dataquest.com/press_gartner/quickstats/ITSpending.html*.

7. Director Force Transformation Office of the Secretary of Defense, "The Implementation of Network-Centric Warfare," Washington, DC: Office of the Secretary of Defense, Office of Force Transformation, 2005.

8. Command and Control Research Program, *About the Program*, Command and Control Research Program, Office of the Secretary of Defense, 2005 [accessed September 5, 2005]), available from *www.dodccrp.org/html2/about_program.html*. The Command and Control Research Program (CCRP) within the Office of the Assistant Secretary of Defense, NII focuses upon (1) improving both the state of the art and the state of the practice of command and control, and (2) enhancing DoD's understanding of the national security implications of the Information Age. It provides "Out of the Box" thinking and explores ways to help DoD take full advantage of the opportunities afforded by the Information Age. The CCRP forges links between the operational and technical communities, and enhances the body of knowledge and research infrastructure upon which future progress depends.

9. Alberts, Garstka, and Stein, *Network Centric Warfare: Developing and Leveraging Information Superiority*.

10. Arthur K. Cebrowski and John Garstka, Jr., "Network Centric Warfare: Its Origins and Future," *Proceedings: U.S. Naval Institute* 124, No. 1, 1998, in Alberts, Garstka, and Stein, *Network Centric Warfare: Developing and Leveraging Information Superiority*, p. 88.

11. David S. Alberts, *Information Age Transformation: Getting to a 21st Century Military*, Washington, DC: Department of Defense Command and Control Research Program, 2002, p. 43.

12. *Ibid.*

13. Director Force Transformation Office of the Secretary of Defense, *Network Centric Operations Case Studies*, Office of the Secretary of Defense, Office of Force Transformation, 2005 [accessed September 6, 2005], available from *www.oft.osd.mil/initiatives/ncw/studies.cfm*.

14. David S. Alberts and Richard E. Hayes, *Power to the Edge: Command, Control in the Information Age*, *Information Age Transformation Series*, Washington, DC: CCRP Publication Series, 2003.

15. *Ibid.*, p. 5.

16. C-SPAN, "Military Restructuring Efforts [Videorecording]/National Defense University," in *C-SPAN Archives*, USA: 2002.

17. John Garstka, *Defense Transformation and Network Centric Warfare*, Office of the Secretary of Defense, Office of Force Transformation, September 2 2002 [accessed September 2, 2005], available from *navyleague.org/membership/NCW.pdf.*

18. John Garstka, J. and David S. Alberts, "Network Centric Operations Conceptual Framework Version 2.0," Vienna, VA: Evidence Based Research, Inc, 2004, p. 2.

19. *Ibid.*, p. 20.

20. *Ibid.*, p. 59.

21. Daniel Gonzales *et al.*, *Network-Centric Operations Case Study: The Stryker Brigade Combat Team*, Santa Monica, CA: Rand, 2005.

22. David Mawby, Ian McDougall, and Greg Boehmer, "A Network-Centric Operations Case Study: US/UK Coalition Combat Operations During Operation Iraqi Freedom," Washington, DC: Evidence Based Research, Inc and PA Consulting, UK, 2005; See the Office of Force Transformation web site for all available NCW cases studies: *www.oft.osd.mil/initiatives/ncw/studies.cfm* .

23. Director Force Transformation Office of the Secretary of Defense, "The Implementation of Network-Centric Warfare," p. 15.

24. See for example, Edmund Blash, "Network-Centric Warfare Requires a Closer Look," *Signal Magazine*, May 2003; Robert H. Scales, "Human Intel Vs. Technology," *Washington Times* 2004; Vego, "Net-Centric Is Not Decisive."

25. Director Force Transformation Office of the Secretary of Defense, "The Implementation of Network-Centric Warfare," p. 3.

26. *Ibid.*, p. 16.

27. *Ibid.*, p. 20.

28. *Ibid.*, p. 19, chart available at *www.oft.osd.mil/library/library_files/document_387_NCW_Book_LowRes.pdf*, accessed December 2007.

29. *Ibid.*, p. 33.

30. *Ibid.*, p. 34.

31. Gonzales *et al.*, *Network-Centric Operations Case Study: The Stryker Brigade Combat Team*, p. xxi.

32. Director Force Transformation Office of the Secretary of Defense, "The Implementation of Network-Centric Warfare," p. 16.

33. John Keller, "Defense Spending Set to Increase for Electronics and Electro-Optics Programs in 2007." *Military & Aerospace Technology*. March 2006, pp. 18-20.

34. Director Force Transformation Office of the Secretary of Defense, "The Implementation of Network-Centric Warfare," p. 2.

35. Anonymous, "Giambastiani: Networked Force Is 'Not a Luxury'," *Defense News*, 2005 [accessed April 5, 2005], available from *www.defensenews.com/story.php?F=740965&C=america.*

36. Geoff Fein, "Info Sharing Will Be Vital in Future Combat Operations, Hagee Says," *Defense Daily*, March 31, 2005.

37. William S. Wallace, "Network-Enabled Battle Command." *Military Review* LXXXV, No. 3, 2005, 5.

38. *Ibid.*, p. 5.

39. Director Force Transformation Office of the Secretary of Defense, "The Implementation of Network-Centric Warfare," p. 57.

40. *Ibid.*, p. 43.

41. Tommy Franks, "Impact of the Network on Operation Iraqi Freedom," Presentation at the Network Centric Warfare 2004, Washington, DC, 2004; Nick Justice, "Situational Awareness in OIF/OEF Via FBCB2-Blue Force Tracker," presentation at the Network Centric Warfare Conference, Washington, DC, January 22, 2004.

42. Tisserand, "U.S. V Corps and 3rd Infantry Division, Mechanized) During Operation Iraqi Freedom Combat Operations, Mar-Apr 2003, Volume III: Network Centric Warfare Insights."

43. Marilyn Quagliotti, "Moving to a Net-Centric Environment" Presentation at the Network Centric Warfare 2005, Washington, DC, 2005.

44. Jason Miller, *DoD's GIG-BE Reaches Full Operational Capability*, Government Computer Network, 2005 [accessed August 9, 2007], available from *www.gcn.com/online/vol1_no1/37848-1.html*.

45. ADM Cebrowski, USN, Ret., stated in an interview, "We have mountain of evidence now, ranging from simulations, to experimentation, to real world combat experiences, that verify the power of networking." See Anonymous, "The Power of Information Comes from the Ability to Share," *Defender*, April 29 2005. This study has already commented on the impressive results of the *Network-Centric Operations Case Study: The Stryker Brigade Combat Team* conducted by RAND. Also, there are seven case studies being published by the Office of Force Transformation that will further document the potential of NCO. The Center for Strategic Leadership, U.S. Army War College is completing a case study that examines network centric operations involving V Corps and 3 Infantry Division during Operation IRAQI FREEDOM. The initial findings indicate, "New information systems, sensors, and extended connectivity improved combat effectiveness. This extended connectivity allowed V Corps and 3 ID to both fight widely dispersed over extended distances and rapidly task organize and fully integrate newly arrived units into combat operations. . . ." See Dennis Murphy, *Network Enabled Operations in Operation Iraqi Freedom: Initial Impressions*, 2005, Center for Strategic Leadership, U.S. Army War College, *www.carlisle.army.mil/usacsl/Publications/06-05.pdf*, accessed May 9, 2005.

46. See, for example, Thomas P. M. Barnett, "The Seven Deadly Sins of Network-Centric Warfare," *Proceedings: U.S. Naval Institute*, Vol. 125, 1999, pp. 36-39; Edmund Blash, "Network-Centric Warfare Requires a Closer Look,." *Signal Magazine*, May 2003, pp. 56-57; Thomas X. Hammes, *The Sling and the Stone: On War in the 21st Century*. St. Paul, MN: Zenith Press, 2004; Alfred Kaufman, "Caught in the Network: How the Doctrine of Network-Centric Warfare Allows Technology to Dictate Military Strategy," *Armed Forces Journal*, February 2005, pp. 20-22; and Milan Vego, "Net-Centric is Not Decisive," *Naval Institute Proceedings* 129, No. 1, 2003, pp. 52-58; and Frederick W. Kagan, *Finding the Target: The Transformation of American Military Policy*, 1st edition, New York: Encounter Books, 2006.

47. See Vego, "Net-Centric Is Not Decisive." The first five bullets paraphrase Dr. Vego's concerns about NCW.

48. Alfred Kaufman, "Caught in the Network: How the Doctrine of Network-Centric Warfare Allows Technology to Dictate Military Strategy," *Armed Forces Journal*, February 2005.

49. Thomas X. Hammes, *The Sling and the Stone: On War in the 21st Century*, St. Paul, MN: Zenith Press, 2004.

50. Douglas A. Macgregor, *Transformation under Fire: Revolutionizing How America Fights*, Westport, Connecticut: Praeger, 2003, p. 257.

51. Gonzales *et al.*, *Network-Centric Operations Case Study: The Stryker Brigade Combat Team*; Mawby, McDougall, and Boehmer, "A Network-Centric Operations Case Study: US/Uk Coalition Combat Operations During Operation Iraqi Freedom."

52. Mawby, McDougall, and Boehmer, "A Network-Centric Operations Case Study: US/UK Coalition Combat Operations During Operation Iraqi Freedom," Appendix G.

53. Gonzales *et al.*, *Network-Centric Operations Case Study: The Stryker Brigade Combat Team*, pp. 109-11.

54. John Keller, "Transformational Communications," *Military & Aerospace Electronics*, May 2005.

55. *Ibid.*, p. 28.

APPENDIX I

CONTRIBUTORS

J. BOONE BARTHOLOMEES, JR. (Ph.D., Duke University, 1978) is Professor of Military History in the Department of National Security and Strategy at the U.S. Army War College. He is the course director for the core course Theory of War and Strategy and a former holder of the Dwight D. Eisenhower Chair of National Security Studies. He is a retired Army Colonel and the author of *Buff Facings and Gilt Buttons: Headquarters and Staff Operations in the Army of Northern Virginia, 1861-1865.* He edited *The U.S. Army War College Guide to National Security Policy and Strategy*, 2004, and the 2d edition published in 2006.

TAMI DAVIS BIDDLE (Ph.D., Yale University, 1995) is Professor of Strategy and Military History at the U.S. Army War College. She was the 2005-2007 George C. Marshall Professor of Military Studies at the College, and the 2001-2002 Harold K. Johnson Visiting Professor of Military History at the U.S. Army's Military History Institute. Prior to that she taught in the Department of History at Duke University, where she was a core faculty member of the Duke University of North Carolina Joint Program in Military History. She received her Ph.D. in history from Yale, and has held fellowships from Harvard, the Social Science Research Council, and the Smithsonian Institution's National Air and Space Museum. Her research focus has been warfare in the 20th century, in particular the history of air warfare. Her book, *Rhetoric and Reality in Air Warfare: The Evolution of British and American Ideas about Strategic Bombing, 1914-1945* (Princeton: Princeton University Press, 2002) was a *Choice* Outstanding Academic Title for 2002, and was added to the Chief of Air Staff's Reading List, Royal Air Force.

CLAYTON K. S. CHUN (Ph.D., RAND Graduate School, 1992) is Chairman of the Department of Distance Education at the U.S. Army War College and holds the General Hoyt S. Vandenburg Chair of Aerospace Studies. He was previously the Professor of Economics in the Department of National Security and Strategy. Dr. Chun is a retired Air Force officer with missile, space, command and control, strategy, and education assignments. He has published on a number of national security, economics, and space related issues.

G. K. CUNNINGHAM (MA, Duquesne University, 2004) is Professor of Joint Land Operations and Doctrine in the Department of Military Strategy, Planning, and Operations at the U.S. Army War College. He is also the Deputy Director for the Joint Force Land Component Commander Course. He is a retired Marine Corps colonel with a wide background of command and staff positions in contingency planning, joint operations, and interagency programs. He has written and presented on humanitarian de-mining operations and was a military delegate to the Ottawa Convention on the prohibition of antipersonnel landmines.

JEFFREY A. FARNSWORTH (MS, U.S. Army War College, 2006) is the Space Control Division Director, National Security Space Office. After 11 years of successful service as an Army Corps of Engineers Officer, to include duty in Operations DESERT SHIELD/DESERT STORM and SOUTHERN WATCH, Colonel Farnsworth was selected as an Army Space Operations Officer. His space assignments include Exchange Officer to Naval Space Command, where he served in N5 (Space Plans and Policy) and N3 (Chief, Marine Corps Space Support Team); Headquarters Space and Missile Defense Command (SMDC), as the Deputy for Space Operations and Plans;

Headquarters Department of the Army, Deputy Chief of Staff G-3/5/7, as the Space Policy Branch Chief; Commander 1st Space Battalion, U.S. Army Strategic Forces Command; and Deputy for Space Concepts and Architectures, at the TRADOC Army Capabilities Integration Center and SMDC Future Warfare Center. His professional military space education includes the Inter-Service Space Fundamentals and Intelligence Operations Courses, the Space Applications Advanced Course, Army Space Operations Officer Qualification Course, and the Space 300 Course. Colonel Farnsworth holds a BS in Civil Engineering from Norwich University and a Master of Strategic Studies from the U.S. Army War College. He wrote this paper as his Strategy Research Paper while at USAWC.

REED J. FENDRICK (MA, Cornell University) is a senior Foreign Service Officer with the U.S. Department of State where he has served since 1974. He served with the Department of National Security and Strategy at the U.S. Army War College from 2002 to 2004. A graduate of the University of Wisconsin-Madison, he received the M.A. degree in Government from Cornell University. Among his diplomatic assignments, he has been Deputy Chief of Mission and Charge d'Affaires at the American Embassy in The Hague, the Netherlands; Political Counselor at the American Embassy in Pretoria, South Africa; Deputy Director of the Office of Central African Affairs; Pearson Fellow assigned to the Office of International Relations of the Governor of Hawaii; Political Officer in the American Embassy in Paris, France, Pretoria, South Africa, the American Embassy in Bridgetown, Barbados, and the United States Mission to the United Nations; Deputy Principal Officer at the American Consulate-General in Alexandria, Egypt; Junior Officer at the American Embassy in Rabat, Morocco and Staff Assistant to the Assistant Secretary of State for African Affairs. In July 2004, he joined the United States Mission to the United Nations where he serves as Counselor for Political Affairs.

JEFFREY L. GROH (D.Sc., Robert Morris University, 2003) is the Professor of Information and Technology in Warfare in the Department of Distance Education at the U.S. Army War College. He is a retired Armor officer. Prior to his retirement in 2004 he served in the 11th, 3rd, and 2nd Armored Cavalry Regiments. He also served as the Deputy Division Chief, J-5 NATO Policy Division in the Office of the Joint Chiefs of Staff. He has been a member of the U.S. Army War College faculty since 1999. He holds the U.S. Army War College General Colin Powell Chair for Military and Strategic Studies.

JAMES F. HOLCOMB (Colonel, Infantry, retired) is a Faculty Instructor in the Department of Distance Education at the U.S. Army War College. Commissioned from West Point, he served in a variety of Infantry, Special Forces and Russian/East European Foreign Area Officer assignments. Prior to his retirement from the Army in 2002, he taught for five years as Director of Military Strategy in the Department of National Security and Strategy. He also teaches the elective in Grand Strategy and the Strategic Art to the Resident and Distance Education Courses at the War College.

DAVID JABLONSKY (Ph.D., Kansas University, 1979) was the Professor of National Security Affairs in the Department of National Security and Strategy at the U.S. Army War College until his retirement in 2007. A graduate of Dartmouth College and the U.S. Army War College, he received a MA from Boston University in international relations and holds MA and Ph.D. degrees in European history from Kansas University. He held the Elihu Root Chair of Strategy, the George C. Marshall Chair of Military Studies, and the Dwight D. Eisenhower Chair of National Security Studies while at the Army War College. He is the author of five books, eight monographs and numerous articles and book chapters dealing with European history and international relations. He is a retired Army colonel.

ANK L. JONES (MPA, State University of New York at Albany, 1978) is Assistant Professor of curity Studies at the U.S. Army War College. A retired member of the Senior Executive Service with more thirty years of government service, he served in several positions within the Office of the Secretary of Defense including Deputy Assistant Secretary of Defense for Special Operations Policy and Support and as Principal Director for Strategy, Plans and Resources in the Office of the Assistant Secretary of Defense for Homeland Defense. From 2006-2007, he was a fellow at the Homeland Security Institute, the Department of Homeland Security's federally-funded research and development center, where he worked on national response planning and maritime security issues. He has written several book chapters and journal articles on such subjects as national security policymaking, homeland defense, and terrorism.

JANEEN M. KLINGER (Ph.D. University of California, Berkeley, 1990) is Professor of Political Science with the Department of National Security and Strategy, U.S. Army War College. She taught previously at the Command and Staff College of Marine Corps University and at Franklin and Marshall College. She also worked as an analyst for the Central Intelligence Agency specializing in issues related to international political economy.

DENNIS M. MURPHY (MS, Pennsylvania State University, 1984) the Director of the Information in Warfare Group at Center for Strategic Leadership, U.S. Army War College, where he teaches information operations and strategic communication elective courses and conducts workshops focused on the information element of power. He served in a variety of command and staff positions over his 27 years of U.S. Army service to include command of a direct support artillery battalion forward deployed to Germany and an associate professorship at West Point. Professor Murphy was appointed as the first George C. Marshall Fellow for Political-Military and Diplomatic Gaming at the Department of State's Foreign Service Institute in 1999. His work in information operations (IO) and strategic communication includes a tour as senior observer-trainer for the Battle Command Training Program, Operations Group Delta (Joint Task Force and Combatant Command trainers) where he trained NATO multinational forces on IO prior their initial deployment to Bosnia. He has written on information operations, strategic communication and national security issues and published in *Military Review*, *Field Artillery Journal*, *Foreign Service Journal*, *NECWORKS Journal*, and *Parameters*, among others. His most recent article, "The Trouble with Strategic Communication(s)" appears in the winter 2008 issue of *IO Sphere*.

R. CRAIG NATION (Ph.D. Duke University, 1976) has served as Professor of Strategy and Director of Russian and Eurasian Studies with the Department of National Security and Strategy, U.S. Army War College, since 1996. His most recent major publication, a history of the Balkan conflict of the 1990s, is entitled *War in the Balkans, 1991-2002*.

LOUIS J. NIGRO, JR. (Ph.D., Vanderbilt University, 1979) is a career diplomat and a member of the Senior Foreign Service of the United States. From 2004-2006, he was seconded to the U.S. Army War College faculty as Professor of International Relations. In the Department of State since 1980, he has served overseas at U.S. Embassies in The Bahamas, Chad, Haiti, The Holy See, Guinea, and Cuba. He was Deputy Chief of Mission in the last three postings. In Washington, he has served in the Department of State's Operations Center, Policy Planning Council, Office of Western European Affairs, and Office of Canadian Affairs. For his service in Haiti, he won the Department of State's Superior Honor Award. Before joining the Foreign Service, Mr. Nigro was a Fulbright-Hays Research

Fellow in Italy and taught modern European history at Stanford University. He is the author of *New Diplomacy in Italy: American Propaganda and U.S.-Italian Relations, 1917-1919* (New York: Pe Lang, 1999.)

JOHN F. TROXELL (MPA, Princeton University, 1982), is an Associate Professor in the Center for Strategic Leadership at the U.S. Army War College and holds the General George S. Patton Chair of Operational Research and Analysis. Prior to assuming his current position he was the Director of National Security Studies in the Department of National Security and Strategy at the Army War College. He has also been a faculty member of the Department of Social Studies at the United States Military Academy. He is a retired Army colonel and has served in a variety of operational and staff assignments to include the Department of the Army War Plans Division and as a force planner for the Assistant Secretary of Defense for Strategy and Requirements. He has published articles and monographs with the Strategic Studies Institute, *Parameters*, and *Military Review*.

HARRY R. "RICH" YARGER (Ph.D., History, Temple University, 1996) is the Professor of National Security Policy in the Department of National Security and Strategy at the U.S. Army War College. Currently he teaches courses in: Fundamentals of Strategic Thinking, Theory of War and Strategy, National Security Policy and Strategy, and Terrorism. His research focuses on national security policy, strategic theory, and the education and development of strategic level leaders. Dr. Yarger has also taught at the undergraduate level at several local colleges. A retired Army colonel, he is a Vietnam veteran and served in both Germany and Korea.